The Study of Liturgy

Valerie Perris-Taylor.

The Study of Liturgy

Edited by
Cheslyn Jones, Geoffrey Wainwright
Edward Yarnold, SJ

LONDON
SPCK

First published 1978
Second impression 1978
SPCK
Holy Trinity Church, Marylebone Road
London NW1 4DU

Printed in Great Britain by
William Clowes & Sons Limited, London, Beccles and Colchester

ISBN 0 281 03581 4 cased
ISBN 0 281 03578 4 paper

CONTENTS

Contents

ILLUSTRATIONS

PLATES

Thanks are due to the photographers and organizations cited for permission to reproduce these plates.

Illustrations

FIGURES

We are grateful to the authors, publishers, and organizations cited for permission to base these figures on copyright originals.

Illustrations

Drawings by Denys Baker

CONTRIBUTORS

The Revd R. T. Beckwith, Warden of Latimer House, Oxford.

The Revd Dr Paul F. Bradshaw, Director of Studies, Chichester Theological College.

The Revd Peter G. Cobb, Librarian of Pusey House, Oxford.

The Revd Dr J. H. Crehan, SJ, Editor of *A Catholic Dictionary of Theology*.

The Revd J. D. Crichton, formerly Editor of *Life and Worship*.

The Revd Dr G. J. Cuming, Lecturer in Liturgical Studies, King's College, London.

The Revd Kevin Donovan, SJ, Lecturer in Liturgical Studies, Heythrop College, London.

The Revd Alan Dunstan, Canon Residentiary of Gloucester Cathedral.

The Revd Canon J. D. C. Fisher, Vicar of St John Baptist, Hove.

The Revd Dr J. Gelineau, SJ, Centre Sèvres, Paris.

W. Jardine Grisbrooke, Esq., Lecturer in Liturgiology, The Queen's College, Birmingham.

The Revd Dr R. J. Halliburton, Principal of Chichester Theological College.

The Revd Frank Hawkins, Vicar of St Mary's, East Grinstead, Sussex.

The Revd Dr Peter Hinchliff, Fellow and Chaplain of Balliol College, Oxford.

The Revd Dr D. M. Hope, Principal of St Stephen's House, Oxford.

The Revd Clifford Howell, SJ, writer and lecturer on liturgical subjects.

The Revd Canon C. P. M. Jones, Principal of Pusey House, Oxford.

The Revd Dr K. W. Noakes, Priest-in-charge of Marhamchurch, Bude, Cornwall.

The Revd D. H. Tripp, Methodist Minister in the Manchester (Cheetham Hill and Prestwich) Circuit.

The Revd Dr Geoffrey Wainwright, Lecturer in Systematic Theology, The Queen's College, Birmingham.

The Revd Hugh Wybrew, Vicar of Pinner, Middlesex.

The Revd Dr E. J. Yarnold, SJ, Tutor in Theology, Campion Hall, Oxford.

PREFACE

This book on the Study of Liturgy has a two-fold parentage. On one side it is a successor to *Liturgy and Worship*, produced by SPCK in 1932, in the aftermath of the 1927/28 projected revision of the 1662 Book of Common Prayer; this composite volume, edited by Dr W. K. Lowther Clarke and Dr Charles Harris, has been the mainstay of Anglican ordination candidates and other students of liturgy for over 40 years. It is neither surprising nor discreditable, in a time of such widespread liturgical interest and development, that this work should be in need of revision; nor that it was difficult to find a scholar of the calibre of the late Dr Lowther Clarke to undertake a second edition.

On the other side, the present work owes its origin to a group of members of the Oxford Theology Faculty, who were at first gathered together by Dr G. D. Kilpatrick, Dean Ireland Professor of the Exegesis of the Holy Scriptures, for the study of the history and theology of liturgies (in fact, of the Eucharist), aspects liable to be neglected in many Christian circles in the discussion and practice of liturgical reform. After two years the group decided to enlarge its aims and membership, and, with the encouragement of SPCK, to set about the production of a book which could go some way towards taking the place of *Liturgy and Worship*.

The child does not exactly take after either parent. In particular it differs from *Liturgy and Worship* in two important aspects. First, *Liturgy and Worship*, though by no means oblivious of other churches and traditions, was primarily a work by Anglican authors for Anglican readers in all branches of the Anglican Communion. The contributors and editors of this book represent a larger slice of Christendom; as well as Anglicans (R. T. Beckwith, P. F. Bradshaw, P. G. Cobb, G. J. Cuming, A. L. Dunstan, J. D. C. Fisher, R. J. Halliburton, F. J. Hawkins, P. B. Hinchliff, D. M. Hope, C. P. M. Jones, K. W. Noakes, H. Wybrew) we include Roman Catholics (J. H. Crehan, J. D. Crichton, K. Donovan, J. Gelineau, C. Howell, E. J. Yarnold) and Methodists (D. H. Tripp and Geoffrey Wainwright), who also hold a watching brief for the other Protestant Churches. Although our provenance and concerns are predominantly 'Western', we have tried to make sure that the Eastern liturgical tradition is never overlooked; indeed one of our contributors is himself Orthodox (W. J. Grisbrooke). We have tried as far as possible to produce an introduction to the study of liturgy for students in all our churches throughout the English-speaking world.

Secondly, *Liturgy and Worship* covered not only all the services of the Book of Common Prayer, but also, in supplementary essays, rites such as the coronation of a sovereign and the consecration of a church, and activities like extempore prayer and liturgical silence. The essay on the visitation of the sick covers a wide area of pastoral concern. Ours is a smaller book, and we have not tried to treat the whole field. We have limited ourselves to the central corporate rites of the Christian assembly; and we have given no clear and specific consideration to the more personal and pastoral rites, such as marriage and burial, while recognizing that they too have an 'ecclesial' character. They require fuller treatment, liturgical and pastoral, as we find, for instance, in the SPCK series, the Library of Pastoral Care.

So we have limited ourselves to Initiation, Eucharist, Ordination, Office, and Calendar. Each of these subjects has been the responsibility of its own panel of authors, and they are presented historically under five main divisions: Jewish and New Testament, patristic, medieval, reformation and counter-reformation, and contemporary (i.e. the reforms of the last twenty years). The historical account of these rites is preceded by a general introduction, in the form of a series of notes giving background information on subjects, like Hippolytus or Cranmer, which recur in the study of all the rites.

But we do not wish to present liturgy in isolation. We are anxious to make clear its theological foundations and connections; the theological introduction is an essential part of our intention. We are also anxious to show that the study of liturgy, even in its historical aspects, is not irrelevant to the present concerns of Christians, pastoral as well as liturgical; and so the concluding pastoral orientation is for us as important as the theological introduction.

It was also our ambition, in each phase of historical exposition, to show the connection between liturgy and other aspects of Christian activity and interest. We hoped to make full use of the vivid historical reconstruction of liturgical life, pioneered in English by Edmund Bishop in *Liturgica Historica* (1918), and followed by Dom Gregory Dix in *The Shape of the Liturgy* (1945), e.g. pp. 42ff, 659ff, 744–5. Unfortunately space has forced us to limit ourselves severely in this respect, and readers have generally been left to the resources of their own imagination.

Space has also imposed on us another most unwelcome self-denying ordinance. If we could not include full-blooded and dramatic reconstructions of each rite, at least we hoped to be able to include the main texts of the rites. They are, however, readily available for modern students in such collections as E. C. Whitaker's *Documents of the Baptismal Liturgy*, R. C. D. Jasper and G. J. Cuming's *Prayers of the Eucharist: early and reformed*, H. B. Porter's *Ordination Prayers of the Ancient Western Churches*, which, along with the *Dictionary of Liturgy and Worship*, edited by J. G. Davies, are indispensable companions to this volume.

As this book is intended to encourage further study, we have aimed at providing adequate bibliographies for each section. Unfortunately this has proved difficult in the case of the most recent period, when much liturgical literature has been produced all over the place, often ephemeral or provisional in content and presentation.

We have not tried to impose upon contributors any rigid uniformity in style or treatment. Varying levels of academic intensity will be found among the contributions; and we have encouraged this variety, so that students may gain some understanding of the range of scholarship that is possible in this field. Diligent readers, especially if they consult the index, will also detect traces of theological pluriformity, as in the differing interpretations of *anamnesis* (pp. 25–7, 49, 154, 205).

Our thanks are due to Dr Kilpatrick for his initial impetus and continued interest; to our contributors and to Mr Robin Brookes and all at SPCK for their co-operation, encouragement, and patience, and to the Revd F. V. A. Boyse, who has acted as copy editor; to the Very Revd Kallistos Ware, Spalding Lecturer in Eastern Orthodox Studies and Fellow of Pembroke College, Oxford, for generous advice and help with the Orthodox sections; to Père Gelineau for agreeing to co-operate in this Anglo-Saxon symposium, and to Mr David Wulstan, of Magdalen College, Oxford, for help with the English tradition of liturgical music; to Mr A. W. Lancaster and Mrs B. Strologo for secretarial assistance and to the Board of the Oxford Theology Faculty for a grant in aid.

CHESLYN JONES   GEOFFREY WAINWRIGHT   EDWARD YARNOLD   *Editors*

December 1977

ACKNOWLEDGEMENTS

Thanks are due to the following for permission to quote from copyright sources:

A. & C. Black Ltd: *A Synopsis of the Gospels, Part 1*, by H. F. D. Sparks

Geoffrey Chapman (Publishers): *Christian Celebration: The Mass* by J. D. Crichton

Oxford University Press: *The Parson's Handbook* by Percy Dearmer

Verlag Friedrich Pustet: Article by J. Pascher in *Aus der Theologie der Zeit*, edited by G. Söhngen.

ABBREVIATIONS

AC	Alcuin Club
ACW	Ancient Christian Writers, ed. J. Quasten *et al.* Westminster, Maryland and Longmans Green 1946ff
AH	*Adversus Haereses*, Irenaeus, ed. W. W. Harvey. CUP 1857
AIR	*The Awe-Inspiring Rites of Initiation*, E. J. Yarnold. St Paul Publications 1972
Anal. Boll.	*Analecta Bollandiana*. Paris and Brussels 1882ff
Ap. Const.	*Apostolic Constitutions*
Ap. Trad.	*The Apostolic Tradition*, Hippolytus, references according to the edition of G. Dix and H. Chadwick. SPCK 1968
AT	Author's translation
AV	Authorized Version
Bapt. Inst.	*Baptismal Instructions*, John Chrysostom, ed. and tr. P. W. Harkins. ACW 1963
BCP	Book of Common Prayer
BM	British Museum
BVM	Blessed Virgin Mary
Cat.	*Catecheses*, Cyril of Jerusalem
CC	Corpus Christianorum. Turnhout 1953ff
CCPC	*Christian Celebration: The Prayer of the Church*, J. D. Crichton. G. Chapman 1976
CDT	*A Catholic Dictionary of Theology*, ed. J. H. Crehan *et al.* Nelson 1962
CIPBC	Church of India, Pakistan, Burma, and Ceylon
CL	Constitution on the Liturgy
CNI	Church of North India
COCU	Church of Christ Uniting *also* Consultation on Church Union

xxi

C of E	Church of England
CQR	*Church Quarterly Review*, 169 vols. London 1875–1968
CR	Corpus Reformatorum. Brunswick *et al.* 1834ff
CSCO	Corpus Scriptorum Christianorum Orientalium. Paris etc. 1903ff
CSEL	Corpus Scriptorum Ecclesiasticorum Latinorum. Vienna 1866ff
CSI	Church of South India
Cuming, *History*	*A History of Anglican Liturgy*, G. J. Cuming. Macmillan 1969
CUP	Cambridge University Press
DACL	*Dictionnaire d'archéologie chrétienne et de liturgie*, ed. F. Cabrol and H. Leclercq. Paris 1907–53
DBL	*Documents of the Baptismal Liturgy*, E. C. Whitaker, 2nd edn AC SPCK 1970
de Bapt.	*de Baptismo*, Tertullian *or* Augustine
de Myst., de Sac.	*de Mysteriis, de Sacramentis*, Ambrose
Did.	*Didache*
Dix, *Shape*	*The Shape of the Liturgy*, G. Dix, 2nd edn Dacre Press 1945
DLT	Darton, Longman and Todd
DLW	*A Dictionary of Liturgy and Worship*, ed. J. G. Davies. SCM 1972
DO	*L'office divin: histoire de la formation du bréviaire*, P. Salmon. LO 27, 1959
DS	*Enchiridion Symbolorum, Definitionum et Declarationum*, ed. H. Denzinger and A. Schönmetzer, 33rd edn Barcelona etc., 1965
DTC	*Dictionnaire de théologie catholique*, ed. A. Vacant *et al.* Paris 1903–50
ECQ	*Eastern Churches Quarterly*. Ramsgate 1936–64
Egeria	*Egeria's Travels*. tr. and ed. J. Wilkinson. SPCK 1971
EL	*Ephemerides liturgicae*. Rome 1887ff
EO	*Echos d'Orient*, 39 vols. Paris 1897–1942

EP	*Eglise en prière*, ed. A. G. Martimort. Paris etc. 1965; ET, *Introduction to the Liturgy*. Irish University Press 1968
Ep.	*Epistle*
ERE	*Encyclopaedia of Religion and Ethics*, ed. J. Hastings. T. & T. Clark 1908–26
ET	English translation
EWJ	(ET) *The Eucharistic Words of Jesus*, J. Jeremias. SCM 1966
Ex. T	*Expository Times*. Edinburgh 1889ff
FP	Florilegium Patristicum. Bonn 1904–41
GCS	Die griechischen christlichen Schriftsteller der ersten drei Jahrhunderte. Leipzig 1897–1941; Berlin and Leipzig 1953; Berlin 1954ff
Gee-Hardy	*Documents Illustrative of English Church History*, ed. H. Gee and W. J. Hardy. Macmillan 1896
HBS	Henry Bradshaw Society
HE	*Historia Ecclesiastica*
Hom. cat.	*Homélies catéchetiques*, Theodore of Mopsuestia, ed. R. Tonneau and R. Devreesse. ST 1949
HTR	*Harvard Theological Review*. New York 1908f; Cambridge, Mass. 1910ff
ICC	International Critical Commentary. Edinburgh 1895ff
ICEL	International Committee for English in the Liturgy
ICET	International Consultation on English Texts
JB	Jerusalem Bible. DLT 1966
JEH	*Journal of Ecclesiastical History*. London 1950ff
JLW	*Jahrbuch für Liturgiewissenschaft*. Münster 1921–41
JQR	*Jewish Quarterly Review*. London 1888–1908; Philadelphia 1910ff
JTS	*Journal of Theological Studies*. London 1900–5; Oxford 1906–49; N.S. Oxford 1950ff
LACT	Library of Anglo-Catholic Theology, 97 vols. J. H. Parker 1841–63

LCC	Library of the Christian Classics. SCM and Westminster, Philadelphia 1953ff
LEW	*Liturgies Eastern and Western*, ed. F. E. Brightman, vol. 1. Clarendon Press 1896
LMD	*La Maison-Dieu*. Paris 1945ff
LO	Lex Orandi. Paris 1944ff
LP	*Le Liber Pontificalis*, ed. L. Duchesne, 2 vols. Bibliothèque des Ecoles Françaises d'Athènes et de Rome 1886–92
LQ	Liturgiegeschichtliche Quellen. Münster 1918–27
LQF	Liturgiegeschichtliche Quellen und Forschungen, and Liturgiewissenschaftliche Quellen und Forschungen. Münster 1928–39, and 1957 ff
LS	*Liturgical Studies*, E. C. Ratcliff, ed. A. H. Couratin and D. H. Tripp. SPCK 1976
LThK	*Lexikon für Theologie und Kirche*, 2nd edn, ed. J. Höfer and K. Rahner. 10 vols. and Index. Freiburg 1957–67; 3 supplementary vols., *Das zweite vatikanische Konzil*, 1967–8
LW	*Liturgy and Worship*, ed. W. K. Lowther Clarke and C. Harris. SPCK 1932
LXX	The Septuagint
M	Mishnah
MD	*The Manual of Discipline*
MF	*Missale Francorum*
MGH	Monumenta Germaniae Historica. Hanover etc. 1826ff
Misc. Ag.	Miscellanea Agostiniana. Rome 1930–1
MRR	(ET) *The Mass of the Roman Rite*, J. A. Jungmann. New York 1951–5
MSR	*Mélanges de science religieuse*. Lille 1944ff
Myst. Cat.	*Mystagogic Catecheses*, attributed to Cyril of Jerusalem
NEB	New English Bible. OUP and CUP 1970
Nov. T	*Novum Testamentum*. Leiden 1956ff
NRT	*Nouvelle revue théologique*. Louvain 1869ff

NT	New Testament
NTRJ	*The New Testament and Rabbinic Judaism*, D. Daube. Athlone Press 1956
NTS	*New Testament Studies*. Washington D.C. 1923–33
OC	*Oriens Christianus*. Leipzig and Wiesbaden 1901ff
OCA	*Orientalia Christiana Analecta*. Rome 1935ff
OCP	*Orientalia Christiana Periodica*. Rome 1935ff
ODCC	*The Oxford Dictionary of the Christian Church*, 2nd edn. OUP 1974
ODMA	*L'office divin au moyen âge*, P. Salmon. LO 43, 1967
OECT	Oxford Early Christian Texts. Clarendon Press 1971ff
OR	*Ordo Romanus*, ed. M. Andrieu. Louvain 1931–61
OT	Old Testament
OUP	Oxford University Press
Pap. Oxy.	Oxyrhynchus Papyri
PBA	Prayer Book Association
PE	*Prex Eucharistica*, ed. A. Hänggi and I. Pahl. Fribourg 1968
PECUSA	(Protestant) Episcopal Church of the USA
PEER	*Prayers of the Eucharist: Early and Reformed*, ed. R. C. D. Jasper and G. J. Cuming. Collins 1975
PG	Patrologia Graeca, ed. J.-P. Migne. Paris 1857–66
PL	Patrologia Latina, ed. J.-P. Migne. Paris 1844–64
PO	Patrologia Orientalis, ed. R. Graffin and F. Nau. Paris 1907ff
Procat.	*Procatechesis*, Cyril of Jerusalem
Procter and Frere	*A New History of the Book of Common Prayer*, F. Procter, ed. W. H. Frere. Macmillan 1901
PS	Parker Society
RAC	*Reallexikon für Antike und Christentum*, ed. T. Klauser. Stuttgart 1950ff
R Bén	*Revue bénédictine*. Maredsous 1885ff

RC	Roman Catholic
Rech SR or *RSR*	*Recherches de science religieuse.* Paris 1910ff
RevSR	*Revue de sciences religieuses.* Strasbourg *et al.* 1921ff
RevThPh	*Revue de théologie et de philosophie.* Lausanne 1868ff
RG	*Romano-German Pontifical*
RGG	*Die Religion in Geschichte und Gegenwart*, 3rd edn by K. Galling. Tübingen 1957–65
RHE	*Revue d'histoire ecclésiastique.* Louvain 1900ff
RSV	Revised Standard Version
RTAM	*Recherches de théologie ancienne et médiévale.* Louvain 1929ff
RV	Revised Version
Sarapion	*Euchologium*, ed. F. X. Funk. Paderborn 1905
SC	*Sources chrétiennes.* Paris 1942ff
SCM	Student Christian Movement Press (Publishers)
Serm.	Sermon
SJT	*Scottish Journal of Theology.* Edinburgh 1948ff
SL	*Studia Liturgica.* Rotterdam 1962ff
SP	*Studia Patristica.* Berlin 1957ff
SPCK	The Society for Promoting Christian Knowledge
ST	Studi e Testi. Rome 1900ff
Strack-Billerbeck	*Kommentar zum Neuen Testament aus Talmud und Midrasch*, H. Strack and P. Billerbeck. Munich 1922
St. Th.	*Studia Theologica.* Lund 1952ff
TDNT	*Theological Dictionary of the New Testament* (ET of *Theologisches Wörterbuch zum Neuen Testament*, G. Kittel). Grand Rapids, Michigan 1964ff
Theo. Mops.	Theodore of Mopsuestia
TL	*Travaux liturgiques*, B. Capelle. Louvain 1955–67
TU	*Texte und Untersuchungen zur Geschichte der altchristlichen Literatur* begründet von O. von Gebhardt und A. Harnack. Leipzig *et al.* 1882ff

URC	United Reformed Church
VC	*Vigiliae Christianae*. Amsterdam 1947ff
VT	*Vetus Testamentum*. Leiden 1951ff
WCC	World Council of Churches
ZNTW	*Zeitschrift für die neutestamentliche Wissenschaft und die Kunde des Urchristentums*. Giessen 1900–32; Berlin 1933ff; Beihefte, Giessen 1923–34; Berlin 1936ff

PART ONE

A Theology of Worship

A THEOLOGY OF WORSHIP

J. D. CRICHTON

GENERAL

Bouyer, L., (ET) *Rite and Man*. Burns and Oates 1963.
Grainger, R., *The Language of the Rite*. DLT 1974.
Otto, R., (ET) *The Idea of the Holy*. Penguin 1959.
Parrinder, G., *Worship in the World's Religions*. 2nd edn Sheldon 1974.
Smart, N., *The Concept of Worship*. Macmillan 1972.

ROMAN CATHOLIC

Bouyer, L., (ET) *Life and Liturgy*. Sheed and Ward 1956.
Casel, O., (ET) *The Mystery of Christian Worship*. DLT 1962.
Daniélou, J., (ET) *Bible and Liturgy*. DLT 1964.
Davis, C., *Liturgy and Doctrine*. Sheed and Ward 1960.
Guardini, R., (ET) *The Spirit of the Liturgy*. Sheed and Ward 1930.
Lash, N., *His Presence in the World*. Sheed and Ward 1968.
Panikkar, R., *Worship and Secular Man*. DLT 1973.
Schillebeeckx, E., (ET) *Christ the Sacrament*. Sheed and Ward 1963.
Segundo, J. L., (ET) *The Sacraments Today*. Orbis 1974.
Vagaggini, C., (ET) *Theological Dimensions of the Liturgy*. 2 vols., Collegeville
  1959.
Verheul, A., (ET) *Introduction to the Liturgy*. Burns and Oates 1968.

EASTERN

Schmemann, A., *Introduction to Liturgical Theology*. Faith Press 1966.
Schmemann, A., *The World as Sacrament*. DLT 1966.
Verghese, P., *The Joy of Freedom: Eastern Worship and Modern Man*.
  Lutterworth 1967.

LUTHERAN

Brilioth, Y., (ET) *Eucharistic Faith and Practice—Catholic and Evangelical*.
  SPCK 1930.
Brunner, P., (ET) *Worship in the Name of Jesus*. Concordia, London and
  St Louis 1968.
Vajta, V., (ET) *Luther on Worship*. Philadelphia 1958.

REFORMED

Abba, R., *Principles of Christian Worship*. OUP 1960.
von Allmen, J. J., (ET) *Worship—its Theology and Practice*. Lutterworth 1965.
von Allmen, J. J., (ET) *The Lord's Supper*. Lutterworth 1969.
Arndt, E. J. F., *The Font and the Table*. Lutterworth 1967.

Hageman, H. G., *Pulpit and Table*, John Knox, Richmond Va. 1962.
Leenhardt, F. J., *Parole visible*. Neuchâtel 1971.
Thurian, M., (ET) *The Eucharistic Memorial*. 2 vols., Lutterworth 1960-1.

ANGLICAN

Davies, J. G., *The Spirit, the Church and the Sacraments*. Faith Press 1954.
Davies, J. G., *Worship and Mission*. SCM 1966.
Davies, J. G., *Every Day God*. SCM 1973.
Dillistone, F. W., *Christianity and Symbolism*. Collins 1955.
Mascall, E. L., *Corpus Christi*. 2nd edn Longmans 1965.
Quick, O. C., *The Christian Sacraments*. Nisbet 1927.
Underhill, E., *Worship*. Nisbet 1936.

METHODIST

Kay, J. A., *The Nature of Christian Worship*, Epworth 1953.
Ryder Smith, C., *The Sacramental Society*. Epworth 1927.
Wainwright, G., *Eucharist and Eschatology*. Epworth 1971.
White, J. F., *The Worldliness of Worship*. OUP New York 1967.

BAPTIST

Clark, N., *An Approach to the Theology of the Sacraments*. SCM 1956.
Clark, N., *Call to Worship*. SCM 1960.

UNITED

Garrett, T. S. (CSI), *Christian Worship*. 2nd edn OUP 1963.
Hahn, W., (ET) *Worship and Congregation*. Lutterworth 1963.

ECUMENICAL

Report on Worship presented to the Fourth World Conference on Faith and Order, Montreal 1963, WCC Faith and Order Paper no. 39.
One Baptism, One Eucharist, and a Mutually Recognized Ministry, WCC Faith and Order Paper no. 73 (1975).
Wainwright, G., 'The Eucharist as an ecumenical sacrament of reconciliation and renewal' in *SL* 11 (1976), pp. 1-18.
Wainwright, G., 'Recent thinking on Christian beliefs: Baptism and the Eucharist' in *Expository Times*, 88 (1976-7), pp. 132-7.

THEOLOGY OF PREACHING

von Allmen, J. J., (ET) *Preaching and Congregation*. SCM 1962.
Botte, B., *et al.*, *La parole dans la liturgie*. Paris 1970.
Browne, R. E. C., *The Ministry of the Word*. 2nd edn SCM 1976.
Fuller, R. H., *What is Liturgical Preaching?* SCM 1957.
Keir, T. H., *The Word in Worship*. OUP 1962.
Knox, J., *The Integrity of Preaching*. Abingdon/Epworth 1957.

Milner, P., (ed.), *The Ministry of the Word*. Burns and Oates 1967.
Ott, H., (ET) *Theology and Preaching*. Lutterworth 1965.

Several approaches to the subject of worship are possible. It can be regarded as a branch of *historical* studies and there is a long tradition of so treating it in England. The results can provide the raw material of theology. Or you can adopt what is an *ethical* rather than a religious approach: God is the supreme being, the creator, to whom we *owe* a debt of homage, praise, adoration, thanksgiving, etc.; but since, in the phrase of Aristotle, man is a social animal, he does this and needs to do this communally; hence public worship. Then there are the immensely important findings of the *anthropologists*, the value and true significance of which were obscured by an imperfect philosophy. Progress was made by the students of comparative religion (and worship) when they adapted to their purpose the methods of phenomenology (R. Otto, G. van der Leeuw, Mircea Eliade).[1]

One of the results of these studies is that worship is seen to have a value and significance of its own that cannot be explained or explained away as superstition or magic or the expression of fear. Worship is a *religious* phenomenon, a reaching out *through* the fear that always accompanies the sacred to the *mysterium* conceived as *tremendum* but also *fascinans*, because behind it and in it there is an intuition of the Transcendent.[2] But if in this sense worship is profoundly religious it is also profoundly human. One of the most constant features of human history is the ritualization of the great events of human life, birth, marriage, and death. But it is important to understand that this ritualization was not a sacralization of these events. Primitive man regarded the whole of life as sacred.[3] The sacred and the rite are not imposed on the profane and the 'natural'. Rather, the great events of life were regarded as in some sense mysterious, not wholly under the control of man, and the rite is witness to man's need to refer them to a higher power on which he felt dependent. But these events were important at the purely human level. Birth meant entrance into the life of the tribe, clan, or community. Marriage, often surrounded by elaborate customs and laws, was of peculiar importance. It was necessary for the continuance of the community and must therefore be controlled in one way or another. The rites of marriage, the giving

---

[1] See *ODCC* s.v. 'Phenomenology' (p. 1078): 'Acc. to Husserl phenomenology is a descriptive science concerned with the discovery and analysis of essences and essential meanings' but which excludes metaphysical questions. Cf. also L. Bouyer, *Rite and Man*, pp. 21–30.
[2] See Otto, *The Idea of the Holy*, and L. Bouyer, *Rite and Man*, p. 26.
[3] See L. Bouyer, *Rite and Man*.

away of the bride and the sealing of the contract by gifts, have survived into modern times. Death was the ultimate mystery, a passage into the unknown or into a 'known' that was fraught with peril, and from the earliest times it was an event always accompanied by ritual. Rite, then, which has been described as corresponding 'to a basic human need'[1] is embedded in the human situation, but at the same time reaches out beyond it.

But rite also enabled man to relate to the community of which he was part[2] and all primitive worship was communal worship. In this context perhaps the sacred meal was of even greater importance than the 'rites of passage'. The meal is at the heart of human living. By it man lives, and in primitive societies he had to provide the materials of the meal from his very livelihood, the results of his hunting or growing. This meal was at once the expression of the sacredness of life and the expression of the realization that the community depended on the sources of life: 'It is in the sacred meal that man sees the sacredness of life, of his own life, and as a result apprehends himself as being dependent upon one who is almighty and all good, or, to express it more accurately, upon the singular and superabundant fruitfulness of the divinity. To recognize the sacredness of a meal as being the highest form of human activity is to recognize man's total dependence, both for his creation and continued existence, upon a God who is at the same time apprehended as the one who possesses the fulness of life.'[3]

Worship, then, can be seen as at once reaching out to the Transcendent and as embedded in human life. By the sacred meal especially it was the means by which the community expressed its corporate life, which it saw as essentially dependent on the divine, however that may have been conceived. A further quality is that it engaged the whole being of man. Actions, gestures, symbols expressive of a reality they could but dimly grasp, song, and dance were the means he felt necessary to express his worship. Unlike modern industrialized man he did not see the need for a rational system of thought which would justify his actions. He went to meet what he conceived to be reality with the whole of his being, and if reality was to be glimpsed through symbolic gestures, that is the way he would have it. It was in accordance with his nature. In any case he was in touch, or wished to be in touch, with a reality that went beyond the values of this world and that could best be apprehended by poetry (*poiesis*) and drama, a *dromenon*, an action in which he was involved.

[1] David Martin, in R. Grainger, p. ix.
[2] David Martin, op. cit., pp. ix–xi.
[3] L. Bouyer, *Rite and Man*, p. 84.

6

At the heart of the *dromenon*, the ritual action, was the *myth*, though whether the myth came before the rite or, as seems more probable,[1] the rite came before the myth, is a question that does not concern us here. The myth was a sacred narrative, whether true or fictional, which gave an account of, or 'explained', the origins of human life or of the community. The events had taken place in a kind of timeless time (*in illo tempore*),[2] and since they 'explained' how the community came to be, it was vital to keep in touch with them if the community was to retain its cohesion. Hence the, usually annual, re-enactment of the myth, for which ritual, with fixed patterns allowing of repetition, was the predestined instrument. The story was retold, though the word-element seems to have been small, and the actions were re-enacted as if for the first time. The past event was in a way made present, so that the community could come into contact with it and restore its life.[3] Finally, in the more primitive religions the whole community acted out the sacred drama. It was an essentially communal thing.

All this may seem a far cry from Christian worship, but Christian worship does not deny the values to be found in more primitive kinds of worship. It purifies them, puts them into an entirely new context, and enhances them.

CHRISTIAN WORSHIP

Because it is God who always takes the initiative, Christian worship is best discussed in the terms of *response*. In worship man is responding to God and this is true of the whole of the liturgy, whether it be praise, thanksgiving, supplication, or repentance, whether it be Eucharist or baptism, or liturgical prayer or the celebration of the Church's year. If this is so, worship must be seen in the context of saving history, which is the record of the divine initiative.

For our purposes here it is necessary to set out the extent of the history of salvation and to suggest its meaning. Conventionally it begins with the calling of Abraham, 'our father in faith'; though the liturgy includes in its scope the creation epic of Gen. 1 and 2, and like 1 Peter sees the story

---

[1] See L. Bouyer, *Rite and Man*.

[2] See Mircea Eliade, *Myths, Dreams and Mysteries* (ET Collins Fontana 1968), pp. 30–1.

[3] For a more extended treatment, see not only the various works of Mircea Eliade but also *The Mysteries*, being the *Eranos* Yearbooks, 1936, 1939, 1940–1, 1942, 1944, ed. Joseph Campbell (Routledge and Kegan Paul 1955). The various matters are frequently related to Christian worship in this volume: e.g. Hugo Rahner, 'The Christian Mystery and the Pagan'.

of Noah as relevant to saving history (baptism). The whole of OT history in its main vicissitudes and in a variety of ways is seen as the preparation for the coming of the Messiah. He and his redeeming work of passion, death, and resurrection are the culmination of saving history, which is carried forward, by the operation of the Holy Spirit, in the Church, which awaits the *eschaton*, the summing up of all things in Christ at the end. This pattern underlies the whole of the Christian liturgy. There is the proclamation of God's word in the OT lessons, which prepare the way for the *kerygma* of the NT lessons, culminating in the reading of the gospel. The Eucharist is set in the context of the passover festival and of the making of the covenant in the desert. The paschal mystery of Christ's passion, death, and resurrection is the very heart of the Eucharist, which by *anamnesis* recalls it and makes its power present to the people here and now. In its celebration and in that of the other sacraments the Church looks on to and reaches out to the fulfilment of all things in Christ. The liturgical year from Advent to Pentecost follows the same course.

But the history of salvation is not to be seen as a series of disparate events or as the mere recording of what once happened. It is the record of God's self-disclosure, made in and through the events, the disclosure of a God who gives himself. This is the deepest meaning of salvation-history. The whole record can be seen as the self-giving of God, who takes the initiative, who approaches mankind to bring men nearer to himself, to make them his own people, and by covenant, which is the expression of his love,[1] to bind them to himself. In this perspective Abraham is a figure of crucial importance. God called him to make him the father of many peoples; he responded with faith and in that faith entered upon an unknown destiny (cf. Heb. 11.8). It was this response of faith that made him pleasing to God (righteous) and on account of it that God made covenant with him (Gen. 17.19; cf. 22.17; Rom. 4.11). The same was true of all the great figures of the OT (Heb. 11.11–40). It was by faith that Moses accepted his vocation to become the leader of his people, it was by faith that he led them out of Egypt, it was by faith that he kept the passover, and above all it was by faith that he responded to the God who revealed to him that he is the God who acts, the God who saves.

The story can be briefly continued. God showed his love for his people in the saving events of the passover, in the rescue from Egypt, in the passage through the Red Sea, but above all in the covenant, when the people bound themselves to God who is ever faithful to his promises. So close was this union intended to be that the later writers of the OT could call the covenant the marriage-union or even the love-match between

[1] *Ḥesed* = mercy = (in most modern translations) love.

8

God and his people, thus foreshadowing the Pauline and Johannine teaching on the Church as the bride of Christ (Eph. 5.22–32 and Rev. 21.1, 2). The role of the prophets was to recall to the people God's faithful love, shown to them in the Exodus events which for them spelt 'salvation', and to renew the response of faith of the people. As we know, all was in vain. The response of faith that God sought for, a response that would result in total commitment, was refused and it looked as if the divine purpose of salvation was frustrated.

Then in the appointed time God sent his Son, 'born of a woman, born under the law, to redeem the subjects of the Law' (Gal. 4.4). God had looked for the response of faith from his people, for their Yes to his saving love. They were unable to give it, but Jesus, the second Adam, gave that radical assent to his Father's saving will: 'In him it is always Yes. For all the promises of God find their Yes in him. That is why we utter Amen through him, to the glory of God'.[1] The response of Jesus Christ is the correlative of the 'faithful love' of his Father, or in other words the whole meaning and intent of his life is to do the will of the Father who sent him. But the radical change for the Christian is that now he is able to make the response of faith, to say Yes to God in and through the response of Christ, whose Yes we endorse with Amen 'to the glory of God'. Here we come very close to a definition of worship, for the glorifying of God, the response in faith which issues into praise, thanksgiving, and supplication is exactly what we are doing in worship. This response is also prompted by the Holy Spirit (Rom. 8.27), so that through Christ in the Spirit we respond to the Father's love. This is the ground-pattern of all Christian worship.

In the OT, as we have seen, God approached man in event and word, the word usually coming after the event to unfold its meaning. The word of God is proclaimed in the Law, it is heard in the institution of the covenant, above all it is proclaimed by the prophets who recall to the people the primordial events by which they were made God's people, and who, by so doing, attempt to deepen the people's understanding of these events so that they may turn or turn back to the God who has made himself known to them. But coming through all the words is God's word, calling, inviting, urging the people to respond to him with the word of faith, to commit themselves totally to himself. They respond to the Law by trying to keep it, they respond with a word of obedience at the institution of the covenant (Exod. 24.6–8), they respond with praise, blessing, and supplication in the psalms that were sung to accompany the

---

[1] 2 Cor. 1.19, 20 (RSV). Cf. JB, ibid. 'However many the promises God made, the Yes to them all is in him'.

sacrifices of the Temple and the service of the word in the synagogue. To God's inviting word, they responded with the words that his prophets and writers put on their lips. Both in the Old Testament and the New, words play a peculiarly important role (in contrast to primitive worship where the action is dominant and the word seems to have little role at all), first because faith comes by hearing—the word must be proclaimed—and secondly because response in words is the specifically human way by which man makes known to himself and to others that he has received the word. It has been said that 'faith itself is prayer, the basic form of prayer',[1] a statement that is equally significant when it is reversed: 'prayer is uttered faith'.

But though the word of God was never wanting to the people of the OT,[2] they were unable to make an adequate response of faith. Something more and, we may say, something different was needed. When the Son of God became man, when the transcendent God involved himself in the human predicament, there took place a self-communication that resulted in an 'enfleshment', 'the Word became flesh' (Jn. 1.14), and, if the term may be used, the 'religion' that Christ brought into the world was, by the very exigencies of the case, an 'enfleshed' religion, or, in other words, a sacramental religion.[3] In the first place, Christ *embodied* the supreme and necessary response or Yes to his Father: 'in him it is always Yes'. Because of this, man can now make his response of faith in word and sacrament, and this is what he is doing in the liturgies, however various, of the Christian Church.

But if the word is indispensable, sacrament is of unique importance. Man is not just a reasoning mind, much less a mass of emotion. He is a body-soul creature or, as it has been said, 'Man is not a spirit lodged in a body, he is a being in which the body is consubstantially united to the spirit.'[4] Man is a unity; you can indeed mentally distinguish in him body and soul, but when he acts, he acts in the wholeness of his personality. He lays hold of the faith with the whole of his being, assisted by revelation and institutions like the family and the Church. When in worship he responds to God in faith, in praise and thanksgiving as well as with love, he does so with his whole being and feels the need to express his worship, his out-going from self to God, in words and song and gesture. If then it is true that man approaches God human-wise, it is also true that God has

---

[1] *The Common Catechism* (ET Search Press 1975), p. 357.

[2] Except perhaps in the last 150 years.

[3] See the present writer's *Christian Celebration: The Mass* (G. Chapman 1971), p. 7.

[4] M. D. Chenu, 'Anthropologie de la liturgie', in *La Liturgie après Vatican II* (Paris 1967), p. 161.

approached man in a human manner, giving himself in his incarnate Son through whom we know him ('Philip, he that has seen me has seen the Father') and are able to give ourselves to him. That is why the Christian religion and the worship that is its expression is essentially 'incarnational' or, what comes to much the same thing, sacramental. But we must add immediately, this is not to the detriment of the word, for word and sacrament are inseparably united and man's worship is his embodied response to God.

Through the centuries of the OT God was offering his love to the people but they did not 'know' him, he did not reveal his inner nature. Jesus came as the revelation of the Father (Mt. 11.25–27). The mystery of God, hidden for ages and generations, is now made manifest (Col. 1.26), and the essence of that mystery is that God is love (1 Jn. 4.8). This Jesus made plain by his life, his words and his passion, death, and resurrection. That is why he has been called 'the sacrament' of the Father,[1] the showing forth of the Father and the revelation of his saving purpose, adumbrated throughout the ages but now made known in Jesus Christ.

But Jesus is not only the revelation of the Father, he is in himself the communication of the Father's love, the primary and supreme gift of God to men. Christ makes God present to men with all his redeeming power and love and this he did principally in his passion, death, and resurrection. In the terminology of St Paul, Christ is the mystery (*musterion*)[2] 'which is in (*en*) you, the hope of your glory' (Col. 1.27). Christ, then, makes effective among men the self-giving of God, who calls and urges them to respond to him in self-giving of faith and love through the word and sacrament of the liturgy. In the dialogue that is set up, in the exchange that takes place, we meet God and are able to enter into union with him; which is the end-purpose of all worship.[3]

The culmination, however, of God's self-revelation and self-giving in Christ was the passion, death, and resurrection, to which we must add, as the liturgies do, his ascension into heaven, the apparent end of the Lord's earthly work of redemption. All this has been called the paschal mystery,[4] and the term is useful as putting Christ's redeeming work in the context of the passover. The passover of Christ fulfilled and transcended the

---

[1] Vatican II, *Constitution on the Church*, n. 2, though the term is not used here; and cf. E. Schillebeeckx, *Christ the Sacrament*.

[2] The Vulgate regularly translates the word by *sacramentum*.

[3] *Christian Celebration: The Mass*, pp. 7, 8.

[4] Cf. *Constitution on the Liturgy* (*CL*), 5: 'He [Christ] achieved his task principally by the *paschal mystery* of his blessed passion, resurrection from the dead and the glorious ascension whereby "dying he destroyed our death and rising he restored our life"' (the quotation is from the Easter Preface of the Roman rite).

Jewish Passover. It is in the passover context[1] that the Eucharist was instituted, thus indicating that it is through the Eucharist that the passover of Christ, his redeeming work, is made available to men. It is of the passover of Christ that the Eucharist is the *anamnesis* or *memoria*.[2] Just as the paschal mystery was the culmination of Christ's redeeming work, so the Eucharist becomes the culmination and centre of Christian worship.

If that sufficiently explains the use of the word 'paschal', 'mystery' also deserves attention. It can be readily agreed that in the NT 'mystery' is not a cultic term and most modern exegetes do not see it as a borrowing from the mystery religions (see p. 54). Nonetheless it has a long history in liturgy, especially in the Roman liturgy but also in the Eastern, and indeed it marks a point of convergence between them.[3] Keeping to purely NT sources we can see that the mystery exists on three levels:

(1) There is the mystery that is God 'dwelling in light inaccessible' (1 Tim. 6.16) and in a plenitude of love that is always giving itself, always being communicated from Father to Son and Holy Spirit and back again. This love God freely communicated outside himself first in creation and then in the redemption so that all could share in it.

(2) The mystery, as we have seen, exists in the historical order. As we read in 1 Tim. 3.16, Christ is the mystery of God:

Great indeed, we confess, is the mystery of our religion (*eusebeias*):
He (*hos*) was manifested (*ephanerothe*) in the flesh,
vindicated in the Spirit,[4]
seen by angels,
preached among the nations,
believed on in the world,
taken up in glory.

Here Christ is called the mystery of 'our worshipful attitude'[5] towards God, and a summary content of the mystery is given in the lines that follow.

Mystery here evidently means event, in the terms of Eliade the primordial event, namely Christ's redeeming work by which the Church

---

[1] This statement is not meant to prejudge the question whether or not the Last Supper was a passover meal. See pp. 160–2.

[2] Cf. Lk. 22.19 (longer reading); 1 Cor. 11.24, 25.

[3] See for instance the introduction by G. Florovsky to *The Festal Menaion*, ET Mother Mary and Archimandrite Kallistos Ware (Faber 1969).

[4] RSV: 'vindicated': *aliter* 'justified', and cf. JB 'attested'.

[5] *Eusebeia*, or 'piety' in the older and deeper sense, meant 'dutifulness with love' and of course it extended to living but then so does worship. Cf. Rom. 12.1.

came into existence. It looked back to the past which it interpreted and on to the future when God's plan will have been fully worked out and revealed and all things will be renewed in Christ, who 'was taken up in glory', the firstborn from the dead (Col. 1.18).

(3) The third level at which the mystery exists is the liturgy. It is concerned with past events, the saving work of Christ, but it is not concerned with them *as past*. It seeks to bring about an encounter between the worshippers and the saving mystery. If an event is to be experienced, it has to be experienced *as present*. As Dom Odo Casel liked to say (and apparently Kierkegaard before him), Christ has to become man's contemporary. This is perhaps best expressed by Leo the Great, who in a sermon on the Ascension said: *Quod...redemptoris nostri conspicuum fuit, in sacramenta transivit* (what our Redeemer did visibly has passed over into the sacraments).[1] He is considering how, after the forty days of Christ's resurrection-life, he was lifted up to remain at the right hand of his Father until he should come again. *Now* all that he did in his earthly life is to be found in the *sacraments*, the liturgy that he and his hearers were celebrating.[2]

Let us take two other examples from the Roman liturgy if only because the word 'mystery' is used.[3] An ancient prayer for Holy Week asks that what we are doing *in mysterio* we may lay hold of in reality. The second is a collect for Good Friday, when the major part of the service consists of words (OT, a Pauline epistle and the singing of the passion according to St John). There is no Eucharist, simply the giving of Holy Communion from the reserved sacrament, and after it we pray: 'Almighty and merciful God, you have *renewed us by the blessed passion and death of your Christ*; preserve in us *the work of your redemption* (*operis misericordiae*) that by our partaking of this *mystery* we may always live devoted to your service'. These texts and a hundred others that could be cited show the Church's conviction that when Christians celebrate the liturgy they encounter Christ in his passion, death, and resurrection and are renewed by it.

What then is the particular significance of the use of 'mystery' in this third sense? First, it is a link between the past and the present, or rather it looks to the past to recover the power of the primordial event and makes

---

[1] Sermo 74, *De Ascens.* (PL 54.398).

[2] This is not to the detriment of the word, wherein also we find Christ, and in the time of Leo (died 461) there were three lessons in the Eucharist. In any case, he was engaged in the ministry of preaching.

[3] Leo also made much use of the word *mysterium*, particularly in his sermons on the liturgical year (See M. B. de Soos, *Le mystère liturgique d'après Saint Léon le Grand*, LQF, Heft 34 (Münster 1958)).

its power present in the here and now so that the worshipper can encounter the redeeming Christ. What gives it a particular quality is that it does this through symbols which manifest the presence and activity of Christ, and because they are the sacraments to which he committed himself; he through them can convey the saving power of his passion and resurrection.[1] The liturgical mystery can be seen as *l'entre deux mondes*, and that is part of the difficulty in understanding it. It is not simply an historical event (though its celebration takes place in time), and it certainly does not seek to reproduce historical events. It will have nothing to do with the allegorizing of the writers of the ninth and subsequent centuries, least of all with John Beleth and William Durandus for whom the Eucharist became a sacred drama where the physical events of the passion were thought to be discernible in the rite. Nor is it sufficient to say that the mystery is a way of remembering the past, as if one were recalling the Diamond Jubilee of Queen Victoria. By the liturgical mystery we are *actualizing* the past event, making it present so that the saving power of Christ can be made available to the worshipper in the here and now.

The purpose of this view of the liturgy is at once to preserve the realism of the liturgical action (it is not *mere* remembering) and to give it a depth that goes beyond merely verbal or psychological reactions. If it is to be defined, it must be said to be a sacramental-symbolic action in the strong sense of the word 'symbolic'. It is an action that uses signs, themselves pregnant with reality, and the principal symbols of the liturgy are those chosen by Christ himself: water and bread and wine. Each of these has its own natural significance, but when they are taken up into the liturgy they acquire a deeper significance and indeed a different purpose. Bread sustains life and wine does likewise, but when they are used in the Eucharist they become symbols, pregnant symbols, of Christ and the life he offers us. But in the Christian liturgy they are effectual symbols only because they exist by the ordinance of Christ, derive from him and are totally dependent on him.

A further advantage of seeing the liturgy in this way is that it meets the needs of man. 'Man, in the whole richness of his being, wishes to meet God, desires that God should be real and present to him. He achieves this in the first instance by faith but it is in the symbolic-liturgical action that faith is expressed and in a telling way concretized. The Church in the celebration of the liturgy is declaring its faith that Christ the Redeemer is present and active, and man through his involvement in the celebration

---

[1] All the foregoing is based on *Christian Celebration: The Mass*, pp. 27–8 and *The Church's Worship*, pp. 24–6.

14

can make encounter with the living God who comes to him in symbol, sacrament, in a word *in mysterio'*. Man can respond with the whole of his being, with mind and body, with his senses, in word and song and movement.

'Perhaps the whole matter of the liturgical mystery can best be expressed by saying that it is the concrete (symbolic) and manifold expression of God's presence and action in Christ among his people now.'[1]

The reader should be warned that not everyone is agreed about the above mystery-theory of the liturgy. There are those who dislike the associations of the word 'mystery'; it seems to suggest mystery religions (see pp. 54–5). It came into use for the liturgy in the fourth century when the mystery religions were already dying. Others object to the mystery-theory of Dom Odo Casel (see bibliography), who, it is alleged, was unduly influenced by his studies on the mystery religions of the Greco-Roman empire. Theologians also have difficulties in accepting his particular view of the 'presence' of Christ's mysteries in the liturgy. For the very lengthy controversy see Theodore Filthaut, Fr. trans. *La théologie des mystères. Exposé de la controverse*, Desclée 1954. I have tried to be neutral and have, as I believe, conveyed the teaching found in the Vatican II *Constitution on the Liturgy*, especially 2, 5 and cf. 102: the celebration of the liturgical year makes present 'in some way' the mysteries of Christ. It was Dom Casel's contention that in his mystery-presence theory he in no way wished to say that the past *historical* events were made present. What he meant was that the *reality* of those events was made present by the liturgy which is so much more than a mere 'remembering'. The Christian has to come into contact with the redeeming Christ if he is to enter into, or be 'plunged into' (an expression Casel liked to use) the paschal mystery. For him the liturgy was not just a means of 'conveying' grace to the participant: it was the place (or moment) where the Christian could meet Christ in the fulness of his redeeming activity. According to him, it is the genius of the liturgy regarded as mystery-sacrament-symbol that it can do this. By its very nature it transcends time and can therefore effect the encounter with Christ who is made present, or perhaps better, who makes himself present. There is no question of the *repetition* of past events—Christ died and rose again once for all—and Casel liked to say that the only thing that was in the power of the Church was to initiate the celebration of the rite.

---

[1] The foregoing two paragraphs are from *Christian Celebration: The Mass*, p. 29, slightly revised.

But because Christ is the head of the Church and committed himself to the liturgy he inaugurated, in response to the Church he always makes himself present in the liturgy. M. de la Taille (*Mysterium Fidei*, 1921) said much the same thing in reference to the Eucharist: 'The *newness* of the Mass-sacrifice is to be found only in the part of the Church' (p. 296), and all the Church can do is to celebrate the rite.

The core of Casel's theory is not new, though he gave a dynamism to liturgical celebration that had been wanting. St Thomas Aquinas spoke of the Eucharist as a *re-praesentatio* of the passion and the Council of Trent used the term *repraesentatur*, which, I think, should be translated as 'actualize'. CL uses the term 'perpetuate'—the Church perpetuates what Christ did at the Supper and on the cross—which is to be seen as a neutral term, leaving the options open. But it also uses the term *memoria*: 'Christ left to his Church a *memorial* of his death and resurrection' (47); and this I think must be regarded as the key word. *Anamnesis*, it is widely maintained nowadays, means much more than just remembering a past event: it recalls into the present the reality of a past event. This is the sense of the term in the four eucharistic prayers of the Roman rite and also, I take it, of the *anamnesis* prayer of the C of E's Series 2 and 3. All told, when we are talking about the liturgy as mystery making present the reality of the past events of Christ's redeeming work, we are talking about *anamnesis*. The reader can find further discussion of the term *anamnesis* elsewhere in the book, though he will observe that the authors are not unanimous in their interpretation (pp. 25, 49, 154, 205).

The liturgy, then, is the making present in word, symbol and sacrament of the paschal mystery of Christ so that through its celebration the men and women of today may make a saving encounter with God. However, if we leave the matter there, we shall have excluded a whole dimension of saving history as well as of Christian worship. If the Pentecost-event has never formed part of the anamnesis of the Eucharist, the giving of the Spirit is always in view. In the liturgical context, the ascension (which *has* normally been one of the events mentioned in the anamnesis) can be seen as the bridge between the paschal mystery of Christ and the giving of the Spirit. This is based on the NT perspective: Christ returns to his Father that he may send upon his Church the Spirit he promised (Acts 2.33, etc.). But the presence of the Spirit in the liturgical celebration is not to be seen simply in the terms of the epiclesis, as if he comes into the action only at a certain point. The liturgy is always celebrated in the power of the Holy Spirit.[1] Just as prayer is made in the Spirit (Rom. 8.26–7), so is

[1] See Boris Bobrinskoy in *LMD* 121 (1975), p. 73.

the celebration of the liturgy. If it looks *back* to Christ in his redeeming work, it looks to Christ as he now is, filled with the Spirit, and Lord.

His presence in the Eucharist can be traced in all its great phases. The people are called and become the *oikos pneumatikos*, the 'spiritual house', or perhaps the 'house of the Spirit', and here they are to offer *pneumatikas thusias*, 'spiritual sacrifices', which are acceptable because they are offered through Jesus Christ (1 Pet. 2.5–9). He is present in the prayers which so often end with the phrase 'in the unity of the Holy Spirit', a reminder at least that the Spirit is prompting the prayer of the community. He is present in the lessons which are not so much a giving of information as the proclamation of God's word, which is always done in the Spirit (cf. Lk. 4.18). He is present in the action of the Eucharist, as is made plain by the twofold invocations of the Spirit in the eucharistic prayers II, III and IV of the Roman rite and in the thanksgiving prayer of Series 3 in the C of E. He is present in the moment of holy communion when, as the oldest form of epiclesis makes clear,[1] he is invoked to make the communion fruitful.[2]

When the full implications of the ascension are realized, its mention in the anamnesis suggests another dimension of the liturgy. He is seated at the right hand of the Father, 'a minister (*leitourgos*) in the sanctuary', a high priest and forerunner on our behalf (Heb. 8.2; 6.20) where he is ever living to make intercession for us (Heb. 7.25). However mysterious it may be, the teaching of the Letter to the Hebrews is that Christ continues his priestly role, mediator of a better covenant (Heb. 8.6), and that through him and through his action mankind can achieve salvation. The whole central section of Hebrews (3—10) is so much about the heavenly sacrifice of Christ that one is tempted to think that for the writer it was the one that matters above all. But here, as in Revelation (5.6; 19.9; 21; 22), the writer is showing the awareness of the primitive Church that the earthly liturgy is but the counterpart of the heavenly and that it is from the latter that it receives all its saving power. This sense of the presence of the heavenly sacrifice has always been particularly strong in the Byzantine liturgy, so much so that it has influenced the design of the Byzantine church. But it has never been lacking in the Roman rite, witness the prayer after the

---

1 The eucharistic prayer of the *Apostolic Tradition* (see pp. 173–4, 247), now adapted to the Roman rite.

2 See the present writer's article in *Life and Worship*, 176 (1973), pp. 12–20. Also appearing in *Pastoral Liturgy: a Symposium*, ed. H. E. Winstone (Collins 1975). Cf. also the remarks of B. Bobrinskoy, art. cit., p. 74: 'This prayer [the Lord's Prayer] is indeed said by us in Jesus Christ by the Holy Spirit. But the fruit of the prayer of Christ, of his heavenly and permanent epiclesis, is the coming of the Holy Spirit. Christian prayer (and the liturgy is always prayer) is then the prayer of Christ in the Church, not only by the Spirit and in the Spirit but for (the coming of) the Spirit.'

consecration which asks that God's angel may take the sacrifice to the altar in heaven (i.e. Christ; cf. Heb. 13.10: 'We have an altar'; see p. 192), that as the worshippers receive 'from this altar' (the one in church), they may be 'filled with every grace and blessing'. In this perspective it should not be surprising that the Roman, the Byzantine, and no doubt other liturgies celebrate the Eucharist in the company of St Mary and the other saints. It is a practice which reveals that the Church believes it is 'in communion'[1] with the members of the heavenly Church.

If the demythologizers will allow us to say that the liturgy looks up, it is also true that the liturgy looks on to the future, the *eschaton*. Almost all eucharistic prayers in their anamneses 'look forward to the coming of the Lord in glory', and the season of Advent is strongly marked by the same theme. It is the theme too of the acclamation to be found in the Roman rite and in Series 3: 'Christ has died, Christ is risen, Christ will come again'; or, as it is sometimes expressed, 'Christ has come, Christ comes, and Christ will come again'. In the Christian liturgy, then, we have an anticipation of the Second Coming; the reality of that event is being slowly and gradually achieved by the celebration of the Eucharist, as well as by the whole action of the Church. The Church, in other words, has transferred to its liturgy the teaching of the parables of the banquet which foreshadow the heavenly banquet of the Book of Revelation. This is marked in the current Roman liturgy by the phrase that is spoken immediately before holy communion: 'Happy are those who are called to his supper'.[2]

To come closer to the eucharistic texts of the NT, Mark 14.25 (and par.) and 1 Cor. 11.26, if, as I believe,[3] they refer to the 'time of the Church', which throughout the ages celebrates the eschatological banquet, they also refer to the final summing up of all things in Christ. This is particularly clear from 1 Corinthians: 'For as often as you eat this bread and drink this cup, you proclaim the Lord's death until he comes'. Perhaps it would not be too much to say that the celebration of the Eucharist 'realizes' or begins to realize what is to happen in its fulness at the *eschaton*.[4]

Looking back from the point at which we have arrived, it is possible to see that the Christian liturgy is patterned on the history of salvation. There is the original initiative of God, who throughout the ages offers

---

[1] Cf. *Communicantes* of the Roman Canon.

[2] Rev. 19.9. It is a pity that the marriage symbol was not kept: 'Blessed are those who are invited to the marriage supper of the Lamb'.

[3] See Max Thurian, *The Eucharistic Memorial*, Part II, pp. 66–7: 'The Church *already* sits at table with Christ to eat and drink with him....'

[4] See Geoffrey Wainwright, *Eucharist and Eschatology* (Epworth 1971).

man his love. The history is carried forward by the redeeming events of Christ the Son of God, who on the cross gives himself totally to his Father and for the salvation of mankind. He ascends to the Father and sends upon his Church the Holy Spirit so that his *ecclesia* may continue in time and space and by the power of the Holy Spirit his redeeming work. The Church looks on to the consummation of all things when Christ will hand all things to his Father so that he may be all in all things (1 Cor. 15.28). To the Father through the Son and in the Holy Spirit, is the underlying pattern of the history of salvation. So is it too of the liturgy. In the eucharistic prayer we give praise and thanksgiving to the Father through the Son, whose redeeming acts are recalled, and in the Holy Spirit, who is invoked on the offering (*epiclesis*). The doxology at the end of the prayer expresses the whole truth succinctly but explicitly. Almost all collects begin with an ascription of praise to the Father, make petition through the Son and conclude with a mention of the Holy Spirit.[1] The phrase serves to remind us that the aim of the whole liturgy is entrance into communion with God, a communion in the divine life and love that constitute the Trinity.[2]

THE CHURCH THE WORSHIPPING COMMUNITY

In the liturgy there is a vertical movement, the out-going of man to God. But there is also a horizontal movement. Liturgy is celebrated *with* others and the relationships between the members of the worshipping community are of the highest importance. *Private* acts of *public* worship are a contradiction in terms, as a statement in *CL* suggests: 'Liturgical services are not private functions but are celebrations of the Church, which is the sacrament of unity' (26). At the practical level all liturgical rites are arranged for the participation of the community. Rite, as we have seen, enables people to relate to each other (the kiss, the handshake—both symbolic gestures) and also to the community. One can become part of it or enter more deeply into its life. The sociologists tell us that for true community there must be a face-to-face relationship, and for the Christian this means that the members of the community are *persons* bound together by faith and love. In principle they are already related to

[1] The phrase 'in the unity of the Holy Spirit', regarded by Jungmann as referring to the unity of the Church, is held by Botte to refer to the unity of the three Persons of the Trinity and he is almost certainly right. Cf. for Jungmann (ET) *The Place of Christ in Liturgical Prayer* (G. Chapman 1965), p. 204; and for Botte *LMD* 23 (1950), pp. 49–53.
[2] The difficulty of making the Trinity the direct object of worship can be seen in the unsatisfactory texts of even the revised Roman rite for the feast. It is a late-comer to the liturgical year, eleventh century. Up till that time the older pattern was invariable.

one another. In the worshipping community this relationship is deepened and enhanced—or will be, if the members try to act as a community.

This—and faith and love apart—is the human dimension of community whose values are of course to be found in the Christian worshipping community, though its origin and its essential qualities are to be found in a source outside itself, namely Christ.

Of all the great figures used of the Church,[1] body, mystery, sacrament, the people of God, the last is the most useful to begin with. The people of the OT were called by God, were formed into a people and united to him by a covenant which was the sign of union and the proof of God's abiding love. The covenant, celebrated annually in the passover meal, was the centre of their religious life. It was to a people that God made his self-disclosure and it was from this people that he chose the Messiah who would bring into existence a new people (the 'Israel of God'; Gal. 6.16). To them he revealed himself as the Son of his Father first by word and then by deed. He adumbrated the formation of this new people by the choice of the Twelve (Mt. 10.1–8, par., cf. Rev. 21.12–14), representing the twelve tribes of Israel, and to them he committed the continuation of his word and of the 'liturgy' that he inaugurated. Just as the covenant with all its sacrificial associations was the centre of OT religion, so he made the new covenant in his own blood the centre of the religion of the new people of God. This covenant between God and the people was brought into existence by his sacrifice (Eph. 5.2, etc.) in which he offered himself, as one of the human race, as *head* of the human race, that he might take away the sin of the world and reconcile it to his Father. If the term 'priest' is only implicit in most of the NT writings,[2] it becomes explicit in the Letter to the Hebrews, where Jesus is spoken of as 'high priest after the order of Melchizedek' precisely in the context of his passion (5.7–10), wherein he is mediator of the new covenant (8.1–13).

The Fourth Gospel yields a similar teaching. Jesus is making his passover (13.1, 3), he commits to his disciples his word which is a word of love, he dedicates himself to his self-offering (17.19) to be made the next day, and as he dies he 'hands over' the spirit (*paredoken to pneuma*). This, combined with the piercing of his side whence flowed blood and water (the symbols of the Eucharist and baptism), has been seen from a very early time, perhaps by the writer of the Gospel himself, as the moment when the Church, the people of God and the Spirit-filled body of Christ,

---

[1] Cf. Vatican II, *Constitution on the Church*, nos. 2, 5, 6, 7.

[2] Though see X. Léon-Dufour, ET *A Dictionary of Biblical Theology* (G. Chapman 1973), s.v. 'priesthood'.

was brought into existence.[1] In the words of an ancient collect,[2] 'the wonderful sacrament of the Church' thus came into existence.

By the very condition of its origin this Church is a priestly Church. It is born of Christ, the priest who offers himself in sacrifice. It is to this Church that Christ commits the 'memorial' of his sacrifice and commands his followers to do what he had done until the end of time. The people of the OT were described as 'a kingdom of priests and a holy nation' (Exod. 19.6). Now through the high priest of the new covenant, but only through him, the new Israel of God is made a priestly people who are a spiritual house, a holy priesthood who offer 'spiritual sacrifices acceptable to God through Jesus Christ' (1 Pet. 2.4–9).[3] As we have observed above, the adjective '*pneumatikos*', applied to both the 'house' and the 'sacrifices', suggests that the house is the house of the Spirit and the offering it has to make is made 'in the Spirit'. Since the Church is the Spirit-filled body of Christ, this is completely comprehensible: the Church and its worship correspond with each other. This is how the author of the *Mystagogic Catecheses* in the fourth century saw the Eucharist he was celebrating: 'after the spiritual sacrifice (*ten pneumatiken thusian*), the [act of] unbloody worship, has been accomplished, we invoke God for the peace of the Church, etc.'.[4] Finally, we may note that this priestly people is also a missionary community: they are a chosen race, a royal priesthood, a holy nation, God's own people, who are to declare 'the wonderful deeds of him who called you out of darkness into his marvellous light' (1 Pet. 2.9).

The Pauline teaching on the Church as 'body' emphasizes at once the closeness of the relationship between Christ and the people—they are members, limbs, of the body—and the horizontal relationships between the members of the body (1 Cor. 12.12ff). In other words, perhaps more strongly than before, it is indicated that the priestly people is also a community, the community of Christ with which he has a vital relationship. He is the source of all its life; it is totally dependent on him as the branches of a tree are on its trunk (Jn. 15.1ff). And the relationships of faith and love between its members are in the first instance created by Christ, though they are to be realized and strengthened by

---

1 See B. F. Westcott, *The Gospel of St John* (1898) in loc. 19.30, and for the patristic evidence, Additional Note, pp. 284–6. Cf. also 1 Jn. 5.6.

2 Old Roman rite of the Easter Vigil.

3 Y. Congar in *Le mystère du temple* (Paris 1958), pp. 207–10, has pointed out that the context of this passage is strongly liturgical: v. 2 'neophytes', just baptized; v. 3 the reference to Psalm 33 (34), used from an early date for communion; and even v. 4 'come to him' which Congar says is a liturgical term. Cf. Rev. 1.6; 5.10 for other references to the priestly people: *hiereis kai basileian*.

4 *Myst. Cat.* (attributed to Cyril of Jerusalem), 5.8. See pp. 61–2.

A Theology of Worship

Eucharist, which is the sacramental sign of *koinonia*, of communion, the union of minds and hearts in faith and love. If the Church can be said to 'make' the Eucharist, in a much deeper sense the Eucharist makes the Church. But the depth and richness of the relationship is best seen in Ephesians 5, where Christ is said to be the head of the Church of which he is also Saviour; and this Church is his bride (vv. 25–6), which he brought into existence by the 'fragrant offering and sacrifice' that he offered to his Father (v. 2).[1]

It is this people, then, the priestly people, the body of Christ and the community of Christ, who are the 'subject' of liturgical celebrations. In other words, it is they who celebrate the liturgy, and the form of the liturgy must be of such sort as to make this possible. The Christian liturgy by its nature cannot be the monologue of a single participant. It is the action of a whole community. On the other hand, it is not an unstructured community. Each member, and indeed each group of members (e.g. the choir), has its role to fulfil and all by fulfilling these functions are exercising the priesthood that they share with Christ and his ministers. In the Catholic tradition of the eastern and western Churches, an indispensable part of this structure is the priesthood, which is a ministry, a *diakonia*, of the priesthood of Christ and is in no way opposed to the priesthood of the people but is complementary to it. There is but one priesthood, that of Christ, which the whole Church exists to serve and make actual in the here and now. In the liturgical assembly the ministers of Christ have a special role of leading, of presiding, of preaching and of uniting all in self-offering with Christ.[2] For their part, the people not only act and offer *through* the priest-celebrant, they act and offer *with* him. By virtue of their baptism, they share in the priesthood of Christ and, as we have seen from 1 Pet. 2.4–9, they have their various roles to perform.

But neither they nor the ministerial priesthood act independently. By reason of their relationship to Christ and because *together* they are the

---

[1] A treatment of the bridal theme would draw out the truth that the liturgy is a dialogue between the Bride and the Bridegroom, and this is particularly true of the Divine Office. In the Christian interpretation of the psalms the Church is frequently addressing the *Kyrios* who is also the Bridegroom.

[2] 'Through the proclamation of the gospel, the people of God is called together and assembled so that when all who belong to this people have been sanctified by the Holy Spirit, they can offer themselves as "sacrifice, living, holy, pleasing to God" (Rom. 12.1). Through the ministry of priests, the spiritual sacrifice of the faithful is made perfect in union with the sacrifice of Christ, the sole Mediator' (Vatican II, *Decree on the Ministry and Life of Priests*, 2). For further treatment see *Christian Celebration: the Mass*, pp. 36–7, and David Powers, *Ministers of Christ and his Church* (G. Chapman 1969), chs. 8 and 9.

body of Christ, the whole liturgical action and every liturgical action is also the action of Christ who is head and high priest of the body. The closeness of the union between head and members, and the identity of the action of the Church with that of Christ is best illustrated by the saying, 'When the Church baptizes it is Christ who is baptizing', which is a paraphrase of a statement of Augustine, who said that the Lord baptizes through his ministers.[1] The ultimate subject of the liturgical celebration, then, is neither the ordained ministry nor yet the people, nor indeed both together, but Christ who acts in and through his Church. Obviously his action is invisible, but the people of God, his body, is a visible and structured community and over the whole range of its liturgical action, which, to repeat, consists of both word and sacrament, manifests Christ's presence, shows forth the nature of his activity, which is redemptive, and by his power makes his redeeming work effectual and available to men and women of today. It is for these reasons that the Church is called the 'sacrament of Christ'. Like him it is both visible and invisible and its sole *raison d'être* is to mediate his saving love to mankind.

From Christ, the sacrament of the Father and of his saving purpose, to the Church, which is the sacrament of Christ, and then to the liturgy, which exists to manifest and convey the redeeming love of God, the line is clear. The liturgy then is essentially and by its nature sacramental. This is the order of reality in which it exists. It is neither simply intellectual, addressing itself to disincarnated reason, nor moralistic, exhorting men to do better, though it contains both these elements, but deriving as it does from Christ, who is both divine and human and who is the invisible priest of the visible Church, the liturgy addresses itself to the whole man and seeks to draw him into union with God by means that are consonant with human nature. It addresses a word to him but it *embodies* this word in actions, gestures and symbols; and if 'the supernatural saving reality, veiled in historical events and surrounded by the darkness of mystery, is present to us only in earthly form (*sacramentum*), and demands the revealing word',[2] the gesture or thing (water, bread, wine) forces us to attend to the word, enables us to grasp its import and to appropriate its content. If man cannot live by bread alone, neither can he live by word alone.

---

[1] *In Joann. Ev. Tract.* V.1; PL 35. 1417 and cf. 1419: 'The Lord Jesus Christ did not wish to give his baptism to anyone; not that no one should be baptized with the baptism of the Lord, but that *the Lord himself should always baptize*. So it was that the Lord would *baptize through his ministers* so that those whom the ministers were to baptize, the Lord would baptize.'

[2] Schillebeeckx, 'The Sacraments: An Encounter with God', in *Christianity Divided* (Sheed and Ward 1961), p. 246.

To say that the liturgy is sacramental is to say that it is symbolic, though its symbols are not merely decorative but purposeful.[1] The principal symbols of the liturgy are scriptural, ordained by Christ: the pouring of (or dipping in) water, which signifies death and resurrection in Christ (Rom. 6.3, 4), entrance into the kingdom (Jn. 3.5), and adoption into the family of God (Rom. 8.14, 15; Gal. 4.5, 6); the taking of the bread and wine, the making of the *anamnesis* over them and the eating and drinking of 'the bread of life and the cup of salvation', which refer us to the sacrificial death which we thereby proclaim (1 Cor. 11.25–27; cf. 10.21, 22). The use of anointing, in the Roman, Byzantine, and other eastern liturgies, must be seen against the vast and rich teaching of the Bible if it is to be understood. In the OT, apart from being used to make certain people sacred, it signified abundance of life, and in the NT it is the symbol of the fulness of divine life, whose source is Christ, the Anointed, and which is communicated by his Spirit.[2] In all three cases there is a correlation between the gesture (and the thing) and its natural significance. Water spells life and cleanliness, bread and wine are the nourishment and vital support of human life, and oil signifies richness, abundance, and healing. But the symbol has a certain darkness or opacity, and precisely because of that it arrests the senses, gives pause to the mind, and at the same time refers us to the greater reality of which it is the symbol and to which it would draw us. But the very darkness and indefiniteness of the symbol means that it has a very wide range of significance. Water can and does suggest both life and death—we cannot live without it and yet we can lose our life in it. So the symbol suggests and invites rather than states, and since in the liturgy we are confronted with the mystery of God and of his ways with us, it is a peculiarly appropriate means to lead us to that mystery. But it is also clear that the word has a role of crucial importance. In the phrase of Schillebeeckx, it is first 'the revealing word'; it indicates what is happening. But secondly, it is the defining word, for it shows us that it is this kind of action that is taking place (confirmation and not baptism) and not another. For Augustine the combination of the element with the word constituted the sacrament.[3]

---

[1] Nor are they to be confused with allegory of which we have had more than enough in liturgy in the past.

[2] See *DLW*, the present writer's article 'Unction', pp. 358–60.

[3] *Accedit verbum ad elementum et fit sacramentum. In Joh. Tract.* 80.3; PL 35. 1840. Cf. B. Neunheuser, ET *Baptism and Confirmation* (Burns and Oates 1964), p. 117. For further treatment on symbolism see F. W. Dillistone, *Christianity and Symbolism*, pp. 185ff; for the symbolism of the sacraments: *Christian Celebration: The Sacraments*, ch. 2.

The Church, then, is the worshipping community, the priestly people of God and the body of Christ, which by the ordinance of Christ celebrates the liturgy that he inaugurated. But it is legitimate to ask: where does this Church exist? In recent years there has been a considerable emphasis on the local church. The Church is seen not so much as a vast institution whose model is the empire or a secular undertaking but as the union of churches bound together by a common faith and love. It is a community of this sort that constructs the sacrament-sign of the great Church and, in the sense that it makes present to this gathered community the saving word and work of Christ, brings that Church into existence in the order of action. Or, to put it in another way, the celebration of the liturgy by the local community actualizes the great Church. It is here at this level that the Church is visible, here that it is really in action. This is well expressed by CL (n. 41), which sees the diocese as the local church. It calls the celebration of its liturgy 'the pre-eminent manifestation of the Church', when there is the full active participation of all God's people 'in the same liturgical celebrations, especially in the same Eucharist, in a single prayer at one altar, at which there presides the bishop surrounded by his college of priests and ministers'. Here the Church can be seen for what it really is, uniquely concentrated on the *opus Dei*, which has been entrusted to it and reaching out to the whole community, who by the power of Christ are lifted up in one common act of worship so that they may give praise to God and make an encounter with the living Christ. And when the members of the community seek to live out in their daily lives what they profess in their worship, then they can make the mystery of Christ manifest to others (*CL* 2). Of other groupings the same document says that 'in some manner they represent the visible Church constituted throughout the world'. It is here that the Church is at work, it is here that in fact people hear the Good News of salvation, it is here that they are incorporated into the Church, it is here that they are nourished by the body and blood of Christ so that they may bear witness to him in the world.

Can we come a little closer and see how this happens? To do so it will be useful to return to the theology of the sacrament-mystery-*anamnesis*. Every sacramental and liturgical act is a participation in the paschal mystery of Christ; perhaps this can best be illustrated by the sacraments of initiation, though what is true of them is true of all. Thus in Penance we rise from the death of sin and are restored to new life in the risen Christ who reconciles us with the Father. Marriage is the sacrament-sign of the union between Christ and his Church, a union that was the fruit of his redeeming sacrifice (Eph. 5.2, 25, 26). Christian death is a dying in the Lord that we may share in his resurrection.

25

Baptism is the celebration of Christ's death and resurrection and through it men and women die (symbolically) with him in the waters and they are raised up from the waters to the new life of which the risen Lord is the source (Rom. 6.3–4; Col. 2.12). In the words of Paul they are united to him in his death and they 'will be certainly united with him in a resurrection like his' (Rom. 6.5). Through the celebration of baptism, then, men and women are able to participate in the death and resurrection of Christ. They are able to make the mystery their own and it is their vocation to live by what they have received (vv. 5–11). In a word, by the making of the anamnesis of the death and resurrection of Christ by water and word we can be incorporated into the body of Christ.

If confirmation cannot so easily be seen as a celebration of the paschal mystery, that no doubt is because it is totally dependent on baptism. But, as we observed above, the paschal mystery of Christ issued into the giving of the Spirit to the Church so that it could bear witness to the risen Christ. If confirmation is understood as the establishing of the Holy Spirit in the baptized individual, we can see that it 'confirms' his relationship to Christ and enables him to bear witness to Christ in his passion and resurrection.

When we come to the Eucharist we are confronted with a liturgical action which, perhaps it is not too much to say, is defined by anamnesis. It is the sacrament of anamnesis, and because it is, it is the supreme celebration of the mystery of Christ. But if we are to understand how this is so, we must give some further consideration to anamnesis. It is a term (and a reality) that is found in both the Old and New Testaments, and in its first movement it is a recalling before God by men of the past events of his saving mercy. Through making the memorial of the events we are asking that their saving power may be made present to us here and now. In the Eucharist we are recalling before the Father the saving deeds of his Son; and because we do so according to the command of Christ and because he and his Father are faithful to their covenanted promises, Christ makes himself present in all his redeeming activity. In the words of Max Thurian, the Eucharist 'is not just a liturgical action that makes the Lord present, it is a liturgical action that recalls as a memorial before the Father the unique sacrifice of the Son, and this makes him present in his memorial, in the presentation of his sacrifice before the Father and in his intercession as heavenly High Priest'.[1] Through the celebration of the Eucharist the Christian is able to make a living encounter with the Lord who died and rose again, to join the offering of himself and his life (Rom.

---

[1] (ET) *The Eucharistic Memorial*, Part II, pp. 35–6. Not all scholars agree that this is the meaning of anamnesis in the Bible (see e.g. p. 49); but the theory does not stand or fall by the exegesis of particular texts.

12.1) to that of Christ, who enfolds it in his own and presents it to his Father. Through this encounter and through his reception of Christ in Holy Communion, he is able to enter into and share in the paschal mystery of Christ. He makes or begins to make the passover of the Lord the passover of his own life.

The same principle of anamnesis is applicable, *mutatis mutandis*, outside the strictly sacramental sphere, whether the dominical sacraments be thought of as two, seven, or more. For if all liturgy is ecclesial, *of* the Church, all liturgy is 'Christic', centred upon Christ and done in his name. The liturgical year, as we have seen, looks back to the saving events of the OT, is a recalling and actualizing of the redeeming work of Christ, and looks on to the consummation of all things in him. But no more than the Eucharist is the liturgical year a mere remembering. Through its celebration Christ makes himself present and that presence, it is interesting to note, is largely made through words which may be those of holy scripture or those of the poets who, together with the music that their words have evoked, have enriched our worship throughout the centuries. These patterns of words, music, gesture, and movement, sometimes of great beauty, have formed the setting of the eucharistic action on whose content in one way and another they have thrown light. Together they have manifested the Christ who makes himself present. Likewise, the prayer of the Church, whether it is called the Divine Office or Mattins and Evensong, which are so largely scriptural, recalls the past, speaks through Christ who is present, and constantly looks on to the end. For this we have the promise of Christ who, speaking of prayer, said: 'Where two or three are gathered together in my name, there am I in the midst of them' (Mt. 18.20).

Man's posture before God is one of receptivity. It is because God first gives himself that man can respond in faith and self-gift. Since, as we have seen, worship is primarily response in faith, a response that can only be made in Jesus Christ, who is the definitive Yes to the Father, our worship is grounded in Christ. Through him response can express itself in praise, thanksgiving, repentance, and supplication, and this is to say that all our worship is made through him to the Father in the power of the Holy Spirit. But just as God revealed himself first to the people of the OT, in word and deed, so does he to the new people whom he brought into existence through the Son, the second Adam, the head of the body, the mystery of the Father and of his redeeming love. By his life, teaching, passion, death, and resurrection, he made that love present among men and effective of their redemption. Through him the people, now constituted as the community of Christ, can respond with him in thanksgiving and in the making of the memorial, the anamnesis, of the sacrifice he offered in love to his Father and for the salvation of mankind. One with Christ, as members of his body, a body that is visibly existing in space and time, the Church can make present the reality of his redeeming work to men and women of every succeeding generation. Because Christ has willed that he should be with his Church and because as high priest of the unique sacrifice of salvation he has chosen to unite the Church to himself, it is able to offer itself with him in thanksgiving and supplication. For what it has to handle is the *sacramentum* of Christ's self-offering that makes present to the body the reality of that self-offering. In the words of Augustine: 'Of his self-offering (*oblatio*) Christ willed that the Church's sacrifice should be the daily *sacramentum*, and since she is his body, she learns to offer herself through him'. She begins to become what Christ would have her be: 'In that which she offers, she herself is offered'.[1]

Itself the sacrament of Christ, making him present by word and sacrament, the Church perpetually recalls the saving paschal mystery. To incorporate members, the Church can do no other than through word and water recall and celebrate the paschal mystery of Christ in which they are inserted into his death that they may share in his new life. For it is he who is active through his Church in the sacramental celebration. When men and women are reconciled to the body after sin, it is through the celebration of the passion and resurrection that they are reconciled. When one is healed and strengthened by the anointing of the oil of the sick, it is Christ who is communicating his strength and his compassion to the patient. When the Church is proclaiming the word of God, 'Christ is still proclaiming his gospel' (*CL* 33). When the Church prays, he is present in the midst of them and makes that prayer his own. Thus the sacrament-Church is the perpetual sign of the presence of the redeeming Christ among men and makes available to them the reality of his unfailing love.

Liturgy does not lend itself to definition, but if one is to be attempted it could be stated as follows: it is the communal celebration by the Church, which is Christ's body and in which he with the Holy Spirit is active, of the paschal mystery. Through this celebration, which is by nature sacramental, Christ, the high priest of the community, makes present and available to men and women of today the reality of his salvation.

It may be thought that the latreutic aspect of the liturgy has not been sufficiently emphasized in the foregoing. This suggests a question about the final purpose of liturgy. It has been said that the purpose of liturgy is 'to give glory to God', but this expression needs examination. Sometimes the 'glory' has been interpreted in purely human terms suggesting that

---

[1] *De Civ. Dei*, 10.20 and 10.6.

28

worship, elaborate ceremonial, somehow impresses people and makes them think that God is a great and splendid being. If this was ever so, it is not so now. People are not impressed by a splendid ceremonial performed by people whose lives do not reflect what their worship expresses. It is seen nowadays (though St Benedict said it long ago) that glory can be given to God only through the *lives* of those who worship him. It is through the witness of the lives of Christians that glory is given to God, and it is they who, expressing in their lives the mystery of Christ, manifest it to others (*CL* 2). In short, it is redeemed man who is responding to God in worship and life, it is man who is sanctified by the redeeming love of Christ, who gives glory to God. In the phrase of Irenaeus, 'It is the living human being who is the glory of God' (*Gloria Dei vivens homo*).

PART TWO

The Development of the Liturgy

I
GENERAL INTRODUCTION

1 The Periods of Liturgical History

GEOFFREY WAINWRIGHT

The historian's division of the past into periods always raises problems of delimitation, yet the fact remains that culture and events have combined to give to varying stretches of human history the character—discernible at least in retrospect—of an age. Liturgical historians have sometimes presented their subject by taking samples of worship at different times and places. Thus J. G. Davies describes *Holy Week* (Lutterworth 1963) as celebrated in Jerusalem in the late fourth century, at Salisbury in the later Middle Ages, and in the Churches of Rome and England in our own time. For G. A. Michell, in *Landmarks in Liturgy* (DLT 1961), the principal staging-posts in his history of the Eucharist are the rite outlined by Justin Martyr, the western Mass of the later Middle Ages, and the English service of the Prayer Books. Our own aim, in the historical part of this book, has been to tell a fairly connected story for each of the main liturgical actions of the Church: initiation, Eucharist, ordination, and the divine office. In face of all the structural continuities of ritual history, however, it is important to recognize that the living performance, the religious 'feel', and the theological understanding of the rites have varied in different ages and places, in keeping with the general evolution of the Church's life and thought and of its social and cultural context.

Liturgical history may roughly be divided into these periods: (1) the apostolic age; (2) the patristic period; (3) the medieval (early, high, and late); (4) the Reformation and beyond; (5) the Counter-Reformation and baroque; (6) the modern and contemporary. If we may allow the reader to glean supporting or corrective detail from his subsequent study, these periods may for the moment be sweepingly characterized in the following way.

1 THE APOSTOLIC AGE

Our primary source is obviously the New Testament. Surveys of the material may be found in two books of identical title, *Worship in the New Testament*, by G. Delling (1952; ET DLT 1962) and C. F. D. Moule (Lutterworth 1961); two other studies are also virtually limited to the NT

33

period: R. P. Martin, *Worship in the Early Church* (2nd edn Marshall, Morgan and Scott 1974), and F. Hahn, (ET) *The Worship of the Early Church* (Philadelphia 1973). The evidence is either fragmentary or indirect and has to be interpreted in the light of later practice. The problem here is to find the *juste milieu*: on the one hand, one must beware of importing too easily into the apostolic age elements whose certain attestation dates only from the second or third centuries; on the other hand, one must give due weight to the possibility that some theological statements in the NT reflect liturgical practices that were already current in the very early days. What is to be gathered about the words spoken at baptism from Mt. 28.19; Acts 2.38; 8.16, 37; 10.48; 19.5; 22.16; Rom. 10.9? Did initiation include an anointing with oil (2 Cor. 1.21f; Eph. 1.13; 4.30; 1 Jn. 2.20, 27)? Are the eucharistic institution narratives more 'rubrical' or more 'textual' in character? What are the meanings of the various impositions of hands (Acts 6.6; 8.17; 9.17; 13.3; 19.6; 1 Tim. 4.14; 5.22; 2 Tim. 1.6; Heb. 6.2)? Do Lk. 24.13–35 and Acts 20.7–11 reflect a service of word and sacrament? Is Acts 2.42, 46 an historical or an idealized picture of the worship of the primitive Jerusalem church? What precise form did the troublesome Corinthian assemblies take (1 Cor. 11 and 14)? What was the place of the 'hymns' which scholars have found embedded in the NT writings? How was 'the first day of the week' observed, and from when (Mk. 16.2 and pars.; Jn. 20.19, 26; Acts 20.7; 1 Cor. 16.2; cf. Rev. 1.10)?

An important question is that of liturgical continuities and discontinuities as the Church gradually defined itself over against Judaism. That question was not settled even by the close of the apostolic age. 'There was a continuing relation between Christianity and Judaism which involved both attraction and repulsion.'[1] What are we to make of the participation, recorded in Acts, of the primitive Church in the worship of the Jerusalem Temple? Why do early Christian writers and liturgies mention Abel, Melchizedek, and Abraham—all figures from before the Mosaic legislation—as those who made acceptable sacrifices to God? What is the implication of the frequent quotation by Christians of Mal. 1.11? Is L. Finkelstein right to see the 'spiritualized' version of the *birkat hamazon* in *Did.* 10 as a deliberate slur upon Judaism?[2] Was the use of the common cup a Christian innovation ... which the Jews then adopted?[3] Was the *Sanctus* borrowed from the synagogue and, if so, when (cf. Rev. 4.8; 1 Clem. 34)? How was the Christian Easter related to the

---

[1] C. K. Barrett, *The Gospel of John and Judaism* (SPCK 1975), p. 69.
[2] *JQR* n. s. 19 (1928–9), pp. 211–62.
[3] H. Schürmann, *Der Paschamahlbericht Lk. 22, (7–14.) 15–18* (2nd edn Münster 1968), pp. 60–65.

Jewish Passover (1 Cor. 5.7; the Quartodeciman controversy)? What of the recurrent tendency among Christians to make the sabbath a liturgical day?[1]

2 THE PATRISTIC PERIOD → *Greg. the Great*

The patristic period, particularly when the western Church is in view, may conveniently be delimited according to the title of J. A. Jungmann's book, *The Early Liturgy to the time of Gregory the Great* (Notre Dame 1959; DLT 1960). An important question was the definition of Christian worship over against pagan religion. R. Perdelwitz argued that 1 Pet. 1.2–5—the whole epistle is closely associated with baptism—was already presenting the Christian initiatory rite as superior to the *taurobolium* of the Cybele cult.[2] Clement of Alexandria summons the devotee of the pagan mysteries to come to the Church and find the true mysteries (*Protrepticus*, 12.119f). Jungmann has shown how the early Church took into its worship many features of pagan religion and filled them with Christian significance: the language and style of prayers; the symbols used in catacomb painting and sculpture; the kissing of holy objects; the bridal crown; the funeral meal and the *refrigerium*; the dates of processions and festivals.... It was in this way that the liturgy, with increasing effect from the fourth century, played its part in the 'transformation of pagan society'.

The conversion of Constantine marks a watershed in the patristic period. In the second and third centuries, the Church was a relatively private community, suffering from time to time the threat and the actuality of imperial persecution and looking for the End of the world. Its worship took place in houses. We know from Justin Martyr the bare outline of its initiation rite and its Sunday assembly for word and sacrament in the middle of the second century; but the prayers were extempore. As the second century passes into the third, we can add details and possibly texts from Tertullian and (problematically) the document identified as *Ap. Trad.* Of developments in the third century we know little. With the conversion of Constantine, however, the Church 'went public', and from the second half of the fourth century onwards we possess fairly full information about Christian worship. The Church now borrowed much from the civil magistracy: the basilican building, the clothes, the processions, the lights, the incense.... The ritual structure of initiation and Eucharist became fixed in this classical period: we have the

---

[1] See A. A. McArthur, *The Evolution of the Christian Year* (SCM 1953), pp. 22–8.
[2] *Die Mysterienreligion und das Problem des 1. Petrusbriefes* (Giessen 1911).

detailed evidence of the mystagogical catecheses (see p. 61) and of the chief eucharistic liturgies of both East and West, whose principal features—and sometimes even the texts—go back to this time. It is now that the Church, in a process vividly described by Gregory Dix,[1] makes itself at home in history; and the eschatological expectancy of the early period is almost lost.

3 THE MIDDLE AGES

Structurally, the classical shapes of the Christian rites remained firm, even in the case of an initiation which was now predominantly administered to infants (this is certainly true in the East, but allowance must be made for the more or less accidental 'disintegration' of the pattern of initiation in the West).[2] But the basic structures became overlaid, chiefly perhaps as the result of a new separation between ministers and people that had been unknown before the conversion of the Empire (T. Klauser calls it 'the dissolution of the liturgical community').[3] In the new church buildings, clergy and *plebs* were often separated by a balustrade, a curtain, a screen (iconostasis in the Byzantine East), or even a wall. Religiously, this separation expressed or encouraged a new sense of the 'terrifying' nature of the holy mysteries.[4] At the Eucharist, the two parts of the congregation 'met' only at such high points of the liturgy as the Scripture readings (but in what language?), the bringing of the gifts to the altar (the East created the Great Entry, but nothing really replaced the declining offertory procession in the West), parts of the great eucharistic prayer (the rest was 'secret'), and communion (though lay communion also became less frequent). Meanwhile, the now numerous clergy got on with the liturgy *plus* certain ministerial devotions, and the people busied themselves at best with their individual meditation and prayers or listened to the complicated choral singing that covered the real action. Thus for both clergy and people the fundamental structure of the rite and the basic unity of the assembly grew obscure. Medieval commentators on the liturgy see it largely as an allegorical representation of the life of Jesus or of the mystical ascent of

[1] *Shape*, pp. 303ff.
[2] See J. D. C. Fisher, *Christian Initiation: Baptism in the Medieval West* (SPCK 1965).
[3] T. Klauser, ET *A Short History of the Western Liturgy* (OUP 1969).
[4] See E. Bishop, in R. H. Connolly, *The Liturgical Homilies of Narsai* (CUP 1909), pp. 92–7. J. A. Jungmann discerns throughout the medieval developments the dogmatic factor of an initially anti-Arian stress—first in the East and then in the West—on the divinity of Christ ('The defeat of Teutonic Arianism and the revolution in religious culture in the early Middle Ages' in (ET) *Pastoral Liturgy* (Challoner 1962), in particular pp. 12–14, 59f, 62f).

the soul. There is, at least in the West, little sense of the Eucharist as the present *parousia* of the Lord who came and who is to come: the sight of the elevated host was a poor substitute for the Bride's communion with her Master. Mass was offered *for* the people (hence also private Masses), not celebrated *by* the people. By the eve of the Reformation, the Mass had become an elaborate performance: 'there is a very rich façade, but behind it a great emptiness yawns' (Jungmann).[1]

4 THE REFORMATION AND BEYOND

If the high medieval scholastics tried to define theologically what, amid the welter of liturgical detail, was the essential form and matter of the sacraments, the Reformers in turn sought at the practical level to concentrate each rite on the single, simple action that they judged to lie at its heart. By the pruning of ceremonial and by the multiplication of explanatory words, they reduced baptism to a water rite, the Eucharist to communion, ordination to the laying on of hands (they would have said 'restored', for—though they remained in some ways imprisoned in the medieval framework—they aimed at the primitive). Helped by the vernacular language, the printed book, and the long sermon, worship became in each territory the vehicle for direct doctrinal instruction of the people. Justifiable though these moves may have been in a Church needing reform, their price was paid in the loss of the sacramental dimension and the growth of didacticism which have characterized Protestant worship. From time to time there were short-lived sacramental revivals (English examples would be the Caroline and the Wesleyan). Ritually, a novel feature of Protestant worship was the giving of independent value to hymns in the structure of the service.

5 COUNTER-REFORMATION AND BAROQUE

The Roman Breviary (1568), Missal (1570), Pontifical (1596) and Ritual (1614) start the period of what T. Klauser calls 'rigid unification' and 'rubricism', and J. A. Jungmann 'unyielding uniformity' and '*Geschichtslosigkeit*'.[2] It is the age of the Congregation of Rites (founded

---

[1] 'The state of liturgical life on the eve of the Reformation', in *Pastoral Liturgy*, pp. 64–80; cf. A. H. Couratin, 'The Eucharist in the Middle Ages' in J. Daniélou, A. H. Couratin and J. Kent, *The Pelican Guide to Modern Theology. Vol. 2: Historical Theology* (Penguin 1969), pp. 215–30. See also B. L. Manning, *The People's Faith in the Time of Wyclif* (CUP 1919). It is only fair to state that there is something of a reaction among medievalists against the black picture painted above.

[2] T. Klauser, op. cit., pp. 117ff; J. A. Jungmann, 'Liturgical life in the Baroque Period', in *Pastoral Liturgy*, pp. 80–9.

1588). By art and music and vestments, the baroque period made of the Mass a splendid thing to watch and listen to, and the often tattered traces of that style persisted until Vatican II. Preaching and the people's communion were largely divorced from the Mass. The Mass was centred on the consecration; the real presence would be perpetuated in the tabernacle; exposition and benediction were the popular devotions. For J. A. Jungmann the symbol of the baroque period is the sun-shaped monstrance and the Corpus Christi procession: liturgical life in general was characterized by a 'move towards the periphery'. Paraliturgical activities flourished: the Stations of the Cross, the rosary, the cult of the Sacred Heart.

6 THE MODERN AND THE CONTEMPORARY

In many ways the nineteenth century and the first half of the twentieth constitute a desiccated period for the liturgy in both Catholicism and Protestantism. Yet there were early precursors of that liturgical movement of renewal which has been gaining momentum with the twentieth century.[1] In France, Dom P. Guéranger refounded the abbey of Solesmes, whose Gregorian chant and whose publication *L'Année Liturgique* betokened a desired return to purity. The modern Liturgical Movement is, however, conventionally dated from Dom L. Beauduin's address to the Malines conference of 1909,[2] whence pastoral interests gained the upper hand over the archaeological (though sound history was still pursued). In the twenties, the German abbey of Maria Laach, with Abbot I. Herwegen and Dom O. Casel, worked at providing a theology of worship to undergird the liturgical renewal. In France, the Parisian *Centre de Pastorale Liturgique* (founded 1940), with its periodical *La Maison-Dieu*, fused theory and practice into one. The Liturgical Movement has spread beyond the bounds of the European continent and of the Roman Catholic Church (a sign of this is the international and ecumenical journal *Studia Liturgica*). Since the second world war, many Anglican and Protestant Churches have both revised their service-books and renewed their pastoral ministry according to the principles of the Liturgical Movement: worship is 'the work of the people', and the Eucharist is its focal expression. But the culminating point so far has been the new rites of initiation and the new missal that have been composed on the basis of Vatican II's *Constitution on the Sacred Liturgy*. The Orthodox Churches have remained relatively untouched by the Movement.

[1] H. E. Chandlee, 'Liturgical Movement' in *DLW*, pp. 216–22.
[2] A. Haquin, *Dom Lambert Beauduin et le renouveau liturgique* (Gembloux 1976).

2 The Jewish Background to Christian Worship

R. T. BECKWITH

At its origin, Christianity was a Jewish religion. Jesus Christ was a Jew, and his first followers were Jews. The Judaism of the first century, especially in the dispersion but also in Palestine, had been considerably influenced by Greek thought, culture, and language, but its roots were still in the OT, and its basic languages were still Hebrew and Aramaic. The teaching of Jesus had, of course, great originality, but whatever in it was traditional it owed to Judaism rather than to any other source. Moreover, in their practice, Jesus and his first followers conformed to a large extent to Jewish customs. When, therefore, the question is asked against what background Christian worship arose, the only answer that can be given is Jewish worship. Such Greek influences on Christian worship as had not first affected Jewish worship are mainly of later date. From the outset, the originality of Christianity is seen in its worship, but so is the traditional, Jewish character of Christianity.

SOURCES OF INFORMATION

Our sources of knowledge about Jewish worship in the first century are varied. The most reliable are those which were written in or before the first century, but these supply us with only partial information. The OT is, of course, basic, as containing the written law of Jewish worship. Of the intertestamental literature, Judith, Maccabees, Jubilees, 1 Enoch, the Testament of Levi, Joseph and Asenath, the Sibylline Oracles and the Dead Sea Scrolls, though sometimes hard to date, record significant developments. In the first century A.D., we get our first substantial evidence of the pattern of synagogue worship, in incidental references made by Philo, the NT and Josephus; and further facts about the Jewish calendar emerge from the *Didache* and from the earliest surviving rabbinical document, the Megillath Taanith. Moreover, Christian worship, as described in the NT and the *Didache*, is itself a witness to Jewish worship, because of the indications it gives of Jewish influence.

When one moves into the field of post-first-century literature, the evidence is more ample, but its applicability to the first century becomes somewhat problematical. The rest of the rabbinical literature began to be written down about the end of the second century, the date usually given to the Mishnah. The Tosefta, Targum Neofiti and the Halakic Midrashim are also relatively early, and so are the *baraitas* (sayings quoted from old rabbinic compilations other than the Mishnah) in the two Talmuds.[1] Moreover, the fact that the rabbinical literature is a record of oral tradition, first handed down by word of mouth and only later reduced to writing, means that there is a good chance of its statements being applicable to a period one or two centuries earlier than the date of writing. In some of the works mentioned we find a lot of evidence about Jewish worship in the Temple, the synagogue and the home, and this is far earlier than that provided by Jewish Prayer Books, which began to appear only in the ninth century.[2] Since the breach between the Church and the synagogue took place before the end of the first century, the likelihood is that, where the resemblances between Jewish and Christian worship are striking, they are due to the influence which the former exerted upon the latter in the first century. Exceptions to this rule might be found in ancient Syria and Palestine, where geography and language led to a longer period of Jewish influence, in individuals with an unusual knowledge of Judaism (such as Hippolytus, Origen, Epiphanius, and Jerome), or in relatively modern times, when the cultural dominance of Christianity led to the reverse process, whereby Jewish worship was in some respects influenced by Christian. But even when Christianity and Judaism have been in close contact, antagonism between them has generally been such as to limit any influence, and in ancient Syria and Palestine this influence seems to have been largely conservative in its effects.

There are two further factors which complicate the handling of post-first-century material. One is the fact of the destruction of the Temple in A.D. 70. This must have strongly affected Jewish Christians, who had previously tried to practise Jewish worship in addition to Christian (temple sacrifice as well as Christian sacrament, circumcision as well as

---

[1] In references to passages of the Mishnah, the Tosefta, and the Jerusalem and Babylonian Talmuds, they will be abbreviated to M., Tos., Jer. and Bab. respectively. For ET of most of the ancient (non-biblical) Jewish texts mentioned in this section, see E. W. Brooks, *Joseph and Asenath* (SPCK 1918); R. H. Charles, *The Apocrypha and Pseudepigrapha of the OT* (Clarendon Press 1913); F. H. Colson *et al.*, *Philo* (Loeb edn, 12 vols., Heinemann 1929–62); H. Danby, *Tractate Sanhedrin: Mishna and Tosefta* (SPCK 1919); *The Mishnah* (Clarendon Press 1933); I. Epstein, *The Babylonian Talmud* (35 vols., Soncino 1935–52); A. Diez Macho, *Neophyti 1* (Madrid 1968 etc., continuing); H. St. J. Thackeray *et al.*, *Josephus* (Loeb edn, 9 vols., Heinemann 1926–65); A. L. Williams, *Tractate Berakoth: Mishna and Tosefta* (SPCK 1921); S. Zeitlin, 'Megillat Taanit as a Source for Jewish Chronology and History' (*JQR* 1918–20). There is a French translation of the Jerusalem Talmud by M. Schwab (10 vols., Paris 1871–90) but no ET.

[2] See I. Z. Idelsohn, *Jewish Liturgy and its Development* (New York 1932), p. 56. This is the easiest reliable textbook on Jewish liturgy for students pursuing the subject further.

baptism, the sabbath as well as the Lord's Day);[1] but it undoubtedly affected non-Christian Jews no less profoundly. It meant for them that the synagogue became not just a complement to the Temple but a substitute for it. The synagogue had already become something approaching a substitute to the Jews of the dispersion and the excommunicated Essenes, but it now became the same to the influential Pharisees of Palestine, whose influence was still more enhanced by the fact that the Temple had been the sole centre of influence possessed by the Sadducees. The emphasis on teaching and prayer as the only important elements of worship apart from circumcision and ceremonial washings now became all-pervasive, and though the hope remained that the Temple would be restored, in the meantime a hint was taken from Ps. 50.13f; 51.16f; Is. 66.20, etc., and the sacrificial law was simply spiritualized.[2] It is also significant that the great annual holy days had previously centred on sacrifice. How far the passover meal was affected by the fact that it was no longer confined to Jerusalem and no longer had as its main dish an animal which had been sacrificed is an open question, but it certainly became more of a domestic, family, occasion, with women and minors regularly involved, as among the Jews of the dispersion (Philo, *De Vita Mosis*, 2.224f etc.).[3]

The other factor is the fluidity of ancient liturgical texts. The rabbinical literature indicates that the structure of services and the themes of prayers were fixed before their actual wording was.[4] A standard form of words there might be, but worshippers were permitted and even encouraged to paraphrase it. This is exactly what we find in early Christian worship also (Justin, 1 *Apol.*, 65, 67; Hippolytus, *Ap. Trad.*, 10.3–5). In such a situation, a very general correspondence between certain features of Jewish and Christian worship may be the only indication left of a very definite influence, but in the nature of the case it is an obscure indication, not a clear one.

THE CENTRES OF JEWISH WORSHIP

The main centres of Jewish worship at the birth of Christianity were three: the Temple, the synagogue and the home. The Temple was primarily concerned with sacrifice, which was normally permitted nowhere else; but, because of God's promise to meet Israel there, it was

Temple

---

[1] See the evidence of Acts, Rom., Gal., Phil., and Col.; and Eusebius, *HE* 3.27.5.

[2] See Idelsohn, op. cit., p. 26f; I. Elbogen, *Der jüdische Gottesdienst in seiner geschichtlichen Entwicklung* (Hildesheim 1962), p. 251.

[3] See J. B. Segal, *The Hebrew Passover from the Earliest Times to A.D. 70* (OUP 1963).

[4] See Idelsohn, op. cit., pp. xvii, 28.

also the place at which, or towards which, the Jews said their prayers (1 Kgs. 8.28ff; Lk. 1.10, etc.). Moreover, teaching took place there (Lk. 2.46f), a custom followed by Christ and the apostles. The sacrifices offered there were those prescribed in the Pentateuch, and fell into three main categories: the burnt (or whole) offering, in which the complete sacrifice was a gift to God consumed by fire; the sin and guilt offerings, of which the priest but not the guilty party was allowed to eat, and in which there were special regulations about the atoning application of the blood; and the peace (or shared) offering, of which the lay worshipper himself was allowed to eat a share, as a guest of the Lord. The sin offerings of the Day of Atonement were a variation on the second type, and the passover sacrifice a variation on the third. All these were primarily animal sacrifices, but there were also vegetable sacrifices, such as the shewbread and the incense. The Law prescribed sacrifices morning and evening on every day of the year, with additional sacrifices on sabbaths, new moons, annual festivals, and the annual fast of the Day of Atonement. Pious Jews tried to get to Jerusalem at least for the festivals of Passover, Pentecost, and Tabernacles, in accordance with the Law (Ex. 23.17 etc.). The Gospels show Christ visiting the Temple for the festivals, including the intertestamental feast of the rededication of the Temple (Jn. 10.22f), and on his last visit he specifically gives directions for the offering of the passover lamb. Consequently, although in the NT (as in the writings of the Qumran separatists) the Temple is reinterpreted as signifying the people of God, it is not surprising that the Christians of Jerusalem followed Christ's example and continued to frequent the Temple and its sacrifices until they were excommunicated or the Temple was destroyed.

Whether the synagogue began as a substitute for the Temple, during the exile, or as a supplement to the Temple, developed for the benefit of those who because of distance could only go there infrequently, it has in its history fulfilled both roles. Its services have always been non-sacrificial. The reading and exposition of the Scriptures in the synagogue on the sabbath is recorded in the NT (Lk. 4.16–27; Acts 13.15, 27; 15.21) and by Philo and Josephus, and the name *proseuche* which Philo, Josephus, and Egyptian papyri and inscriptions use for the synagogue, shows that prayer was offered there; but none of these early authorities say anything about services on weekdays, except special occasions. According to the Mishnah, some synagogues had services on Mondays and Thursdays (Megillah 1.3; 3.6–4.1), and for two weeks in the year the lay *maamad* (embryo congregation) corresponding to a particular priestly course held daily services in a selected synagogue (Taanith 4.1–5, etc.). Apart from these exceptions, synagogue services in the first century were probably confined to sabbaths and holy days. Christ regularly took part in

42

the sabbath-day services of the synagogue and taught there, and
wherever his disciples carried the gospel we find them associating
themselves with the synagogue for as long as they are allowed to, and
trying to found the local church on a Jewish nucleus. It seems probable,
therefore, that when a local church first had to separate from the
synagogue, as in Acts 19.8f, it regarded itself as a synagogue, like the
congregations called 'synagogues' in Jas. 2.2 and the *Shepherd of Hermas*
(Mandate 11.14), and modelled its worship on what it had been used to in
the synagogue, though with the addition of the Christian sacraments and
charismata, and with an increasing tendency to meet for worship on the
Lord's Day rather than the sabbath. In the first clear descriptions of a
Christian service as a whole (Justin, 1 *Apol.* 65, 67), the influence of
synagogue services is plain; and there is another token of influence in the
fact that the Jewish synagogue, like the Christian congregation, seems to
have been the broad context in which the initiation and instruction of
converts took place.

The home was the scene of Jewish family worship. The duty of
circumcising sons had always rested upon the parent (Gen. 17.12; 21.4;
Ex. 4.24–26) and it had remained a domestic ceremony (Lk. 1.58f). It
was not transferred from the home to the synagogue until many centuries
after Christ. The parent also had the duty of instructing the child
(Gen. 18.19; Ex. 13.8; Ps. 78.3–6 etc.), and it is significant that two of the
first-century references to private Bible reading are concerned with the
instruction of children (4 Macc. 18.10–19; 2 Tim. 3.15). Sabbath meals
were particularly joyful family occasions; and according to the Mishnah
(Berakoth) grace was said several times at meals, over each main dish,
over bread and over wine; and when people were eating together, most
benedictions were said by one person for all, and a responsive grace was
added at the end of the meal. This pattern corresponds to the two graces
recorded at the Last Supper, and the three graces of the agape-cum-
Eucharist in *Didache*, 9f. Before evening meals, a benediction for the light
was also said at the bringing in of the lamp. This too was carried over into
the Christian agape (*Ap. Trad.*, 26.18–27), and may be the source of the
ancient Greek vesper hymn 'Hail, gladdening Light'.

Individual worship also belonged mostly to the home, but was not
private to the extent that Christ's teaching made it (Mt. 6.5f). The daily
hours of individual prayer were three (Ps. 55.17; Dan. 6.10), connected
with the hours of daily sacrifice in the Temple (Ez. 9.5ff; Dan. 9.20f;
Judith 9.1ff; Lk. 1.10). One of the three hours, as we know from Acts
3.1; 10.3, 30, was the ninth hour (3 p.m.), the time of the evening sacrifice
in the first century (Josephus, *Antiquities*, 14.65; M. Pesahim 5.1), and
this was adopted as one of its daily hours of prayer by the Church

(Tertullian, *On Fasting*, 10; *Ap. Trad.*, 36.5f, etc.). At these three hours the most ancient of the traditional Jewish prayers, the *Tefillah*, was recited (M. Berakoth 4.1): hence the corresponding Christian rule in *Didache*, 8 that the Lord's Prayer is to be said three times a day. Thanksgiving was customary twice a day, at rising and retiring (Josephus, *Ant.* 4.212), and on those occasions the most ancient of the traditional Jewish thanksgivings, the *Shema'*, was used (M. Berakoth 1.1f). Another type of individual worship was ceremonial washing, required by the Pentateuch in connection with various natural accidents (Lev. 11—15; Num. 19), to which others had been added by the Pharisees.

Sects which were out of communion with the predominant schools of the Pharisees and the Sadducees had their own centres of worship. To say nothing of the Samaritans, there were the Essenes, who lived communally (not unlike the early Jerusalem church) and followed their own interpretation of the Law, laying great stress on ceremonial washings. They refused to offer sacrifices at the Temple under prevailing conditions, and had consequently been excommunicated (Josephus, *Ant.*, 18.19). The Qumran community, who followed the divergent calendar of Jubilees and 1 Enoch, were very likely the marrying Essenes mentioned by Josephus (*War*, 2.160f). The Therapeutae of Egypt, described by Philo (*De Vita Contemplativa*), who regarded Pentecost as the chief festival, seem to have been a related body.

JEWISH INFLUENCE ON BAPTISM

At three places in the NT, Jn. 3.22–6, Heb. 6.2 and Heb. 10.22, Christian baptism seems to be classed with Jewish cleansing ceremonies, and in the first passage John's baptism is included as well. Two of the terms used here are *katharismos* (cf. Mk. 1.44; Lk. 2.22; Jn. 2.6) and *baptismos* (cf. Mk. 7.4; Heb. 9.10). *Baptizo* itself is used of Jewish cleansings in Lk. 11.38.

The link is provided by proselyte baptism and John's baptism. (But for a different view, see p. 81.) The former had been added to circumcision for heathen converts, because they had not previously observed the laws of ceremonial purity (Greek Testament of Levi, 14.6; Sibylline Oracles, 4.165–7; Joseph and Asenath; M. Pesahim 8.8). The first and third references show that it was applied to women as well as men, and this means to children too, who were likewise liable to contract uncleanness (M. Tohoroth 3.6; M. Niddah 5.3–5; M. Zabim 2.1). The second and third references show that it was spiritualized to denote forgiveness of sins and rebirth, as well as ceremonial cleansing. The *baraita* in Bab. Yebamoth 47 a–b describes the rite. Candidates were questioned about their motives, told some of the laws they would have to observe, and if they consented were circumcised immediately. When healed, they immersed themselves naked, while two learned men instructed them further in the laws. In the case of women, they were put in the water by other women, while the sages taught them the laws from a distance. The *baraitas* in Bab. Kerithoth 8b–9a show that a sacrifice had afterwards to be offered.

In three respects, John's baptism carried the matter further. He completed the reinterpretation of the baptism as for forgiveness of sins; he therefore applied it to Jews, not just to Gentiles; and he administered it himself.

The points of comparison with Christian baptism are many. (a) Children were candidates for circumcision and proselyte baptism as well as adults. The probability that household baptism in the NT (Acts 16.15, 31–34; 18.8; 1 Cor. 1.16) included infants is therefore strong, and infant baptism in the Church is explicitly attested from the second century.[1] (b) John's baptism, like Christian, signified the forgiveness of sins; and this signification and that of rebirth were becoming attached to proselyte baptism also. (c) Proselyte baptism (unlike circumcision) was only given in the first generation, since converts would observe the laws of cleanness thereafter; but forgiveness of sins was needed in every generation, which accounts for Christian practice. (d) Forgiveness of sins was needed by Jews and Gentiles alike; hence the scope of Christian baptism. (e) The interrogation about motives is paralleled in Hippolytus (*Ap. Trad.*, 16.2). (f) The delay before proselyte baptism, while circumcision healed, may account for the delay for instruction and fasting in *Didache*, 7, out of which grew the catechumenate. There was also a long period of probation among the Essenes, and the catechetical theme of the Two Ways in *Didache*, 1–6 is paralleled in the Dead Sea Scrolls. However, there is no such delay in the NT, either for Jewish or Gentile converts (Acts 2.41; 8.12, 16, 36; 9.18; 10.47f; 16.33; 18.8; 19.5; 22.16). There, immediate circumcision has been replaced by immediate baptism. (g) Naked immersion, and the consequent special provision for women, are paralleled in the Syrian *Didascalia*, 16, where the women who put them in the water are deaconesses, and the men who pronounce the requisite words are clergy. The directions in *Ap. Trad.* 21.3, 5, 11, and the separate baptistery in Christian basilicas, probably also reflect baptism received naked. Not all Jewish lustrations were immersions, however (Lev. 14.7; Num. 8.7; 19; Ezek. 36; M. Yadaim), and the mass open-air baptisms by

---

[1] See J. Jeremias, (ET) *Infant Baptism in the First Four Centuries* (SCM 1960); (ET) *The Origins of Infant Baptism* (SCM 1963). For a different view see K. Aland, (ET) *Did the Early Church Baptize Infants?* (SCM 1963).

John, Jesus, and Peter recorded in Jn. 3 and Acts 2 probably followed another mode. The symbolism of Rom. 6.4; Col. 2.12 suggests immersion, but that of Tit. 3.5f pouring. (h) Self-administration was normal in Jewish lustrations, but not universal (Ex. 29; Num. 8; Num. 19). John did not observe it, nor did the early Christians normally, though it may be hinted at in the middle voice used in Acts 22.16; 1 Cor. 6.11; 10.2. (i) Running water is prescribed in Lev. 14.5–7; 15.13; Num. 19.17, and is preferred in *Didache* 7. Compare also the river baptisms of the NT.

JEWISH INFLUENCE ON CONFIRMATION AND ADMISSION TO COMMUNION

The three references which the NT contains to the laying-on of hands in initiation, symbolizing the baptismal gift of the Spirit (Acts 8.15–17; 19.5f; Heb. 6.2), are not known to have any antecedents in Jewish initiation ceremonies. This was probably a new ceremony, suggested by Dt. 34.9.

The same may be true of anointing in initiation. This is somewhat later attested, occurring first in second century Gnostic texts, but could very well have been suggested by the links between anointing and the Spirit in 1 Sam. 16.13; Is. 61.1; Zech. 4; 2 Cor. 1.21f, and between anointing and ceremonial cleansing in the washing and anointing of the priests (Ex. 29; Ex. 40; Lev. 8). Moreover, the Christian mode of anointing the baptized, by pouring and crossing (*Ap. Trad.*, 22.2f), closely conformed to Jewish tradition about the mode of anointing the priests (see *baraita* in Bab. Kerithoth 5b etc.). Alternatively, it is not impossible that anointing formed part of proselyte baptism, and as such was silently taken over by the Church in the first century. This possibility is suggested by the widespread custom, shared by the Jews, of using oil after taking a bath (Ruth 3.3; 2 Sam. 12.20; Ezek. 16.9; Sus. 17). If so, the ceremony was probably at first a mere incidental of Christian initiation, which began to be mentioned only after it had been given a symbolic interpretation. A third possibility is that the anointing is of Essene origin. One of the first witnesses to anointing is the second-century Gnostic *Gospel of Philip*, which teaches initiation by baptism, anointing, and first communion, much as Hippolytus and Tertullian do early in the next century, though the latter add laying-on of hands. The *Gospel of Philip* is associated with Syria, but Valentinus, whose disciple the author appears to be, came from Egypt, and it is therefore interesting that Essene Judaism, both in Palestine and in Egypt, appears to have practised initiation by anointing, washing, and eating bread and wine (Palestine—Greek Testament of

Levi 8.4f), or by washing, eating bread and wine, and anointing (Egypt—Joseph and Asenath). Circumcision would have preceded these in the case of males.

The interval between baptism and anointing or the laying-on of hands in later western practice has no known precedent in the early Church or Judaism. An interval between baptism (cum confirmation?) in infancy and first communion at a later age is definitely attested, however. Origen, about A.D. 235, when permanently resident in Palestine, states that children are not given communion (*Homilies on Judges*, 6.2), and what he says may well apply to his homeland of Egypt too. There is no clear evidence to the contrary anywhere before Cyprian, writing in N. Africa about 250 (*On the Lapsed*, 9, 25). Third century Syrian support for Origen is found in *Didascalia*, 9, in a passage beginning 'Honour the bishops ...' (ed. Connolly, p. 94), where a long period of Christian education intervenes between baptism and admission to communion. The earliest Syrian evidence to the contrary is in the *Apostolic Constitutions*, and the earliest Egyptian evidence still later. Now, it may well be that the primitive practice of Palestine, Syria, and Egypt in this matter goes back to Judaism. The Mishnah states that 'at thirteen one is fit for the fulfilling of the commandments' (Aboth 5.21; Niddah 5.6), and Segal holds that when Jesus went up to Jerusalem at the age of twelve (Lk. 2.41ff) it was to prepare him for admission to the passover meal a year later (cf. M. Yoma 8.4).[1] The Essenes even delayed admission to the passover meal till the age of twenty (Jubilees 49.17). Whether, at either age, there was a ceremony of admission to adult religious responsibilities, comparable to the later Jewish *bar-mitzvah* rite or 'confirmation', is uncertain; but, even without this, the Reformers' belief that they had a precedent for their confirmation practice in the early Church and Judaism can be seen to be far less wide of the mark than is usually stated.

JEWISH INFLUENCE ON THE ANTE-COMMUNION AND THE DAILY OFFICES

The three daily hours for saying the *Tefillah* and the two for saying the *Shema'* were of course also observed on the sabbath, and on that occasion they were apparently combined into three public synagogue services, which about A.D. 100 were extended to weekdays.[2] The changing of the daily hours of private prayer among Christians into daily public services was a parallel but later development (see p. 362). On the sabbath there was a fourth hour of prayer, corresponding to the additional sabbath

[1] Op. cit., pp. 254, 257f etc.
[2] See Idelsohn, op. cit., pp. xviiif, 27f, 118f.

sacrifice (Num. 28.9f), and this too was kept as a synagogue service (M. Berakoth 4.1, 7 etc.). The reading and exposition of Scripture was also added, so public worship filled most of the day (Philo, *Hypothetica*, 7.13; Josephus, *Against Apion*, 1.209). This throws light on the number of Sunday services among early Christians, and the first statement on the point, that in Bithynia about 112 they had more than one (Pliny, *Ep.* 10.96, *to Trajan*, see pp. 51–2), should be given its full weight. The *Shema'*, the *Tefillah* and even the lections (M. Megillah 4.1f) all had benedictions attached, but only the first is primarily praise or thanksgiving. The *Tefillah*, also called the *'Amidah* or the 18 Benedictions, is primarily petition, but the link of each petition with praise is a significant parallel to the mixture of the two in the eucharistic prayers of the *Didache*, Justin and Hippolytus. Written liturgical prayers of various kinds, mainly for the tabernacle and temple services, and older than the *Shema'* or *Tefillah*, are found in Num. 5.19–22; 6.23–27; Dt. 21.6–8; 26.3–10, 13–15, and in the Psalter, for the liturgical use of which see 1 Chr. 16.7–42, the Psalm titles (especially LXX), M. Tamid 7.4 etc. To the Psalms, the Qumran community added its book of Hymns, and the singing of both kinds of composition in early Christian services is indicated in 1 Cor. 14.26; Eph. 5.19; Col. 3.16. Out of such elements the ante-communion, and more slowly and obscurely the daily office, developed, though the *Shema'* was replaced by the thanksgiving prayer of the communion proper.[1]

JEWISH INFLUENCE ON THE COMMUNION PROPER

The actions and words of our Lord at two points in the Last Supper, recorded by the synoptists and in 1 Cor. 11, follow the normal pattern of a Jewish meal as seen in the feedings of the five thousand and the four thousand, in Acts 27.35f, and in the earliest description of the passover meal (M. Pesahim 10). Graces are normal: only our Lord's interpretative and eschatological words and command to repeat (Mk. 14.22, 24f; 1 Cor. 11.24f) are new. J. Jeremias has powerfully argued that the larger meal in which Christ was taking part was the passover meal (*The Eucharistic Words of Jesus*, (ET) SCM 1966), as the synoptists state. How the evidence of John is to be reconciled with this is uncertain: possibly Jn. 18.28 uses 'eat the passover' in the extended sense of Dt. 16.3. At all events, the general setting was the passover season. The background of

[1] For texts of the *Shema'* and the *Tefillah*, see W. O. E. Oesterley, *The Jewish Background of the Christian Liturgy* (Clarendon Press 1925), pp. 42–67; and for further information C. W. Dugmore, *The Influence of the Synagogue upon the Divine Office* (Faith Press 1964); A. Sendrey, *Music in Ancient Israel* (Vision Press 1969). For further discussion of the synagogue services, see pp. 353–6.

the interpretative words is probably the interpretation of various items on the passover table by the head of the household as commemorative of the Exodus (M. Pesahim 10.5). The Passover was essentially commemorative, and commemoration (or reminding) is the sense of Christ's word *anamnesis* (Lk. 22.19; 1 Cor. 11.24f; cf. Philo, *De Congressu*, 39–43), the reminder being primarily directed towards men (Ex. 13.3, 9; Dt. 16.3), which accounts for Paul's paraphrase *katangello* (1 Cor. 11.26). The claim that *anamnesis* and its Semitic equivalents in the Passover denote the making present or effective of a past event is without linguistic or Jewish support.[1] The larger meal grew into the Christian agape, which is still combined with the Eucharist in 1 Cor. 11 and *Didache* 9f but has become a separate event by the time of Justin and Hippolytus. Meals eaten together had covenanting significance for the Jews (Gen. 26.28–31; Ps. 41.9; Ob. 7; Jn. 13.18), especially meals upon a sacrifice, at which God was the host (Gen. 31.44–54; Ex. 24.5–11); hence the language about *koinonia* between God and all the communicants in 1 Cor. 10.16–22. Meals were also joyful occasions (Dt. 12.6f, 17f; 27.7; 1 Chr. 29.22; Lk. 15.23, 29; Acts 2.46f); hence the appropriateness of the Eucharist as an anticipation of the blissful heavenly 'feast' (Mt. 26.29; Lk. 22.30; 1 Cor. 11.26; cf. Is. 25.6; Mt. 8.11; Rev. 19.9). The sacramental language of Joseph and Asenath about the initiate 'eating the blessed bread of life' and 'drinking the blessed cup of immortality' is likewise relevant background, but so too are non-cultic sayings such as Ecclus. 24.21ff, where the divine Wisdom is eaten and drunk through the book of the Law, and Targum Neofiti Ex. 16.15, where Moses the lawgiver is said to be the heavenly manna (cf. Jn. 6.31ff; 1 Cor. 10.3f).

The texts of the graces over bread and wine, and the introduction to the responsive grace over 'the cup of the blessing' afterwards, are known to us from M. Berakoth 6.1; 7.3. The themes of the responsive grace are given in *baraitas* (Jer. Berakoth 7.2; Bab. Berakoth 48b) and Jeremias prints a critical text (op. cit., p. 110). This long grace, which combines praise and petition, is a possible model for Hippolytus' unified eucharistic prayer, the institution narrative corresponding to the festal addition which (at any rate later) became customary.[2] The confession of sin (*Didache* 4, 14) may have been suggested by Jewish confessions, such as that of Lev. 16.21, as well as by Paul's warning in 1 Cor. 11.27–34. The Sanctus, which when it first appears in the fourth century is found in a non-eucharistic context and a more Jewish form (*Ap. Const.*, 7.35) as well as in the consecration prayer, is doubtless derived from the *Kedusha*

---

[1] But for another view, see pp. 16, 25, 154, 205.

[2] See L. Ligier, 'The Origins of the Eucharistic Prayer', *SL* 9 (1973). On blessings in the Eucharist, see p. 154. On Jewish graces, see also p.43.

(Is. 6.3 plus Ezek. 3.12) of the synagogue liturgy, first mentioned in the Tosefta (Tos. Berakoth 1.9).

JEWISH INFLUENCE ON ORDINATION

For whatever reason, the duty of the priests and levites to teach the Law (Lev. 10.11; Dt. 17.11; Mal. 2.5–7 etc.) had by the first century passed to the lay 'scribes' (Scripture-experts), 'teachers of the Law', 'lawyers' or 'rabbis', who taught on occasion in the Temple (Lk. 2.46) but had their great centre of influence in the synagogue (Mt. 23.6; Mk. 1.21f; Lk. 5.17; 6.6f), and are almost invariably linked in the NT with the Pharisees. The synagogue also had one or more 'synagogue-rulers', responsible for discipline there (Lk. 13.14) and for choosing who should preach (Acts 13.15), read the lessons, or lead the prayers; and an attendant (Lk. 4.20). The 'elders' of the synagogue (Lk. 7.1–5) were the rabbis. They had the tasks of ruling, judging, and teaching. As teachers, the elders expound the Scriptures on the sabbath in Philo, *Hypothetica*, 7.13. Consequently, the first Christian 'elders' normally have teaching as well as ruling responsibilities (Acts 20.28; 1 Tim. 5.17; Tit. 1.9; cf. 1 Tim. 3.2). Whether the other Christian titles of 'bishop' and 'deacon' are derived from Judaism is less certain, but for this possibility see Epiphanius, *Panarion*, 30.11; T. H. Gaster, *The Scriptures of the Dead Sea Sect* (1957), pp. 308–10. The synagogue-ruler and attendant seem to have been purely local appointments, but the scribe, being ordained, had a wider scope for his ministry, though he settled and earned his living by a trade. Ordination was originally by the laying-on of hands (Tos. Sanhedrin 1.1; see p. 296), which explains Christian practice (Acts 6.6; 1 Tim. 4.14; 5.22; 2 Tim. 1.6); and according to the Talmud a rabbi originally ordained his own pupils, though in the second century A.D. this right was concentrated in the national patriarch (Jer. Sanhedrin 1.2–4), rather in the same way as, among Christians, it was then being concentrated in the monarchical bishop.[1]

JEWISH INFLUENCE ON THE CALENDAR

The basic Mosaic calendar, outlined on p. 42, had been amplified by the first century with the addition of Purim (Est. 9), the rededication of the Temple (1 Macc. 4) and the other post-biblical festivals and fasts recorded in Judith 8.6, Megillath Taanith and M. Taanith. There is no

[1] See further Elbogen, op. cit., pp. 482–92; E. Ferguson, 'Laying on of Hands: its Significance in Ordination' (*JTS*, Apr. 1975), and the literature there cited.

compelling evidence that the Church continued to observe any part of the Jewish calendar after the breach with the synagogue, though forms of Passover and Pentecost, with Christian meanings, are apparent in the course of the second century, and a form of the sabbath, temporarily, in the fourth century. The greatly simplified ceremonial of the Church (baptism-cum-confirmation and Eucharist) was matched by a greatly simplified calendar, and the only two new Christian observances of the first century were the Lord's Day (Acts 20.7; 1 Cor. 16.2; Rev. 1.10; *Didache*, 14) and the weekly fasts on Wednesday and Friday (*Didache*, 8). The latter are explicitly stated to be chosen with an eye to the Jewish practice of calling fasts on Monday and Thursday, and the former seems to be influenced by the Jewish sabbath. Like the sabbath, but unlike any other festival, it is geared to the Jewish week; and, among further likenesses, it is a memorial, is the regular day of corporate worship, and bases its worship on the sabbath-day worship of the synagogue.[1]

3 The Letter of Pliny

D. H. TRIPP

Pliny the Younger, Governor of Bithynia and Pontus 111–2 A.D., reported to Trajan (*Letters*, 10.96) his dealings with Christians. Those who had been Christians but were so no longer, 'attested that . . . their custom had been to gather before dawn on a fixed day and to sing a hymn (*carmen*) to Christ as if to a god, and to bind themselves by an oath (*sacramento*) not for any criminal purpose, but to abstain from theft, brigandage, adultery, breach of faith and misappropriation of trust. With this complete, it had been their custom to separate, and to meet again to take food—but quite ordinary, harmless food' (AT).

Many liturgiologists decline to seek evidence here for the growth of Christian worship, because this is at least a second-hand account, and because of the supposed rule of secrecy surrounding early Christian rites. This secrecy is not attested before the fourth century (see p. 109), and there is no reason to expect apostates to observe it if it existed at all. Pliny is clearly trying to be both exact and complete in his account.

The older view (Voss, Bingham) was that this refers to a morning Eucharist and to an evening Agape. In this context, *sacramentum* cannot

[1] See further R. T. Beckwith and W. Stott, *This is the Day* (Marshall, Morgan and Scott 1978); 'The Day, its Divisions and its Limits, in Biblical Thought' (*Evangelical Quarterly*, Oct. 1971).

mean a religious rite as such, but only 'an oath of allegiance'. Another suggestion, that we have here a reference to a Christian version of the synagogue service, with use of the Decalogue, is open to the objection that the recital of the Decalogue is not naturally taken as an oath, and also that it is by no means sure that the Decalogue in the synagogue service was general outside Palestine.

The most satisfactory view is that put forward by H. Lietzmann (*Geschichtliche Studien Albert Hauck* (Leipzig 1916), pp. 34–8 = TU 74 (1962), pp. 48–53), that the *sacramentum*, and perhaps also the *carmen*, is a baptismal vow in some form, the food taken later being the (baptismal?) Eucharist. If baptism was administered in a river or stream, the new Christians would have to leave the spot to join the congregation for the Eucharist. Recent studies of Jewish–Christian baptism (such as that of Erik Peterson, *Frühkirche, Judentum, Gnosis* (Rome 1959), pp. 221–35) support this view, as does also a consideration of the 'Two Ways' document in the *Didache* (see pp. 55–7) as a pre-baptismal course of instruction, based on the Decalogue. Important indirect evidence for this conclusion lies in the fact that Pliny is clearly very interested in initiations. The former Christians, as he reports them, say both that they are Christians and that they are not (*esse se Christianos dixerunt et mox negaverunt*). This odd turn of phrase can best be explained if Pliny's question was something very like: 'Have you been initiated as a Christian?'

Even if Lietzmann is right, it remains unclear whether the baptismal Eucharist is here indicated as following hard upon the baptism.

4 Gnosticism

D. H. TRIPP

'Gnosticism' is the traditional name given to a group of sects associated with the Christian Church from at least the second century. It has been assumed that the rites of Valentinians and Marcionites were close to those of the orthodox Christians; this is well attested for Marcion (see Tertullian, *adv. Marcion.*), but is less clear in the other case. The Ophite sects, represented by the Coptic texts in the Bruce and Askew codices, clearly had developing systems of initiations in which baptisms and sacred dances with incantations were, if perhaps previously derived from Christian practice, progressively elaborated to match the sects' cosmological and astrological theories. Irenaeus preserves (*AH* 1.21.3) an account, too detailed to be invented, of the goings-on of one Marcus. Marcus is often called a Valentinian, but without satisfactory reasons. His initiations used garbled Aramic formulae, which seem to be Jewish–Christian in origin. His other rites included glossolalia to order, invocation to call down into cups of water the 'blood of Charis' (an echo of 'Let grace come' in the *Didache?*) and an initiation-rite called the 'Bridal Chamber'; what Irenaeus suspected of this, need not be said, and Marcus has all the appearance of a mountebank (which Irenaeus does not suggest of his other targets), so that these suspicions are not unreasonable. A related rite, using marriage symbolism, may be found in Hippolytus' account of the Naassenes (*Ref.*, 5.8–9 and 26–7); Widengren links this with enthronement, which seems too remote from common affairs.

Some of these elements may be adapted from Christian ways, as was generally thought of Gnosticism as a whole. Since Reitzenstein and Bousset (whose ideas were popularized by Bultmann) suggested that Gnosticism is in fact a pre-Christian phenomenon, it has been argued that Gnostic rites are also pre-Christian. Thus Anz suggested that Gnostic baptism goes back to Babylonia, in association with the myth of the ascent of the soul. A 'gnostic' origin of the Eucharist has even been mooted (Schmithals). Although these suggestions point to non-Christian origins for many features of developing Gnosticism, they have been heavily criticized on historical grounds. In any case, the creative surge of the second century A.D. would explain most of these developments.

The Coptic Nag Hammadi texts have not yet been fully examined, but they may illuminate the problem. Traces of 'Bridal Chamber' rites have been suggested in the *Gospel of Philip*, and an initiation-homily in the *Gospel of Truth*; there may be a ritual curse in the *Book of Thomas the Contender*.

Gnosticism has been suggested as a path along which pagan (especially mystery-) rites found their way into the Church. Much is unclear, this point not least.

For a recent treatment of Gnosticism, see R. M. Grant, *After the New Testament* (Philadelphia 1967), especially chs. 12–13.

The sources may be studied in the following works: L. Fendt, *Gnostische Mysterien* (Munich 1922); G. R. S. Meade, *Pistis Sophia* 2nd edn (Watkins 1921); J. Doresse, (ET) *The Secret Books of the Egyptian Gnostische Mysterien* (Munich 1922); G. R. S. Meade, *Pistis Sophia* 2nd C. Black 1960); R. McL. Wilson, *The Gospel of Philip* (Mowbrays 1962); articles in *Eranos*-Yearbooks, esp. 1944; *Acts of Thomas*, in collections of NT Apocrypha.

5 The Mysteries

D. H. TRIPP

The mystery-religions (or more correctly 'mystery-cults', for they were not independent systems and were easily amenable to syncretistic absorption) were prominent features of pagan religion in late antiquity. The cults were associated either with sacred sites, such as Eleusis, or with deities of a suitable character, such as Orpheus, Dionysus, Attis, Isis, Mithras, Serapis, or the Cabiri.

The cults differed greatly, and little can be said with certainty, for they had in common a rule of secrecy. Christian writers often allege them to have been immoral, but such charges must be treated with reserve. The impression that they were obscene would not be surprising if their themes referred much to fertility, as seems to have been the case. Current opinion regards all information upon their rites as dubious, because of the effectiveness of their rule of secrecy. Certain common features can, however, be picked out.

A mystery-religion may have been either in origin a cult of a small ethnic group submerged by invasion and tenaciously clinging to its identity through inherited ritual, or at the other extreme a virtually synthetic cult imposed by decree (as with Serapis). In any case, the practice of the cult would be voluntary in most cases, and in any event a predominantly individual matter, unlike the waning official cults of the city-states. Whether the deity concerned was a fertility-god or not, the core of the rite was a unification of the worshipper with the god in a way not otherwise possible, i.e. a *mystical* union or bond. This experience touched upon the deepest issues of life and death, whether in nature or in the individual man. Three stages were usually to be expected: a period of purification and probation (perhaps with lustrations, fastings, self-mutilation, sacrifices, etc.); a moment of initiation or a series of initiations into succeeding grades, which filled the initiate with the life of the god or led him to share the knowledge of the god; and the crowning *epopteia* or vision, which seems to have been regarded as both an external ceremony and a moment of inward enlightenment.

Christianity knew no secret rites, until the fourth century (see p. 109); even at that stage, when various decorative features like those of the mysteries were added to Christian rites, it is not certain that any corresponding theological changes were made at any profound level. Suggestions that Christian worship in the fourth century was deeply influenced, or its nature seriously altered, by the mysteries or other pagan cults run the risk of reading back into the mysteries elements which were compatible with Christianity, or even original to it, but much later became the subject of controversy.

The following works are informative: S. Angus, *The Mystery-Religions and Christianity* (John Murray 1925); R. Reitzenstein, *Die hellenistischen Mysterienreligionen* 2nd edn Leipzig 1920: to be used with great caution; N. Turchi, *Fontes historiae mysteriorum aevi hellenistici* (Turin 1923); A. Mylonas, *Eleusis and the Eleusinian Mysteries* (Princeton 1961); F. Cumont, (ET) *The Mysteries of Mithra* (Dover edn, New York 1956); M. J. Vermaseren, (ET) *Mithras, the Secret God* (Chatto and Windus 1963); W. F. Otto, (ET) *Dionysus, Myth and Cult* (Bloomington, Indiana, and London 1965); G. Wagner, (ET) *Pauline Baptism and the Pagan Mysteries* (Oliver and Boyd 1967); A. D. Nock, *Conversion* (OUP 1933); H. Rahner, (ET) *Greek Myths and the Christian Mystery* (Burns Oates 1963).

6 The *Didache*

FRANK HAWKINS

The text of the *Didache* was first published in 1883, from a manuscript previously discovered by Metropolitan Bryennios in a library in Constantinople. This manuscript, written in 1056, contains the only known form of the *Didache* complete in Greek. This text is now referred to as H (Codex Hierosolymitanus), though some earlier editors designated it C. The full title of the work is given as *The Teaching of the Lord to the Gentiles through the Twelve Apostles*, though the index to H gives it simply as *The Teaching of the Twelve Apostles*. Today it is known usually as 'The *Didache*'.

The work appears to be a very early form of Church Order consisting of two main sections and a conclusion. The first section (chs. 1–6) contains instruction on the theme of the 'Two Ways': moral teaching which sets out the difference between the 'Way of Life' and the 'Way of Death'. The second section deals with liturgical matters and particular aspects of church discipline. It includes instructions on baptism (ch. 7), fasting and prayer (8), 'eucharistic' prayers (9, 10), the ministry of apostles and prophets (11–13), the Sunday Eucharist (14), and the status of bishops and deacons (15). In conclusion there is a brief section setting out the eschatological background of the Christian life (16).

The *Didache* contains evidence of Christian life and discipline from an early period which (in the case of the oldest traditions) may be the NT period itself. The precise significance of its contents depends to some extent on questions of internal analysis and criticism and their bearing on the final date of the compilation. More important is the fact that there is evidence of the wide popularity of the *Didache* in the early Church. It is incorporated into later Church Orders; in whole (e.g. *Ap. Const.*, 7.1–32) or in part (e.g. the Ethiopic version of the *Apostolic Canons*).

The date of the *Didache* remains uncertain. Three main solutions have been proposed:

(a) That the *Didache* is a genuine Church Order from a very early period. The distinctive nature of its contents (relative to NT material) is due to the fact that it derives from a Christian community remote from the 'mainstream' Christian churches and traditions of the first century. Such views generally date the work c. 80–100, or even earlier.

(b) That the *Didache* is a compilation of the middle or late second century based on genuine or fictional elements from an older period. It was compiled to give the impression of issuing from and illustrating genuine apostolic Christian life and practice.

(c) That the *Didache* is a composite document, containing elements from different backgrounds and stages of development, but originating from the first century. J-P. Audet, the major exponent of this view, considers that some original material may be as early as A.D. 60.

The origin of the *Didache* is equally difficult to determine. The internal evidence is not decisive since the older material (especially the 'Two Ways' and the liturgical prayers) could well have originated outside the community using the developed compilation. General indications favour Syria, particularly in possible indications of a connection with Antioch (e.g. use of Matthaean-type gospel tradition; ministry of wandering prophets and teachers, cf. Acts 11.27ff, 13.1ff, 15.30ff). But against this must be set the indications of the external evidence: the lack of conclusive parallels in Ignatius of Antioch or in Theophilus, and the fact that later use of the *Didache* (*Ap. Const.*; Eth.) and the earliest textual evidence (Pap. Oxy.; Coptic) point rather to Egypt.

Audet provides a complete revised text and a fresh survey of all the textual evidence. He includes complete collations of the Oxyrhynchus fragments, and the Coptic version, together with extant material from the Ethiopic and Georgian versions. His conclusions favour the text derived from *Ap. Const.* Bk 7 and the Coptic over against H (Bryennios). There is a full discussion in Audet, pp. 221–43. Otherwise there is the text of H. Lietzmann (Kleine Texte 6, 1936; 6th edn 1962) and working texts in both the Lightfoot and Loeb editions of the Apostolic Fathers. Audet's views are subjected to critical scrutiny by B. C. Butler in two articles in *JTS* 11 (1960), pp. 265–83 and 12 (1961), pp. 27–38.

The most important edition and commentary is that of J.-P. Audet, *La Didachè*, Paris 1958. ET in the Loeb and ACW series, and in M. Staniforth, *Early Christian Writings* (Penguin 1968).

7 The *Apostolic Tradition*

THE EDITORS

The document known as *The Apostolic Tradition*, ascribed by many scholars to Hippolytus, the schismatic bishop of Rome (ob. A.D. 236, 237?), contains valuable information about church life and order in the early third century. It may be divided for convenience into three parts. The first concerns the ordination of those chosen for the office of bishop, presbyter, and deacon, providing also a full account of the central features of the eucharistic liturgy of the time. The first section deals also with the appointment of confessors, widows, readers, and sub-deacons, and with the consecration of virgins. The second part is mostly concerned with church regulations affecting the laity, covering their training and discipline from their admission to the catechumenate to their baptism. The initiation rite is also described in some detail. The third part relates a medley of ecclesiastical observances, treating such matters as fasting, first fruits, visiting the sick, daily assembly of the clergy, and burial charges. It concludes with recommendations as to the times at which Christians ought to pray.

The history of the transmission of this text is, to say the least, complex and fraught with difficulties. By the beginning of this century it was known largely through Ethiopic, Bohairic, Sahidic, Latin, and Arabic translations, printed from MSS representing a variety of stages in its development. Already it was clear that the document bore close relationship to other church orders, notably to the *Apostolic Constitutions*, the so-called 'Canons of Hippolytus', and to the *Testamentum Domini*. Called by H. Achelis[1] (1891) 'The Egyptian Church Order' and wedged by him between the *Canons of Hippolytus* and *Ap. Const.*, Bk 8 in parallel columns, it was then widely thought to derive from the other Church

---

[1] References to the works of Achelis and the other authors quoted in this section can be found in the bibliographies of Dix and Botte, with the addition of: F. C. Burkitt, *JTS* 31 (1930), p. 261; and J. Magne, '*Tradition apostolique sur les charismes*' et '*Diataxeis des saints apôtres*' (Paris 1975).

Orders. However, the independent researches of E. Schwartz (1910) and R. H. Connolly (1916) brought each to the conclusion that 'The Egyptian Church Order' was in fact used as a source by those presumed to be its parents, that it dated in all probability from the beginning of the third century, and that it should properly be identified with a treatise entitled *The Apostolic Tradition* which Hippolytus of Rome (according to the legend on his statue, unearthed on the Via Tiburtina in 1551) is said to have written. Already Hippolytus had been claimed as the author of the *Canons of Hippolytus*, being regarded as responsible for the *Epitome* of *Ap. Const.*, Bk 8 (or 'Constitutions through Hippolytus'). For reasons of dating alone, he is clearly the author of neither; yet it is significant that his name is introduced into the *Epitome* at the very moment that the compiler begins to make use of the *Ap. Trad.*; in fact it is from both the *Epitome* and from *Ap. Const.*, Bk 8 that a Greek text of the *Ap. Trad.* can be recovered, just as a fragmentary Syriac version may be deduced from its quotation in the *Testamentum Domini* (itself originally a Greek document).

Various attempts have been made to sever the document both from Rome and from Hippolytus as its author. In 1955, A. Salles drew attention to the paucity of contacts and parallels between the *Ap. Trad.* and the later liturgy of the Roman community. Similarly F. C. Burkitt favoured the theory that the Latin version was in fact compiled for one of the Arian communities in North Italy (350–400); J. M. Hanssens has argued valiantly for the thesis that Hippolytus himself was of Alexandrian origins, and that he came to Rome, bringing with him the liturgy of his own country. This would explain the popularity of the document in Egypt and Ethiopia. J. Magne attaches great weight to the fact that there is some evidence which suggests that the document may not have been known in antiquity as the Apostolic Tradition, which he believes to have been the title of a work by Hippolytus on charisms.

However, both G. Dix and H. Chadwick have shown that on internal evidence alone there is more to relate the document to early third-century Rome than to other Christian milieux; B. Botte similarly observes that the parallels with the liturgy of Alexandria can be more than matched with parallels from the liturgy of Rome, and that there is not the shadow of a proof that Hippolytus had a drop of Egyptian blood in him. There is of course no final proof that Hippolytus himself is the author of this text. Its dating would place it well within his life-time; its place of origin is the city in which he exercised his somewhat stormy ministry. Moreover, if Hippolytus is not responsible for this influential Church Order, it is difficult to conjecture why it should have been fathered on one who was scarcely the most reputable of ecclesiastical figures of the third century. It is clearly safe, therefore, to use this document as evidence for early third century Rome; and its value is not seriously impaired, if we wish to dissociate it from the martyr bishop who witnessed a good confession in the mines of Sardinia.

The best text is in B. Botte, *La Tradition Apostolique de Saint Hippolyte* (Münster 1963). ET and introduction in G. Dix, *The Treatise on the Apostolic Tradition of St Hippolytus of Rome*, 2nd edn rev. H. Chadwick (SPCK 1968). References will be given in the present work according to Dix. A translation with simplified apparatus can also be found in G. J. Cuming, *Hippolytus: a text for students* (Grove Books 1976).[1]

8 Church Orders

E. J. YARNOLD, SJ

The Church Orders were collections of practical directives concerning Christian living; and as these include regulations concerning the method of performing the Church's rites, and some of the texts of the rites themselves, the Church Orders are liturgical books, codes of canon law, and moral treatises combined. The history of the text of these documents is complicated and far from certain, for many of them have survived not as separate works but in combination with others, and often not in their original language. In order to add weight to their prescriptions, most of these Orders, as the titles show, adopted the convention of claiming apostolic authority, sometimes even putting all their contents on the lips of the apostles themselves.

Two of the most important of these Orders, the *Didache* and the *Apostolic Tradition*, receive special treatment elsewhere.[2] Of the others the following particularly merit attention:

The *Didascalia* (or, to give it its full title, *The Catholic Teaching of the Twelve Holy Apostles and Disciples of our Saviour*) is generally thought to have originated in Syria in the first half of the third century. Its original language was probably Greek, but it survives in full only in Syriac, though parts of the Greek, and of a Latin version, have survived through inclusion in other collections. ET in R. H. Connolly, *Didascalia Apostolorum: the Syriac version translated and accompanied by the Verona*

---

[1] The Editors wish to thank J. H. Crehan and others who have helped with the writing of this section.

[2] See pp. 55–9.

Latin fragments, with an Introduction and Notes (Clarendon Press 1929). The surviving Greek text is contained in F. X. Funk, *Didascalia et Constitutiones Apostolorum* (Paderborn 1905).

The *Apostolic Constitutions* is also probably of Syrian origin, dating from the second half of the fourth century. The original Greek text is extant. Books 1–6 consist of a reworking of the *Didascalia*; Book 7 comprises a version of the *Didache* followed by additional liturgical material; Book 8 begins with a treatise on charisms followed by an elaboration of the *Apostolic Tradition*, concluding with 85 *Apostolic Canons*. The earlier books contain several versions of the ceremonies of initiation, and the last book preserves a very full text of the Antiochene Eucharist. Funk's edition is contained in his work quoted above. The unequivocally Arian character of the liturgies contained in the *Apostolic Constitutions* has been shown by C. H. Turner in articles in *JTS* 15 (1913–14), pp. 53–65; 16 (1914–15), pp. 54–61, 523–38; 31 (1929–30), pp. 128–41.

The *Testamentum Domini* is another elaboration of the *Apostolic Tradition* roughly contemporary with the *Apostolic Constitutions*. Its original language is thought to have been Greek, but it survives only in translations in Syriac and other languages. Its place of origin is probably Syria. Outdoing the other Church Orders, it places its instructions on the lips, not of the apostles, but of Christ himself. ET with introduction and notes in J. Cooper and A. J. MacLean, *The Testament of the Lord* (T. and T. Clark 1902).

There is a useful account of the various Church Orders in B. Botte, *La Tradition Apostolique de Saint Hippolyte* (Münster 1963), pp. xvii–xxviii.

9 The *Euchologium* of Sarapion

E. J. YARNOLD, SJ

At the end of the last century G. Wobbermin (TU 17.3b (1898)) published a *Euchologium*, or collection of prayers in Greek, which was attributed in the MS to Sarapion, the Bishop of Thmuis in Egypt about 339–63 to whom St Athanasius addressed several letters on the divinity of the Holy Spirit. The collection includes a complete anaphora as well as prayers to be used in the rites of initiation. F. E. Brightman (*JTS* 1 (1899–1900), pp. 88–113 and 247–77) re-edited the text and re-arranged the prayers in a more logical order, which is followed in the edition of F. X. Funk, *Didascalia et Constitutiones Apostolorum*, vol. 2 (Paderborn 1905). J. Wordsworth published an ET with full introduction entitled

Bishop Sarapion's Prayer-Book 2nd edn (SPCK 1910), but does not follow Brightman's re-arrangement, retaining the order of the MS. Recently B. Botte, in an article entitled 'L'Eucologe de Sérapion est-il authentique?' (*OC* 48 (1964), pp. 50–6), has argued that what survives is a modification of Sarapion's prayers by an Arian hand fifty to a hundred years later. The *Euchologium* retains nevertheless a great importance in the history of the liturgy.

10 Baptismal Catechesis

E. J. YARNOLD, SJ

Among the large number of fourth-century baptismal instructions that have survived, many take the form of explanations of the rites of initiation. As the rites included first communion as well as baptism, these baptismal homilies provide accounts of the main sacraments which are of great value to liturgical scholars, especially as they often quote *verbatim* long sections of the prayers. The most important examples are those attributed to St Cyril of Jerusalem, St Ambrose, St John Chrysostom and Theodore of Mopsuestia.

Cyril of Jerusalem's baptismal sermons fall into three classes: the *Procatechesis* (the sermon preached to those who had just enrolled for baptism); the eighteen *Catecheses*, or instructions in the Christian faith preached in preparation for baptism after the procatechesis; and the five *Mystagogic Catecheses*, the sermons explaining the ceremonies of baptism after the event. All three sets of sermons are included in the edition that until recently provided the only reliable text available, that of G. Reischl and J. Rupp (Munich 1848 and 1860). Recently A. Piédagnel has edited a critical text (SC 126) of the *Myst. Cat.*; the earlier edition of F. L. Cross (*St Cyril of Jerusalem's Lectures on the Christian Sacraments* (SPCK 1951)) contains the Greek text of the *Procat.* and *Myst. Cat.*, with ET and valuable introductory material.

All scholars accept the fact that Cyril wrote the *Procat.* and the *Cat.*, but strong doubt has been expressed about the *Myst. Cat.* The arguments against the Cyrilline authorship are most readily available to English readers in A. A. Stephenson's introduction to his translation of the *Myst. Cat.*; the argument rests on (i) the MS attributions (the early MSS do not attribute the work to Cyril alone, but to John, who was Cyril's successor in the see of Jerusalem, or to John and Cyril, or to no one); (ii) the differences in style and theology between the *Cat.* and the *Myst. Cat.*;

(iii) the dating of various features of the eucharistic liturgy described by 'Cyril' (such as the inclusion of the Lord's Prayer, the emphasis on the sense of awe).[1] However, the MS attributions are too inconsistent to prove anything; and the last two arguments need indicate no more than an interval between the composition of the *Cat.* and that of the *Myst. Cat.* The one figure that Cyril gives (and that a vague one) suggests a date of about A.D. 348 for the *Cat.*, which would be shortly before or after he became bishop.[2] It is possible that the *Myst. Cat.* were composed by Cyril at a date much closer to his death in 387. It is even possible, as Stephenson suggests (pp. 147–8), that the *Myst. Cat.*, as we have them, were preached by John on the basis of a text originally composed by Cyril. At all events, the summary of the rites to be received which Cyril gave at the end of the last *Cat.* (18.33) corresponds very closely to the *Myst. Cat.* that we possess; and it has been argued that St Ambrose, in his *de Sacramentis* (delivered about 391), shows familiarity with the *Myst. Cat.*, or at least with an earlier form of them.[3] Moreover, Egeria's account of her pilgrimage, which according to Devos and Wilkinson took place in 381–4,[4] describes a form of initiation-rite which corresponds with that in the *Myst. Cat.* Hence in these pages we shall give the name Cyril to the author of the *Myst. Cat.*, even though they may have been modified by a later hand, perhaps that of John, and we shall assume that the baptismal ceremonies at the middle of the century took more or less the form which Cyril describes, even though certain details may have been introduced later. The fact that the Old Armenian Lectionary lists the same scriptural readings as Cyril for both the *Cat.* and the *Myst. Cat.*, even though the versions of the Lectionary which we have came seventy years or more after Cyril preached his *Cat.*, shows that the framework of these instructions was very firmly fixed in tradition.[5]

Scholars have never entertained serious doubts about the authenticity of St Ambrose's *de Mysteriis*, but his other work of this kind, the *de Sacramentis*, has come under serious suspicion at various times. Both works are edited by O. Faller (CSEL 73). B. Botte's edition (SC 25 bis)

---

[1] *The Works of Saint Cyril of Jerusalem* (The Fathers of the Church, vol. 64) (Washington 1970), pp. 143–9. Cf. also Cross, pp. xxxvi–xxxix.

[2] *Cat.*, 6.20, where Cyril says that there were people still living who had seen the heresiarch Mani, and that his heresy had begun under the reign of Probus (276–82) 'as much as seventy years ago' (*pro ... holon hebdomekonta eton*). In fact Mani died in 276.

[3] Cf. E. J. Yarnold, 'Did St Ambrose know the Mystagogic Catecheses of St Cyril of Jerusalem?', *SP* 12 (1975), pp. 184–9; the same author's article on the authorship of the *Myst. Cat.* will be published in *Heythrop Journal* 19.2 (1978).

[4] Wilkinson, pp. 237–9. See below, pp. 64–5.

[5] Wilkinson, pp. 253–60, with references to the works of A. Renoux on lectionaries, see pp. 66–7.

provides a useful introduction and notes, as well as a French translation. The arguments against the authenticity of the *de Sac.* are similar to the ones brought against Cyril's *Myst. Cat.*, which we have discussed above: the attribution to Ambrose is much less clear in the MSS than that of the *de Myst.*; the literary style and the description of ceremonies are said to show differences in the two works; some of the ceremonies described in the *de Sac.* are said not to fit in with what is known of Milanese liturgical practice at the time. However, O. Faller and R. H. Connolly, working independently, proved by very many examples that the *de Sac.* contains distinctive expressions, ideas, and translations of scriptural quotations which are also to be found in other works of Ambrose; the cumulative evidence is so strong that practically all scholars take the authenticity for granted.[1] It is generally believed that *de Sac.* is the text of six mystagogic catecheses which Ambrose preached in Easter Week to the newly baptized, and fulfils the same function as the *Myst. Cat.* of Cyril; since the sermons show signs of improvisation, it is plausibly suggested that the text that we have was not intended for publication, but is the version taken down from the lips of the preacher by a shorthand-writer. The *de Myst.* will then be an abbreviated and polished version for publication, omitting the parts which would fall under the *disciplina arcani* (see pp. 109–10), and running the six sermons together as a single continuous work. The probable date of both works is about 391; the rites they describe must be very close to those by which St Ambrose baptized St Augustine in 387.

We possess three sets of baptismal sermons by John Chrysostom. The Greek texts are dispersed among three collections: *Huit Catéchèses Baptismales*, ed. A. Wenger, SC 50; *Varia Graeca Sacra*, ed. A. Papadopoulos-Kerameus (St Petersburg 1909); and PG 49.223–40, ed. B. de Montfaucon. They are conveniently gathered together in English translation, with introduction and notes by P. W. Harkins (ACW vol. 31). Of these twelve, the second and the eleventh[2] describe the baptismal ceremonies; but, unlike the mystagogic sermons of Cyril and Ambrose, these sermons were preached before baptism. There are grounds for thinking that Chrysostom did not deliver them in his see of Constantinople, but as a simple priest in Antioch about 390.[3]

---

1 The issue is discussed with many references in the introductions of the editions of Faller and Botte. Recently, however, K. Gamber (*Die Autorschaft von De Sacramentis*, (Regensburg 1967)) has attempted to disprove the Ambrosian authorship, but against the weight of the evidence adduced by Connolly and Faller his arguments carry no conviction.

2 Wenger 2 and Papadopoulos-Kerameus 3.

3 Cf. Harkins, pp. 15–18.

There are extant sixteen baptismal sermons of Theodore of Mopsuestia, of which the last four describe the rites of initiation, giving systematic quotations from what seems to be an established ritual. The first two of these describe baptism before it is received; the third and fourth describe first communion (received immediately after baptism as part of the ceremony of initiation) and were delivered on the two days after the sacraments were received. These sermons survived only in a Syriac translation of the original Greek.

Theodore became Bishop of Mopsuestia about 392, but some scholars maintain that he preached the sermons, like Chrysostom, at Antioch as a priest.[1] If that is so, they must be almost contemporaneous with Chrysostom's; the ceremonies the two preachers describe are almost identical. The differences that there are (see pp. 101, 106) suggest that Theodore's are the later.

The Syriac text is published in *Woodbrooke Studies* (ed. Mingana) vols. 5–6 with an ET; and in *Studi e Testi* (ed. R. Tonneau and R. Devreesse), vol. 145 with a French translation.

The *Mystagogic Catecheses* of Cyril, the *de Sacramentis* of Ambrose, the last four catechetical homilies of Theodore, and a baptismal instruction of Chrysostom are given in ET with introduction and notes in *AIR*.

11 Egeria's *Pilgrimage*

E. J. YARNOLD, SJ

The work now generally called the *Itinerarium Egeriae* was one of the earliest of several accounts of pilgrimages to the Holy Land and other sacred places; it dates perhaps to the years 381–4, though some scholars would prefer to set it twenty or more years later.[2] It has been known under various titles, since the title-page of the one surviving MS is missing. The earliest editions and studies identified the authoress with the Silvia of Aquitaine mentioned by Palladius (*Historia Lausiaca*, 55.1). Later scholars preferred the claims of a female pilgrim who was the subject of a seventh-century encomium in the form of a letter by Valerius, the abbot of a Spanish monastery; her name was given variously as

---

[1] Cf. Tonneau-Devreese, p. xvi. On the relation between the two almost contemporary rites of Chrysostom and Theodore, cf. *AIR* pp. 208–9, n. 65. However Tonneau's arguments are rejected by B. Botte, *Miscellanea Liturgica in onore di S.E. il Card. G. Lercaro* (Rome etc. 1967), pp. 805–6.

[2] Cf. Wilkinson, pp. 237–9.

Aetheria, Eucheria, and Egeria. Recent research in the MSS favours the form Egeria, and so we shall call her here.[1] She appears to have been a member of a religious community in a place close to the Atlantic, probably Spain or Gaul, who was writing for her sisters in religion an account of her three-year pilgrimage round the Holy Places from the Nile to Ephesus.[2] Her report is of great interest, especially in its description of the Holy Week liturgy at Jerusalem, in the course of which she describes some of the ceremonies of initiation; if the earlier date suggested above is right, we are given an eye-witness account of Cyril of Jerusalem's initiation-ceremonies to supplement the description of them in the *Mystagogic Catecheses* which are attributed to him.

The best edition is in the collection of *itineraria* in vol. 175 of the CC series. J. Wilkinson, *Egeria's Travels* (SPCK 1971) gives an ET and a wealth of fascinating illustrative material. There is another ET in ACW no. 38.

12 Liturgical Books

D. M. HOPE

The Sacramentary was the Celebrant's book. This contained the necessary texts for the celebrating of the Eucharist—collect, prayer over the offerings, proper preface (if one was necessary), and post-communion prayer. Generally the Canon was also included (see plate 2). In addition, texts for the administration of baptism, various formulae for blessings, the rite of ordination, and other prayers were also to be found in the sacramentary. The origins and development of this type of book are difficult to trace; however, the fore-runner of the sacramentary appears to have been smaller collections of Mass formulae, known as *libelli*.[3] The earliest example of the sacramentary-type book is the Verona Codex 85,[4] commonly but misleadingly called the Leonine Sacramentary. It is little more than a collection of libelli, arranged haphazardly in places, and with no clear evidence that it was ever used as a formal Mass book. Other popes, in particular Gelasius and Gregory the Great, have their names attached to sacramentaries, again somewhat misleadingly, since the matter is not quite so simple or straightforward, as we shall see below

---

[1] Cf. Wilkinson, pp. 235–6. The text of Valerius' letter is edited, with introduction, by Z. García, *Analecta Bollandiana*, 29 (1910), pp. 377–99.
[2] Cf. Wilkinson, p. 3.
[3] See A. Stuiber, *Libelli Sacramentorum Romani* (Theophaneia 6, Bonn 1950).
[4] L. C. Mohlberg, and others, *Sacramentarium Veronense* (Rome 1955).

(pp. 224–7). Sacramentaries, by the tenth and eleventh centuries, had begun to multiply in number, so that by the twelfth and thirteenth centuries almost every church, certainly every monastery, had its own sacramentary or set of sacramentaries; very rarely did one copy match another exactly.

In connection with the sacramentary, it may be worthwhile noting that much of what is commonly written on the history and development of the western liturgy is dependent upon reconstructions, the supposed archetypes of earlier years. The codex Vat. Reg. lat. 316 is a good example—for this is supposed to encapsulate an 'old-Roman' core of a sacramentary, the contents of which must be arrived at by critical analysis of the text. F. L. Cross, in his article 'Early Western liturgical manuscripts',[1] quite rightly makes the point that liturgical manuscripts are not manuscripts of an historical kind. They were in constant use and so provide immediate evidence of what was being *done*, when, and where. Following a cursory survey of K. Gamber's *Codices Liturgici Latini Antiquiores*, he is unable to support the view that sacramentaries, as that word is commonly understood, could have existed much before A.D. 700.

The Lectionary was the book which contained the Scripture readings for the Eucharist. In general, until the Middle Ages, it was the custom that readings be taken, not from collections of selected passages, but directly from the Bible according to a list giving the beginning (*incipit*) and end (*explicit*) of the extract. Such lists could be found in lesson indexes, or catalogues, called capitularies. For the most part, these give us the most useful information of the system which governed the eucharistic lections during the early period. Thus the lectionary, originally and for some considerable time, consisted only of biblical references.

It is fortunate, however, that a number of manuscripts of old lectionaries have survived and these provide information about the various readings for the eucharistic assemblies; usually three readings— one from the OT, one from the NT, and then a narrative from the Gospels. The most ancient lectionary surviving from Rome is the Comes (a word from the civil sphere indicating a book from which one drew instruction) of Würzburg,[2] compiled in the eighth century, written in insular script, yet whose contents indicate seventh-century usage. In Spain the *Liber Comicus* is to be found in four or five great centres, and in

---

[1] *JTS* 16 (1965), pp. 61–7.
[2] G. Morin, 'Le plus ancien "Comes" ou lectionnaire de l'Eglise romaine', in *R Bén.*, 27 (1910), pp. 40–74. Also, W. H. Frere, *Studies in Early Roman Liturgy*, iii, The Roman Epistle Lectionary (AC 32, 1935).

Gaul the most complete account is the lectionary of Luxeuil.[1] Mgr Martimort[2] writes that 'customs noted in all these have many points of contact in spite of their differences'.

The Antiphonary or the *Liber antiphonarius* belonged properly to the *schola cantorum* and contained those parts of the Mass (and office) which were sung. Of the pre-Gregorian period fragmentary evidence only survives. However, preserved in manuscripts of the Carolingian period is a book, a complete work, which Jungmann[3] asserts can be traced to Gregory the Great. In the older manuscript no melodies are written, indeed it is not until the tenth century that the melodies are written in neums. Until that time it is likely that much of the chant was learned by heart and passed down through successive generations of singers. The antiphonary, strictly speaking, contained only those chants which were sung antiphonally; the *cantatorium* was a collection of pieces assigned to a cantor who intoned them from the ambo—the gradual, alleluia, and tract. The people joined in a short responsory verse. However, this later came to be incorporated into the choir's repertoire, when the whole of this section became the responsibility of soloist and choir alone. Of great interest and importance is the only surviving liturgical evidence of the choir office in the Celtic church, the Antiphonary of Bangor.[4] This was written at the monastery of Bangor in Ireland, towards the end of the seventh century; the manuscript is now at the Ambrosian Library at Milan.

The Missal did not emerge until the period between the end of the tenth century and the thirteenth century. Certainly by the end of the thirteenth century the *Missale Plenum* had displaced the sacramentary. The appearance of the Missal marked the gradual disappearance of the Antiphonary, Lectionary, and Sacramentary, for these three separate volumes were fused into the one book, the Missal. The new tendency to regard the celebration of the Eucharist less as a communal activity than as an almost private act of the priest meant that all the necessary texts (which the celebrant now needed to recite himself) had to be collated in one book. In an Ordo of the Lateran[5] in the twelfth century, we find for

[1] *The Lectionary of Luxeuil* (Par., Bib. Nat. lat. 9427), ed. P. Salmon (Collectanea Biblica Latina, vii and ix, Rome 1944–53).

[2] A. G. Martimort, *The Church at Prayer: The Eucharist* (Irish University Press 1973), p. 99.

[3] J. A. Jungmann, *MRR* 1.64–5.

[4] Critical edition by F. E. Warren (HBS 4 and 10; 1893–5).

[5] L. Fischer, *Bernhardi cardinalis et Lateranensis ecclesiae prioris Ordo officiorum ecclesiae Lateranensis* (Munich 1916), pp. 80–1.

the first time the celebrant and assisting ministers reciting for themselves the chants and readings. Hence the influence of the purely 'private' Mass in the public and solemn worship of the Church.

Quite alone in its period is the *Bobbio Missal*,[1] so called, which whilst it does not contain any of the Mass-chants, does include the texts of the readings with the celebrant's prayers.

More recently, the latest edition of the *Missale Romanum* has reverted to more ancient use, in that it has been published without the Scripture readings; these are collected in a separate lectionary.

The Breviary emerged, for the Divine Office, as a single compilation from hitherto independent volumes: the psalter, antiphonal and hymnal—in the same way that the Missal appeared, incorporating three books formerly necessary for the celebration of the Eucharist. By the early Middle Ages, the contents of the separate books of the Breviary had become lengthy, diverse and elaborate—impossible in fact for the easy recitation of the Office except within the monastic church. Thus the demand for a shorter and comprehensive volume, a demand which became a necessity as the office became obligatory for all clergy, secular as well as religious.

The Ordines Romani contain instructions and directions concerning the actual performance of each liturgical function. Originally pertaining to the rites as they were performed in Rome, they were frequently copied and used as guides in centres other than Rome itself. Consequently, the original text has in many cases been altered and interpolations inserted, to satisfy regional or local customs. Their composition is set over a long period of time, from the seventh century to the fifteenth, and as with the sacramentaries, those of Roman origin have been edited and amplified to fulfil the needs of the Gallican churches.

The name of M. Andrieu[2] will always be associated with the *Ordines Romani*, for it was he who produced, not only a critical edition, but also numerous researches into the evaluation of this complex set of texts. Before Andrieu, who identified fifty '*ordines*', Mabillon, in his *Musaeum Italicum*,[3] had published a collection of fifteen.

The *Ordines* themselves contain certain instructions, not only for the celebration of the Mass by the Bishop of Rome (I–X), but also for a wide

---

[1] *The 'Bobbio Missal'*, ed., by E. A. Lowe (HBS 53, 58, 1917–20), with notes and studies by A. Wilmart, E. A. Lowe, H. A. Wilson (ib., 61, 1924).

[2] M. Andrieu, *Les Ordines Romani du haut moyen âge* (Louvain 1931–61).

[3] J. Mabillon, *Musaeum Italicum*, vol. ii (Paris 1689).

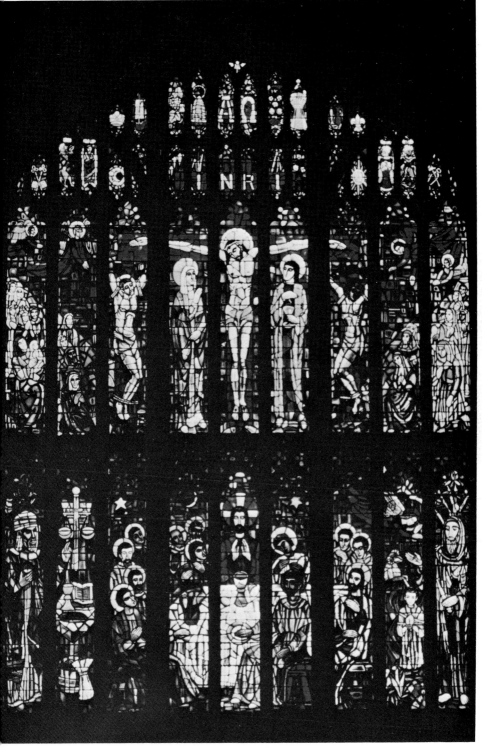

1 Eton College Chapel, east window, by Evie Hone, 1952
The Last Supper is flanked by the priest-king Melchizedek (left) and the sacrifice of Isaac
and surmounted by the crucifixion (see p. 160)

2 From the Gellone Sacramentary, eighth century,
showing the conclusion of the preface, *Sanctus*,
and the beginning of the Canon (*Te Igitur*) with the T elaborated into a crucifix,
in red and black script, with Greek characters for the *Sanctus*

(see p. 65)

variety of matters connected with liturgical celebration—special arrangements for the chant and lections in the liturgical hours (XII–XIV), regulations for the hours of prayer and for meals in the monasteries of Rome (XIV and XVIII), points connected with the ordination of bishops and priests, also the liturgy of the Ember season in respect of the ordinations (XXXIV–XL), a description of the way in which churches in Rome were consecrated, special mention being made of the deposition of relics (XLI–XLIII), the rites for the dying and instructions concerning the corpse (XLIX), also the order to be observed at the coronation of the emperor (XLV–XLVIII). By far the most important for the development of the Western eucharistic liturgy is the first of the series, going back as it does to the eighth century, and even being attributed by some to Pope Gregory the Great. Certainly it suffices for a full description of the papal Mass as it would have been celebrated in Rome about the beginning of the eighth century, at the end of the Gregorian period of liturgical reorganization.

The Liber Pontificalis is a collection of lives of the early popes, written in a fairly systematized manner, and arranged in strict chronological order. Brevity is characteristic of the earlier lives, whilst those of the ninth and tenth centuries and beyond, are more detailed and lengthy. The statements it contains must be treated with great reserve. Forming a kind of preface to the whole work there is an apocryphal letter of Pope Damasus which he supposedly sent to Jerome, asking him to furnish a list of the popes, together with a brief biography of each, from St Peter to his own time. The work appeared as a series of collected lives, and additions were made from time to time. Mgr L. Duchesne produced the critical edition.[1]

Further information on the whole of this section can be found in L. C. Sheppard, *The Liturgical Books* (Burns and Oates 1962).

---

[1] *Le Liber Pontificalis* (Bibliothèque des Ecoles Françaises d'Athènes et de Rome, 2 vols., 1886–92).

13 Thomas Cranmer and the Prayer Book

R. T. BECKWITH

Thomas Cranmer (1489–1556), Archbishop of Canterbury from 1532 until his degradation and execution as a heretic in the reign of Mary, was the creator, virtually single-handed, of English vernacular liturgy. Cranmer's career has been the subject of much recent study and very diverse judgements. His latest biographer, who is no undiscriminating admirer, points to his belief in royal supremacy and his dread of revolution and disorder, even in the Reforming interest, as the clues to the apparent inconsistencies of his conduct (Jasper Ridley, *Thomas Cranmer* (Clarendon Press 1962), p. 11f). A cautious man, at one time firmly convinced of transubstantiation and other medieval doctrines, the progressive change in Cranmer's views, culminating in his conversion to Ridley's eucharistic beliefs (about 1546), made him the chief promoter of liturgical, doctrinal, and disciplinary reform both in Henry VIII's reign and in Edward VI's. The decision to set up the English Bible in every church (1538), to have it read at the Sunday offices and the Mass (1543, 1547) and the provision of the First Book of Homilies (1547) must be attributed mainly to Cranmer's influence; and it is probable that five of the Homilies, the first English Litany (1544), the Order of the Communion (1548), and the two Edwardian editions of the Book of Common Prayer and Ordinal (1549–50, 1552) are substantially Cranmer's own compositions.[1] Outside the liturgical sphere, the Forty-two Articles (1552), on which the Thirty-nine were later based, were probably drafted by Cranmer; and his controversial treatises on the Lord's Supper provide an important commentary on his liturgies.

Cranmer was not only a cautious man but a peaceable man. Faced with the necessity of making great changes, he followed Luther in not making greater ones than he could help; moreover, he made them by stages, not all at once. Thus, the 1552 Communion service was the fourth stage in a process which began with the first introduction of English into the Latin

---

[1] That others than Cranmer played some part in the preparation of the Order of the Communion and the two editions of the Book of Common Prayer is of course true, though very likely they did nothing more than comment on his drafts (see F. E. Brightman, in *LW* pp. 153–5, 169, 174). The theory of C. W. Dugmore that the 1552 Book was produced by Zwinglian opponents of Cranmer (in A. M. Ramsey *et al.*, *The English Prayer Book 1549–1662* (SPCK 1963), ch. 2) cannot even be reconciled with the evidence which he himself adduces. The belief of G. G. Willis that the 1552 Book differs from that of 1549 in not observing the rules of linguistic *cursus* ('Liturgical English', in *The Anglican Catholic*, Winter 1972), if true, shows a change of practice but not a difference of authorship.

Mass in 1547. Similarly, the 1552 services of Morning and Evening Prayer were the fifth stage in a process which began with the first introduction of English into the Latin offices in 1543 and the two draft revisions of the Breviary, before the publication of the two Prayer Books. His concern in all this was not simply the concern of the Tudor monarchy for national political unity (though this was doubtless a factor, and even so the 1549 Book provoked a rebellion in the South West), but also a concern for the spiritual unity of the Church, to which he gives expression in the preface 'Of Ceremonies' and in Article 34, as had earlier been done in the royal proclamation accompanying the 1548 Order of the Communion. The same twin motives, together with the threat of private revisions,[1] led to the quest for a national uniformity more complete than the growing influence of the Sarum use had hitherto achieved. The possibility cannot be excluded that, had Edward VI lived longer, there would have been yet another stage of liturgical revision, though the evidence that Cranmer intended anything of the kind is confined to a rumour reported in *The Troubles at Frankfort* (1575) and to certain indications of future rubrical change (but perhaps nothing more) which D. G. Selwyn has kindly pointed out to the writer in the posthumous *Reformatio Legum Ecclesiasticarum* (1571), a joint-work by Cranmer and others.

The once-popular view that the 1549 Prayer Book reflected Cranmer's true mind, and that the changes in 1552 were changes for the worse made under the malign influence of continental Protestantism, is today very hard to maintain. Five pieces of evidence have combined to discredit this view. In the first place, the royal proclamation accompanying the 1548 Order of the Communion expressed the intention 'from time to time, further to travail for the reformation and setting forth of ... Godly orders'. In the second place, the 1549 book, as well as that of 1552, is deeply marked by the influence of continental Protestantism. In the third place, the report of the House of Lords debate in December 1548 on the forthcoming 1549 Prayer Book shows the reforming bishops already voicing their mature eucharistic opinions. In the fourth place, there is a letter extant, written from Lambeth itself by Bucer and Fagius on 26 April 1549, just before the 1549 Book came into use, stating that the book is only an interim measure, designed to make change less difficult to accept (*Original Letters*, PS, vol. 2, pp. 534–7). In the fifth place, between the publication of the two Prayer Books Cranmer's literary controversy with Bishop Gardiner on the Lord's Supper took place; and in this Cranmer refuses to admit the legitimacy of any of Gardiner's appeals to

---

[1] See the royal proclamation just mentioned and the 1549 Act of Uniformity.

the 1549 Book in favour of unreformed doctrine, constantly maintaining that it was intended to express the views which he now holds. Each of the passages invoked by Gardiner was altered in the 1552 revision, so as to exclude his interpretation.[1] These five facts suggest that the 1549 Prayer Book was intended from the outset as a preliminary step in the direction of something more definite, by a man whose convictions were already formed. Consequently, the statements in the 1551 Act of Uniformity that the 1549 Book was 'a very godly order ... agreeable to the word of God and the primitive church', but had now been further revised 'as well for the more plain and manifest explanation ... as for the more perfection', should not be referred simply to problems that had arisen since the 1549 Book was introduced, such as Gardiner's misinterpretations and Bucer's criticisms.

One reason for Cranmer's cautious and conservative leanings was the respect for antiquity which comes to expression in his preface 'Of Ceremonies' and his controversial writings. He did not, however, cultivate antiquity for its own sake, as some of his successors in liturgical revision were to do. This would have conflicted with his principle of avoiding unnecessary change. The only points at which Cranmer recognized a necessity for change were points where the liturgy had gone astray from scriptural teaching, or was understood in an unscriptural sense, and there indeed antiquity often provided the best model for change (hence the reference to the primitive Church in the preface now called 'Concerning the Service of the Church', the Commination service, and the 1551 Act of Uniformity). But the Fathers were no absolute norm for Cranmer: as chs. 2 and 7 of his *Confutation of Unwritten Verities* show, he recognized faults in their teaching which were not to be imitated. The idea taken up by the 1958 Lambeth Conference (resolution 74c) that the 'recovery of the worship of the Primitive Church' was 'the aim of the compilers of the first Prayer Books of the Church of England' is a mistaken one. And the argument by which this idea is often supported, that Cranmer was so ignorant of patristic liturgy that he imagined his Prayer Books to be much nearer to it than they were, is quite at variance with the facts. The combined evidence of his controversial writings, his library and the parliamentary debate on the 1549 Prayer Book show that he knew the liturgical evidence of Justin Martyr, Tertullian, Cyprian, the *De Sacramentis*, pseudo-Dionysius, Isidore and other of the Fathers, the Liturgy of St Chrysostom, the Mozarabic Missal and the epicleses from the eastern liturgies. As I have written elsewhere, 'he certainly knew enough for us to be sure that if he had made the worship of the early

[1] For the passages in the 1549 Book on which Gardiner based his arguments, and for editions of the 1548 parliamentary debate, see pp. 265–6, below.

church a model for close imitation he would have got much nearer to it than he did. His omission of sacrificial language in regard to the elements from the communion service, though he knew it to be universal in antiquity, is a case in point. And the epiclesis he actually discarded in 1552, after having himself introduced it in 1549' (*Services of Baptism and Confirmation* (Marcham 1967), p. 29).

All in all, Cranmer was a child of the Renaissance no less than of the Reformation. And his greatest gifts became apparent when he took a share in the task of reviving English vernacular literature, by creating an English liturgy. The Book of Common Prayer has an originality and power which are often lacking both in Reformation liturgies and in attempts to restore the worship of the primitive Church. His English liturgical style is not the least part of what he accomplished. Though owing something to its Latin antecedents, and sharing the redundancies characteristic of Tudor English, it achieves the difficult art of being contemporary without being colloquial, of having dignity without sacrificing vigour, and of expressing fervour without lapsing into sentimentality.[1]

Cranmer's general liturgical aims are clear from his Prayer Book itself, and especially from the two prefatory statements 'Concerning the Service of the Church' and 'Of Ceremonies'. He seeks to attain intelligibility, edification, and corporateness, by producing, for regular use, a single, simple liturgy in the vernacular, in which the Scriptures are read and expounded in an orderly way, biblical teaching is incorporated throughout, all that is misleading or meaningless is excluded, words are audible, actions are visible, and congregational participation in speaking, singing, and reception of the sacrament (in both kinds) is encouraged. In pursuing these aims, there were limits to what he achieved. Like other students of the Bible, he had his blind spots. Being confronted with a largely illiterate Church, and long-standing habits of infrequent lay communion, he was not able to implement his principle of congregational worship as fully as he wished, and he had to carry simplicity to lengths which restricted variety and freedom, and sacrificed some of the riches of the pre-Reformation liturgy. He curbed music and ceremonial to an extent which may have been necessary at the time, but was not permanently desirable. He made rather too much use of exhortations. Yet, when all necessary deductions have been made, his achievement remains extraordinary. When compared with the state of the liturgy at the beginning of Henry's reign, Cranmer's Prayer Books show the

---

[1] For a discussion and appreciation of Cranmer's liturgical language, see especially Stella Brook, *The Language of the Book of Common Prayer* (Deutsch 1965), and C. S. Lewis, *English Literature in the Sixteenth Century* (Clarendon Press 1954), pp. 215–21.

following significant changes: the language has been altered from Latin to English; a multiplicity of service books has been reduced to one; a number of regional uses has been reduced to one national use; the rubrics have been pruned (even to excess), simplified, and fully integrated with the liturgical texts; the lectionary has been reformed; preaching has been revived; the congregation has been given a considerable part in the service; the cup has been restored to the laity, and the rule of receiving the sacrament once a year has been increased threefold; an impressive new structure has been given to the Communion service; the eight daily offices have been combined into two; the biblical content of most services has been greatly increased; and traditional doctrines and practices which Cranmer judged to be in conflict with biblical theology (notably the sacrifice of the Mass, transubstantiation, reservation, the confessional, the invocation of saints, and petition for the departed) have been reformed or entirely removed. The fact that his second Prayer Book received only minor revisions in 1559, 1604, and 1662, and in its 1662 form is still widely used in England and other parts of the world, is a tribute to his achievement which is not easy to gainsay.[1]

14 The Prayer Book after Cranmer

R. T. BECKWITH

In the twelve months following the introduction of the 1552 Prayer Book, Edward VI died, Mary ascended the throne, and the 1552 book was abolished by her First Act of Repeal. It was reintroduced in 1559, after Elizabeth became queen, with a few small changes, especially in the Communion service; also a table of Sunday lessons was added and an undiplomatic petition against the papacy in the Litany was omitted. The Puritan movement became influential during Elizabeth's reign, and at the accession of James I the Puritans presented him with the Millenary Petition, which led to the Hampton Court Conference between the Puritans and the bishops, with the king presiding. The Puritans desired the abolition of various ceremonies and ornaments (notably the sign of the cross in baptism, the marriage-ring and the surplice), the interrogation of infants, baptism by women and the use of the Apocrypha, and wished confirmation to be replaced by a stricter communion discipline. In the event, the 1604 Prayer Book, issued by royal proclamation without an Act of Uniformity such as had accompanied the

[1] For a short modern life of Cranmer, students should consult G. W. Bromiley, *Thomas Cranmer, Archbishop and Martyr* (Vine Books 1956).

previous three Prayer Books, made few changes beyond stressing the desirability of an ordained minister at private baptisms where possible, and adding to the Catechism the section on the sacraments, abridged from Alexander Nowell's *Catechism* (PS) by John Overall. A more important outcome of the Hampton Court Conference was the (so-called) Authorized Version of the Bible (1611).[1] In 1645, during the Commonwealth, the Prayer Book was again abolished and was replaced by the non-liturgical Westminster Directory (see pp. 259–60). Before it was restored by Charles II in 1662, under a new Act of Uniformity, there was a second conference between bishops and Puritans, at the Savoy, where a similar but longer list of objections was submitted, together with a substitute liturgy prepared by Richard Baxter. The Laudian bishops John Cosin and Matthew Wren also had long lists of changes prepared, many of them based upon the 1637 Laudian Prayer Book for Scotland.[2] In the event, the 1662 Prayer Book strongly resembled its English predecessor. Some additions, notably the adult baptism service, were made, and far too many small changes to be listed here: they are conveniently summarized in the 1662 'Preface'. Also, the requirement of episcopal ordination was made absolute. The 1662 Act of Uniformity continued in force until 1975, though its provisions had long been modified by legislation for the relief of Protestant Nonconformists and Roman Catholics. It has now been replaced by the Worship and Doctrine Measure, which preserves the 1662 Prayer Book as a norm of doctrine and as a permanent option in worship, but allows the General Synod to authorize additional forms of worship at will.

The Book of Common Prayer was fairly rapidly introduced into the whole of the British Isles and the British dependencies abroad, and with the colonial expansion of the British crown and the missionary expansion of the Anglican church, especially from the eighteenth century onwards, it was carried to many parts of the world. Translations into French (for the Channel Islands and Calais), into Welsh, into Irish, and into Manx appeared at intervals between 1553 and 1765, and the first three were revised after 1662; translations into other languages have followed. In Scotland, owing to the prevalence of Presbyterianism, the Prayer Book made little headway until the separate organization of the Scottish

---

[1] For the records of the Hampton Court Conference, see E. Cardwell, *A History of Conferences connected with the Book of Common Prayer* (OUP 1840).

[2] For the background of the 1637 and 1662 Prayer Books, see pp. 268–71. The 1637 book can be studied in G. Donaldson, *The Making of the Scottish Prayer Book of 1637* (Edinburgh U.P. 1954) and W. J. Grisbrooke, *Anglican Liturgies of the Seventeenth and Eighteenth Centuries* (SPCK 1958). For the records of the Savoy Conference, see E. Cardwell, op. cit., and for Baxter's liturgy P. Hall, *Reliquiae Liturgicae* (Binns and Goodwin 1847), vol. 4.

Episcopal Church in William III's reign, and it was not translated into Gaelic until 1794.[1] A separate Prayer Book for Scotland was prepared in 1619,[2] and the Laudian one was actually introduced, only to be rejected by the Kirk, in 1637. Especially significant was its Communion service, which returned in various points of order and content to the 1549 rite, as more in accordance with patristic liturgy, and introduced an offering of the unconsecrated bread and wine. Enthusiasm for patristic liturgy became the foremost liturgical consideration for the 'Usager' party among the Nonjurors, who separated from the Church of England and the Church of Scotland after the accession of William III in 1688, because of their conscientious inability to take the oaths to the new king in the lifetime of James II, and because of the abolition of episcopacy in Scotland. A new Communion service was published by Thomas Brett and others in 1718 and a complete service book by Thomas Deacon in 1734. Both included the four ancient 'usages' of the mixed chalice, petition for the departed, the offering of the elements (now in the consecration prayer) and the epiclesis, but Brett preserved the main substance of the Prayer Book service, with additions, subtractions, and rearrangements, whereas Deacon got as close as he could to the fourth century *Apostolic Constitutions*.[3] The Scottish Episcopalian Communion service of 1764 was much more on the lines of the former than of the latter, and did not even give expression to two of the usages (the mixed chalice and petition for the departed). The same is true of the service in the first American Prayer Book of 1790, produced in consequence of the War of Independence, which was based on the Scottish service but was more cautious still;[4] and likewise of that in the second American Prayer Book of 1892.

In England, meanwhile, an unsuccessful attempt had been made in 1689 to revise the Prayer Book, with a view to uniting Anglicans and the

---

[1] On translations of the Prayer Book, see *LW*, pp. 813–33. Modern vernacular versions are in use in many missionary provinces of the Anglican world. The Irish, American, and Canadian revisions of the Prayer Book have also been translated into other languages.

[2] Text in G. W. Sprott, *Scottish Liturgies of the Reign of James VI* (Blackwood 1901).

[3] Text of the two Communion services in W. J. Grisbrooke, *Anglican Liturgies of the Seventeenth and Eighteenth Centuries* (SPCK 1958), and of Deacon's complete book in P. Hall, *Fragmenta Liturgica* (Binns and Goodwin 1948), vol. 6.

[4] Text of the Scottish service in W. J. Grisbrooke, op. cit., and of the American also in J. Dowden, *The Annotated Scottish Communion Office* (Grant 1884). For the further history of the Prayer Book in America, see E. L. Parsons and B. H. Jones, *The American Prayer Book: its origins and principles* (New York 1937); M. H. Shepherd, Jr., *The Oxford American Prayer Book Commentary* (New York 1950); and J. W. Suter and G. J. Cleaveland, *The American Book of Common Prayer: its origin and development* (New York 1949).

more moderate Nonconformists in a single non-Roman church. A good many further concessions to Puritan scruples would have been made in this revision than were granted in 1662, but its Latitudinarian promoters were unable to overcome the High Church opposition.[1] A second unsuccessful attempt was made almost two centuries later, this time prompted by domestic Anglican motives. A number of unobtrusive changes in the Prayer Book had been made meanwhile by Parliament, latterly with the help of Convocation. There had been the substitution of new Easter tables and a new lectionary and the removal of some of the state services, but one piece of legislation not reflected in the text of the book was the Act of Uniformity Amendment Act (1872), permitting a shortening of the daily offices on weekdays. In the *Convocation Prayer Book* (Murray 1879), these last provisions were formally inserted, together with a number of other small changes, such as the inclusion of an explanatory statement on the meaning of the Athanasian Creed and a rubric encouraging non-communicants to leave after the ante-communion, now that the increased number of celebrations had made non-communicating attendance more likely. There were, however, various disagreements on the proposals between the two Convocations, and the project was allowed to lapse.[2]

The patristic enthusiasm of the Nonjurors and their Scottish and American successors was linked with high doctrines of tradition and episcopacy, and with a eucharistic doctrine of a peculiar type, which was fully expounded in John Johnson's *Unbloody Sacrifice and Altar* (LACT), published in 1714–18, and was answered in the writings of Daniel Waterland. It was a sort of virtualism, which asserted a real presence of the *Holy Spirit* in the consecrated bread and wine, making them virtually but not really the body and blood of Christ when offered to God and when received by the communicants. The nineteenth-century Oxford Movement, however, brought with it a bolder return to pre-Reformation doctrine, as well as to pre-Reformation liturgy, which has been reflected in greater or lesser degree in most of the revised Prayer Books produced since the turn of this century: namely, in the second and third Scottish books of 1912 and 1929, the third American book of 1928, the South African book of 1954, the Japanese and second Canadian books of 1959, and the CIPBC book of 1963. Exceptions are the second Irish book of 1926 and the first Canadian book of 1918, which (like the first Irish book of 1878, produced in the wake of disestablishment) keep

---

[1] Text in T. J. Fawcett, *The Liturgy of Comprehension 1689* (Mayhew-McCrimmon 1973).

[2] Further information in R. C. D. Jasper, *Prayer Book Revision in England 1800–1900* (SPCK 1954).

closely to the doctrine and ethos of 1662, and are simply concerned with adaptation to local and contemporary needs.[1] The Broad Church movement which followed on the heels of the Oxford Movement has also had its effect on many of the revised Prayer Books of this century, leading to a dilution of their biblical content. In some cases, the changes have been facilitated by the modern principle of doctrinal comprehensiveness, the use of 1662 being permitted alongside the revised book, or parts of 1662 being included as options within the revised book. This policy has been followed in Scotland, South Africa, and the former CIPBC, and was proposed for England in the third abortive English revision, that of 1927–8.[2] In no case, however, was the text of 1662 set on one side. It was rearranged, adapted, supplemented, and expurgated, but its main substance was retained.[3] What is different about present-day experiments in revision is that (while in many cases, though not all,[4] reflecting the same doctrinal tendencies as the revised Prayer Books of a few years ago) they usually abandon 1662 apart from odd details, and instead draw their basic materials straight from the ancient liturgies, modifying them according to current habits of thought, and rephrasing them in the idiom of the day. Examples of the earlier policy do still occur—for instance, *Alternative Services, First Series* (SPCK 1965), based on the 1928 proposals, and *Sunday Services Revised* (Sydney 1973), an adventurous paraphrase of 1662 in modern English, which has been followed rather more cautiously in Kenya (*Modern English Services* (Nairobi 1975)); but whether a widespread resurgence of this policy may be looked for depends mainly on theological and ecumenical factors. The modern experimental services have now begun to be combined into Prayer Books (the USA and Australia leading the way), but whether these will in any province replace the existing Prayer Book, or simply become an alternative to it, is not yet certain.[5]

[1] There have also been certain diocesan Prayer Books in different parts of the world, but these are of less importance.

[2] For further information on the 1927–8 revision, see pp. 274–6.

[3] This is written in virtual ignorance of what is contained in the Japanese Prayer Book. If the translation of its Communion service in B. J. Wigan, *The Liturgy in English* (OUP 1962), is anything to judge by, it departs rather further from 1662 than other revised Prayer Books of its era.

[4] Australia, Tanzania, Kenya and the diocese of Chile have now produced liturgies which adhere resolutely to the doctrine of 1662, but these are exceptions. See the article 'A Turning Point in Prayer Book Revision', in *The Churchman*, April 1975.

[5] For further information on the history of the BCP, students may consult Cuming, *History*, or D. E. W. Harrison, *Common Prayer in the Church of England* (SPCK 1969). Useful collections of texts are B. Wigan, *The Liturgy in English* (OUP 1964), and P. J. Jagger, *Christian Initiation 1552–1969* (SPCK 1970). Many of the revised Prayer Books from outside England are obtainable via SPCK.

II
INITIATION

GENERAL

Brockett, L., *The Theology of Baptism*. Mercier 1971.

Couratin, A. H., *The Pelican Guide to Modern Theology*, vol. 2 (Penguin 1969), pp. 131–239.

Davies, J. G., *The Architectural Setting of Baptism*. Barrie and Rockliff 1962.

Hamann, A., *Baptême et confirmation*. Paris 1969.

Kretschmar, G., *Die Geschichte des Taufgottesdienstes in der alten Kirche*, Leiturgia, vol. 5. Kassel 1970.

Milner, A. P., *The Theology of Confirmation*. Mercier 1972.

Mitchell, L. L., *Baptismal Anointing*. AC SPCK 1966.

Lampe, G. W. H., *The Seal of the Spirit*. 2nd edn SPCK 1967.

Neunheuser, B., (ET) *Baptism and Confirmation*. Herder, Burns Oates 1964.

Schmemann, A., *Of Water and the Spirit*. New York 1974, SPCK 1976.

Schlink, E., (ET) *The Doctrine of Baptism*. St Louis 1972.

Stenzel, A., *Die Taufe: eine genetische Erklärung der Taufliturgie*. Innsbruck 1958.

Studia Liturgica, 12 (1977), nn. 2–3.

Wainwright, G., *Christian Initiation*. Lutterworth 1969.

Wainwright, G., 'The rites and ceremonies of Christian initiation: developments in the past', *SL*, 10 (1974), pp. 2–24.

Whitaker, E. C., *Documents of the Baptismal Liturgy*, 2nd edn AC SPCK 1970, =*DBL*.

Whitaker, E. C., *The Baptismal Liturgy: an Introduction to Baptism in the Western Church*. Faith Press 1965.

1 From New Testament Times until St Cyprian

K. W. NOAKES

THE NEW TESTAMENT PERIOD

Beasley-Murray, G., *Baptism in the New Testament*. Macmillan 1962.
Dunn, J. D. G., *Baptism in the Holy Spirit*. SCM 1970.
Flemington, W. F., *The New Testament Doctrine of Baptism*. SPCK 1948.
Schnackenburg, R., (ET) *Baptism in the Thought of St Paul*. Blackwell 1964.

THE EARLY PATRISTIC PERIOD

Benoit, A., *Le baptême chrétien au IIe siècle*. Paris 1953.
Hamann, A., (ed.), Alba Patristic Library 2. *Baptism, Ancient Liturgies and Patristic Texts*. Staten Is. 1967.
Jungmann, J., (ET) *The Early Liturgy*. DLT 1959.
Wainwright, G., 'The baptismal Eucharist before Nicaea', *SL* 4 (1965), pp. 9–36.

The letters of St Cyprian are quoted by CSEL numbers, but they can be found in Migne thus: 64=PL 3.1047ff, 69=3.1183ff, 72=3.1083ff, 73=3.1155ff, 74 = 3.1173ff Ad Demetrianum = 4.561ff.

The ministry of John the Baptist stands at the beginning of the gospel for all four evangelists. Prefaced in Matthew and Luke by nativity stories, the ministry of John is the immediate precursor of the ministry of Jesus in each Gospel. Behind the figure of the Baptist there lies a long history of the use of water in the religion of Israel; water was used to cleanse from impurity[1] and the prophets looked forward to a sprinkling with pure waters in the messianic age.[2] Amongst John's contemporaries, the members of the sect at Qumran, lustrations were important; they thought of their lustrations as a means of moral and religious cleansing, when combined with penitence, and they cherished ardent eschatological expectations, conceiving their own task to be that of preparing the Way of the Lord.[3]

John may have had contact with groups such as the Qumran sectarians, but he is best seen as a follower in the tradition of the prophets who would often make use of symbolic actions.[4] His baptism expresses repentance and conversion; it is a baptism of repentance for the remission of sins

[1] Numerous references in Lev., e.g. 15.5; 16.24, 26; 17.15. For the Jewish antecedents of baptism, see pp. 44–7.
[2] E.g. Ezek. 36.25; Zech. 13.1; Is. 4.4.
[3] Beasley-Murray, op. cit., p. 39.
[4] See Lampe, op. cit., pp. 19–32.

(Mk. 1.4). John's ministry is not self-sufficient but points forward to the One who comes after him and who will administer a baptism in Spirit and fire (Mk. 1.7f and parallels). All are to experience the purgative act of messianic judgement, which will mean destruction for the unrepentant and, for the repentant, a refining prior to participation in the messianic kingdom. John's baptism is a preparation for the messianic baptism;[1] it is the initiatory rite which brings together the messianic people.

One of the best attested facts about Jesus is that he was baptized by John in the Jordan. This incident is reported in the synoptics and alluded to in the Fourth Gospel.[2] That the propriety of Jesus' baptism by John was a problem for some in the early Church is shown by Matthew's account (Mt. 3.14f). Luke, on the other hand, emphasizes the Lord's solidarity with the publicans and sinners and all the people (Lk. 3.21). For the evangelists the baptism of the Lord inaugurated his ministry; the descent of the Spirit which closely followed his baptism meant that the new covenant had been entered upon, a new epoch begun.

Although the baptism of Jesus as the inauguration of his messianic ministry was obviously unique, yet from the time of the resurrection[3] it seems that baptism was the mark of belonging to the Christian community.[4] It is reasonable to suppose that Christian baptism derived from the baptism of John. However, the content of the Christian rite was much richer, since it was not merely a baptism of repentance for remission of sins, but also a means of sharing in Christ, a means of dying with him, of being baptized into him, of becoming a member of his Body, of receiving his Spirit.

If we look at the writings of the NT we shall find much about the significance of baptism, but little liturgical detail. The NT writings were not intended to give a comprehensive survey of church life but were each written for some particular purpose, for a particular group of Christians in a particular situation. Couratin has rightly stated: 'It is what the NT

---

[1] The thoroughly eschatological character of John's baptism makes it unlikely that it derived from Jewish proselyte baptism; besides, direct evidence of proselyte baptism is lacking before the latter part of the first century A.D. (However for a different view, see pp. 44–5.) On the question of proselyte baptism see Beasley-Murray, op. cit., pp. 18–31 and H. H. Rowley, 'Jewish Proselyte Baptism and the Baptism of John' in *From Moses to Qumran* (Lutterworth 1961), pp. 211–35.

[2] Mk. 1.9–11 and parallels; Jn. 1.32ff.

[3] In John's Gospel alone is there mention of Jesus or the disciples baptizing during the Lord's ministry (3.22f; 4.1–3).

[4] In Mt. 28.16–20 the risen Lord directs the eleven to evangelize all the nations, baptizing men into the name of the Father and of the Son and of the Holy Spirit; cf. Mk. 16.15f, part of the later, additional, ending of that Gospel.

writings presuppose that is of greater importance than what they actually describe.'[1]

If we look at the earliest stratum of NT writings, the epistles of Paul, we find that the apostle is always highly conscious of the change effected by Christ in his own life and in the lives of fellow Christians. Thus he frequently contrasts the two modes of life: in the old Adam and in the new (Rom. 5.12ff, cf. 6.12—7.6; 1 Cor. 15.20ff, cf. 6.9–11), according to the flesh and according to the Spirit (Gal. 5.16ff). Throughout his letters, Paul assumes that to become a Christian one is baptized; the 'once-for-all-ness' of baptism is a basic presupposition of Paul's thought, as of all subsequent thought about baptism. Baptism is the frontier between two worlds, between two entirely different modes of life, or, rather, between death and life. Faith and baptism are inextricably linked; in their baptism believers confess Christ as Saviour (Rom. 10.9).

In a striking phrase Paul speaks of baptism as a burial with Christ;[2] 'Do you not know that all of us who have been baptized into Christ Jesus were baptized into his death? We were buried therefore with him by baptism into death, so that as Christ was raised from the dead by the glory of the Father, we too might walk in newness of life' (Rom. 6.3f). The old solidarity in sin, which in the previous chapter Paul had spoken of as a solidarity in Adam, has been replaced by a new solidarity in righteousness, solidarity in the new Adam, Christ. 'For if we have been united with him in a death like his, we shall certainly be united with him in a resurrection like his' (Rom. 6.5 RSV). The believer has put off the old man with his doings and put on Christ (Col. 3.9f; Gal. 3.27).

Alongside his talk of baptism into Christ Jesus (Rom. 6.3; Gal. 3.27), Paul also speaks of baptism in the Holy Spirit (1 Cor. 12.13). The life of the Christian is life in the Spirit, entered upon at baptism (cf. 2 Cor. 1.22). It is the gift of the Spirit which means participation in the new covenant (2 Cor. 3); baptism in the Spirit incorporates a man into the Body of Christ.[3]

In the Epistle to the Ephesians Christians are described as those sealed with the promised Holy Spirit for the day of redemption (1.13; 4.30). Presumably this 'sealing' occurred when a person was initiated into the Christian community. In 5.25–7 the author apparently speaks of baptism in terms of a prenuptial bridal bath ('the washing (*loutron*) of water with

---

[1] Op. cit., p. 139.

[2] The theme of baptism as burial with Christ recurs in Col. 2.12; Christians are those who have 'died with Christ', Col. 2.20.

[3] In 1 Cor. 6.11 Paul juxtaposes the name of the Lord Jesus and the Spirit of our God as agents of the deliverance effected through baptism.

the word') which cleanses and sanctifies. The word *loutron* recurs in the allusion to initiation as rebirth and renewal in Tit. 3.5f; according to his mercy he saved us, 'by the washing of regeneration and renewal in the Holy Spirit, which he poured out upon us richly through Jesus Christ our Saviour'.

Among 'the elementary doctrines of Christ' the author of the Epistle to the Hebrews includes 'the instruction about ablutions (*baptismoi*)' and 'the laying on of hands' (6.2). Presumably this instruction about baptisms in the plural refers to basic teaching wherein Christian baptism was contrasted with other lustrations. Later in the Epistle the author mentions the two complementary aspects of baptism, inward and outward; 'let us draw near with a true heart in full assurance of faith, with our hearts sprinkled clean from an evil conscience and our bodies washed with pure water' (10.22).

Even if one does not accept the view that 1 Peter is a baptismal homily,[1] one cannot deny the wealth of allusion to the quality of Christian life made possible by the redemption achieved by Christ and made effective through baptism; the recipients are addressed as 'newborn babes' (2.2), they have been 'born anew' (1.3, 23). However, there is only one direct reference to baptism in the Epistle, namely in 3.21, where the author draws an analogy between the waters of the Flood and the water of baptism; 'Baptism, which corresponds to this (i.e. the waters of the Flood), now saves you, not as a removal of dirt from the body but as an appeal to God for a clear conscience, through the resurrection of Jesus Christ. . . .'

As well as a number of possible allusions to baptism,[2] John's Gospel contains the account of the meeting of Jesus and Nicodemus (ch. 3), where baptism is definitely in view. The Lord insists that a man must be born from above if he is to see the Kingdom of God. This birth is of water and the Spirit; except a man be born of water and the Spirit he cannot enter into the Kingdom of God (3.5). Water and the Spirit are co-ordinated here as elsewhere in John's Gospel (7.38f; cf. 4.14); together they are agents of heavenly birth.

---

[1] See arguments in F. L. Cross, *1 Peter, A Paschal Liturgy* (Mowbray 1954); C. F. D. Moule, 'The Nature and Purpose of 1 Peter', *NTS* 3 (1956), pp. 1–11; T. C. G. Thornton, '1 Peter, A Paschal Liturgy', *JTS* 12 (1961), pp. 14–26.

[2] E.g. in the discourse at the well of Jacob (ch. 4), at the healing of the paralytic (ch. 5) and of the man born blind (ch. 9), in the water (and the blood) from the side of the Crucified (19.34). Scholars differ widely in their estimation of the extent of sacramental allusions in John's Gospel; thus O. Cullmann, *Early Christian Worship* (SCM 1953), sees a wealth of sacramental references, whereas Bultmann regards them as later interpolations. There is a useful survey, 'The Sacramentalism of John', on pp. cxi–cxiv of R. E. Brown's Anchor Bible *Commentary on John* (G. Chapman 1971).

In 1 John reference is made to the *chrisma*, the anointing from the Holy One which Christians have received (2.20; 2.27); this anointing, no doubt conferred at initiation, is the Spirit who abides in believers and teaches them. The 'water and the blood' of 1 Jn. 5.6–12 are often interpreted sacramentally as referring to baptism and Eucharist, and T. W. Manson[1] suggested that the triad of witnesses in verse 8, the Spirit, the water, and the blood, refers to three stages of initiation, i.e. reception of the Spirit, baptism and Eucharist. However, in view of the anti-docetic tone of 1 John it seems best to interpret the water and the blood as referring to key events (baptism, death) in the incarnate ministry of Jesus; as such they join with the Spirit in bearing witness to the reality of that earthly ministry.

Although there is a wide spectrum of views on the question of the historical value of Acts, it is certain that this work was never intended to be a liturgical handbook or guide to the practice of the early Church. The aim of Acts is to show how the gospel was spread throughout the Empire from Jerusalem to Rome, and so the author concentrates on the major turning-points in this saga and not on details of church life and organization. However, the initiation of converts, especially when they are representatives of new categories of believers, is an important element in this drama of the widening spread of the mission of the Church. Therefore from Acts we can learn something of the author's understanding of initiation and possibly we may learn something of the practice of the apostolic Church with regard to initiation.[2]

It seems likely that the author of Acts intends the imperative of Peter in 2.38 to establish the pattern and norm for entry into the Church. After his Pentecost sermon the hearers said to Peter and the rest of the apostles '"Brethren, what shall we do?" And Peter said to them, "Repent, and be baptized everyone of you in the name of Jesus Christ for the forgiveness of your sins; and you shall receive the gift of the Holy Spirit"'. There are three important and directly related elements in this process of entry into the Church: repentance, baptism in water, and reception of the Spirit.

When one examines the accounts of initiation in Acts the relation between the gift of the Spirit and baptism in water does not seem to be consistent. Sometimes one finds the sequence of 2.38, as in the case of the Ephesians who were baptized into the name of the Lord Jesus, had hands laid upon them and received the Holy Spirit (19.5f). Sometimes the sequence is inverted, as in the case of Cornelius, who received the Holy Spirit while Peter was still speaking and was then baptized (10.44–8; cf.

[1] 'Entry into Membership of the Early Church', *JTS* 48 (1947), pp. 25–33.
[2] Dunn, op. cit., provides an illuminating exegesis of the important passages in Acts.

perhaps the case of Paul, 9.17f). In other instances the reception of the Spirit and baptism in water seem quite unconnected, as in the case of Apollos (18.25; cf. also the account of Pentecost, 2.4).

If there is a consistent point of view underlying these ambiguities, it is that for the author of Acts the one thing that makes a man a Christian is the gift of the Spirit; repentance and baptism in water are necessary, but it is the reception of the gift of the Spirit which is the decisive mark of the Christian. Thus, in the case of the Samaritans (8.4ff), they are not really Christians until the Spirit comes upon them at the laying on of the apostles' hands. Their response to Philip's preaching was a mere parallel to their response to Simon the magician, as the narrative makes clear. Simon himself believed and was baptized and 'continued with Philip'; he was in the same situation as the other Samaritans who had gone through the form but had not experienced the reality. Likewise in the story of the twelve Ephesian disciples, these 'disciples' only become Christians when they receive the Spirit (19.6). In 19.2 Paul is not asking Christians whether they have received the Spirit, but is asking disciples who profess belief whether they are Christians. The story of Apollos makes an illuminating contrast; he did not need rebaptism because he possessed the Spirit already (18.25).

For the author of Acts, therefore, there are three necessary elements in initiation—repentance, baptism in water and the gift of the Spirit—but the most important of these is the gift of the Spirit.

Having made a brief survey of the main evidence of the NT concerning initiation, we can tentatively explore the content and nature of initiation in the apostolic age.

The initiatory rite consisted in:

  (i) preparation,
 (ii) dipping in water with mention of the name of Jesus or of the Trinity,
(iii) possibly anointing and/or, in some churches, laying on of hands.

The candidates would have been adult, although it is possible that children might have been among those baptized when whole households were converted.[1]

With regard to (i), it is difficult to determine how much elementary instruction the candidates would have received before baptism. We

[1] For discussion of whether the early Church baptized infants see J. Jeremias, (ET) *Infant Baptism in the First Four Centuries* (SCM 1960); (ET) *The Origins of Infant Baptism* (SCM 1963); K. Aland, *Did the Early Church Baptize Infants?* (SCM 1963). For Jewish precedents, see p. 45.

cannot tell, for example, how much of the instruction to converts alluded to by Paul in 1 Thess. was delivered before baptism and how much afterwards. Perhaps there is some indication of the contents of baptismal instruction in Heb. 6.1f, where 'the elementary doctrines of Christ' are listed as 'a foundation of repentance from dead works and of faith towards God, with instruction about ablutions, the laying on of hands, the resurrection of the dead and eternal judgement'. It has been plausibly suggested that the ethical instruction which has a common content and pattern in the various Pauline and non-Pauline epistles derives from baptismal catechesis.[1]

A profession of belief was an integral part of baptism. It seems that this profession was made by the candidate expressing assent to a question put to him by the minister of baptism, either a question about belief in Jesus (hence baptism 'in the name of Jesus', cf. Acts 2.38; 8.16; 10.48; 19.5; Rom. 10.9; 1 Cor. 6.11) or, in some congregations, a threefold question about belief in Father, Son, and Holy Spirit (cf. Mt. 28.19). It is important to note that all the evidence points to the fact that the minister of baptism posed the question, 'Do you believe in . . . ?', and did not use the baptismal formula familiar to us, 'I baptize you in the name of . . .'.[2] The baptismal confession in answer to interrogation is probably alluded to in Rom. 10.9 and is mentioned explicitly in 1 Tim. 6.12 and Heb. 4.14.[3]

Baptism would have been performed in a river or pool or in a domestic bath-house. There can be no certainty in the matter of whether baptism in the NT period was by immersion or by affusion. Nor have we much evidence of the identity of the minister of baptism. In Acts the missionary apostles are presented as baptizing their converts. However, in 1 Cor. 1.12–17, Paul, while by no means disparaging baptism, expresses gladness that he had baptized only a few Corinthians, since this would have led to even more partisanship, and, besides, his ministry was not that of baptizing but of preaching the gospel.

Whether the most primitive rites of initiation included any element

---

[1] See P. Carrington, *The Primitive Christian Catechism* (CUP 1940); E.G. Selwyn, Commentary on *1 Peter* (Macmillan 1946), especially Essay 2, pp. 363–466.

[2] The western text of the story of the Ethiopian eunuch presents us in Acts 8.37 with a declaration of faith on the part of the baptized, 'I believe that Jesus Christ is the Son of God', but all the western liturgies until the fourth century require assent to a question, not a declaration of faith.

[3] On baptismal interrogation see J. N. D. Kelly, *Early Christian Creeds* (3rd edn Longman 1971), pp. 40–9; also E. C. Whitaker, 'The Baptismal Interrogations', *Theology* 59 (1956), pp. 103–12, 'The Baptismal Formula in the Syrian rite', *CQR* 161 (1960), pp. 346–52, 'The History of the Baptismal Formula', *JEH* 16 (1965), pp. 1–12.

other than mere baptism in water is a much disputed point. Lampe,[1] for instance, has insisted that the initiation-rite originally consisted simply of water-baptism. Other edifying ceremonies, anointing and laying on of hands, may have been added later in some circles but played no essential role in the rite. However, the NT evidence strongly suggests that, in some congregations at least, laying on of hands was an important element in baptism and was the means whereby the Spirit was conferred. Thus, in Heb. 6.2 baptism and laying on of hands are very closely linked.[2] The laying on of hands is also presented as an integral part of initiation in Acts 19.5f and 8.14ff; the imposition of hands is portrayed as the climax of a single initiatory process. Lampe has argued[3] that the two incidents of the Samaritans and the Ephesians should be seen not as providing evidence for normal liturgical practice but as vital turning-points in the spread of the gospel at which an important new category of convert was welcomed into the Church and associated by the laying on of hands with its apostolic, missionary task. This explanation has little plausibility with regard to the Samaritans and it does not fit the case of the Ephesians.

It is always difficult to assess to what extent contemporary liturgical practice affected the shape of any incident in the Gospels, but it has been reasonably suggested that the account of the baptism of Jesus provides an instance of reflection of current liturgy. As the baptism of Jesus consisted of two closely related but distinct events, the baptism in the Jordan and the descent of the Spirit, so, it is suggested, the early initiation-rite was not a simple undifferentiated process, but rather, contained two elements, baptism in water and laying on of hands. The one incorporation into the new people of God was achieved by a double rite which emphasized and effected the two aspects of initiation, the 'negative' aspect of death to the past and to the old Adam and the 'positive' aspect of the gift of new life in the Spirit.[4]

Was there an actual anointing in the primitive initiation-rite? Some would regard 2 Cor. 1.21f as not merely metaphorical; here God is said to have anointed us, sealed us, and given us the earnest of the Spirit in our hearts. The other references to sealing (Eph. 1.13; 4.30), the seal of God on the foreheads of the righteous (Rev. 7.2ff; 9.4, cf. 14.1; 22.4), and anointing (1 Jn. 2.20; 2.27) might also be understood literally. It must be admitted, however, that the evidence for laying on of hands as an integral

---

[1] Op. cit., passim.
[2] Dunn, op. cit., p. 207, writes on Heb. 6.2, 'As to the relation between baptism and laying on of hands the very unusual use of *te* (instead of *kai*) suggests that what is envisaged is a single ceremony like that in Acts 19, the single rite of initiation'.
[3] Op. cit., pp. 66–77.
[4] Tit. 3.5 may reflect this duality within the one rite of initiation.

part of the rite of initiation in the earliest period is much stronger than the evidence for anointing.[1]

When we pass from the New Testament to the literature of second-century Christianity we find numerous allusions to initiation and its effects, but only two descriptions of the rite; that in the *Didache*, 7 (see pp. 55–7), and that of Justin (1 *Apol.*, 61 and 65), who was born in Syria, but wrote in mid-second-century Rome (*DBL* 1–2).

Evidence is scanty and no doubt the details of the initiation-rite varied from place to place, but we can note a number of interesting developments from the most primitive rite:

(i) Preparation for baptism has become more formally organized. Fasting, by the candidates, the one who baptizes and the congregation, is enjoined as part of the preparation in both our sources:

> But before the baptism let him that baptizes and him that is baptized fast, and any others also who are able; and you shall order him that is baptized to fast a day or two before. (*Didache*)

> As many as are persuaded and believe that what we teach and say is true, and undertake to be able to live accordingly, are instructed to pray and to entreat God with fasting for the remission of their sins that are past, we praying and fasting with them. (Justin)

In the *Didache* the instruction on baptism is preceded by 'The Two Ways', moral instruction based on a Jewish source (chs. 1–6). It has commonly been supposed that the two ways were used in pre-baptismal catechesis in the congregation from which the *Didache* stems. However, the link between ch. 7 and the preceding material, 'having first recited all these things', may be a secondary addition to the original text, as Audet has argued.[2]

(ii) The threefold form of baptismal interrogation has become the norm; as the candidate assents to each question he is dipped in the water. Presumably Justin alludes to the actual form of the interrogations when he speaks of baptism 'in the name of God the Father and Lord of the universe', 'and in the name of Jesus Christ who was crucified under Pontius Pilate, and in the name of the Holy Spirit who through the prophets foretold all things about Jesus'.

There would have been no special church buildings, the Eucharist being celebrated in private houses, and, as in the NT period, baptism would often be performed outdoors at a natural source of water. Justin

---

[1] See L. L. Mitchell, *Baptismal Anointing* (SPCK 1966), pp. 15–29. On the possible Jewish origins of anointing as an initiation-rite, see p. 46.

[2] J.-P. Audet, *La Didachè, instruction des apôtres* (Paris 1958), pp. 58–62.

simply writes, 'Then they are brought by us where there is water', but the *Didache* gives more precise directions, '. . . baptize in the name of the Father and of the Son and of the Holy Spirit in living [i.e. running] water. But if you have not living water, then baptize in other water, and if you are not able in cold, then in warm. But if you have neither, then pour water on the head thrice in the name of the Father and of the Son and of the Holy Spirit'.[1]

(iii) Baptism leads into the Eucharist. In the NT writings it is implied throughout that baptism means entry into the Body of Christ and hence baptism conveys the right to participate in the Eucharist. This link between baptism and Eucharist, which can perhaps be observed in the *Didache*, 9.5 and 10.6 (but see pp. 170–1 for another view), is made explicit in the initiation-rite described by Justin, where initiation leads directly to the Eucharist; after the baptismal dipping the candidate is introduced into the congregation, common prayers are said for Christians everywhere and especially for the newly baptized, the kiss of peace is given and the Eucharist begins.

In neither the *Didache* nor Justin are we told who is the minister of baptism. However, it is certain that, as the second century progressed, initiation became increasingly the prerogative of the local bishop, as is already stated early in the century by Ignatius, who writes that everything must be under the bishop's control; 'it is not lawful apart from the bishop either to baptize or to hold an *agape*' (*ad Smyrn.*, 8).

Did the initiatory rites of the second century include either an unction or imposition of hands for imparting the Holy Spirit? The *Didache* makes no mention of unction or imposition of hands.[2] Justin's account is problematic in that he fails to mention the gift of the Spirit at initiation and he does not seem to mention any action within the rite other than dipping in water. This apparent silence is not, however, conclusive proof that Justin knew nothing of the gift of the Spirit mediated either through hand-laying, or unction, or both. It has been argued that Justin may have left his account deliberately incomplete; it was not his purpose to go into great detail in matters of liturgy since he was writing to stress primarily the harmlessness of Christian rites. E. C. Ratcliff has proposed that

---

1 See T. Klauser, 'Taufet in lebendigem Wasser! Zum religions- und kulturgeschicht-lichen Verständnis von Didache 7.1–3', in *Pisciculi* (Festschrift für Dölger) (Münster, 1939), pp. 157ff.

2 At the end of 10.7 the Coptic version of the *Didache*, followed by *Ap. Const.*, inserts an instruction about blessing oil at the Eucharist. This is almost certainly a secondary addition to the text. Anyway, there is no necessary connection between this blessing of oil and its use at baptism. See Audet, op. cit., pp. 67–70.

prayer for the descent of the Holy Spirit on the candidate at the laying on of hands may be referred to amongst the petitions for the newly baptized ('enlightened') before the Eucharist in 1 *Apol.* 65.[1]

We have much more evidence of the use of anointing in heterodox circles than in orthodox. For example, we learn of the use of anointing in Marcionite initiation[2] (Tertullian, *adv. Marcionem*, 1.14; 1.28; 3.22), amongst the Marcosians (Irenaeus, *AH* 1.14.2f) and in the Valentinian gnostic circles reflected in the *Gospel of Philip*.[3] Lampe has suggested that anointing was a subsidiary ceremony in initiation first developed among gnostics and only after the end of the second century borrowed by orthodox Christians. However, considering the mutual antagonism, it seems unlikely that such borrowing occurred. The use of oil in initiation would not have been strange since oil was normally used when a person had a bath, and also the anointing of kings was a familiar feature of the Old Testament, the Spirit being bestowed on David at his anointing by Samuel (1 Sam. 16.13). In view of this background, the references to the anointing of Christians in orthodox writers of the latter part of the second century (Irenaeus, *AH* 3.9.3; Theophilus, *ad Autol.*, 1.12) may not be merely metaphorical, but may refer to a ceremony within initiation.

There has been considerable controversy over the meaning of 'seal' and 'sealing' in the early patristic literature.[4] On examination of the second-century evidence Dix concluded that the seal means the consignation of the forehead with chrism at baptism for the bestowal of the Holy Spirit, whereas Lampe decided that the seal means the seal of the Spirit conveyed by baptism in water with no further ceremonies. It should be noted, however, that the seal in this period does not always bear the same meaning and often has no evident association with the Holy Spirit; frequently it is best interpreted as referring to the signing of the baptized with the cross during initiation.

For the rite of initiation in the West in the early third century there are two important sources: Tertullian's works, especially his *de Baptismo*,

[1] E. C. Ratcliff, 'Justin Martyr and Confirmation', *LS* 110–16 = *Theology* 51 (1948), pp. 133–9. A. H. Couratin, 'Justin Martyr and Confirmation—a note', *Theology* 55 (1950), pp. 458–60, attempts to show from the typology used in *The Dialogue with Trypho* that Justin knew of an anointing after baptism.

[2] From Tertullian, *adv. Marcionem* 1.14, it appears that Marcionite initiation consisted in baptism in water, anointing, signing with the cross, giving of milk and honey, and Eucharist.

[3] Lampe, op. cit., pp. 120–8, gives a detailed survey of gnostic evidence.

[4] On the seal see G. Dix, *The Theology of Confirmation in Relation to Baptism* (Dacre Press 1946); 'The Seal in the Second Century', *Theology* 51 (1948), pp. 7–12; J. E. L. Oulton, 'Second Century Teaching on Holy Baptism', *Theology* 50 (1947), pp. 86–91; Lampe, op. cit., *passim*.

and the *Apostolic Tradition* of Hippolytus of Rome (*DBL* 2–10). The *de Baptismo* (*c.* 200) is not intended to provide a balanced survey of the rite of initiation in north Africa in Tertullian's day but is a polemical work written in defence of baptism against the pestilential views of a gnostic sect led by a 'certain female viper' (*de Bapt.*, 1). However, from the *de Baptismo* and from references to initiation in his other works we can reconstruct with fair accuracy the rite known to Tertullian. For the *Apostolic Tradition*, see pp. 57–9.

Before we look at the pattern of initiation in the time of Hippolytus and Tertullian there are four important general observations to be made. First, baptism is normally to take place at Easter. Tertullian writes that although every time is suitable for baptism, nevertheless Easter is the most fitting time and, after that, Pentecost (*de Bapt.*, 19). It must be remembered that before the fourth century the great celebration of redemption was not split into Good Friday and Easter Day but instead on the eve of Easter there was a celebration of the Christian Pasch, a representation of the whole drama of salvation. Secondly, it is made explicit that the normal minister of baptism is the bishop, although his function can be delegated to presbyters, deacons, and even laymen according to Tertullian (*de Bapt.*, 17). In the *Ap. Trad.* it is laid down that a presbyter performs the anointing, before and immediately after baptism, and the baptism itself, while to the bishop is reserved the imposition of hands. Thirdly, although adult baptism is still normal, the baptism of infants is also practised. In the *Ap. Trad.* it is stated that children are to be baptized first (21.4); Tertullian knows of the practice of infant baptism but is opposed to it (*de Bapt.*, 18). Fourthly, the catechumenate had a much more developed form.[1] The *Ap. Trad.* gives a considerable amount of information about this matter. There was to be an initial inquiry into the character and mode of life of potential candidates; there is a long list of professions forbidden to Christians. After three years of instruction there was a further examination before entry upon the final preparation for baptism which consisted of exorcisms and fasting (*Ap. Trad.*, 20). From *de Bapt.*, 20 we learn that candidates are 'to pray with repeated prayers, fasts and bendings of the knee and night vigils'; they are to confess their past sins.

The pattern of initiation indicated by Hippolytus and Tertullian is as follows:

    (i) Catechumenate and immediate preparation for baptism.
    (ii) Blessing of water (*de Bapt.*, 3 and 4; *Ap. Trad.*, 21.1).

---

[1] On the early history of the catechumenate see B. Capelle, 'L'introduction du catéchumenat à Rome', *RTAM* 5 (1933), pp. 129–54.

(iii) Threefold renunciation of the devil (of the devil, his pomp, and his angels/works) (Tertullian, *de Corona*, 3; *de Spectaculis*, 4; *Ap. Trad.*, 21.9). Hippolytus alone refers to an anointing for exorcism at this point.

(iv) Threefold dipping at threefold interrogation (Tertullian, *adv. Praxean*, 26; *de Corona*, 3; *Ap. Trad.*, 21.12–18). The candidate replies '*Credo*' to each of the three questions. Tertullian's words in *de Corona*, 3, 'Then we are three times immersed, making a somewhat fuller reply than the Lord laid down in the gospel', are best understood as referring to the fact that the officiant's questions were now fuller and longer than the simple formulae implied in Mt. 28.19.

(v) Anointing (*de Bapt.*, 7; *Ap. Trad.*, 21.19), probably of the whole body, since in *de Corona*, 3 it is stated that the newly baptized refrain from the daily bath for seven days.

(vi) Laying on of the bishop's hand accompanied by prayer for the descent of the Spirit (*de Bapt.*, 8; *Ap. Trad.*, 22.1). The 'laying on of the hand' means that the bishop stretched out his hand over the candidate during the prayer (cf. Tertullian, *de Res. carn.*, 8, 'the flesh is overshadowed by the imposition of the hand'). Hippolytus alone adds a final unction by the bishop (*Ap. Trad.*, 22.2).

(vii) Signing with the cross; this occurs before the laying on of hands in Tertullian, *de Res. carn.*, 8.

(viii) Paschal Eucharist. Tertullian refers to the drinking of milk and honey before the Eucharist (*de Corona*, 3) while Hippolytus refers to the bringing of milk and honey at the offertory in the Eucharist (*Ap. Trad.*, 23.2).[1]

This initiatory rite is a unity, although we can see clearly within it the elements which will in time become 'Confirmation' (anointing, laying on of hands, signing with cross). According to Tertullian the Holy Spirit is active throughout the whole rite; baptism in water by the operation of the Holy Spirit gives cleansing and remission of sins, while the ensuing hand-laying imparts the gift of the Spirit (*de Bapt.*, chs. 3, 4, 6, and 8; *de Res. carn.*, 8).

In the rite described by Hippolytus the text of the prayer said at the imposition of the bishop's hand is problematic. The Latin version contains no explicit mention of the giving of the Spirit, while other versions have a slightly longer prayer with a petition that the Holy Spirit be given. It has been argued that a line has dropped out of the Latin text

[1] There is also reference to milk at baptism in an early third-century work from north Africa, *Passio Perpetuae* (*The Acts of the Christian Martyrs*, OECT), ch. 5.

at this point; the parallel with Tertullian's rite certainly suggests that the longer text should be preferred.

The post-baptismal anointing (by a presbyter with oil of thanksgiving consecrated by the bishop at the start of proceedings, according to *Ap. Trad.*, 21.19) was held to confer membership in Christ, the anointed one (*de Bapt.*, 7; the unction is 'in the name of Jesus Christ', *Ap. Trad.*, 21.19).

Writing in the middle of the third century, Cyprian, Bishop of Carthage, dealt with a number of controversial questions concerning initiation, although he did not describe the rite in full (*DBL* 10–12). His letters reflect his involvement in debates about the timing of infant baptism, about clinical baptism (baptism at the sick-bed; from *kline*, bed) and about heretical baptism.

Unlike Tertullian, Cyprian was a supporter of infant baptism, which was becoming increasingly common. In north Africa there was debate whether baptism should take place as soon as possible or be performed, like circumcision, on the eighth day after birth. A certain Fidus had taken the latter view but Cyprian in his reply (*Ep.* 64) tells him that 'our council thought very differently'; baptism, which confers remission of original sin, should not be delayed.

A controversy had arisen between the north African church and Rome over the treatment of those who had been baptized by heretics but who now wanted to join the Catholic Church. Unfortunately the letters of Stephen, Bishop of Rome, on this subject are no longer extant, but it is apparent that the Roman practice was to receive schismatics and heretics into communion by hand-laying alone, whereas Cyprian followed the established north African tradition (cf. Tertullian, *de Bapt.*, 15) of requiring that heretics and schismatics should be initiated fully. The north Africans regarded heretical and schismatic baptism as invalid on the ground that the Holy Spirit is not to be found outside the Catholic Church; the heretical minister of baptism cannot convey what he does not possess, the Holy Spirit.

In his comments on this subject Cyprian makes it clear that the Holy Spirit is conferred at hand-laying in initiation. Heretics and schismatics ought to be baptized because 'it is not enough that the hand should be laid on them for the receiving of the Holy Spirit without receiving also the Church's baptism' (*Ep.* 72.1). Cyprian obviously regarded the Roman hand-laying on heretics as equivalent to the hand-laying in initiation, although it is probable that for the Romans themselves the hand-laying was regarded not as initiatory but as reconciliatory, 'for penitence' (*Ep.* 74.1).

The initiatory rite which Cyprian knew was an integral whole, consisting of baptism in water, anointing,[1] hand-laying, consignation[2] and Eucharist.[3] However, as Tertullian tended to distinguish the effects of baptism in water and imposition of hands, so Cyprian speaks of baptism in water as conferring remission of sins (*Ep.* 73.6), causing renewal and spiritual birth (*Ep.* 74.5 and 7), and as preparing a temple ready for occupation by the Holy Spirit (*Ep.* 74.5), while the gift of the Spirit is conferred by the immediately ensuing laying on of hands (*Ep.* 73.6; 69.11; 74.5 and 7). He refers to the Samaritan episode in Acts 8 as a pattern for contemporary practice: 'Because they [i.e. the Samaritans baptized by Philip] had obtained the legitimate baptism of the Church, it was not fitting that they should be baptized again; but only what was lacking was done by Peter and John, namely, that prayer being made for them, with laying on of hands, the Holy Spirit should be invoked and poured upon them. Which now also is done among us, those baptized in the Church being brought to the bishops of the Church and by our prayer and laying on of hands they receive the Holy Spirit and are perfected with the seal of the Lord' (*Ep.* 73.8). However, it would be wrong to suppose that in Cyprian's view the Spirit is active only in the latter part of the rite; he is active throughout since water cannot cleanse without the Holy Spirit (*Ep.* 73.7). Like Tertullian, Cyprian believed that the baptismal rite is imbued with the Holy Spirit, but in reply to a question about clinical baptism he opposed a crude, quantitative view of the Spirit's presence which would make aspersion, the method used at the sick bed, less effective than the normal baptism by dipping (*Ep.* 69.13f).

[1] Unction conferred membership in Christ (*Ep.* 70.2); cf. Tertullian.
[2] *Ad Demetrianum*, 22; there are references to 'seal' and 'sealing' in *Ep.* 73.6 and 9.
[3] Baptized infants received Holy Communion (*de Lapsis*, 9 and 25).

2 The Fourth and Fifth Centuries

E. J. YARNOLD, SJ

Atchley, E. G. C. F., *On the Epiclesis of the Eucharistic Liturgy and in the Consecration of the Font.* AC 1935.

Finn, T., *The Liturgy of Baptism in the Baptismal Instructions of St John Chrysostom.* Washington 1967.

Kretschmar, G., *Die Geschichte des Taufgottesdienstes.*

Rahner, H., (ET) *Greek Myths and Christian Mystery.* Burns Oates 1963.

Riley, H. M., *Christian Initiation.* Washington 1974.

Wilkinson, J., *Egeria's Travels.* SPCK 1971.

Yarnold, E. J., *The Awe-Inspiring Rites of Initiation: Baptismal Homilies of the Fourth Century* = *AIR*.

Yarnold, E. J., 'The Ceremonies of Initiation in the *De Sacramentis* and *De Mysteriis* of St Ambrose', *SP* 10 (1970), pp. 453–63.

Ysebaert, J., *Greek Baptismal Terminology: Its Origins and Early Development.* Nijmegen 1962.

When we reach the fourth century we are presented with a great wealth of evidence concerning the sacraments of initiation. It is striking that, although (as we shall see later) great changes were made in the rites of initiation during the fourth century, the ceremonies all over the Christian world continued to have many features in common. The individual ceremonies that made up the rites of initiation were put together in different orders in different localities, and these individual ceremonies were performed in different ways with different interpretations; nevertheless many of these individual ceremonies remained recognizably the same everywhere. The ceremonies of initiation took place generally in three stages:

A Admission to catechumenate;
B Enrolment as a candidate and preparation for baptism;
C The rites of initiation.

A ADMISSION TO THE CATECHUMENATE

The regular baptism of children is attested by Origen, Tertullian, the *Apostolic Tradition*, and Cyprian in the third century, and by Asterius about 340, although the evidence does not show whether this practice was universal or whether Christian parents could without censure postpone the baptism of their children to maturer years. Towards the middle of the fourth century, however, the baptism of children, apart from emergency baptisms, seems to have become the exception. The evidence is presented in J. Jeremias, *Infant Baptism in the First Four Centuries* ET (SCM 1960), pp. 11–18. (See above, p. 85, n. 1.) Towards the end of the fourth century there begins to be a return to the practice of child-baptism: Gregory of Nazianzus recommends child-baptism (but not infant-baptism), and St Augustine, in the early fifth century, proposes a theological justification of the baptism of those who are too young to have faith. Tertullian gives reasons for the postponement of baptism: the child's sponsors are held responsible if he fails to fulfil the obligations of Christianity when he grows up; and, besides, little children are sinless, and do not require the forgiveness of sins which baptism confers. (Cf. Gregory of Nazianzus, *Or.* 40 on Baptism, 28 (PG 36.400); Augustine, *Ep.* 98; Tertullian, *de Bapt.*, 18, *DBL* 9; Jeremias, op. cit., pp. 94–7.)

The motives for the postponement, however, were not always so innocent: St Augustine refers to the common belief that it is best to prolong the period before baptism, so that a person may sin with the assurance that he will receive forgiveness at baptism: 'let him alone, let him do as he pleases; he is not yet baptized.' (*Conf.*, 1.18. Cf. Tertullian, *de Paen.*, 6; Jeremias, op. cit., pp. 87–9.) The less cynical would say that it was better to wait until the individual was prepared for a total conversion of life; the passionate years of youth, or a position of civic authority which might involve the taking of life, were good reasons for postponing the sacrament. The list of saints who were themselves children of good Christian parents, but were not baptized until late in life, is impressive: e.g., Ambrose, Augustine, Chrysostom, Gregory of Nazianzus (the son of a bishop), Jerome, Paulinus of Nola.

Consequently, since baptism was put off until later in life, the need was felt for an earlier ceremony which would establish a person in some looser and less privileged association with the Church. To meet this need a new significance came to be read into the ceremony of admission to the catechumenate. The word 'catechumenate' is a modern one, derived from the term 'hearers' (of instruction, or of the word of God) (*katechoumenoi, audientes, auditores*), by which people who had taken this first step towards Christian membership were described (cf. Finn, p. 31). In the second half of the fourth century, as baptism was deferred, admission to the catechumenate was advanced, and seems sometimes to have been regarded less as a first preparation for baptism than as admission to a second-class membership of the Church. In some churches the ceremony seems to have had four elements: the sign of the cross traced on the candidate's forehead, salt placed on his tongue (to signify healing, preservation, and the seasoning of wisdom), the laying on of hands and an exorcism. The first two parts of the rite were often repeated: St Augustine says, 'I began to receive the sign of his cross and the seasoning of his salt straight from my mother's womb' (*Conf.*, 1.18); the salt seems to have been a substitute for the Eucharist. The catechumens were entitled to attend the eucharistic assembly and hear the sermon, but they were dismissed after the prayer offered for them during the Prayer of the Faithful, and so were not present at the eucharistic rites themselves. (Cf. *Ap. Const.*, ed. Funk, 8.6.14; and on all this section *AIR* 4–7; *DBL* 99–100).

B ENROLMENT AS A CANDIDATE AND PREPARATION FOR BAPTISM

As early as Tertullian's time, it was considered appropriate to confer baptism at the feasts of Easter or Pentecost, although the sacrament could also be administered with less solemnity on other days; one such in Cappadocia was the Epiphany. However the baptismal catecheses of Cyril, Ambrose, Chrysostom and Theodore (see pp. 61–4) assume no date other than Easter. The following process can be reconstructed, mainly from their writings:

(1) Those who wished to be baptized had to *give in their names* at least forty days in advance. Those who wished to be baptized at Easter had to do this at the beginning of Lent (see pp. 412–13), and it was to such newly enrolled that Cyril of Jerusalem addressed his *Procatechesis*: when people were baptized at Pentecost a similar forty-day period seems to have been required (cf. Siricius, *Letter to Himerius*, PL 13.1134–5). The ceremony was called 'enrolment' (*onomatographia*), and the phrase 'to enrol' (*onoma dounai, nomen dare*) gained a specific meaning in reference to it (cf. Cyril, *Procat.*, 1, *DBL* 24; Ambrose, *de Sac.*, 3.12, *AIR* 126). In Jerusalem, and probably in other churches too, this enrolment took place in two stages. *Egeria* (45, *DBL* 41–2) recounts how the candidate gives his name to the presbyter before Lent; he then has to appear at the beginning of Lent with his sponsor (i.e. godparent, a godfather for a man, a godmother for a woman) before the bishop, who takes evidence of the candidate's behaviour and, if he is satisfied, registers his name. (On Egeria, see pp. 64–5.) The enrolled (*apographentes*) were now called 'applicants' (*competentes*), 'chosen' (*electi*) or 'destined for illumination' (*photizomenoi, illuminandi*).

(2) This ceremonial investigation in the presence of the bishop which Egeria described is known to have taken place in many different churches, and was called the *scrutinies*. In Jerusalem they seem to have taken place once only, on the first day of Lent, but it seems to have been the Roman practice to repeat them three times, according to the eighth canon of the Synod of Rome (*c*. A.D. 402; *DBL* 229).

(3) The scrutinies concluded with an *exorcism*.[1] The details of this dramatic ceremony probably varied in different churches, but at least some of the following actions would be performed: the candidate stood barefoot on sackcloth of goat's hair, then knelt, his face was veiled, his head bowed, his hands outstretched, his outer garment removed; one of the ministers breathed on the candidate, to fill him with a purifying fear and to drive away the devil; he heard the words by which he was freed from Satan's power. The exorcism, which had first taken place when he was admitted to the catechumenate, was repeated several times after the scrutinies, daily, in fact, according to the *Ap. Trad.*, 20.3 (*DBL* 4; cf. *Egeria*, 46.1; *AIR* 8–11, *DBL* 42).

(4) Throughout Lent the candidates were expected to attend daily *instructions*. For the first part of Lent (the first five weeks, according to Egeria) the instruction dealt with scripture, the resurrection and faith; in Milan, according to Ambrose, moral questions were discussed on the basis of Old Testament readings. The extant eighteen catecheses of Cyril do not include the expositions of scripture; perhaps the other twenty-two or so needed to make up the Lenten number of about forty were less formal and consequently were not preserved.[2]

(5) In the second part of Lent the instruction focused on the creed and in some places the Lord's Prayer. In some western churches the creed was taught in three stages, called the handing-over, explanation and repetition of the creed (*traditio, explanatio, redditio symboli*). The first of these ceremonies took place one Sunday towards the middle of Lent: the catechumens, who up till now had not been allowed to hear the creed, now had to repeat it phrase by phrase after the bishop or catechist or sponsor; they were not allowed to have it in writing. In Rome this ceremony took place on the third Sunday, in Egeria's account on the

---

[1] Cf. F. J. Dölger, *Der Exorzismus im altchristlichen Taufrituel* (Paderborn 1909).

[2] Egeria, *Pereg.*, 46.2: 'During the forty days he goes through the whole Bible, beginning with Genesis, and first relating the literal meaning of each passage, then interpreting its spiritual meaning. He also teaches them at this time all about the resurrection and the faith.' (trans. Wilkinson, p. 144; cf. Ambrose, *de Myst.*, 1.) But the fifth-century Old Armenian Lectionary, which prescribes almost exactly the same readings for the pre- and post-baptismal catechesis as Cyril, with one exception gives no readings for these twenty-two pre-baptismal catecheses which are missing from Cyril's collection. This suggests that in Jerusalem the instruction on these other days did not take the form of a systematic exposition of the faith based on a reading. (Cf. Wilkinson, pp. 253–77). Examples of Lenten catechesis are Ambrose, *de Elia et Ieiunio* and *de Abraha*, and Augustine, *Serm.*, 212–6. On church orders and baptismal catechesis, see pp. 59–64.

fifth; on at least one occasion St Ambrose performed it as late as the Sunday before Easter (cf. *Egeria*, 46.3, *DBL* 42–3; Ambrose, *Ep.* 20.4).

The handing over of the creed was followed by the explanation of its clauses. Sometimes this was done in the same sermon in which the candidates were taught to recite the creed, as in Ambrose's sermon entitled *Explanatio Symboli*; Cyril however spread the instruction on the creed over thirteen sermons (*Cat.*, 6–18).

Ambrose tells his candidates that they will have to repeat (*reddere*) the creed, but he does not add any details about the ceremony of repetition (*Ex. Symb.*, 9). Egeria describes this ceremony as it took place on the seventh Sunday (46.5). Cyril and others speak of the candidate's need to learn the creed by heart, without saying anything of a *redditio* (*Cat.*, 5.12, *DBL* 27). St Augustine, in a sermon, fills in details of the ceremony of *redditio*; he may also be referring to it in his description of the convert Victorinus making his profession of faith 'on a rostrum, in the sight of the faithful people'.[1]

Augustine (*de Symbolo*, 1) speaks of a similar handing over of the Lord's Prayer the Sunday after the *traditio symboli* (this prayer, like the creed, was also kept secret), with a *redditio* the following Sunday; Theodore (*Hom. Cat.*, 11.19) speaks of the *traditio* without mentioning the *redditio*: both teachers provide an *explanatio* of the prayer. Cyril and Ambrose, however, make their explanation of the prayer part of their exposition after baptism of the ceremonies of the Eucharist, in which the Lord's Prayer is included; they seem to have had no formal *traditio* of the prayer.

(6) The candidates had to observe the fast of forty days; in some places the fast applied not only to food, but also to the legitimate use of marriage. The pleasure of the bath was also renounced, but the candidates were allowed a bath on Maundy Thursday to make themselves decent for baptism. (Cf. Augustine, *de Fide et Operibus*, 8; *Ep.* 54.10; Ambrose, *de El. et Iei.*, 79; *Ap. Trad.*, 20.5, *DBL* 4).

---

[1] *De Symbolo*, 11; *Miscellanea Agostiniana*, ed. Morin, 1.449–50; *Conf.*, 8.5. See other quotations from St Augustine in *DBL* 103. A. Wenger, *Jean Chrysostome: Huit Catéchèses Baptismales* (SC 50), p. 94, suggests that Chrysostom alludes to a repetition of the creed on Maundy Thursday (which would be consistent with the fact that Ambrose taught the creed on the previous Sunday); cf. Chrysostom, *Bapt. Inst.*, Harkins, 11.15 = *DBL* 36. The translation however in both Harkins and *DBL* should run: 'Therefore, my sermon today is called "faith", and I require you to say nothing more until you shall say "I believe."' It seems more likely that Chrysostom's words refer not to the *redditio* but to the profession of faith made shortly before baptism; see below p. 103.

C THE FINAL RITES OF INITIATION

These rites comprised many ceremonies, but no church performed them all, and the order varied. One can, however, distinguish between preparatory rites, centred on the renunciation of the devil, and baptism itself with its accompanying ceremonies. At Easter (much less is known of the rites at other times) the celebration took place in the context of the Easter vigil, which was kept by all the faithful, and not only by the candidates for baptism. Most sources indicate that the rites took place in the night between Holy Saturday and Easter Sunday, though Chrysostom seems to be speaking of preparatory rites that take place on the Friday (cf. *AIR* 167, n. 34). In the *Ap. Trad.* (21.1; *AIR* 265, *DBL* 4) the ceremonies begin at cockcrow.

(1) The rites begin in an outside room of the baptistery. The subsequent entry into the baptistery thus becomes itself a rite (cf. Cyril, *Myst. Cat.*, 1.2, 11; 2.2; Ambrose, *de Sac.*, 1.4, 10; *AIR* 68, 73–4, 101, 103; *DBL* 27–9, 128–9).

(2) *The Opening (apertio)* was a ceremony known only in the West. The bishop touches the candidate's nostrils and ears, repeating the words of Mk. 7.34 in Aramaic and Latin: '*Effeta*, that is, be opened': the purpose of the rite was to confer understanding of the baptismal ceremonies and a share in the 'good odour of Christ' (Ambrose, *de Sac.*, 1.2 quoting 2 Cor. 2.15; *AIR* 100; *DBL* 128).

(3) *Stripping*, which was a practical necessity for the total anointing and the immersion, was made a ceremony in its own right, recalling Christ's naked entry into life and departure from it, the discarding of the old man, and a return to the innocence of Paradise (cf. Cyril, *Myst. Cat.*, 2.2; *AIR* 74; *DBL* 29; Ambrose, *in Ps. 61*, 32). In the Syrian rites as early as the third century deaconesses attended to the women for the sake of decency (cf. *Didascalia*, 16, Connolly, p. 146; *DBL* 13).

(4) *A prebaptismal anointing of the whole body with olive oil.* In the *Ap. Trad.* (21.10; *AIR* 266; *DBL* 5) this anointing constitutes an exorcism; indeed the oil is called 'oil of exorcism'. In later rites the connection with exorcism remains, even though it is less explicit. Ambrose, for example (*de Sac.*, 1.4; *AIR* 101; *DBL* 128), recalls the anointing of an athlete, and sees the rite as a preparation for the struggle against the devil. Cyril (*Myst. Cat.*, 2.3; *AIR* 75; *DBL* 29), while recalling the power of the anointing to drive away the devil and remove traces of sin, adds that it also signifies a share in Christ, the true olive. In Chrysostom and Theodore, however, this anointing occurs after the anointing of the head.

3 Calendar and Lectionary from Cranmer's liturgical projects
with corrections in Cranmer's own hand
(see p. 390)

4 Baptistry, Dura Europos, Syria, with font for immersion, third century (see p. 103)

(5) *Renunciation of the devil.* The basic form of this ceremony is the renunciation of Satan, his followers, and everything connected with him. Like the foregoing anointing, therefore, it provides the negative condition necessary for the receiving of the new life of Christ in baptism; it also looks forward to the spiritual conflict after baptism. These rites, like all liturgical ceremonies, tended to grow. Some growths obscured the essential meaning of the sacrament, but these preliminary rites emphasize the negative aspect of baptism, the death to sin, and the struggle against it.

The basic form of the renunciation is elaborated in various ways:

(a) The list of the devil's following is variously expressed. The simplest form is that given by Tertullian (*de Spectaculis*, 4) 'the devil and his following (*pompae*) and his angels'. (*DBL* 9 wrongly reads 'works' instead of 'angels'.) There are, however, more elaborate forms, such as that of Theodore: 'Satan, all his angels, all his works, all his service, all his vanity and all his worldly enticements' (*Hom. Cat.*, 13, synopsis; *AIR* 176; *DBL* 47 gives a shorter form).

(b) In the East the candidate addresses Satan ('I renounce you, Satan. . . .'), with the exception of the formula given by Theodore of Mopsuestia, in which there is the plain statement, 'I renounce Satan, all his angels. . . .' In the West the renunciation takes the form of question and answer: 'Do you renounce Satan (or 'the devil')?' 'I do renounce him', etc.[1]

(c) In some Eastern rites the candidate faced west in order to address Satan, the Lord of darkness. It is sometimes said that the westward-facing position and the subsequent turn to the east were not adopted in the Latin Church; however, it is implied in Ambrose's description of the candidate turning to the east for the following ceremony of the contract with Christ.[2]

(6) *Contract with Christ* ('adhesion'). In many rites, after the renunciation the candidate turns to the east and pledges his loyalty to Christ. Sometimes this pledge takes the form of a direct declaration: 'I

---

[1] East: Cyril, *Myst. Cat.*, 1.4; Chrysostom, *Bapt. Inst.*, Harkins, 2.20 (but see 11.19); Theodore, *Hom. Cat.*, 13, synopsis; *AIR* 69, 166, 176; *DBL* 28, 39, 47. West: Ambrose, *de Sac.*, 1.5; *AIR* 101; *DBL* 128. The *Ap. Trad.* (21.9; *AIR* 266; *DBL* 5) in the third century used the vocative form: so did Ambrose in another place (*Hexameron*, 1.14), possibly under the influence of an Eastern source. Jerome also gives a formula in which the devil is addressed in the vocative, but this probably represents Palestinian usage (*Ep.* 130.7, 14).

[2] *De Myst.*, 7; *DBL* 131. (Cf. E. J. Yarnold, 'Ceremonies', p. 457.) For the practice in the Greek Church of facing west to make the renunciation cf. Cyril, *Myst. Cat.*, 1.4; *AIR* 69; *DBL* 28.

enter into your service, O Christ' (cf. Chrysostom, *Bapt. Inst.*, Harkins 2.21; *AIR* 166; *DBL* 40); the verb is *suntattomai* (noun *suntaxis*), in contrast with the verb 'I renounce' (*apotattomai*, noun *apotaxis*). In other places the pledge consists of a trinitarian act of faith (cf. Cyril, *Myst. Cat.*, 1.9; Theo. Mops., *Hom. Cat.*, 13, synopsis; *AIR* 73, 176; *DBL* 28). This act of faith, even though it does not involve the use of the verb *suntattomai*, can still be described as a *suntaxis* (cf. Cyril, *Myst. Cat.* 1.8; *AIR* 72; *DBL* 28).

(7) *Blessing of the baptismal water.* Although in an emergency ordinary water could presumably be used, proper practice required that the water should be consecrated; indeed it was commonly held that 'not all waters have a curative power; only that water has it which has the grace of Christ' (Ambrose, *de Sac.*, 1.15; *AIR* 105). The rite of consecration could have three parts:

(a) An *exorcism* of the water, which was necessary because, in Tertullian's words, 'the profane angel of evil frequents the company of this element to ruin men' (*de Bapt.*, 5; cf. Ambrose, *de Sac.*, 1.15, 18; *AIR* 105–6; *DBL* 129).

(b) An *epiclesis*, by which the power of God is called down upon the water. More is said elsewhere in this book about the eucharistic epiclesis (see pp. 175–6), but its use is not limited to the Eucharist. In the most trinitarian form of epiclesis, God the Father is asked to send the Holy Spirit upon the sacramental matter so that the Holy Spirit may exert his power through it; in the Eucharist the Spirit's action makes Christ present, thus completing the trinitarian pattern (cf. Cyril, *Myst. Cat.*, 5.7; *AIR* 91; *PEER* 53). In the baptismal epiclesis, the prayer to God (the Father) that the Spirit may descend on the water occurs as early as Tertullian (*de Bapt.*, 4; *DBL* 7). Sarapion, however, gives his characteristic epiclesis not of the Spirit but of the Word (see p. 200); the Father is asked that the Word may descend on the water and fill it with the Holy Spirit, so that the baptized may become spiritual (*Euchologium*, 19(7); *DBL* 83). In the *Ap. Const.* the epiclesis, like those over the oil and ointment (*myron*), is set in a prayer of thanksgiving (7.43–4; cf. 7.27; *DBL* 33–4). This setting of the epiclesis became most common in the Eucharist and the ordination service.

(c) *A sign of the cross* is associated with the water; perhaps the bishop traced the sign in the water with his hand or dipped his cross into it (cf. *AIR* 24), or poured oil into it crosswise (cf. *DBL* 64).

(8) *Immersion.* In the fourth and fifth centuries the fonts were like baths let into the floor of the baptisteries: a few steps led down into the water. Frequently the water was constantly running into and out of the font.

J. G. Davies (*Architectural Setting*, pp. 23–6) has shown that the fonts were generally too shallow to permit of easy total immersion. Contemporary representations of the baptism of Christ point to the same conclusion, for they normally show the water reaching below the waist, sometimes scarcely covering Christ's ankles (see plate 5).[1] Theodore of Mopsuestia describes how the bishop placed his hand on the candidate's head and pushed him under the water (*Hom. Cat.*, 14, synopsis; *AIR* 189; *DBL* 49); but the iconographical and archaeological evidence suggests that in some places the bishop poured water over the candidate standing in the water of the font, or made water from the inlet pipe run over his head (Cf. Davies, *Architectural Setting*, pp. 25–6).

The fonts of Dura Europos (see p. 474 and plate 4) and Nazareth, which are perhaps the earliest surviving fonts, were rectangular, and this seems to have been the earliest shape, once the practice was abandoned of baptizing in streams in the open air. By the fifth century eight-sided fonts set within baptisteries of the same shape became common; the shape was meant to symbolize the eighth day (after the seven days of creation), namely the day of the resurrection. It is argued that the extant baptistery and font in Milan were the first to be built in this form, and were constructed by St Ambrose about 386, but there are reasons for thinking this date too early.[2]

It seems to have been the universal practice to immerse the candidate in water three times, in conjunction with the naming of the three Persons of the Trinity. The Antiochene Church in the fourth century used the formula: 'N. is baptized in the name of the Father and of the Son and of the Holy Spirit'. In the West, however, the words took the form of a profession of faith by means of question and answer: 'Do you believe in God the Father almighty?' 'I believe'. This exchange was followed by the first immersion; the process was repeated for the Son and the Holy Spirit. The questions were sometimes elaborated into a rudimentary creed. This

---

[1] Cf. J. G. Davies, *The Early Christian Church* (Weidenfeld & Nicolson 1965), plates 5 and 14.

[2] Ambrose, *de Sac.*, 3.1 (*AIR* 120; *DBL* 130), speaks of the tomb-like shape of fonts; these words could be a description of a rectangular font, which resembled a tomb hollowed out of the stone wall of a catacomb, or the free-standing circular, hexagonal or octagonal baptistery, resembling a mausoleum, in which Western fonts were generally set. In a poem attributed to Ambrose the symbolism of the eight sides is explained; but it is notable that the *de Sac.* and *de Myst.* are totally silent on this subject. On the baptistery on the site of the basilica of the Annunciation at Nazareth, see P. B. Bagatti, *Gli Scavi di Nazaret* (Jerusalem 1967), vol. 1, pp. 115–19, and figs. 70–2. For the Milanese baptistery, cf. two articles in *Recherches Augustiniennes*, 4 (1966): 'Il Battisterio di Sant' Ambrogio a Milano' by M. M. Roberti, and 'Dove fu battezzato Sant' Agostino' by A. Paredi. On the general subject, cf. Davies, *Architectural Setting*, pp. 1–42.

is the third point in the ceremonies at which an act of faith could be made; the other two were the repetition of the creed and the contract with Christ.[1]

(9) *An anointing of the head*, with either olive-oil or *myron* (the symbolism of *myron* will be discussed later).[2] As Ambrose (*de. Sac.*, 3.1; *AIR* 120; *DBL* 130) described the rite, the oil is poured over the head; Chrysostom and Theodore speak instead of the tracing of the seal (sign of the cross) on the forehead.[3] In some places this rite is performed before baptism. The rite is said to symbolize priesthood (Ambrose, *de Myst.*, 30; *DBL* 132), or eternal life (Ambrose, *de Sac.*, 2.24; *AIR* 119; *DBL* 130), or membership of Christ's flock or army (Theo. Mops., *Hom. Cat.*, 13.17–20; *AIR* 186–8; *DBL* 47–8) (presumably because of the mark traced on the forehead); some preachers attribute to this rite also the power of exorcism.

(10) *The washing of the feet.* In many churches in both East and West, when the candidate had come up from the font, his feet were washed by the bishop, assisted by the clergy.[4] The reading of Jn. 13 linked this ceremony with the Washing of the Feet at the Last Supper. In most places the purpose seems to have been to remind the neophytes to perform works of humble charity; but Ambrose insisted that the rite had a sacramental effect, namely to protect the neophyte from the tendency to sin inherited from Adam (*de Sac.*, 3.7; *AIR* 123–4; *de Myst.*, 32; *DBL* 132).

(11) After the immersion and the washing, the candidate was dressed in a *white garment*, as a sign of innocence, and a symbol of the wedding-garment. It is known that by the fifth century the neophytes wore their baptismal robes for the whole of Easter week, changing back into their

---

[1] Antioch: Theo. Mops. *Hom. Cat.*, 14, synopsis; *AIR* 189; *DBL* 49. West: Ambrose, *de Sac.*, 2.20; *AIR* 117; *DBL* 129–30. On baptismal creeds: J. N. D. Kelly, *Early Christian Creeds* (3rd edn Longman 1972), pp. 30–52.

[2] Cf. p. 107. In *Ap. Trad.*, 21.19 (*AIR* 267, *DBL* 6) the anointing at this point is performed with 'oil of thanksgiving', in contrast with the 'oil of exorcism'.

[3] Chrysostom, *Bapt. Inst.*, Harkins, 2.22; *AIR* 166; *DBL* 40. Theodore, *Hom. Cat.*, 13.17–20; *AIR* 186–8; *DBL* 47–8. Tertullian (*de Bapt.*, 7; *DBL* 8), by referring to the anointing of Aaron (Lev. 8.12), shows that in his rite too oil was poured on the head. On the seal see F. J. Dölger, *Sphragis* (Paderborn 1911).

[4] For a list of churches in which this rite was practised, cf. *AIR* 27. For St Augustine's practice see *DBL* 104. In some of these places it is possible that the Gospel was simply read without any accompanying ceremony of washing. It has been suggested that the little fonts which have been found beside the main fonts in some churches were for this ceremony (cf. J. G. Davies, *Architectural Setting*, p. 26). But a contrary view is expressed in *AIR* 28 and Yarnold, 'Ceremonies', pp. 460–1.

ordinary clothes on Low Sunday (*in depositis albis*). There are indications that as early as the fourth century the robes were worn for the week.[1]

(12) *The gift of the Spirit*, which later evolved into the western rite of *confirmation*, took place under many different forms (see pp. 115–6). According to Tertullian the rite for the conferring of this gift took the form of a laying-on of hands and a blessing; in *Ap. Trad.*, the bishop also pours consecrated oil, lays his hand again on the neophyte's head, seals him on the forehead and gives him the kiss of peace. Cyprian speaks of a laying-on of hands and a sealing. Ambrose simply speaks of a 'spiritual sealing' through which the Holy Spirit is received with his seven gifts, though from another passage it appears that the sealing involves the tracing of the sign of the cross, and that an anointing also is involved (*de Sac.*, 3.8–10; 6.6–7; *AIR* 124–5, 151; *DBL* 131). In Jerusalem Cyril describes briefly a post-baptismal anointing with chrism on the forehead, ears, nostrils, and breast for the giving of the Spirit (*Myst. Cat.*, 3.4; *AIR* 81–2; *DBL* 30).[2]

In the Eastern church, however, the rite for the gift of the Spirit is not so consistently located, nor indeed always easy to identify. In many early Syrian liturgies the rites of initiation consist solely of an epiclesis over oil and water, and an anointing and signing with oil followed by baptism. This pattern can be observed in the *Acts of Judas Thomas* (third century) and the *History of John the Son of Zebedee* (about A.D. 400).[3] No attempt is made to distinguish between the effects of anointing and immersion. In the *Didascalia* similarly the rite of initiation consists of anointing followed by baptism; the neophyte can be said to have been filled with the Holy Spirit through baptism, but in this phrase the word 'baptism' is meant to include the whole ceremony, and not to refer to immersion as distinct from the preceding anointing (chs. 16 and 26; Connolly, pp. 146–7, 242, 246; *DBL* 12–13, where however only part of ch. 16 is included).

---

[1] Cyril, *Myst. Cat.*, 4.8; Chrysostom, *Bapt. Inst.*, Harkins 4.3, 6.23–24; Theo. Mops., *Hom. Cat.*, 14, synopsis; *AIR* 87, 189; *DBL* 49. More references are given in *AIR* 29, n. 158. The earliest hint comes from Asterius in the fourth century.

[2] For the use of chrism for the sealing, and the refusal to allow anyone but the bishop to seal, cf. Innocent I, Letter to Decentius of Gubbio, 3.6 (PL 20.554–5). See L. L. Mitchell, *Baptismal Anointing*, pp. 93–6. For an explanation of the symbolism of the seal, cf. Lampe, *Seal*, pp. 7–18. Soldiers in the Roman army were sometimes given a seal, which was a cross-shaped tattoo or brand on the forehead (see plate 6).

[3] *DBL* 13–19; 21–3. This pattern is found more consistently in the Syriac version of the *Acts of Judas Thomas* (ed. A. Klijn, Leiden 1962) than in the Greek version (ed. Lipsius-Bonnet, Leipzig 1891). In the *Acts of J.T.* the sealing is performed, not by tracing a mark on the forehead, but by pouring oil over the head; it should be remembered however that some of the liturgical features of this work may be due to gnostic influence.

There is however a second understanding to be found in some Syrian sources, to the effect that it is the pre-baptismal anointing which confers the Spirit. This is true of the *Ap. Const.* (7.22; cf. 3.16; 7.42; *DBL* 30–3), where it is the pre-baptismal anointing, not the immersion or the post-baptismal sealing with *myron*, which gives a 'share of the Spirit' (though 'if there be neither oil nor *myron*, the water is sufficient'). The same is true of the fifth-century theologian Narsai (*Homily* 22; Connolly, pp. 41–5; *DBL* 52–4) (though apparently there is no post-baptismal sealing; the oil is applied both by tracing the seal on the forehead and anointing the whole body): the oil is the 'drug of the Spirit'. In this interpretation the anointing retains its force as an exorcism; the gift of the Spirit is the positive effect which corresponds with the expulsion of the devil from the candidate.

There is also a third Syrian understanding of the rite, which is apparent in the sermons of Chrysostom (*Bapt. Inst.*, Harkins 2.22–6: *AIR* 166–9; *DBL* 40–1). His rite contains both a sealing with *myron* and an anointing of the whole body with oil before baptism, but neither of these ceremonies is connected with the gift of the Spirit, except that the oil is called 'spiritual'. There is no anointing or sealing after baptism; it is in baptism itself that 'by words of the bishop and by his hand the presence of the Holy Spirit flies down upon you'. It seems that this laying-on of hands is none other than the bishop's action in pushing the candidate down under the water. Proclus of Constantinople gives a rite which follows the same pattern as Chrysostom's, and he too associates the Spirit with the immersion: '... how you lay aside your corruption in the font, which is a tomb; how, made new, you rise again to life in the Spirit' (AT: Wenger, p. 101; Harkins, p. 228).

A fourth Syrian version of the rite appears in Theodore of Mopsuestia. He comments, like Chrysostom, on the pre-baptismal sealing of the forehead and total anointing without linking them especially with the Holy Spirit, except to say that, after the sealing, 'You may receive the rest of the sacraments and so acquire the full armour of the Spirit' (*Hom. Cat.*, 13.20; cf. 13.17–19; 14.8; *AIR* 186–8, 194; *DBL* 48). Theodore seems to connect the gift of the Spirit with a sealing with oil after baptism (*Hom. Cat.*, 14.27; *AIR* 207–9; *DBL* 49–50); but this ceremony is not said to confer the Holy Spirit, but to be a sign that the Holy Spirit came upon the candidate at the moment of immersion (*DBL*'s quotation ends before these words). I have presented arguments elsewhere (*AIR* 208–9, n. 65) for this view, which contradicts those suggested by L. L. Mitchell (who expounds the theory that the whole of this section in Theodore is a later interpolation, perhaps by the sixth-century Syriac translator) and G. W. H. Lampe (who thinks that there is no ceremony of sealing here, and that Theodore is speaking of anointing and sealing in a metaphorical sense).[1]

The rite of Cyril of Jerusalem, which, as we have seen above, follows the Western pattern, affords a fifth Syrian type.

Presumably these five types are all derived from one original Syrian form, but liturgical scholars do not agree what that form was. E. C. Whitaker may well be right in his conjecture that 'confirmation originated in a development within the early Church by which the oil at the baptismal bath came to share the sacramental association of the water' (p. xxii; cf. pp. xv–xxi). But he does violence to the evidence in trying to fit the majority of the rites into the third category listed above (that exemplified by Chrysostom), just as T. Thompson and E. C. Ratcliff do violence to the evidence in regarding the second type as the norm.[2] The only conclusion that the evidence permits is that, whatever the original form of the giving of the Spirit in the Syrian rite, by the fourth century it became differentiated into five distinct types.

There is no unanimity among the Fathers about the effect of the gift of the Spirit. Some link the gift with strength for the fight against the devil and purification from sin (cf. Cyril, *Myst. Cat.*, 3.4; *AIR* 82); some stress the sevenfold gifts of the Spirit (cf. Ambrose, *de Sac.*, 3.8; *AIR* 124–5; *DBL* 131); some treat it eschatologically, seeing it as an anticipation of heaven (cf. Theo. Mops., *Hom. Cat.*, 14.27, *AIR* 209); some regard it as a 'completion' or 'perfecting' of baptism (cf. Ambrose, *de Sac.*, 3.8; Theo. Mops., *Hom. Cat.*, 14.19; *AIR* 124, 202). But until confirmation became separated from baptism there was little need to define exactly the nature of the new grace which was added by the gift of the Spirit (see pp. 115–116).

As has been seen, in some churches the Spirit was given in a rite of sealing with a scented unguent called *myron* or chrism. In connection with the pre-baptismal sealing, Chrysostom explains its symbolism as follows: 'The chrism is a mixture of olive oil and *myron*; the *myron* is for the bride, the oil for the athlete.' (*Bapt. Inst.*, Harkins 11.27: AT; *DBL* 37). Irenaeus is the first to mention an anointing with *myron* or balsam in describing a gnostic rite: 'Then they anoint (*myrizousi*) the initiate with balsam juice, for they maintain that this *myron* is a sign of the universal good odour' (*AH* 1.21.3). There is no evidence of its use in orthodox

---

[1] L. L. Mitchell, *Baptismal Anointing* (AC 48, 1966), p. 41; Lampe, *Seal*, p. 202, n. 4.

[2] T. Thompson, *The Offices of Baptism and Confirmation* (CUP 1914), p. 31. E. C. Ratcliff, 'The Old Syrian Baptismal Tradition', *SL* 140–2 = *Studies in Church History*, ed. G. J. Cuming, vol. 2 (Nelson 1965), pp. 26–8. For other versions of the same theory (e.g. that of G. Dix), cf. Lampe, *Seal*, pp. vii–xiv.

circles until the time of Chrysostom, Ambrose (*de Sac.*, 3.1; *AIR* 120; *DBL* 130; *de Myst.*, 29) and the *Ap. Const.* (7.27, 44; *DBL* 34).

In both East and West the rite associated with the gift of the Holy Spirit could be performed only by the bishop. Innocent I traced this belief back to Acts 8:

> Concerning the signing of children, it is clear that this may not be performed by anyone except the bishop. ... This is evident, not only from the Church's practice, but also from the passage in the Acts of the Apostles which states that Peter and John were sent to confer the Holy Spirit on those who were already baptized.[1]

(13) From the second century baptism was in some areas called 'illumination'. It was appropriate therefore that the neophyte should be given a *lighted candle or lamp* to carry. The custom is described by Proclus of Constantinople in the first half of the fifth century. Pseudo-Ambrose also refers to the ceremony, and there seem to be allusions to it in earlier writers.[2]

(14) Initiation was now completed by the entry into the church of the neophytes, dressed in white and carrying their candles. They now for the first time attended the whole of the Eucharist, during which they made their first communion. In some churches in the West, after receiving the eucharistic bread and wine, the neophytes also received a drink of milk and honey. This was said to symbolize the promised land, baby-food and the sweetness of Christ's word.[3]

In Milan, however, there was one privilege of the faithful in which the neophyte was not allowed to share until Low Sunday, namely, taking part in the procession of people bringing their offerings to the altar (Ambrose, *in Ps.* 118, Prologue 2).

---

[1] *Ep.* 25, ad Decentium, 3.6; *DBL* 229. The newly baptized were commonly called 'children' or 'infants' because they had been reborn, whatever their age in years.

[2] Proclus quoted in Wenger, p. 101; Harkins, p. 228. Pseudo-Ambrose, *de lapsu Virginis*, 5.19; PL 16.372. Cf. Syriac and Greek *Acts of Judas Thomas*, *DBL* 14. Gregory of Nazianzus, *Orat.* 40.46; cf. 45.2; PG 36.425, 624. Ephrem, *Hymn for Epiphany*, 7.9; CSCO 82.163-7; ET, Nicene and Post-Nicene Fathers, 13.274-6. The ceremony soon appears in the Armenian rite; cf. G. Winkler, 'Das armenische Initiationsrituale in seiner historischen Entwicklung', soon to be published in Rome. I owe her thanks for her helpful comments.

[3] Cf. *Ap. Trad.* 23.2-3; *AIR* 269 (there is mention also of another chalice containing water); Tertullian (*Adv. Marc.*, 1.14.3). The rite was still practised in Rome in the sixth century: cf. John the Deacon, *Ad Senarium*, 12 (PL 59.405; *DBL* 157-8); *Leonine Sacramentary*, Mohlberg, p. 26; Feltoe, p. 25; *DBL* 153-4. There is a possible reference also in Ambrose, *de Sac.* 5.15; *AIR* 147. Cf. Yarnold, 'Ceremonies', p. 463.

THE *DISCIPLINA ARCANI*

A striking feature of the celebration of the initiation-sacraments of the fourth and early fifth centuries was the practice of shrouding in secrecy the facts concerning baptism, the Eucharist, the creed, and the Lord's Prayer. Scholars were to give to this practice the name of *disciplina arcani*. Although its roots may consist of such New Testament texts as 'Do not give dogs what is holy; and do not throw your pearls before swine' (Mt. 7.6, RSV), there is not much evidence for its observance until the middle of the fourth century. Then examples occur with great frequency, which show that the practice was observed all over the Church, in some places almost ostentatiously. A preacher will hint at a secret topic, and then break off with such words as 'Those who have been initiated will know what I mean' (cf. *AIR* 50–4).

The *disciplina arcani* was closely linked with the custom of withholding instruction on certain matters until a catechumen had given in his name for baptism and become a *competens*; in some places, as we have seen, instruction on baptism itself and the Eucharist was not given until these sacraments had already been received. The catechumen had to leave the assembly after the Liturgy of the Word, before the Eucharist proper began (see p. 187). Candidates for baptism were frequently reminded of the need to observe the secrecy very strictly (cf. Cyril, *Procat.* 12; *DBL* 26). Some people were extremely scrupulous in their observance of it; for example, Epiphanius of Salamis feels it necessary to describe the Last Supper in these cryptic terms: 'he stood up at the Supper, took these things and gave thanks, saying: "This is my this"' (*Ancoratus*, 57; PG 43.117).

Besides reverence, the desire to arouse the catechumen's curiosity seems to have been a motive. It is also possible that there was the wish to imitate the secrecy of the Greek and Roman mystery-religions. It is certain that at this time there appears in baptismal sermons an emphasis on the awe (an emotion typical of mystery-religions) which the Christian mysteries of baptism and the Eucharist aroused;[1] and it was not long since Constantine had provided the Church with Christian mystery-sites at Jerusalem, the place where the Christian God (like Persephone at Eleusis) died and rose again. Jerusalem indeed was the source from which several liturgical innovations seem to have spread (cf. Dix, *Shape*, pp. 350–3).

---

[1] The words *phriktos*, *phrikodes* (spine-chilling, hair-raising, awe-inspiring) were often used in this connection, e.g. by Chrysostom, *Bapt. Inst.*, Harkins 6.15. Cf. E. J. Yarnold, 'Baptism and the Pagan Mysteries in the Fourth Century', *Heythrop Journal*, 13 (1972), pp. 247–67, esp. p. 247.

Obviously the *disciplina arcani* could flourish only at a time when infant baptism was not normally practised. If children were let in on the secret, it could not remain a secret for long. Consequently from the middle of the fifth century, as infant baptism became normal, the practice of mystagogic catechesis and the *disciplina arcani* became redundant and lapsed, even for adult converts.

3 The West from about A.D. 500 to the Reformation

J. D. C. FISHER

E. J. YARNOLD, SJ

ROMAN

Andrieu, M., *Les Ordines Romani du haut moyen âge*. Louvain, vols. 2 (1948), 3 (1951), 5 (1961).

Lietzmann, H., *Das Sacramentarium Gregorianum nach dem Aachener Urexemplar* (commonly called the *Hadrianum*). Münster 1921.

Mohlberg, L. C., *Liber Sacramentorum Romanae Ecclesiae Ordinis anni circuli* (*Sacramentarium Gelasianum*). Rome 1958.

Wilmart, A., *Analecta Reginensia*. Città del Vaticano 1933.

GALLICAN

Lowe, E. A., *The Bobbio Missal*. HBS 1923.

Mohlberg, L. C., *Missale Gallicanum Vetus*. Rome 1958. *Missale Gothicum*. Rome 1961.

SPANISH

Férotin, M., *Liber Ordinum*. Paris 1904.

Hildephonsus of Toledo, *de Cognitione Baptismi*, in PL 96.

Isidore of Seville, *de Ecclesiasticis Officiis*, in PL 83.

IRISH

Warner, G. H., *The Stowe Missal*. HBS, 1915.

MODERN WORKS

Chavasse, A., *Le sacramentaire gélasien*. Tournai 1958.

Fisher, J. D. C., *Christian Initiation: Baptism in the Medieval West*. SPCK 1965. (The beginner could well start with this book.)

Van Buchem, L. A., *L'homélie pseudo-eusébienne de pentecôte*. Nijmegen 1967.

TO THE END OF THE EIGHTH CENTURY

In the sixth and following two centuries initiation continued to be celebrated with full solemnity at certain great festivals, although the rule restricting it to the vigils of Easter and Pentecost was more strictly observed in central Italy, where dioceses were small and bishops relatively numerous, than in Gaul or Britain.

In Rome in the second half of Lent the candidates, now assumed to be infants, were assembled at first on Sundays and later on weekdays for three scrutinies, later increased to seven. No longer an examination of the candidates' personal faith or morals, these scrutinies were designed to ensure that the evil spirit departed from them, and consisted therefore mainly in prayer and exorcism. An order for the making of a catechumen, in which the candidates were enrolled and formally accepted for initiation, was combined with the first scrutiny, and included prayer, consignation, and the placing in the infant's mouth of exorcized salt, with the formula: 'N, receive the salt of wisdom for a token of propitiation unto eternal life'. During this period the creed and the Lord's Prayer were recited to the infants, in theory for them to learn. Early on Holy Saturday came the *Effeta*, when the noses and ears of the candidates were touched with saliva, the anointing of breast and back with exorcized oil together with the renunciation of Satan, and finally the reciting of the creed on behalf of the infants, who had in theory now learnt it.

The initiatory rite proper began with the blessing of the font by the bishop, in the Lateran by the pope himself. The most significant words in the long prayer of blessing are these:

> May the power of thy Holy Spirit descend into all the water of this font and make the whole substance of this water fruitful with regenerating power.

Through consecration the water became the sacramental means by which the spiritual blessings of baptism were conveyed; whatever the rationale of lay baptism the implication of this rite is that baptism in unconsecrated water would have been a merely physical washing. The ceremonial became gradually more complex, there being at first a signing of the water and later an insufflation, the infusion of chrism, and the dipping of a candle in the water.

The actual baptism consisted in a threefold question and answer and dipping of each infant, the requirement of Mt. 28.19 being fulfilled in this way without a recitation by the officiant of the now traditional trinitarian formula, which was not introduced into the Roman rite until the eighth century.[1]

[1] See Fisher, p. 17.

Immediately after the baptism the infants were anointed on the head by a presbyter, who said: 'Almighty God ... himself anoints thee with the chrism of salvation in Christ Jesus unto eternal life.' This was commonly believed to confer membership in the royal and priestly body of Christ, but not to impart the Holy Spirit.

The infants were then vested and presented to the bishop, who prayed over them:

> Almighty God ... who hast regenerated thy servants by water and the Holy Spirit, and hast given to them forgiveness of all their sins'—a succinct summary of the blessings just bestowed at the font—'send, Lord, upon them thy Holy Spirit, the Paraclete, and give them the spirit of wisdom and understanding....

The sevenfold graces of the Spirit enumerated in Is. 11.2 were in this prayer invoked upon the candidates, each of whom was then signed on the forehead by the bishop with chrism, and received the *pax*. The purpose of this chrismation was to convey to the baptized that gift of the Holy Spirit which Isaiah had prophesied would rest upon the Messiah, which was in fact bestowed upon Jesus the Messiah at his baptism, and was initially outpoured upon his church at Pentecost.

The rite came to a climax with the mass of the Paschal vigil, at which the candidates were communicated for the first time.[1]

In other parts of the West the rites had much in common with the Roman rite, but also some notable differences. In the Gallican missals there was an unusual trinitarian formula of baptism, which included some anti-Arian polemic.[2] In Spain for a time there was a single instead of a threefold dipping.[3] In northern Italy, Gaul, and Ireland the vesting of the candidates was followed by the *pedilavium* (foot-washing).[4]

But the most significant difference is that in the Gallican missals (see pp. 228–34) of this period and in the Irish *Stowe Missal* (*DBL* 213–21) there was no post-baptismal consignation of the forehead by the bishop. Two explanations have been offered. Either these books were intended for the use of presbyters and therefore omitted those parts of the rite which presbyters were not competent to perform, or the rites in these

---

[1] All the above information can be found in Mohlberg's edition of the *Gelasian Sacramentary*, pp. 32–97 (*DBL* 166–96), in Lietzmann's edition of the *Hadrianum*, pp. 45–54, and in Andrieu's edition of *Ordo Romanus XI*, vol. 2, pp. 417–47 (*DBL* 196–204). An earlier description of the Roman rite is given by John the Deacon (*c.* A.D. 500) in his Letter to Senarius; ed. Wilmart, ST vol. 50; PL 59; *DBL* 154–8. See Fisher, pp. 1–29.

[2] *Missale Gallicanum Vetus*, ed. Mohlberg, p. 42; *Bobbio Missal*, ed. Lowe, p. 75; *DBL* 204–13; Fisher, pp. 50–1.

[3] See Fisher, p. 91.

[4] Ambrose, *de Sac.*, 3.4; *DBL* 130. See Fisher, pp. 32–3, 36–7, 44–5, 84.

books are complete rites of initiation performed in their entirety by presbyters, in which case, even if the accompanying formulae do not specifically say so, the one unction after baptism was *inter alia* the sign of the giving of the Spirit (cf. Fisher, pp. 52–7, 84).

Now it had long been the rule that candidates should not be reserved for initiation at one of the customary seasons if there was any risk that they might die in the meantime. Consequently initiation was required at many times of the year, and in considerable haste, for the great number of newly born infants who were not expected to survive. In these situations, there being no time to secure the presence of a bishop, the local presbyter, who was instantly available, performed as much of the rite as he could— that is, he baptized and gave communion in the expectation that, if the child recovered, the missing consignation of the forehead would be supplied at the next episcopal visitation. Those who were thus baptized in haste and died unconfirmed were not held to have been thereby deprived of eternal salvation; but if they recovered, they were supposed to receive confirmation at the next opportunity.

An order for the initiation of the sick is given in the *Hadrianum*, that version of the *Gregorian Sacramentary* which Pope Hadrian I gave to Charlemagne in 784 or soon after.[1] It is necessarily brief, consisting only of the blessing of the water, baptism, and the unction of the head, after which 'you communicate and confirm him', the word 'confirm' here meaning administer the chalice. Significantly nothing is said of any episcopal anointing of the forehead. Thus, although initiation at the Paschal vigil was still in principle the norm, there were in practice many departures from the norm (Fisher, p. 28).

When in 789 Charlemagne ordered the Roman rite to be used throughout his empire,[2] the consequences were twofold. First, the Gallican churches had to pay more attention than hitherto to the rule that the proper seasons for initiation were the vigils of Easter and Pentecost; and secondly, if the rite was to be administered in its entirety, a bishop had to be present to perform the chrismation of the forehead, that part of the rite which was traditionally associated with the giving of the Holy Spirit.

Hence where and when the Roman rite prevailed, the episcopal ceremonies now known as confirmation had to be omitted for the time being from the many initiations where no bishop was present.

Many such initiations, being administered in sudden emergency to infants in imminent danger of death, could be regarded as abnormal. But in time the norm changed. For in large dioceses initiation began to be

[1] *MGH, Epp. Merovingici et Karolini Aevi*, i. p. 626.
[2] *Capit.* of 789, c. 23, *MGH, Cap. Legum Franc.*, i. p. 64.

required at the customary seasons in other churches besides the see-church with the result that in these other baptismal churches even the solemn initiations had of necessity to take place in the absence of a bishop. Thus in the Gallican *Supplement* to the *Hadrianum*, formerly ascribed to Alcuin, there are some variations from the Roman use, including this rubric:

> The infant is clothed with his robe: if a bishop is present he must immediately be confirmed with chrism and then communicated, and if there is no bishop present, he shall be communicated by the presbyter.[1]

Hence the traditional sequence of baptism–confirmation–communion became changed to baptism–communion–confirmation, as is found in the early eighth century *Sacramentary of Prague*, where baptism takes place at Easter and confirmation eight days later. Similarly the rite of initiation described by Alcuin[2] and Rabanus Maurus, Abbot of Fulda and later Archbishop of Mainz,[3] is the Roman rite of Paschal initiation with the episcopal hand-laying, signing with chrism, and prayer coming a week after the candidates have been baptized and 'confirmed with the Lord's body and blood'.

Since Alcuin and Rabanus believed that the first post-baptismal unction by the presbyter conferred the gift of the Spirit, they had to find some meaning for the episcopal chrismation and hand-laying which traditionally also conferred that gift. They said that through the imposition of the bishop's hand the baptized received the Spirit of sevenfold grace so that they might be strengthened to preach to others. The influence of their teaching encouraged the later common belief that the grace of confirmation should be understood primarily in terms of strengthening. Alcuin and Rabanus were dealing with a situation where many candidates for initiation might be adults. Magnus of Sens, however, in a diocese where infant baptism was normal said that the episcopal hand-laying supplied strength to persevere in the true faith.[4] In the fifth century, Faustus of Riez had said that the strengthening was 'for the fight', and the notion of such a *robur ad pugnam* also gained currency throughout the Middle Ages (see note below).

Those for whatever reason baptized in the absence of a bishop were intended to receive confirmation at the next possible opportunity. Such an opportunity, however, might not present itself soon, because in large dioceses bishops had great distances to travel, some bishops were not

[1] H. A. Wilson, *The Gregorian Sacramentary* (HBS 1915), p. 163; Fisher, pp. 71–2.
[2] *Ep. 134 Odoino Presbitero, MGH, Epp. Karolini Aevi*, ii (Berlin 1895), pp. 202f.
[3] PL 107.312f.
[4] PL 102.983f.

good visitors, and some had inroads made into their time by state duties. In addition many parents were negligent in presenting their children for confirmation when the opportunity did arise. This was to cause Archbishop Peckham at the Council of Lambeth in 1281 to complain of the damnable negligence of confirmation, to obviate which he ordered that none be admitted to the sacrament of the Lord's body and blood, save if in danger of death, unless he had been confirmed, or reasonably prevented from receiving confirmation.[1] Furthermore the unsettled state of parts of western Europe during much of this period made systematic visitation of a diocese impossible.

Hence confirmation was in actual practice coming more and more to be separated in time from baptism, and the interval was becoming longer; it was acquiring the appearance of an independent sacrament, and was no longer an indispensable preliminary to the receiving of communion. Thus the way was paved for the belief that confirmation is the sacrament of adolescents.

'CONFIRMATION' AS A LITURGICAL TERM

The noun *confirmatio* is first found as a liturgical term in a well known sermon preached by Faustus of Riez on Whitsunday about the year 460. The cognate verb is found earlier still because the Council of Riez in 439 spoke of confirming neophytes, an expression whose meaning was already well understood in southern Gaul. In this part of Gaul there was now very commonly an interval of time between baptism, which could be administered by a presbyter, and the ensuing ceremony, which conferred the Holy Spirit and which could only be performed by a bishop. When the last part of the rite of initiation began to be separated from baptism itself, it also began to acquire a new name, confirmation.

Faustus' sermon is important because it represents the first known attempt to base a theology of initiation on a disintegrated rite. Faustus said that as regards innocence baptism is complete, but as regards grace there is in confirmation an increase; while the regeneration conferred in baptism suffices for those who die forthwith, confirmation is a necessary equipment of those who live to a full age to face the struggles of this world; in baptism we are reborn to life, after baptism we are confirmed for combat; in baptism we are washed, after baptism we are strengthened. Faustus equated the gift conveyed by confirmation with the gift of the Spirit initially outpoured at Pentecost.

[1] F. M. Powicke and C. R. Cheney, *Councils and Synods with Other Documents relating to the English Church* (OUP 1964), p. 897.

At this time 'confirm' meant complete, baptism being completed, sealed, or consummated by the gift of the Holy Spirit in confirmation. When Faustus said that in confirmation we are strengthened, he used a different verb (*roboramur*). When 'confirm' was first used, confirmation was a sacramental act conferring grace, and had nothing to do with the renewal of baptismal promises.

Faustus' teaching on the relation of confirmation to baptism became standard doctrine in the West in the Middle Ages because it was quoted by the author of the *False Decretals*, which were read by leading authorities including St Thomas Aquinas and Gratian, the great compiler of the canon law.[1]

FROM CHARLEMAGNE TO THE REFORMATION

In the foregoing pages we began to consider some of the regional types of initiation-rite. For convenience they can be loosely classified as Roman, Milanese, Gallican (including German), English, Celtic, and Spanish (Mozarabic) types (see pp. 228–30). Thus in Spain the candidate was immersed only once; in Gallican and Milanese usage a foot-washing rite was included. From time to time efforts were made to induce the regions to conform to the Roman pattern. Augustine of Canterbury, for example, introduced Roman usage into Britain early in the seventh century, and Charlemagne imposed it throughout his empire early in the ninth. In Spain, however, the Mozarabic rite continued in use until the eleventh century, and the Celtic rite, exemplified by the Stowe Missal (*c.* 800), was not replaced by the Roman until the twelfth. Despite these repeated attempts to impose uniformity, local variations continued to develop. Thus the Sarum rite (*DBL* 231–53) was in common use in the late Middle Ages throughout England, Wales, and Ireland; but even so it had more in common with Roman practice than with the earlier regional types. A particular subject for local variation was the practice of confirmation by presbyters. In the sixteenth century, however, the Council of Trent led to the imposition of a fairly general uniformity.

By that century infant baptism had become so common that liturgical books ceased to include any specific rite for adults. In many places regulations had been laid down insisting on an interval of not more than a week between birth and baptism. One consequence of this was that baptism began to be regarded as the child's naming-ceremony; another was that some baptismal rites (such as those of Sarum) included an admonition to the godparents to teach the child its prayers and to see that

[1] The outstanding work on this subject is by L. A. Van Buchem (see bibliography).

it was confirmed. In addition, though Easter and Pentecost could still be described as the 'solemn' times for baptism, most children were baptized on other occasions. Of the rites of the catechumenate, some, such as the scrutinies and the handing over of the creed and the Lord's Prayer, were obviously inappropriate for infants and were discarded; others, such as the reception of the child at the church door, the giving of salt and the exorcisms, were retained, but were included with baptism in a single service instead of forming a preparation on an earlier day. The triple immersion took place while the trinitarian formula 'I baptize thee in the name ...' was recited once, after the triple interrogation concerning faith. Baptism by a presbyter had become the standard practice; the gift of the Holy Spirit was linked with confirmation, which was to be conferred by the bishop when the child was at least seven years old. (However in the Sarum rite confirmation was given at once if the bishop was present; accordingly Elizabeth I was confirmed immediately after baptism.) Reverence for the eucharistic species led to the postponement of first communion to a similar age. (In some places for a time blessed bread was given instead of holy communion.) By this process the three parts of the rites of initiation, baptism, confirmation, and communion, became separated one from another. English practice insisted that a child should not be admitted to communion before confirmation; the purpose of this regulation was simply to ensure that parents took the trouble to get their children confirmed (see p. 115).

4 The Byzantine Rite

W. JARDINE GRISBROOKE

Schmemann, A., *Of Water and the Spirit* (a theological commentary on the Byzantine rite).

The oldest surviving liturgical documents of the Byzantine rite are to be found in the Greek MS known as the Barberini *Euchologion*, probably a work of the late eighth or early ninth century.[1] The euchologion contains two sets of texts relating to the liturgy of initiation.

The first comprises two catechetical exhortations or homilies, and the renunciation, profession of faith, and declaration of adhesion to Christ, which marked the conclusion of the preparation of adult catechumens to be baptized at Easter; this rite takes place under the presidency of the archbishop (i.e. the patriarch) on Good Friday. The second set comprises two prayers connected with infancy, the prayer for the making of a catechumen, the pre-baptismal exorcisms, the renunciation, profession of faith and the adhesion, and then the order of baptism itself. Apart from the first two of these prayers, the whole is evidently arranged for use in either infant or adult initiation.[2]

A comparison of the content of this second set of texts with the modern Byzantine baptismal rite reveals that there has been little change for the last eleven hundred years—and probably, from such indications as we have, since long before that.[3] The following summary, therefore, is of the modern rite, only major changes from earlier practice being noted.

The service falls into two distinct parts, the Order for the making of a catechumen, and the Order of holy baptism, each of which is printed separately under its own title.

The Order for the making of a catechumen comprises: (i) the prayer for the admission of a catechumen, which is preceded by a triple breathing upon the candidate and a triple signing of him with the sign of the cross on brow and breast, and commences with a laying on of hands in

---

[1] Vat. MS. Barberini Gk. 336. The sets of text here referred to are at fol. 260ff and 170ff. Cf. A. Jacob, 'La tradition des manuscrits de la liturgie de S. Jean Chrysostome VIIIᵉ–XIIᵉ siècles', *LO* 47 (1970), pp. 109–38.

[2] *DBL* 69–82 gives both sets, but appears to assume that the first set of texts is incomplete, and that it should continue with an actual baptismal liturgy. But an examination of the Constantinopolitan arrangements for Good Friday and Holy Saturday in Mateos, *Le Typikon de la Grande Eglise*, vol. 2, pp. 79, 85, suggests that this is a misapprehension.

[3] Cf., e.g. Mateos, op. cit. vol. 2, p. 79, n. 6. And there is nothing of any consequence in the rite which is incompatible with such references as are to be found in earlier writers.

the name of the Trinity; (ii) the exorcisms, four in number, although the third and fourth are printed together in the books, the fourth being accompanied by a breathing upon the brow, mouth, and breast of the catechumen; (iii) the renunciations—the catechumen, turned towards the west, and with arms upraised, three times renounces Satan, his angels, his works, his worship and his pomp, confirms the renunciation, and blows and spits as an expression of final contempt for all that he has renounced; (iv) the profession of faith, consisting of the Nicene-Constantinopolitan Creed, preceded and followed by a declaration of adhesion; (v) a concluding prayer for the grace of baptismal renewal and enlightenment.

The Order of holy baptism comprises: (i) the hallowing of the baptismal water, consisting of a diaconal litany, during which the priest prays *secreto* for the divine assistance in the administration of the sacrament, and a lengthy prayer of anaphoral form, commencing with a thanksgiving for creation and redemption, continuing with an epiclesis for the descent of the Holy Spirit upon the water, and concluding with a petition for the fruits of this hallowing of the water and a doxology; the epiclesis is accompanied by a triple breathing on the water in the form of the cross at an appropriate point; (ii) the pre-baptismal anointing, on brow, breast, and back, preceded by the blessing of the 'oil of gladness' corresponding to the western 'oil of catechumens', and a triple signing of the water with this oil; (iii) the baptism itself, the candidate being placed upright in the font, and immersed three times, once at the naming of each person of the Trinity, with the formula; 'The servant of God N. is baptized in the name of the Father, Amen; and of the Son, Amen; and of the Holy Spirit, Amen.'; (iv) the clothing, preceded by Psalm 31 (32).

The administration of the sacrament of chrismation (corresponding to the western confirmation) follows at once for infants as well as for adults. Its administration, like that of baptism, is delegated to the priest, although he uses episcopally (in modern practice patriarchally or primatially) consecrated chrism. The celebrant says a prayer giving thanks for baptism and beseeching the gifts of the seal of the Holy Spirit and participation in the Eucharist, after which he anoints the newly-baptized on brow, eyes, nostrils, mouth, ears, breast, hands, and feet, saying at each anointing 'The seal of the gift of the Holy Spirit, Amen'.

The baptismal rites are concluded with a brief form of the synaxis, with an appropriate epistle and gospel. There is no provision in the modern books for the celebration of the eucharistic liturgy as an integral part of the baptismal rite, and this is the most marked change from the rite as given in the Barberini *Euchologion*; the other apparent major change is that in the older form chrismation is even more closely integrated with baptism than it is in the modern service, but this may be due to a minor accidental transposition in the manuscript.

5 Lutheran, Anglican, and Reformed Rites

J. D. C. FISHER

Barkley, J. M., 'Baptism: Reformed', *DLW* pp. 60–3.

Calvin, J., *Institutes of the Christian Religion*. (ET) Philadelphia and London 1935.

Fisher, J. D. C., *Christian Initiation: the Reformation Period*. AC SPCK 1970.

Hermann, Archbishop of Cologne, *A Simple and Religious Consultation*, ET by J. Daye, 1547 and 1548.

Hubert, F., 'Die Strassburger Liturgischen Ordnungen', in *Zeitalter der Reformation*. Göttingen 1900.

Knox, J., *Works I–IV*, ed. D. Laing. Edinburgh 1846 etc.

Luthardt, C. E., in *Zeitschrift für kirchliche Wissenschaft und kirchliches Leben*, 10. Leipzig 1889.

Luther's Works, 53. Philadelphia 1965.

Maxwell, W. D., *The Liturgical Portions of the Genevan Service Book*. Faith Press 1965.

Ollard, S. L., 'Confirmation in the Anglican Communion', in *Confirmation, or the Laying on of Hands*. 2nd edn SPCK 1934.

Procter, F., *A New History of the Book of Common Prayer*, rev. W. H. Frere. Macmillan 1901.

Repp, A. C., *Confirmation in the Lutheran Church*. St Louis 1964.

Richter, A. L., *Die Evangelischen Kirchenordnungen*. Weimar 1846 and 1871.

Sehling, E., *Die Evangelischen Kirchenordnungen des XVI Jahrhunderts*. Leipzig 1902 etc.

Whitaker, E. C., *Martin Bucer and the Book of Common Prayer*. AC 1974.

Zwingli, U., *Works*, CR 88–94.

The sixteenth-century Reformers criticized the medieval Latin rite of baptism on five main counts. (1) Since it could be shown from scripture that by divine appointment baptism must be administered with water in the name of the Trinity, nothing else was essential to the rite, the blessing of the font and the use of oil, candles, salt, and spittle being unnecessary additions introduced by men. (2) These additions gave rise to superstition. (3) The prevalent custom of baptizing children at any time in an almost empty church detracted from the honour due to a holy sacrament, and obscured the ecclesial element in baptism. (4) Not enough care was taken to choose suitable godparents. (5) The service was not meaningful because it was in Latin.

Although they greatly emphasized the need for personal faith in all who would be Christians, the Reformers for the most part retained the practice of infant baptism. Relying solely on the authority of scripture, they had to go to the Bible to justify the baptism of infants against the criticism of the Anabaptists. To this end they relied on five principal arguments. (1) Since God had made a covenant with Abraham, promising to be his God and the God of his seed, therefore the children of Christian parents, coming within the scope of his new covenant, were eligible for the sacrament which conferred membership in God's people. (2) Since the infant sons of Jews were received into God's people by circumcision, therefore the infant children of Christians should be received into the new Israel by baptism, the Christian counterpart of circumcision. (3) Since our Lord welcomed and blessed the little children brought to him, the Church should likewise welcome little children by baptism. (4) If the children of one believing parent were deemed holy, so also were the children of two believing parents. Being therefore holy, they were eligible for baptism. (5) Some of the households which the New Testament shows to have been baptized must have included some little children.

The year 1523 saw the first stage in baptismal reform when the Latin rites began to be put into the vernacular. More radical revisions were introduced in Luther's second *Taufbüchlein* (1526), by Zwingli in Zurich (1525), and by Bucer in Strassburg (1525).

Luther's rite of 1526 opens with an exorcism and signing of the child's forehead and breast, as in the Latin Magdeburg *Agenda*. The next prayer, 'Almighty and eternal God . . . I invoke thee upon this thy servant *N* . . .', is the corresponding prayer in the *Agenda*, adapted because there is now no giving of salt. Next follows the Flood-prayer, so called from its typology. The child is then exorcized in the name of the Trinity, the Gospel (Mk. 10.13–16) is read, and the Lord's Prayer is said by all. Then the child is brought to the font for the actual baptism. After the renunciation of Satan and the interrogations concerning the faith, the child is dipped in the font by the priest, who at the same time recites the trinitarian formula. Finally at the vesting of the child in a white robe there comes this prayer: 'The almighty God and Father of our Lord Jesus Christ, who has regenerated thee by water and the Holy Spirit, and has forgiven thee all thy sins, strengthen thee with his grace unto eternal life.' This is the prayer at the presbyteral unction in the old Latin rite, modified now that there is no anointing.[1]

[1] For the full rite see Luther's Works, vol. 53, pp. 106–9.

Zwingli's order of baptism was one from which 'all additions which have no foundation in scripture have been removed'. A prayer resembling Luther's Flood-prayer is said, the Gospel (Mk. 10) is read, the child is named and baptized by the minister, who pronounces the trinitarian formula, and is finally vested in a white robe, called a chrisom.

In Bucer's rite the minister delivers an exhortation, after which all say the Lord's Prayer and the Apostles' Creed. After a prayer for the child the Gospel (Mk. 10) is read. The godparents are charged 'to teach this child Christian order, discipline, and fear of God'. Then the minister, having asked the godparents to name the child, pours water upon it, at the same time pronouncing the trinitarian formula. Opportunity is provided for a sermon, which may be short or long according to the circumstances.

Thus in these three Protestant orders of baptism, of which Luther's is the most conservative and Bucer's the most full of exhortation, the act of dipping in water and the trinitarian formula are made to stand out as the only essential matter and form of baptism.

Bucer ordered the clergy to baptize only on Sundays so that the baptism of the child, the presentation and entrusting of him to the Church with the prayers for him might take place with due solemnity and reverence in the presence of God's people.[1]

In the *Pia Deliberatio* or *Consultation*, which he and Melanchthon produced in 1543 at the request of Hermann von Wied to assist him in the reform of the church of Cologne of which he was archbishop, Bucer said that the ancient custom of baptizing only at Easter and Whitsun could not be restored; instead

> We will that baptism be ministered only upon the Sundays and holy days, when the whole congregation is wont to come together, if the weakness of the infants let [i.e. prevent] not the same, so that it is to be feared that they will not live till the next holy day, for our mind is that the handling of the sacrament of Christ's body and blood called Eucharistia may be joined with baptism, and that they which bring the infants to baptism may use the body and blood of our Lord Jesus Christ after the manner and institution of the primitive church.[2]

In 1542 Calvin drew up an order of baptism for his church in Geneva. Children are to be brought to baptism either on Sunday afternoon at the time of the catechism or on weekdays after the morning sermon. The minister delivers a long discourse in which the meaning of baptism is expounded: through it God incorporates us into his Church; in it he testifies before us his forgiveness of our sins; water is the sign that he

[1] F. Hubert, pp. 37f.
[2] ET J. Daye, fol. 153.

wishes to cleanse our souls; baptism is a sure testimony that God wishes to be a merciful father to us and to assist us by his Holy Spirit to combat the devil, man, and the desires of the flesh; the benefits of baptism are received by us if we do not by ingratitude destroy the force of the sacrament; opportunity is taken to justify infant baptism out of scripture, and the Matthean version of the blessing of the little children is read. There follow a prayer for the child and the saying of the Lord's Prayer. The ensuing charge to the godparents leads into the saying of the Apostles' Creed. Finally the child is baptized in the threefold name. In this extremely simple rite, which reveals the influence of Bucer, Calvin believed that, in abolishing the many ancient ceremonies which were not commanded by God, he had recovered a form of baptism such 'as Jesus Christ has ordered, as the apostles have preserved and followed, as the primitive church has used'.[1]

The rite used by John Knox when he was in Geneva from 1555 to 1559 is very similar.[2] The opening address covers the same ground as Calvin's, and ends with a charge to the godparents and congregation to see that their children are brought up as Christians. The father, or godfather, recites the Creed; a prayer for the child and the Lord's Prayer are said. Then the minister takes water in his hand and lays it upon the child's head, at the same time pronouncing the trinitarian formula. In Knox's view baptism is 'the seal of justice and the sign of regeneration, but neither the cause, neither yet the effect and virtue'. The seal once received 'is durable, and needeth not to be iterate, lest that by iteration and multiplication of the sign, the office of the Holy Spirit, which is to illuminate, regenerate, and to purge, be attributed to it'.[3] Thus for Calvin and Knox the washing in water is a demonstration and proof of the benefits which God wills to confer rather than the instrumental means by which he confers them.

In the Prayer Book of 1549 (see pp. 70–74) Cranmer used the *Consultation*, but not exclusively. He followed Bucer in requiring baptism to be administered on 'Sundays and other holy days when the most number of people may come together', except that he ordered the baptismal party to be ready at the church door not at the beginning of the Eucharist but before the last canticle at Morning or Evening Prayer. The first part of the service, a relic of the old order for the making of a catechumen, takes place at the church door immediately before the actual baptism, whereas in the *Consultation* it could take place the day before. It consisted in a fairly free version of the Flood-prayer, which was in the

[1] CR 34, cols. 185–92.
[2] See Maxwell, pp. 105–11.
[3] *Works*, ed. D. Laing, 4.122.

Consultation, the signing of the child on forehead and breast 'in token that thou shalt not be ashamed to confess the faith of Christ crucified . . .',[1] an exorcism taken from the exorcisms in the *Sarum* rite, the reading of the Gospel (Mk. 10), a brief exhortation, the saying of the Lord's Prayer and the Apostles' Creed. The final prayer, 'Almighty and everlasting God . . . we give thee humble thanks . . .', is taken entirely from the *Consultation*. The priest then conducts the child by the right hand into church for the actual baptism.

The priest dips the child 'discreetly and warily' three times in the water, saying the trinitarian formula. If the child is weak, baptism by affusion is permitted. Although in the *Consultation* Bucer had omitted both these ceremonies, the child is then vested in a chrisom and finally anointed on the head. The accompanying prayer is an adaptation of the old prayer at the presbyteral unction after baptism:

> Almighty God, the Father of our Lord Jesus Christ, who hath regenerated thee by water and the Holy Ghost, and hath given unto thee remission of all thy sins, he vouchsafe to anoint thee with the unction of his Holy Spirit, and bring thee to the inheritance of everlasting life.

The service ends with a charge to the godparents to see that the child is brought up to know what a solemn vow, promise, and profession he has made through them; in particular they are to see that he hears sermons, and learns the Creed, Lord's Prayer, and Ten Commandments in English. The final rubric requires children to be presented for confirmation so soon as they can say in the vulgar tongue the articles of the faith, the Lord's Prayer, and the Ten Commandments, and have further been instructed in the catechism.

The form for the blessing of the font is placed by itself after the service of private baptism, because the water in the font once consecrated can be reserved up to one month for future use. The first prayer, after referring to the descent of the Spirit upon our Lord, includes a petition, 'Send down, we beseech thee, the same thy Holy Spirit to assist us, and to be present at this our invocation of thy holy name: sanctify this fountain of baptism, thou that art the sanctifier of all things . . . .' The water is signed with the cross. There follow a number of short prayers taken from the Mozarabic *Missale Mixtum*. The concluding prayer, 'Almighty ever-living God, whose most dearly beloved Son . . . did shed out of his most precious side . . .', includes a statement that the water has been 'prepared for the ministration of thy holy sacrament'.

Among the criticisms of this rite made by Bucer in his *Censura* are

[1] This prayer is derived partly from the *Sarum Manual* and partly from Luther's *Taufbüchlein*.

these: (1) Baptism should not take place during Morning or Evening Prayer but 'when the congregation is still present in the greatest numbers, before the administration of the Holy Supper is begun'. (2) The service at the church door is 'possessed of enough decency, order, and edification' for it to take place inside the church in the hearing of the congregation. (3) The prayer at the signing of the child, the questions concerning the renunciation and the interrogative creed are all addressed to the child who cannot understand. (4) Inanimate objects such as water ought not to be blessed. (5) Exorcism is appropriate only in the case of demoniacs. (6) The giving of the white robe and the anointing, though ancient signs, are no longer edifying, serving more 'for the maintenance and increase of superstition and show than of piety and religion'.[1]

In the second Prayer Book of 1552 some notice was taken of these criticisms. While the opening rubrics continue to incorporate baptism into Morning or Evening Prayer, the service at the church door has been abolished, everything now taking place at the font. This entailed some rearrangement of the material. After an opening exhortation there comes a revised version of the Flood-prayer, which, however, retains the statement that by his own baptism our Lord sanctified the flood Jordan and all other waters to the mystical washing away of sin, although Bucer had alleged that it was unscriptural, and encouraged a 'superstitious belief that a kind of power of sanctifying in the waters is imposed upon the baptism of Christ'.[2]

The prayer at the signing of the child is no longer addressed to the child: the signing of breast and forehead becomes a signing of the forehead only, and is transferred to a point immediately after the actual baptism and in such close proximity to it that it has often been taken for the essential matter and form of baptism. The exorcism is abolished. The words of renunciation, now shortened, and the creed are addressed to the godparents. All that survives of the blessing of the font is placed immediately before the actual baptism; four of the short prayers are retained, and also the final prayer, which, however, no longer declares the water to have been prepared for the ministration of the sacrament. There is no consignation and no invocation of the Holy Spirit, the intention plainly being to avoid any suggestion that the water is consecrated.

The child is dipped in the water, it seems, only once. The child's name is no longer used in the preliminaries of baptism, and is now used once only, at the very moment of baptism, so encouraging the mistaken notion that christening and naming are synonymous. The giving of the white robe and the use of chrism are abolished.

[1] See E. C. Whitaker, *Martin Bucer and the Book of Common Prayer*, pp. 82–100.
[2] Ibid., p. 88.

After the baptism there now come the Lord's Prayer, a prayer of thanksgiving formerly in the service at the church door, and the charge to the godparents.

The order of baptism in the Prayer Book of 1662 is substantially that of 1552 with some verbal alterations. Among the differences may be noted the following. The godparents are asked to renounce the devil, but in the name of the child. Although the prayer before the baptism has no invocation of the Holy Spirit, it now includes the petition, 'sanctify this water to the mystical washing away of sin'. The final rubric of 1552 requiring the child in due time to be confirmed is now the concluding part of the charge to the godparents. Two rubrics are added at the end. (1) 'It is certain by God's word that children which are baptized, dying before they commit actual sin, are undoubtedly saved.' The doctrinal implication of this rubric becomes apparent when it is compared with the statement in the *Bishops' Book* of 1537 that 'infants and children dying in their infancy shall undoubtedly be saved thereby, and else not'. But in the Prayer Book rubric the reference is also to baptized infants who die unconfirmed. (2) The sign of the cross at baptism is justified by reference to Canon 30 of the Canons of 1604.

All the time that candidates for initiation were baptized in the nude, and all the time that some candidates for initiation might be adults, baptism itself was not a public act but for obvious reasons took place in the privacy of the baptistery, a building detached from the main body of the church. At the solemn initiations in the presence of the bishop the candidates after their baptism were vested in their white robes and escorted into church where all the faithful were gathered together to celebrate a great festival. The need for privacy, however, ended where and when it could be assumed that all candidates for baptism were infants. Hence in the Middle Ages in the baptismal churches fonts large enough to permit the dipping of an infant in the water began to be erected, usually at the west end of the church near the door in order to signify that the infant by baptism was admitted into the fellowship of the church. In some churches the space round the font was enclosed by a screen or railing to form a baptistery within the church. In the sixteenth century Anglican churches retained the medieval fonts at the back of the church. Basins placed near the pulpit or table were used in Calvinistic churches, while the Lutherans preferred to place the font at the east end and near the table and pulpit so that the word and the sacrament could be ministered in full view of the whole congregation.

For the attitude of the Prayer Book to adult baptism, see p. 134.

PRIVATE BAPTISM

The *Saxon Church Order* of 1539 forbade private baptism except in grave emergency, when it sufficed to say the Lord's Prayer and then baptize in the threefold name; a child thus baptized did not need to be baptized again. At the reception into church of one privately baptized the pastor had to ask who was present at the baptism, who performed it, whether the Lord's Prayer was said, whether water and the trinitarian formula were used. If the answers were in the affirmative, the Gospel (Mk. 10) was read, followed by a brief prayer; if, however, the answers were uncertain, the child was to be baptized.[1]

This rite was closely followed by Bucer in the *Consultation*,[2] which in turn was followed by Cranmer. In the Prayer Books of 1549 and 1552 private baptism, forbidden except in grave necessity, consists in the saying of the Lord's Prayer and baptism in the threefold name. A child thus baptized is, if he recovers, to be brought to church, when the same questions are asked about the baptism. If all has been done correctly, the Gospel (Mk. 10) is read, the minister and godparents say the Lord's Prayer and the Creed, and then follow the renunciation and confession of faith and (in 1549 only) the giving of the chrisom. The service concludes with the thanksgiving and charge to the godparents. If there is any doubt whether the baptism has been correctly performed, conditional baptism, although rejected by the Lutherans, is required.

The opening rubric orders the clergy frequently to warn their people not to defer the baptism of their children longer than the Sunday or holy day next after birth.

In 1662 a number of alterations were made. Baptism must now not be deferred beyond the first or second Sunday after birth. The Lord's Prayer and such other prayers from the service of public baptism as time permits are to be said before the baptism, and after it is to be said the prayer of thanksgiving for the regeneration of the child. If the child recovers, the same procedure is to be followed when he is brought to church, except that after the response to the creed and the promise to keep God's holy will and commandments, the priest receives the child into the congregation of Christ's flock and signs him with the sign of the cross, as in the service of public baptism. Conditional baptism is again enjoined where doubt has arisen.

---

[1] E. Sehling, 1.264–8.
[2] Daye, fols. 167–71.

CONFIRMATION

Luther rejected the medieval rite of confirmation on the ground that it was a merely human invention, not divinely instituted, and consequently neither a sacrament nor a means of grace; to say that it conferred the Holy Spirit was to detract from baptism; where in Scripture it is said that the apostles laid their hands on the baptized, the Holy Spirit was given with outward signs causing them to speak in other languages in order to preach the gospel; but this only happened for a time. So Luther produced no order of confirmation as such, but issued a shorter and longer catechism to be learnt by children before they were admitted to communion.

Hence in some Lutheran churches the instruction of the children in the catechism concluded with the examination of them by a pastor without any ceremony to mark the occasion, and their admission to communion.

However, in the *Ziegenhain Order of Church Discipline* which Bucer compiled in 1538 at the invitation of Philip, Landgrave of Hesse, children were to be presented in church at one of the great festivals to be examined in the faith by the pastor. When they had answered the questions, the pastor asked the prayers of the congregation that the children might have perseverance and an increase of the Holy Spirit; finally he laid his hands upon them, confirming them in the name of the Lord and establishing them in the Christian fellowship. They were then admitted to the Lord's table.[1]

In 1539 the *Cassel Church Order*, embodying the regulations of Ziegenhain, included an order of confirmation and laying on of hands to be used in all parishes at Christmas, Easter, and Pentecost at the time of public preaching. The children answered the questions in the catechism, promised to be faithful in their attendance at church, to bring alms for the poor, and obey the elders. Then came a long prayer followed by a hand-laying and the petition, 'receive the Holy Spirit, protection and guard against all evil, strength and help to all goodness, from the gracious hand of God the Father, Son, and Holy Spirit'.[2] It is open to dispute whether Bucer believed the hand-laying to be an ordinary blessing or to convey an objective gift of the Holy Spirit similar to that imparted in the Latin rite of confirmation. Thus, whether Bucer intended it or not, the hand-laying could be interpreted in a fully sacramental sense. Clearly in his treatment of confirmation Bucer was more conservative than Luther.

In the *Consultation*[3] Bucer said that because those baptized in infancy

[1] Sehling, 8.102ff.
[2] Ibid., pp. 124ff.
[3] Daye, fols. 171-5.

cannot at their baptism confess their faith or give themselves to the obedience of Christ, they must do this when they have been well instructed and understand the great benefits of baptism. When they do this the congregation must be present to pray for them and ask for them the increase of the Holy Spirit so that they may persevere in the faith. The sign used is laying-on of hands in accordance with the example of Christ and his apostles. Whereas in former times the minister of confirmation was the bishop, now dioceses are so large that the bishop cannot pay an annual visit to every parish in his diocese to confirm those who have been catechized; therefore it is better that confirmation be administered by visitors than that it be deferred.

The confirmation service begins with the catechizing of the children. Next after a long prayer for their spiritual welfare the pastor lays his hands on them and says another prayer, of which the chief petition is:

Confirm this thy servant with the Holy Spirit, that he may continue in the obedience of the gospel and strongly resist the devil and his own weakness, and not grieve the Holy Ghost, or trouble or offend thy Church with slanders, but that his whole life may serve to the praise of thy glory, his own health, and common profit of thy congregation....

The use of oil has been abandoned on the ground that this sign has been abused most superstitiously. This rite, rejected in the church of Cologne for which it was designed, is of interest today only because of its influence upon Cranmer and the *Book of Common Prayer*.

In the Prayer Book of 1549 confirmation is to be administered only to such as can say in their mother tongue the Creed, Lord's Prayer, and Ten Commandments, and can answer such questions out of the catechism as the bishop may ask them. This rubric put an end to the confirmation of infants, which, although rare in the later middle ages, had been permitted as late as 1533 when the Princess Elizabeth was baptized and confirmed three days after birth.

The candidates, having come to years of discretion, openly before the Church ratify and confess the promises made for them at their baptism. Because by imposition of hands and prayer they receive strength and defence against temptation to sin, confirmation should be administered at that age when children begin to be in danger of falling into sin. The deferment of confirmation does not imperil the salvation of young children, because it is certain by God's word that children baptized, if they depart this life in their infancy, are undoubtedly saved.

The bishop is the only minister of confirmation. After the catechizing of the candidates the service proper begins with versicles translated from the rite in the *Sarum Manual*, after which the bishop says the prayer for the sevenfold Spirit, the traditional confirmation-prayer of the West, which expresses the intention of the rite, '...send down from heaven...upon them thy Holy Ghost the Comforter with the manifold gifts of grace....' There follows this prayer, 'Sign them, O Lord, and mark them to be thine for ever by the virtue of thy holy cross and passion. Confirm and strengthen them with the inward unction of the Holy Ghost mercifully unto everlasting life.' Then the bishop signs the candidates on the forehead and lays his hand on their heads, saying, '*N*, I sign thee with the sign of the cross and lay my hands upon thee in the name....' Finally he gives the *pax*.

The closing rubrics order the parish priest to instruct in the catechism for half an hour before Evening Prayer at least once in six weeks the children, servants, and prentices whom their parents, masters, and dames are enjoined to send along to him. None is to be admitted to the holy communion until he has been confirmed.[1] In this way it is hoped that all communicants would approach the sacrament with understanding.

This rite, the most conservative rite of confirmation in any church of the Reformation, is 'reformed' in so far as it begins with the catechizing of the candidates, but is 'catholic' in that it is virtually the *Sarum* rite put into English, but with the use of chrism abolished.

In the Prayer Book of 1552 the catechizing continued to form the beginning of the rite, but the confirmation itself was drastically revised. The signing of the forehead with its accompanying formula and the *pax* were abolished; and one significant change was made in the confirmation prayer, the main petition being altered to read, '...strengthen them... with the Holy Ghost, the Comforter, and daily increase in them thy manifold gifts of grace....' This emendation plays down the idea that there is any objective giving of the Holy Spirit at the moment of the hand-laying, turning the prayer rather into a petition that the confirmed may henceforward grow in the grace of the Spirit.

As he lays his hand on each candidate the bishop prays, 'Defend, O Lord, this child with thy heavenly grace, that he may continue thine for ever, and daily increase in thy Holy Spirit more and more, until he come unto thy everlasting kingdom.' As Cosin said, 'This prayer seems to be rather a prayer that may be said by any minister than a confirmation that was reserved only to the bishop.'

In this revision the influence of Bucer and the *Consultation* are evident. The result was a rite noticeably more Lutheran in character.

---

[1] This rubric can be traced back through the *Sarum Manual* to the Council of Lambeth (1281), where, however, the intention was to ensure that all baptized children were confirmed.

In the Prayer Book of 1662 the Catechism is printed separately from the Order of Confirmation. The priest, who has been ordered to catechize the children of his parish on Sundays and holy days after the second lesson at Evensong, presents to the bishop those whom he considers ready to be confirmed. The rite begins with an introduction derived from the opening rubrics in the earlier books. Instead of questioning them in the catechism the bishop asks the candidates to 'renew the solemn promise and vow that was made in your name at your baptism, ratifying and confirming the same in your own persons....' The confirmation service itself is as in 1552. To the final rubric on admission to communion there is added, 'or be ready and desirous to be confirmed', suggesting that in some places episcopal visitations were infrequent.

Calvin denounced the medieval rite of confirmation as a pretended sacrament nowhere recommended in Scripture: the medieval teaching that confirmation armed the Christian to fight the battles of life lopped off half the efficacy of baptism, because all who had been baptized into Christ had put on Christ with his gifts: the rule that only bishops might confirm was unscriptural because Ananias, a disciple, laid his hands on Paul: in Acts 8 the laying on of hands was a sign which lasted only for a time, ceasing when the effects ceased.

Calvin believed that as far back as apostolic times it was customary for the children of Christians to be baptized in infancy and on coming to years of discretion to be presented to the bishop in order to make the promises required of adult candidates for baptism; and to add dignity to this exercise the laying on of hands was practised; thus a youth, having given satisfactory evidence of his faith, was dismissed with a solemn blessing.[1]

Now Calvin believed this procedure to be the pure and original form of confirmation before it became corrupted with additions such as the use of chrism. This belief, it seems, was widely held in the sixteenth century, since there is evidence of it, for instance, in the writings of Bucer,[2] Cranmer,[3] Jewell,[4] and Whitgift.[5] Nevertheless it was quite mistaken, being a reading back into the primitive era of the practice of a much later age. (For some qualifications, see p. 47.)

Although Calvin wished this supposedly primitive practice to be restored, he did not in fact restore it in his church in Geneva. Knox, too, dispensed with a rite of confirmation as such, admitting children to

---

[1] See *Institutes*, 4.19.4–13.
[2] Daye, fol. 171.
[3] PS 2, p. 419.
[4] PS 2, p. 1125.
[5] PS 3, pp. 479f.

communion as soon as they could say the Lord's Prayer, Creed, and Ten Commandments.

The great merit of the rites of the Confirmation in the churches of the Reformation is that they restored to Christian initiation that element which is missing at the baptism of infants, namely, the personal confession of faith in Christ, which in the New Testament is an essential part of baptism.

6 The Radical Reformation

D. H. TRIPP

Bender, H. S., 'Baptism', in *Mennonite Encyclopaedia*, I (Hillsboro, Kansas, 1955), pp. 224–8.

Zeman, J. K., *The Anabaptists and the Czech Brethren in Moravia 1526–1628 = Studies in European History* XX. The Hague and Paris 1969.

Hubmaier, B., *Schriften* in *Quellen zur Geschichte der Täufer* IX (1962).

West, W. M. S., 'The Anabaptists and the rise of the Baptist movement', in *Christian Baptism*, ed. A. Gilmore (Lutterworth 1959), pp. 223–72.

Williams, G. H., *The Radical Reformation*. Philadelphia 1962.

Windhorst, C., *Täuferisches Taufverständnis: B. Hubmaiers Lehre zwischen traditioneller und reformatorischer Theologie*. Leiden 1976.

The Hussites and the Czech Brethren used infant baptism, with a simple rite of extempore prayer and singing, and baptized adults only in the case of converts from Roman Catholicism and the Utraquist communities. Even as late as 1526, the Conference of Czech Brethren and German Evangelicals at Austerlitz did not question infant baptism, although the Czech custom of infant communion was there severely attacked. The Czech Brethren gave up the practice of rebaptism in 1534 (partly under political pressure) but continued with infant baptism from then into the present.

Among the 'radical elements' of the Reformation, the critique of infant baptism seems to have begun only in 1524 with Conrad Grebel. Rebaptism and a consistent discipline of adult baptism began in that year at Zollikon and elsewhere in the area of Zürich. The Anabaptist preacher Reublin took the campaign to Waldshut in 1524, where the local Reforming leader Hubmaier was himself rebaptized on 15 April 1525.

The typical rite began with the candidate confessing his sins before the preacher and others (either at an open service or at home) and asking for baptism. The preacher asked those present if they had any objections. If there were none, the candidate knelt, and the officiant poured on water from a ladle or his hand: 'I baptize you in the name of God the Father, God the Son, and God the Holy Spirit'.

Baptism by immersion was rare in the extreme until the Baptists of England and the Low Countries began to influence the older Anabaptist communities, particularly in the second half of the eighteenth century.

Pre-baptismal catechesis became general among Anabaptists, and their baptisms begin with an examination of the candidate's grasp of basic doctrine. No rite of confirmation is included, but the rite often concludes with a gesture of welcome into the Church.

7 The Modern Period

PETER HINCHLIFF

von Allmen, J. J., *Worship: its Theology and Practice*. Lutterworth 1965.
Crichton, J. D., *Christian Celebration: the Sacraments*. G. Chapman 1973.
Davies, J. G., ed., *DLW*, article 'Baptism'.
Faith and Order, Louvain 1971. WCC, Geneva, 1971.
Howell, C., *The Constitution on the Sacred Liturgy*. Whitegate Publications 1963.
Jagger, P. J., *Christian Initiation, 1552–1969*. AC SPCK 1970.
One Baptism, One Eucharist, and a Mutually Recognized Ministry. WCC, Geneva, 1975.
Pocknee, C. E., *The Rites of Christian Initiation*. Mowbray 1961.
Principles of Prayer Book Revision. SPCK 1957.
SL 12 (1977), nn. 2–3.
Whitaker, E. C., *The Proposed Services of Baptism and Confirmation Reconsidered*. SPCK 1960.

If the baptismal rites of the Reformers corrected some of the failings of the medieval Church, they did not deal with all of the problems and difficulties. There were, indeed, aspects of the matter which became far worse after the Reformation. It was taken for granted, for instance, in most of Christendom that the practice of dividing the initiation rite into a service of baptism for infants and some form of confirmation later, was not only normal but basic. (In the East the ancient practice of combining baptism with water, anointing with episcopally consecrated oil in confirmation, and the Eucharist, in one single ceremony, was continued. The whole, single rite was administered to infants.) In the West the term 'baptism' was used to refer exclusively to the first part of initiation, administered in infancy except by Anabaptists. The Roman Church continued to administer confirmation and first communion as separate rites and not necessarily in that order. In the Church of England confirmation was normally a precondition for admission to communion. The idea that this rite was chiefly an opportunity for the candidate to renew the baptismal promises on his own account once he had reached the age of discretion, tended to overshadow any sacramental theology about the gift of the Spirit. The baptism of infants with water was identified with everything said in the New Testament about baptism. Confirmation tended to become something added, no longer initiatory but almost a rite of passage to Christian adulthood. The same thing might be said, perhaps with even more force, about the confirmation services of most of the Churches of the Reformation and of the Free Churches in England. Those Churches which rejected infant baptism did so principally on the ground that a personal affirmation of faith was essential to the rite. In these traditions confirmation, viewed as a renewal of baptismal promises, could have no place. There was, therefore, a wide variety of 'solutions' to the problems caused by the fragmentation of the original initiatory rite. The western fragmentation led some to treat confirmation as a separate and second giving of the Spirit; others to treat it as a renewal of vows and regard water-baptism as the complete and only sacrament of initiation; yet others to insist on water-baptism of believers, reject infant baptism, and abandon confirmation.

Rigid and separate theologies of baptism, therefore, developed in the Churches and the rites used did not always directly reflect the theologies. In the Prayer Book of 1662, for instance, a service for the baptism of adults was included for the benefit of those who, through the growth of Anabaptism, had grown up during the Commonwealth and had not been baptized as infants, and of adult native converts in the plantations. But it was assumed that infant baptism was still the norm, in theology as well as practice. The adult rite was modelled on that for infants, not vice versa. It was simply adapted for candidates who could speak for themselves. This meant that the vestiges of the medieval admission of catechumens, transferred in 1552 to a point immediately after the actual immersion or affusion, were retained in that position, and the baptismal vows, though made by an adult candidate himself (the godparents are witnesses), still had to be renewed by him at confirmation without any recognition of the fact that he had already made a personal affirmation of faith. This was to create immense liturgical confusion in those parts of the Anglican Communion which were in a genuinely missionary situation. Their converts were adults. Several of the provinces wished to revive a service for the admission of catechumens. They then found that they were repeating some liturgical features in the admission service and in baptism, in baptism and in confirmation.

Real discomfort over this divergence and confusion was not felt until the nineteenth century. The Oxford Movement caused some Anglicans to take a new interest in liturgical matters, often in an archaic form, and to wish to stress the sacramental importance of confirmation. Dom Guéranger and his work in the abbey of Solesmes led to a revival of liturgical scholarship in the Roman Church of the same period; and early in this century came the beginnings of the Liturgical Movement. Since the concept of the Church as the people of God and Body of Christ was at the heart of the movement, the initiatory rites were bound to be seen as something more than a private ceremony for the benefit of the individual. Baptism, confirmation, and the ceremonies of Holy Week began to acquire a new importance as expressions of the nature of the Church. Moreover, in all Churches, the missionary expansion of the nineteenth and early twentieth centuries compelled a new interest in adult baptism and a tendency to recover the belief that baptism and confirmation, as a single rite of Christian initiation administered to adult believers, should be the theological norm even if not the usual practice.

It was, nevertheless, a long time before these ideas affected actual liturgical revision. The 1928 Prayer Book made few significant changes in the practice of the Church of England except to allow for a greater emphasis to be placed upon the sacramental character of the rite. In the thirties most of the Anglican provinces adopted rites based on the pattern of 1928. Those provinces where Anglo-Catholic traditions were strong tended to use Acts 8.14–17 as the lection at confirmation and made chrismation at least an optional addition to the laying-on of hands, thus implying that the rite was essentially for the giving of the Holy Spirit and raising a further theological issue about the nature of water-baptism: has the baptized infant received the Holy Spirit? If he has, what is the difference between baptism and confirmation?

After the Second World War, when the 'modern' period can be held to have begun, the progress of the Ecumenical Movement led to a new interest in the theology of baptism. There was a general expectation that a study of baptism might lead to a greater unity because the Churches recognized each other's baptism and because baptism was widely regarded as that which bound all Christians together. When the Faith and Order Commission met at Louvain in 1971 it received a report on 'Baptism, Confirmation and Eucharist'[1] which represented the results of

---

[1] Printed in *Faith and Order, Louvain 1971*, Faith and Order Paper No. 59, WCC, pp. 35ff. For some of the theological background see also G. Wainwright, 'Développements baptismaux depuis 1967', *Études théologiques et religieuses*, 49 (1974), pp. 67–93.
Information about baptism in various traditions, but concerning practice rather than the rite itself, may be found in the article 'Baptism' in *DLW*.

a study conducted under the auspices of the World Council of Churches and stretching back to the fifties. The report revealed that there is far less ecumenical agreement than had been supposed and that there is considerable confusion within each Church about the meaning and practice even of its own rites. As between the Churches the confusion is even greater. 'Baptism' can mean the whole initiatory process or simply the act of sacramental laving with water. 'Confirmation' can mean chrismation (by bishop or priest), the laying-on of hands, or the renewal of baptismal vows, or two or more of these together. The point in the process at which a person can be said to become a member of the Church varies from tradition to tradition. Sometimes being 'a member of the Church' is not the same as being 'a full member'. The Churches differ about whether the whole process, or a part only, is necessary for admission to communion. They also differ about whether the actual eucharistic rite should be part of the liturgical form for initiation.

Some of the confusion is terminological. Some clarification can be achieved by an agreement to use 'baptism' to describe baptism with water alone, while 'initiation' is used for the whole rite including confirmation. But that degree of clarification immediately reveals the greater confusion. Baptists and Orthodox will be able to agree upon the statement, 'Initiation is a single act after which a person is fully a member of the Church'. By that statement Baptists will mean that initiation is water-baptism performed upon persons old enough to make an avowal of faith. The Orthodox will mean that baptism, chrismation, and communion can be administered in one single rite even to tiny babies. Anglicans and Methodists might agree on the statement, 'Baptism makes one in some sense a member of the Church but full membership comes at confirmation', and could mean very different things by 'confirmation'.

Additional complexity is introduced by two recent developments. Pentecostal experiences have begun to appear, and to be valued, in all Christian traditions. Some members of the movement talk of speaking with tongues as if it were to be identified absolutely with the 'gift of the Spirit', and of the reception of that gift as 'baptism in the Spirit'. This cuts right across more conventional thought and language about confirmation.[1] Moreover, the practice of some independent African churches has been to repeat the act of baptism several times upon the same person, for healing, and for forgiveness of sins. This not only conflicts with the once-for-all character traditionally ascribed to baptism, it also cuts across the role more often ascribed to the rites of the Easter vigil or to sacramental penance and unction.[2]

[1] W. J. Hollenweger, *The Pentecostals* (SCM 1972), pp. 9ff.
[2] B. G. M. Sundkler, *Bantu Prophets in South Africa*, rev. edn (OUP 1961), pp. 201ff.

The confusion is more than terminological, as the last examples show. There is a real theological difference between denominations and within them, which has been partially obscured by the terminological similarities. The Churches may agree that, 'Our common baptism is thus a basic bond of unity by which we are called as one people to confess and serve one Lord in each place and in all the world.'[1] They will not necessarily be saying the same thing. Efforts towards a 'consensus' are still being pursued. In 1974 the Faith and Order Commission produced the Accra Statement on *One Baptism, One Eucharist, and a Mutually Recognised Ministry*. Responses were sought from the Churches, and it is hoped that a revision of the statement will help a fuller agreement to emerge.

A further complicating factor is that liturgical revision has probably never been such a self-conscious or highly technical process as it is at present. In fact committees and commissions are not so much revising old liturgies as creating new ones. In the field of initiation-rites the experts are attempting to reduce the confusion by producing forms which express a coherent understanding of the meaning of baptism and confirmation. This understanding has sometimes been based upon a particular theological viewpoint or, perhaps more often, upon the belief that the practice of a particular period, or the pattern exhibited by a particular liturgical document, ought to be treated as normative. In either case the committee is able to produce a rite which is neat, consistent and capable of being explained logically. The committee, however, seldom has the power to authorize the use of the rite. Modifications are introduced by those who have that power but not the expertise: the pattern is destroyed once more.

All this makes it difficult to treat the profusion of modern rites systematically or thoroughly. Each revision is almost *sui generis* and it is impossible even to treat them in 'families' in the manner which once used to be popular when dealing with ancient eucharistic liturgies. There are similarities between rites, of course, but they are due to a common dependence upon theological ideas and an eclectic borrowing from one another rather than to a generic descent. There is no discernible geographical or even denominational grouping which overrides other patterns. Any given rite may exhibit features common to so many other types as to defy any kind of classification at all.

Anglican revisions show this wide variety, while also exhibiting sufficient common characteristics to allow some classification.[2] In the

[1] *Faith and Order (Louvain 1971)*, p. 52.

[2] Peter J. Jagger, *Christian Initiation, 1552–1969*, SPCK 1970, a collection of Anglican and other texts, is essential for a study of the period. For a survey of recent Anglican revision see articles by R. C. D. Jasper, L. Weil, and D. Holeton in *SL* 12 (1977), nn. 2–3.

fifties many of the provinces were still catching up on the pattern set by 1928. CIPBC, for instance, produced proposed rites in 1951 which were markedly influenced by the 1928 Prayer Book in spite of the fact that the synod of bishops had asked for *new* rites to be drawn up.[1] As was appropriate to a 'missionary' context, rather more prominence was given to the fact that there might be adult candidates for baptism. In the confirmation-rite provision was made for chrismation as an alternative to the 1662 form of laying on of hands and the introduction to the service was modelled on the presentation of candidates at an ordination. When the revised Book of Common Prayer was officially approved in 1960[2] the 1928 pattern became even more obvious because the chrismation, together with the giving of a white garment and a lighted taper at baptism, was relegated to a supplement. The influence of the ordination-rite remained the one distinctive element.

South Africa provides another example of the process. The revised Prayer Book of 1954[3] contained rites of the 1928 pattern with a form for the admission of catechumens. An attempt in 1963 to produce an interim rite[4] for the baptism-confirmation of adults merely served to reveal how much repetition and confusion there was in the existing rites. A completely new liturgy of initiation was, therefore, prepared.[5] The first, and normative, rite[6] in the series was a single form for the baptism and confirmation of an adult; all the other forms were adaptations of this. Their most distinctive feature is that the Matthean formula is replaced by a threefold affirmation of faith. Conservative opinion so disliked this 'innovation' that even before the form was printed a declaratory formula had to be inserted so that the celebrant proclaims that the candidate '... is baptized in the Name of the Father, and of the Son, and of the Holy Spirit'. At confirmation, the laying-on of hands takes place in silence.

The Series 2 revision in England, authorized in 1968, also took baptism–confirmation of adults as the single, normative rite.[7] It was,

[1] Jagger, op. cit., pp. 67ff.

[2] *The Book of Common Prayer ... according to the use of the CIPBC* (SPCK 1961), Part ii. See also Jagger, op. cit., pp. 95ff.

[3] Jagger, op. cit., p. 77, describes the initiatory rites as '1954', the date of the publication of the South African Prayer Book in a single volume. The rites were actually authorized in the twenties. For an account of the revision see P. Hinchliff, 'Revising Christian Initiation Rites', *SL* 2 (1963), pp. 273–84.

[4] Hinchliff, op. cit. pp. 283f.

[5] *Proposals for the Revision of the Rites of Baptism and Confirmation*, Liturgical Committee of the Church of the Province of SA 1967, and Jagger, op. cit., pp. 113ff.

[6] I.e. the forms do not appear in the order in which Jagger prints them.

[7] See *Baptism and Confirmation, A Report submitted by the Church of England Liturgical Commission* (SPCK 1967); *Baptism and Confirmation* (Alternative Services: Second Series); and Jagger, op. cit., pp. 138ff.

however, a much less radical revision, modernizing language rather than embodying a new liturgical pattern. Nor was repetition entirely eliminated. An adult candidate baptized and confirmed on successive days makes exactly the same promises at both services. It is not clear what confirmation is, on those occasions when it is neither part of the single, complete initiatory rite nor the fulfilment in adult life of baptism administered to an infant. At the confirmation itself, the laying on of hands is accompanied by the formula, 'Confirm, O Lord, thy servant [N.] with thy Holy Spirit.' (A similar, but rather longer, version of this formula is to be found in the West Indian rite of 1964 and the Welsh rite of 1968.)[1]

Within two years of the authorization of the Series 2 forms of service, the English archbishops appointed a commission to consider the whole theology and practice of initiation. The commission's report of 1971 made certain radical proposals.[2] Baptism in water was seen as complete sacramental initiation; communion was envisaged 'at an earlier age than is now considered normal'; confirmation would be reserved for maturer years as 'a commissioning of the fully instructed and responsible Christian adult for the work of ministry and mission in the world to which he is thereby committing himself'. The Liturgical Commission's draft *Initiation Services: Series 3* (1977) in fact retain a confirmation that is more in keeping with customary Anglican understandings. The draft includes provision for 'the baptism of families'. It also offers a service of 'thanksgiving for the birth of a child', which could be used whether or not the infant was to be baptized.

In the PECUSA *Proposed Book of Common Prayer* (1977), the baptismal rite is designed for use in a eucharistic context and is a composite form for both adults and infants.[3] Historically, the revisers were persuaded by the thesis that Cranmer's post-baptismal consignation was intended as sacramental confirmation. In the new baptismal rite, the consignation is accompanied by the formula 'N., you are sealed by the Holy Spirit in Baptism and marked as Christ's own for ever'; and if a priest makes the consignation an anointing, he must use chrism consecrated by the bishop. It appears that it was originally intended that this 'enriched' baptism should be the only initiation-rite. The companion form was for the affirmation of baptismal vows and a 'dedication to mission', but this has been modified and made once more a kind of confirmation so that the logic of the rite is again far from clear.

[1] Jagger, op. cit., pp. 111 and 153f.

[2] *Christian Initiation etc.*, General Synod of the Church of England 1971 (generally known as the 'Ely Report').

[3] For earlier drafts, see *Prayer Book Studies 18* and *26*, PECUSA Standing Liturgical Commission 1970 and 1973.

Roman Catholic revision has been much more systematic. In the first place the theological issues were dealt with before the revision was undertaken and at an extremely authoritative level. This has considerable advantages over a system which allows the revising liturgical committee to deal with the theology in passing. The process has, moreover, been centrally directed and there is consequently far less variation from one part of the world to another, though the process of translation into the vernacular and the effect of local custom and regulation has modified this somewhat.

The Second Vatican Council enacted the *Constitution on the Sacred Liturgy* in December 1963. Though baptism and confirmation do not occupy a very prominent position in the document, many of the general principles enunciated obviously applied to those rites and some very clear directives were given. It was laid down, for instance, that in any future order for the baptism of infants the questions and promises were to be phrased in such a way as to make it clear that they were directed to and made by the godparents and not as if by the baby himself. The *Constitution* also envisaged the restoration of the baptism of adults to a pastorally and liturgically central position.

The immediate practical effect of the *Constitution* was the translation of the existing Roman rite into various vernacular languages.[1] A 'consilium' was appointed to proceed with the actual work of revising the rites, applying the theological principles of the *Constitution* to the creation of archetypal liturgies. The initiation-rites were considered quite early in the life of the consilium, and a remarkable feature of the work was the presence of observers from other Churches at some of the sessions, an ecumenical approach which was further evidenced when an early draft of the proposed rites was shown to a WCC theological commission on worship.

Of the actual revised rites, the *Ordo Baptismi Parvulorum* was issued first, in 1969. In addition to an introduction to the particular rite itself, it was issued with a general introduction to the whole proposed liturgical complex of initiation setting out the theological principles behind revision. The International Committee on English in the Liturgy produced its translation at the end of the same year.[2] The new rite is very simple. The exorcism is in the form of a prayer that the candidates may be delivered from the power of sin rather than a direct abjuration of the devil. There is an anointing with oil immediately following and then a eucharistic blessing of the font which includes an epiclesis. After this come the promises made by the godparents. The actual baptismal

[1] For the English text see Jagger, op. cit., pp. 224f.
[2] See Jagger, op. cit., pp. 275ff., and *The Rite for Baptism of Children* (G. Chapman 1970).

formula is in the traditional Matthean form with a triple immersion or pouring. The Effeta ceremony (see p. 100) has become a prayer and has been moved to the end of the service after the giving of the white garment and the lighted candle. It is now also optional and, at least in England, is hardly used at all. Perhaps the most important pastoral feature of the revised rite is that the parents have specifically to declare that they wish the child to be baptized and brought up in the Christian faith. The parish priest is directed to discuss this undertaking with them beforehand and to refuse to baptize unless there are good grounds for thinking that it will be fulfilled.

The new rite of confirmation was instituted by the bull *Divinum Consortium Naturae* of 1971,[1] which asserts that its prime significance is to complete the process of initiation and to endow the candidates with the Holy Spirit for the task of sharing in the apostolic witness. The rite is designed to be used in the setting of the Mass, immediately after the gospel. After a homily comes the renewal of the baptismal vows. The bishop and the attendant priests 'impose hands over' the candidates collectively as an explanatory symbolic action invoking the Holy Spirit. The bishop says a prayer that the candidates may receive the sevenfold gift and this is followed by the essential of the rite, which consists of the tracing of the sign of the cross with chrism on the candidate's forehead with the words, 'N., be sealed with the gift of the Holy Spirit'. This rite is considered to constitute the essential laying on of hands.[2]

The *Ordo Initiationis Christianae Adultorum*[3] of 1972, although it was the last of the documents to be issued, should be regarded as the theological and liturgical norm, and the form of adult baptism which it contains as the order for baptism as such. This is a matter of some importance because the wording of the questions put to godparents in infant baptism (discussed above) has been criticized in some quarters on that ground that it appears to make a profession of faith no longer an essential part of the rite. The *Ordo* of 1972 makes it clear, at least by implication, that the baptism of believing adults (in which the candidate does make a profession of faith) is the norm, and the fact that the ceremonies of the catechumenate have been restored in a form which is spread over several weeks reinforces this.

Another matter of importance is that the permission for priests to

---

1 ET by ICEL is contained in *The Rite of Confirmation* (St Paul Publications 1976); cf. the 1964 form in Jagger, op. cit., pp. 229ff.

2 Cf. the Australian Anglican rite in Jagger, op. cit., p. 133; PECUSA comments in *Prayer Book Studies 26*; and the COCU rite discussed below.

3 For a discussion of the document see J. D. Crichton, *Christian Celebration: the Sacraments* (G. Chapman 1973), pp. 29–64.

confirm, which existed in certain cases even before Vatican II, has been extended. Priests may share in confirming some of the candidates, with chrism received from the bishop, when the latter is presiding at the confirmation of large numbers. The *Ordo Initiationis Christianae Adultorum*, moreover, directs that when a priest presides at the sacramental initiation of an adult he should also confirm him, indicating the intention that confirmation should always follow as closely as possible upon baptism and should precede communion.

Anglicans and Roman Catholics are not, of course, the only Churches which have revised the initiatory rites in recent years. The 1960s and 1970s were, in fact, particularly fertile years for study and revision in the field of baptism and confirmation.[1] In 1962 a first attempt was made to provide agreed orders of baptism and confirmation for eight North American Lutheran churches.[2] Much further work was done before the 1978 *Lutheran Book of Worship*, in which we may note the re-introduction of a 'Flood-prayer' into a composite order of baptism for adults and children, which includes also an imposition of hands and a consignation (optionally with oil), with the formula 'N., child of God, you have been sealed by the Holy Spirit and marked with the cross of Christ for ever'. In some Protestant churches, unofficial forms of service may be preferred[3] or one may be devised *ad hoc*. It would appear, however, that there are two broad generalizations that may be made about at least such official rites as have been produced in Britain.[4] First, they appear to favour the incorporation of a version of the 1662 prayer 'Defend, O Lord . . .'[5] with or without an act of laying on of hands. This suggests that there has been a general tendency for other 'English' rites to conform to an Anglican pattern for confirmation or, at least, to assume that confirmation is a quite separate and specific quasi-sacramental office. This view is reinforced by a second fact, that, in those cases in which a single rite for baptism of adults and their reception into full membership

---

[1] E.g. *SL* 3 (1964), p. 57 (Swiss proposals); *SL* 3 (1964), p. 123 (English Presbyterian revision); *SL* 3 (1964), p. 254 (Congregational); *SL* 3 (1964), pp. 245ff (Church of Scotland); *SL* 4 (1965), p. 181 (Lusitanian).

[2] *Occasional Services and Additional Orders*, Joint Commission on Liturgy and Hymnal 1962; see also Jagger, op. cit., pp. 218f and *SL* 1 (1962), pp. 28ff.

[3] E.g. E. A. Payne and S. F. Winward, *Orders and Prayers for Church Worship*, published by the Baptist Union with some unofficial status (Jagger, op. cit., pp. 205ff) and the more experimental C. Micklem ed., *Contemporary Prayers for Public Worship* (SCM 1967).

[4] The texts in Jagger, op. cit., are almost all drawn from British sources.

[5] See Jagger, op. cit., p. 203 (English Presbyterian 1948), p. 254 (English Presbyterian 1968), p. 216 (Moravian 1960), p. 243 (Methodist 1967; retained in the 1975 *Service Book*), p. 264 (Church of Scotland). The prayer is sometimes said after rather than at the laying on of hands.

is provided,[1] it includes an act of confirmation. This act cannot, therefore, simply be regarded as a renewal of baptismal vows. It must be conceived to have some separate character and purpose of its own.

The revised *Methodist Service Book*, authorized by the British Conference and published in 1975, illustrates the ecumenical tendencies of much modern revision. The rite for the baptism of infants, like the R.C. *Ordo* of 1969, lays much stress on the preliminary pastoral preparation. After the lections and prayers come the promises, which are in an unusual form. The parents are asked to promise to provide a Christian home and upbringing, to help the infant to renounce evil and to trust in Christ, and to encourage him to enter into full membership of the Church and to serve Christ in the world. The sponsors are then asked to assist the parents in these undertakings. In other words, the questions are—as they had been since the Methodist *Book of Offices* of 1936—a means of eliciting from the parents and sponsors a declaration of what they intend to do for the child, rather than promises made on the child's behalf. It can be argued that they are the real questions that need to be put and that they make the meaning of what is being done quite explicit; and, since the Apostles' Creed follows immediately afterwards, it can also be argued that a confession of faith is still made on the infant's behalf. On the other hand, since the promises made at the baptism of an adult are in the traditional form, the difference is bound to raise very sharply the question whether infant's and believer's baptism is the same sacrament in any real sense.

The baptismal formula, in both cases, is the Matthean one. In the case of the baptism of infants it is followed by a prayer based on the 1662 form for the reception of the child into the congregation of Christ's flock, but modifying it so that the ambiguities of 1662 are removed and it is made plain that it is baptism itself which 'receives' the child into the Church. In the form for baptism of adults the actual baptism with water is followed immediately by the 'reception into full membership or confirmation'. This rite, whether it follows upon adult baptism or upon the making of promises by those baptized in infancy, consists of a prayer for the sevenfold gifts of the Spirit and the formula (which is a development of the Series 2 formula with echoes of the prayer 'Defend, O Lord,...'), 'Lord, confirm your servant N., by your holy Spirit that he may continue to be yours for ever.' The laying on of hands at confirmation is optional.

The tendency for modern revisions of all kinds to move towards a similar pattern raises the question of the effect of ecumenism on liturgical practice. There has been much agreement. The WCC Accra Statement

[1] Jagger, op. cit., pp. 214ff (Moravian), 243ff (Methodist; similarly in the 1975 *Service Book*) and 266ff (Church of Scotland).

lists elements which it is held 'should find a place within any comprehensive order of baptism'. Nevertheless it is clear that the effect of the Ecumenical Movement has been patchy and erratic but sometimes very fruitful.[1] Negotiations for reunion have occasionally produced liturgical forms for common use, either to provide a positive means for the growing together of participating Churches or with an eye to the practice of the united Church in the future. The Churches of East Africa produced such a baptismal liturgy, based on that of South India[2] and the Consultation on Church Union in the United States has prepared draft proposals for a rite of initiation of a more radical kind.[3] This latter rite is plainly intended as a single act of initiation, for use with both infants and adults. After baptism with water and the name of the Trinity it proceeds immediately to the laying on of hands (with an optional chrismation) accompanying the words 'You are sealed by the Holy Spirit...'.

Of all the 'reunion' rites it is, of course, those of the CSI which are of most interest because it is possible to arrive at some sort of assessment of the way in which they are being used.[4] The rites themselves are not at all radical.[5] One gets the impression that infant baptism is still regarded as the norm. Though provision is made in the 'Directions to Ministers'[6] for combining baptism and confirmation in the case of adult candidates, there is no attempt to impose any rationale upon the liturgy of initiation as a whole. Theological questions about when the Spirit is given or when the candidates becomes a 'full member' of the Church are left open. The baptismal rite begins with an exhortation and a lection; then follow the profession of faith (the Apostles' Creed), the promises and prayer for the candidates, then the baptism with water and the name of the Trinity, the reception into the Church (adapted from 1662), optional ceremonies of the giving of a lighted taper and a white garment and concluding prayers of thanksgiving. Confirmation is 'for the reception of baptized persons into the full fellowship of the Church'. The renewal of baptismal vows is extended so that the candidates make promises to be faithful in matters such as prayer, bible-reading and almsgiving. The laying on of hands is performed by a presbyter with a prayer which is an adaptation of 'Defend, O Lord...'. There is a separate and emphatic act of reception

[1] See L. A. Creedy, 'Baptism in Church Union Negotiations', WCC FO/70.49 1970.
[2] Jagger, op. cit., pp. 317ff.
[3] *An Order for the Celebration of Holy Baptism* (preliminary draft), Consultation on Church Union 1972.
[4] See e.g. T. S. Garrett, *Worship in the CSI* (Lutterworth 1958), and S. M. Gibbard, 'Liturgical Life in the CSI', *SL* 3 (1964), pp. 193ff.
[5] *The Book of Common Worship* (OUP 1963). Leaflets containing separate services were published before 1962, see *SL* 1 (1962), p. 74.
[6] *The Book of Common Worship*, pp. xiff and n.b. p. xx.

into the fellowship of the Church with a welcome said by the whole congregation and the giving of the peace. The form for 'Believer's Baptism', though it is printed first, together with an office for 'Making a Catechumen', appears to be an adaptation of the rites for infant baptism, rather than the other way round. For instance, when the rites of baptism and confirmation are combined, the candidate is 'received into the congregation of Christ's flock' immediately after baptism with water and then, at the end of the whole service, is 'received' again 'as partner in the common life of the Church'. None of the repetition or dislocation appears to have been eliminated.

The new united Church of North India and that of Pakistan contain those who conscientiously hold (as former Baptists) that baptism ought to be administered only to candidates who are able to make a conscious profession of personal faith, and those who, equally conscientiously, hold that it is right to baptize infants.[1]

Forms of service which will hold together these divergent views on baptism and yet avoid ambiguity and confusion are obviously not easy to devise. For this reason the Order of Confirmation approved for use in the Church of North India in 1974 is obviously an important document. The service begins with a salutation and an exhortation, which declares that the purpose of confirmation is that the candidates (who have already been baptized) may publicly accept for themselves God's promise of salvation and that, through the laying on of hands, they may *increasingly experience* the grace and power of God's Holy Spirit. Thus, while the reality of infant baptism is asserted, confirmation becomes much more than a renewal of baptismal promises. The same theme is expressed again in the bishop's address to the candidates, which follows. He refers to the fact that they will be giving their own 'free and deliberate assent to the pledge which was then made in your name', but adds, 'You have come to declare your faith in the Lord Jesus Christ, your acceptance of him as your Saviour, and your commitment to him for ever.' This is entirely in line with statements made by the Baptists at the time of union, that they were able to accept the provision of infant baptism on the understanding that confirmation would provide an opportunity for precisely this kind of public profession of faith. The same note reappears later, after the lections, in three successive sections of the service called 'the profession of personal discipleship', 'the declaration of faith', and 'the promises'. In the first of these the bishop puts three questions to each candidate individually, beginning '[N.] ... do you accept Jesus Christ as your Lord and Saviour?' and including a renunciation of evil. The second consists

[1] *Plan of Church Union in North India and Pakistan* (Christian Literature Society 1965), p. 7.

of three questions, as in Series 2, concerning 'belief and trust' in the Trinity and the recitation of the Apostles' Creed. The third follows the CSI pattern in extending the promises to cover prayer and bible-reading, attendance at public worship and proper stewardship of material possessions. This part of the service ends with an act of self-dedication. Then follows the actual confirmation, consisting of a prayer that those who in baptism were made God's children and members of his Church by the water of rebirth and the power of the Holy Spirit may be granted 'the fullness of the same Spirit, the Spirit of wisdom and understanding...' and so on, through the sevenfold gifts. The bishop then lays his hands on the head of each candidate with the formula, 'Confirm, O Lord, your child ... in your Holy Spirit', and, after all have been confirmed, he says a slightly modified version of the prayer 'Defend, O Lord ...'. The service ends with the Lord's Prayer, another prayer, and an act of receiving and welcoming the newly confirmed into the congregation.

It would seem that, at the cost of making the service very long, and somewhat overburdened with questions and promises, the compilers have done a good job. The rite is clear and coherent, recognizes the validity of infant baptism while requiring an unequivocal public profession of personal commitment and faith. This apparent coherence is somewhat spoiled, however, by a note at the end of the service which permits the rite to be used 'immediately after believer's baptism, if all the candidates have been specially prepared to be baptized and confirmed at the same service.' The note directs that, in that case, the bishop's address to the candidates at the beginning of the service, and the prayer which follows it, 'must be appropriately modified'. Reference back to those sections quickly reveals that almost everything that is said about baptism there is entirely inappropriate to the case of adult believers who have just that moment been baptized.

NOTE

A final trend to be noted, particularly in North America, is the provision of liturgical opportunity for the 'renewal' of a baptism whose permanency it is not intended to contest. In 1976 the United Methodist Church published an 'alternate text' for *Baptism, Confirmation and Renewal*. Confirmation is seen as 'the first renewal of the baptismal faith', and 'other renewals of the baptismal covenant' may take place among whole congregations or in individual cases. The 1978 *Lutheran Book of Worship* includes confirmation, reception into membership from other denominations, and restoration of membership all under *Affirmation of Baptism* (confirmation is distinguishable by the imposition of hands, though *Contemporary Worship 8* had in 1974 tried to move away from an unrepeatable quasi-sacramental confirmation). The final Lutheran pattern is close to that of the Episcopal *Proposed BCP* (1977) at 'confirmation, reception, or reaffirmation'. Several Churches now provide for 'the renewal of baptismal vows' by the congregation at an Easter Vigil, after the manner introduced by the Roman revision of the Paschal Vigil in 1951–5.

III

THE EUCHARIST

Baumstark, A., (ET) *Comparative Liturgy*. Mowbray 1958.
Bouyer, L., (ET) *Eucharist*. Notre Dame 1968.
Brightman, F. E., *LEW*.
Brilioth, Y., (ET) *Eucharistic Faith and Practice: Evangelical and Catholic*. SPCK 1930.
Crichton, J. D., *Christian Celebration: the Mass*. G. Chapman 1971.
Dix, G., *Shape*.
Jasper, R. C. D., and Cuming, G. J., *PEER*.
Jungmann, J. A., (ET) *The Early Liturgy to the Time of Gregory the Great*. DLT 1960.
Jungmann, J. A., (ET) *The Eucharistic Prayer*. Challoner 1956.
Jungmann, J. A., (ET) *The Liturgy of the Word*. Burns and Oates 1966.
Jungmann, J. A., (ET) *MRR*.
Jungmann, J. A., (ET) *The Place of Christ in Liturgical Prayer*. G. Chapman 1965.
Jungmann, J. A., (ET) *Public Worship*. Challoner 1951.
King, A. A., *Concelebration in the Christian Church*. Mowbrays 1966.
Klauser, T., (ET) *A Short History of the Western Liturgy*. OUP 1969.
Lietzmann, H., (ET) *Mass and the Lord's Supper, a Study in the History of the Liturgy*. Leiden, 1953–76.
Martimort, A. G., (ET) *The Church at Prayer—the Eucharist*. Irish University Press 1973.
Righetti, M., *Manuale di Storia Liturgica*. 3rd edn Milan 1966.

1 The New Testament

C. P. M. JONES

GENERAL

Benoît, P., (ET) *Jesus and the Gospel*, vol. 1 (DLT 1973), ch. 6, pp. 95–122.
Bouyer, L., (ET) *Eucharist* (Notre Dame 1968), chs. 2–5, pp. 15–113.
Cirlot, F. L., *The Early Eucharist*. SPCK 1939.
Concilium, vol. 10, no. 4 (Dec. 1968) (devoted chiefly to the Eucharist in the NT).
Cullmann, O., (ET) *Early Christian Worship*. SCM 1953.
Dalman, G., (ET) *Jesus-Jeshua* (SPCK 1929), chs. 11–16, pp. 86–184.
Daube, D., *He that Cometh* (1966) and *Wine in the Bible* (1974). London
 Diocesan Council for Christian-Jewish Understanding
Dix, G., *The Shape of the Liturgy* (Dacre Press 1945), ch. 4, pp. 48–102.
Farrer, A. M., 'Eucharist and Church in the New Testament', ch. 4 in *The
 Parish Communion*, ed. A. G. Hebert (SPCK 1937), pp. 75–94.
Higgins, A. J. B., *The Lord's Supper in the New Testament*. SCM 1952.
Jeremias, J., (ET) *The Eucharistic Words of Jesus*. SCM 1966 (*EWJ*)
Jungmann, J. A., (ET) *The Early Liturgy* (DLT 1959), chs. 2–4, pp. 10–38.
Lietzmann, H., (ET) *Mass and Lord's Supper* (Leiden 1953–76), chs. 13–17, pp.
 172–215 (fasc. 3 and 4).
Ligier, L., 'From the Last Supper to the Eucharist', ch. 8 of *The New Liturgy*,
 ed. L. Sheppard (DLT 1970), pp. 113–25.
Moule, C. F. D., *Worship in the New Testament* (Lutterworth 1961), ch. 2, pp.
 18–46.
Schürmann, H., *LThK* (2nd edn) I, 26–31 (Abendmahl).
Schweizer, E., *RGG* (3rd edn) I, 10–19 (Abendmahl im NT).
Srawley, J. H., *The Early History of the Liturgy*, 2nd edn (CUP 1947), ch. 1, pp.
 1–17.
Thurian, M., (ET) *The Eucharistic Memorial* (part 2: the New Testament).
 Lutterworth 1961.
Wainwright, G., *Eucharist and Eschatology*. Epworth 1971.

INTRODUCTION (see pp. 150–1)

Bultmann, R., (ET) *Theology of the NT* (SCM 1952), in vol. 1, pp. 144–151.
Couratin, A. H., in *The Pelican Guide to Modern Theology* vol. 2, ed. R. P. C.
 Hanson (Penguin 1969), pp. 131–40, 145–56.
Cullmann, O., *Early Christian Worship*, pp. 7–36.
Schnackenburg, R., (ET) *God's Rule and Kingdom*, 2nd edn (Burns Oates 1968),
 pp. 249–58.

ST PAUL AND CORINTH[1] (see pp. 151–6)

Barrett, C. K., *The First Epistle to the Corinthians*, Black; NT Commentaries
 (Black 1968), pp. 218–24, 229–38, 258–77.

[1] For the fullest treatment of the Eucharist in St Paul, see Paul Neuenzeit, *Das
Herrenmahl, Studien zur paulinischen Eucharistieauffassung* (Munich 1960).

148

Bornkamm, G., (ET) *Early Christian Experience* (SCM 1969), pp. 123–79.

Conzelmann, H., (ET) *1 Corinthians* (Philadelphia 1975), pp. 164–74, 192–203.

Farrer, A. M., in *Eucharistic Theology then and now* (SPCK 1968), pp. 15–33.

Käsemann, E., (ET) *Essays on N.T. Themes* (SCM 1964), pp. 108–35.

ST MARK AND ST PAUL (see pp. 160–2)

Baker, J. A., in *Thinking about the Eucharist* (SCM 1972), pp. 38–58.

Davies, W. D., *Paul and Rabbinic Judaism* (SPCK 1955), pp. 242–53.

Dibelius, M., (ET) *From Tradition to Gospel* (Ivor Nicholson & Watson 1934), pp. 205–11.

Kuhn, K. G., 'The Lord's Supper and the Communal Meal at Qumran', in *The Scrolls and the New Testament*, ed. K. Stendahl (SCM 1958), pp. 65–93.

Marxsen, W., 'The History of the Eucharistic Tradition in the New Testament' in *Word and Sacrament*, ed. R. R. Williams (SPCK 1968), pp. 64–73.

Schweizer, E., (ET) *The Good News according to Mark* (SPCK 1971), pp. 293–305.

Taylor, V., *Jesus and his Sacrifice* (Macmillan 1937), pp. 114–42, 201–17.

ST LUKE AND ACTS (see pp. 162–4)

Benoît, P., 'Le récit de la cène dans Lc. XXII 15–20', in *Exégèse et théologie* I (Paris 1961) pp. 163–203.

Chadwick, H., 'The Shorter Text of Luke XXII 15–20', *HTR* 50, 4 (Oct. 1957) pp. 249–58.

Kenyon, F. G. and Legg, S. C. E., 'The Textual Data' in *The Ministry and Sacraments*, ed. R. Dunkerley (SCM 1937), pp. 272–86.

Kiddle, M., 'The Passion Narrative of St Luke's Gospel', *JTS* (July 1935), pp. 267–81.

Kilpatrick, G. D., 'Luke XXII. 19–20', *JTS* 47 (Jan. 1946), pp. 49–56.

Rese, M., 'Zur Problematik von Kurz- und Langtext in Luk. xxii 17 ff', *NTS* 22 (1975), pp. 15–31.

Richardson, R. D., 'The Place of Luke in the Eucharistic Tradition' in *The Gospels Reconsidered* (Blackwell 1960), pp. 118–30.

Schürmann, H., *Concilium*, Dec. 1968, pp. 61–7, and his works there cited.

Williams, C. S. C., *Alterations to the Text of the Synoptic Gospels and Acts* (Blackwell 1951), pp. 47–51.

ST JOHN (see pp. 164–6)

Cullmann, O., op. cit., pp. 37–119.

Evans, C. F., 'Eucharist and Symbolism in the N.T.', in *Thinking about the Eucharist*, supra pp. 59–68.

Giblet, J., 'The Eucharist in St John's Gospel' in *Concilium* vol. cit. pp. 32–6.

Hoskyns, E. C., and Davey, F. N., *The Fourth Gospel* (Faber & Faber 1940), pp. 309–47.

Lindars, B., *Behind the Fourth Gospel* (SPCK 1971), pp. 43–9; *The Gospel of John*, New Century Bible (Oliphants 1972), pp. 234–6, 254–72.

Wilckens, U., 'Der eucharistische Abschnitt (Jn. 6. 51–8)', in R. Schnackenburg's Festschrift, *N.T. und Kirche*, ed. J. Gnilka (Freiburg 1974), pp. 220–48.

1 PETER, HEBREWS, AND REVELATION (see pp. 166–8)

Couratin, A. H., 'The Sacrifice of Praise', *Theology* 58 (Aug. 1955), pp. 285–91.

Williamson, R., 'The Eucharist and the Epistle to the Hebrews', *NTS* 21 (1975), pp. 300–12, and references there.

Shepherd, M. H., *The Paschal Liturgy and the Apocalypse*. Lutterworth 1960.

INTRODUCTION

As we set out to assess the evidence for the Eucharist in the NT our task seems delicate and difficult, yet very important: delicate, because we are not concerned with sacramental doctrine in general but with liturgical rites and practice, and yet in either case we have to rely on the same rather slender evidence; difficult, because, in addition to the hazards in establishing Jewish custom in the first century AD,[1] the NT evidence is, in Dr Wainwright's words (p. 34), either fragmentary or indirect. We have the fragmentary evidence of the institution narratives in the synoptic Gospels and 1 Cor. 11, with two references in 1 Cor. 10, and perhaps the references to the 'breaking of bread' in Luke-Acts. We have indirect evidence in the discourse of Jn. 6 and in the gospel accounts of the miraculous multiplication of loaves and fishes; together with some oblique allusions in 1 Pet., Heb. and Rev. No wonder that A. H. Couratin allows no history of the liturgy before the fourth century, but only a skeletal 'pre-history' (p. 157), small pieces of evidence, to be pieced together, 'knowing that many of the bits are irretrievably lost' (pp. 154, 155). And yet 'it is what the NT writings presuppose that is of greater importance than what they actually describe' (p. 139). R. P. C. Hanson can even say of this period 'liturgy did not exist';[2] if this was really so, our task would be impossible.

Nevertheless our assignment is of the greatest importance in assessing the nature of Christianity in and through its chief recurrent liturgical rite. Is it a mystery religion, only accidentally attached to Jesus of Nazareth? or has this rite a historical and personal origin in Jesus, which exercises

---

[1] See R.T. Beckwith above, p. 39, and J. Neusner, *The Rabbinic Traditions about the Pharisees before 70* (Leiden 1971), vol. I, pp. 1ff.

[2] In *The Times* (4.12.1976), 'Liturgical uniformity did not exist because liturgy did not exist.' This sentence is probably intended to be understood as a summary of his earlier *article*, 'The Liberty of the Bishop to improvise prayer in the Eucharist', *Vigiliae Christianae* 15 (1961), pp. 173–6.

some kind of control on its development? These questions, if they can be answered at all, can only be approached through the evidence of the NT.

At a time of great uncertainty among NT scholars, particularly about the nature and historical value of the Gospels and the Acts of the Apostles, we will try a purely historical approach, taking the references in a rough chronological order, as they were written. Starting with St Paul (1 Cor.), we then consider the earliest evangelist, St Mark, together with his follower St Matthew; then the Lucan writings; then, by way of the gospel feeding stories, the Fourth Gospel: concluding with 1 Peter, Hebrews, and Revelation. We can then see whether a coherent story emerges, linking the events of the Upper Room with the Church's Eucharist as it is first described by Justin Martyr (*c.* AD 150).

ST PAUL AND CORINTH

St Paul's importance as a historical source can hardly be exaggerated.[1] His overt references to the Eucharist are limited to chs. 10 and 11 of the first letter to Corinth, written in AD 53 or 54, just over twenty years after the crucifixion and more than ten years before the earliest extant Gospel. 1 Cor. 10.1–4 and 15–22 occur in the course of the long section on eating meat associated with pagan sacrifice (8.1—11.1); 'strong' Christians had claimed the right to eat anything in any context, regardless of this association and of weaker brethren's scruples. But great privilege imposes great responsibility and self-restraint; St Paul himself voluntarily forgoes some of his apostolic rights (ch. 9). In ch. 10 he turns to the community, using the type of 'our fathers', the Israelites of the exodus and the wilderness; they too had their initiation 'into Moses' in the cloud and the sea; they had their *pneumatic* food and drink; but, as terrible warning to the Corinthian Christians, they were not immune from temptation, sin, rejection and death (10.1–13). 'This is the only passage in the NT in which the two sacraments are mentioned together' (Robertson and Plummer, ICC *ad loc.* p. 202), and both sacramental actions are twofold. The *pneumatic* food is the manna of Exod. 16, the drink is the water from the rock of Exod. 17.1–7 and Num. 20.1–13 and 21.16–18. In this first surviving allusion to the Christian Eucharist, the manna analogy takes up many OT references[2] and anticipates the fuller treatment of Jn. 6.30–51; the *pneumatic* water from the *pneumatic* rock (a type of Christ) takes up a rabbinic explanation of the three references to miraculous

---

[1] See further my essay in *Christian Believing*, Report of the Doctrine Commission of the Church of England (SPCK 1976), pp. 91ff.

[2] Esp. Ps. 78.24f; Neh. 9.15; Wisd. Sol. 16.20. See G. Wainwright, op. cit., p. 22 and note.

water.[1] What does Paul mean by *pneumatic*? For some it refers to the substance of the special food and drink, conceived as made of *pneuma*, spirit, as of a refined ethereal element;[2] others understand it as symbolical or archetypal (cf. Gal. 4.24 and Barrett p. 222). St Paul's usage is flexible. Perhaps the best meaning is God-given, divinely or supernaturally provided (cf. Rom. 7.14 of the Law); this best fits the OT incidents. For ourselves we note that both elements are mentioned together and in parallel terms (contrast 11.24, 25); and that the sacramental food is so taken for granted that it can be referred to casually in this indirect way.

In the next section (10.15–22) the reality of the sacrament is not only presumed but is made the basis of the argument. St Paul changes his tack. Hitherto he has agreed with those who refuse to take idols seriously and risk scandalizing weaker brethren; now he draws on another OT tradition, viz. that the idols represent pagan deities and demons, and they and their rites must be taken seriously. The Eucharist establishes a fellowship (*koinonia*) between Christ and the Christians, analogous to the Jewish and pagan sacrifices, and 'you cannot drink the Lord's cup *and* the demons' cup; you cannot share in the Lord's table *and* the demons' table' (21). The Lord is a jealous God. St Paul can appeal to the Corinthians' intelligence (15) and to their eucharistic practice (16): 'The cup of the blessing [over] which we bless [God], surely it is a common sharing in the blood of Christ? the bread which we break, surely it is a common sharing in the body of Christ?' The pneumatic food and drink now reappear more closely defined as the Body and Blood of Christ; although the ultimate basis of this definition will be given later (11.23–26), St Paul can assume it as common ground shared with his audience, strong enough to support the further argument. He mentions the cup before the bread (cf. Lk. 22.17 and 19a and *Did.* 9.2, 3); this does not necessarily reflect a local liturgical deviation. The cup comes before the bread, because a further point is to be made about the bread (17); the common sharing of the particles of the one, broken, loaf symbolizes and effects the union of the participants not only with Christ but also with one another. The eucharistic body creates the ecclesial body (cf. *Did.* 9,4). St Paul calls the cup '*the* cup of the blessing', *one* cup as in 11.25; 'the cup of *the* blessing', signifying a specific act of praise; but not 'the cup of the thanksgiving' as we would expect from 11.25. Partaking of the cup is partaking of Christ's Blood; this clarifies the meaning of 11.25. The cup mediates the Blood of

---

[1] The legend has been reconstructed by E. E. Ellis, *Paul's Use of the Old Testament* (Oliver and Boyd 1957), pp. 66–70; and *JBL* 76 (1957), pp. 53–6.

[2] Wainwright, pp. 99f; Käsemann, pp. 114–19.

Christ's covenant sacrifice. In this one verse (16), the later problems of eucharistic sacrifice and communion are already posed.

Again, as in 10.3, 4, the two elements are mentioned together, and in sentences of parallel structure. In addition to consumption there are hints of antecedent rites, the breaking of the bread and the blessing over the cup. In both passages the elements are contiguous; this suggests that they were closely associated in the contemporary rite. But this was not always so, as ch. 11 shows.

The next four chapters are concerned with the (weekly?) assembly (*ecclesia*) or assemblies of the Corinthian community; chs. 12—14 deal with their charismatic anarchy, while in ch. 11 St Paul deals with irregularities due to neglect of two of his *traditions*, both of which seem to have universal force (cf. 11.16 and 23), about ladies wearing head-dress during the gathering (11.3–16) and about the Lord's Supper (11.17–34). 'When you assemble together it is not [possible] to eat the Lord's supper' (20); they come together for the worse rather than the better (17), even for condemnation (34). The clique-prone Corinthians have brought their divisions into the gathering, though the divisions here seem to be more social than theological (22, contrast 1.10–13). The gathering includes a meal, to which all contribute; but the richer cliques are going ahead with their picnics, and even getting drunk, leaving nothing for the poor who are likely to arrive late after work. In reply he solemnly repeats the tradition of the acts and words of 'the Lord Jesus in the night in which he was being handed over', in obedience to which alone the community meal can be the supper *of the Lord*, held under his authority, in his memory, even under his presidency. From neglect of this, sacrilege has been committed and judgement has been severe (27–31). Earlier scholars[1] regarded the sacrilege as treating the bread as ordinary bread, not discerning in it the Lord's body (29). More recent scholars have suggested quite the opposite, taking a wider view of the 'body';[2] far from taking a 'low' view of the sacrament, the leading Corinthians held a very 'high' view of the sacramental action (as we would expect from ch. 10). The fraternal fellowship of Christians in assembly is quite irrelevant; 'it is the Mass that matters', and all is well if the poor are in time for this great climax. On either view St Paul's remedy is the same. It is mainly contained in the institution narrative, which he reproduces not only as the *ground* of the rite but also as the *pattern* for its performance. To this he adds two riders (33, 34): all must wait till all are assembled before the meal and gathering begin, and purely social eating and drinking should

---

[1] E.g. Lietzmann, op. cit., p. 208.
[2] E.g. Bornkamm, op. cit., pp. 127–9.

be done at home. 'And any remaining matters I will rule on when I come' (34).

We are now in a position to sketch out the rite of the Lord's Supper as St Paul had bequeathed it to Corinth and as he wished it to be maintained. It is a plenary session and may not begin until all are assembled. It is a real meal, to which all (or at least the well off) contribute food and drink. It opens with the customary Jewish blessing of God over the bread, which is then broken in pieces and distributed to all, probably with words of interpretation or distribution identifying the bread as the Body of Christ (11.24). By this the gathering is constituted as the ecclesial Body of Christ (10.17). The meal continues, and at the end 'the cup of the blessing' is produced and the thanksgiving is said before all drink of it. It would seem that during that thanksgiving the death of the Lord, the risen, victorious ever-present Lord of the community, is *proclaimed* 'until he come' (11.26). The action is not an acted parable that needs no explanation; it needs a *verbal*[1] proclamation, for which there is no satisfactory place in Jewish tradition other than the extended thanksgiving after the meal, the *birkat ha-mazon*.[2] The content of this thanksgiving and proclamation is the recalling of the wonderful works of God in creation, election, and providence, and now in his Son and all he has done through his death and resurrection; in this way the whole eucharistic action is performed 'for my memorial (*anamnesis*), *because* ... you proclaim. ...'[3] Thus the 'memorial' is raised to God through the thanksgiving of those who are mindful and grateful; and yet men are enjoined to 'do this', that they may remember.[4] 'Until he come'; these words are of more than chronological significance and have the force of a final clause 'until (the goal is reached that) he may come'. This clause seems to be a paraphrase of the Aramaic *Maranatha*, still preserved in the

---

[1] See *TDNT*, I, pp. 71, 72 on *katangello*.

[2] For the text, as reconstructed by L. Finkelstein, see *EWJ*, p. 110; *PEER*, pp. 9, 10. See also J. P. Audet, 'Literary Forms and Contents of a Normal Eucharistia in the First Century', in *The Gospels Reconsidered* (Blackwell 1960), pp. 16–35. For the *birkat ha-mazon* as the origin of the eucharistic prayer, see L. Ligier, op. cit., pp. 121ff; L. Bouyer, op. cit.

[3] For this understanding of *anamnesis*, see G. D. Kilpatrick's article 'ANAMNESIS', *Liturgical Review* 5 (May 1975), pp. 35–40.

[4] *Anamnesis*. The reference is Godward ('that God may remember me', *EWJ*, pp. 251–5), and manward (see R. T. Beckwith *supra* p. 49); both are possible (D. R. Jones, *JTS* n.s. 6 (1955), pp. 186–7); as in the Psalms (105 entire; and cf. 77.10ff with 25.6, 7; also 111.3ff, see Käsemann, op. cit., pp. 120–1f). Also N. A. Dahl, *Studia Theologica* 1 (1948) pp. 82–7. Compare the rabbinic teaching on the Passover: In every generation a man must so regard himself as if he came forth himself out of Egypt (*Pes.* 10.5; Danby, *Mishnah*, p. 151); see C. J. A. Hickling, *Liturgical Review*, 4 (Nov. 1974), p. 20; G. Wainwright, op. cit., pp. 6off.

Corinthian liturgy (16.22; cf. *Did.* 10.6; Rev. 22.20). The death of the risen Lord is so proclaimed that his return is invoked and anticipated; his *parousia* is both presence and arrival.[1]

With ch. 11 we seem to have finished with the Eucharist; but the next three chapters are still concerned with the Corinthian assembly, even though St Paul is mainly concerned with the balance of *charisms*. But the question arises, did the Corinthians have *one* (weekly?) assembly, or *two*, one for the supper and one for the instruction and charisms? We cannot answer definitely; I would only suggest that it may have been difficult or impossible to hold two plenary sessions a week, and that St Paul is describing two aspects or phases of the one assembly. There is notable continuity between ch. 11 and 12—14, particularly in the elaboration of the body-image of 10.16, 17 as taken up in 11.23, 24, 29, 33 and applied to the diversity-in-unity of the Corinthian fellowship in 12.12–30. This famous passage presupposes the eucharistic teaching and practice of the previous chapters. In his practical application (ch. 14) St Paul insists on order and succession instead of the spontaneous simultaneity of their charismatic chaos; he encourages intelligible speech in preference to *glossolalia*; only so can the uninstructed add his corroborative Amen to your thanksgiving (*eucharistia*; 14.16–19). The thanksgiving is singled out but not further defined; it could well include, and could not exclude, the special thanksgiving over the cup (11.25, 26). In that case there would be no clear demarcation between the Lord's Supper and the charismatic assembly; the meal ended, the Spirit-guided session of psalmody, teaching, prophecy (26) would follow, and the thanksgiving over the cup and its circulation would occur in the course of it, or at its beginning. Thus the Spirit-session, following the meal, could take the place of the wine session (*symposion*) which the Jews were adopting on festal occasions.[2] It would appear that, at least at Corinth, the meal *preceded* any ministry of the word.[3]

Finally, who *presided* at Corinth? On Jewish precedents the father of the house would have said the opening blessing over the bread; the thanksgiving over the cup, according to later Jewish evidence, could be delegated to a privileged guest. We do not know whether Pauline churches inherited these customs. At any rate all are not equal in the Christian assembly, in which God has ordained an embryonic hierarchy:

---

[1] 'Until he come'—see *EWJ*, p. 253; Bornkamm, pp. 147–52. *Maranatha:* on the possible meanings, see *TDNT* IV, pp. 466–72; H. Conzelmann, op. cit., p. 202; C. J. A. Hickling, ibid. pp. 21–2; G. Wainwright, op. cit., pp. 68ff.

[2] *Concilium*, Dec. 1968, p. 61; H. Schürmann, with references. Cf. also Col. 3.12–17 and Eph. 5.15–20, esp. 18. The situation at Corinth was not unique, but exaggerated.

[3] See O. Cullmann, op. cit., pp. 20–5; C. F. D. Moule, op. cit., pp. 61–6; G. Bornkamm, op. cit., pp. 161–79; G. J. Cuming, *infra* (356).

'1. apostles, 2. prophets, 3. teachers' (12.28), all ministers of the word in some sense, underlining the connection we have traced between the proclamation of God's redeeming acts and the eucharistic thanksgiving. Nor do we know who actually enforced the difficult discipline imposed on those who spoke with tongues and their interpreters (14.27–33). Perhaps all was in the hands of St Paul's special agents in Corinth (16.15, 16), to whom obedience is expected.

ST PAUL AND THE TRADITION

So much for Corinth, and we could leave the matter there, if it were not for St Paul's citation of a version of the narrative of the Last Supper (11.23–25, cf. synopsis p. 158–9), verses which go behind the Corinthian situation to the very origins of the Eucharist, which he says he received 'from the Lord'. H. Lietzmann (op. cit. p. 208) understood this as a personal revelation of the Lord, pointing to a new and special connection between the ordinance and his death. This hypothesis is without parallel and is unnecessary; the clearest affinity of this passage is not with St Paul's records of his supernatural experiences (e.g. 2 Cor. 12.1–10), but with the other recitation of earliest tradition in the same epistle (15.1ff). The catechetical tradition of Christ's redemptive death and resurrection he had received from those who were in Christ before him; the eucharistic tradition had its origin in Christ himself. (And it belonged to the teaching tradition rather than the liturgical; the citation would have had no force in Corinth if the narrative was already included in the eucharistic rite).[1] The affinity with 1 Cor. 15.1ff is important and illuminating; both are in line with accepted rabbinic precedents for the transmission of authoritative teaching.[2] Many scholars, under the influence of the Acts of the Apostles, assume that St Paul assimilated the traditions of the church at Antioch; his own testimony suggests that his source was Peter at Jerusalem, whom he 'visited to get information from', within three years of his conversion.[3] He is passing on a tradition which

---

[1] Following A. M. Farrer, 'The Eucharist in 1 Corinthians', in *Eucharistic Theology Then and Now* (SPCK 1968), p. 19, in contrast to G. D. Kilpatrick, *RevThPh* 1964, pp. 1–2 and *Liturgical Review* 5, May 1975, pp. 37ff. See also J. A. Baker, op. cit., p. 55.

[2] Cf. B. Gerhardsson, *Memory and Manuscript* (Lund 1961), pp. 288–302, 320–3; *EWJ*, pp. 101ff.

[3] G. D. Kilpatrick, 'Galatians 1. 18: *historesai Kephan*', in *New Testament Essays* (in memory of T. W. Manson), ed. A. J. B. Higgins, (Manchester University Press 1959), pp. 144–9. St Paul's apostolic commission, authority, and jurisdiction are direct from Christ and unmediated (Gal. 1.1–12; 2. 7–9); details of the historic tradition would be received from Peter and the Jerusalem community (1 Cor. 15.1–5). With a Cephas faction in Corinth, Paul could not risk contradiction and would have to take especial care to be accurate.

was fully formed before his conversion; it is the earliest surviving account of the Last Supper, and there is a *prima facie* case for its authenticity. This impression is supported by the following facts:

1. The action and words concerning the bread precede the meal; those concerning the cup follow it. This pattern accords well with Jewish meal customs on solemn occasions. The bread-words accompany the normal action over the bread; the wine-words accompany the thanksgiving over the cup. The single, common cup, so essential to the symbolism, may not have been contemporary custom, but Jesus' own idea (Schürmann, *Concilium*, Dec. 1968, p. 64 and note).

2. Because the two actions are separated by the meal and are in no way interconnected, *two* commands to repeat the action as *anamnesis* are required; as Dix asserts 'It is pure recollection, or it would never have retained those words "Do this for the re-calling of Me" over the broken bread, *absolutely necessary at that point on that one occasion, and absolutely superfluous on any other*' (Shape, p. 69). This point needs to be emphasized in the face of widespread scepticism, which rejects the command to repeat and regards it as a Pauline insertion. The twice repeated *hosakis* (as often as) in connection with the cup recognizes that wine was not usual at ordinary meals, but was added on special occasions.

3. The bread-saying and the cup-saying are independent of each other and are not parallel. The cup-saying is based on the passage in Jeremiah (31.31–34), which authorizes the concept of a new covenant, but provides no means for its inauguration; Jesus offers his blood for this purpose after the pattern of the inauguration of the first covenant (Exod. 24.4–8). But the saying refers to the cup explicitly and to its contents implicitly, thus respecting the Jewish abhorrence of drinking blood.

4. Many Jewish customs are presumed and not stated; there are no commands to take or eat or drink.

As well as one or two phrases reminiscent of Paul's own style, there are a number of un-pauline features which suggest the presence of an earlier source (*EWJ*, pp. 101–5). Our investigation seems to support the view that there is a *prima facie* case for considering this narrative to be close to the original event.

THE INSTITUTION NARRATIVES

Matt. 26.26–29	Mark 14.22–25	Luke 22.15–20	1 Cor. 11.23–26
26 And as they were eating Jesus	22 And as they were eating he	15 And he said unto them, With desire I have desired to eat this passover with you before I suffer: 16 for I say unto you, I will not eat it, until it be fulfilled in the kingdom of God. 17 And he received a cup, and when he had given thanks, he said, Take this, and divide it among yourselves: 18 for I say unto you, I will not drink from henceforth of the fruit of the vine, until the kingdom of God shall come	23 For I received of the Lord that which also I delivered unto you, how that the Lord Jesus in the night in which he was betrayed
took ᵃ bread, and	took ᵃ bread, and when he had	19 And he took ᵃ bread, and when he had given thanks	took bread; 24 and when he had given thanks
blessed and brake it; and he gave to the disciples, and said, Take, eat; this is my body.	blessed he brake it, and gave to them, and said, Take ye: this is my body	he brake it, and gave to them, saying This is my bodyᵇ which is given for you: this do in remembrance of me.	he brake it, and said, This is my body, whichᵃ is for you: this do in remembrance of me.

THE INSTITUTION NARRATIVES (*Cont.*)

Matt. 26.27–29	Mark 14.23–25	Luke 22.20	1 Cor. 11.25–26
27 And he took[b] a cup,	23 And he took a cup,	20 And the cup in like manner after supper,	25 In like manner also the cup, after supper,
and gave thanks and gave to them,	and when he had given thanks he gave to them: and they all drank of it.		
saying Drink ye all of it; 28 for	24 And he said unto them,	saying,	saying,
this is my blood of [c]the [d]covenant,	This is my blood of[b] the [c]covenant	This cup is the new[c] covenant in my blood, even that which is poured out for you.	This cup is the new [c]covenant in my blood:
which is shed for many unto remission of sins.	which is shed for many		this do, as oft as ye drink it, in remembrance of me.
29 But I say unto you. I will not drink henceforth of this fruit of the vine, until that day when I drink it new with you in my Father's kingdom.	25 Verily I say unto you, I will no more drink of the fruit of the vine, until that day when I drink it new in the kingdom of God.		26 For as often as ye eat this bread, and drink the cup, ye proclaim the Lord's death till he come.

a. Or *a loaf*
b. Some ancient authorities read *the cup*.
c. Or, *the testament*.
d. Many ancient authorities insert *new*.

a. Or, *a loaf*
b. Or, *the testament*.
c. Some ancient authorities insert *new*.

a. Or, *a loaf*
b. Some ancient authorities omit *which is given for you. . .which is poured out for you.*
c. Or, *testament*

a. Many ancient authorities read *is broken for you*.
b. Or, *testament*

(*based on H. F. D. Sparks, A Synopsis of the Gospels, Part I* (A. & C. Black 1964), pp. 201–2.)

ST MARK

St Mark's narrative of the Last Supper is embedded in his Passion story. Moreover the Supper seems to be the Passover, a detail not mentioned by St Paul; this can be inferred from 14.12–16, where we find the only paschal allusions in the Gospel. The words and actions with the bread and cup (14.22–25) occur in the course of the meal, 'and as they were eating' (22, cf.18). The two actions follow one another without a break; the two sayings have a parallel form, 'This is my body/blood'. There is no hint of repetition. Jesus takes a cup, any cup (contrast 1 Cor. 11.25); its contents are designated as 'my covenant-blood which is being poured out for many', based on Exod. 24.8 and Is. 53.12. There are details not mentioned by Paul: they are told to take the bread; he 'gave them the cup and they all drank of it' before the interpretative words.

Such details are elaborated by Matthew (26.26–29), who in all other respects follows Mark exactly. 'Take, eat'; 'drink of this all of you'. His only significant addition is the phrase 'for the remission of sins' to the cup-saying, underlining the atoning power of Jesus' blood.[1]

In both these Gospels we can understand the bread and cup episode as an important, indeed essential, part of the Passion narrative.[2] On the night before the crucifixion he lays bare his own inner purpose in approaching and accepting death; he makes it into a sacrificial offering, to provide the blood for a new alliance between God and the twelve-fold Israel (cf. Exod. 24.4) and for 'many' (=all, cf. Is. 53.12) by the twofold sign; by accepting the bread and cup the disciples accept his intention and their own share in it. The last verse (Mk. 14.25; Mt. 26.29) looks beyond the Passion to his vindication and glorification to be celebrated in the Kingdom of God with new wine ('with you', Mt.). This interpretation does not exclude the Christian Eucharist, neither does it require it (see plate 1).

We may also suppose that Mark's version reflects the Eucharist of his own time and church, some years after St Paul committed to writing the earliest liturgical pattern. The tendencies already noticeable at Corinth have developed in the opposite direction to that enjoined by the apostle. The sacramental actions no longer envelop the meal; they have been linked together and take place during it. The interpretative words have

---

[1] *EWJ*, pp. 113, 114. The phrase is omitted in his account of the Baptist's preaching (Mt. 3.1, cf. Mk. 1.4) and transferred here, perhaps as a corollary to the new covenant (cf. Jer. 31.34; also Heb. 8.12; 10.17, 18).

[2] J. A. Baker, ibid. p. 51; K. G. Kuhn, op. cit., 'Originally they were only the words by which Jesus explained the twin parable' (p. 88); 'Even as all present at the meal partake of the bread and the wine, so will they all share in the atonement of his death, of his body to be given and his blood to be shed' (p. 93).

become words of administration. The emphasis is on body and blood, halfway to St John's flesh and blood (6.53f). We have moved some way from the framework of the Jewish meal and its graces, perhaps to a purely gentile milieu. Those who hold that Mark has preserved the original tradition have to look elsewhere for their models: to 'the blessed bread of life', 'the blessed cup of immortality and 'the chrism of incorruption' in *Joseph and Asenath*,[1] to the Essene meals as described by Josephus (*Wars* II, 139–43), or to the solemn formal meals at Qumran, of which none may partake until the priest has blessed the bread *and* the wine.[2]

ST PAUL AND ST MARK

We have already compared these two basic texts in some detail; but there are still some outstanding issues. Was the Last Supper the Passover meal or not? Is Paul or Mark nearer to the event or to Jesus' intention? There are many difficulties.

The first is the problem of chronology, well summarized by G. Ogg (*Historicity and Chronology in the NT* (SPCK 1965), pp. 75–96). The question is wider than the nature of the Last Supper; it includes the dating of the whole Passion story. Mk. 14.12–16; Mt. 26.17–19; Lk. 22.7–16 assert that the meal is the Passover meal, taken on the evening before the festival; therefore for them the trial and crucifixion take place on the Passover. On the other hand, the Fourth Gospel insists that Jesus was crucified *before* the Passover and died along with the lambs (cf. Jn. 18.28; 19.14, 36). Jeremias has argued strenuously not only that the supper was the Passover but also that the crucifixion could have taken place legitimately on the festival (*EWJ*, pp. 15–88); but on this last point he has convinced few (see J. B. Segal, *The Hebrew Passover* (OUP 1963), pp. 244–5).

On the paschal rite itself, Jewish scholars differ as to how much we can actually know about the full extent of procedure in the first century A.D. Jeremias, Dix, Daube (opp. cit. and *The NT and Rabbinic Judaism* (Athlone Press 1956), pp. 163–6) and Billerbeck (Strack-Billerbeck IV, pp. 41–76) all follow Dalman in presuming a maximum knowledge of the rites, thrown back from the Mishnah and later, and in detecting the maximum correspondence with NT details. On the other hand Segal (op. cit. p. 241) warns that 'in analysing passages of the NT relevant to the Passover, scholars may have been too readily disposed to seek in them the reflection of later Jewish practice. . . . Some of the rites that play so

[1] G. D. Kilpatrick, *Ex.T* 64 (Oct. 1952), pp. 4–7; K. G. Kuhn, ibid. pp. 74–7.
[2] K. G. Kuhn, ibid. pp. 65–72; also G. Vermes, *The Dead Sea Scrolls in English* (Penguin 1962), pp. 81, 121.

central a part in the Seder service are intended to symbolize and commemorate the service of the Temple after its destruction'. Even if the paschal character of the Supper were established, the fact remains that Jesus did not select and sacramentalize any distinctively paschal feature (the unleavened bread, the lamb, the bitter herbs), but only the bread and cup of normal festal custom.

In the earliest Christian allusion to Passover St Paul wrote (1 Cor. 5.7): Our passover is sacrificed, that is Christ; therefore let us keep festival. . . . Perhaps this basic image, thrown out with no further explanation, was interpreted in two ways, and applied by St John to the death and by the synoptists to the meal at which the death was designated as a sacrifice.

There are also linguistic difficulties. Assuming that Jesus spoke Aramaic and that his genuine sayings can be readily translated back into Aramaic, Jeremias has attempted to rediscover the *ipsissima verba* of Jesus through analysis of semitic features detectible in St Mark. But Aramaic is an awkward language to dogmatize about, as new texts yield new usages.[1] Mark's semitisms are a constant factor in his style throughout the Gospel.[2] It is likely that Jesus and his circle spoke more than one language, and it is possible that Greek equivalents of Aramaic expressions were worked out from the beginning.

If the evidence is weighted in favour of St Paul, we are in agreement with W. Marxsen (op. cit. pp. 66ff); but when he goes on to claim that when the pattern of the Eucharist as a covenant meal was changed into a purely sacramental rite, its original character was completely destroyed, we need not follow him; for it is clear that, even at Corinth, the two sacramental elements and actions had always had special status (1 Cor. 10.3, 4, 16), even when they enclosed the meal.

ST LUKE AND ACTS

'The Lucan account of the Last Supper is a scholar's paradise and a beginner's nightmare' (G. B. Caird, *Saint Luke* (Penguin 1963), p. 237). Read carefully Lk. 22.15–20 in the synopsis, noting that verses 19 and 20

---

[1] Cf. Jeremias' acceptance of 'my covenant-blood', *EWJ* p. 193, n. 2; similarly on *guph* (*soma*), meaning person as well as corpse, see C. J. A. Hickling, *Liturgical Review* 5 (May 1975), pp. 56, 61.

[2] N. Turner, *JTS* n.s. 8 (1957), pp. 108–11. It is in Mark's favour that he uses *eulogein* for the blessing over the bread and *eucharistein* for the thanksgiving over the cup; but in the feeding stories he has *eulogein* at 6.41, and *eucharistein* at 8.6. Though originally distinct in meaning they had become interchangeable. Paul likewise uses *eucharistein* of bread and cup (1 Cor. 11.23), but *eulogein* also of the cup (1 Cor. 10.16). Cf. 1 Cor. 14.16, both in one verse.

are in brackets, signifying that they are absent in some MSS. (There is a wider range of variations affecting the whole passage; they are set out fully by Kenyon and Legg, op. cit. pp. 284–5). The brackets were inserted in their 1881 edition of the NT by Westcott and Hort, who judged them to be a 'Western non-interpolation' or omission. Although the bracketed section is absent from a very small number of MSS, the shorter version attracted the support of a large number of scholars, including a critical defence by Kilpatrick (art. cit.). Many scholars (e.g. Benoît, Kenyon, Jeremias, Williams) have returned to the support of the longer text, while Schürmann maintains that Luke has preserved the earliest account of the Last Supper in a form previous to Paul. It is difficult to detect any rational unity in either version, particularly the shorter (see H. Chadwick, art. cit.).

Any attempt to unravel this problem must take into account the distinctive theology and outlook of this evangelist, as author of both volumes.[1] In the Acts we find references to the 'breaking of bread' at Christian gatherings (2.42, 46; 20.7, possibly 27.33–6).[2] In the Gospel the Lord is made known to the two at Emmaus through the breaking of the bread (Lk. 24.30, 31, 35). We also know, both through his own writing and through his omissions from Mark, that he neglects, to say the least, the early concept of salvation or redemption through the efficacy of the precious blood of Christ (cf. Lk. 24.47); only once can we find a phrase expressing this conviction (Acts 20.28), in St Paul's farewell speech to the presbyters of Ephesus at Miletus, perhaps included in deference to St Paul's own theology. Let us look at both versions of the supper in the light of these facts.

The shorter version has no reference to 'my body *given for you*', or to the 'new covenant in my blood which is being poured out for you'. A cup precedes the bread, but it has no sacramental association. The inverted order may reflect a local usage; but there is no command to repeat any rite. The passage has no hint of atonement, or of the cup-saying which might express it.[3]

Both versions combine features of Mark, particularly the eschatological saying (14.25), with Luke's own material which mainly concerns the Passover; the longer version incorporates a good deal of 1 Cor. 11.23–25. Lk. 22.15–18 definitely portrays a farewell Passover, represented by

---

1 Schürmann admitted that he had taken no account of 'redaction criticism' in his close textual work; see note added to the reprinted edition, *Der Paschamahlbericht* (Münster 1968), p. ix.
2 See E. R. Goodenough, 'The Perspective of Acts' in *Studies in Luke-Acts*, ed. L. E. Keck and J. L. Martyn (SPCK 1968), pp. 51–2.
3 See M. Kiddle, art. cit. pp. 277–8; and, more fully, M. Rese, art. cit.

paschal lamb (15, 16) and cup (17, 18); when this is concluded, the Eucharist is instituted (19, 20). At first sight it appears that only the bread rite is to be repeated, as he drops St Paul's command to repeat the cup rite; but on closer inspection we find that the one command applies to both. By a subtle movement of the word *hosautos* (likewise) he rephrases Paul and says: 'also the cup — equally after the meal — saying. . .'. Both eucharistic rites are joined together after the meal. In this case we have a further liturgical development: the Eucharist has become a special and separate rite after the meal.[1]

ST JOHN

On the sacramental doctrine of the Fourth Gospel two extreme views have been put forward. R. Bultmann's commentary presupposes, without argument, that the Gospel, as we now have it, has been through the hands of one or more redactors, to whom we owe *all* the sacramental references (*The Gospel of John* (ET Blackwell 1971), p. 11). O. Cullmann, on the other hand, sees sacraments everywhere; John's main concern is 'to set forth the line from the life of Jesus to the Christ of the community, in such a way as to demonstrate their identity. Because the Christ of the community is present in a special way in the sacraments, this line leads us in many, even if not in all the narratives, to the sacraments' (op. cit., p. 117). On Bultmann's view, we would have nothing to say; on Cullmann's, we could never stop.

Despite John's great elaboration of the Last Supper scene (chs. 13–17) it contains no reference to the institution of the Eucharist. But there is also no Transfiguration and no real Gethsemane, and yet we cannot say that these mysteries are entirely absent. Christ is constantly manifesting the glory of God (Jn. 1.14, 18; 2.11; 12.23; 13.31, 32; 17.4–8, 24–26); he is continually occupied in doing the Father's will (4.34; 5.19; 6.38; 8.29; 17.4; 19.30). Equally the institution narrative may be lying somewhere beneath the surface, perhaps in the chapter (6) on the Bread of Life. This long discourse (26–59) is attached to the record of two signs, Jesus' feeding of the five thousand (5–13) and his mysterious coming and going across the lake (16–25), linked together as closely as in Mark (6.35–52). The account of the feeding has many features in common with the

---

[1] M. Dibelius, op. cit., pp. 210–1; P. Benoît, op. cit., pp. 196–203. St Luke's doctrine is akin to that of St Thomas Aquinas in his eucharistic hymns, e.g. Meekly with the law complying,/First he finished its command,/Then, immortal food supplying,/Gave himself with his own hand (English Hymnal 326). Any assessment of Luke's eucharistic theology must also take into account his reference to the twelve thrones and the eschatological banquet in 22.29, 30.

6 Sphragis: a Roman commander bearing a cruciform seal on his forehead; a sarcophagus in Museo delle Terme, Rome (see p. 105)

7 Baptism by total immersion in a cow trough, South India

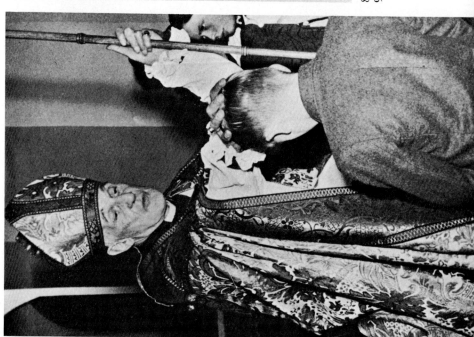

8 Confirmation by an Anglican bishop
9 The Ardagh Chalice, early eighth-century Celtic (Irish) work, in beaten silver adorned with gold and enamel

synoptic accounts (Mk. 6.41, 42; 8.6–8; Mt. 14.19, 20; 15.36, 37; Lk. 9.16, 17); while they, with their references to taking, blessing (Mk. 6.41; Mt. 14.19; Lk. 9.16) or giving thanks (Mk. 8.6; Mt. 15.36), breaking and distribution, anticipate or reflect the institution of the Eucharist and its later practice; or, through their common dependence on Jewish custom, reflect the continuity between the Last Supper and all the preceding meals taken together by Jesus and his followers. The dialogue and discourse have caused difficulty, as 53–8 undoubtedly allude to the Christian sacrament, through the specific reference to eating (chewing) flesh and drinking blood, while the earlier part of the discourse does not necessarily do so, with its more general talk of Christ as the bread of life which satisfies hunger (*and* thirst, 35, cf. the vine image, 15.1ff).

Modern exegetes (e.g. Lindars, Wilckens, etc.) see the discourse as an exposition of the text *He gave them bread from heaven to eat* (31, a synthetic text; cf. Exod. 16.4, 15; Ps. 105.40; and those cited in n. 2, p. 151). In the first half (up to 51b) Christ is presented as the true manna, God's own gift to the world (cf. 3.16), from heaven itself, not just from the sky, designed to impart and sustain *eternal* life, not just a *viaticum* for the limited journey through the wilderness. But as *living* bread (cf. 5.26; 6.57a), the Son is not just the gift of the Father to the world, but must equally give himself; and so 'the bread which I will give is my flesh on behalf of the life of the world' (51c). This sentence is the visible pivot of the discourse; before it, Christ speaks of himself as bread, after it, he speaks of his flesh *and* blood. The invisible pivot is the narrative of the Last Supper in the synoptic tradition, where Christ pledges himself to a sacrificial death by imparting himself to his disciples in a double sign. So understood, the dialogue has a progressive and dramatic unity as well as coherence. Even so there is a clear break at 51c, between the general symbolism of the manna and the specific symbolism of the sacrament. Perhaps we have more here than a meditation on the bread of life and the Eucharist; we may have a meditation on the liturgy of the evangelist's time, with the reading of the word and its exposition preceding the commemoration of the passion (51c) and the communion in two kinds (53–6), anticipating the order given by Justin Martyr (p. 172).

Further we note that by now the two elements are not only parallel but are complementary; *flesh* (not *body*) and blood signify human nature in its totality (cf. Gal. 1.16; Mt. 16, 17; Heb. 2.14).[1] Moreover the flesh on its

---

[1] Cf. St Thomas Aquinas' hymn: In twofold form of sacrament/He gave his flesh, he gave his blood/That man of twofold substance blent/Might wholly feed on mystic food (English Hymnal 330); and Cranmer's prayer 'that our sinful *bodies* may be made clean by his *body*, and our *souls* washed through his most precious *blood*'. (See *infra*, p. 266). See A. M. Farrer in *The Parish Communion*, p. 88 n. 4; *contra EWJ*, p. 199.

own is powerless unless quickened by the Spirit; the sacramental actions operate in virtue of the spirit and life of Jesus' sayings (63). Later, after the crucifixion, the water and blood from Christ's side are quickened by his Spirit to provide baptism and Eucharist (19.34, 35, in the light of 19.30; 7.39 and 1 Jn. 5.6–8).

This leads to further imaginative speculation about the last half of the Gospel (13—20), which falls roughly into two sections, discussion and action, the discourses after supper and the narrative of the passion and resurrection. The discourses (14—16), with their revelation and teaching about the relation of Jesus and his disciples, reflect the ministry of the word; then in the long prayer (17) Christ offers his return to the Father, and sanctifies himself on behalf of his disciples. The passion follows, leading up to its climax in his death (19.30), with its victorious cry (cf. 17.4) and the exsufflation of the Spirit. Perhaps we have here also a reflection on the liturgy of word and sacrament of the author's time.

1 PETER, HEBREWS, AND REVELATION

Although 1 Peter has many allusions to baptism and has been considered to be a paschal treatise, or even liturgy, it contains no explicit reference to the Eucharist; nevertheless the newly reborn are attached to Christ as to a living stone, and are expected, 'as living stones themselves, to be built up as a *pneumatic* house, into a holy priesthood, to offer up *pneumatic* sacrifices that are to be acceptable to God through Jesus Christ' (1 Pet. 2.5). This is a beautiful description of the Church as eucharistic community with its eucharistic prayer, but in a general and not a sacramental sense; and yet the sacramental sense aptly fits, and fulfils, the words (as in Col. 1.12ff; 3.17; Eph. 1.6f).

Hebrews and Revelation are less simple in this respect. Hebrews has been acclaimed both as the supreme authority for, and as the final condemnation of, eucharistic sacrifice in the NT. For all its interest in biblical (but not contemporary Jewish) patterns of sacrifice and atonement, its references to *Christian* worship are enigmatic and obscure. For all its interest in Melchizedek, as a foil for levitical priesthood and as an archetype of Christ, no mention is made of the fact that he 'brought forth bread and wine' (Gen. 14.18). And yet the author knew the Marcan saying about the covenant blood; 'it is certain that the author of Hebrews has misquoted the text in Exodus in order to make it square with the phrase in Mark' (Exod. 24.8; Heb. 9.20; Mk. 14, 24; Couratin, p. 286; also *EWJ*, p. 170). Perhaps we should distinguish between the author's 'theology' and his 'religion' or Christianity. In his theological exercise, he is trying to unify and streamline the faith around the images of the once-for-all priestly oblation of Christ, which atones for sin and opens the way to the throne of God, and of Christ the forerunner who leads his people into the promised heavenly land, whither they follow in faith to this invisible and future goal. Christ's path is straight, through death to glory; and the Christian path should be the same. His dominant images, however, cannot contain all the material, such as the resurrection of Jesus or his *parousia* (coming); and yet he admits them in a limited way (e.g. 13.20, of the resurrection; 9.28; 10.37, of the parousia). It may be the same with the Eucharist. In line with 6.4–5, the divinely provided food and drink of 1 Cor. 10.3–4 would have been very congenial to his pilgrims; but the author might not have encouraged them to pause to 'participate in the body and blood of Christ' (1 Cor. 10.16) or to 'proclaim the death of the Lord' (1 Cor. 11.26), for either phrase could be construed nostalgically. In the body of the argument, Christ by his death provides the blood which effects the atonement and inaugurates the new covenant. He goes into heaven itself and ever lives to make intercession for us (7.25); but he does not 'plead his sacrifice'. And yet, later (12.22–24), outside the main argument, we are taken to mount Zion, to the celebration of the heavenly host before God and Jesus 'the mediator of a new covenant and the blood of sprinkling which speaks better than Abel', being eternally efficacious (cf. Gen. 4.10). Hebrews here introduces a new factor, which prepares us for the Revelation: the true focus of Christian worship, as also of Christian faith and life, is not here but *there*, in heaven (cf. Mt. 6.9), 'the throne of grace' where we may receive mercy and grace (Heb. 4.16; 10, 19ff). In this light we may make some sense of 13.10–16, an enigmatic passage, where the author is trying to deal with practicalities, and yet links them with his key images of atonement (11, 12) and pilgrimage (13, 14). Having in Christ the heavenly reality of the atonement ritual (Lev. 16), we Christians 'have an altar', the archetype of the mercy seat, which the ordinary levitical priests could not approach, and we have the right to eat at it. It is available to us, because of Jesus' atoning work and sacrifice, offered outside the earthly city and cultic area; we must follow him out, towards the eternal city, where this altar can be found, and through him we can 'offer up a sacrifice of praise to God continually', confessing his name (15); and this also involves well-doing and sharing (*koinonia*), which are also sacrifices well-pleasing to God (16). This passage can be understood non-sacramentally, and has been interpreted anti-sacramentally; but it is also possible that the unexpressed clue to its intricacy lies in a Christian eucharistic assembly, not unlike that presupposed by St Paul, in which the Lord's death was proclaimed in conjunction with the thanksgiving for food and drink, which were then shared in a general meal.

Revelation takes up and develops the imagery of the messianic banquet, as hinted by Christ in Mk. 14.25 (more explicitly in Mt. 26.29 and Lk 22.29, 30), both individually and corporately. For the individual, 'I stand at the door and knock; if any man hear my voice and open the door, I will come in to him, and will sup with him, and he with me' (3.20). Corporately, during the final visions, the great coming of the Lord and his reunion with his elect (cf. 2 Thess. 2.1) is presented under the image of a marriage and its feast; 'blessed are those who are called to the marriage supper of the Lamb' (19.9).

Liturgical practice also lies behind the earlier visions of the heavenly court in chs. 4 and 5. The divine throne with the attendant elders (presbyters) is held to reflect the lay-out of the Christian community assembled for worship; and it is equally possible that the heavenly proceedings reflect the order and contents of the earthly liturgy. The heavenly details are a fusion drawn from Ezek. 1, Dan. 7.10 and Is. 6.1–3. The four living creatures praise God unceasingly, singing the Sanctus, 'Holy, holy, holy . . .'; as in Is. 6.3; but the wording is nearer to that of later liturgies than to the LXX of Isaiah. This suggests that this liturgical custom is already well established (Couratin, pp. 285, 288; also cf. 1 *Clem.* 34.6). The elders respond with a hymn acclaiming God worthy of glory and honour 'because thou didst create all things and they were in existence through thy will and were created' (4.11). The heavenly liturgy is first of all continual praise of God in himself and as creator of all things. The next chapter introduces the sealed book which only Christ can open; the book representing the divine plan for salvation, which Christ has already fulfilled. He is portrayed as a lamb, slain but upright (5.6, cf. 1.18). As he appears and takes the book, the four creatures and the twenty-four elders ascribe to him divine honours, and praise him, in words which match the hymn to God himself (cf. 5.9 and 4.11), 'for thou wast slain and didst purchase for God by thy blood (men) out of every tribe and language and people and race; and didst constitute them for our God a kingdom and priests, and they will reign on the earth' (5.9, 10; cf. 1.6). Their acclamation is taken up by crowds of angels (5.12), while the whole creation voices an ascription of praise and blessing to God and the Lamb (5.13), to which the four creatures reply Amen (5.14). The topics of thanksgiving correspond closely with Justin Martyr's requirements for the eucharistic prayer and with Hippolytus' earliest model text of the prayer.[1]

---

[1] Couratin, pp. 288–90; see *PEER*, pp. 17–23; and *infra*, pp. 171–6.

CONCLUSION

Can we trace a coherent story from the Upper Room to the Church's Eucharist as first described by Justin Martyr? It seems that we can go a good deal of the way. From our earliest account (1 Cor. 11.23–25), on the night before he died, Jesus gave new meanings to the traditional blessing and breaking of bread before the meal and to the thanksgiving over the cup at its close, and asked that these acts should be repeated with the same intention. For a while his followers and their converts held their communal meal within this framework, but with growing instability. Human unsociability and impatience, coupled with the special significance that had always been given to the bread and cup, caused them to join these two elements together in a separate rite, at first in the course of the meal (Mark and Matthew) and later at its close (Lk. 22.19, 20). During this process the words connected with each element underwent increasing assimilation, reaching a climax in the Fourth Gospel.[1] It is then only a small step to abolish the special blessing over the bread, and to incorporate it into the longer thanksgiving over the cup, one eucharistic prayer over both elements, followed by simultaneous distribution, as in Justin Martyr. The earliest Christians, at least at Corinth, seem to have followed the meal with an extended instruction session; in Justin's time the Eucharist was preceded by lessons, sermon, and intercession. How or when this reversal took place we do not know; it turned out to be universal, and so it may have happened quite early, early enough to be reflected in Lk. 24.25–35 and Jn. 6. For the eucharistic prayer itself, we have the Jewish thanksgiving over the cup as a model, 1 Cor. 11.26 as a hint of its Christian transformation, and its possible reflection in Revelation.

It is a coherent story, or rather the framework of a story. But is it history or a fairy story? Our answer in the end will depend on our historical estimate of 1 Cor. 11.23ff as a source and of St Paul as an authority; and a great deal more than liturgy depends on our answer.

[1] See T. A. Burkill, *Mysterious Revelation* (Cornell 1963), p. 279; H. Schürmann, *Concilium*, Dec. 1968.

2 From the
Apostolic Fathers to Irenaeus

K. W. NOAKES

Texts

PE pp. 66–79.
PEER pp. 14–20.

Studies

Audet, J.-P., *La Dìdachè, instruction des apôtres*. Paris 1958.
Barnard, L. W., *Justin Martyr: His Life and Thought* (CUP 1967), pp. 126–56.
Dix, G., *Shape*, pp. 48–155; 222–4.
Jungmann, J. A., *The Early Liturgy*, pp. 39–49.
Jungmann, J. A., *MRR*.
Ligier, L., 'From the Last Supper to the Eucharist', in *The New Liturgy*, ed. L. Sheppard (DLT 1970), pp. 113–50.
Ligier, L., 'The Origins of the Eucharistic Prayer from the Last Supper to the Eucharist', in *SL* 9 (1973), pp. 161–85.
Rordorf, W., (ET) *Sunday* (SCM 1968), pp. 238–73.
Srawley, J. H., *The Early History of the Liturgy*. 2nd edn (CUP 1947), pp. 18–40.

Despite the lack of evidence about how it was celebrated in the first century, there is no doubt that the Eucharist was at the heart of the life of the Church. It was celebrated weekly on the Lord's day and it was the sacrifice prophesied by the Lord through Malachi, 'In every place and at every time offer me a pure sacrifice; for I am a great King, says the Lord, and my Name is wonderful among the nations' (*Did.* 14, quoting Mal. 1.11). In order that their sacrifice might be pure, the *Didache* orders Christians to confess their sins and be reconciled to their brothers before taking part in the Eucharist.

The celebration of the Eucharist in due order is one of the concerns of the author of 1 Clement (chs. 40 and 41). Likewise, Ignatius is concerned with orderly celebration; he sees the Eucharist celebrated by the bishop as the bond which unites men in Christ and writes, 'Be careful to observe one Eucharist' (*Phil.* 4). Since the eucharistic bread is the Flesh of our Saviour Jesus Christ and wine his Blood (*Smyrn.* 6; *Rom.* 7), it is the 'medicine of immortality and the antidote that we should not die but live for ever in Jesus Christ' (*Eph.* 20).

The *Didache*[1] reflects the gradual disengagement of the Eucharist from the meal. Thus, the prayers in ch. 9 and 10 probably belong to a

[1] See pp. 55–7, and Audet, op. cit., pp. 372–433. For ET of the eucharistic texts of the *Didache*, see *PEER* 3.

preceding meal and the words of 10.6 represent the liturgical dialogue introducing the Eucharist proper, in which the baptized ('the holy') are invited to the Eucharist and the non-baptized excluded (cf. 9.5). The meal which preceded the Eucharist had the character of a liturgy of hope in which the mighty acts of God were recalled and his future mighty acts looked forward to. The table prayers (9.2; 9.3; 10.2ff) follow the pattern of the Jewish *berakah*, or benediction, including blessing of the name of God the Creator, thanksgiving for his mighty acts, supplication and doxology (see p. 49). This pattern found in the *Didache*, was to be fundamental in the development of the eucharistic prayer in succeeding centuries.

If the *Didache* presents problems of interpretation, the brief account of Christian worship given by Pliny, governor of Bithynia in 112, presents even more problems. Pliny's few words have received a variety of interpretations from scholars (see pp. 51–2) but it is certain that we can learn very little from him about how the Eucharist was performed.

The earliest reasonably detailed account of the Eucharist is given by Justin (mid second century), who describes two celebrations, one following baptism, and the other an ordinary Sunday service (1 *Apol.*, 65 and 67; *PEER* 4). In neither case is there any survival of the meal. The centre of both accounts is the eucharistic prayer spoken by the President and acclaimed by the people's 'Amen'. This prayer is improvised (cf. *Did.*, 10.7) but the President is to follow a certain pattern, addressing the Father in the name of the Son and of the Holy Spirit and giving thanks for the gifts that we were worthy to receive from him. According to Justin the eucharistic prayer effects the transformation of the bread and wine into the Flesh and Blood of Jesus (1 *Apol.*, 66). Something of the content of the eucharistic prayer can perhaps be filled in by looking at references to the Eucharist in Justin's *Dialogue with Trypho* (chs. 41; 70; 117). There we find the eucharistic bread and cup identified with the pure sacrifice spoken of by Malachi. The Eucharist, enjoined by Christ and offered by Christians throughout the world, is the means of offering God thanks for creation and redemption and is a memorial (*anamnesis*)[1] of the passion (or of the incarnation and passion). Therefore the eucharistic prayer familiar to Justin would have included thanks for creation and redemption and an offering of bread and wine as a memorial of the passion. No doubt the structure of the prayer would have followed closely the pattern provided by Jewish benedictions.

From his two accounts we can list the ingredients of the liturgy known to Justin:

[2] See pp. 16, 49, 154.

1. Readings and sermon (displaced by baptism in the first account). The lector reads from the OT and from the Gospels for as long as time permits and the President delivers a homily.
2. Common Prayer, which would no doubt have included prayer for the Emperor and secular authorities, is recited standing. The kiss of peace, regarded as a seal of prayer, follows.
3. Bread and cup are brought to the President. The cup contains wine mixed with water; in the first account a further cup is mentioned containing water only, probably a peculiarity of the baptismal Eucharist.
4. Eucharistic prayer and Amen.
5. Distribution of the Eucharist by deacons to those present and to those absent.
(6. Collection.)

Items 1 and 2 were probably modelled on synagogue worship. The President of the whole service would have been the bishop (cf. 1 *Clem.*, 44, where the bishop's office is to 'offer the gifts'). A striking feature of Justin's accounts is his stress on the communal nature of the Eucharist and, in particular, on the significance of the Amen as expressing the whole people's participation in and assent to the eucharistic prayer.

Although he is as clear as Justin that the eucharistic elements become the Body and Blood of Christ, Irenaeus stresses that the Eucharist is an offering to God of the first fruits of creation, the oblation of the New Covenant. 'We are bound, therefore, to offer to God the first fruits of his creation, as Moses also says, "You shall not appear in the presence of the Lord your God empty"' (*AH* 4.18.1; cf. 4.18.4). Thus he opposed the views of gnostic contemporaries who held that matter is inherently evil.

Because of their wariness in using the good things of creation, gnostic groups often seem to have received communion in bread alone (e.g. *Acts of John*, 85; 109; *Acts of Thomas*, 27; 29; 49f; 133; these texts are available in Hennecke, *N.T. Apocrypha* II (ET Lutterworth Press 1965)); the cup associated with the bread was often a cup of water (*Acts of Thomas*, 120; *Acts of Paul*, (Hennecke) p. 372; *Acts of Peter*, ibid. p. 280).

3 The *Apostolic Tradition* of Hippolytus

PETER G. COBB

For texts and studies of the *Ap. Trad.* see pp. 57–9. In addition:

Connolly, R. H., *JTS* 39 (1938), pp. 350–69.
Botte, B., *RTAM* 14 (1947), pp. 241–51.
Botte, B., *LMD* 35 (1953), pp. 9–23.
Botte, B., *RTAM* 33 (1966), pp. 177–86.
Botte, B., *Didaskalia*, 2 (1972), pp. 221–33.
Bouyer, L., *Eucharist*, pp. 158–82.
Ratcliff, E. C., *LS* pp. 18–40=*JEH* 1 (1950), pp. 29–36, 125–34.
Richardson, R. D., Supplementary Essay to H. Lietzmann, *Mass and Lord's Supper*, pp. 434–9.

It is obvious from the discussion above (pp. 57–9) that there are many problems connected with the original milieu, the authorship, and integrity of the text usually known as the *Apostolic Tradition* of St Hippolytus. Still, the text as it stands contains one of the earliest complete eucharistic prayers that we possess, if not the very earliest; its date and its influence on later liturgies, both Eastern and Western, give it the utmost importance in the study of liturgy.[1]

The following is a somewhat literal translation of Botte's reconstruction of the text:

BISHOP: The Lord be with you.
PEOPLE: And with your spirit.
BISHOP: Let us lift up our hearts.
PEOPLE: We lift them up to the Lord.
BISHOP: Let us give thanks to the Lord.
PEOPLE: It is right and proper.
BISHOP: We give thanks to you, O God, through your beloved Child Jesus
Christ whom you have sent us in these last days as Saviour,
Redeemer and Messenger of your plan;
who is your inseparable Word,
through whom you have created all things;
and whom, in your good pleasure, you have sent down from heaven
into the womb of a virgin;
and who, having been conceived, became incarnate and was shown
to be your son, born of the Holy Spirit and the Virgin;
who fulfilling your will and acquiring for you a holy people,
stretched out his hands as he suffered to free from suffering those
who trust in you;

[1] See pp. xliv–li of Dix's edition.

who, when he was handed over to voluntary suffering,

in order to destroy death and to break the chains of the devil,

to tread down hell beneath his feet, to bring out the righteous into light,

to set the term[1] and to manifest the resurrection,

taking bread, gave thanks to you and said,

Take, eat; this is my Body which is broken for you;

likewise the cup, saying,

This is my Blood which is shed for you.

When you do this, do it in memory of me.

Mindful, therefore, of his death and resurrection,

we offer you this bread and this cup,

giving thanks to you for accounting us worthy to stand before you and to minister to you as priests.

And we ask you to send your Holy Spirit upon the offering of holy Church.

In gathering [them] together grant to all those who share in your holy [mysteries] [so to partake] that they may be filled with the Holy Spirit for the strengthening of their faith in truth; in order that we may praise you and glorify you through your Child Jesus Christ, through whom be to you glory and honour with the Holy Spirit in holy Church now and throughout all ages. Amen.

The eucharistic prayer is a model, a pattern, for use by a newly consecrated bishop when he concelebrates with his presbyters (4.1–2). The author expressly states that a bishop has the right to pray extempore, although his caveat that the prayer should be orthodox indicates that it was becoming stereotyped (10.3–5).

It opens with the dialogue which has become traditional in the West (see below p. 190, n.6). The bishop then takes up his own last words, giving thanks to God for the work of Christ. This whole section undoubtedly dates from the time of Hippolytus as its terms can largely be parallelled in the *Epistle of Barnabas* and in the works of Irenaeus (see R. H. Connolly, art. cit., and E. C. Ratcliff in *The Study of Theology*, ed. K. E. Kirk (Hodder and Stoughton 1939), pp. 422ff). Its Christology is primitive, too: Christ is referred to as Logos, as Child/Servant and as Angel of Counsel. What is particularly noteworthy is the absence of the Sanctus, and of a thanksgiving for creation, which Justin and Irenaeus both state was part of the substance of the prayer known to them. The brief reference to creation—'through whom you have created all things'—in words which occur in the long thanksgiving for creation in *Ap. Const.* Book 8, which is based on the *Ap. Trad.*, has led some scholars

---

[1] Botte suggests 'to fix the rule [of faith]' but the phrase probably means 'to set a term [to the detention of the souls in hell]'.

to suppose that there was originally a whole section on creation at the beginning of the prayer, which had been omitted by the middle of the fourth century (the presumed date of the form in which we have the text).

The Institution Narrative is an integral part of the Christological thanksgiving. The way it is linked to what precedes is unique in that it is the last of a whole series of dependent clauses—'We give thanks to you . . . through . . . Christ whom . . . you have sent . . . who is your Word . . . who . . . in order to destroy death . . . taking bread gave thanks to you and said "Take, eat . . ."' Very probably the narrative was originally briefer. (See W. E. Pitt, 'The Anamneses and Institution Narrative in the Liturgy of *Apostolic Constitutions* Book 8', *JEH* 9 (1958), pp. 1–7.)

The prayer then goes on to the prototypal anamnesis-oblation paragraph. The mysteries recalled are only two, Christ's death (*mors* not *passio* as in Ambrose, *De Sac.* 4.27 and in the Gelasian Canon) and resurrection. The second main verb of the whole prayer is the 'we offer' of this passage, but it is followed by a dependent thanksgiving for the priesthood of the Church, one of the three themes of thanksgiving mentioned by Justin (1 *Apol.* 65; *Dial.*, 116f) and it has been suggested,[1] plausibly in view of the eucharistic nature of the prayer in the writings of the early Fathers (see also *Ap. Trad.* 23.1), that originally in the Roman tradition 'thank' was the main verb and 'offer' the dependent participle. Be that as it may, the idea that the Eucharist is a spiritual sacrifice, the pure sacrifice of Mal. 1.11, had already been expressed in terms of offering in Justin (*Dial.* 41) and it is explicit in the anamneses of all classical liturgies, East and West, with the single exception of Addai and Mari. (See B. Botte, 'Problèmes de l'anamnèse', *JEH* 5 (1954), pp. 16–24.)

The text as it stands in its mid-fourth-century form, however different it may have been originally, then continues with an epiclesis or petition for the descent of the Holy Spirit into the oblation and for the fruits of communion and a doxology. Dix believed that the petition for the descent of the Holy Spirit should be excised on textual as well as historico-liturgical grounds, but Botte has shown that his textual argument is ill-founded. Ratcliff, in a masterly article in *JEH* 1950, whilst tacitly accepting Botte's demonstration, nevertheless wishes to remove the whole of this last section. He agrees with Dix's other argument that an epiclesis accords ill with what is known of Hippolytus' theology and would have been anachronistic at the beginning of the third century, and puts forward his much disputed but not disproven hypothesis that the prayer originally culminated in the Sanctus. Meanwhile it must be

[1] G. A. Michell, *Eucharistic Consecration in the Primitive Church* (SPCK 1948), p. 12, n. 12.

pointed out that the epiclesis as it stands is very similar to the epiclesis in Addai and Mari; it is not a consecratory epiclesis as in *Ap. Const.* Book 8 (*PEER* 13) but rather a prayer for the unity of the Church and the fruits of communion: and that to remove it from Hippolytus' prayer would rob us of an intelligible basis for the development not only of the epiclesis but also of intercessions within the Canon which are such a marked feature of later Eastern liturgies in particular.

In the *Ap. Trad.*, the eucharistic prayer is still the only prayer in the liturgy of the faithful. There is no mention of the Lord's Prayer as a communion devotion or of a post-communion prayer. The text as we have it does give some words of administration: 'The bread of heaven in Christ Jesus'. 'Amen' (23.5) but these are almost certainly not contemporary with Hippolytus. It is more likely that the formula used in his time was that implied as in use in mid-third-century Rome by Eusebius (*HE* 6. 43.18f; cf. Tertullian, *De Spec.* 25) and witnessed by Ambrose (*De Sac.* 4.25; *AIR*, p. 138) at the end of the next: 'The Body of Christ'. 'Amen'. It is significant that they appear in the so-called *Canons of Hippolytus* (ed. R. Coquin, PO 31.385).

4 The Anaphora of Addai and Mari

PETER G. COBB

Text

Macomber, W. F., *OCP* 32 (1966), pp. 335–71.
ET in *PEER* 6.

Studies

Botte, B., *OCP* 15 (1949), pp. 259–76.
Botte, B., *Sacris Erudiri*, 6 (1954), pp. 48–72.
Botte, B., *L'Orient Syrien*, 10 (1965), pp. 89–106.
Bouyer, L., *Eucharist*, pp. 146–58.
Cutrone, E. J., *Theological Studies*, 34 (1973), pp. 624–42.
Engberding, H., *OC* 41 (1957), pp. 102–24.
Macomber, W. F., *OCP* 37 (1971), pp. 55–84.
Raes, A., *Orientalia Christiana Analecta*, 186 (1970), pp. 1–8.
Ratcliff, E. C., *LS* pp. 80–90=*JTS* 30 (1928), pp. 23–32.
Ratcliff, E. C., *LS* pp. 66–79=*Biblical and Patristic Studies in Memory of R. P. Casey*, ed. J. N. Birdsall and R. W. Thomson (Freiburg-in-Breisgau 1963), pp. 235–49.

Richardson, R. D., Supplementary Essay to H. Lietzmann, (ET) *The Mass and the Lord's Supper*, pp. 445–69.
Vellian, J., *Le Muséon*, 85 (1972), pp. 201–23.

In recent years there has been growing interest in the East Syrian anaphora named after Addai and Mari, the traditional founders of the Church of Edessa, an interest stimulated by the recent discovery by William Macomber of a MS some five centuries older than the sixteenth-century version used hitherto. The importance of the anaphora lies in the fact that imbedded in it there is to be found the eucharistic prayer of the ancient Church of Edessa, whose position outside the Roman Empire ensured its relative detachment from developments in Greek-speaking Christendom although it also contributed to its becoming schismatic and Nestorian. However, what the MSS contain is probably an original text modified in the light of the *Catechetical Homilies* of Theodore of Mopsuestia (see p. 64) and also the Nestorian anaphora attributed to him (probably mid-sixth century in its present form), the Liturgical Homilies of Narsai (d. 502), and the Maronite anaphora of St Peter III. Some light is thrown on it too by various early Gnostic prayers. (See G. A. Michell, *Eucharistic Consecration in the Primitive Church* (SPCK 1948), pp. 22–5.)

The anaphora consists of an opening dialogue, preface, thanksgiving for the incarnation and redemption, commemoration of the 'fathers, who have been pleasing in your sight in the commemoration of the Body and Blood of your Christ, which we offer upon the pure and holy altar according as you have taught us'. Then, after intercessions for peace and that all men may know the Father and that he sent the Son, this central paragraph occurs:

> And we also, Lord, your lowly, weak and miserable servants, who have gathered and stand before you, and have received through tradition the form which is from you, rejoicing, glorifying, exalting, commemorating and celebrating this great mystery of the passion, death, and resurrection of our Lord Jesus Christ . . . .

Next comes an epiclesis of the Holy Spirit on the oblation, and a final prayer of thanksgiving.

The problems connected with this anaphora are manifold. The text is clearly corrupt in places; there is no main verb in the central paragraph, for example. It has also clearly been edited; the prayer is addressed to the Trinity at the beginning and to the Father at the end, but another paragraph is addressed to Christ, whilst the central paragraph vacillates between the Father and the Son. This led Ratcliff, followed by Dix and most other writers, to postulate that the whole prayer was originally addressed to Christ, but Botte thinks that it was originally Monarchian, which would make it very primitive, perhaps as early as the first half of the third century. Certain features of it are unique: the absence of an Institution Narrative[1] and the position of the intercessions.

Almost all commentators follow Ratcliff in supposing that the Sanctus is an interpolation but there is disagreement about the intercessions. Ratcliff and Dix want to excise them altogether; Engberding thinks they were borrowed from the anaphora of Theodore, whilst Botte holds that they are a more primitive form of those found there. Botte also believes that Theodore has preserved their original position, between the anamnesis and epiclesis (see art. cit. in *Sacris Erudiri*, 1954).

The central paragraph has caused the most speculation: Botte, following Lietzmann and supported by Bouyer, holds that it is an anamnesis, dependent on a peculiar East Syrian form of the Institution Narrative including the words 'Do this as my memorial *when you are gathered together* (in my name)' and he consequently adds such an Institution Narrative in his reconstruction of the text;[2] Engberding thinks that it is a continuation of the intercessions and Raes suggests that it is an introduction to the epiclesis which follows. Dix, Raes, and Richardson see no necessity for an Institution Narrative, or for any more explicit reference to the Last Supper than the phrase 'have received by tradition the example that comes from you'.

The epiclesis is also the centre of a controversy. Ratcliff argues that it is an addition to bring *Addai and Mari* into line with Greek ways of thought; but noting that it is of the same type as that in *Ap. Trad.*, not a consecratory epiclesis but rather a prayer for the fruits of communion, he suggests that it was originally a communion devotion, only later incorporated into the anaphora itself. Botte has come very close to this position: he stresses that the epiclesis is archaic in type and Semitic in style, but agrees that it is a secondary element which has been introduced clumsily into a prayer whose unity it breaks. Dix surprisingly thinks that it is an integral part of the text.

The final paragraph, according to Ratcliff and Botte, follows on from the central paragraph. It is a suitable enough ending to the prayer, but Ratcliff, in his article of 1963, suggested that originally *Addai and Mari*

---

[1] It is also absent from another fragmentary East Syrian anaphora edited by R. H. Connolly in *OC Neue Serie* 12–14 (1925), pp. 99–128.

[2] Botte's argument was thought by many to be conclusive, but Cutrone points out that the omission of the words 'in my name' from the recently discovered MS considerably weakens it. Macomber, however, is inclined to accept that there was originally an Institution Narrative in the prayer and believes that the Maronite version witnesses both to its original position (after the commemoration of the dead in the intercessions) and to the substance of its contents.

culminated, like the *Ap. Trad.*, in the singing of the Sanctus. Richardson, however, has criticized this thesis very severely.

5 The Liturgy of the Word in the Early Church

PETER G. COBB

GENERAL

Amiot, F., *History of the Mass*, (ET). 2nd edn 1963 (Faith & Fact Books 109).
Botte, B., *et al.*, *La parole dans la liturgie*. Paris 1970.
Denis-Boulet, N. M., 'Analysis of the Rites and Prayers of the Mass' in *The Church at Prayer. Vol. 2 The Eucharist*, ed. A. G. Martimort (ET Irish University Press 1973), pp. 73–193.
Capelle, B., *Travaux liturgiques de doctrine et d'histoire*, Louvain 1955–67 = *TL*.
Eisenhofer, L. and Lechner, J., *The Liturgy of the Roman Rite* (ET Herder-Nelson 1961), pp. 271–334.
Kucharek, C., *The Byzantine-Slav Liturgy of St John Chrysostom*. Allendale, Canada, 1971.
Mateos, J., *La célébration de la parole dans la liturgie byzantine (OCA 191)*. Rome 1971.
Michell, G. A., *Landmarks in Liturgy*. DLT 1961.

THE INTROIT

Callewaert, C., 'Introitus', *EL* 52 (1938), pp. 484–9.
Leclercq, H., 'Introit' in *DACL*, 7.1212–20.

THE KYRIES

Bishop, E., 'Kyrie Eleison: a Liturgical Consultation' in *Liturgica Historia* (1918), pp. 116–36.
Callewaert, C., 'Les étapes de l'histoire du Kyrie', *RHE* 38 (1942), pp. 20–45.
Capelle, B., 'Le Kyrie de la messe et le pape Gélase', *R Bén.* 46 (1934), pp. 126–44 = *TL* 2, pp. 116–34.

THE GLORIA IN EXCELSIS

Blume, C., 'Der Engelhymnus Gloria in Excelsis Deo' in *Stimmen aus Maria-Laach*, 73 (1907), pp. 43–62.
Capelle, B., 'Le texte du Gloria in excelsis Deo' in *RHE* 44 (1949), pp. 439–57 = *TL* 2, pp. 176–91.
Maranget, P., 'Le Gloria in excelsis', *Cours et conférences des semaines liturgiques*, 6 (1927), Louvain.
Stapelmann, W., *Der Hymnus angelicus. Geschichte und Erklärung des Gloria*, Heidelberg 1948.

The Eucharist

THE COLLECT

Bruylants, B., *Les oraisons du missel romain, texte et histoire*. 2 vols., Louvain 1952 (*EL* 1).

Capelle, B., 'Collecta', *R Bén.*, 42 (1930), pp. 197–204 = *TL* 2, pp. 192–9.

Casel, O., 'Beiträge zu römischen Orationen', *JLW* 11 (1931), pp. 35–45.

Kiesling, C., *Before His Majesty—A Study of the Spiritual Doctrine of the Orations of the Roman Missal*. River Forest, Ill. 1965.

Willis, G. G., *Further Essays in Early Roman Liturgy*, AC 50 (1968), pp. 103–21.

THE READINGS

Texts

Burkitt, F. C., 'The Early Syriac Lectionary System', *PBA* 10 (1921–3), pp. 301–38.

Conybeare, F. C., *Rituale Armenorum* (Clarendon Press 1905), pp. 507–27.

Garitte, G., *Le calendrier palestineo-géorgien du Sinaiticus 34*. Brussels 1958.

Dold, A., *Das älteste Liturgiebuch der lateinischen Kirche. Ein altgallikanisches Lektionar des 5–6 Jhs.* (*Texte und Arbeiten* 26–8). Beuron 1936.

Morin, G., 'Le plus ancien "Comes" ou lectionnaire de l'Eglise romaine', *R Bén.* 27 (1910), pp. 41–74.

Perez de Urbel, J. and Gonzalez y Ruiz-Zorrilla, A., ed., *Liber Commicus* (*Monumenta Hispaniae Sacra, Series Liturgica*, 2, 3). Madrid 1950–5.

Renoux, A., *Le codex arménien Jérusalem 121*, PO 35.1, 36.2.

Salmon, P., ed., *Le lectionnaire de Luxeuil* (*Collectanea Biblica Latina*, 7 and 9). Rome 1944, 1953.

Tarchnischvili, M., *Le grand lectionnaire de l'Eglise de Jérusalem (5–8e siècles)*. 2 vols., Louvain 1959, 1960, CSCO 188–9, 204–5.

Studies

Baumstark, A., *Comparative Liturgy*, pp. 120–9.

Capelle, B., 'Note sur le lectionnaire romain de la messe avant S. Grégoire', *RHE* 34 (1938), pp. 556–9 = *TL* 2, pp. 200–3.

Chavasse, A., 'Les plus anciens types du lectionnaire et de l'antiphonaire romains de la messe', *R Bén.* 62 (1952), pp. 3–94.

Dubois, R., 'Hatte die römische Messe je eine dreigliedrige Leseordnung?' *Heiliger Dienst*, Salzburg, 18 (1964), pp. 129–37.

Frere, W. H., *Studies in Early Roman Liturgy. The Roman Gospel Lectionary*, AC 30, 1934; *The Roman Epistle Lectionary*, AC 32, 1935.

Godu, G., 'Epîtres', 'Evangiles', *DACL* 5.245–344, 852–923.

Gy, P. M., 'La question du système des lectures de la liturgie byzantine', *Miscellanea liturgica in onore di Giacomo Lercaro* (vol. 2 Rome 1967), pp. 251–61.

Lamb, J. A., 'The Place of the Bible in the Liturgy', in *The Cambridge History of the Bible*, vol. 1, ed. P. R. Ackroyd and C. F. Evans (CUP 1970), pp. 563–86.

Rahlfs, O. G. A., *Die alttestamentlichen Lektionen der griechischen Kirche*. Göttingen 1915.

van Dijk, S. J. P., 'The Bible in Liturgical Use', in *The Cambridge History of the Bible*, vol. 2, ed. G. W. H. Lampe (1969), pp. 220–51.
Willis, G. G., *St Augustine's Lectionary*, AC 44, 1962.

CHANTS BETWEEN THE READINGS

Froger, J., 'L'Alleluja dans l'usage romain et la réforme de saint Grégoire', *EL* 62 (1948), pp. 6–48.
Gelineau, J., *Antiphona. Recherches sur les formes liturgiques de la psalmodie aux premiers siècles.* Paris 1968.
Lamb, J. A., *The Psalms in Christian Worship.* Faith Press 1962.
Martimort, A. G., 'Origine et signification de l'alleluia de la messe romaine', *Kyriakon, Festschrift J. Quasten 2* (Münster 1970), pp. 811–34.

THE SERMON

Olivar, A., 'Quelques remarques historiques sur la prédication comme action liturgique dans l'église ancienne', *Mélanges liturgiques offerts au R.P. Dom B. Botte O.S.B.* (Louvain 1970), pp. 429–43.

THE CREED

Capelle, B., 'Alcuin et l'histoire du symbole de la messe', *RTAM* 6 (1934), pp. 249–60 = *TL* 2, pp. 211–21.
Capelle, B., 'L'introduction du symbole à la messe', *Mélanges J. de Ghellinck*, 2 (Louvain 1951), pp. 1003–27 = *TL* 3, pp. 60–81.

THE DISMISSAL OF THE CATECHUMENS

Borella, P., 'La "missa" o "Dismissio catechumenorum" nelle liturgie occidentali', *EL* 53 (1939), pp. 60–110.

THE PRAYERS OF THE FAITHFUL

Baumstark, A., *Comparative Liturgy*, pp. 71–80.
Connolly, R. H., 'Liturgical Prayers of Intercession', *JTS* 21 (1920), pp. 219–32.
Grisbrooke, W. J., 'Intercession at the Eucharist', *SL* 4 (1965), pp. 129–42.
Molin, J. B., 'L'Oratio Communis Fidelium au moyen âge en occident du Xe au XVe siècle', *Miscellanea Liturgica in onore di Giacomo Lercaro*, vol. 2 (Rome 1967), pp. 313–468.
Willis, G. G., 'The Solemn Prayers of Good Friday', in *Essays in Early Roman Liturgy*, AC 46 (1964), pp. 1–48.

From the earliest descriptions of the Eucharist, it is clear that it could be divided into two parts, either of which might on occasion be held independently, or in a different church-building from the other (Justin, 1 *Apol.* 65; *Ap. Trad.* 4; *Egeria* 27.6; Augustine, *Serm.* 325.2, PL 38.1448; Socrates, *HE* 5.22, PG 67.640). The first part is derived from the synagogue reading and prayer service and the second from the Lord's words and actions at the Last Supper. These two parts are usually called the 'Mass of the Catechumens' and the 'Mass of the Faithful' although the terms were not actually used in this way until the eleventh century (Jungmann, *MRR*, 1, 261, n. 1). The oldest terms known are those used by Tertullian: the Ministry of the Word and the Offering of the Sacrifice ('aut sacrificium offertur aut Dei verbum administratur'. *De cultu fem.* 2.11).

Until the end of the fourth century, in both East and West, the service formally began, after a call to order by the bishop or deacon, with the reading of the lessons (Augustine, *De civ. dei* 22.8; *Ap. Const.* 8.5.11).

INTRODUCTORY MATERIAL

No doubt from the earliest times, Christians had sung, or had had read to them, other material whilst waiting for the whole congregation to assemble (e.g. *Egeria*, 24.8). From the fifth century on, some of this became an invariable part of the structure of the liturgy. It was common for an Office immediately to precede the Eucharist, but other material, some connected with the preparation of the ministers, usually of a penitential character, and some with the preparation of the elements, particularly in the East, was also used. It is impossible to discuss much of this introductory material because of its diversity but in view of the influence of the Roman rite in the West, we shall base our study on the material in that rite.

In the description of the papal stational mass in Ordo Romanus Primus which dates from the late seventh century (see p. 68) the readings are preceded by four distinct items, the Introit, the Kyries, the Gloria, and the Collect. We shall look at each in turn.

The Introit

The purpose of the singing of a psalm at this point was to cover the entrance of the ministers, which at a solemn papal mass in a large basilica would take some time. If the *Liber Pontificalis* (see p. 69) is rightly interpreted, it was introduced by Pope Celestine I (422–32) (*LP* 1.230).

The Kyries

These are the vestigial remains of the Litany introduced into the Roman rite, probably by Pope Gelasius (492–96), in imitation of the East, where the form first appeared in the fourth century (*Ap. Const.* 8.6; *Egeria* 24.5, 6). The original Roman form of this *Deprecatio Gelasii* has in all probability been preserved in a ninth century MS (text in G. G. Willis, *Essays in Early Roman Liturgy* (AC 46, 1964), pp. 22–4), but a letter from Gregory the Great to John of Syracuse in 598 (Registrum vol. 9, Ep. 26,

PL 77.956) reveals that in his time, on weekdays, the petitions were omitted and only the responses used. It was not until the eighth century that this was the practice at all Masses. The responses were first stylized into the familiar nine-fold pattern of three Kyries, three Christes and three Kyries in the Gallican tradition (*OR*.XV n. 16).

The Gloria in Excelsis

This is one of the few surviving *psalmi idiotici*, popular hymns modelled on the psalms and canticles, of which *Phos Hilaron*[1] is another. Two Greek and a Syrian version have come down to us. The oldest Latin text in the seventh-century Antiphonary of Bangor (HBS 1893, fol. 33) is an almost exact translation of the version in the Codex Alexandrinus of the Bible. In the East it was used in the Office, and when introduced into the West, probably by St Hilary (*c*. 315–67), it was sung at Lauds, at any rate in Gaul in the time of St Caesarius (*c*. 470–542). It could therefore be the case that the Gloria in Excelsis is really part of the Morning Office which was commonly celebrated immediately before Mass, but, according to a not improbable tradition, it was first used at the Eucharist by the Pope at the Christmas Midnight Mass and its use was extended to Sundays and feasts by Pope Symmachus (498–514). For several centuries its use at Mass was a privilege confined to bishops.

In the seventh century, a priest could sing it, but only at Easter (*OR* II, p. 116). In Gaul, possibly because of the Gloria's use in the Office, the Benedictus was sung at the Mass after the Kyries in the sixth century (Gregory of Tours, *Hist. Francorum* 8.7 (Penguin Edition 1974, p. 439)).

The Collect

The *oratio prima* of the Roman rite was apparently introduced by Leo I (440–61) or his immediate predecessor. It was not a feature of the liturgy in the time of Celestine I (422–32) (*LP* 1, p. 230) but some extant collects date from that of Leo.[2] The name derives from the Gallican rite: *collectio*, later *collecta*; and refers to the *function* of the prayer, to its collecting or summing up of the people's intercessions, not to the *occasion* of its use, at a collection or gathering of the people before a procession, as was once thought (Willis, Further Essays, p. 106f).

Views differ as to its purpose. Some hold that it is to conclude the entrance procession, and it is indeed of the same liturgical and literary style as the prayer over the offerings and the post-communion prayer (see pp. 190, 194), which were introduced about the same time, and which

[1] See E. R. Smothers, 'Phos Hilaron', *RechSR* 19 (1929), pp. 266–83. Cf. p. 186.
[2] Cf. F. L. Cross, 'Pre-Leonine Elements in the Proper of the Roman Mass', *JTS* 50 (1949), pp. 191–7.

conclude the offertory and communion processions (Jungmann, *MRR*, 1.265–7, 359f. *Public Worship*, pp. 94f). Others hold that it originally concluded the Litany, but its introduction seems to pre-date that of the Litany. Others again hold that it is to introduce the readings and point to a prayer in such a position in the Egyptian and Syrian rites in the late fourth century (Willis, op. cit., p. 112).

The style and form of the collects is, however, peculiarly Roman. They are, in fact, related to the literary and devotional traditions of pagan Rome.[1] The classical collects of the fifth and sixth centuries are 'extremely well-balanced, economical of words and direct' (Willis, op. cit., p. 118). They are written in majestic prose according to the rules of cursus. All are addressed to God the Father in conformity with the primitive tradition enforced by the Council of Hippo in 393 and this remains true of those in the Roman rite until about the year 1000. Originally they were free compositions, and improvisation continued on occasion until at least the sixth century (Augustine, *De cat. rud.*, 9.13, PL 40.320).

Their form consists of:

(i) an address to God;
(ii) a relative or participial clause referring to some attribute or saving act of God;
(iii) the petition;
(iv) the purpose for which we ask;
(v) the conclusion,

although (ii) on occasion and (iv) much more frequently are omitted. The original conclusion was simply 'per Christum Dominum nostrum': all the collects in the Leonine Sacramentary and almost all those in the Gelasian end thus.

The primitive Roman rule was that there should be only one collect at the Eucharist, and this was observed at Rome itself until about the end of the tenth century; but elsewhere in the West the number multiplied, although not usually beyond seven (Amalarius, *Liber Officialis*, Prooemium 2, ed. Hanssens, 2.13).

THE LITURGY OF THE WORD

THE READINGS

The reading of passages from the Scriptures was one of the elements of worship taken over by the Christians from the Jews (Lk. 4.16–21, Acts

---

[1] See C. Mohrmann, 'Le latin liturgique', *LMD* 23 (1950), pp. 5–30.

13.27. See p. 48). As early as Justin's time, readings were a feature of the pre-eucharistic service: 'The memoirs of the apostles or the writings of the prophets are read as long as time permits'. (1 *Apol.*, 67). In the fourth-century Antiochene tradition there were two lessons from the Law and the Prophets (as in the synagogue) followed by one from the Epistles or Acts and finally one from the Gospel (*Ap. Cons.*, 8.5.11), but the use of three lessons, one OT and two NT, was far more common. This was the custom in Gaul and Spain until the seventh century and in the ancient Masses in Milan. It was probably the original practice in Rome (Jungmann, *MRR*, 1.395f, A. Chavasse, *Le sacramentaire gélasien* (Tournai 1958), pp. 190–7) but the third lesson was being dropped in the fourth century. It then became customary to have two NT readings on Sundays and one OT reading and the Gospel on ferial weekdays. The Byzantine liturgy since the seventh century has also had only two readings, but always both from the NT.

Occasionally non-scriptural texts were used.[1] Readings from the Acts of the Martyrs were allowed at Mass on the appropriate feast days by the Third Council of Carthage in 397 and Augustine frequently quotes from them in his sermons (see Willis, *St Augustine's Lectionary*, p. 11 and n. 9). The practice survived longest in the Gallican rite.

It is often held that the Scriptures were read continuously in the early Church, as the books of the Law, although not of the Prophets, were in the synagogue. This seems to be proved by commentaries of the Fathers on the books of the Bible which were originally delivered as sermons, and certainly Egeria's repeated exclamations about the appropriateness of the choice of lesson for the day or occasion in Jerusalem (e.g. 29.2) indicates that she was not used to such selection. Efforts have been made to find traces of this *lectio continua* in later lectionaries of the East (S. Salaville, *An Introduction to the Study of Eastern Liturgies* (Sand 1938), pp. 190–2) and of the West (Jungmann, *MRR*, 1.399ff). However, Willis claims that the selection of readings was originally dependent on the bishop's choice 'which was sometimes exercised with a view to providing schemes of consecutive reading' (op. cit., p. 10). St Augustine's writings provide ample evidence of a bishop's selecting his own readings in the fifth century (op. cit., p. 7). On the other hand, they also indicate that the lessons were fixed for certain great feasts and could not be changed (*Serm.* 232.1, PL 38.1108).

The Eastertide lections were probably the first to be fixed; Acts seems to have been read in both East and West (Augustine, *Serm.* 6 on St John;

[1] See B. de Gaiffier, 'La lecture des actes des martyrs dans la prière liturgique en Occident', *Anal. Boll.*, 72 (1954), pp. 134–66.

John Chrysostom, *Serm.* 1 on Acts, *Cur in Pentecoste Acta legantur*, PG 60.22), and then, during the fourth century, those for the feasts of Christmas, Epiphany, and Ascension Day. Sundays began to acquire fixed lessons in Antioch in Chrysostom's time (*Serm.* 11 on St John, PG 59.77). The period between Pentecost and Advent was the last to have fixed lessons. The choice of readings was determined by various criteria—by their appropriateness for some ceremony in the catechumenate, by some catchword suitable to the season, by the situation of the Roman stational church or the history of their martyrs or by the proximity of the feast of some great saint honoured in Rome (e.g. see Jungmann, *MRR*, 1.402f).

There were no authoritative lectionaries until the mid-fifth century when Venerius, the bishop of Marseilles, had one drawn up for the feast days of the whole year but not, apparently, for ferial days (Gennadius, *De script. eccles.* 79, PL 58.1104). The first complete lectionaries date only from the seventh century.

CHANTS BETWEEN THE READINGS

As early as Tertullian we have evidence of the Christian use of the Psalter in the Ministry of the Word (*de anima*, 9), although it is not until the fourth century that there is clear evidence of psalms being sung responsorially, that is by one cantor with the people repeating a refrain, between the lessons (*Ap. Const.*, 2.57.6; Athanasius, *de fuga*, 24, PG 25.676; Augustine, *Enarr. in ps. 119.1*, PL 37.1596; Chrysostom, *in ps. 117 expos.* 1, PG 55.328). This method was derived from Jewish practice and contrasts with the antiphonal method used for the more recent chants of the Introit, Offertory, and Communion, whereby two choirs sing alternately. Psalm-singing probably became much more important with the disappearance of the *psalmi idiotici* in the third century (see p. 183). At first, and even in the time of St Augustine, the psalm could be regarded as a lesson in itself and not as a mere response (e.g. Augustine, *Serm.* 176, PL 38.950).

The position of the psalm in the Roman rite, as in *Ap. Const.* 2, was between the first two lessons, but this was not the case everywhere. At Hippo, when there were three lessons, the psalm was sung between the last two; there was apparently nothing between the first two (Willis, *St Augustine's Lectionary*, p. 21).

The Alleluia is used in all rites except the Ethiopian and Gallican and always in connection with the Gospel. At Milan it was apparently sung during the Gospel procession but in the Mozarabic rite it was sung after the Gospel. At Rome, in the mid-fifth century, it was used only on Easter Day (Sozomen, *HE* 7.19, PG 67.1476), (although Augustine in Africa knows of it on all Sundays), but by the sixth century it was used throughout Eastertide (John the Deacon, *Epist. ad Senarium* 13, PL 59.406) and Gregory the Great extended its use still further (*Ep. to John of Syracuse*, Registrum Bk. 9.26).

THE SERMON

The homily was one of the constituent parts of the liturgy from the earliest times, being one of the elements inherited from Judaism (Acts 13.15; Justin 1 *Apol.*, 67). Its essential function was to expound and explain the Scriptures which had just been read.

It was the duty of the bishop, the privilege of a priest, to preach in the liturgy. By the fourth century it had become the general practice in the East that all priests present who wished to do so should preach and, after them, the bishop himself (*Ap. Const.*, 2.57.9; *Egeria* 25.1). In the West the danger of heresy led to priests being forbidden to preach (Socrates, *HE*, 5.22, PG 67.640; Sozomen, *HE*, 7.19, PG 67.1476; Celestine I, *Ep.* 21, PL 50.528–30) but exceptions were made, of Augustine when he was a priest, for example. This was acceptable in North Africa and Italy, where dioceses were small, but north of the Alps, where they were large, it was intolerable. In Gaul the Council of Vaison in 529, at the instance of St Caesarius, gave priests the right to preach (Canon 2; Mansi 8.727).

THE CREED

The recitation of the Creed belongs originally and essentially to baptism but in the struggles against the Christological heresies it came to be used in the Eucharist itself. In the Byzantine liturgy it was recited after the Great Entry and was always said, never sung, by the people, usually in the plural form (see p. 212). The custom spread to the West when the Visigoths renounced Arianism at the end of the sixth century, but they recited the Creed before the Lord's Prayer as a preparation for communion. Two centuries later Charlemagne, no doubt advised by Alcuin, introduced the Creed with the addition of the *filioque* clause into the liturgy at Aachen in yet another place, immediately after the Gospel, and from there, under imperial influence, it spread throughout the West and was eventually adopted by Rome itself after the visit of Henry II in 1014 (Berno of Reichenau, PL 142.1060f). In the West it rapidly became the custom for the people to sing the Creed although by the tenth century the clerical choir had arrogated it to itself.

THE DISMISSAL OF THE CATECHUMENS

Originally, it seems that the non-baptized had to leave the Christian assembly before the Prayers and the exchange of the kiss of peace (Justin,

1 *Apol.*, 65; *Ap. Trad.*, 18–19). The earliest practice probably was for them to do this in silence, but by the fourth century the congregation first prayed for them and the president gave them a blessing (Chrysostom, *in 2 Cor. hom.* 2.5, PG 61.399; *Ap. Const.*, 8.6; Sarapion (Funk), 3–4). Later opposite tendencies seem to have been at work: in Gaul and Spain they were evidently sent out before the Gospel, as councils in the fourth and fifth centuries needed to forbid the practice, whilst elsewhere they stayed for part of the Prayers of the Faithful and only having been prayed for and blessed did they depart.

With the disappearance of the catechumenate the formal dismissal of the catechumens was naturally omitted or at least contracted. It was dropped from the Roman rite but continued in Milan, Gaul, Spain, and north Africa and survives in the Byzantine rite to the present day.

THE PRAYERS OF THE FAITHFUL

According to Justin Martyr (1 *Apol.*, 65), whose evidence is corroborated half a century later by Hippolytus (*Ap. Trad.*, 22.5), the first act of the newly baptized was to join in the common prayers of the faithful. Tertullian in north Africa mentions some of the subjects of intercession (*De Orat.*, 29). Until the recent revision, the Roman Solemn Prayers of Good Friday virtually preserved the early form of the intercessions in the West, in which the bishop or priest asked for prayers for the various orders of the Church and for other objects and then, after an interval of silent prayer on their knees, the people were called upon to stand and the bishop or priest said a collect—

President:	Bidding.
Deacon:	'Let us kneel'.
	Silent prayer.
Deacon:	'Arise'.
President:	Collect.

In almost all the Eastern rites the intercession is in the form of a litany which consists of brief biddings sung by the deacon, to each of which the people respond Kyrie Eleison, and a concluding collect sung by the bishop or priest. (For origins see above p. 172.) The litany is usually in the same position as the Roman Solemn Prayers but is often duplicated at the beginning of the liturgy. Pope Gelasius was responsible for substituting a litany for the Solemn Prayers at Rome (see p. 182), but they survived in Gaul at least until the sixth century.

6 The Liturgy of the Faithful in the Fourth and Early Fifth Centuries

E. J. YARNOLD, SJ

Botte, B., *Le canon de la messe romaine*, Louvain 1935.

Brightman, F. E., *LEW*.

Dix, G., *Shape*. (This work contains partial translations of many of the liturgies discussed here.)

Grisbrooke, W. J., 'Anaphora', *DLW* pp. 10–17.

Jungmann, J. A., *MRR*.

Jungmann, J. A., (ET) *The Place of Christ in Liturgical Prayer*.

Klauser, T., *A Short History of the Western Liturgy*.

Lietzmann, H., *Mass and Lord's Supper*.

McKenna, J. H., *Eucharist and Holy Spirit: the eucharistic Epiclesis in 20th-century Theology*. AC Mayhew-McCrimmon 1975.

Srawley, J. H., *The Early History of the Liturgy*. 2nd edn CUP 1947.

Vagaggini, C., (ET) *The Canon of the Mass and Liturgical Reform*. G. Chapman 1967.

Here the exposition, begun in the previous section, is continued from the point after the dismissal of the catechumens and the prayers of the faithful. We shall discuss in turn three main regional types: the Western, the Syrian, and the Egyptian; no such classification, however, is entirely satisfactory.

I THE WESTERN TYPE

The *de Sacramentis* of St Ambrose (see pp. 62–3) contains the earliest Latin text of the central part of the eucharistic prayer. Apart from this we have to rely on secondary sources and fragments (see p. 191, n. 1).

1. The Kiss of Peace should logically come before the offertory, as it was seen to be the reconciliation before offering prescribed in Mt. 5.24 (cf. Justin, 1 *Apol.* 65). By the fifth century however it had become a preliminary to communion at Rome, though some other Western churches kept the old position (cf. Innocent I, *Ep.* 25.4, PL 20.553).

2. The offertory. In the fourth century the practice of earlier times was continued: the bishop 'offered' the gifts 'offered' by the faithful. The people themselves brought their gifts up to the altar, but there is at this time no evidence whether or not there was a formal offertory procession,

or at what point in the Eucharist (or before it) this offering took place.[1] The fact that in some areas it was necessary to forbid the bringing up of offerings apart from those of bread and wine suggests that outside the Eucharist other offerings were made for the poor.[2] St Augustine reminds the newly-baptized that they are themselves identified with the eucharistic offerings on the altar;[3] but more usually the emphasis is on the fact that these are offered in thanksgiving, in propitiation, or on behalf of the dead. The reading of the names of those who had made the offerings, already mentioned in the *Ap. Trad.* (28) outside the Eucharist, is frequently attested in the fourth and fifth centuries, sometimes within the eucharistic rites. This publication of names appears to have taken place originally at its logical place when the gifts were offered; but Western practice, stemming probably from Rome, transferred the reading of the names to the eucharistic prayer itself, where it became a prayer for the offerers, enhanced by its conjunction with the offering of Christ's own sacrifice. By the time of St Augustine (*Retract.* 2.11) an offertory psalm was sung. Pope Innocent I speaks of a prayer of 'commendation' of the offerings, and St Augustine of an '*oratio*' before the Sursum Corda; these may be references to a prayer over the offerings.[4] Ambrose appears to refer to the use of incense at the offertory.[5] There is no Western evidence as early as this for a lavabo-rite at this point in the service.

3. The eucharistic Prayer (*anaphora*) consisting of the following parts:
   (a) A dialogue introducing the Prayer, as in the *Ap. Trad.* 4.3; cf. p. 173.[6]
   (b) The Preface, which introduces the eucharistic Prayer with a

---

[1] Ambrose, *in Ps. 118*, prologue 2; Augustine, *Ep.* 111.8; Council of Elvira (A.D. 305), can. 29 (Mansi 2.10; PL 84.305). Cf. A. Clark, *EL* 64 (1950), pp. 309–44.

[2] Council of Hippo (A.D. 393), can. 23 (Mansi, 3.922; PL 56.426); however, milk and honey for the baptismal Mass and first-fruits of grapes and wheat could be included in the offerings. A fourth- or fifth-century mosaic at Aquileia is generally thought to represent an offertory procession, in which other goods, such as birds, are carried as well as bread and wine; a eucharistic angel is included in the scene (cf. p. 192, and H. Lietzmann, *ZNTW* 20 (1921), pp. 249–52).

[3] 'Vos estis quod accepistis.' 'Panis dominicus facti estis.' (*Serm.* 227 and 229) Cf. *Serm.* 6 (Denis), *Misc. Ag.*, 1.30; PL 46.835.

[4] Innocent, *Ep.* 25.5; Augustine, *Serm.* 227. There is also a possible reference to a prayer over the offerings in Ambrose, *de Sac.* 4.14, if the passage is punctuated to read: 'laus deo, defertur oratio, petitur pro populo . . .'; but see p. 191.

[5] *In Luc.* 1.28.

[6] Cf. Augustine, *Serm.* 227; *Misc. Ag.* 1.31 (PL 46.836); 1.463–4. A form of the dialogue may already have been in existence when St Paul wrote 2 Thess.1.3. It has been suggested that the source of the phrase 'Lift up your hearts' is Lam.3.41. There are also possible echoes of Col. 3.1–2 and Jn. 11.41.

reference to the last words of the dialogue, 'Let us give thanks. . . .' A fourth-century fragment of an Arian polemical work quotes from two such Latin Catholic prefaces; the first begins: 'it is worthy and just for us here and everywhere to give you thanks, holy Lord, almighty God', and the second has a similar beginning. The fact that the fragment quotes two versions suggests that there were already a number of variations.[1]

(c) Sanctus. Already in this period some Eastern liturgies concluded the Preface with the Sanctus (see p. 195), but there is no evidence for this practice in the West until about 400, when it is referred to in connection with Is. 6.3 in a pseudo-Ambrosian work, which states that the acclamation 'Holy, holy, holy' is recited in nearly all the Eastern and several Western churches.[2] The second Preface of the Arian fragment, however, appears to run straight through to the next stage of the anaphora without a Sanctus (*PEER* 20.1). It seems therefore that the use of the Sanctus was in the process of spreading through the West at the beginning of the fifth century.

(d) The commendation of the offerings. The second preface of the Arian fragment contains a prayer of this nature in somewhat harsh Latin: '. . . as we ask your great and compliant mercy to accept this sacrifice, which we offer to you as we stand in the sight of your divine majesty through Jesus Christ our Lord and God. . . .' Innocent I spoke of the commendation of the offerings (*Ep.* 25.5); it may be this prayer rather than an *oratio super oblata*, as suggested above, that he has in mind (see p. 190); the phrase of *de Sac.* 4.14, *defertur oratio*, may have the same reference. At this point in the liturgy the 'offerings' or 'sacrifice' are still apparently considered as the people's offerings rather than Christ's sacrifice.

(e) The Commemorations. Innocent I (*Ep.* 25.5) insisted that the names of those who had made the offerings should be recited after the commendation of the offerings, 'during the sacred mysteries';[3] his

---

[1] The Arian fragment is contained in *Sacramentarium Veronense*, ed. Mohlberg (Rome 1956), p. 202; *PE* 422; PL 13.611–12; C. Vagaggini, *Canon*, pp. 31–2. Vagaggini reconstructs the early Roman canon of A.D. 378–416 from this fragment, the fourth book of Ambrose's *de Sac.* (*PEER* 19; *PE* 421–2), and a Mozarabic *post pridie* (cf. M. Férotin, *Le Liber Mozarabicus Sacramentorum* (Paris 1912), col. 641; *PEER* 20.2; *PE* 428). *PEER* 20 gives another reconstruction.

[2] *Libellus de Spiritu Sancto* (PL 17.1010; ed. Chavoutier, *Sacris Eruditi*, 11 (1960), p. 149). On the date of the *Libellus*, and of the introduction of the Sanctus into the Roman liturgy, see pp. 151–63 and 180–91 of the same article. For another view, see E. C. Ratcliff, 'The Sanctus and the Pattern of the Early Anaphora' in *LS* pp. 18–40=*JEH* I (1950), pp. 29–36, 125–34.

[3] Cf. Jerome, *in Jer.* 2.109 (CC 74.116; PL 24.755–6); *in Ez.* 6.18 (CC 75.238; PL 25.175). Cf. W. J. Grisbrooke, 'Intercession at the Eucharist', *SL* 5 (1966), pp. 20–44.

correspondent was evidently familiar with what was probably the earliest position for the recitation of the names, i.e. during the offertory. St Augustine (*Serm.* 159.1) attests also that at the altar the martyrs were honoured, and prayers offered for the dead.

(f) Epiclesis over the offerings. There is no explicit epiclesis in the *de Sacramentis* or the Arian fragment. Ambrose does, however, speak of an invocation of the Holy Spirit over the oblations in a work of earlier date than the *de Sacramentis* (*de Spir. Sanct.* 3.16), but must be referring either to an earlier stage of development of the Milanese liturgy, or else to the liturgical practice of other churches. There is evidence for the existence of an epiclesis of the Spirit in Africa about the time of Ambrose,[1] and perhaps even in Rome at the time of Pope Gelasius I (492–6) (Thiel, fr. 7). What may correspond to the epiclesis of the Spirit in some Western rites is a prayer to the Father before the institution narrative asking him to make the offering 'approved, spiritual, pleasing, the figure of the Body and Blood of our Lord Jesus Christ'.[2] The same may be true of the Prayer of Offering after the institution narrative ((j) below).

(g) Supper narrative and words of Institution, after which, in the *de Sacramentis*, the people make the acclamation 'Amen' (*de Sac.* 4.25).

(h) Anamnesis: 'therefore we *call to mind* his most glorious passion, his resurrection from hell and his ascension into heaven' (*de Sac.* 4.27).

(j) Prayer of offering: 'we offer you this spotless sacrifice, this spiritual sacrifice, this bloodless sacrifice, this holy bread and chalice of eternal life, and we beseech and pray you to take up this offering by the hands of your angels to your altar on high, just as you were graciously pleased to receive the gift of your just servant Abel, the sacrifice of our father Abraham, and the offering the high priest Melchizedek made to you.' (*de Sac.*, 4.27, see plate 13). Some scholars, noting that the 'Gelasian' canon reads 'angel' in the singular, think the last part of the prayer is an epiclesis in which the angel stands for Christ or the Spirit. But this theory is weakened by the fact that 'angels' appears to be the earlier and the commoner reading.[3]

[1] Optatus of Milevis, *de Schism. Donat.* 6.1. So too, perhaps, Augustine, *de Trin.* 3.4.10.

[2] *De Sac.* 4.21. The Mozarabic prayer referred to above contains similar words. The use of the word 'figure' does not imply that the bread and wine are only empty symbols; figures, types, and antitypes were often thought to contain the reality they symbolized. Cf. p. 207 and *AIR*, pp. 93–4, n. 23; 136–7, n. 44.

[3] Cf. Ambrosiaster, *Qu. vet. ac nov. Test.* 109.21 (CSEL 50; PL 35), where Melchizedek is taken as standing for the Holy Spirit. Cf. Botte's note on the passage in his edition of the *de Sacramentis* for further references; also *AIR*, pp. 139–40, n. 54. Righetti (3.411; plate 62) reproduces a sixth-century mosaic from S. Vitale in Ravenna of angels offering the eucharistic lamb.

4. Communion

(a) The Kiss of Peace. It began to be given at this point rather than at the offertory towards the end of the period we are studying, as Innocent I (*Ep.* 25.4) and Augustine (*Serm.* 227) attest for Rome and Africa respectively.

(b) The fraction, or breaking of the bread. The Western writers of the period do not often mention this rite, for it was still regarded simply as a practical necessity for communion.[1]

(c) The *fermentum* (i.e. leaven). It was the Roman practice by the time of Innocent I (*Ep.* 25.8) that a piece of the bread consecrated at the Pope's Mass was taken round on Sundays to each of the local churches as a sign of unity.

(d) The mixing of a particle of the consecrated bread with the eucharistic wine. This rite came to be called 'consecration', and appears to have been practised at Rome as early as the pontificate of Sixtus II (257–8).[2]

(e) The Lord's Prayer had a place in the liturgy in Africa at least as early as the beginning of the fourth century.[3] The use by several Fathers of the word 'dare' (*tolman, audere*) in connection with the Lord's Prayer, suggests that it was introduced by such a phrase as 'audemus dicere'.[4] However, the liturgical service in question may not have been the Eucharist. St Augustine however was able to say that in nearly every church the prayer was said after the fraction in preparation for communion (*Ep.* 149.16; *Serm.* 17.5); but in the *de Sacramentis* the prayer seems to follow communion and to conclude with a doxology (6.24).[5]

---

[1] 'Ad distribuendum comminuitur', Augustine, *Ep.* 149.16.

[2] St Laurence is said to have protested when the Pope was being taken to martyrdom without his deacon, Laurence himself, 'to whom you entrusted the consecration (*consecrationem*) of the Lord's Blood.' (Ambrose, *de Off.* 1.204; PL 16.84–5).

[3] Cf. Jungmann, *MRR* 2.277, n. 1, quoting Optatus' description of a Donatist service of penance before the altar, during which the Lord's Prayer was recited (*de Schism. Donat.* 2.20; CSEL 26).

[4] Jerome, *adv. Pelag.* 3.15 (PL 23.585); Augustine, *Serm.* 110.5. A phrase of Cyprian's seems to echo the first half of the Roman introduction to the Lord's prayer, *praeceptis salutaribus moniti*: 'inter cetera salutaria sua monita et praecepta divina ... etiam orandi ipse formam dedit' (*de Dominica Oratione* 2; CSEL 3.267; PL 4.537). Cf. Tertullian, *de Or.* 11: 'memoria praeceptorum viam orationibus sternit'. *A priori* one would expect that Christians would wish to include the Lord's Prayer in their celebration of his Supper.

[5] The order of Ambrose's treatment favours this conclusion. (1) 'Quid superest nisi oratio?', he asks after explaining communion (*de Sac.* 5.18). (2) He apparently does not regard the prayer as part of the 'sacraments' (5.17, 24). (3) The prayer certainly comes after the words of institution (5.24). (4) Yet he does not give the straightforward explanation that the phrase 'Give us this day our daily bread' is a request for the grace of communion—presumably because it comes after communion (5.26).

(f) Communion. St Augustine speaks of the communicants receiving at the altar-rails (*cancelli*) (*Serm.* 392.5), though the newly-baptized seem to come right up to the altar (*Serm.* 224.4). According to Ambrose, the bishop says to each communicant, 'The Body of Christ', to which the communicant replies 'Amen' (*de Sac.* 4.25). It appears from a remark of Augustine's (*Contr. ep. Parm.* 2.7.13) that the Bread was received in the joined hands. He also informs us that the custom had recently been introduced at Carthage of having psalms sung by a cantor during the distribution of communion (*Retract.* 2.37(11)).

(g) A blessing, accompanied by a spoken prayer, which the people received with bowed heads. St Augustine's description suggests that this blessing was given before communion.[1]

(h) A post-communion prayer of thanksgiving (*Ep.* 149.16).

II SYRIAN LITURGIES

The fullest liturgical texts are the *Apostolic Constitutions* (*AC*) and the *Testamentum Domini* (*T*). The *AC* in fact contains two accounts of the Eucharist: the first, in Book 2, is a slightly adapted version of the short account contained in the third-century *Didascalia*; the second, in Book 8, is much fuller. The *Mystagogic Catecheses* (*MC*) attributed to Cyril of Jerusalem and the *Catechetical Homilies* (*HC*) of Theodore of Mopsuestia also contain many extracts from current liturgical texts. Other writings also contribute to our knowledge of the rites as practised in this part of the world, especially those of John Chrysostom.[2] From these sources it is apparent that about the end of the fourth century a liturgy of the following type was celebrated in the area around Jerusalem and Antioch, though there were of course local variations, and the pattern was constantly evolving:[3]

[1] Augustine, *Ep.* 149.16; Ambrosiaster, *Qu. vet. ac nov. Test.* 109.3.

[2] See the discussion of Church Orders, pp. 59–60. The *Didascalia* is quoted according to the translation of R. H. Connolly, *Didascalia Apostolorum* (Clarendon Press 1929); the *Testamentum* according to that of J. Cooper and A. J. MacLean (T. and T. Clark 1902), an edition which contains useful notes. *T*'s liturgy is eclectic, and has certain affinities with Egyptian rites, so that some scholars prefer to class it as Egyptian. For a reconstruction of Chrysostom's liturgy (as opposed to the later Byzantine liturgy that bears his name), see Brightman, *LEW* 1.470–81. When quoting from Chrysostom I have for convenience given references to the notes contained in those pages of *LEW*. *PE* contains most of these eucharistic prayers in Greek and in Latin translation: *AC*, Bk. 8: *PE* 82–94; *T*: *PE* 219–22; *HC*: *PE* 214–18; *MC*: *PE* 206–8. *HC* and *MC* are also contained in *AIR* in English translation. *LEW* contains the full text, not only the canon, of *AC* (pp. 3–30) and *MC* (pp. 464–70). *PEER* contains ET of the eucharistic prayers of *AC*, Bk. 8 (*PEER* 13); *HC* (*PEER* 14); *MC* (*PEER* 11).

[3] I am following here Theodore's order, though adding the rites which he does not mention.

1. The bringing of the offerings to the altar. There is no offertory procession of the people as in the West. The people's offerings referred to in *AC* 8.47.2–4 must have been given in, with little formality, before the Mass began; birds and other exotic offerings may not be brought. Now the deacons, with much ceremonial, brought the bread to the altar, spread a cloth, and placed the bread on it (*HC* 15.25–6). *T* lays it down that the altar must be veiled from the congregation; those who have contributed the offerings are present within the veil together with the clergy, widows, etc. According to *T*, the bishop, together with the presbyters, lays hands on the loaves that have been placed on the altar (1.23); after the deacon has called the people to attention, the bishop says aloud over the offerings a prayer of thanksgiving, to which the people reply 'Amen' (*HC* 15.30–3).

2. The Kiss of Peace, introduced by the dialogue: 'Peace be with you'; 'And with thy spirit'.[1]

3. The Lavabo, a sign of the need of purity for the holy acts which are to follow.[2]

4. Commemoration of the living and the dead; their names were read from the 'diptychs', the tablets inscribed with the names of those for whom prayers were offered (*HC* 15.43).

5. Eucharistic Prayer.
    (a) Introductory dialogue, similar to that in the western rite.[3]
    (b) Preface, expressing praise, adoration, and thanksgiving in union with the angels.[4]
    (c) Sanctus: 'Holy, holy, holy . . .', derived from Is. 6.3.[5]
    (d) In *AC* there then follows a prayer extolling God's 'holiness' (8.12. 29–34).
    (e) The Supper-narrative and words of institution are found in *AC*, *T* and Chrysostom. *T* has two peculiarities: first the Lord's command 'Do this' is given in the form 'When ye shall do this, ye make my resurrection'; secondly, the words over the chalice are not recited, and the bishop simply says, 'Also the cup of wine which he mixed he gave for

---

[1] *HC* 15.34–5; 39. *T* 1.23. The position before the offering, as in *AC* 8.11.9, is more logical; cf. p. 189. It is not clear whether the kiss described in *MC* 5.3 comes before or after the placing of the offerings on the altar.

[2] *HC* 15.42; *AC* 8.11.12; *MC* 5.2.

[3] *HC* 16.2–4; *AC* 8.12.4–5; *MC* 5.4–5; *T* 1.23.

[4] *HC* 16.5; *AC* 8.12.6ff; *MC* 5.6; *T* 1.23.

[5] *HC* 16.6; *AC* 8.27; *MC* 5.6. *T* has no Sanctus, but Chrysostom's liturgy has (*LEW*, nn. 20–1). See p. 191.

a type of the Blood which he shed for us'. Cyril and Theodore quote no Supper-narrative or words of institution, but some scholars think that these Fathers' comments suggest that this rite was present in their liturgies. It might be respect for the *disciplina arcani* which led them to omit the words from their published accounts.[1]

(f) Anamnesis. This is contained in *AC* (8.12.38) and *T* (1.23), but there is no mention of it in Theodore, Cyril, or Chrysostom.

(g) The prayer of offering, which is logically connected with the anamnesis, is found in the same sources.

(h) The epiclesis appears to be included in all five sources.[2] Theodore's epiclesis has two distinct parts: the Holy Spirit is called down first on the offerings and then on the assembly. The same two elements, though less clearly separated, are discernible also in *AC* and Chrysostom. *T*'s epiclesis, if it can fairly be described as such, is simply a prayer that the communicants may be made one with God and filled with the Holy Spirit. It has another peculiar feature: whereas in the other four sources God is asked to send down his Spirit, in *T* the whole Trinity is petitioned to make the coming communion fruitful for the recipients. In Theodore the epiclesis is the moment when the risen Christ becomes sacramentally present by the power of the Holy Spirit, who descends on the bread and wine. Chrysostom, however, maintains that it is the speaking of the words of institution which effects this transformation.[3]

(i) Prayers for the living and the dead.[4]

(j) Commemoration of the saints (Cyril, *MC* 5.9).

(k) Doxology and people's response 'Amen'.[5]

7. Communion.

(a) The Lord's Prayer comes at this point in Cyril and Chrysostom; both hint at the formula of introduction, 'We dare to say'.[6]

(b) The fraction is not mentioned by *AC*, *T*, or Cyril, presumably because these sources attached no significance to the rite, regarding it simply as a functional necessity. Chrysostom (*LEW*, n. 29) refers to it

---

[1] *AC* 8.12.35–7; *T* 1.23; Chrysostom, *LEW*, n. 22. *HC* 16.10: 'When he was about to go to meet his passion, he bequeathed this food to his disciples.' *MC* 4.6: 'It is the Body and Blood of Christ according to the Lord's saying.' Cf. the anaphora of Addai and Mari (pp. 176–9).

[2] *HC* 16.11–13; *AC* 8.12.39; *MC* 5.7; *T* 1.23; Chrysostom, *LEW*, n. 23.

[3] Chrysostom, *de prod. Jud.* 1.6 (*LEW*, n. 22; PG 49.380): [the bishop] 'says, "This is my body"; this utterance transforms (*metarruthmizei*) the offerings.' Cf. Ambrose, *de Sac.* 4.14–17.

[4] *HC* 16.14; *AC* 8.12.40–9; *MC* 5.8–10; *T* 1.23; Chrysostom, *LEW*, nn. 25–6.

[5] *AC* 8.12.50–1; *T* 1.23; Chrysostom, *LEW*, n. 27.

[6] *MC* 5.11; Chrysostom, *LEW*, n. 28.

10 Reformed Lord's Supper, with table lengthwise in chancel and minister at its north side (see p. 267)

11 Holy Communion being administered to a child with a spoon by an Orthodox priest

12　Concelebration during the Canon, in a tenth-century German ivory panel

briefly, and contrasts it with the fact that Christ's limbs were not broken on the cross. Theodore, however, describes the rite in detail (after the bread is broken, the bishop makes the sign of the cross with it over the chalice), and gives an elaborate theological explanation, recalling that the Body and Blood were separated on Calvary, and that Christ parcelled himself out, so to speak, to his apostles in the resurrection appearances (*HC* 16.15–20).

(c) The mixing. Theodore alone describes this rite, explaining that it symbolizes the fact that the Body and Blood confer a single grace (*HC* 16.17).

(d) Another set of prayers for the Church: in Theodore, especially for the offerer, in *AC* for the living and the dead, and in commemoration of the saints.[1]

(e) The dialogue before communion. In Theodore (*HC* 16.22–3) it takes the following form:

Bishop: 'Peace be with you'.
People: 'And with thy spirit'.
Deacon: 'Let us attend'.
Bishop: 'What is holy for the holy'.
People: 'One holy Father, one holy Son, one Holy Spirit. Glory be to the Father. . . .'

Cyril (*MC* 5.19) substitutes for the last words the following: 'One is holy, one is Lord, Jesus Christ'. *AC* (8.13.11–13) adds a miniature *Gloria in excelsis* and a Hosanna. Chrysostom gives the detail that the doors (*amphithura*) or curtains (*parapetasmata*) separating the sanctuary from the people are opened and the sacrifice brought out (*LEW*, nn. 29–31).

(f) Communion. The Bread is received in the outstretched hands: the bishop says, 'The Body of Christ', 'The Blood of Christ', to which the people reply 'Amen'. Theodore instructs the communicants to adore the Bread, and to apply it to their eyes and lips before eating it. Cyril tells the people to bow in worship, and to touch their eyes, forehead, and other senses with the wine remaining on their lips.[2]

(g) A psalm is sung during communion. *AC* (8.13.16) and Cyril (*MC* 5.20) specify Ps. 33(34).8: 'Taste and see'; Chrysostom (*LEW*, n. 32) speaks of Ps. 144(145): 'I will extol thee'.

(h) According to *AC*, what is left over after communion is conveyed into the sacristy.[3]

---

[1] *HC* 16.21; *AC* 8.13.1–10; perhaps Chrysostom, *LEW*, n. 29.
[2] *HC* 16.27–8; *AC* 8.13.14–15; *MC* 5.21–2; *T* 1.23.
[3] *AC* 8.13.17. But see 8.31.2, where the *eulogiai* that are left over are distributed later to the clergy. This second text seems to refer to the bread and wine that were offered but not used for the Eucharist. See Funk's note to his edition of the *AC*, p. 533.

(i) Thanksgiving. *AC* (8.14.1—15.9) and *T* (1.23) give a form of thanksgiving (ending with a doxology) said by the bishop after the deacon has spoken a bidding; *HC* (16.29) seems to envisage a silent prayer; Chrysostom (*LEW*, n. 34) refers to 'hymns of thanksgiving'.

(j) A dismissal, 'Go in peace', was spoken by the deacon (*AC* 8.15.10; Chrysostom, *LEW*, n. 35).

III THE EGYPTIAN TYPE

The developed Egyptian liturgy in Greek is known as the Liturgy of St Mark (*PEER* 10); the earliest MSS of it are as late as the twelfth century. The following sources, however, throw light on the earlier stages of the Greek Egyptian liturgy: the fourth- or fifth-century Strasbourg papyrus 254 (*S*), which contains a long section of a eucharistic prayer; the sixth- or seventh-century Dêr Balizeh papyrus (*D-B*); the sixth-century Manchester parchment (*M*); and a Louvain Coptic fragment of a sixth-century eucharistic prayer (*L*). In addition, the *Euchologium* attributed to Sarapion of Thmuis (Sar.) contains a complete anaphora, apparently of the fourth century, which differs in many respects from the other Egyptian versions, but still has enough in common with them to make a joint treatment illuminating. Finally, many facts can be gleaned from the observations of the Fathers of the period.[1]

1. The Kiss of Peace, which, according to Origen, took place after the Intercessions (*LEW*, n. 11).

2. The Offertory, which seems to have had more in common with the Western offertory procession than did the Syrian rite of bringing in the bread and wine already offered by the people. Cyril of Alexandria speaks of the holy vessels in which each brings up (*prosagonton*) the sacrifices (*LEW*, n. 13).

---

[1] See the reconstruction in C. Vagaggini, *Canon*, pp. 67–76. Strasbourg 254: M. Andrieu and P. Collomp, *Rev SR*, 8 (1928), pp. 489–515; the Greek text is on pp. 500–1, and in *PE* 116–8; ET in *PEER* 9a. Dêr-Balizeh: C. H. Roberts and B. Capelle, *Bibliothèque du Muséon*, 23 (1949); *PE* 124–7; ET in *PEER* 9c. The Manchester parchment: C. H. Roberts, *Catalogue of the Greek and Latin Papyri in the John Rylands Library, Manchester*, vol. 3 (1938), pp. 25–8; *PE* 120–3. The Louvain fragment: see the retroversion from Coptic to Greek by L. Lefort, *Muséon*, 53 (1940), p. 24; *PE* 140; ET in *PEER* 9d. For Sarapion: see pp. 60–1, with the warning concerning authenticity; *PE* 128–33, whose numeration I am following here; ET in *PEER* 8; cf. B. Capelle, *Muséon*, 59 (1946), pp. 425–43. For authors of the fourth and fifth centuries, see *LEW*, 1.504–9; my references are to the notes there. G. J. Cuming, *JTS* 25 (1974), pp. 117–24, argues for counting Cyril of Jerusalem's liturgy as Egyptian rather than Syrian.

3. Eucharistic Prayer.

(a) The Preface. Sar. (1) begins with the words 'It is worthy and just'. Presumably therefore it was introduced with the same formula ('Lift up your hearts', etc.) as the other liturgies. Several peculiar features are found in Egyptian Prefaces: first, a prayer of offering (with the verb in the present tense) (*S* r 11–18); secondly, petitions: in Sar. (6–7), a brief prayer for the Spirit; in what remains of *D-B* (II r 1–5), a short, more personal prayer; *S* is much fuller, including prayers for the living and dead, a reading of names from the diptychs and a commemoration of the saints. *S* ends here with a doxology; *D-B* (II r 6–24) and Sar. (8–10) link the Church's praise with that of the angels, and run into a Sanctus. *M* evidently begins immediately after the Sanctus, echoing a phrase from that prayer: 'Heaven and earth are indeed full of your holy glory'—a phrase which was to find a place in the later liturgies of St Mark and the Jacobite Copts (*LEW*, 1.132.11–13; 176.5–7). *L* begins with the last words of the Sanctus, and a similar echoing phrase to that of *M*.

(b) Epiclesis *before* the words of institution. Sar.'s epiclesis (11) is undeveloped, being the simple request that God should fill the sacrifice which the people *have* offered (*prosenenkamen*) with his power and sharing; the act of offering is thus regarded as already completed before the Eucharistic Prayer.[1] In *M* (r 2–4) God is asked to fill the sacrifice with the Holy Spirit, but neither here nor in Sar. is it said explicitly that the result will be to change it into the Body and Blood. *D-B*'s epiclesis has three parts: first, God is asked, 'Fill us too with the glory that comes from you'; secondly, he is asked to send his Holy Spirit on the offerings, and to make the bread Christ's Body and the chalice his Blood; thirdly, in terms that recall the *Didache*, God is besought to gather his Church together as the bread distributed on the mountains became one body, and the wine of the holy vine of David and water from the spotless Lamb were mixed to become one mystery (II r 25–v 11). Sar. has a similar passage at a later point in his eucharistic prayer (13).

(c) An offering-prayer occurs at this point in Sar. (11–12), in which the bishop recalls that 'we have offered to you this living sacrifice, the bloodless offering. . . .' The past tenses should again be noticed. *L* gives a phrase expressing offering (in the present tense) and anamnesis before the epiclesis (*PE* 140.5).

(d) Words of Institution. In Sar., *D-B*, and *M* the words are introduced by the causal particles *hoti* (Sar. 12; *M* r 4) or *gar* (*D-B* II v 12), presumably because the institution explains why the offering is not mere bread and wine, but is the likeness of Christ's Body (Sar.), or to be

---

[1] On the significance of this past tense, see H. Lietzmann, *Mass and Lord's Supper*, pp. 152–60 (186–97 in the German); A. D. Nock, *JTS* 30 (1928–9), pp. 382–4.

filled with the Holy Spirit.[1] Sar. contains two unique features: (i) a prayer of offering and for mercy and unity between the words over the bread and those over the chalice (it is here that he places the prayer derived from the *Didache* referred to under (b)); (ii) there is no command to 'do this', or statement 'as often as you do this . . .' (13). *D-B* adds the words 'drank' after 'he took the cup, blessed'; there is the same insertion in Irenaeus' account of the last Supper (*D-B* II v 22; *AH* 5.33.1).

(e) The Anamnesis is much less explicit in the Egyptian liturgies. Sar. simply has the phrase, 'we too making the likeness of the death'; (13); in *D-B* the Lord's words 'As often as you eat this bread and drink this cup, you proclaim my death and make *anamnesis* of me', are followed at once by the declaration, 'We announce your death, we confess your resurrection' (*D-B* II v 26–31). *M*'s structure seems basically similar (r 16–24).

(f) A prayer of offering, again in the past tense—'we have offered' (*proethekamen* or *prosenenkamen*)—is given in Sar. (13–14) and in the later Liturgies of Mark and the Coptic Jacobites (*LEW*, 1.133.30–1; 178.15–16; *PE* 114.4; 138.3). Sar. indeed gives two prayers of offering, after the institution of the bread and after the institution of the chalice. *D-B* has no prayer of offering here at all, but apparently runs straight into the second epiclesis (II v 32).

(g) Second epiclesis. In *M* God is now asked to send his Spirit on the bread and chalice and to make them become the Body and Blood of Christ, so that the people may enjoy various spiritual gifts, which are spelt out at length (r 25–v 6). *D-B* (II v 32–III r 6) appears to contain an extended epiclesis ending with the prayer that the people may be granted certain gifts of the Spirit. Sar's epiclesis is peculiar, for it is a prayer that God's word may come upon the bread and chalice so that they may become the Body of the Word and the Blood of Truth. (Sar.'s baptismal rite contains an epiclesis of the word over the water: see p. 102.) Sar. alone gives the intercession for the living and dead and the reading of the diptychs at this point, rather than in the typical Egyptian position during the Preface (15–19).

(h) Concluding doxology.[2]

(5) Communion.

(a) and (b). The fraction came between the anaphora and communion (*LEW*, n. 21); at some point the Lord's Prayer was recited (*LEW*, n. 25). Sar. (Funk 14) adds a prayer for purity and wisdom.

---

[1] On the causal particles, see A. D. Nock, op. cit., pp. 385–7.

[2] *M* v 7–9; *D-B* III r 7–8; Sar. 19. Mark: *LEW*, 1.134.26–32; *PE* 114.25–9. Coptic Jacobite: *LEW*, 1.180.7–12; *PE* 139.19–21.

(c) The communion of the clergy, followed by a blessing of the people (Sar., Funk 15).

(d) The announcement 'Holy things for the holy', (*LEW*, n. 26).

(e) Communion. The people came up to the altar and stretched out their hands to receive. It was customary for them to take home some of the Bread for communion during the week (*LEW*, nn. 22, 27).

(f) Sar. (Funk 16) gives a post-communion prayer.

(g) Dismissal (*LEW*, n. 28).

7 The Patristic Theology of the Eucharist

R. J. HALLIBURTON

The student is well advised to begin with J. N. D. Kelly, *Early Christian Doctrines* (5th edn Black 1977), pp. 211–16, 440–55. The earlier studies by D. Stone, *A History of the Doctrine of the Holy Eucharist*, vol. 1 (Longmans 1909); and by C. Gore, *The Body of Christ* (John Murray 1901), contain much valuable material, as does P. Batiffol's *Etudes d'histoire de théologie positive: Ser. 2., L'Eucharistie*, Paris 1905. Cf. also G. Dix, *Shape*, pp. 208–302; M. Goguel, *L'Eucharistie des origines à Justin Martyr* (Paris 1909); J. Betz, *Die Eucharistie in der Zeit der griechischen Väter* (Freiburg 1955 ff); B. Winslow, 'Some leading ideas in the primitive liturgies' in *ECQ* 4 (1940–1), pp. 47–52; W. J. Grisbrooke, 'Anaphora' in *DLW;* and much useful reference in J. Jungmann, *The Place of Christ in Liturgical Prayer*. M. de la Taille's *The Mystery of Faith* (ET Sheed and Ward 1941), is a systematic study of eucharistic doctrine and makes frequent reference to patristic teaching. Articles in: *ERE* (J. Srawley, s.v. 'Eucharist—to the end of the Middle Ages'), *RAC* (F. Hauck, s.v. 'Messe'), and *DTC* (A. Gaudel s.v. 'Messe; le sacrifice de la messe dans l'Eglise latine'). See also bibliography in *ODCC* (2nd edn) s.v.

Another approach is to study the principal themes of the eucharistic prayer. Cf. here on the *Institution Narrative* W. E. Pitt, 'The Anamneses and Institution Narratives in the Liturgy of *Apostolic Constitutions* Book VIII', in *JEH* 9 (1958), pp. 1–7; R. Rios, 'The liturgy and reunion; the words of consecration in the tradition of the eastern churches' in *ECQ* 4 (1940–1), pp. 97–104; S. Salaville, 'La consécration eucharistique d'après quelques auteurs grecs et syriens' in *EO* 13, pp. 321–4. On the *epiclesis*, a vast literature amongst which of note are C. Atchley, *On the Epiclesis of the Eucharistic Liturgy and on the Consecration of the Font* (AC OUP 1935); H. W. Codrington, 'The Heavenly Altar and the Epiclesis in Egypt', in *JTS* 39 (1938), pp. 141–50; G. Dix, 'The Origins of the Epiclesis', in *Theology*, 28 (1936), pp. 125–37 and 187–202; C. Kern, 'En marge de l'épiclèse', in *Irenikon*, 24 (1951), pp. 166–94; C. Kern and H. W.

Codrington, 'The Epiclesis', in *ECQ* 9 (1951–2), pp. 198–205; J. H. McKenna, *Eucharist and Holy Spirit* (AC Mayhew-McCrimmon 1975); G. A. Michell, 'Firmilian and Eucharistic Consecration', in *JTS* 5 (1954), pp. 215–20; C. C. Richardson, 'The origin of the epiclesis' in *Anglican Theological Review* (1946), pp. 148–53; B. Botte, 'L'épiclèse de l'anaphore d'Hippolyte' in *RTAM* 14 (1947), pp. 241–51. On the *anamnesis*, O. Casel, *Das Gedächtnis des Herrn in der altchristlichen Liturgie* (Ecclesia Orans, 2), (Freiburg 1918).

Most histories of the liturgy are concerned with theology as well as rite and should be consulted together with the above.

A comparative shortage of texts, a variety of theological and liturgical emphases in different areas and in different periods, and a steadily developing theology together make the task of reconstructing a portrait of the patristic Eucharist both complex and formidable. Further, it should be remembered that the Fathers will not always yield to the questions we ask them out of our own preoccupations in eucharistic theology today, but serve us best in being allowed to express their own eucharistic faith in their own terms. Despite this, however, it is clearly possible to trace certain lines of development in the patristic theology of the Eucharist which will at least afford the outlines of a portrait; nor shall we in this commit the Fathers to a uniformity which they would not own, though we shall nonetheless be able to discern their common faith in the one Christ of the eucharistic mystery.

1 EUCHARIST AND CHURCH

From the earliest times, the Eucharist has been a public and not a private affair, the assembly of the people of God and not the private devotion of a series of individuals.[1] In the Epistle to the Hebrews (10.25), Christians are warned not to 'forsake the assembling of (themselves) together'.[2] The account of the Eucharist at Corinth (1 Cor. 11.17ff) clearly envisages a corporate act of the local church, and Ignatius of Antioch similarly exhorts Christians to take care to assemble more frequently to give thanks (*eucharistein*) and praise to God.[3] For Ignatius, the Eucharist is a sign of the unity of the people of God—there is one Eucharist as there is one flesh of our Lord Jesus Christ, one Church, one bishop, one altar.[4] In the *Didache* too (in a passage which may refer to the Eucharist), Christians pray that the bread now broken and 'scattered upon the mountains'

---

[1] Cf. L. Bouyer, *Life and Liturgy*, ch. 3. on Jewish Qahal and Christian Ecclesia.
[2] Which may, in view of the reference to 'the day drawing nigh', have a eucharistic association. Cf. A. Snell, *A New and Living Way* (SPCK 1959), p. 130.
[3] *Eph.* 13.1.
[4] *Phil.* 1.4; cf. *Mag.* 7, *Smyrn.* 8.2.

(referring to the scattering of Israel, cf. Nah. 3.18) may be reassembled and reunited into one;[1] and for Augustine, Christians are to see in the many grains, ground by the prayers of exorcism, moistened by the waters of baptism and now united in the one eucharistic loaf, the image of themselves as the Body of Christ, the Church.[2] For many of the Fathers, the eucharistic assembly is thus an image of the Church, the people of God assembled with their Head both receiving and awaiting their final redemption. Hence it is but natural that disunity among Christians (the formation of parties or sects) should have as one of its first signs the establishment of a separate altar with a separate bishop[3] and that the reunion of Christians after schism (or with due penance performed after lapsing) should be symbolized by the invitation to share in one another's Eucharist[4] or, in the case of the penitents, to return to the sacraments.[5]

2 THE EUCHARIST AND REDEMPTION

For the Fathers, salvation lay within the Church; in fact no sure salvation could be found outside. It is understandable, therefore, that at the heart of patristic ecclesial life (in the central prayer of the Eucharist) should be found the solemn thanksgiving for (commemoration of) God's redeeming action in Christ (and in the world before Christ's coming), an action through which, moreover, the Christian community both apprehended and experienced the continuing benefits of God's redeeming love, once and for all shown and effected in the life and passion, death, and resurrection of Christ. *Thanksgiving* (*eucharistia*) and *commemoration* (or memorial, *anamnesis*) are terms which must be examined and understood in the peculiar context of their times; each is closely associated with the notion of *sacrifice*.

(a) *Thanksgiving*

The association between the Christian Eucharist and Jewish forms of thanksgiving (in particular Passover thanksgivings) has already been discussed.[6] In the patristic period, the term *eucharistia* is used to denote either the action of the president in reciting the eucharistic prayer (with its themes of thanksgiving for God's work in creation and redemption), or for the service as a whole, or to describe the consecrated species. Justin

---

[1] *Did.* 9.1.
[2] *Serm.* 262.
[3] Cf. Gregory of Nyssa, *Ep. 3 ad Eustathium.*
[4] Cf. Irenaeus in Eusebius, *HE* 5.24.
[5] Cyprian, *De lapsis, passim.*
[6] pp. 49, 154.

Martyr, for example, relates that the president of the Eucharist *gives thanks* 'at considerable length';[1] for Ignatius, the only term he knows to describe the liturgical assembly is the 'eucharistia';[2] and for the ante-Nicene Church in particular, *eucharistia* is the usual word for the reserved sacrament.[3] Justin Martyr too describes the eucharistic species as either *eucharistia* or 'eucharistized bread' (1 *Apol.* 65). The thanksgivings of the early Church (as we know them through the extant prayers and commentaries of the Fathers) have, for their theme, like the Jewish thanksgivings, the mighty acts of God for his people in the world, and range from the simple directives supplied, e.g. by Hippolytus for celebrants at the Eucharist to a detailed résumé of the divine activity from the creation to the redemption in Christ (as in *Ap. Const.* Bk. 8). The purpose of such thanksgivings (again like Jewish thanksgivings) is not only to render due return of gratitude from the creature to the Creator, but also to ask for a continued blessing and a continuing redemption. In the majority of eucharistic prayers, the series of thanksgivings, culminating in the thanksgiving for the work of Christ (of which special memorial is made—see next section) is followed by a petition that the worshippers may receive the fruits of this saving work in communion. Here again this resembles the Jewish thanksgivings; the theme in short is 'Blessed art thou O Lord . . . . Have mercy upon us O Lord'.[4]

(b) *Memorial*

There is clearly some awareness in the patristic period of the Jewish understanding of memorial, particularly of the passover memorials,[5] and the Fathers in relation to the Eucharist understood memorial in a technical sense closely akin to this (and not in our modern popular sense of remembrance). Thus, for Justin the bread of the Eucharist was prescribed by the Lord 'in remembrance of the suffering which he endured'.[6] Again 'he gave us the bread in remembrance of his being made flesh and the cup in remembrance of his own blood';[7] and later he speaks

---

[1] 1 *Apol.* 65.

[2] *Eph.* 13.1.; *Smyrn.* 7.1.; *Philad.* 4.1.; cf. Justin, *Dial.* 14.1.; Irenaeus, *AH.* 4, 18; Basil, *De Spir. Sanct.* 66.

[3] Cf. Irenaeus' letter already quoted (in Eusebius *HE* 5.24) in which he relates that some non-Quartodeciman presbyters sent the Eucharist (*eucharistian*) to some Asia Minor Quartodecimans).

[4] Cf. *PEER* 1; L. Bouyer, (ET) *Life and Liturgy* (Sheed and Ward 1956), ch. 9; L. Ligier, 'From the Last Supper to the Eucharist', in *The New Liturgy*, ed. L. Sheppard (DLT 1970), pp. 113–50.

[5] See pp. 16, 25, 49, 154; also Methodius, *Symp.* 9.1; Chrysostom, *Pasch.* 4; Theodoret, *qu. 12. in Ex.*

[6] *Dial.* 41.1.

[7] Ibid. 70.4.

of the 'memorial of solid and liquid food in which the suffering of the Son of God is remembered'.[1] John Chrysostom says that 'the aweful mysteries. . . are called a sacrifice of thanksgiving because they are the commemoration of many benefits and signify the sum of God's care for us'.[2] Similarly, he compares the memorials of Judaism to the memorials of Christians, the former being of the shedding of blood to preserve the firstborn, the latter of the shedding of blood for the sins of the whole world.[3] To make memorial of the mighty acts of God (as is done in most eucharistic prayers of this period in the section generally known today as the anamnesis) is much the same as giving thanks for these same mighty acts.[4] The purpose of such memorials, like that of the thanksgiving, is on the one hand to evoke a response of gratitude, and on the other to secure a continued blessing.

The theme of the anamnesis, then, is briefly: 'We commemorate (show forth, proclaim, confess) . . . (then) we offer . . . we pray that . . . .'[5]

(c) *Sacrifice*

For the Fathers, the Eucharist was the Christian sacrifice. This is a term which may have been avoided during the sub-apostolic age, but which from the second century onwards is commonly used to refer to the principal act of worship of the Christian Church. Though clearly *prosphora/oblatio* can be seen in patristic literature to refer to the offering of material gifts,[6] to the offering of thanks and praise and to the Christian's willing surrender of himself in heart and mind,[7] the act which most properly provides the Eucharist with the name of sacrifice is the sacrifice of Christ himself of which solemn memorial is made at each eucharistic celebration. By the end of the fourth century, there is a strong sense in some writers that the worshipper at the Eucharist stands in the presence of Christ sacrificed. John Chrysostom, for example, speaks of 'the most awesome sacrifice' and of 'the Lord sacrificed and lying there and the priest bending over the sacrifice and interceding'.[8] Theodore of Mopsuestia sees certain details of the passion, e.g. the burial, represented by the ritual of the bringing of the gifts to the altar.[9] Cyril of Jerusalem

---

[1] Ibid. 117.3.

[2] *Hom. in Matth.* 25.4.

[3] Ibid. *Hom.* 82.1.

[4] Cf. Jungmann, *MRR* s.v., and our quotations from Justin above.

[5] For the kind of vocabulary used in anamneses it is useful to parallel the anamneses of early patristic prayers printed in *PEER*.

[6] Cf. *Ap. Trad.* quoted on p. 174.

[7] As e.g. in Augustine, *de civ. Dei.* 10.6.

[8] *De Sacerdotio* 6.4.; 3.4.

[9] *Hom. cat.* 15.25–6 (*AIR* 227–8).

can say that 'we offer Christ sacrificed on behalf of our sins';[1] and Gregory of Nyssa refers to the severing of the Lord's body and blood by 'the bloodless cutting of the voice of the priest'.[2] The language to modern ears is indeed on the verge of the bizarre, but it is the notion of being in the presence of Christ both priest and victim that is perhaps most fundamental.[3] How this is possible (i.e. to be present at an event which happened once in history) is expressed by the Fathers in one of two ways. (i) The one is to stress the eternal or trans-temporal quality of the Eucharist;[4] for the Christian Eucharist not only looks back but looks forward to the second coming, it is celebrated on the first day of the new creation,[5] and the events which gave rise to it inaugurated the last age. Hence, it is the sacrifice of the last days.[6] The type of the eucharistic sacrifice in patristic literature is not uncommonly the sacrifice of Melchizedek, himself a trans-temporal figure.[7] In sacred time, in the last age, there is, so to speak, no punctuation,[8] an event at the beginning is as present throughout as it was at the outset. Hence, the Christ is present throughout as Lord of the Last Age, present in all his mysteries, incarnate, crucified, and risen, perpetually making available his redeeming work until his last mighty act in the Second Coming. (ii) On the other hand the same understanding is conveyed by the imagery of the heavenly. We should note here with special caution that none of the Fathers in their discussion of the heavenly work of Christ or of the heavenly altar speaks of Christ's sacrifice being perpetually offered in the heavens.[9] Origen speaks of the eternal high priest *making intercession* for us at the heavenly altar;[10] Byzantine art represents Christ as the Lamb of God *once* slain but now triumphant above the images of the sacrifice of Abel and Melchizedek.[11] So there is no question of a repeated sacrifice or a sacrifice to which something may be added. This 'cosmic' language about the

---

[1] *Myst. Cat.* 5.10.

[2] *Ep.* 171.

[3] Cf. Jungmann, *The Place of Christ in Liturgical Prayer*, pp. 239ff—of especial interest for the development of the sense of awe and fear at the Eucharist which is related to the Christian's consciousness of his presence in the realm of the heavenly.

[4] Jewish celebrations after all possess such transtemporal qualities—cf. Strack–Billerbeck, ad. Lk. 22.19.

[5] Justin, *Dial.* 41.

[6] Cf. *Didascalia*, 26.

[7] Cf. J. Daniélou, *The Bible and the Liturgy* (ET, DLT 1960), pp. 144–7.

[8] Cf. O. Cullmann, *Christ and Time* (ET, SCM rev. edn 1962), ch.5; and A. Schmemann, *Introduction to Liturgical Theology* (Faith Press 1966), ch. 1.

[9] Cf. G. Aulén, *Eucharist and Sacrifice* (ET, Oliver and Boyd 1960). pp. 152–3.

[10] *In Lev. hom.* 6.2.; 7.2.; 9.1,3,4,5,6,9,10; *In Jud. hom.* 7.2.

[11] E.g. as in the presbyterium of San Vitale at Ravenna. See also plate 13.

Eucharist simply seems to stress the perpetual availability of the sacrifice of Christ (understood as his whole redeeming work) at any time and at any place; and the rite whereby Christians both perceive and receive redemption in Christ is thus suitably described as sacrifice, which the Church can be said to offer or to make memorial of—for Chrysostom the terms are synonymous[1]—always rembering that 'in that which she offers, she herself is offered'.[2]

3 THE FRUITS OF COMMUNION

In general, the Fathers are completely unequivocal in their belief that what is received in communion is the Body and Blood of Christ; and despite reference to the eucharistic elements as the symbols (*figurae/ typoi, antitypoi*) of Christ's Body and Blood, despite also the Alexandrian tradition which tends to stress the spiritual realities received through the act of communion, there is at the same time a realization that the figure, type, or symbol is closely to be identified with that which it symbolizes, and that spiritual interpretations of the benefits of receiving the sacrament are not incompatible with belief in the objective identification of the elements with the Body and Blood of Christ.[3] Not until the fourth century, however, do we have any evidence of interest in the notion of 'change', i.e. of speculation as to what happens to the eucharistic elements by the 'word of prayer' during the eucharistic action. A number of words are used to indicate that a change or conversion is in fact effected in the bread and wine: Cyril of Jerusalem speaks of a *metabole*, John Chrysostom prefers *metarruthmizo*, Gregory of Nyssa *metastoikeo* or again (with Chrysostom) *metaskeuazo;* Cyril of Alexandria suggests *methistemi*, and in the west, Ambrose proposes *convertere, mutare, fieri* or *transfigurare*. The conversion or change is of course the work of God himself acting through his Spirit (Cyril of Jerusalem) or his Word (Sarapion of Thmuis) in response to the prayer of the celebrant (Gregory of Nyssa) in order that the faithful may receive the fruits of communion. It is important that this kind of language should be understood in its context. For many of the Fathers (from Justin onwards), there was a close analogy between the Word's assumption of flesh at the Incarnation and the divine action at the Eucharist. The argument roughly speaking is that as human nature was transformed by its union with the Word (through the action of the Spirit), so the eucharistic elements are transformed in order that we too may be

[1] *Hom. in Heb.* 17.3.
[2] Augustine, *De Civ. Dei* 10.6.
[3] This is convincingly argued in Kelly, *Early Christian Doctrines*, pp. 212–3.

transformed and saved from incorruption (the best illustration of this theme perhaps being in Theodore of Mopsuestia's lectures on the Eucharist).[1] The motif is in fact soteriological rather than magical; which goes some way towards accounting for the spiritual counsel found in writers such as Origen and indeed Augustine in the attempt to direct us towards the reality of that which we receive and the manner in which we ought to receive it. For what is received is not a thing but a person, a dynamic and outgoing redeemer who demands a response from those who would approach him. The act of communion after all is but the consummation of the eucharistic memorial; and if by this memorial our redemption is brought nigh, then it is in communion of the Body and Blood of the Redeemer that we receive the fruits of this redemption.

8 The Byzantine Liturgy from the *Apostolic Constitutions* to the Present Day

HUGH WYBREW

Text

Brightman, F. E., *LEW*, vol. 1, pp. 309–44.
Trembelas, P. N., *Hai Treis Leitourgiai*. Athens 1935.
   (ET) *The Orthodox Liturgy*. SPCK: Fellowship of SS. Alban and Sergius, 1935.

Liturgical Commentaries

Bornert, R., *Les commentaires byzantins de la divine liturgie*, Archives de l'Orient chrétien 9. Paris 1966.
   Theodore of Mopsuestia, *Catechetical Homilies*, in *AIR*, pp. 211–63.
Maximus the Confessor, *Mystagogia*, French tr. in Hamman, A., *L'initiation chrétienne*, Lettres chrétiennes 7. Paris 1963.
Nicolas Cabasilas, (ET) *A Commentary on the Divine Liturgy*, J. M. Hussey and P. A. McNulty. SPCK 1960.

Studies

Kucharek, C., *The Byzantine-Slav Liturgy of S. John Chrysostom*. Allendale 1971.
Mateos, J., *La célébration de la parole dans la liturgie byzantine*, *OCA* 191. Rome 1971.
Salaville, S., *An Introduction to the Study of Eastern Liturgies*. Sand 1938.

[1] *Hom. cat.* 15 and 16, *AIR* pp. 211–63.

Schmemann, A., *Introduction to Liturgical Theology*. Faith Press 1966.
Schmemann, A., *The World as Sacrament*. DLT 1966.
Schulz, H.-J., *Die byzantinische Liturgie*. Freiburg in Breisgau 1964.
Taft, R. F., *Évolution historique de la liturgie de saint Jean Chrysostome*, Pt. 1,
  'Entrée des mystères', *Proche-Orient chrétien*, 22 (1972), pp. 3–4; 24 (1974),
  p. 1.
Taft, R. F., *The Great Entrance*, OCA 200. Rome 1975.

The eucharistic rite of Constantinople derived from the West Syrian tradition. Byzantium had no special ecclesiastical importance until the Council of Constantinople of 381 recognized it as the New Rome, and it had so far come within the sphere of influence of Antioch. In the fourth century it had a series of bishops from Syria and Cappadocia, among them John Chrysostom, a native of Antioch. Such details of the rite of Constantinople as can be gleaned from the writings of Chrysostom suggest that it followed the main lines of the Antiochene rite, as it is reflected in *Ap. Const*. The prestige of Constantinople enabled its rite first to influence, and finally to replace, local rites within the Empire, just as in the West the rite of Rome eventually ousted other rites. In 1194 the distinguished Byzantine canon lawyer Theodore Balsamon declared the continuing use of the Alexandrian rite of St Mark and the Jerusalem rite of St James unlawful: 'All the churches of God ought to follow the custom of New Rome, that is, Constantinople'.[1] The Byzantine rite spread beyond the Empire, too, to the countries converted by Byzantine missionary activity, and became the sole rite used by all the national Orthodox Churches.

BASIL, CHRYSOSTOM, AND THE BYZANTINE EUCHARIST

In later Byzantine usage two rites were used for the celebration of the Liturgy, as the eucharistic rite came to be called in the East. One came to bear the name of John Chrysostom, the other that of Basil the Great, Bishop of Caesarea in Cappadocia. There is no direct evidence to connect either bishop with the rite named after him. The name of Basil is attached to several eucharistic prayers, among them one used in the Coptic Church. A strong case has been made in favour of the view that the Byzantine eucharistic prayer, or anaphora, is an expansion of the Coptic

---

[1] Cf. Dix, *Shape*, p. 546, n. 1. The rite of St James survived in Jerusalem on his feast-day, on which it is now often used elsewhere.

one, and that the expansion was the work of Basil himself.[1] The historical and literary evidence for the connection between Basil and the Byzantine Liturgy has generally been thought a good deal stronger than that for the traditional link between Chrysostom and the Liturgy. But recently it has been argued that, as in the case of Basil, the prayers of the central core of the rite of Chrysostom must go back to his time, and may reasonably be ascribed to him.[2] In both cases only the anaphora and other prayers belonging to the older stratum of the rite are in question, and at least in the case of the anaphora both Basil and Chrysostom no doubt worked on the basis of existing traditions.

THE BYZANTINE LITURGY IN THE SEVENTH CENTURY

The first text of the Byzantine Eucharist is given in the Barberini Codex at the end of the eighth century. The main evidence for the rite before then is the description of the Liturgy given by Maximus the Confessor in his *Mystagogia*, written about 628–30.[3]

(a) *The Liturgy of the Word*—'*Liturgy of the Catechumens*'

The bishop and the people entered the church together, and the bishop went to his place in the sanctuary. The entry was accompanied by the chanting of the Trisagion. In both East and West the entry of the bishop became more ceremonious in the course of the fifth century, and came to be accompanied by chant. The Trisagion was first mentioned at the Council of Chalcedon in 451, where it was used as an antimonophysite battle-cry.[4] It was almost certainly a liturgical piece before that, though it cannot be shown that it was used as an entrance chant before the beginning of the sixth century, and it may originally have come between the OT and NT readings.[5] According to Dionysius the Areopagite, about A.D. 500, the bishop censed the whole church before the Liturgy began.[6]

The Liturgy of the Catechumens had developed little from the end of the fourth century. After the bishop's greeting, 'Peace be with you', came

---

[1] Cf. *Un témoin archaïque de la liturgie copte de S. Basile*, by J. Doresse and E. Lanne (Louvain 1960). En annexe: *Les Liturgies 'basiliennes' et saint Basile*, by B. Capelle.

[2] Cf. Georg Wagner, *Der Ursprung der Chrysostomusliturgie*, Liturgiewissenschaftliche Quellen und Forschungen, Heft 59 (Münster 1973), pp. 1–138.

[3] Cf. *Opera*, ed. Combefis (Paris 1675), 2.489ff; PG 91. French tr. by M. Lot-Borodine in *L'initiation chrétienne*, ed. A. Hamman (Paris 1963) (first published in *Irénikon*, 13 (1936) –15 (1938).

[4] Cf. Mansi, 6.936 C.

[5] Cf. Marcellinus Comes, *Chronicum* for year 512, PL 51. 937C–938B.

[6] Cf. *Ecclesiastica Hierarchia*, III.3.3 (PG 3.428D–429B).

the scripture readings. In the seventh century both Old and New Rome followed the same pattern. There were three readings: an OT lesson, followed by a responsorial psalm, the *Prokeimenon;* an Epistle, followed by the Alleluia interspersed between the verses of a psalm or part of a psalm; and the Gospel. The readings were followed by the sermon, after which those not allowed to remain for the Liturgy of the Faithful were dismissed. Since there could have been few catechumens in Constantinople at this time, it is probable that the dismissals were a survival from earlier practice. The doors of the church were then closed.

(b) *The Liturgy of the Sacrament—'Liturgy of the Faithful'*

Maximus does not mention the Intercession. But it is reasonable to suppose that a litany led by the deacon, of the kind found in the rite of *Ap. Const.* (see p. 188), existed in the Byzantine Liturgy at this time in the same place. There follows what Maximus calls the entry of the holy and venerable mysteries. The bread and wine are brought to the altar, presumably from the place where they had been kept since they were handed in by the people as they came into church. In the East there seems never to have been a people's offertory procession at this point, as in the West. In the third century the Syrian *Didascalia* says that the people hand in their offerings as they come into the church.[1] Their transfer to the altar at the beginning of the Eucharist proper was at first done simply by the deacons, but in time developed into the 'Great Entrance', the ceremonial high-spot of the Byzantine Liturgy. Maximus gives no details of this transfer, but it is clear from the name he gives it that it was of more than practical significance. At the end of the fourth century Theodore of Mopsuestia had interpreted this transfer, accomplished in a splendid procession, as symbolizing Christ going to his passion.[2] Further east, in the latter half of the fifth century, Narsai gives in his Liturgical Homilies a similar interpretation of an equally impressive procession.[3] Maximus does not describe the Great Entrance in detail. But in the sixth century Patriarch Eutychius of Constantinople (552–65, 577–82) protested against the splendour of the procession, whose accompanying chant gave people the impression that the King of Glory himself was being received.[4] The Church of the Holy Wisdom built by Justinian in 532–37 was the ideal setting for ceremonial development, and Maximus' brief reference probably covered a procession as impressive as that described by Theodore and Narsai. Certainly the procession was accompanied by a

[1] *Didascalia* ed. Connolly, 2, 57 (see pp. 59–60).
[2] *Hom. Cat.*, 15.25–9; *AIR.* pp. 227–30.
[3] *The Liturgical Homilies of Narsai*, by Dom R. H. Connolly, (CUP 1909), p. 3.
[4] *Sermo de paschate et sanctissima eucharistia*, 8 PG 86. 2400–1.

chant, of which Maximus makes no mention. The Cherubic Hymn was introduced, according to Cedrenus in the eleventh century, by Justin II in 574.[1] It fits in with the kind of interpretation of the Great Entrance found already in Theodore, and it may have been to it that Eutychius refers. The significance of the Great Entrance in the Byzantine Liturgy is quite other than that of the Roman offertory procession.

The Great Entrance is followed by the Kiss of Peace, and the Nicene Creed. The use of the Creed in the Eucharist in the East began in 476 as a monophysite practice, designed to emphasize loyalty to the decisions of Nicaea. Its introduction into the rite of Constantinople by Patriarch Timothy (511–17) separated the anaphora from the Great Entrance, and so obscured the original structure of the Eucharist at this point.[2]

Maximus does not describe the anaphora in any detail. If the arguments connecting the Byzantine eucharistic prayers, or anaphoras, with Basil and Chrysostom are accepted, it will have been one of the two formulae given in the Barberini Codex at the end of the eighth century. The greater part of the anaphora was said by the celebrant in a low voice. The spread of this habit marks a significant change in eucharistic worship. It began, apparently, in East Syria, for the *Liturgical Homilies* of Narsai imply that the whole of the prayer was said secretly, except the words which introduced the people's responses, like the Sanctus.[3] The practice was spreading in the Byzantine Church in the time of Justinian, who felt it necessary to legislate against it. His Novella 137 of the year 565 orders all bishops and priests to say the prayers used in the Divine Oblation and in Holy Baptism not inaudibly, but in a voice that can be heard by the faithful people.[4] Justinian's law did not prevent the spread of the practice, which by the end of the seventh century had been adopted at Rome for the part of the prayer after the Sanctus. The result was that the anaphora ceased to be the prayer of the whole people, uttered by the priest as their spokesman; it became a prayer of the priest alone. Various explanations have been attempted for this development. Probably it had its origin in the devotional attitude formed by the growing stress on the awesomeness of the mysteries which spread from the fourth century onwards.[5] Other prayers in the Byzantine Liturgy also came to be said secretly by the priest.

The anaphora is followed by the Lord's Prayer, which in other rites at

---

[1] Cedrenus, *Historiarum Compendium*, PG 121. 748B.
[2] Theodore the Lector, *Historiae Ecclesiasticae Fragmenta*, 2.32 (PG 86. 201A).
[3] Narsai, op. cit. pp. 12ff.
[4] *Corpus iuris civilis*, ed. Mommsen et al., vol. 3 (Berlin 1895), pp. 695–9.
[5] Cf. E. Bishop, 'Fear and Awe attaching to the Eucharistic Service', in Narsai, op. cit., Appendix, pp. 92–7.

this time came only after the fraction. This Byzantine custom was imitated by the Roman Church under Gregory the Great at the end of the sixth century, with the result that the prayer came to be separated from the distribution of communion, for which it was originally the preparation (see pp. 193, 196, 200, 234).

The elevation of the consecrated elements is accompanied by the invitation, 'Holy things for holy people', to which the people reply, 'One is holy, one is Lord, Jesus Christ, to the glory of God the Father'. Maximus makes no mention of the ceremony of the *Zeon*, the addition at this point of a little hot water to the chalice. Whether or not it was part of the rite of Constantinople at this time is uncertain. But it was certainly a practice among the Byzantines by the end of the sixth century, for the Armenian Catholicos Moses II rejected an invitation to a theological conference with the Byzantines issued by the Emperor Maurice (582–602), since he declined 'to eat leavened bread and drink hot water' with them.[1] The origin of this ceremony is quite obscure. It seems likely that from the beginning it had a symbolic rather than a practical function, and was perhaps connected with the belief of the Aphthartodocetae that the body of Christ never lost its warmth between the cross and the resurrection.[2]

The distribution of communion is accompanied, as in the West, by a chant, consisting of a psalm. At this time communion was still received in the traditional manner, the bread in the hands, followed by the cup. But although Maximus includes communion in his commentary, the practice of frequent communion had by this time died out in the East. From the end of the fourth century it declined rapidly in both East and West, except in conservative churches like Rome. The stress on the holy and terrifying character of the consecrated elements, which first appears in Cyril of Jerusalem, with the consequent insistence that only those suitably prepared should approach them, discouraged most communicants. The inclusion of temporary abstinence from the use of marriage as one of the prerequisites for communion, under OT influence, played a large part in this decline in both East and West. Infrequent communion of the laity, which still largely persists in the Orthodox Churches, produced a radical change in the balance of eucharistic worship. Liturgical texts, in East and West alike, still presupposed the ancient view that communion was an integral part of the rite. But the devotion of the people had to be focused elsewhere.

After communion, the hymn 'Let our mouth be filled with thy praise'

[1] PG 132. 1248–9.
[2] Cf. L. H. Grondijs, *L'iconographie byzantine du Crucifié mort sur la croix* (Brussels 1941), pp. 76f.

was sung. It was introduced, according to the *Chronicon Paschale*, by Patriarch Sergius in 624.[1] The Liturgy ended with the dismissal of the people, probably preceded by a prayer asking God's blessing on them, of the kind found in *Ap. Const.*

The Byzantine Liturgy of the seventh century still preserved the relatively simple structure of the fourth-century rite. It had become elaborated, as all rites tended to become, at the entry of the clergy, the preparation of the bread and wine before the anaphora, the distribution of communion, and the conclusion of the service. But two changes of great importance had occurred: the decay of lay communion, and the silent recitation of the anaphora.

THE BYZANTINE LITURGY IN THE NINTH CENTURY

The first textual evidence for the Byzantine Liturgy is the Codex Barberini gr 336, from about 800, which includes the Liturgies of St Basil and St Chrysostom, although the latter is not so named.[2] The first formula given is that of Basil, which at this time was the more commonly used. The MS gives only the prayers needed by the celebrant. A comparison with the rite of the seventh century shows that important changes have taken place in the intervening years. Chief among them are the ceremonial preparation of the elements before the Liturgy begins, and the addition of a short office of antiphons and prayers before the Liturgy of the Catechumens. A survey of the rite at this period, which was described in later versions of the *Historia Ecclesiastica*, ascribed to Germanus, Patriarch of Constantinople, who died in 733, reveals the main developments.[3]

(a) *The Preparation of the Elements*

At some time during the eighth century the preparation of the bread and wine was transferred from before the Great Entrance to before the Liturgy as a whole. The Barberini MS provides for each Liturgy a prayer to be said by the priest in the sacristy when he puts the bread on the paten. The wine and water were put into the chalice at the same time. By the beginning of the ninth century, the sign of the cross was made in some places over the bread, and sometimes over the chalice. The prayers recited at this preparation, or *Proskomidia*, anticipate petitions to be

---

[1] *Chronicon paschale,* ʼ390 (PG 92. 1001).
[2] Text in Brightman, *LEW* 1. 309-44.
[3] N. Borgia, ed., *Il commentario liturgico di s. Germano Patriarca Constantinopolitano e la versione latina di Anastasio Bibliotecario* (Grottaferrata 1912).

made later in the anaphora. That in Basil asks that the bread may be blessed and received at the heavenly altar, that in Chrysostom closely resembles the epiclesis of the Holy Spirit in the anaphora, asking that the Holy Spirit may be sent to make the bread and wine the Body and Blood of Christ. They were probably first introduced when the preparation took place before the Great Entrance: the prayer in Basil is found in the Liturgy of St James accompanying the chant covering the Great Entrance. In their new place they could be understood to reinforce the popular Byzantine view that the elements were in some sense consecrated before the rite began (see plate 14).

(b) *The Antiphons*

The Barberini MS gives prayers for three antiphons before the Liturgy of St Basil. These antiphons were psalms, with refrains sung between their verses. They are first mentioned in the *HE*. They represent what was in origin a short office of three psalms with refrains, sung at the stations made during processions on certain great days in Constantinople. Each antiphon had a corresponding prayer, recited either out loud or silently, with a concluding doxology said out loud. It became the custom to perform this office on other days, when there was no procession. This practice had begun by the eighth century, but the antiphons were not considered an integral part of the Liturgy until the tenth century, and there were occasions when they were not sung.[1]

It seems probable that by the eighth century the entrance chant in the Byzantine rite was no longer the Trisagion, but a psalm with a refrain, as in the Roman rite. The refrain, called a *troparion*, varied according to the feast. It was perhaps the existence of this entry antiphon, executed in the same way as those of the stational office, which attracted to itself two more, to form an office modelled on that of the stations.

The antiphons appear at about the same time as the Proskomidia. It is tempting to suppose that the two are in some way connected, and that the antiphons were added to the introit to give time for the preparation of the elements, before the Liturgy of the Catechumens began.

(c) *The Liturgy of the Word*

These developments meant that the Liturgy now began not with the entry of clergy and people into the church, but with the entry of the clergy into the sanctuary. In this procession, which came to be called the Little Entrance, was carried the book of the Gospels. Only the entry of the bishop into the church during the third antiphon marked this as the

[1] On this and on the development of the Liturgy of the Catechumens see J. Mateos, *La célébration de la parole*.

original beginning of the whole rite. The Barberini MS provides an entry prayer, perhaps originally said out loud.

The great *Synapte*, or litany, then followed. Some time previously, it had been removed from its position after the dismissals, and inserted here. It is interesting to notice a similar shift in the place of the intercession in Rome. At the end of the fifth century the old Solemn Prayers after the sermon were replaced by a litany of Eastern type at the beginning of the Mass.

The Trisagion followed, displaced from its original function as an entry chant by the newer antiphon. A prayer is recited secretly by the celebrant in connection with the chant.

By the ninth century the readings, in Byzantium as in Rome, had been reduced to two. The disappearance of the OT reading left the Prokeimenon standing alone in front of the Epistle.

After the sermon follows the *Ectenie*, so-called from the Greek adjective applied to this litany, meaning insistent or fervent. This Ectenie is not mentioned in earlier sources, and was presumably inserted between the seventh and ninth centuries, which saw so many changes in the Byzantine rite. It appears to have been a form of prayer used during the penitential processions in Constantinople. On solemn rogations it was used after an office of readings, after the Gospel. This usage probably prompted its inclusion in the normal Liturgy. It is reasonable to suppose that it was put in only after the Synapte had been removed from a place after the dismissals to one before the Trisagion.

(d) *The Liturgy of the Sacrament*

The dismissal of the catechumens is followed in the Barberini MS by two prayers of the faithful. In origin these prayers seem to have been designed to accompany the Synapte which formed the intercession. The first was said silently by the bishop during the Synapte, the second, recited out loud, was the conclusion of the litany. Subsequently, the two prayers of the faithful were used in connection with two short litanies. These represent the ancient intercession, divided into two and generally abbreviated. The abbreviations presumably were made when the full Synapte was sung before the Trisagion, though a full litany was recited here in some places until the fourteenth century. In a somewhat shortened form, it is still used in the Russian Church when there is a deacon officiating with the priest.

The entry of the prepared elements follows. *Basil* contains a private prayer of the priest, said before the entry. Cast in the first person singular, it belongs to the category of private devotions of the priest which in both East and West came to be given formal expression within the eucharistic rite. Both formulae in the Barberini MS contain an offertory prayer to be said by the priest once the elements are on the altar. Like corresponding Western prayers, they anticipate some of the petitions of the anaphora with regard to the elements. It is likely that the offertory litany sung now at this point was already in the rite at this time. It includes a petition for the gifts, as well as petitions for the worshippers.

The anaphora follows, preceded by the Kiss of Peace and the creed. The Barberini MS gives the earliest text of the two Byzantine anaphorae. Both follow the general pattern of the Syrian tradition.[1]

The anaphora is followed by a litany, as in *Ap. Const.*, which is a repetition of the offertory litany, with the inclusion of a petition for the acceptance of the gifts. The priest meanwhile recites secretly a prayer, whose conclusion leads into the Lord's Prayer. The greeting 'Peace be with you' is followed by the diaconal injunction 'Let us bow our heads'. The priest says silently a prayer of blessing. After the elevation with its traditional formula, a portion of the consecrated bread is put into the chalice with the formula 'For the fulness of the Holy Spirit'. Barberini MS gr 336 does not mention the Zeon.

Communion, accompanied by a chant, was beginning in the ninth century to be given by means of a spoon. When communion is finished, the priest gives a blessing, 'O Lord save thy people and bless thine heritage', and the '*Plerotheto*' is sung. A diaconal litany of thanksgiving is sung while the priest says secretly a prayer of thanksgiving. The deacon's dismissal of the people is followed by the Prayer behind the Ambo. This formula of blessing was at this time a variable prayer, and ended the Liturgy.

In all essentials the Liturgy in the ninth century had reached its present structure. A period of considerable development had modified its previous structure in important ways. In particular, the ceremonial preparation of the elements before the Liturgy of the Catechumens added a new item to the traditional order, which had no equivalent in the Roman rite. The Liturgy of the Catechumens itself became more complex with the addition of the *Enarxis*, a rite of litanies and antiphons before the Little Entrance. Additional litanies at various points in the rite further interrupted its traditional sequence. Only in the Proskomidia was further significant development to take place, before the Byzantine Liturgy reached the form in which it has been preserved subsequently in the Orthodox Churches.

---

[1] On the anaphoras, cf. works cited on p. 210, nn. 1, 2. Cf. also H.-J. Schulz, *Die Byzantinische Liturgie*, pp. 18–28.

THE COMPLETION OF THE
BYZANTINE LITURGY

By the fourteenth century the Byzantine eucharistic rite reached the term of its evolution. Local variations in detail had always existed, although the rite in all essentials was the same throughout the Byzantine Church and its offshoots. The fourteenth century saw the first attempt to attain uniformity of detail, when Patriarch Philotheos (1354–76) compiled his Constitutions.[1] These prescribed the manner of celebrating the Liturgy in all its details. They won their way gradually in the local Orthodox Churches, although certain local variations have continued to exist, or have sprung up subsequently.

(a) *The Proskomidia*

The preparation of the elements by the fourteenth century had become very complex. Already in the ninth century the priest pierced the small bread used for the Liturgy, the *Prosphora*, with a liturgical spear, so symbolizing the passion of Christ. Later, it became the custom to remove from the bread a portion called the Lamb, which alone was consecrated. The number of breads used increased, in connection with the commemoration of the Blessed Virgin Mary, the saints, the living and the dead, for whose memorial small particles were cut out and placed on the paten alongside the Lamb. The Constitutions of Philotheos fixed the number at five. The commemoration of the dead and the living in this way appears to go back to the ninth century, that of the saints to the eleventh. The ceremonial and accompanying formulae of the Proskomidia reflect a two-fold symbolic interpretation of this part of the rite. What is done with the Lamb from the ninth century, enacts in symbols the passion of Christ. From the eleventh century, the Proskomidia is also understood as symbolizing the birth and early life of Christ: the star-shaped frame put over the paten to support its veil represents the star which brought the Magi to the Christ.

This way of interpreting the Proskomidia belongs to a long tradition in the Byzantine Church of understanding the Liturgy as a representation in symbols of the life of Christ, whose beginnings can be seen in Theodore of Mopsuestia. Varied in its development, which can be traced in the Byzantine commentaries on the Liturgy, it was given some coherence by Theodore of Andida in the eleventh century. He saw the Liturgy as a presentation of the whole life of Christ: the Proskomidia represented the birth and hidden life, the Liturgy of the Catechumens

[1] PG 154. 745–66.

the public appearance and ministry, and the Liturgy of the Faithful the passion, death, and resurrection of Christ.[1]

(b) *Private Prayers of the Clergy*

From the eleventh century prayers were provided for the priest and deacon to say as they entered the church to prepare for the Liturgy. They were comparatively simple. In time their number increased. They were said before the icon-screen, and include prayers of penitence, and the veneration of the icons of Christ and the Virgin. As in the Western rite, so from the thirteenth century the Byzantine Liturgy provided prayers to be said as each of the vestments was put on. After vesting, the priest washes his hands, saying part of Ps. 25. This washing was originally connected with the offertory, as in other rites. It remained there until the thirteenth century, even though the Proskomidia had been transferred to the beginning of the rite. But it then became part of the preliminary preparation of the priest, except at an episcopal Liturgy, when the bishop completes the Proskomidia, and so washes his hands ceremonially, immediately before the Great Entrance.

Devotions before communion for the clergy begin to appear about the ninth or tenth century, as they did in the Roman rite. Fixed forms of previously personal devotion, they tended to increase in number, and to vary from place to place. They have never been completely standardized. Other formulae, said silently by the celebrant, owed their introduction to the tradition of interpreting the Liturgy symbolically.

With the addition of these elements the Byzantine rite reached the form in which the Orthodox Churches use it today. Historical conditions made it not only an expression of Eastern eucharistic piety, but also an expression of the national cultures of the Orthodox peoples under Turkish rule. So deeply has it become rooted in their life that it is more resistant to pressures towards change than Western rites. In a few places there are trends towards less infrequent communion; and some experiments with reciting prayers out loud, and eliminating repetitions, are being made. But it is impossible at present to foresee anything in the Orthodox Church resembling the liturgical movement in the Western Churches.

[1] Cf. R. Bornert, *Les commentaires byzantins de la divine liturgie* (Paris 1966).

9 The Medieval Western Rites

D. M. HOPE

CANON OF THE MASS

Botte, B., *Le canon de la messe romaine*. Louvain 1935.
Botte, B., and Mohrmann, C., *L'ordinaire de la messe, texte critique, traduction et études*. Paris, Louvain, 1953.
Eisenhofer, L., *Canon missae romanae, Pars 1, Traditio textus*. Rome 1954. *Canon missae, Pars 2, Textus propinqui*. Rome 1966.
Jungmann, J. A., *MRR* 2. 101–274.
PEER 21.

VERONA SACRAMENTARY

Text

Mohlberg, L. C., *Sacramentarium Veronense*. Rome 1956.

Studies

Cabrol, F., in *DACL* 8. 2549–73.
Callewaert, C., 'Saint Léon le Grand et les textes du Léonien', in *Sacris Erudiri*, 1 (1948), pp. 35–132.
Hope, D. M., *The Leonine Sacramentary*. OUP 1971.
Stuiber, A., *Libelli Sacramentorum Romani*, Theophaneia, 6. Bonn 1950.

'GELASIAN' SACRAMENTARY

Texts

Cod. Vat. Reg. lat. 316
Mohlberg, L. C., *Liber Sacramentorum Romanae Ecclesiae Ordinis anni circuli* (Rome 1960), pp. 183–6.
Cod. Sangall. 348
Mohlberg, L. C., *Das frankische Sacramentarium Gelasianum* (Cod. Sangall. 348). Münster im Westfalen 1939.

Studies

Moreton, B., *The Eighth-Century Gelasian Sacramentary*. OUP 1976.
Chavasse, A., *Le sacramentaire gélasien*. Tournai 1958.

'GREGORIAN' SACRAMENTARY

Texts

Cod. Cambrai 164
Lietzmann, H., *Das Sacramentarium Gregorianum nach dem Aachener Urexemplar*, in *Liturgiegeschichtliche Quellen* 3. Münster im Westfalen 1921, reprinted 1967.

Padua D 47

Mohlberg, L. C., *Die alteste erreichbare Gestalt des Liber Sacramentorum anni circuli der romische Kirche*, ib. 11–12. Münster im Westfalen 1927, reprinted 1967.

Wilson, H. A., *The Gregorian Sacramentary under Charles the Great*, HBS 49. London 1915.

Studies

Ashworth, H., 'The Influence of the Lombard Invasions on the Gregorian Sacramentary', in *Bulletin of the John Rylands Library*, 36 (1954), pp. 305–27.

Bourque, E., *Etude sur les sacramentaires romains*. Rome 1948.

Cabrol, F., in *DACL* 6, cols. 1766–96.

Capelle, B., 'La main de S. Gregoire dans le sacramentaire gregorien', *R Bén.* 49 (1937), pp. 13–28.

CELTIC

Gougaud, L., in *DACL* 1, cols. 2969–3032.

MacCarthy, B., in *Transactions of the Royal Irish Academy*, 27 (1886), pp. 135–268.

Warner, G. F., *The Stowe Missal*, HBS 31–32, 1906–15.

Warren, F. E., *Liturgy and Ritual in the Celtic Church*. Clarendon Press 1881.

GALLICAN

Duchesne, L., (ET) *Christian Worship*. SPCK 1903.

Mohlberg, L. C., *Missale Gothicum*. Rome 1961.

Porter, W. S., *The Gallican Rite*. Mowbray 1958.

PEER 17.

Other important texts are the Bobbio Missal, Missale Gallicanum vetus and Missale Francorum.

MOZARABIC

Bishop, W. C., *The Mozarabic and Ambrosian Rites*. AC 1924.

Cabrol, F., (ET.) The Mass of the Western Rites. Sand 1934.

Cabrol, F., in *DACL* 12, cols. 390–491.

Férotin, M., *Le Liber Mozarabicus Sacramentorum et les manuscrits mozarabes*. Paris 1912.

Férotin, N., *Le Liber Ordinum en usage dans l'église wisigothique et mozarabe d'Espagne du Ve au XIe siècle*. Paris 1904.

King, A. A., *Liturgies of the Primatial Sees* (Longmans Green 1957), pp. 457–631.

PEER 18.

ORDINES ROMANI

Andrieu, M., *Les Ordines Romani du haut Moyen-Age*, i–v. Louvain 1931–61.

Atchley, E. G. C. F., *Ordo Romanus Primus* (Library of Liturgiology and Ecclesiology for English Readers 6), (London 1905), pp. 58–114.

PEER 22.

GENERAL

Bishop, E., *Liturgica Historica*. Clarendon Press 1918.

Bourque, E., *Etude sur les sacramentaires romains*. Rome 1948.

Cabrol, F., *The Mass of the Western Rites*.

Capelle, B., 'Le Kyrie de la Messe et le pape Gélase', in *R Bén* 46 (1934), pp. 126–44.

Chavasse, A., 'Les plus anciens types du lectionnaire et de l'antiphonaire romains de la messe', in *R Bén* 62 (1950), pp. 3–94.

Gamber, K., *Sakramentartypen*, Texte und Arbeiten, 49/50. Beuron 1958.

Gamber, K., *Codices Liturgici Latini Antiquiores*, Spicilegii Friburgensis Subsidia. Freiburg 1963.

Jungmann, J. A., *MRR* and *The Early Liturgy*.

King, A. A., *Liturgies of the Primatial Sees*.

King, A. A., *Liturgies of the Past*. Longmans 1959.

Klauser, T., (ET) *A Short History of the Western Liturgy*. OUP 1969.

Lejay, P., 'Ambrosienne (Liturgie)', *DACL* 1, cols. 1373–442.

Mohrmann, C., *Liturgical Latin; its Origins and Character*. Burns Oates 1959.

Martimort, A. G., *The Church at Prayer—The Eucharist*.

Srawley, J. H., *The Early History of the Liturgy*. CUP 1947.

Willis, G. G., *Essays in Early Roman Liturgy*. AC SPCK 1964.

Willis, G. G., *Further Essays in Early Roman Liturgy*. AC SPCK 1968.

Much of our knowledge concerning the development of the Western liturgy is still uncertain and obscure. It is not until the MSS of the eighth and ninth centuries that we can be sure of Western liturgical forms, and even then, many of these same MSS are of non-Roman origin. With the aid of textual analysis and literary criticism, it is just possible to trace the development of the liturgy back into the sixth century, but hardly much beyond the fifth.

By the beginning of the fifth century the most important development had been the fixing and establishing of the core of the Canon of the Mass. All the evidence points to the Canon's completion by the end of the sixth century at the latest. Jungmann[1] suggests that the fourth century saw the working out of the basic text of the Canon by an anonymous author and that there are certain similarities between this more ancient, shorter, version and the anaphoras of the Orient, in particular that of the Egyptian liturgy.

The text of the Canon as it is preserved in the old Gelasian, codex Vat. Reginensis lat. 316,[2] is prefaced by the rubric 'Incipit canon actionis' and there follows at once the introductory dialogue 'Sursum corda' etc., Sanctus, Te igitur, and so on. In the same way as the prayer in Hippolytus (see pp. 173–4), the Canon comprises a single unit beginning

[1] *MRR* 1.51. See also above, pp. 190–2.
[2] Cf. Mohlberg, *Liber Sacramentorum*, pp. 183–6.

with the dialogue 'Sursum corda' and concluding with the final doxology 'Per ipsum et cum ipso et in ipso'. However, in many of the MSS between the eighth and tenth centuries, and beyond, it is clear that 'Te igitur' is the formal opening of the Canon; indeed this is presupposed in Ordo I of the Ordines Romani. The 'T' in these MSS stands out in great prominence, very often being highly decorated and much ornamented (see plate 2). In some MSS it has taken over a whole page.

It is this Great Prayer which is absolutely essential and quite indispensable in the celebration of any Eucharist. The prayer itself is addressed to God the Father, through Jesus Christ his Son, and is made in the name of the whole community. The celebrant bids the people 'have their hearts lifted to the Lord' in the dialogue which introduces the Canon. The same basic features are discernible in all the traditional anaphoras, both in the East and in the West. In the first place thanksgiving is made, primarily Christological, though in general for creation, redemption, and sanctification. The Sanctus[1] is said/sung by the whole community, priest and people. Before the narrative of the Lord's institution of the Eucharist, prayer (epiclesis or invocation) is made to God that the offerings be accepted, that they be consecrated through his power and that the participants be granted unity. The anamnesis/oblation follows, during which the Dominical words of institution are recited; the Lord's saving passion and death, his resurrection and his ascension, are recalled; often with some reference being made at this point to the second coming. Prayer is made for the living and the dead, thus recalling the oneness of the earthly Church with the heavenly, and all Christians now departed. The Canon closes with the doxology in praise of the triune God and the people signify their assent by joining boldly in the final 'Amen'.

The fact of the one fixed central point, namely the Canon of the Mass, and the stability with which it provided this part of the liturgy is in marked opposition to the tendency of other parts to diversification and alteration. As the Canon reached its final shape, it was only the Preface which remained subject to such variation, being alterable in accordance with feast or circumstance. In other parts of the Mass, however, provision was made for more and variable prayers: the collect or collects, said at the beginning; the act of offering the gifts is highlighted and emphasized by a prayer at that point; and the communion concluded by a post-communion prayer. Thus the Mass rite was generally rounded, expanded, and polished.

Since the fourth century, the hymn 'Gloria in excelsis Deo' has been

---

[1] On the date of the introduction of the Sanctus, see p. 191 and Martimort, p. 145.

known throughout much of the Christian world (see p. 183). It was not until the seventh century that 'the simple priest' could sing it, and then only at the Easter Vigil.[1] By the eleventh century it became an integral part of the Mass rite on every feast day, whoever the celebrant was.

As far as the end of the fifth century, the general prayer for the Church had been included in the Western liturgy after the reading of the Gospel. This intercession was divided into various sections—for the Church, the Pope, (the Emperor), catechumens, heretics, etc. Following the pontificate of Felix III (483–92) there is no further sign of it. On the other hand, an intercessory kyrie-litany of oriental origin was introduced just before the lections by Gelasius (492–6). It is traditionally known as the 'deprecatio Gelasii'.[2]

By the beginning of the sixth century the framework of the Western liturgy had been essentially determined, so far as the public prayer of the celebrant is concerned.[3] The same could also be said of the singing. In this comparatively early stage, when forms and order were still being evolved, provision was made for simple chanting between the lections; also processional chants of a modest nature were employed at the beginning, at the offertory and at the conclusion of the service. Naturally, with the passage of time, such music became more sophisticated and the texts to be sung more formalized and systematized.

A further consequence of the movement towards fixed forms was the production of liturgical books, the most important and interesting of which for our present study are the sacramentaries. Albert Stuiber[4] has shown that there were in existence, in the papal archives at the Lateran, liturgical sketches which the popes had made for themselves of the variable prayers of the Eucharist. He also provides evidence that the presbyters attached to the titular churches in Rome had made collections of groups of these prayers on a number of sheets of parchment or 'libelli', and that a number of such 'libelli' were the fore-runners of what has come to be called the Leonine Sacramentary, but now more correctly, the Verona Sacramentary.[5] In fact both the words 'Leonine' and 'sacramentary' are misnomers for this MS no. lxxxv to be found in the Chapter Library at Verona, though it cannot be denied that Pope Leo was himself responsible for some of the prayer formulas within this collection.[6] A

---

[1] A. Chavasse, *Le sacramentaire gélasien*, p. 100. On this night he was allowed to sit like a bishop in the middle of the apse!

[2] See p. 182, and Jungmann, *MRR* 1.336–9.

[3] Cf. Jungmann, *MRR* 1.58.

[4] *Libelli Sacramentorum Romani*.

[5] Cf. Mohlberg, *Sacramentarium Veronense*.

[6] Cf. Hope, *The Leonine Sacramentary*.

single MS, to be dated about A.D. 600, it contains material from various sources and spreading over some two hundred years. The first part, which would have covered the period from January to April, is missing; and the MS contains no evidence of the Canon of the Mass. The arrangement is in a two-fold system, namely by the ecclesiastical and by the civil year. Undoubtedly the formulas contained within the MS are Roman in origin, though according to Lowe and Bischoff the MS itself was written in Verona. Verona lxxxv is a collection of Mass prayers, often with more than one set for a particular feast, and sometimes with very many sets of prayers, as for the feast of SS. Peter and Paul, where there are no less than twenty eight! The author, whoever he was, has put together the formulas very casually, and occasionally misplaces sets of prayers. This collection cannot be reckoned to be anything other than a purely private venture and ought never to be termed a 'sacramentary' (see p. 65). In addition, it is difficult to see what use many of the formulas would be with their intensely personal and local references, outside the group or community for which they were so obviously first intended. From the evidence that the Verona MS gives us of the situation in the fifth and sixth centuries, one cannot but conclude that there must still have been a good deal of fluidity about these elements in the Western liturgy to which the manuscript bears testimony, and that any definitively fixed book of formulas was not yet possible.

The appearance of the Gelasian Sacramentary brings us to the first 'sacramentary' of the Roman church, though again the word 'Gelasian' is misleading, since Pope Gelasius had no real connection with its composition or compilation. Liturgical scholars are careful to distinguish two forms of this sacramentary, an older and then a later form. The older form, *the* Gelasian, is preserved in one MS only, the codex Reginensis 316 of the Vatican Library.[1] This MS was part of the great collection of Queen Christina of Sweden and it came to Rome only when the Vatican acquired her library; the country of the MS's origin is more likely to have been France. Both Lowe and Bischoff[2] have suggested that it was written about A.D. 750 and that its place of origin is a convent at Chelles near Paris. Many of the formulas within the codex are undoubtedly Roman in origin, but equally there are certain elements which could not possibly have come from Rome. In addition to the fact that a large number of non-Roman saints' feasts are indicated and that the stational notices are missing, evidence of Gallican material is clear; two examples are the

---

[1] See above, p. 66.
[2] B. Bischoff, *Die Kölner Nonnenhandschriften und die Skriptorium von Chelles*, in *Karolingische und Ottonische Kunst*, ed. F. Gerke and others (Forschungen zur Kunstgeschichte und christlichen Archäologie, 3; Wiesbaden 1957), pp. 395–411.

saints' names in the Canon and the prayer for the Emperor on Good Friday. It is not impossible, however, to extricate the Roman material, and Jungmann,[1] suggests that either in the form of a complete book, or in small collections, this material of Roman origin must have found its way into France at the very latest in the first half of the seventh century. The book itself, which is made up of 245 folios, is divided into three distinct sections: (1) temporale, (2) sanctorale, and (3) sets of prayers not covered by (1) or (2). This last section (3) begins with the phrase 'Incipit Canon actionis' which precedes the Sursum corda, Preface and Sanctus. Antoine Chavasse,[2] following the methods of Stuiber, has been able to show that the Gelasian Sacramentary was produced in much the same way as Verona lxxxv, but whereas the libelli were arranged in a very arbitrary fashion in that codex, in the Gelasianum the material has been carefully edited and given shape and order. As has already been pointed out, the sacramentary has nothing to do with Pope Gelasius, indeed it has little to do with papal authors at all—those who composed it and those who used it were the Roman presbyters; and in contrast to the 'papal' Gregorianum, this may best be described as a Roman presbyters' sacramentary.

In common with other liturgical books around the year 700, including the Gregorian sacramentary, this Roman presbyters' sacramentary was imported into France by the Frankish clergy. Once there, it was inevitable that borrowing and exchanging of forms would take place, not only with the Gallican material already in use, but also with the Gregorianum. Hence there came into existence in France about the first half of the eighth century another type of sacramentary, a 'mixed' work, generally known as the Gelasians of the eighth century. This type is preserved in several MSS, but the best known is that of St Gall 348, written about the year 800[3] at St Gall. In this sacramentary, movable and immovable feasts are not preserved separately, but are intermingled as one unit.

The same may be said for the Gregorian Sacramentary which, so far as the MS tradition is concerned, is for the most part Frankish and except for some fragments, no earlier than the ninth century. Lietzmann,[4] in 1921, produced an edition of the 'authentic' Gregorianum, at that time in Aachen, from some early copies of it which have been only slightly edited, and which have fortunately survived; the most important and basic of these being the MS Cambrai 159 (164). This book comprises what is

[1] *MRR* 1.62.
[2] *Le sacramentaire gélasien.*
[3] Cf. Mohlberg, *Das frankische Sacramentarium Gelasianum.*
[4] See bibliography.

generally termed the Hadrianum. All the Sundays after Pentecost and the Sundays after Christmas are missing, also some of the feasts introduced in Rome during the seventh and eighth centuries. The temporale and sanctorale are mixed together, except for the period from Septuagesima to Easter. Holy Week is included, with the blessing of the oils on Thursday, the Solemn Prayers of Good Friday, and the blessing of the font on Easter Eve. Clearly this original Gregorianum had been a papal book, indeed a stational book, with the Roman basilicas where the pope celebrated the feasts marked at the beginning of the respective Masses.[1] Not unnaturally, so far as the presbyters' celebration of the liturgy was concerned, and also the liturgical year itself, the sacramentary was incomplete.

During the mid-seventh century, however, much of what was lacking for presbyteral celebration came to be included in a 'revised' form of the Gregorian. For example, provision is made for five Masses after Epiphany, four after the octave of Easter and five after Pentecost. The Memento of the dead, not included in the papal sacramentary since the dead were not commemorated on Sundays or on the days of stational Masses, is included in the Canon. This presbyteral type of the Gregorian is best represented by a MS in the library of Padua number D47,[2] dating from the mid-ninth century and copied in Belgium, possibly at Liège, and then brought to Verona in the tenth century.

The whole task of imposing liturgical conformity and attempting to create some form and order in matters liturgical in the West came not by way of papal authority or decree, but initially by Pepin, though somewhat unsuccessfully because of a lack of 'Roman' books in the Frankish kingdom; and then more forcefully by Charlemagne between the years 785 and 790. Following his visit to Rome in 781, the emperor requested Pope Hadrian I for a copy of the sacramentary currently in use in the church of Rome, since he was anxious that the Roman rite should be obligatory throughout his lands. The letter containing Charlemagne's request has not survived, but the papal reply has.[3] In his letter Pope Hadrian states that the copy which he is sending is pure 'immixtum' Roman use. However, as we have already noted, such a sacramentary was of little use to the parish clergy within Charlemagne's territories; hence the addition of a substantial supplement, preceded by an explanatory

---

[1] For a vivid description of the papal stational Mass as described in Ordo Romanus Primus, see Atchley, *Ordo Romanus Primus*, pp. 58–114 or Klauser, *A Short History of the Western Liturgy*, pp. 59–68.

[2] Mohlberg, *Die älteste erreichbare Gestalt des Liber Sacramentorum anni circuli der römische Kirche*.

[3] *MGH*, Ep. III, p. 626.

preface.[1] The preface was placed carefully between the papal Hadrianum now corrected and the supplement in order to make a clear distinction between these two books. After this there is a list of the contents of the supplement with some 140 titles, most of them of Gallican origin—the text of the Exultet for Holy Saturday at the blessing of the Paschal Candle; prayers to fit the Gallican lessons for the vigils of Easter and Pentecost; prayers for catechumens, and, most important for the clergy of the Frankish lands, the addition of Mass formulas for the thirty-seven Sundays of the year not provided for in the Hadrianum, because they were not Sundays of the papal stations. Much of this new material was clearly derived from the eighth-century Gelasian tradition.

From time to time in this present study, the word 'Gallican' has appeared. Perhaps this is the point at which we ought to turn aside for a moment and investigate more carefully what is meant by 'Gallican' liturgy. Jungmann,[2] in dealing with the development of the Western liturgy, concludes that there are two main streams of tradition (1) Roman/African, and (2) Gallic. For the most part we have been considering so far the development of the former. The Gallic category he further sub-divides into four useful sections a. Gallican, b. Celtic, c. Mozarabic, or Old Spanish, and d. Milanese/Ambrosian.

The Gallican liturgical tradition and forms are perhaps best typified in the Missale Gothicum (Vat. Reg. lat. 317).[3] This MS had its possible origins at the end of the seventh century, and was perhaps written in the scriptorium of Luxeuil. It is important to realize that there was no Gallican rite as such—a Mass rite formalized and imposed. Nevertheless one can speak of Gallican liturgy and thereby include the many and diverse forms of 'Gallican' types which abounded in the Frankish lands during the late seventh and eighth centuries. In addition to the independence of Rome which these Gallican forms display, there is also a definite leaning towards splendour and ceremonial; there is too a wide diversity of variable prayers exhibiting a strong Byzantine influence. Edmund Bishop has described the early Roman rite as sober and restrained.[4] Quite the opposite is true of the Gallican type. The prayers are often long and prolix, the rhetoric exuberant and diffuse, the thought-forms ornamental and involved. The theological ideas expressed in a

---

[1] On the question of the 'Supplement', once attributed to Alcuin, but now considered to be the work of St Benedict of Aniane, see J. Deshusses, 'Le "Supplement" au sacramentaire grégorien: Alcuin ou saint Benoît d'Aniane?' in *Archiv für Liturgiewissenschaft*, 9 (pt. 1; 1965), pp. 48–71.

[2] *MRR* 1.44f.

[3] Cf. Mohlberg, *Missale Gothicum.*

[4] *Liturgica Historica*, p. 12.

13 Abel, Abraham, and Melchizedek with their respective offerings, fore-shadowing the Christian eucharist, in the basilica of S. Apollinare in Classe, Ravenna, sixth century (see p. 192)

14 The Prothesis
The preparation of the elements before the Orthodox liturgy
(see p. 215)

number of prayers, chiefly their being addressed to Christ rather than the Father, reflect the fact that Christological conflict in the form of anti-Arianism was not far beneath the surface.

Clearly questions have been raised as to the centre of such liturgical forms, for it is presupposed that such an important type as the Gallican must have had some focal point in western Europe and manifestly that focus was not Rome. Duchesne[1] proposed Milan as such a centre. The emperors during the fourth century took up their residence there; in ecclesiastical matters the influence of Milan was great, extending as far as Spain. Also, if one supposes that the bishops of Milan took the lead in establishing this liturgical type, the name of Auxentius (355–74) springs to mind. His Cappadocian origin could explain many of the oriental features and similarities which distinguish Gallican liturgical praxis from the Roman. However, such a thesis, whilst attractive in many aspects, is difficult to sustain, especially since at least the Canon of the Mass cited by St Ambrose (see pp. 189–92) is essentially Roman. A further possibility, ventured by Cabrol[2] but later much modified, is that Gallican liturgy was endemic to the West, abandoned later by Rome and Milan, but retained in the Frankish lands. This view also is difficult to accept, in that the Gallican liturgical type emerges in a comparatively late stage of development. In any case there are no signs whatever at Rome itself of 'Gallican' features, during the early period of the development of the liturgy. No one theory of the origins of the Gallican type has yet won universal acceptance among scholars, but perhaps the least unsatisfactory possibility is that at the time when forms of prayer began to be composed and written more fully, the Gallican temperament asserted itself in its own prayer forms and ways of worship.

The Celtic liturgical forms were the result of the indefatigable travels of many of the Scottish and Irish monks across Europe, who when returning to their native lands combined what they had found abroad with what already existed. Clearly, they had no intention of creating a new liturgy, but they felt free to combine elements from various sources. The Stowe Missal[3] is one such collection. From this and other surviving documents it is clear that the Celtic type was indeed a *mélange* of foreign elements, Roman, Gallican, Mozarabic and oriental patterns, together with any indigenous liturgical compositions. Only in the very widest sense, if at all, is it possible to speak of a distinct liturgy.

The Mozarabic or Old Spanish liturgy (the term Mozarabic is really a misnomer, for properly it only refers to that part of Spain overrun by the

[1] *Christian Worship*, p. 91.
[2] *The Mass of the Western Rites*, p. 156.
[3] The best edition of the text is that of B. MacCarthy.

Moors after 711) continues principally in the Mozarabic chapel of the cathedral of Toledo which Cardinal Ximenes had established about the beginning of the sixteenth century. However, the rite was already almost fully developed by the end of the sixth century. It further developed and expanded until the late seventh century, and many of its formulas show markedly the influence of anti-Arian polemic. It is well to remember that, about the beginning of the fifth century, Spain was invaded by those strong contenders for Arian Christianity, the Visigoths; not until the end of the sixth century was this same group committed to orthodox Catholicism. In the meantime there had been much persecution and bitter controversy, and this influence not unnaturally continued for some considerable time. The prayers of the Mozarabic liturgy reflect the subject of this dispute, in that very rarely is the mediatorship of Christ mentioned—only in the very oldest forms is this to be found. Prayers are addressed indifferently to God the Father and to God the Son; always the consubstantiality of the Father and the Son is carefully maintained. At the conclusion of a prayer the Holy Trinity is often addressed, rather than the formula to which we are now accustomed 'per Jesum Christum' etc. A number of these prayers found their way, through Ireland, into the Roman liturgy, such as the Proper Preface for the feast of the Holy Trinity. Two found a permanent place in the old *Missale Romanum*, in the Order of the Mass, namely 'Suscipe, Sancta Trinitas' and 'Placeat tibi, Sancta Trinitas'. To a large extent the Mozarabic rite was a national one and many of its formulas are to be attributed to the Spanish bishops Eugenius II, Ildefonsus, and Julian. The diversity, richness, and particularity of the prayer-forms are the most noticeable features and these can be found in such liturgical books as the *Liber Ordinum* and the *Liber Mozarabicus Sacramentorum*.[1] With documents such as these, it is possible to reconstruct the Mozarabic rite of the seventh or eighth century.

The preparations for the Mozarabic liturgy consisted of a number of rites and prayers: the washing of hands, four 'Aves' before and after vesting, appropriate prayers for each vestment, the psalm 'Judica' with the anthem 'Introibo ad altare Dei', the confession of sins, the absolution, the prayer 'Aufer a nobis', the signing of the altar with the cross and kissing it (formerly the kissing of the cross present on the altar), and the preparation of the chalice. On this last point there seems to be no clear guidance: in the *Missale Mixtum* (1561) the oblata may be prepared 'before the *Officium* of the Mass begins, or before the Gospel, or before the Offertory, as the priest wishes'.

[1] The editions of Férotin are listed in the bibliography.

The liturgy began with the 'Officium', the equivalent of the Roman introit. This comprised an anthem, the verse of a psalm and a doxology, taken either from Scripture or from the Acts of the saint whose feast is that day commemorated. In outline the Officium is closer to the Roman Introit than is the Ambrosian 'Ingressa'. There was no Kyrie eleison, and the Gloria in excelsis was enclosed at beginning and end by the 'per omnia saecula saeculorum'. Later the Gloria was prohibited on Sundays in Advent and Lent. After the final 'per omnia', the Deacon said 'Oremus' and the collect prayer. Very often the prayer was addressed directly to Christ and would display a two-fold form: a bidding prayer or invitation to pray, sometimes of great length, almost in the form of a homily, and then a collect which would sum up the subject for intercession. A greeting followed this prayer: 'Dominus sit semper vobiscum. Et cum spiritu tuo'.

After the greeting there was a reading from the OT. There would be also the Epistle and the Gospel, though this structure was not invariable—during Lent there were four lessons, two from the OT and two from the NT. From Easter to Pentecost the first reading was taken from the Apocalypse, that from the OT being suppressed. As the reader announced the lesson, the people responded 'Deo gratias', making the sign of the cross. After the reading they answered simply 'Amen'. The celebrant added a further greeting, as before.

The canticle Benedicite, with the first verse of the psalm 'Confitemini' (105), was sung and then the Psallendo—a responsory sung by the precentor from a pulpit. The ancient Mozarabic books contain a Tract, which was sung from the ambo by the psalmist. After the Psallendo the *Missale Mixtum* contains a rubric requiring the priest to prepare the chalice by putting in wine and water, to place the host upon the paten and to put that on the chalice; then to say the 'preces'. According to St Isidore, it was the place of the deacon to prepare the chalice and to say the prayers. (Note what was said above about the point at which the chalice was prepared in this rite.)

Following the singing of the Psallendo and the diaconal prayers, the celebrant calls for silence—'Silentium facite'—and the deacon read the Epistle, though originally it had been read by a lector. Again the people said 'Amen' at its conclusion and the Gospel continued, with no chant intervening, after the salutation by the celebrant. Like the Epistle, in Spain the Gospel was first read by the lector; only later was this function reserved to the deacon. The diaconal prayer 'Munda cor meum' was said, and the deacon received the celebrant's blessing. Having returned to the altar the Deacon said 'Laus tibi', the people continuing, 'Domine Jesu Christe, Rex aeternae gloriae'. The book of the Gospels was accompanied by lights and incense, the Gospel was announced in the usual way, and the people responded 'Gloria tibi, Domine' and made the sign of the cross. 'Amen' was the response at the end of the Gospel-reading. The book was kissed by the celebrant who said, 'Ave verbum divinum, reformatio virtutum et restitutio sanitatum'.

The 'Lauda', which followed the Gospel, was composed of the Alleluia and a verse taken generally from a psalm. It was sung by the cantor, and this custom of singing such a verse and alleluia after the Gospel is found in other Gallican-type liturgies. At this point, there was formerly a prayer for the penitents, and their dismissal, as well as that of the catechumens. So ended the first part of the Mass, which in general and in its principal features may be said to be much the same as the Gallican and even the Roman synaxis.

During the chant of the 'sacrificium' which followed, the offering of bread and wine by the people took place in the Old Mozarabic rite. The 'pallium' covering was removed from the altar and the corporal spread. The celebrant then received the gifts of the people, the bread in a linen cloth and the wine in a large cruet or other receptacle. Deacons poured the wine into a large chalice and with it mixed some water; also as much as was needed of the offerings was placed upon the altar and covered with a veil of silk known as the 'coopertorium', 'palla', or 'palla corporalis'. There was a proper prayer, 'ad extendendum corporale'. The offertory finished, the celebrant returned to his throne and washed his hands. The deacon performed this service, whilst the sub-deacon offered water to the other sacred ministers present. The signal for the conclusion of the 'sacrificium' was given by the celebrant, whereupon he went to the altar and said the prayer 'Accedam ad te. . .'.

The customary salutation 'Dominus sit semper vobiscum' marked the beginning of the second part of the service. This was followed by a proper known as the 'Missa'—an opening prayer to prepare the faithful for the eucharistic celebration. It is sometimes an invocation to the Father, or the Son; sometimes a series of pious exclamations; sometimes a lyrical chant in honour of the mystery of the saint whose feast is being celebrated. After the 'Missa', the clergy or choir responded 'Hagios, hagios, hagios, Domine Deus Rex aeterne, tibi laudes et gratias'. A very compressed form of the litany prayers followed the Hagios, and these intercessions were concluded with a response from the choir.

The 'Oratio post nomina' was the name of the prayer after the reading of the names of the living and the departed for whom the Eucharist was being offered. Usually the deacon read out the names, or the celebrant himself; occasionally it could be done by one of the cantors. It was a variable prayer—according to the mystery or saint of the day.

The prayer 'ad pacem' and the kiss of peace in the Mozarabic and Gallican rites occurred before the dialogue leading to the Canon, as in the Byzantine liturgy. The introductory dialogue itself was very different. The celebrant said, 'I will go in to the altar of God. To God who gives joy to my youth.' He then laid his hands on the chalice, saying 'Aures ad Dominum. Habemus ad Dominum'. He then continued 'Sursum corda...'.[1] With hands lifted up towards heaven he would say the 'Illatio'; like the Roman Preface or the Gallican 'Contestatio', this was concluded by the Sanctus, which in its turn led into the prayer 'Post Sanctus', and also the consecration. A further prayer was the 'Post pridie' and the 'Confirmatio sacramenti'. The priest then took the consecrated host on the paten, held it over the uncovered chalice and elevated both to show to the people.

The Spanish were the first in the West to introduce the Nicene Creed into the Mass. In the East the custom existed already, and in 568 Justinian the Younger had made it binding. (See pp. 187 and 212.) Unlike the Greeks and Orientals, the Spanish placed the Creed at the end of the Canon and before the Lord's Prayer.

The fraction was a somewhat complicated affair. The host was divided into two; one half placed on the paten, the other half further divided into five parts. The celebrant then divided the first part into four. Thus nine pieces were obtained and these were arranged in the form of a cross, and each received the name of one of the mysteries of Christ: 'corporatio, nativitas, circumcisio, apparitio, passio, mors, resurrectio', and separately, 'gloria', and 'regnum'. The fraction was placed after the Creed and before the Lord's Prayer. After the Lord's Prayer there followed the embolism ('For thine is the kingdom...'), not variable as it is with the Gallican forms. The priest then took the particle 'regnum' and placed it in the chalice with the appropriate words for the commixture. The rite of Blessing in Spain, as in Gaul, took place after the Mixing (see p. 193). The people were blessed with a variable formula interspersed with Amens. Communion was given according to rank and the whole rite ended with a proper 'completuria' and dismissal.[2]

The remaining sub-division is the liturgy of Milan,[3] which has been classified as Gallican, though strictly speaking it ought properly not to be allocated to any particular group. The Roman Canon was used with only minor changes, but then this had been established as early as Ambrose; non-Roman features are clear, particularly in the order of the Eucharist and a number of its prayers; for example the Offertory with procession

[1] Give your ears to the Lord. We have given them to the Lord. Lift up your hearts....
[2] For further detail see King, *Liturgies of the Primatial Sees*, pp. 457ff.
[3] See King, op. cit., pp. 286–456.

took place before and not after the Creed. This Ambrosian rite is still used; in 1976 it was adapted to the norms of Vatican II.

All these are sub-divisions of what may broadly be termed Gallican liturgies. In other rites, as well as in the Eucharist, the Gallican liturgies are in marked contrast to that which was to be found at Rome. Their more significant features will have emerged in the course of our comments: their exuberance and prolixity, their tendency towards greater ceremonial and splendour, similarities to parts of the Byzantine liturgy, the strong anti-Arian content of some of their prayer-formulas. With the many and varied styles of liturgical performance in the Frankish kingdoms, it is hardly surprising that some measure was needed to restrict the escalating chaos; hence the directive of Charlemagne, and his insistence upon the introduction of the Roman rite within his territories.

Four further points regarding the development of the eucharistic rite remain for brief comment. When Gregory the Great was ill, he made a passing comment in one of his letters that the Eucharist which he himself celebrated could last in those days anything up to three hours (PL 77.956ff). Gregory's reform was aimed at cutting down and streamlining the rite which he had inherited. In the first part of the Mass he was not prepared to do without a sermon, as some of his predecessors had done! Rather, he shortened the litany and dispensed with the deacon's part in the litany on ferial days, thus reducing this merely to the Kyrie eleison, Christe eleison. Within the Canon, as we have already seen, the second part of the Hanc igitur, namely the clause 'diesque nostros' was added by Gregory the Great. And finally he raised the Lord's Prayer to its proper dignity by directing that it be recited immediately after the Canon (cf. p. 213). The Agnus Dei introduced a quite alien note into the Roman liturgy. Indeed it was an importation from an Eastern source by Pope Sergius (687–701), who himself had an ancestry of Sicilian and Syrian background.[1] In the Roman rite it was sung at the time of the Fraction (see p. 193).

During the course of the ninth century and the years following, the initiative and liveliness in matters liturgical passed from Rome to the Franco-German churches. From the end of the ninth century and beyond it is well known that conditions in Rome were becoming extremely difficult. The papacy itself fell into disrepute; moreover the popes very rarely performed their liturgical duties at all, or they celebrated the liturgy in so perfunctory a way as to cause offence to both clergy and people. Little wonder that Rome ceased to hold the high position she had once attained in the liturgical life of the Western church.

[1] L. Duchesne ed., *Le Liber Pontificalis*, 1, 376.

By the end of the tenth century, the process of liturgical development had been reversed. Following his massive work on the Ordines Romani (see pp. 68–9), Andrieu remarks that, at least in the administration of the sacraments, it was the newer rites such as had been developed in France in the eighth, ninth, and tenth centuries which were now being used in Rome itself. Not very long after the year 1000, Rome had received back its liturgy, but no longer was it the austere, epigrammatic, and sober liturgy of the old Roman rite. There had been a radical change following the reshaping and undoubted enrichment it had received in the Franco-German lands. Klauser[1] goes so far as to say that in this very critical period for the development of the Western liturgy, 'the Franco-German church succeeded in saving Roman liturgy, not only for Rome itself, but for the entire Christian world of the Middle Ages'.

Now fundamentally the order of the Mass which had supplanted the local form in Rome itself and had replaced it with a Gallicized version, even at the very centre of Christendom, was only one type out of many. There was still a good deal of variation permitted, not only at regional level, but also at local. Except for those parts of the eucharistic liturgy which had been inherited from the older sacramentaries, variation abounded from country to country, from church to church, from monastery to monastery, even from MS to MS. There are many hundreds of such texts still in existence; scarcely one of them agrees with another in detail. Private prayers of the celebrant were beginning to find their way into the public celebration of the Mass, some of these to the extent of being copied into the official text of the particular Mass-book.

Clearly there was urgent need for some sort of rationalization of so many diverse variations within the order of the Mass. Initially, the impetus came from the larger reformed monastic communities—Cluny, the Cistercians, the Carthusians, and the Premonstratensians: each had made provision for the careful, detailed, and disciplined regulation of the eucharistic celebration. If such reform had been necessary to secure uniformity in the liturgical tradition of static orders, it was imperative that the itinerant orders, much more vulnerable to the liturgical idiosyncrasies of the day, should be equipped with a more stable rite. By the mid-thirteenth century, the Dominicans, under their General, Humbert de Romans, had determined, with care and detail, the order of the Mass rite which was to be used throughout the Order. Much more important and extensive in its effects, however, was the decision of the Franciscans to adopt the *Missale secundum usum Romanae curiae*. Under Innocent III, the Roman curia, already powerful and influential in its

---

[1] T. Klauser, *A Short History of the Western Liturgy*, p. 77.

organization, had determined for its own use its own type of Roman Mass-book based on that which had certainly been used in the old basilicas. The order of the Mass contained therein was extremely simple. J. A. Jungmann[1] comments on the rapidity of the change from sacramentary to missal. The Franciscan Missal and the *Missale secundum consuetudinem Romanae curiae* were to all intents and purposes identical; it was this which was carried into all parts of the world by the wandering friars, and as a result, this soon became the predominant type of Mass-book in use throughout Western Christendom. The invention of the printing process only served to strengthen its influence and its prevalence in the Latin West until the reform under Pius V.

During the course of the later Middle Ages special rites could be found for use in particular churches. This would be true of such a rite as a solemn pontifical Mass in a cathedral; 'ordines' from Laon, Soissons, Châlons-sur-Saône give further knowledge of them. For non-solemn Masses there was practically no direction since generally these would be quite simple and plain. Certain centres such as Lyons, Salisbury, Hereford, York, etc. developed their own rites and often influenced the liturgical celebration and order of the area within which such centres were to be found.[2]

The 'Use of Sarum' in the later Middle Ages became increasingly influential throughout England, Wales, and Ireland. Indeed in 1543 the use of the Sarum Breviary was imposed on the whole of the southern Province, and it was from the books of the Sarum Rite that the architects of the First Prayer Book of Edward VI took most of their material. On the eve of the Reformation, the output of Sarum books was enormous; this fact, in itself, indicating the position, influence and importance of this rite in England. It was to Richard Poore, sometime Dean of Salisbury, or to his influence, that the compilation of the two key books have been ascribed: the *Consuetudinarium*—codification of the various rules and regulations affecting those members of the church involved in the choir and sanctuary; and the *Ordinale*—regulations covering the services throughout the year and the way in which the various service books were to be combined. About the mid-fourteenth century this 'Ordinale' was completely revised and the 'New Use of Sarum' came into being.

In essence the Sarum Rite was a 'local medieval modification of the Roman rite in use at the cathedral church of Salisbury'. Archdale King[3] writes:

---

[1] *MRR* 1.101, see p. 67 above.
[2] For more detailed information see A. A. King, *Liturgies of the Past*.
[3] Op. cit., p. 316.

The elaborate splendour of Sarum ceremonial, as carried out in the cathedral church in the centuries immediately preceding the Reformation, contrasted vividly with the comparative simplicity of the practice of the Roman Church. Three, five or even seven deacons and subdeacons, two or more thurifers, and three crucifers figured on solemnities; while two or four priests in copes ('rectores chori') acted as cantors. There was the censing of many altars, and even during the lessons at matins vested priests offered incense at the high altar. Processions were frequent, and those before High Mass on Sundays were especially magnificent. On the altar itself there were rarely more than two lights, but on feasts there were many others, either standing on the ground or suspended from the roof.

As has already been indicated, the rite was fundamentally 'Roman' but in its performance there were important divergences from the order usually associated with 'Roman' usage. During the Epistle, the chalice might be taken into the sanctuary and the corporals unfolded on the altar by an acolyte. The Gradual and Sequence were often elaborate, being sung by two groups, during which the subdeacon washed his hands and prepared the offerings. The water was blessed by the celebrant, still sitting at the sedilia. The Gospel (with procession) and Creed, when ordered, followed. The deacon then brought the vessels to the celebrant, and the bread and wine were offered with a single prayer. Bidding prayers were offered on Sundays in parish churches, after the Gospel and Offertory: in cathedrals and collegiate churches they were said in procession before the High Mass. The Canon followed in the usual order, except that at particular points there were more elaborate ritual gestures. After the Lord's Prayer and the embolism, suffrages ordered for any special purpose might be said, such as psalms and prayers for peace. The Pax and Agnus Dei followed, after which (not before the Agnus) the mixing took place. The Mass concluded in the usual way, again with differences in ceremonial and often with quite different texts for the prayers: thus, for example, at the communion there was no 'Domine non sum dignus', and the words said by the celebrant at his own communion were peculiar to Sarum: 'Hail for ever, most holy flesh of Christ, my highest delight before and above all things. May the Body of our Lord Jesus Christ be my way and my life, sinner that I am. In the name of the Father. . . .' There was no blessing, and the celebrant returned to the sacristy reciting the opening verses of St John's Gospel.

In general, very little seems to have emerged from the right of dioceses or of ecclesiastical provinces to regulate and supervise the liturgy. Earlier the political power of the Romano-German empire, though indirect, had been considerable. One example of direct influence in the shaping of the Roman liturgy had been the request of Henry II in 1014 at his coronation, when he asked that at Rome also the Creed be sung during the course of the Mass, as had for a long time been the northern practice. Now, however, little interest or initiative appeared to be forthcoming from official sources in the matter of co-ordinating and rationalizing liturgical praxis; thus it was that the names of various individual liturgists appear as influential in this regard. In Germany, the *Micrologus*[1] of Bernold of Constance, written at the beginning of the eleventh century, contained a short explanation of the Mass, with a special chapter (23) devoted to the correct text (according to Bernold) of the Ordo Missae. It is interesting to note that in the Canon, Bernold insisted that nothing be added, not even the names of saints. By the beginning of the twelfth century, the Hungarian bishops, in a formal decree, enjoined the arrangement to be found in the *Micrologus* as of obligation in their territory. Of similar importance for France was the short account of the Mass by Bishop John of Avranches, in his explanation of the liturgy, which was mostly concerned with rubrical direction.[2] The influence of this work, however, was not as widespread as that of the *Micrologus* of Bernold.

From the beginning of the eleventh century various changes of far-reaching consequence had begun to take place in the Roman liturgy. The very way in which the liturgy had been celebrated, with its emphasis on community celebration—singers, readers, congregation, and celebrant with their respective parts, the celebration taking place around a simple table and the celebrant facing the people: this familiar pattern was soon to disappear. In its place, the altar came to be more commonly against the rear wall of the church (a practice which had appeared in the sixth century), and thus the priest celebrated Mass with his back to the people. From about 1000, candles became permanent features of altar furnishings, and from the thirteenth century, with the devotional emphasis on the Lord's passion becoming more popularized, a crucifix. More and more the Mass was coming to be regarded as an almost exclusively priestly function, and because the people could no longer hear anything of the Great Prayer, the Canon, they were reduced to the state of mere spectators, looking upon the backs of the ministers as they performed the sacred drama at the alter. An already rich ceremonial came to be further elaborated with a multiplication of signs, gestures, genuflexions, strikings of the breast, kissing of the altar, kissing of the missal and so on, and these were then invested with sacred allegorical significance. Thus the triple silence, of the Secrets, during the Canon and after the Paternoster,

[1] PL, 151.973–1022.
[2] John of Avranches in PL 147.27–62.

represented the three days of the Lord in the tomb. The five-fold turning of the celebrant towards the people called to mind the five appearances of the Lord after his resurrection. The three crosses after the *Te igitur* of the Canon were symbolic of the three times the Lord was mocked before the high priests, Herod, and Pilate respectively, and so on. The high point of this tremendous and intense drama of the Holy Sacrifice was the moment of the elevation of the sacred host just after the consecration; indeed to view the host became at times the sole object of Mass devotion. Folk went from church to church in order to see this moment as often as they could, often rushing in just before and leaving as hurriedly as they had come. A consequent decline in the receiving of Holy Communion ensued.

A highly significant factor which influenced greatly the development of the medieval Mass was the emergence of the private Mass, originating first in the monasteries about the mid-eighth century, and being taken over later by secular priests. Since their inception, monastic communities had normally comprised lay monks and only very much later had they come to accept the possibility of the priest-monk. Once this had happened, naturally the priest-monk wished to exercise, within the community, the office and function for which he had been ordained. The daily private Mass thus became the norm in such monasteries.

The private Mass posed several problems in regard to liturgical books and the ceremonies to be observed in its performance. The celebrant himself now had the task of reciting those parts of the Mass which were normally sung, and he too had to be responsible for reading the appointed lections. Hence the appearance of what is now accepted as normative, the missal, which by the thirteenth century had almost entirely displaced the sacramentary, the antiphonary, and lectionary (see pp. 65–7). Side altars where such Masses were celebrated were often small and space limited; no longer could there be processions to and from the lectern or ambo for the readings from Scripture. Instead the celebrant had to content himself with moving from 'epistle side' to 'gospel side'. The impressive and often lengthy offertory processions became a few steps from the centre of the altar to the credence at its right hand side, where the server would wait with wine and water.

From the 'private' Mass, there spread to the solemn or high Mass the practice of the celebrant's reading to himself the portion of Scripture chanted by the sub-deacon and deacon; also of reading all those texts of the Mass normally sung by the choir. Thus the missal became the indispensable book for the celebration of any Eucharist. In connection with private Masses there had also arisen the practice of reciting private prayers, such as prayers by way of preparation, or on vesting. Since the vesting for a private Mass, more often than not, took place at the altar at which the Mass was to be celebrated, it is not an unexpected development that these came to have more official status as prayers 'at the foot of the altar', and became a part of the prayer formulas for use at a solemn Mass also. Private prayers which had been recited by the celebrant during the lengthy offertory procession, often in the first person singular (including the *'apologiae'*—prayers of personal confession) also became part of the solemn Mass, as well as being taken into the offertory 'complex' of the private Mass.

Once the private Mass had become the norm, inevitably there was a great multiplication of Masses and, along with this development and almost as a concomitant, an unprecedented increase in the number of clergy, of which the greater part derived their whole living from Mass stipends. They celebrated votive Masses or Masses for the dead, the latter being especially popular and in great demand. Without doubt the plethora of Masses had its effects upon the rites and ceremonies. However, even by the late twelfth century dissenting voices were being raised: Peter Cantor suggested that there would have to be fewer churches, fewer altars, fewer and better priests (PL 205.102–7). Several German mystics spoke in a similar vein, among them Meister Eckhart:[1] 'note that neither blessedness nor perfection consists in saying or hearing a lot of Masses'. Thus by the eve of the Reformation we find that such abuses of the Eucharist, except for some very rare exceptions, had continued unabated. J. A. Jungmann writes:

> The holiest of the Church's possessions remained, it is true, the centre of genuine piety. But alas, the clouds and shadows surrounding this centre brought matters to such a pass that the Institution of Jesus, that well of life from which the Church had drawn for 1500 years, became an object of scorn and ridicule and was repudiated as a horrible idolatry by entire peoples.[2]

---

[1] A. Franz, *Die Messe im deutschen Mittelalter. Beiträge zur Geschichte der Liturgie und des religiösen Volkslebens* (Freiburg 1902), p. 298f.
[2] *MRR* 1.132.

10 From Trent to Vatican II

CLIFFORD HOWELL, SJ

Amiot, F., (ET) *Short History of the Mass.* Faith and Fact. Burns Oates 1959.
Crichton, J. D., *Christian Celebration: the Mass.*
Jungmann, J. A., (in addition to books listed in the general bibliography) (ET)
Liturgical Renewal in Retrospect and Prospect. Challoner 1965.
Martimort, A. G., *The Church at Prayer—the Eucharist.*
Sheppard, L., *Blueprint for Worship.* DLT 1964.
Sheppard, L., ed., *The New Liturgy: a comprehensive introduction.* DLT 1970.

In one sense it is true to say that there is no history of the Mass liturgy between the Councils of Trent and of Vatican II; there is history only of the way in which the Tridentine liturgy was performed. The 1570 Missal fixed the texts and rites, and the Sacred Congregation of Rites was founded for the express purpose of preventing any changes. Thus Trent ushered in four centuries of rigidity and fixation; it was an era of rubricism.

To understand this phenomenon, unprecedented in liturgical history, we must look at some of the reasons for it. Trent was a council of the Church under attack. There were heresies to be combated and abuses to be corrected, many of which concerned liturgical praxis. One of the evils—the absolute chaos which existed in liturgical books—involved so many details that the Council itself could not be delayed over them. Reform of the Missal was put into the hands of a new commission which produced the Missal of Pius V in 1570.

A new missal was beyond all doubt very necessary. Before printing was invented all liturgical books were manuscripts; not only were they full of copyists' errors, but they did not even profess to be copies. They were local productions according to local ideas and customs. Every country, every diocese, almost every church throughout the West had its own way of celebrating Mass, for there was no close control from any central authority. Everywhere the Mass did indeed retain its traditional 'shape'—opening rite, scripture readings, preparation, consecration and distribution of the sacrificial gifts, and a concluding rite. But the details within each section varied enormously, and some of the prayers which had crept in were of doubtful orthodoxy. The Council decided that this could be cured only by the imposition of uniformity, an aim which could now be achieved through the printing of a reformed missal.

What sort of a missal? The commission, made up of the best scholars then available, was told to aim at returning to the liturgy of the city of

Rome as it had been in former times: the Mass was to be restored *ad pristinam sanctorum Patrum normam ac ritum*. The basic elements were to be disengaged from all the distorting accretions they had suffered since about the time of Gregory the Great. The result was to be imposed throughout the Western Church on all who could not demonstrate an uninterrupted custom of two hundred years for their current rite. (Thus certain religious orders and a few dioceses were permitted to retain their own rite.)

The ideal was excellent, but was not achieved. For this we should not blame the commission, for they lacked the means for achieving it. In the sixteenth century very little was known of the liturgy prior to the eleventh or tenth centuries; the science of liturgiology had not even been born; vast numbers of liturgical manuscripts were still lying unknown in the recesses of cathedral and monastic libraries. Commission members had not the least suspicion of something very important which has been discovered since their time, namely, that the Gregorian Sacramentary from the Vatican Library was not authentically Gregorian (see pp. 226–227). Thus the Tridentine Commission preserved in their 'reformed' missal many texts and rites that were in fact foreign to 'the original norm and rite laid down by the holy Fathers'.

An even more serious obstacle to success was the whole concept of liturgy which prevailed in the sixteenth century (and long afterwards). It was this concept of liturgy which, in fact, stood in even greater need of change than did the extant texts. For in those days the liturgy of the Mass appeared to be (and was regarded as) an exclusively clerical activity, a holy ritual to be performed by priests and their trained assistants. However, both theology and history show clearly that in truth the Mass is a celebration by the whole Christian community, even though one member of it, the ordained priest, has a unique part to play. Hence the liturgy ought to be such as to express this truth, not only in theory but also in practice. The people should have full, active, intelligent participation in the celebration. The reform really needed was therefore a reform that would elicit such participation. And this, precisely, is something that was not even envisaged—still less achieved—by the 1570 missal. It was based on a defective concept of liturgy.

For this also we should not blame the commission which produced the Tridentine Missal, nor the Council which ordered its production nor the Pope who promulgated it. The true concept of liturgy could never have entered the minds of any of them; all were victims of the circumstances which, centuries before their time, had falsified the concept. The liturgy had been regarded in early days as 'something we all do together' because that was the way it had come into being, and that was the way it was done.

Gradually during the ninth and subsequent centuries it came to be regarded as 'something done by clerics and watched by the people' because that was the way it had *come* to be done.

This change of outlook was caused by several factors, but the chief one was the retention of Latin as the sole liturgical language long after it had ceased to be the language of the people. A secondary cause was the development of a Mass-form, the 'Low Mass', in which all the parts formerly done by deacon, lector, choir, and people were taken over by one single agent—the priest. The Mass had come to look like a 'one-man sacrifice'. This form, called into being by the practice of private celebration (unknown till about the eighth century) gradually ousted the social form ('High Mass') even in public celebration. The Tridentine commission adopted the simpler form, Low Mass, as basic and regarded High Mass as an elaboration of this. Historical facts prove the exact contrary.

The liturgy that was inherited by the Church of the sixteenth century (and which had formed the concept or outlook on liturgy prevalent at that time) was indeed given a reform which tidied up the chaos of its texts and rites, and gave them order and uniformity. But this reform did nothing to eliminate the most fundamental of its defects—unintelligibility and exclusion of the laity. Given the circumstances of those evil times, this is not surprising.

As regards unintelligibility, the Reformers were clamouring for the use of the vernacular. If the Council of Trent had conceded the vernacular for the perfectly sound reasons by which, indeed, it could be justified, the concession would have been misinterpreted at that time as pandering to heresy. Thus, even though some Council Fathers favoured the vernacular for orthodox reasons, the majority decided that the time for granting it had not yet come. Surely they were wise in the circumstances then prevailing.

As regards exclusion of the laity from any active participation, it was again the prevalence of heresy which prevented the Fathers from rectifying that defect. Indeed because of the concept of liturgy then generally held, they did not even see it as a defect. The theological basis for active participation by the people in the liturgy is the doctrine of the general priesthood of the laity. But Reformers were maintaining that this was the only priesthood given by Christ to his Church; the ministerial priesthood, according to them, was a mere invention of power-seeking men. The Council, of course, had to defend the ministerial priesthood, and did so with such emphasis (quite necessary at that time) that any understanding of the general priesthood—if, indeed, any remained after centuries of an exclusively clerical liturgy—faded out from popular consciousness.

And so from 1570 onwards the liturgy entered a period of stagnation. Nothing in the liturgy itself could be changed or developed. Every word printed in black had to be uttered, every action printed in red had to be performed. Thus, and thus only, was the Mass to be celebrated, and a vigilant Sacred Congregation of Rites ensured that it was so. A special branch of knowledge was developed for this purpose—the science of rubrics.

This science soon came to occupy a key position in the minds of post-Tridentine clergy. Pius V's Missal was introduced by three long documents, *Rubricae Generales*, *Ritus Servandus*, and *De Defectibus*, laying down in the minutest detail what a celebrating priest must do. There are only two mentions of the people, and they are merely incidental. All the rest of this gigantic collection of verbiage refers to the priest. It did but confirm the prevailing idea that the priest was the sole offerer of the Mass.

The rubrics made no provision whatever for external active participation by the people in the performance of the liturgy. Yet at public Masses they had to be occupied somehow. In the past their piety had been nourished by various forms of allegory, but in an age which saw the beginnings of empiricism and scientific study, this had lost its appeal. Prayer books in the vernacular could help only the small minority of the faithful who could read. The more usual and more successful method was to teach them to say communal prayers (such as the rosary) or to sing hymns at Low Mass. Often these had nothing to do with what was going on at the altar, but they were at least filled with pious thoughts and did occupy the people.

At High Mass a source of interest was the music sung by the choir. Rubrics controlled the texts sung, but not their settings. The arts of harmony and counterpoint grew to elaborate proportions; the turn of the sixteenth century saw the rise of the great polyphonic school of composers; the next two centuries brought the organ and other musical instruments into the service of the Church. Courts of Princes and choirs of great Cathedrals vied with each other in the production of magnificent works involving at times two or more choirs answering each other or combining with large orchestras in masterpieces by Mozart, Beethoven, and other men of genius. Artistically this was a marvellous enrichment of Christian culture, but liturgically it was disastrous. For music had become the mistress, rather than the handmaid, of liturgy; it submerged the whole Mass in a beautiful sea of sound, in which the liturgy was carried on unobtrusively in the depths, without any significance, coming to the surface of attention only when the music paused briefly at the Elevation.

In this Baroque age not only the ear, but also the eye, was entranced with beauty that was not liturgy but merely occasioned by liturgy. The churches became great halls scintillating with marble and gold, adorned with paintings and sculptures of saints arrayed in whirling draperies, angels playing harps and blowing trumpets while seated on clouds of heavenly glory. The liturgy had degenerated into a sort of opera looked at by the nobility from galleries and boxes near the sanctuary while choirs and orchestras displayed their talents from other galleries in the nave. The people down below gazed and listened.

Sooner or later there was bound to be a reaction. It came towards the end of the seventeenth century when some early sacramentaries and *ordines* came to light and revealed that in patristic times the liturgy was genuinely a communal celebration. Some attempts were made in France, others in Germany, to restore some active participation by the people in the liturgy itself, but they were suppressed by authority, partly because in those days it was held that whatever was not prescribed by rubrics was forbidden, and partly because some of them were sponsored by men of doubtful orthodoxy. A few prayerbooks containing translations of the Mass prayers were published; they, too, were condemned. The first real success came in Germany where the singing of vernacular hymns during Low Mass had long been customary. Both the quality and relevance of the hymns were improved; the words were paraphrases of the Mass prayers, and escaped condemnation because they were not strictly translations. Very popular at Low Mass, they gradually invaded High Mass. For example, the people would sing a German 'Gloria hymn' or a 'Sanctus hymn', but the law was kept because the priest said the obligatory words in Latin. Thus came into being the so-called 'German High Mass', celebrated as the Principal Mass on Sundays in almost every town or village church which had no choir.

On the other hand cathedrals and large city churches with choirs kept up the Latin High Mass. Among these a 'Restoration movement' rejected operatic Mass settings and cultivated polyphony and plainsong. But this was never a popular movement; it was confined to intellectuals whose interests were aesthetic and archaeological. A parallel movement developed in France under the leadership of Abbot Prosper Guéranger of Solesmes, and thus was more monastic than the German 'Caecilian Movement'. It did much in limited circles to foster deep study of the liturgy and was concerned not only with ceremonies and plainsong but also with history and theology. More and more people wanted to know what the Mass prayers meant; they wanted translations. Though vernacular missals were on the Index of Forbidden Books (being dropped from the list only in 1897!), some got published and escaped suppression.

It had become impossible to enforce such a law. Early in the present century vernacular missals became widespread, and many people began to read silently in their pews the very prayers the priest was saying at the altar. The 'liturgical movement' had reached the stage of 'following in the missal'. But that was still not involvement in the actual performance of liturgy.

Such involvement came after Pius X's *Motu Proprio* on Sacred Music (1903), which encouraged plainsong for the people. At High Mass they might sing chants of the Ordinary in Latin. Some twenty years later the logic of the situation won from Rome the concession that they might *say* these same parts in Latin at Low Mass. The liturgical movement had now reached the stage of Dialogue Mass, and, in an effort to render the other parts of the Mass intelligible, began to introduce lectors who read the scripture passages (usefully) in the vernacular while the priest read them (uselessly, but satisfying the rubrics) quietly in Latin.

It is worth noting that these and many other practices introduced by the liturgical movement (e.g. offertory processions) were not changes in the text of the liturgy itself. They were changes only in the way it was being used. But practical difficulties involved drove more and more, both among clergy and laity, to the conclusion that further advances towards the ideal would never be possible without a radical reform of the liturgy itself. The liturgical movement had become a reforming movement.

Between the two world wars there had been enormous advances in ecclesiology, patrology, scripture and liturgical studies. These made it glaringly obvious that the post-Tridentine concept of liturgy was defective. The Mass is not a one-man sacrifice to be watched by people who neither understand nor take part in its celebration; it is a celebration of the Church, the Mystical Body of Christ, consisting of priests and people hierarchically ordered, who should all have part in it.

Gradually these views, as set forth by scholars of the highest competence in articles, books, and speeches at international congresses, were recognized by authority. They were encouraged by papal encyclicals, conceded by Roman documents, bore fruit in the Holy Week reforms of 1955, and culminated in the Constitution on Sacred Liturgy enacted by the Second Vatican Council in 1963. The Council ordered a reform of the liturgy, ruling that 'full active participation by the people, demanded by the very nature of liturgy', should be 'the aim to be considered before all else' as their 'right and duty by reason of their baptism'. The Holy Father appointed a Consilium which finished the work in 1970 when Pope Paul VI promulgated the new Roman Missal to supersede that of 1570 promulgated by Pius V.

It is quite impossible to give in a short space any adequate account of the changes in the Mass liturgy brought about by the Missal of Vatican II. But a brief summary may be attempted by grouping together some of the changes under different headings.

Perhaps the most important of all is the fruit of n. 28 of the Constitution: 'In liturgical celebrations each person, minister or layman, who has an office to perform, should do all of, but only, those parts which pertain to his office by the nature of the rite and the principles of liturgy'. This is technically known as 'differentiation of function' and is the feature of the new rite which, more than any other, makes it clear that the Mass is not a 'one-man sacrifice', but the worship of a hierarchically organized community.

There is also 'differentiation of place'; no longer is everything done at the altar. This most sacred place is reserved for the explicitly sacrificial part of the liturgy. The proclamation of God's word is done from the ambo; there is also the chair, whence the priest presides over the liturgy of the word, says certain non-sacrificial prayers, and leads others in his capacity of president of the community. Thus is fulfilled the aim of n. 50, 'that the intrinsic nature and purpose of the several parts of the Mass, as also the connection between them, may be more clearly manifested'.

The new lectionary fulfils n. 51: 'The treasures of the Bible are to be opened up more lavishly, so that richer fare may be provided for the faithful at the table of God's word'.

'The rites are to be simplified' (n. 50), as has been done at the formerly over-developed offertory, fraction, and the beginning and end of the Mass, as also by the elimination of many small gestures during the eucharistic prayer.

'Elements which have suffered injury through accidents of history' (n. 50) are restored; examples are the penitential rite, the homily and the prayers of the faithful, as also the strong recommendation given to various forms of offertory procession, and to the practice of consecrating at each Mass the hosts which are to be distributed to the people in communion.

The Mass has been greatly enriched by the provision of three eucharistic prayers which may be used as alternatives to the Roman Canon, together with a large number of prefaces for different occasions, and a greatly increased repertoire of collects. In 1974 five more eucharistic prayers were approved, three for children's Masses, and two for Masses of reconciliation.

'In the restoration and promotion of the sacred liturgy, full active participation by all the people is the aim to be considered before all else' (n. 14). Of all the changes introduced for this purpose the most striking, as well as the most valuable, is the restoration of intelligibility through the permission to use the people's own language. Though it was possible for the faithful to 'say or sing in Latin those parts of the Ordinary of the Mass which are rightfully theirs' (n. 54), and though they could learn what these parts meant because they are unchanging, it was undoubtedly difficult and required much training; it is beyond question far easier for the people both to take part and to understand in their own tongue. For the changing parts of the Mass, especially the scripture readings and the collects, concession of the vernacular was a clear necessity.

The reformed liturgy is sometimes referred to as 'the new Mass'. That is not accurate. The Mass itself is fundamentally the same as ever; only its mode of celebration has been changed. Its liturgy has been 'restored to the vigour which it had in the days of the holy Fathers'. What the Council of Trent attempted to do, but could not succeed in doing because of the circumstances prevailing at the time, has now been done, and very well done, by the Second Vatican Council.

11 Protestantism and the Eucharist

D. H. TRIPP

Barkley, J. M., *The Worship of the Reformed Church*. Lutterworth 1966.
Brilioth, Y., (ET) *Eucharistic Faith and Practice*. SPCK 1930.
Jasper, R. C. D. and Cuming, G. J., *PEER*.
Maxwell, W. D., *The Liturgical Portions of the Genevan Service Book*, 2nd edn. Faith Press 1965.
Maxwell, W. D., *An Outline of Christian Worship* (OUP 1936), esp. pp. 72–144.
Micklem, N. ed., *Christian Worship*. OUP 1936.
Reed, L. D., *The Lutheran Liturgy: A Study of the Common Liturgy of the Lutheran Church in America*, 2nd edn. Philadelphia 1959.
Reed, L. D., *Worship: a Study of corporate devotion*. Philadelphia 1959.
Thompson, Bard, *Liturgies of the Western Church*. Cleveland and New York 1962.

THE RADICAL REFORMERS

Christian communities in Europe dissenting from the doctrine, discipline, and liturgy of the Roman Church arose long before the sixteenth century. However, evidence as to the rites favoured by Hussites and Lollards is scarce, and must largely be inferred from what is known of later developments among 'Anabaptists', the 'Radical Wing' of the Reformation. In this sphere also information is hard to come by. Sixteenth-century sources afford a picture of gatherings for worship at which families gathered for a day of exposition and prayer, each man being free to expound any passage which had impressed him and then to lead the group in extempore prayer. As far as the Eucharist was concerned: the Institution Narrative was read, and then the bread was passed round, and all ate together. A cup was then passed round similarly, each worshipper nodding to his neighbour as it came to him, and again before handing it to the next. The reading apart, the action took place in silence. Later developments among Anabaptists included variation in the posture for communion: sitting in one's place, sitting by groups at the table (under Reformed influence?), and the insertion of devotional exhortations and prayers, which were increasingly preserved for future use in manuscript and later in printed manuals for presiding ministers. This development was faster among Mennonites and other continental Anabaptists than with Baptists in Britain, America, and elsewhere.

The radical Protestant tradition came for the most part to be submerged in the upheavals of the sixteenth and seventeenth centuries, and (particularly in England) came to have the reputation of being an eccentric variant on the great 'Folk-Churches' of the Reformation. The radical groups survived, even if in attenuated forms, but their influence was both widespread and profound. Their rites reflected and encouraged a determination to tear away from the Eucharist every accretion of the ages and to go to its simple essence by reproducing the Last Supper as faithfully as might be. This sharp insistence on pristine simplicity was to affect virtually all Protestant liturgiography. It was and is especially attractive to troubled minds in times of dispute and change, both religious and secular. Such aspirations spread by 'stimulus diffusion' across national and confessional barriers, and that at a level where scholars, synods, and hierarchies enjoy little attention.

The content of the rite suggests a very simplistic but perennially popular version of the Memorialist view of the Eucharist: we do just this, because our Lord told us to; and, as we do it, we think of him. More positively, the Eucharist as Christian fellowship clearly emerges here as a *leitmotif*.[1]

[1] C. Krahn, art. 'Communion' in *Mennonite Encyclopedia*, vol. 1 (Kansas, 1955); G. H. Williams, *The Radical Reformation* (Weidenfeld and Nicolson 1962); B. R. White, *The English Separatist Tradition* (OUP 1971); C. Burrage, *Early English Dissenters* (CUP 1912); E. A. Payne, *Free Churchmen, Unrepentant and Repentant* (Carey Kingsgate Press 1965).

THE UNITAS FRATRUM

The oldest surviving Protestant community is the *Unitas Fratrum*, the Moravian Church, formed in Bohemia in 1457. A eucharistic celebration of the Czech brethren in the fifteenth century is described by Schweinitz: After some three weeks of preparatory services and both private and public confession, the rite opens with a hymn, a prayer, and a sermon. During a further hymn, the priest and deacons (no special vestments) approach the Table, which is already prepared. The people are exhorted to penitence, then kneel for a prayer, Our Father, and a hymn. They rise for the absolution. The Institution Narrative is chanted to consecrate the elements. After priest and deacons have received, the people approach at the priest's invitation, in their several groups (by social and church rank, by sex and age). At first, they communicated standing, but pressure from other Churches led to a kneeling posture. During the communion, hymns on the passion are sung. Thanksgivings, intercessions, and a blessing complete the service.

Even after the appalling vicissitudes of the Brethren through the sixteenth and seventeenth centuries and the refounding of the *Unitas Fratrum* by Christian David and Zinzendorf in Saxony in 1722, the Moravian liturgy largely retained its identity, but has tended to take many features from other traditions which the Moravian Church has met in the course of its expansion.

Typical of Moravian worship is the generous use of singing—eighteenth- and nineteenth-century *Liturgien* of the Brethren are simply hymnals—and proper litanies for special seasons, derived from Lutheran models but full of the tender devotion to Jesus which has marked Moravianism since Zinzendorf.

Moravian worship has had little direct influence on other traditions, except perhaps to encourage hymnography, but through the work of Schleiermacher it has deeply affected Protestant attitudes to worship, giving personal piety a major, even a dominant, place.[1]

THE LUTHERAN CHURCHES

BEFORE LUTHER

The Reformation of the sixteenth century was chiefly led by men of high academic attainments, propagated by the select band of clergy whose main work was preaching, and supported by the city communities (both

---

[1] E. de Schweinitz, *History of the Church known as the Unitas Fratrum* (Bethlehem, Pa., 1885); J. T. and K. G. Hamilton, *History of the Moravian Church* (New York, 1967). There seems to be no monograph, in English at least, on Moravian worship.

bourgeois and artisan). Compared with Anabaptist methods, then, those of the Lutheran and Reformed movements were naturally more conservative, more redolent of Renaissance scholarship, and more closely related to the collective life of society at large and the growing articulate nationalisms of Europe. The liturgies of the great Protestant 'Folk-Churches' reflect these relationships, but also shows signs of kinship with more radical trends: insistence on edification and practical piety, the striving after apostolic simplicity, the use of singing to give the people a voice, the almost universal use of the vernacular, the expurgation of everything 'superstitious' or seemingly meaningless.

After the Indulgences controversy of 1517, Luther was clearly the natural head and spokesman of the movement we call the Protestant Reformation; but he was not the first to produce a Protestant Mass. He advocated one in his *Treatise upon the New Testament* (1519), but took no practical steps (so far as is yet known) until 1523, and even then his *Formula Missae* was still in Latin, and suggests rather a professorial essay than a rite for the Church's use.

Andreas Karlstadt was the first to celebrate in German, at Christmas 1521. In 1522, a German communion-rite for the Carmelites at Nördlingen was produced by Kaspar Kantz, their prior. At the offertory, the priest said penitential prayers and *Veni sancte Spiritus* (from the rite of the diocese of Augsburg). The Canon was much cut down (a form of *Quam oblationem* followed by the institution and Our Father). Nunc Dimittis or Te Deum followed the communion. Luther's *bête noire* Thomas Muntzer sired a less conservative (but still oddly conservative) German Evangelical Mass for Allstedt, where it was used from 1523 to 1533, when it was exported to Brunswick and Erfurt—with Luther's approval. Preface and Sanctus lead into the institution with the elevation, followed by the Lord's Prayer and the fraction, a pattern none too different from Luther's. Other rites which preceded Luther's own German Mass were those of Schwarz at Strasbourg, the Worms Mass of 1524, and that of Döber at Nuremberg in 1525, which last appears to be the parent of the Swedish Lutheran orders.[1]

MARTIN LUTHER

Luther's interim measure, *Formula Missae et Communionis* of 1523, has already been mentioned. Its plan was close to the Roman Mass, the major

[1] See J. Smend, *Die evangelischen deutschen Messen bis zu Luthers Deutscher Messe* (Göttingen 1896). Some information in English in Y. Brilioth, pp. 110ff. On Müntzer, see E. G. Rupp, *Patterns of Reformation* (Epworth 1969), ch. 20, and his sources, especially O. J. Mehl, *Thomas Müntzers Deutsche Messen und Kirchenämter* (Grimmen 1937).

alterations being the excision of the Offertory prayers and most of the Canon. The sermon might come at the very beginning or after the Creed. The content, if not the structure, of the consecration sets what was to be the norm (*PEER* 24a). The Latin preface is used up to *aeterne Deus*, to which follows *per Christum Dominum nostrum*, followed by words of institution (sung).

> Then, when the consecration is complete, the choir shall sing the *Sanctus* and during the *Benedictus* the bread and cup shall be elevated according to ancient custom, for the sake of the weak, who might perhaps be annoyed by so quick a change of the most respected custom in the Mass. (AT)

The Lord's Prayer follows, without the embolism. *Pax domini* is to be said, as a 'truly evangelical word, proclaiming the forgiveness of sins'—a typically Lutheran emphasis. The communion uses the Roman words of administration, and is accompanied by *Agnus Dei*. Two collects, *Benedicamus Domino* with Hallelujah, and a biblical benediction form the conclusion.

This *Formula* was to have great influence in time, but Luther's own preferences developed further. The *Deutsche Messe* of 1526 (*PEER* 24b) has dropped *Gloria in excelsis*, and adopted versified forms of the Creed and Sanctus. The consecration is radically altered. The sermon is followed by a paraphrase of the Lord's Prayer and an exhortation to communicate in devout faith. The Institution Narrative is read. The elevation is kept, not as a bodily elevation of Body and Blood, but as an act of memorial, of proclamation. The communion may be given in two parts, after the appropriate words in the Institution (but how?), and is accompanied by the German Sanctus, *Gott sei gelobet*, John Huss' *Jesus Christus unser Heiland* and *Agnus Dei* in German.

There are conservative elements here, such as the isolation of the *Verba Testamenti* and the use of medieval church music from Meissen and southern Germany; but this rite is more than a simplification of the Latin Ordinary of the Mass. Luther's theology has the decisive word.[1]

OTHER LUTHERAN DEVELOPMENTS

Variants upon the Lutheran theme were astonishingly numerous, mostly because the Reformation took place city by independent city, and each locality had to be provided for as its needs and self-esteem required. For

[1] For translations of Luther's rites, see, besides *PEER*, editions of his Works, and also Bard Thompson, *Liturgies of the Western Church*. On his theology of worship, see A. Allwohn, *Gottesdienst und Rechtfertigungslehre* (Göttingen 1926), and V. Vajta, *Luther on Worship* (ET Philadelphia 1958). Essential background: E. G. Rupp, *The Righteousness of God* (Hodder 1953).

the majority of areas, the plan of Reformation was laid down in a 'Church Order', or *Kirchenordnung*, a large part of which would be devoted to the liturgy. This order might be a slim pamphlet, or a 300-page folio like the scheme produced for Archbishop Hermann von Wied of Cologne in 1543 by Bucer and Melanchthon, the famous *Consultation*. This latter was never used as a liturgy, for it was rejected, with the Protestant cause, by the Cologne clergy and most of the nobles of the area, but it was to play a part in the composition of the English Prayer Book. The relationship between the *Kirchenordnungen* is complex in the extreme. The work of prominent individuals may be traced. Mention may be made of Osiander (Brandenburg-Nürnberg 1533), and especially of Bugenhagen. Johannes Bugenhagen made liturgies for Brunswick (1528), Hamburg (1529), and Lübeck (1531). He provided for a Mass without the Lord's Supper (which oddly kept the Preface, Sanctus and Agnus until 1529), and also made additions of a pastoral nature, such as intercessions and the notices. Bugenhagen was a parish priest as well as a professor, and Luther when he died was still his curate. His work represents what may be called a popularization of *Formula Missae*, which suggests that Luther's *Deutsche Messe* was too far from tradition for many Lutherans.

A unifying factor was Lutheran hymnody. If we may superficially describe Anabaptist song as the voice of the suffering Church, and Reformed hymnody as the cautious versification of the Psalms in a spirit of humble penitence, then the Lutheran hymns from the outset keep the jubilant character of the great doxological texts that they replaced.

Lutheran liturgy varied from conservative richness to Calvinistic austerity, as in Württemberg, where the Protestant Church, led by Brentz, was high Lutheran in theology, but Swiss-Reformed in rite.[1]

Scandinavian Lutheranism was equally varied, and still is. Denmark's *Alterbog* is close to *Deutsche Messe*, contrasting with the richness of Olaus Petri's Mass of 1531[2]

LUTHERAN DEVELOPMENTS:
FROM ORTHODOXY TO THE LITURGICAL MOVEMENT

The settled patterns of Lutheran worship were profoundly disturbed when, after the didacticism of Lutheran orthodoxy (German clergy

---

[1] The Church Orders are collected in the vast work of E. Sehling, *Die evangelischen Kirchenordnungen des 16. Jahrhunderts* (Leipzig 1902–13). See also L. Fendt, *Der lutherische Gottesdienst des 16. Jahrhunderts* (Munich 1923); Rietschl and Graff, *Lehrbuch der Liturgik* (Göttingen 1951–2); useful texts as appendices to G. J. Cuming, *History of Anglican Liturgy*.

[2] See *PEER* 25. Cf. E. E. Yelverton, *The Mass in Sweden* (HBS 1920), and commentary in Brilioth, ch. 7; cf. R. Prenter, *Worship*=ch. 5 in L. S. Hunter, ed., *Scandinavian Churches* (Faber 1965).

almost everywhere adopted the black gown (*Talar*) of the teaching profession), the pressure of scepticism and the counter-measures of Pietism encouraged celebrants to experiment very freely, with results that to later minds appeared catastrophic.

The eighteenth century, especially toward its close, witnessed a bewildering variety of innovations, by way of both private enterprise and also 'modernization'. The psychological needs of the time were pandered to unreservedly. This happened also in Roman Catholic and Anglican circles, but the comparative fixity of their rites prevented the fashions of thought from having a public and lasting effect upon liturgical life. [1]

The first reaction was led by King Frederick William III of Prussia (1770–1840). He wanted order, and he wanted unity among his Protestant subjects. Impressed by the dignity of Anglican rites which he saw while in exile, he set about providing a unitive liturgy for the Old Prussian Union (of Lutherans and Reformed) within his realm. He studied early Lutheran liturgies, which gave rise to a school of liturgical study which still lives. His rites for the Berlin royal churches and his *Agende* for all Prussian Protestants were less successful.

Theological tendencies led to two further liturgical movements. The 'older' movement, of which the chief protagonists were Friedrich Spitta (1852–1924) and Julius Smend (1857–1930), set out to appeal to the sense of creaturely dependence and feeling for beauty, to which Schleiermacher had attached such importance. The 'younger' movement is associated with Rudolf Otto, best known as the author of *Das Heilige* (Marburg 1917; ET *The Idea of the Holy* OUP 1924), and Friedrich Heiler. Otto's own plans to build upon his insight into the sense of the numinous, set out in *Zur Erneuerung und Ausgestaltung des Gottesdienstes* (Giessen 1925), look to *Formula Missae* with many detailed enrichments. Heiler's ecumenical movement stirred up interest in Roman Catholic and other non-Lutheran worship.

The Berneuchen Circle, with the organization to which it gave rise, the Brotherhood of St Michael (1929 and 1931 respectively), has sought to revive the Lutheran vision of the Church as a fellowship living under the Word. Their work has included numerous liturgical texts, down to K. F. Müller and K. B. Ritter's *Ordnung der Messe* (1950), of a high liturgical and literary quality.

The key to Lutheran liturgical revision from Frederick William III to the present has been a continued and many-sided recovery of Lutheran tradition. The historians (Kliefoth, Rietschl, Lietzmann, Holl, Graff,

[1] See P. Graff, *Geschichte der Auflösung der alten gottesdienstlichen Formen in der evangelischen Kirche Deutschlands* 2nd edn (Göttingen 1937–9).

Fendt, Mahrenholz, and the rest) and the theologians (particularly Stählin, Peter Brunner, Harbsmeier) have complemented one another in this process.

THE REFORMED CHURCHES

ZWINGLI AND ZURICH

Zwingli's education was humanistic, not monastic like Luther's. As a result, he was impatient of poor literary style in liturgy, and chary of theological speculation, so that he could not easily conceive of Christ's humanity as being both in heaven and substantially present in the eucharistic species. He did not, in his own mind, reduce the Eucharist to a mere act of remembrance, but affirmed a spiritual impartation of Christ in the sacramental action, although his doctrine was never clear to Luther (nor to many others, in his own time and since). He also introduced a new emphasis on the Eucharist as an act of fellowship, in which Anabaptist influence may perhaps be seen.

His first liturgical scheme, *De Canone Missae Epicheiresis* of 1523 (*PEER* 23a), laid violent hands on the Canon of the Mass, as its title promised. The rest of the rite was lightly revised, but the Canon was replaced by four prayers: a recapitulation of redemption, with the Our Father; a prayer for feeding on the Bread of Heaven; for the grace to imitate Christ's sacrificial devotion, and for Christian unity in him; for worthy communion, with the Institution Narrative. His developed scheme appeared in 1525. The normal Sunday worship was to be a preaching-service, based on the medieval prone (as in J. U. Surgant's *Manuale Curatorum*, 1502). The Eucharist would be held four times a year (four times as often as medieval laity had been obliged to communicate). The *Action oder Bruch des Nachtmals* (*PEER* 25b) opens with a prayer for fitting celebration and the Pauline Institution Narrative, which is followed by the *Gloria in excelsis*. John 6.47–63 is read, as a caution against making too much of external things. After an exhortation to devout communion, the Our Father and a pre-communion prayer are said. The Institution is recited, and the elements are carried round in silence to the people in their seats. Ps. 113, a brief thanksgiving and a dismissal end the celebration. The reading of John 13ff was inserted to fill the silence during the distribution in 1535.

FAREL, AND FRANCE AND FRENCH SWITZERLAND

A Reformed rite closely comparable with Zwingli's, and perhaps linked in some way with the Bernese variant of it, is the *Manière et Fasson* of Guillaume Farel. It seems to have been compiled at Montbéliard in 1524;

it was printed at Neuchâtel in 1533. A little less bare than Zwingli's, this rite is still a didactic monologue. After the Institution and before the distribution, there occurs an exhortation that was to recur in Calvin, in Knox, and even in a nineteenth-century Methodist service:

> Therefore, lift up your hearts on high, seeking the heavenly things in heaven, where Jesus Christ is seated at the right hand of the Father; and do not fix your eyes on the visible signs which are corrupted by usage. In joy of heart, in brotherly union, come, everyone, to partake of our Lord's Table, giving thanks unto him for the very great love which he has shown us. Have the death of this good Saviour graven on your hearts in eternal remembrance, so that you are set afire, so also that you incite others to love God and follow his holy Word.

Among other interesting features are the words of administration (a prayer for the indwelling of Christ) and the emphasis in the post-communion prayers on intercession and mission.[1]

OECOLAMPADIUS AND BASEL

Apparently during his days as a castle chaplain in 1523, Oecolampadius wrote a German liturgy, the *Testament Jesu Christi*, 'commonly called the Mass, and done into German'. It is in essence a rendering of the Latin Mass propers for Maundy Thursday.

His next work (probably compiled in conjunction with others, for many minor features are not typical of him) is the *Form und Gstalt* of 1525, which set the tone for the Basel liturgy thereafter. It is parallel to, but markedly distinct from, the rites of Zwingli and Farel.

After the sermon, there stands a communion-exhortation, the Apostles' Creed, fencing of the table, and intercessions with the Our Father. After the preparation of the elements, a short confession (with Ps. 103.1–8 and the *Kyrie* in German) and a declarative absolution, two readings and an exhortation recall the passion. 'No longer do we desire to be our own, but the Lord's, and servants of his servants.... Think upon (the passion) now, as you sit near Christ and hear of him; who, on the day before he suffered....' Thanksgiving concludes with the Lord's Prayer—an interesting sidelight on Luther's use of this prayer. The communion is preceded by a brief call to self-examination, and followed by an abrupt command to love the brotherhood and the poor, with a concluding benediction. This short ending suggests that Protestants, like

---

[1] On Zwingli, see Bard Thompson, pp. 141ff; original texts in *Corpus Reformatorum* edn of his works (Leipzig 1905–35); and see Brilioth, 160ff, and N. Micklem, ed., *Christian Worship*, ch. 9. For Farel, see Bard Thompson, pp. 216–24; J. G. Baum, ed., *La Manière et Fasson* (Strasbourg 1859); J. Meyhoffer and others, *Guillaume Farel: une biographie nouvelle* (Neuchâtel 1930).

their medieval forebears, tended to drift out of the church before the service was finished.

Despite its memorialist surface, this rite reflects a keen sense of the Real Presence—not just in the minds of the worshippers, but in heaven and in that interface of grace where heaven and believers meet.[1]

STRASBOURG

This city was distinguished among the reforming states by its tolerant atmosphere. The surviving Roman Catholic community was small, but free from harassment; their new bishop, Erasmus von Limberg, was enthroned in a Protestant service! Even Anabaptists were expelled and not executed. This policy was due to the city's exposed position, to its experiences of the troubles of the late Middle Ages, and above all to the urbane piety of the preacher Geiler von Keysersberg, the spokesman of Catholic reform, in whose wake came the city's Protestant reformers, Zell, Capito, Hedio, and Bucer.

The first German Mass was held at St Laurence's on 16 February 1524 by Diebold Schwarz. The rite (subsequently published in at least nine editions) was very Lutheran in character. The Canon contained intercessions before the Institution, and after the *Unde et memores* was devoted to exultation in the assurance of adoption. Although the rite was dropped, and the policy of a full Canon was not revived among Lutherans until Wilhelm Löhe's Bavarian *Agende* of 1856, it served to modify the views of Martin Bucer.

Bucer's *Grund und Ursach* of 1524 recommended a rite like Zwingli's, with modifications: an authoritative declaration of pardon, the reading of the Institution from all four biblical versions(!). His *Psalter mit aller Kirchenübung* (18th edn 1539) (*PEER* 26) was less iconoclastic, and had a richer liturgical character. It is a delicate amalgam of ideas from Schwarz, Luther, Oecolampadius, Zwingli, and no doubt others.

The eucharistic exhortation describes the fall of man and Christ's coming incarnate 'so that there might be a holy flesh and blood' which are now to be received in the Supper. The Prayer mutes the tone of thanksgiving, and the Institution is moved from it to the point before the communion, so that the prayer itself combines intercession with petition for devout communion.

Bucer's rite does not commit its users to either side (or should we

---

[1] The *Testament* has not been translated. Its connection with Oecolampadius has been doubted, but without compelling reason. The later rite is in Smend, pp. 213–19, ET in Bard Thompson, pp. 211–15. See also Rupp, Part I, and Stählin's edn of Oecolampadius' *Briefe und Akten* (=*Quellen und Forschungen zur Reformationsgeschichte* 10 and 19) (Leipzig 1927, 1934).

rather say, any of the various sides?) of the bitter eucharistic controversy which split the reforming movement. It shows some of the possibilities of a mediating liturgical theology, such as the Strasbourg Church urgently needed. It was also to be the foundation of Calvin's rite.[1]

CALVIN, KNOX, AND OTHERS

The Protestant worship which Calvin must first have known in any settled form was Farel's *Manière et Fasson*, which appears to have held sway under Farel's aegis in Geneva from 1536 to 1538. Driven from the city in April 1538, Calvin at last found his way to Strasbourg, where he met and was deeply impressed by Bucer's liturgy. He adopted it, substantially altered it, and published it in French at Strasbourg in 1540, under the title of *La Forme des Prières Ecclésiastiques*.

Calvin himself was recalled to Geneva in 1541, and there introduced a slightly simplified form of his Strasbourg rite in the following year (*PEER* 27). This order was to be the direct or indirect norm for Sunday worship throughout the Reformed world.

Calvin had devoted himself to biblical and dogmatic studies, and was well versed in the Fathers.[2] He set his sights on a weekly celebration of the Eucharist, and was only prevented from the realization of his ideal by the direct veto of the city council, who wished to follow Zurich in a quarterly observance. His eucharistic theology was higher than he is often given credit for, and is close to that of Farel, as we have described it above, but without the negative attitude to the sacramental species.

The preaching-service was to open with 'Our help is in the name of the Lord...', with the Commandments, prayer for help, psalm, prayer, reading, and sermon. Then follows intercessory prayer, after which the Eucharist proper begins with the Apostles' Creed and the Institution Narrative (as a warrant for the action, not as a consecration). The table is 'fenced', i.e. immoral and irreligious persons are warned off. The people are urged to examine themselves, and all the penitent are assured of mercy, for this sacrament promises a mutual indwelling of Christ with the believer. The crescendo of this exhortation is a call to lift up spirit and heart to the heavenly realm, imperfectly signified by these earthly emblems, and so to commune with the Father and the Son (a

---

[1] Texts in F. Hubert, *Die Strassburger liturgischen Ordungen im Zeitalter der Reformation* (Göttingen 1900); J. Smend, *Der erste evangelische Gottesdienst in Strassburg* (Strasbourg 1897); ET in Maxwell, *Outline of Christian Worship* (OUP 1936), pp. 87–98, for Schwartz; Bard Thompson, pp. 159–81 for Bucer; cf. G. J. van de Poll, *Martin Bucer's Liturgical Ideas* (Assen 1954); M. U. Chrisman, *Strasbourg and the Reform* (London and Chicago 1967). Also W. D. Maxwell, *Genevan Service Book*.

[2] See H. O. Old, *The Patristic Roots of Reformed Worship* (Zürich 1975).

development away from Farel's negations). Communion (kneeling or standing) is accompanied by psalms and readings, and followed by a short thanksgiving and the Aaronic blessing.

John Knox met and adopted this rite at Frankfurt. He continued Calvin's development away from Farel by inserting a prayer of thanksgiving between the exhortation and the communion. He published the result as the *Forme of Prayers* at Geneva in 1556 (*PEER* 32), and brought it home with him to Scotland, where in 1562 it supplanted the second Edwardine book as the definitive Scottish use under the title of the *Book of Common Order*. It was itself replaced in 1645 by the *Westminster Directory*, but came back to interest and influence through the Scottish liturgical revival.

Calvin's book itself appeared in England in translation in 1550. The Presbyterians of English Puritanism took it up, by way of Knox, and urged it upon Parliament in 1584 (the 'Waldegrave Liturgy') and in 1586 (the 'Middelburg Liturgy'). The latter was used by exiles in the Low Countries, and perhaps in secret in England.

THE WESTMINSTER DIRECTORY OF 1645

Puritan ascendancy in the Long Parliament (from 1640) brought about a thorough presbyterianization of the Church of England under the Commonwealth. As part of its Genevan programme, the Westminster Assembly of Divines created a *Directory for the Publique Worship of God throughout the three Kingdoms* (*PEER* 34).

Its intercessions came between the reading and the sermon. After the exhortation, the elements were to be 'sanctified and blessed' by the Word (sc., the Institution Narrative) and a prayer of thanksgiving, with penitential earnestness, for Christ and his saving work. The prayer continues:

> Earnestly to pray to God, the Father of all mercies, and God of all consolation, to vouchsafe his gracious presence, and the effectual working of his Spirit in us; and so to sanctify these elements of bread and wine, and to bless his own ordinance, that we may receive by faith the body and blood of Jesus Christ, crucified for us, and so to feed upon him that he may be one with us, and we one with him; that he may live in us, and we in him, and to him who hath loved us, and given himself for us.

The fraction and distribution would be accompanied by the Words of Institution (now used in close imitation of the Last Supper, and neither as a warrant nor to consecrate). Explanatory remarks might be inserted after both consecration and communion. The action closed with thanksgiving.

The rite is still in the heavily didactic strain of its Reformed predecessors (does any other anaphora pause to notice the philosophical problems of predestination and election?), but the development of the eucharistic prayer towards being essentially an act of thanksgiving was now complete; this feature was to endure.

After the reverses of the later seventeenth century, what little remained of Presbyterian Puritanism in England became for the most part Unitarian. Presbyterian revival came about through Scots influence, which in turn disseminated the tradition of the *Directory*. One abortive but in itself valuable attempt to produce an English Reformed liturgy was that of Richard Baxter, whose *Savoy Liturgy* of 1661 built upon Calvin's ground-plan, but inserted prayers for devout communion and for consecration either before or around the Institution Narrative (*PEER* 35).

English Free Church worship of the eighteenth and nineteenth centuries seems to have varied between a simplification of the *Directory* and a total disintegration of liturgical form. The more conservative strain, represented by Doddridge and Watts, was Separatist in constitution but Calvinist (and later Zwinglian) in theology; its liturgical contribution was largely in the field of a very flourishing hymnody, which in turn encouraged similar efforts among Methodists and Anglicans. One freak development was the Catholic Apostolic Church, associated with Edward Irving (1792–1834). This fissiparous body contrived to be at once millenarian (glossolalia included) and expansively ritualistic. Its *Liturgy and Other Offices* (John Bate Cardale, various edns from 1838 to 1880) tried to combine Reformed, Anglican, Roman, and Oriental elements. Its chief significance was that it was a spur to liturgical study, especially in the Church of Scotland. It also helped to encourage other eclectic rites, of which W. E. Orchard's *Divine Service* (Oxford 1919) and its milder descendant *The Free Church Book of Common Prayer* (London 1929) are the principal representatives. In all these schemes, the outline of the Roman Mass is the basis, and an attempt is made to compose a full anaphora.

These last two works were extensively used by Free Church ministers of different schools as ideas-books, as was a less ambitious but more workmanlike book, the *Devotional Services for Public Worship* of John Hunter. Hunter, a Congregational minister like Orchard, had been his predecessor at the King's Weigh House Church, London. His Eucharist was a simplified version of Baxter's, but much more acceptable in its literary style for pastoral use. Most of his suggestions for the enrichment of worship turn for models to the Divine Office (see pp. 399–400).

The Reformed Church in America went through similar stages of

15 Contemporary eucharist during the Canon (see p. 479)

16 Contemporary church interior, almost circular in shape
with altar, font, and lectern in full view of all
(see p. 479)

17 Ordination
The laying-on of hands and delivery of the chalice
from a Roman pontifical, 1520
(see p. 321)

thought and experiment. Thomas L. Harris' *Christian Public Worship* (New York 1928) offers both a theology of worship (Schleiermacher and Otto) and specimens of orders of worship. There are three eucharistic orders: one made up simply of a series of Bible quotations, one derived from the Episcopalian rite with additions from Orchard, and one with the same outline but with material mostly derived from Eastern sources. By contrast, H. S. Coffin's *Public Worship of God* (shortly after 1945), which contains no full orders of worship, brings together doctrinal and pastoral considerations relevant to the leadership of worship, with many practical suggestions, including that of a full-orbed Great Thanksgiving at the Communion.

The Continent of Europe also saw a progressive enrichment of Reformed worship, in which Anglican influence was much felt, as may be seen in the work of Osterwald at Basel (1713) and of Bersier (Paris, Église de l'Étoile, 1874, and many later edns).

The Scottish Church had in the meantime been steadily enriching the pattern derived from the *Directory*. After a revival of liturgiological study and a generation of further reflection, there appeared the Church of Scotland's *Prayers for Divine Service* (1923 and 1929) and the United Free Church's *Directory* (1909) and *Book of Common Order* (1928), as well as a host of private publications. After the two Churches mentioned came together in union, there was compiled the great and influential *Book of Common Order* of 1940. This contains four distinct modes of celebration, in which the Reformed faith and the ancient Western pattern of rite are skilfully combined. Comparable but simpler materials are set out in the *Presbyterian Service Book* for England and Wales (London 1968).

Not all Reformed rites are derived from Switzerland or Strasbourg. The liturgy of the Netherlands Reformed Church goes back to John à Lasco's *Forma ac Ratio totius ecclesiastici ministerii* of 1550, generally similar to Farel's work. The draft *Dienstboek* of 1955 offers now three eucharistic orders, one of which is deliberately framed in the light of current ecumenical knowledge and relationships; its structure restores the ancient Western order.

The English Free Churches have maintained the *Directory* tradition, with many enrichments, in the *Book of Congregational Worship* (London 1920) and in Huxtable, Micklem, and Marsh's *Book of Public Worship* (1948), while C. E. Watson's *Rodborough Bede Book* (privately printed in the 1930s and published in 1943) combined a sturdy inventiveness with the enduring folk-tradition of simplicity. Watson's Eucharist inserts responsive acts of confession, dedication, and converse with the living Christ, between the distribution of the elements and their consumption.

Throughout the growth of the Reformed rites, the custom of sitting for communion has generally prevailed, as a conscious attempt to recapture the atmosphere of a supper. Scots practice required communicants to sit in turn at a designated communion pew around the holy table, until this usage declined under the influence of English Free Churches. In itself a small detail, this has helped the Reformed tradition to satisfy the unspoken popular devotion that was represented by the 'Anabaptist' movement to a degree not possible for Lutheran or Anglican practice.[1]

LUTHERAN AND REFORMED:
THE UNITED EVANGELICAL CHURCHES

The ecumenical ambitions of King Frederick William III and their limited success have been described above. The Church of the 'Old Prussian Union' was created by a monarchical *fiat*, but this decree could not end the need to retain two distinct rites, individual regions, parishes and even pastors seeing themselves as either Lutheran or Reformed. Outside the Royal Prussian lands, however, things went differently. In (for example) the city of Bremen and the Grand Duchy of Baden, church unions were brought about by spontaneous popular request.

In the case of Baden, various accidental factors helped the process. The Lutheran Church of the area had a rite closely similar to the Reformed equivalents. The *summus episcopus* of both Churches, the Grand Duke of Baden, was a Roman Catholic! In response to a deputation of pastors, school-masters, and heads of families, the Grand Duke permitted the union of the two bodies in 1821. A single rite—issued by the Church's own courts and long mulled over before publication—at once began to come into use. The first matters to be elucidated were small ones: the size of the breads, the frequency of celebration related to the size of the parish, the order of clerical precedence (by age). The 1858 *Kirchenbuch* set out a very simple rite, of Reformed character. The 1912 revision added a Preface and Sanctus before the Institution Narrative. In 1930, the *Hosanna* was added, with silent prayer after the Institution Narrative. The 1962 *Agende* has added much material; for example, the Narrative is followed by a thanksgiving, an anamnesis and an epiclesis.

---

[1] On Reformed rites, see texts in Bard Thompson, pp. 185ff (Calvin), 287ff (Knox), 311ff (Middelburg), 375ff (Baxter). See also W. D. Maxwell, *Genevan Service Book*, and his *History of Worship in the Church of Scotland* (OUP 1955); G. B. Burnet, *The Holy Communion in the Reformed Church of Scotland* (Oliver and Boyd 1960); Micklem, ed., *Christian Worship*; H. Davies, *The Worship of the English Puritans* (Dacre/A. and C. Black 1948). On Irving, etc., see A. L. Drummond, *Edward Irving and his Circle* (J. Clarke 1938); P. E. Shaw, *The Catholic Apostolic Church* (New York 1946) and D. H. Tripp in *Scottish Journal of Theology*, 22 (1969), pp. 437–54.

We have here an example of a union-rite, constantly enriched by the great traditions, and yet making its own creative way.[1]

12 The Anglican Eucharist: From the Reformation to the Restoration

R. T. BECKWITH

Addleshaw, G. W. O., and Etchells, F., *The Architectural Setting of Anglican Worship*. Faber 1950.

Cardwell, E., *A History of Conferences connected with the Book of Common Prayer*. OUP 1840.

Cuming, G. J., *A History of Anglican Liturgy*. Macmillan 1969.

Dimock, N., *The History of the Book of Common Prayer in its Bearing on Present Eucharistic Controversies*. Longmans 1910.

Gasquet, F. A. and Bishop, E., *Edward VI and the Book of Common Prayer*. Hodges 1890.

Despite Cranmer's conservative leanings and his policy of reform by stages (see pp. 70–73), the Eucharist when it left his hands was extraordinarily different from the service as it still stood at the death of Henry VIII. In the five years between 1547 and 1552 he stamped his mind upon it. Following a programme planned in broad outline from the beginning (see pp. 71–4), he reshaped the traditional material to give clear expression to his understanding of biblical teaching, and clothed this in a liturgical English which he both created and perfected. From then until the Restoration, and indeed until the twentieth century, the Anglican Eucharist was recognizably Cranmer's service, and all revision took this as its starting-point (see pp. 74–8 and 267–77).

ADAPTATION OF THE LATIN MASS

Cranmer's work went through two main phases, before and after his

---

1 See *Bekenntnisschriften der Vereinigten Evangelisch-Protestantischen Landeskirche in Baden* (Karlsruhe 1956), pp. 3–22. The books of the United Churches of Kurhessen-Waldeck, Hessen und Nassau, and of the Palatinate should be noted as parallels. See R. Hupfeld, *Die Abendmahlsfeier* (Gütersloh 1935), C. Mahrenholz, *Kompendium der Liturgik* (Kassel 1963).

replacement of the Latin Mass. In the first phase, three events are important. (i) The 22nd of Edward VI's Injunctions (1547) required that the epistle and gospel be read at high Mass in English. (ii) Later the same year, the Act against Revilers and for Receiving in Both Kinds restored the cup to the laity. (iii) In March 1548, following up hints given in the Act, there was published on royal authority The Order of the Communion.[1] The work is in English, and consists of an exhortation to be read prior to the day of the celebration, followed by a series of nine devotions[2] to be inserted into the Latin Mass immediately after the communion of the priest, so as to provide an edifying vernacular setting for the communion of the people, now in both kinds. The nine items are all recognizable forms of items in the later Prayer Book service, and the second exhortation may already envisage the 1552 sequence of penitence, thanksgiving, and sacrament. The work concludes with directions that the wafer-bread shall be broken before distribution, and that if the wine runs out more shall be consecrated by the use of the words of institution, but without elevation. The material is partly traditional, partly original, and partly adopted from the NT or from Hermann's *Consultation* (1545), a German church-order drawn up by Bucer and Melanchthon (see pp. 253, 257).

THE FIRST ENGLISH COMMUNION SERVICE

The revision programme announced in the royal proclamation accompanying the 1548 Order of the Communion (see pp. 70-1), and the reference in its rubrics to 'other order' yet to come, reveal plainly its interim character. So does the structural crudity of inserting it bodily, as a single unit, into the text of the old service. And we know that by Dec. 1547 Cranmer had already expressed the desire to have most of the Mass in the vernacular: he was doubtful only about 'certain secret mysteries', perhaps referring to passages which he considered doctrinally misleading, and therefore better veiled in Latin unless they could be revised (*Remains and Letters*, PS, p. 151). Consequently, the appearance of a revised service, wholly in English, in the 1549 Prayer Book is a natural development, and with this the second phase of Cranmer's work begins.

In the 1549 service, which is given the new main title of 'The Supper of the Lord and the Holy Communion', the 1548 material is all used, but is dispersed to three points, so as to integrate it with the rest of the rite. Most of it still comes after the canon, but is put before the priest's

---

[1] Full text in *Liturgies of Edward VI*, PS, pp. 1–8; shortened text in *PEER*, pp. 148ff. Text of the act in Gee-Hardy, pp. 322ff.

[2] Exhortation, invitation, confession, absolution, Comfortable words, Prayer of humble access, double administration, blessing.

communion so that it can serve as his preparation as well as the people's, and the priest and people can receive one after the other. In consequence, the priest's personal devotions, including the mutual confession and absolution of the ministers at the beginning of the service, disappear. The long canon is retained, though with some rearrangement and rewording. Preaching and almsgiving are encouraged. Items judged unedifying are omitted or altered, though with considerable restraint. And (again in the interests of edification) ceremonial and music are reduced. Merbecke's *Book of Common Prayer Noted* (1550), written for the 1549 book, is an illustrious example of the sort of music the Reformers judged most edifying: with its rule 'for every syllable a note', it ensures that the words are never disguised by the music. The text of the 1549 service is reprinted with the whole of the Edwardian Prayer Books in the Everyman edition (Dent 1972), and the second half of it is in *PEER*, pp. 152ff.

The structural changes of 1549 are not unlike those that had been carried out by the more conservative Reformers on the continent. In Brightman's *English Rite* (Rivingtons 1915), vol. 1, pp. xcvii–ciii, is a chart showing the 1549 service in parallel columns with Hermann's *Consultation* (see p. 253) and three earlier Lutheran rites, and the structural similarity is striking. Hermann retains the Gradual, Alleluia etc., which 1549 omits, but has already dispensed with the offertory of the elements and broken up the canon. In the position of the sermon and the inclusion of an exhortation after it, the Prayer Book agrees with the earlier Lutheran rites against Hermann, but in a few features (such as the position of the confession and absolution, in the communion proper, not the ante-communion) it differs from them all.

THE SECOND ENGLISH COMMUNION SERVICE

In the 1552 Prayer Book, Cranmer's long-standing purpose of producing an explicitly reformed service at last reached its goal. But the exact shape in which he achieved his purpose was affected by the suggestions which Bucer and Peter Martyr had made for the improvement of the 1549 service,[1] and by the ways in which it had been misinterpreted by Gardiner. Bucer's *Censura* is not now believed to have been written directly for the archbishop's use, and only one of Peter Martyr's suggestions is recorded; but their friendship with Cranmer doubtless led to their opinions being known to him, and a good number of their proposals were in fact adopted. Enough ambiguous language had been

---

[1] See E. C. Whitaker, ed., *Martin Bucer and the Book of Common Prayer* (Mayhew-McCrimmon 1974), and p. 271, below.

retained in 1549 for Gardiner to draw arguments from it in favour of transubstantiation: he appealed to (i) the epiclesis which Cranmer had introduced,[1] (ii) the words of distribution 'The Body/Blood of our Lord Jesus Christ which was given/shed for thee, preserve thy body and soul unto everlasting life', (iii) the references to Christ's Body and Blood being received 'in' the elements, (iv) the kneeling for the Prayer of humble access between consecration and reception, as implying adoration of the sacrament, and (v) the permission for the 'holding up of hands' at the end of the 1549 book, which Gardiner perversely claimed as authority for elevation (actually forbidden in the book) and therefore for adoration. He also attempted to find support for the sacrifice of the Mass in (vi) the inclusion of the Prayer for the Church in the canon (where the sacrifice was traditionally believed to occur) and (vii) the retention of the word 'altar' as one of the names for the Lord's table. Cranmer in his reply rejects these interpretations, but each of the passages was altered in 1552.[2]

In 1552 the structure and content of the service were changed much more strikingly than in 1549. The introit psalm and the offertory of the elements were omitted, the decalogue was introduced, the *Gloria in Excelsis* was moved from the ante-communion to the post-communion, and the devotional material from the 1548 Order of the Communion was once again shifted. Most of it was now placed at the beginning of the communion proper, so that the gap between consecration and administration could be closed. The Prayer of humble access, however, was placed between the Sanctus and the main body of the canon, thus emphasizing the discontinuity between the two in the Western liturgy. Most important of all, the canon itself was broken up: the Prayer for the Church (now the Church 'militant here in earth', without petition for the dead) was moved to an ancient position at the end of the ante-communion; the Lord's Prayer and the anamnesis or Prayer of oblation were moved to the post-communion, the latter being also made optional

---

[1] It is sometimes questioned whether this is properly called an epiclesis, and E. C. Ratcliff has shown that the language 'with thy Holy Spirit and word vouchsafe to bless and sanctify these thy gifts and creatures of bread and wine' is traditional western theological phraseology, the 'word' referring to Christ's words of institution (*LS*, p. 206 = *Theology* June 1957, p. 232f). But in view of Cranmer's certain knowledge of the early eastern epicleses (see p. 72), his introduction of this language into the canon can hardly be accidental.

[2] All except the appeal to the holding up of hands and the word 'altar' (for which see F. A. Gasquet and E. Bishop, *Edward VI and the Book of Common Prayer* (Hodges 1890), p. 284f; J. T. Tomlinson, *The Prayer Book, Articles and Homilies* (Elliot Stock 1897), p. 32f) come in Gardiner's controversy with Cranmer. See Cranmer, *On the Lord's Supper*, PS, pp. 79, 83; 51, 53, 55f; 62-4, 325, 327; 229f; 84.

(to avoid any suggestion of the sacrifice of the Mass); and what remained was the Institution Narrative, introduced by a strong statement of Christ's finished work on Calvary and a petition that the communicants might be partakers of Christ's Body and Blood. The new structure was impressively clear and purposeful, leading up to a climax: after the ministry of the word and prayer in the ante-communion, there followed penitence, forgiveness, thanksgiving, the ministry of the sacrament, and renewed thanksgiving. Also in 1552 the Lord's table was placed where the people might best hear, the eastward position of the priest was changed to north-side,[1] the medieval rule that the laity must receive communion once a year was trebled, leavened bread was permitted and the Black Rubric (explaining that kneeling reception signified humility and thankfulness, and denying any real and essential presence of Christ in the elements) was added. The 1552 service has been reprinted in the same places as the 1549—in the Everyman edition and in *PEER*, pp. 161ff.

THE 1559 REVISION

After the Marian reaction, the 1552 service was restored in the 1559 Elizabethan Prayer Book, with a few alterations. These have often been supposed to have doctrinal significance, but with small reason, as none of them went back behind 1549, and a leap straight from the pre-Reformation services of Mary's reign to 1552 might have caused problems. The changes were that the Mass-vestments were apparently retained for the time being, with the cope for an alternative, as in 1549; that the 1549 words of distribution (see p. 266) were added to those of 1552 ('Take and eat this in remembrance that Christ died for thee, and feed on him in thy heart by faith with thanksgiving', 'Drink this in remembrance that Christ's blood was shed for thee, and be thankful') so that they reached their familiar 1662 form; and that the Black Rubric was omitted. The Queen herself may well have desired these changes from 1552, as she held a very positive doctrine of the sacrament and liked dignified worship; moreover, she showed an inclination to a few other 1549 features in the further measures she took at the start of her reign.[2]

[1] See plate 10. The substitution of north-side, rather than the continental westward position, has often been explained from the occasional practice of turning the table when moving it nearer the congregation, which is probably wrong: see A. Bennett, *Table and Minister* (Church Book Room Press 1963). Either position would have let people see and hear, but the rubric before the absolution may indicate that Cranmer thought it best for the priest to stand sideways when addressing God in the people's hearing, and only to turn towards the people when addressing them.

[2] One of her Injunctions (1559) seeks to supersede the rubric permitting leavened bread (see Gee-Hardy, p. 440). Her Latin Prayer Book (1560) revives extended communion (see p. 271, n. 4) and a celebration at funerals. Neither work had statutory force.

But at least two additional factors were probably involved. First, it was necessary to answer the Marian bishop Scot, who was opposing the 1552 book on the grounds that it never makes any connection between the bread and the Body of Christ.[1] Untrue though this was, the restoration of the 1549 words of distribution emphasized its falsity. And secondly, the 1552 book was being restored, not continued, and the Black Rubric had never been a statutory part of the 1552 book, having been added at the last minute by the royal council to counter John Knox's preaching against kneeling reception. In many copies of the 1552 book, consequently, as the book was already in print, the rubric did not appear or was only pasted in.

THE 1637 (SCOTTISH) REVISION

The English Prayer Book of 1604 made no alteration in the Elizabethan Communion service, but the abortive Scottish Prayer Book of 1637 made many. The main influence here was the 1549 service, to which Bishop Wedderburn of Dunblane was greatly devoted, as being more primitive, and to which he would have conformed the Scottish liturgy still more closely if Charles I and his Laudian advisers had consented.[2] The service restored the offertory of the unconsecrated elements (adding words of oblation); restored thanksgiving for the saints in the prayer for the Church, and came near to restoring petition for the departed (though the retention of the word 'militant' in the introductory bidding showed that it did not intend to go quite that far); inserted the Prayer of humble access between consecration and reception; reunited the Prayer of oblation and Lord's Prayer (but not the Prayer for the Church) with the consecration prayer; restored the epiclesis; and retained only the 1549 words of distribution, without their 1552 complement. As regards externals, it was concerned for dignity and reverence: in agreement with Laudian policy, it reversed the 1552 requirement for the Lord's table to be moved from the east end of the chancel to the place where people could best hear;[3] it restored the option of singing the creed; and it added regulations about further consecration and consumption of the consecrated remains. The text of the service is reprinted in Donaldson (see note 2) in *PEER*, pp. 168ff, and in W. J. Grisbrooke, *Anglican Liturgies of the Seventeenth and Eighteenth Centuries* (SPCK 1958).

[1] See E. Cardwell, *A History of Conferences connected with the Book of Common Prayer* (OUP 1840), p. 112f.

[2] See G. Donaldson, *The Making of the Scottish Prayer Book of 1637* (Edinburgh University Press 1954).

[3] See G. W. O. Addleshaw and F. Etchells, *The Architectural Setting of Anglican Worship* (Faber 1948), chs. 4—6, 8.

THE 1662 REVISION

When the English Prayer Book was restored by Charles II, after its prohibition during the Commonwealth, there were two distinct groups urging change of a far-reaching kind. The first consisted of the Presbyterian Puritans, who were hoping for a revision of the Prayer Book in the direction of their own current practice. At the Savoy Conference (1661) they put their proposals to the bishops, in two forms: (i) detailed suggestions for change in the 1604 text, to which the bishops replied;[1] (ii) a completely different liturgy drawn up by Richard Baxter (see pp. 75, 260), which was virtually ignored. The second group consisted primarily of two surviving Laudian bishops, Cosin and Wren, to whom the credit for the 1662 revision has often been ascribed. But G. J. Cuming has recently shown that, despite the amount of minor change for which they were responsible, they were unsuccessful in their main objectives, owing to the greater influence of moderates like Bishop Sanderson.[2] Cosin had been making manuscript notes on the Prayer Book since his youth, and Wren had occupied his imprisonment during the Commonwealth in the same way. Their work has been admirably analysed and collated by Cuming in his edition of *The Durham Book* (OUP 1961). Cosin was the more radical of the two, but his opinions had been moderating over the years, as a comparison of his various series of notes (*Works*, LACT, vol. 5) clearly shows, and the extent of his ambitions by the time of the Restoration was to conform the Prayer Book fairly closely to the 1637 Scottish pattern.

In the event, the general character of the 1662 service remained as it had been in England from 1552 onwards. The Laudians' wish to follow 1637 as to the positions of the Prayer of oblation, the Lord's Prayer, and the Prayer of humble access, the inclusion of the epiclesis and the location of the Lord's table was disappointed. Also the words of distribution remained in their 1559 form. On the other hand, the offertory of the elements (without words of oblation),[3] thanksgiving for the faithful departed, and the permission to sing the creed and Sanctus were restored; and rubrics of greater fulness and clarity, which ensured reverent behaviour, were adopted, including regulations about further consecration and the consumption of the consecrated remains. At Puritan

---

[1] For the Savoy records, see E. Cardwell, *A History of Conferences*, ch. 7.

[2] *The English Prayer Book 1549–1662*, by A. M. Ramsey *et al.* (SPCK 1963), ch. 5; Cuming, *History*, ch. 7.

[3] On the view that the word 'oblations' in the 1662 Prayer for the Church refers to the elements, see J. Dowden, *Further Studies in the Prayer Book* (Methuen 1908), pp. 176–222.

suggestion, the 1552 Black Rubric was restored.[1] For two approximations to 1549 the Laudians and Puritans were jointly responsible. These were the restoration of the fraction, though in a new position, with other manual acts, and a return to a more discriminating use of the exhortations, with the 1552 prohibition of non-communicating attendance omitted—this practice having ceased to occur, in an age of infrequent celebration (see *The Durham Book*, p. 151).

THE INTERPRETATION OF THE PRAYER BOOK SERVICE

It is sometimes imagined that only the prohibition of Cranmer's Protestant service in Mary's reign and under the Commonwealth could have endeared it to subsequent generations of Anglicans, but in fact its theology was generally congenial to Anglicans for centuries after the Reformation.[2] Calvinist receptionism and virtualism were the prevailing belief, and Cranmer's own view was neither Lutheran nor Zwinglian but substantially Calvinist, as Peter Brooks has shown.[3] According to the evidence of Cheke, he adopted this view in 1546,[4] and he says himself that he did so not long before translating Justus Jonas's *Catechism* (*On the Lord's Supper*, p. 374). Three editions of this translation appeared between the summer and autumn of 1548, in which the Lutheran eucharistic teaching is progressively modified.[5] In Dec. 1548 Cranmer expressed his new beliefs in the House of Lords debate on the intended 1549 Prayer Book,[6] but his earliest expression of them was in March, when he prohibited elevation in the Order of the Communion. Elevation was for purposes of adoration,[7] and the Lutherans were therefore inclined to retain it.[8] Hermann had omitted it, but Cranmer prohibited it.

---

[1] On the reasons for the change of wording in the 1662 Black Rubric, see R. T. Beckwith, *Priesthood and Sacraments* (Marcham 1964), p. 63 and notes.

[2] See C. W. Dugmore, *Eucharistic Doctrine in England from Hooker to Waterland* (SPCK 1942), and *Priesthood and Sacraments*, as above, ch. 5.

[3] *Thomas Cranmer's Doctrine of the Eucharist* (Macmillan 1965).

[4] See Brooks, op. cit., p. 38.

[5] See D. G. Selwyn, 'A Neglected Edition of Cranmer's Catechism' (*JTS*, April 1964).

[6] The report of the debate is published in Gasquet and Bishop, op. cit., and more accurately in J. T. Tomlinson, *Collected Tracts on Ritual* (Church Association n.d.), vol. 2.

[7] See T. W. Drury, *Elevation in the Eucharist* (CUP 1907), pp. 100–24, 158–64.

[8] It is found, for example, in Luther's *Formula Missae* and *Deutsche Messe* (1523, 1526), Schwarz's Strassburg rite (1524), the Brandenburg Church Order (1540), and the Pfalz-Neuburg Church Order (1543).

It is often said that the 1662 service is Cranmer's text with Laudian rubrics, which is formally correct. Cranmer was negligent about rubrics, but to infer from this that he did not believe in consecration, or thought Christ's institution to consist simply of eating and drinking without thanksgiving or manual acts, is mistaken.[1] In reality, he stressed the importance of thanksgiving in his third exhortation and Prayer of oblation; omitted the fraction only because the incidental reference to it in 1549 was misused by Gardiner;[2] and always adhered to the idea of consecration (*On the Lord's Supper*, pp. 11, 131, 177–83). It is true that for Cranmer, as a receptionist, the elements were not sacramental after their sacramental use was over, and he therefore followed Bucer's advice in letting the remains be turned to common purposes again,[3] and Peter Martyr's advice in abolishing extended communion as well as perpetual reservation;[4] but here his beliefs were at one even with Cosin's,[5] by whose influence (and Wren's) the 1662 rubric for the consumption of the remains was introduced. The motive of the 1662 rubric was not theological but to avoid danger or appearance of irreverence. There is even less reason to read theological changes into those rubrics of 1637 or 1662 which merely made explicit practices like the fraction and concepts like consecration to which Cranmer always adhered.

---

[1] Such ideas were first given currency by Dix (*Shape*, pp. 650–99) and Ratcliff (art. cit. on p. 266; and *The English Prayer Book 1549–1662*, by A. M. Ramsey *et al.*, ch. 4 = *LS*, pp. 222–43). For the evidence against them, see R. T. Beckwith *et al.*, *The Service of Holy Communion and its Revision* (Marcham 1972), pp. 40–8, 60.

[2] For the continuance of the fraction in practice, and Cranmer's adherence to it, see *The Service of Holy Communion and its Revision*, as above, p. 44f.

[3] For Bucer's words, see pp. 40–3 of E. C. Whitaker's edn, cited above, p. 265.

[4] On the view that perpetual reservation was expected to continue under all editions of the Prayer Book, though without actually being mentioned, see *Reservation and Communion of the Sick* (Grove 1972), by R. T. Beckwith *et al.*, ch. 1. Extended communion differs from perpetual reservation in that the elements are taken to the absent on the same day as the celebration in church, and with as little delay as possible.

[5] For evidence that Cosin, by the time of the Restoration, did not regard the elements as sacramental after their sacramental use was over, and was opposed to reservation, see his *Works*, LACT, vol. 4, p. 49; vol. 5, pp. 356f, 481.

13 The Eucharist in Anglicanism after 1662

ALAN DUNSTAN

Bell, G. K. A., *Randall Davidson*. OUP 1935.
Cuming, G. J., *A History of Anglican Liturgy*. Macmillan 1969.
Dowden, J., *The Scottish Communion Office of 1764*. 2nd edn OUP 1922.
Garrett, T. S., *Worship in the Church of South India*. 2nd edn Lutterworth 1965.
Grisbrooke, W. J., *Anglican Liturgies of the 17th and 18th Centuries*. SPCK 1958.
Jasper, R. C. D., *Prayer Book Revision in England 1800–1900*. SPCK 1954.
Parsons, E. L. and Jones, B. H., *The American Prayer Book: its origins and principles*. New York 1937.
Shepherd, M. H., Jr, *The Oxford American Prayer Book Commentary*. New York 1950.
Suter, J. W. and Cleaveland, G. J., *The American Book of Common Prayer: its origin and development*. New York 1949.
Wigan, B., *The Liturgy in English*. OUP 1962.

Possibly no one responsible for the 1662 revision of the Prayer Book expected it to last so long. Doubtless many Puritans remained within the Anglican fold in the hope that a further revision would occur in their lifetime, and indeed a large-scale attempt was made in 1689 after the accession of William and Mary (see p. 76–7). Proposals for the communion service at this time[1] were not extensive but they included re-writing or revision of most of the proper collects (with the apparent intention of making them reflect more closely the theme of the Epistle or Gospel), and the use of the Beatitudes as an alternative to the Ten Commandments. Kneeling for the reception of communion was still to be the norm but it was not to be enforced. The service opened with the rather bald rubric 'when there is no communion, there is not to be any communion service', which meant that the Ante-Communion would take place within the context of the Litany and at the reading-desk rather than the altar. Opposition to the book from within the Church of England proved strong, and when it became clear that it was unlikely to unite Anglicans and Dissenters, the revision was dropped without official discussion.

The events of 1688–9 caused the secession of the Non-Jurors, and they were to produce their own liturgies. The first, that of 1718, bore a strong resemblance to the 1549 rite: the Prayer for the Church and the communion devotions were inserted after the Canon (which included the Prayer of oblation, though separated from the Institution Narrative by a

[1] T. J. Fawcett, *The Liturgy of Comprehension 1689* (Mayhew-McCrimmon 1973).

congregational Amen), and an offertory prayer was included. By now controversy raged between the 'Usagers' (those who wanted to return to certain practices claimed as primitive—the mixed chalice, epiclesis, etc.) and the 'Non-Usagers', who combined a fairly Protestant theology with their political loyalty to the Stuart regime. By 1734 the Non-Jurors' liturgy reflected a markedly Orthodox character with a Consecration Prayer of enormous proportions and a specific role for the deacon throughout the service.[1]

We see therefore two major attempts at revision of the Eucharist, one in the interest of comprehension, and the other with an intention to reflect a doctrinal slant not obvious in the 1662 service. To the latter belongs the Scottish Communion Service of 1764, the story of which has been told by John Dowden, who reconstructed the first part (up to the Exhortation), which had not been printed before 1844. The Ante-Communion included responses to the Gospel, and the Summary of the Law as an alternative to the Ten Commandments. Additional offertory sentences were provided and the rubric ran:

> and the Presbyter shall offer up and place the bread and wine prepared for the sacrament upon the Lord's Table.[2]

Following the Narrative of the Institution came the Oblation:

> WHEREFORE, O Lord and heavenly Father, according to the institution of thy dearly beloved Son, our Saviour Jesus Christ, we thy humble servants do celebrate and make here before thy divine Majesty, with these thy holy gifts, WHICH WE NOW OFFER UNTO THEE, the memorial thy Son hath commanded us to make.[3]

The anamnesis and epiclesis led directly into the first post-communion prayer from the 1662 office. Then followed the intercessions, the Lord's Prayer and the communion devotions. The words used at the delivery of the bread and wine were those of the 1549 office, and after communion a brief exhortation led to the Prayer of Thanksgiving (i.e. the second post-communion prayer of 1662), the Gloria and the blessing. The service reflected somewhat the 1637 Laudian Prayer Book which had met such a dramatic fate in Scotland, but it was also clearly influenced by the work and the writings of the Non-Jurors. It is a rite of considerable importance in the Anglican communion since it was one of the sources of the liturgy of the Protestant Episcopal Church of the USA.

[1] W. Jardine Grisbrooke, *Anglican Liturgies*, has a full survey of those liturgies which might be described as more 'catholic' in character than the Prayer Book and the introductory chapter of R. C. D. Jasper's *Prayer Book Revision* has a useful survey of attempts on revision before 1800.

[2] Quoted in Grisbrooke, p. 170.

[3] Quoted in Grisbrooke, p. 178.

In England there were no official revisions of the liturgy between 1662 and our own day. During the eighteenth century its use in most places was rare and celebration four times only in the year became the norm in many areas. The movement towards more frequent communion arose with the Evangelicals and was vigorously pursued by the Tractarians. The early disciples of the Oxford Movement were staunch defenders of the Prayer Book as it stood, but liturgical alterations began to abound in the second half of the nineteenth century. It became common to publish the Prayer Book rite of Holy Communion with interpolations and additions from the Roman Missal in English. Demands from Anglo-Catholics for revision became louder in the light of ritualistic controversies and litigation. The issues of ecclesiastical discipline and liturgical revision thus became almost inextricably interwoven. The Public Worship Regulation Act 1874 had been one only partially successful attempt to deal with the situation, and in 1904 a Royal Commission was appointed to inquire into alleged instances of indiscipline in public worship. It stated:

> The law of public worship in the Church of England is too narrow for the religious life of the present generation. It needlessly condemns much which a great section of Church people, including many of her most devoted members, value; and modern thought and feelings are characterised by a care for ceremonial, a sense of dignity in worship, and an appreciation of the continuity of the Church, which were not similarly felt at the time when the law took its present shape.[1]

The Commission recommended that Letters of Business should be issued to the Convocations to consider a new ornaments rubric, and to frame modifications in the existing law relating to the conduct of divine service. Hence began the process leading to the 1928 Prayer Book.

Already in 1872 there had been passed the Act of Uniformity Amendment Act. This was afterwards regarded as a skeleton in the Anglican liturgical cupboard. It permitted Mattins, Litany, and Holy Communion to be used as separate services, and this gave to the 1662 Communion Service a character not intended by the makers of the Prayer Book. However, many of the charges levelled against that service (e.g. lack of OT lesson, lack of praise) are less easy to sustain when it is seen in its original context.

The attempt to revise liturgy and to enforce discipline at the same time and by the same process marked the course of revision leading to the 1928 Prayer Book. Anglicans had by no means forsworn the ideal of uniformity

[1] Quoted in Bell, *Randall Davidson*, vol. 1, p. 471.

laid down in 1549, and even if there were to be two forms of the Communion Service, they would be contained within the same book. The fact that there were thus at least two motives for the revision has been cited as one reason for the lack of enthusiasm about the book, if not for its ultimate failure.[1]

The order of 1928 provided a form of devotion (put in an appendix) which could be used before the service by both priest and people. The Ten Commandments (in a shortened form) were required on one Sunday in the month; on others the Summary of the Law and on other days the Kyries. Additional Propers were provided. The Offertory remained in its 1662 position (with additional sentences) and was followed by an extended Prayer for the Church which included reference to educational and missionary work as well as the departed. Then came the communion devotions, with shorter forms suggested for weekdays and with the Prayer of humble access at the conclusion. The consecration began with 'The Lord be with you'. After the Sanctus 'All glory be to thee, Almighty God ... ' led into the substance of the 1662 Consecration Prayer which was followed by anamnesis, epiclesis and the bulk of the Prayer of oblation, the whole prayer being followed by the Lord's Prayer. The full 1662 words of administration were provided, together with directions concerning the way in which they could be shortened, and communion was followed by the Prayer of thanksgiving, the Gloria and the blessing. The service was flanked by a number of rubrics designed to safeguard various positions. The service had to be 'said throughout in a distinct and audible voice' and must not be supplemented by additional prayers. But it was 'an ancient and laudable custom' to receive fasting and 'an ancient tradition' to mingle a little water with the wine. The controversial rubrics about reservation were printed under the heading 'An alternative order for the Communion of the Sick'. It was these as much as any part of the book that moved extreme Evangelicals and extreme Anglo-Catholics to unite in opposition to the proposals. The first were opposed to any provision for reservation and the latter to the severe regulations preventing devotions and ceremonies surrounding it.

Besides the reservation question, the position of the Prayer of oblation was the cause of bitter controversy. Bishop W. H. Frere[2] was very influential in the compilation of the first book (1927) though he withdrew his support from the second attempt in 1928. He had advocated the

---

[1] See Bell, *Randall Davidson*, vol. 2, pp. 1354–60.
[2] His liturgical and historical writing was voluminous but see in particular *Some Principles of Liturgical Reform* (John Murray 1914); *The Anaphora* (SPCK 1938); *Walter Howard Frere: his correspondence on Liturgical Revision and Construction*, ed. R. C. D. Jasper (SPCK 1954).

reintroduction of the epiclesis into the service and had argued that the primitive Church regarded the whole consecration Prayer as consecratory and not any particular part of it. Not until the revision of the sixties did his judgement prevail. Although rejected by Parliament the book was widely used in the Church of England between 1928 and 1965. The Summary of the Law, the Kyries and some of the new Propers became common practices; the Prayer for the Church was widely used; the new Canon was less extensively followed and a more common Anglo-Catholic practice was the 'interim rite' which did little more than join the Prayer of oblation to the 1662 form of consecration.

The English revision of 1928 was paralleled in most parts of the Anglican communion. The Scottish Episcopal rite of 1929 retained the Intercession and communion devotions after the consecration prayer but the 1928 American rite put them in the English position, as did the South African liturgy of 1929, though both of these forms transferred the Prayer of humble access to a place immediately before the communion. The liturgy of Ceylon put the whole penitential section very near the beginning of the service. The Bombay liturgy responded to a plea in 1920 for a service more distinctly Indian by including elements like the Trisagion, the Litany of Chrysostom and 'Holy Things for Holy People'. It also included the Creed within the communion part of the service. The Canadian liturgy of 1918 belongs very much to the 1662 family and that of 1959 represents what we might call the 1928 position. The Anglican Church of Australia and New Zealand continued with the basic 1662 order until a new wave of revisions occurred in the sixties. The same was true of the Church of Ireland which had until recent times made no more than minor amendments to the 1662 form.

There are certain features common to most of the revised orders we have cited. Generally there is some modification of the Ante-Communion with provision for only occasional recitation of the Ten Commandments. The Prayer for the Church is commonly modernized and the eucharistic prayer always includes more than a recollection of Calvary and the rehearsal of the Narrative of Institution. There is normally an anamnesis, sometimes an epiclesis and usually some part of the Prayer of oblation is included. But many of the features that have subsequently been changed by modern revisers still remain. The sermon is usually separated from the Gospel and the offertory from the consecration and not until later revisions is the structure of the service clearly marked and the people's part strongly emphasized.

The publication of the Liturgy of the Church of South India (1950, revised 1954, 1962, 1972) has proved to be one of the most significant liturgical events of this century. Its story scarcely belongs to this article for although it used much material from the Book of Common Prayer and the liturgies of the other parent Churches, they were arranged in a quite new pattern. This liturgy marks the transition from the rites of the Prayer Book to the new liturgies we now have in Anglicanism, and has influenced almost every form of eucharistic revision that has taken place since its publication (see pp. 281–3). For such reasons this essay ends with the South India liturgy (to which the Prayer Book contributed at least linguistically), which begins one stream of the revision outlined in chapter 15.

14 Methodism

D. H. TRIPP

Bowmer, J. C., *The Sacrament of the Lord's Supper in Early Methodism*. Dacre Press 1951.

Bowmer, J. C., *The Lord's Supper in Methodism, 1791–1960*. Epworth Press 1961.

Dunkle, W. F. and Quillian, J. D., Jr, edd., *Companion to the Book of Worship*. Nashville and New York 1970.

Harmon, N. B., *Rites and Ritual of Episcopal Methodism*. Nashville 1926.

Rattenbury, J. E., *The Evangelical Doctrines of Charles Wesley's Hymns*. Epworth 1941.

Rattenbury, J. E., *The Eucharistic Hymns of John and Charles Wesley*. Epworth 1945.

Tripp, D. H., *The Renewal of the Covenant in the Methodist Tradition*. Epworth 1969.

Methodism was a sacramental revival—in the minds of its leaders. The Wesley brothers continued into their itinerant evangelistic ministry their ideals of 'constant communion' and their high eucharistic theology which they had acquired in their Oxford days and clung to while in Georgia. The emphasis on justification by faith which governed their thinking after their spiritual experience of May 1738 did not weaken this policy. Indeed, since the sacraments are divinely appointed means for 'waiting on God' in faith, and since the Christ who saves offers himself sacramentally as the object of faith, eucharistic devotion and preaching for conversions were inseparable. The two brothers celebrated frequently, at least once a week on the average. However, the great majority of early Methodists could hardly have done so. It was seldom that one of the brothers could be at any given point; their clerical collaborators were few; the itinerant assistants were not allowed to preside; where only the parish church was available as a place of sacramental life, they must have been limited to the statutory minimum of three communions a year in most cases. Since Methodists were being repelled from the altars by an appreciable number of clergy, it was only to be expected that the Methodist Societies would want their own ministers to celebrate, and equally to be expected that frequent communion would not be an obvious ideal to cherish.

John Wesley, having since 1747 been convinced that presbyters might validly ordain, as being of the same order in essence with bishops, acted upon his conviction only in 1784. He began to ordain for America, and then for Scotland and finally for England, so that the Methodists might not be quite deprived of the sacraments. After his death, a painful adjustment completed the emergence of a sacramental life independent of the parent church.

Wesley's liturgy, the *Sunday Service of the Methodists* (1784), was an adaptation, and above all an abridgement, of the Anglican Prayer Book. This, slightly revised from time to time (especially in the 1882 *Public Prayers and Services*), remained in use until British Methodism united in 1932. One of the two communion orders in the new *Book of Offices* (1936) was substantially Wesley's rite.

The American Methodists quickly adapted Wesley's scheme, chiefly in dropping any expectation of regular Morning Prayer and Litany. The identity of the rite has been preserved, but great variations have taken place; one nineteenth-century order placed the Preface and Sanctus between the communion of the minister(s) and the communion of the people.

Non-Wesleyan Methodist Churches in Britain dispensed with *Sunday Service*. The Primitive Methodists preferred not to use a liturgy at all, but issued two for optional use (1860, *Forms for the Administration of Baptism*, etc., and *c.* 1890, *Order for the Administration of Baptism and other services*). The Methodist New Connexion loved the communion, but never issued any order for its celebration. The United Methodist Free Churches issued two *Books of Services* (after 1864 and *c.* 1890), after using a lightly revised version of the Wesleyan rite compiled by Theodore Jones in 1851. They and the Bible Christians, whose *Book of Services* (*c.* 1890, 2nd edn 1901) was modelled on theirs, belong very much to the Free Church tradition. This is due to reaction to the Oxford Movement, which tended to make much of sacraments and little of Dissenters and Methodists—or so it seemed to the latter. The older non-Wesleyan books incline to preface the communion with a commemorative exhortation, while the later tend to insert between them a prayer or prayers for devout and fruitful communion. The Bible Christian compiler drew on Knox:

'Let us not dwell too much upon these corruptible elements, that are present to our eyes, but rather let us lift our hearts to heaven where our ascended Lord sits at the right hand of God'. When New Connexion, the Bible Christians, and the Free Methodists united in 1907 as the United Methodist Church, their new rite appeared in their *Book of Services* (1913). After the preaching-service, a prayer of thanksgiving and pre-communion devotion introduces the whole eucharistic action, lessons, exhortation and all. It seems to consecrate (if we put it this way) not only elements but a whole act of devotion within which the communion itself is a determinative but not the sole essential feature. The Institution is read after the lessons (and address on special occasions) and a hymn, and immediately before the distribution.

The non-Wesleyan traditions were provided for in the 1936 book for the wider Methodist Union with a 'second order' for the Communion. After penitential devotions, the Preface and Sanctus introduce a series of formally distinct but closely interlocking prayers, which taken together form an interesting parallel with many ancient anaphoras. The influence of the *Free Church Book of Common Prayer* must be seen here.

The preaching-service, which always precedes the celebration of the Eucharist, grew from being two hymns with a sermon and extempore prayer *ad lib.* to a not very flexible equivalent of the Anglican Office, with hymns in the place of psalms and canticles, as was happening with the Free Church use. The sermon came at the end, as in the Office in the parish church (where of course it had no proper place); in the chapel it was seen as the crown of the service, and the other elements often as mere 'preliminaries' to it. Attempts to enrich the preaching-service drew more and more heavily on the Anglican Office.

Associated with Methodist Communions since 1755 has been the Covenant service, usually held on the first Sunday of the New Year. All British and Commonwealth Methodist connexions used it and issued rites for it. Wesley's own (a long exhortation and a long prayer) came from Puritan sources. The form used since 1936, in origin a private venture of George B. Robson (1921), leads up to the moment of renewed self-dedication through a sequence of responsive devotions. Its customary and required association with the Holy Communion shows one side of popular Methodist sacramental devotion, the theme of self-oblation, which has a prominent position in all Methodist liturgy. The *Methodist Service Book* of 1975 includes a revision of this service.

The Wesleys had a high sacramental doctrine which has not yet been fully interpreted. This became attenuated, as their practice was attenuated after their deaths by shortage of celebrants, but it has been kept in the Methodist mind by the Wesley's hymns, which in every department of worship have been as much the liturgy as anything in the service-books.

15 Recent Eucharistic Revision

GEOFFREY WAINWRIGHT

Since the Second World War, and particularly since about 1960, the modern Liturgical Movement has borne abundant fruit in extensive revision of the Communion service. In virtually every part of Western Christianity, eucharistic liturgies of remarkably similar shape have been produced.

1 THE EXTENT OF EUCHARISTIC REVISION

Principles enunciated in Vatican II's Constitution on the Liturgy took practical form in the Missal of Paul VI (1969/70). The extent of activity in the Anglican Communion can be gauged from the fact that C. O. Buchanan's *Modern Anglican Liturgies 1958–1968* (OUP) contains fifteen such eucharistic rites, to which twenty-two more are added by the same compiler's *Further Anglican Liturgies 1968–1975* (Grove Books). The volume of I. Pahl's forthcoming *Abendmahlsliturgien in den Reformations-kirchen* devoted to the period since 1950 lists some thirty Lutheran Eucharists and as many Reformed.

In the United Kingdom, the Church of England authorized its Series 2 Eucharist for experimental use from 1967 and its Series 3 from 1973; the Church in Wales brought out its experimental *Holy Eucharist* in 1966; the Episcopal Church in Scotland issued its *Liturgy* for permissive use in the same year; the Church of Ireland produced an experimental revision in 1967 and then a rather different alternative service of *Holy Communion* in 1972. The Church of Scotland in 1973 published *The Divine Service: three orders for the celebration of the Lord's Supper* as a contribution towards the revision of the *Book of Common Order*; the Presbyterian Churches in England and Wales had already put out their *Service Book* with three orders of Holy Communion (the third for Wales only) in 1968; and the Presbyterian Church in Ireland its revised *Book of Public Worship*, with two orders for Communion, in 1965. The Methodist Church released its new *Sunday Service* in experimental form in 1968, and the definitive version was approved in 1974. A *Book of Public Worship*, which included four Communion orders, had been 'compiled for the use of Congregationalists' by J. Huxtable, J. Marsh, R. Micklem and J. Todd in 1948; and a eucharistic *Order of Public Worship* was officially published by the Congregational Church in England and Wales in 1970. Two Baptist ministers, E. A. Payne and S. F. Winward, compiled a manual of *Orders and Prayers for Church Worship* (1960) which contained two orders for the Lord's Supper.

In the USA, the Protestant Episcopal Church tried out from 1967 to 1970 a *Liturgy of the Lord's Supper* (Prayer Book Studies XVII), which bifurcated into a contemporary and a traditional form in the green book of *Services for Trial Use* (1970/71), and these were repeated, with optional variants, in the 'zebra' book of *Authorized Services* (1973). The same pattern is followed in what finally became the *Proposed Book of Common Prayer* (1976/77). Eight Lutheran bodies collaborated to produce a new common liturgy in the *Service Book* of 1958; the Inter-Lutheran Commission on Worship in 1970 published *The Holy Communion* as Contemporary Worship Booklet 2; this latter appeared in modified form in *The Lutheran Book of Worship* (1978). The Methodist Church revised its *Book of Worship* in 1964 but followed this with a much more modern 'alternate text' for the Lord's Supper in 1972. Among the Presbyterians, the *Worshipbook* of 1970 provided a 'service for the Lord's day' in variant sacramental and non-sacramental forms.

Revision of the eucharistic liturgy has played a part also in planned and achieved schemes of Church union. The firstfruits was the *Lord's Supper* of the Church of South India (1950; revised 1954, 1962, 1972), which in many ways remained close to the Cranmerian tradition but which was also influenced by Reformed participation in the new Church and which incorporated several features from the ancient Syrian tradition of India.[1] The unsuccessful Nigerian scheme of union included a *United Liturgy* (1965), and the East African Church Union Consultation's *United Liturgy for East Africa* appeared in 1966; both these were indebted to the CSI, the personal link being provided in the former case by T. S. Garrett[2] and in the latter by L. W. Brown and his *Liturgy for Africa* (OUP 1964). In the USA, the Consultation on Church Union (COCU) produced an *Order of worship for the proclamation of the Word of God and*

---

[1] Indian-Syrian features were the hymn 'Holy God, Holy and mighty, Holy and immortal', the second litany ('For the peace that is from above . . .'), the congregational Peace, the *Benedictus qui venit* in the form 'Blessed be he that hath come and is to come in the name of the Lord', and the people's acclamations after the Institution Narrative and the anamnesis. See T. S. Garrett, *Worship in the CSI* (SCM 1958, extensively revised edn 1965). An almost entirely Syrianized liturgy had been prepared with the blessing of the Anglican Bishop of Bombay by J. C. Winslow, E. C. Ratcliff, *et al.*, *The Eucharist in India* (Longmans 1920); but despite repeated authorizations it remained something of a dead (Bombay) duck.

[2] *SL* 5 (1966), pp. 183–6.

the celebration of the Lord's Supper (1968). The South African Church Unity Commission in 1972 issued for experimental use an *Order of Service for Sunday Worship*. The Church of North India published an *Order for the Lord's Supper* in 1973–4. In England and Wales, the new United Reformed Church (Congregational-Presbyterian) of 1972 approved a *Book of Order for Worship on the Lord's Day* in 1974.

The ecumenical monastic community of Taizé created its *Eucharist* in 1959 and revised it in 1971. The German Michaelsbruderschaft has its *Evangelische Messe*. Unofficially produced local and sectional rites are countless.

2 THE SERVICE OF WORD AND SACRAMENT

There has been a growing awareness in the Protestant Churches that the 'normal' service is one of Word *and Sacrament*; this is reflected for instance in the bipartite structure of the British Methodist *Sunday Service* of 1968: 'The Preaching Service' and 'The Lord's Supper'. Churches in the Roman, Lutheran, and Cranmerian traditions have, in the *Word* part of their eucharistic services, restored the OT reading which was common throughout Christendom until the end of the fourth century (the CSI took this initiative already in 1950). The homily has been reinstated in the *Ordo missae* in the Roman Catholic Church.

There would be practically universal acceptance of the service-structure outlined by the semi-official British *Joint Liturgical Group*: OT reading; NT reading(s); Sermon; Intercession; Presentation and Taking of the Bread and Wine; eucharistic Prayer; Fraction and Communion.[1] The only contestable point might be the position of the intercessions, which has greatly varied in liturgical history; so much so that E. C. Whitaker has recently argued that the Prayers are a 'third element' distinct from Word and Sacrament.[2] In Justin Martyr's time they came at what the post-Vatican II *Consilium ad exsequendam constitutionem de sacra liturgia* called the 'hinge' between Word and Sacrament, and it is there that the 'bidding prayers' occur in the new Roman rite;[3] but the fifth-century Roman *deprecatio Gelasii*, of which the Kyries at the start of some eucharistic rites are a fossilized relic (Taizé and the North American Lutheran liturgies of 1958 and 1978 have restored to them their biddings), came before the Scripture readings (the 1964 American Methodist *Book of Worship* puts the intercessions in that position, but it

---

[1] N. Clark and R. C. D. Jasper, ed., *Initiation and Eucharist: essays on their structure* SPCK 1972.
[2] R. C. D. Jasper, ed., *The Eucharist Today* (SPCK 1974), pp. 54–65.
[3] See pp. 172, 182, 246–8.

has not been much favoured in modern liturgical revision); and in the classical liturgies of both East and West, intercessions—sometimes very lengthy—were incorporated into the great eucharistic Prayer, and most modern revisions include at least an element of intercession within the great prayer.[1] Nearly all modern revisions give the people a vocal part in the intercessions, usually by arranging them in some kind of litany form.

While the features listed above constitute the main outline of the Eucharist, most liturgies contain also other features about whose position in the rite there is less agreement. Theological and pastoral arguments have been advanced in favour of all the various placings. Thus the chief penitential section now usually occurs at the very beginning as part of the 'preparation' (CSI, Taizé, Rome 1969, British Methodist 1968/74, American Methodist 1972, COCU 1968, Church of Scotland 1973, URC 1974), but Anglican rites keep it in the 1552/1662 tradition either just before (Series 3), or at the start of (Series 2), the Sacrament part of the service. The Creed may occur either after the sermon (CSI, C of E Series 2 and 3, Rome 1969, American Methodist 1972) or early in the Sacrament service (Michaelsbruderschaft, British Methodist 1968/74, Church of Scotland 1973 first and second orders). The Lord's Prayer has largely disappeared from the Word Service (the British Methodists retain it as a climax to the intercessions): it is said either between the eucharistic Prayer and the Fraction (CSI, Taizé, Rome 1969, COCU, North American Inter-Lutheran 1970 and 1978, American Methodist 1972, Church of Scotland 1973, URC 1974) or between the Fraction and communion (C of E Series 2 and 3). The Peace may be exchanged either before the bringing of the gifts to the altar (CSI, C of E Series 2 and 3, British Methodist 1968/74, American Methodist 1972, URC 1974) or before communion (Taizé, after the Fraction; Rome 1969, between the Lord's Prayer and the Fraction) or even after communion (American Methodist 1964). The COCU rite of 1968 puts the Peace after the sermon, between the Creed and the intercessions.

For Churches in the Cranmerian tradition ('And here we offer and present unto thee, O Lord, ourselves, our souls and bodies ... '), the positioning of the 'self-oblation' of the communicants has posed problems. Much Liturgical Movement teaching in the 1950s and 60s associated this thought with a developed 'offertory procession'. Perhaps because of a damaging remark by A. M. Ramsey about 'a shallow and romantic sort of Pelagianism', there has more recently been a defection

---

1 The Jewish *birkat ha-mazon* contains intercessions and petitions within a *berakah* structure (*PEER* 1). On both theological and pastoral grounds, W. J. Grisbrooke has vigorously defended the place of intercessions within the anaphora, in *SL* 4 (1965), pp. 129–55, and 5 (1966), pp. 20–44, 87–103.

from this view (though it should not be forgotten that the people who bring the fruits of the earth and the produce of their labours *are* baptized and believing Christians):[1] Series 2 and Series 3 keep the self-offering in its 1552/1662 post-communion position, and COCU and the 1968/74 British Methodist service bring it into the latter part of the eucharistic Prayer (which was its place in the C of E rites of 1549 and 1928 and in the Scoto-American Episcopalian tradition).

3 THE FOUR-ACTION SHAPE OF THE EUCHARISTIC MEAL

Throughout the English-speaking world and even beyond, great influence has been exercised by Dom Gregory Dix's book *The Shape of the Liturgy*. Dix emphasized a 'four-action shape' which corresponded, once bread and wine were brought together, to the actions of Jesus at the Last Supper: he *took* the bread and wine, he *gave thanks* over them, he *broke* the bread, he *gave* the bread and wine to the disciples.

In Churches in the BCP tradition, recent revisions have removed the Fraction from the Prayer of consecration, where the 1662 Prayer Book had put it, and have restored it as a distinct 'action' between thanksgiving and communion (the Roman and the Calvinist Churches had never lost this placing): the tendency is *not* (as it long was in the Reformed tradition) to associate the Fraction with the 'breaking' of Christ's body on the Cross (see Jn. 19.36! 'Broken' at 1 Cor. 11.24 is secondary), but rather to see the Fraction, in so far as it is at all symbolic, in terms of the many and the one (1 Cor. 10.16–17) (see pp. 193, 196–7).

Dix himself had seen a correspondence between 'Jesus *took*' and the 'offertory'. This view has largely been abandoned, and some recent rites now distinguish between the *presentation* of the bread and wine and the *taking* of them by the eucharistic president.

On the whole, the 'taking' and the 'breaking' have lately rather receded in importance, their purely 'functional' and preparatory side being stressed; and the great thanksgiving and the communion stand out distinctly as the fundamental actions of the eucharistic meal.

---

[1] The North American *Lutheran* rite of 1978 appears to find no theological problem in saying at the offertory 'Merciful Father, we offer with joy and thanksgiving what you have first given us—ourselves, our time, and our possessions—signs of your gracious love. Receive them for the sake of him who offered himself for us, Jesus Christ our Lord'. I have myself often felt the spiritual power of an offertory *dance* in black Africa.

4 THE GREAT PRAYER OF THANKSGIVING

New eucharistic rites clearly see the 'Canon' as beginning with the *Sursum corda* and ending with the people's Amen that rounds off the concluding doxology. Partly as a result of the study of Jewish liturgy (and cf. 1 Tim. 4.4–5),[1] there is a wide acceptance of the theological principle of 'consecration by thanksgiving'. Modern canons really are *eucharistic* prayers: their 'prefaces' strike and hold the note of praise and thanksgiving as they rehearse the mighty acts of God in creation and redemption.

Study of ancient Christian liturgies[2] (the anaphora in *Ap. Trad.* has been particularly influential, even though it lacks the Sanctus) has persuaded modern revisers that a good eucharistic prayer should contain most, if not all, of the following features: (1) introductory dialogue; (2) preface or (first part of the) thanksgiving; (3) Sanctus; a transition which may either (4) continue the thanksgiving or (5) take the form of a preliminary epiclesis, if not both; (6) narrative of the institution; (7) anamnesis-oblation; (8) epiclesis; (9) intercessions; (10) concluding doxology and Amen. When W. J. Grisbrooke, from examination of ancient anaphoras, had collected the foregoing features and arranged them in the 'logical' order given above, he discovered that the three new anaphoras of the Roman rite corresponded exactly to that sequence.[3]

Although the arrangement may vary slightly, most modern eucharistic prayers contain those elements. Differing formulations of individual parts will, however, reflect differing eucharistic theologies on the part of the writers and their ecclesiastical traditions. The anamnesis-oblation is the most sensitive point, for it will almost inevitably express a particular view of the eucharistic sacrifice—historically and theologically a point of controversy. However, work in biblical theology has led to a more 'real' and 'dynamic' understanding of 'memorial', and liturgical writers have thereby been enabled to find a sufficient *rapprochement* between 'Catholic' and 'Protestant' views for a single formula to embrace both; this happened with the Church of England's Series 3:

> Therefore, heavenly Father, with this bread and this cup we do this in remembrance of him: we celebrate and proclaim his perfect sacrifice made

---

[1] G. A. Michell, *Eucharistic Consecration in the Primitive Church* (SPCK 1948); J.-P. Audet, 'Esquisse historique du genre littéraire de la "Bénédiction" juive et de l'"Eucharistie" chrétienne', in *RBén.*, 65 (1958), pp. 371–99; L. Bouyer, *Eucharist*; and various studies by L. Ligier (see *SL* 9 (1973), pp. 161–85).

[2] See pp. 189–201. For the *Ap. Trad.* see pp. 57–9 and 173–6.

[3] Art. 'Anaphora' in *DLW* pp. 10–17. On the new Roman anaphoras, see L. Sheppard, ed., *The New Liturgy* (DLT 1970), pp. 103–258. Also *LMD* 94 (1968/2) and B. Kleinheyer, *Erneuerung des Hochgebets* (Regensburg 1969).

once for all upon the cross, his resurrection from the dead, and his ascension into heaven ... Accept through him, our great high priest, this our sacrifice of thanks and praise....

Of the new Roman Catholic prayers, IV contains the phrase 'we now celebrate this memorial of our redemption', but it also says 'we offer you his body and blood', thereby making unmistakably clear what II means when it says 'we offer you, Father, this life-giving bread, this saving cup', and III when it says 'we offer you in thanksgiving this holy and living sacrifice'. It is doubtful whether *this* view of the eucharistic sacrifice could ever be accepted by Protestants.

Most Western prayers now include in some form or other an 'Eastern' pneumatological epiclesis. The Holy Spirit may be invoked in connection with the elements, the people, the fruits of communion, or any combination of these.

On the Reformed-Presbyterian front, the Institution Narrative is now usually included in the eucharistic prayer (though this was not formerly the case in that tradition). Its use may also, however, be continued as an initial warrant, or at the Taking, or at the Fraction, or at the communion. The CNI service of 1973-74 allows the omission of the institution narrative from the eucharistic prayer, if it has already been used as an initial warrant.

Many new prayers include an Eastern-style acclamation by the people, usually directly after the Institution Narrative. The most popular is: 'Christ has died, Christ is risen, Christ will come again'.

New rites also provide for variety in the eucharistic prayers. The traditional Western practice of 'proper prefaces' is usually maintained. But a new, and more 'Eastern', feature is the provision of complete alternative anaphoras. Thus the Roman Mass now has four eucharistic prayers, the first still being the old Roman canon. For use on occasions other than the principal Sunday service, the PECUSA book of 1971-3 set out a purely rubrical 'order of celebration', accompanied by four alternative eucharistic prayers printed in full (though the last went so far as to call for the improvisation of the preface and the post-Sanctus thanksgiving—a faculty which persisted into the *Proposed Book of Common Prayer* of 1976/77); by the book of 1973, the third of these eucharistic prayers had become a permissible alternative even on Sundays. The English and Welsh Congregationalist *Order of Public Worship* of 1970 provided six eucharistic prayers, of which the last three placed the Sanctus at the end in accordance with E. C. Ratcliff's theory.[1]

[1] See *LS* pp. 18-40 = *JEH* 1 (1950), pp. 29-36, 125-34. For an account of the influence of Ratcliff's theory on revision in the C of E, see C. O. Buchanan, in R. C. D. Jasper, ed., *The Eucharist Today* (SPCK 1974), pp. 15-18, with notes.

In the USA, the unofficial Committee for a Common Eucharistic Prayer produced an ecumenical text in 1975, and this was taken into the Episcopalian *Proposed Book of Common Prayer* as Prayer D of Eucharist II; the British Joint Liturgical Group in 1978 published proposals for an 'ecumenical canon'.[1]

5 SHIFTS IN THEOLOGICAL EMPHASIS

First, the powerful medieval and Reformation concentration on the cross has been broadened to include the other 'mighty acts' of God in Jesus Christ: the thanksgiving and the anamnesis are now likely to mention the birth, life, passion, resurrection, ascension, and heavenly intercession of Jesus Christ as well as his expected parousia. God's saving history with Israel may also be recalled; so the post-Sanctus of the North American Inter-Lutheran rite of 1978: 'Through Abraham you promised to bless all nations. You rescued Israel, your chosen people. Through the Prophets you renewed your promise.' God may be praised for the creation of the world and of mankind; so in its eucharistic preface the CSI liturgy of 1954/62 made thanksgiving 'through Jesus Christ thy Son our Lord, through whom thou didst create the heavens and the earth and all that in them is, and didst make man in thine own image, and when he had fallen into sin didst redeem him to be the firstfruits of a new creation'.

Second, the new rites, in accordance with a renewed theological emphasis on the Church's earthly vocation in the midst of human society, relate the eucharistic assembly to the Church's total witness to Christ in the world. Thus the C of E Series 2 and 3 both pray after communion that God will 'send us out [into the world] in the power of' his 'Spirit to live and work to' his 'praise and glory'. The dismissals often refer to service in the world.

Third, the new rites open up the rediscovered 'eschatological prospect' in various ways. Most commonly, the second advent is 'remembered' or 'looked for' in the anamnesis. Either in the prayers of the faithful or in the canon, petitions may be made for participation with the saints in the final Kingdom. The post-communion prayer of the 1968/74 British Methodist service thanks God for having 'given us a foretaste of the heavenly banquet prepared for all mankind'.

6 LANGUAGE

The question of liturgical language is discussed later in this book (pp.

[1] *SL* 11 (1976), no. 2/3, is devoted to the eucharistic prayer in modern revisions and compositions.

465–73). Here it is enough, as far as English is concerned, to note the changes which took place in the 1960s and 70s. Earlier versions had kept to a quasi-Cranmerian style. The C of E Series 2 Eucharist of 1966 abandoned the rolling periods and achieved a direct and economical text, rather in an 'old Roman' style; but it still addressed God as 'Thou'. By the Series 3 Eucharist of 1971, God was addressed as 'You'; this style of address had been used by the RC International Committee on English in the Liturgy (ICEL) in its translation of *The New Eucharistic Prayers and Prefaces* (1969), and it gained the day by 1974 in the British Methodist *Sunday Service*. The three orders of *Divine Service* from the Church of Scotland (1973) are deliberately conformed to three different linguistic styles: the first (which is a mild revision of the 1940 *Book of Common Order*) corresponds roughly to the AV, the second to the RSV, and the third to the NEB (except that God is addressed as 'You'). The International Consultation on English Texts (ICET) has worked for an ecumenically agreed version of the common liturgical texts (its *Prayers we have in common* include the Gloria in Excelsis, the Creeds, the Sursum Corda, the Sanctus and Benedictus, the Agnus Dei and the Lord's Prayer), but national and denominational variants have been made.

7 TENSIONS

Recent eucharistic revision has in fact had to take account of historical and geographical tensions. There is the tension between denominational tradition and local ecumenical agreement. For Anglicans, for example, the early test was, how is the CSI liturgy related to the BCP? More recently, it has been a question of English Anglicans tracing the influence of their Series 2 and 3 through much of the Anglican world and into united liturgies such as that of the Church of North India.[1] There is also the tension between the universal and the local within a worldwide Church. It appeared at first that it was chiefly in the minor ceremonial that the Roman Catholic Church intended to allow local variety. But variant eucharistic Prayers are now being composed and tried in many countries. Bold examples of whole rites are found in the experimental *New Orders of the Mass for India*, published by the National Biblical Catechetical and Liturgical Centre, Bangalore (1974).

---

[1] C. O. Buchanan sees in Series 2 and 3 the start of a new 'family' of rites: 'Series 3 in the setting of the Anglican Communion', in Jasper, ed., *The Eucharist Today*, pp. 8–33.

IV

ORDINATION

GENERAL

Andrieu, M., *Les Ordines Romani du haut moyen âge*, vols. 3 & 4. Louvain 1951, 1956.

Bligh, J., *Ordination to the Priesthood*. Sheed and Ward 1956.

Bradshaw, P. F., *The Anglican Ordinal*. AC SPCK 1971.

Daube, D., *The New Testament and Rabbinic Judaism = NTRJ*. Athlone Press 1956.

DLW, art. 'Ordinations'.

Grelot, P., *Le ministère de la nouvelle alliance*. Paris 1967.

Kirk, K. E., ed., *The Apostolic Ministry*. Hodder and Stoughton 1946.

Lightfoot, J. B., *The Epistle to the Philippians* (Macmillan 1868), excursus.

Modern Ecumenical Documents on the Ministry. SPCK 1975.

One in Christ, 1970 (3).

Porter, H. B., *The Ordination Prayers of the Ancient Western Churches*. AC SPCK 1967.

Swete, H. B., ed., *The Early History of the Church and the Ministry*. Macmillan 1921.

1 Orders and Ordination in the New Testament

FRANK HAWKINS

Brown, R. E., *Priest and Bishop: Biblical Reflections*. G. Chapman 1970.

von Campenhausen, H., (ET) *Ecclesiastical Authority and Spiritual Power in the Church of the First Three Centuries*. A. and C. Black 1969.

Carey, K., ed., *The Historic Episcopate* (Dacre Press 1954), especially essays by W. H. Vanstone and K. J. Woollcombe.

Gore, C., *The Church and the Ministry*. 2nd edn rev. C. H. Turner. Longmans 1919.

Hennecke, E., (ET) *New Testament Apocrypha* (SCM 1974), pp. 35–87.

Lecuyer, J., *Le sacerdoce dans le mystère du Christ* (Paris 1957), pp. 9–123.

Lightfoot, J. B., *The Epistle to the Philippians* (Macmillan 1868), excursus.

Schmithals, W., (ET) *The Office of Apostle in the Early Church*. SPCK 1971.

Schweizer, E., (ET) *Church Order in the New Testament*. SCM 1961.

Vatican II, Decree on the Priesthood (*Presbyterium Ordinis*), with commentaries.

de Vaux, R., (ET) *Ancient Israel* (DLT 1961), on OT priesthood.

The study of orders and ordination in the NT and early Church is beset with many problems which have been explored in great depth. In recent years it has become apparent that to talk of ministry in the NT even in the most general terms raises particular problems not only of history but also of method. Such evidence as there is must be evaluated against a wider background including relevant material from rabbinic Judaism (cf. p. 50), from the Qumran documents, and from the recently discovered collections of Gnostic documents (cf. pp. 52–3). The NT material itself includes primary evidence of obvious value and relevance, but it is misleading to lump together miscellaneous texts or passages to convey an impression of what is meant by ministry in the NT. The NT material shows signs of internal development and has in any case to be related to the tradition of orders and ordination in the life of the Church as a whole in the first two centuries.

The most obvious (and important) feature of the NT material is the evidence it provides of the diversity of forms of what may be loosely called 'ministry'.[1] The term itself should be understood in the light of its

---

[1] All Christian ministry has its origins in the ministry of Christ, who came not to be ministered to but to minister (Lk. 22.27; cf. Jn. 13.1–17). It is Christ who fulfils the priestly ministries of the Old Covenant and transcends them, becoming High Priest of a new order (Heb. 7.11ff), who is the apostle of this new order (Heb. 3.1), and who is himself commissioned by the Father for his mission in the world (Jn. 20.21). Cf. A. Gelin, 'The Priesthood of Christ in the Epistle to the Hebrews', in *The Sacrament of*

basic meaning of 'service'; for the most part there is no implied distinction between clerical and lay forms of ministry. There is then no single form or pattern of ministry apparent in the NT, nor is there (directly) a single or unified theological basis for one. We see rather a fairly random distribution of names, titles, and functions in relation to ministry, and theological appreciations of its significance which vary considerably.[1]

This fact is reflected in the different ways that forms of ministry are seen to originate in the NT. Some ministers are commissioned directly by Jesus or given gifts of ministry by the Spirit, some are appointed by other Christians, while for other ministries there is no evidence about how they came into being at all. This is not to say that the NT as a whole is indifferent as to how or by whom Christian ministries were appointed, authorized, or recognized. There is certainly evidence of a tendency to develop a unified theological view, but this does not emerge clearly in the NT documents themselves. This unified view is neither established nor fully expressed until the end of the NT period: well into the second century. But the seeds of development are there, and their growth needs fuller explanation than the supposition that they progressed accidentally into later historical forms.

The basic NT evidence can be expressed under four heads: (a) 'The Twelve', (b) the significance of the apostle, (c) the evidence of the major 'charisms': apostles, prophets, and teachers, and (d) the evidence about particular Christian community leaders.

THE TWELVE

The significance of these rests on their calling by, and close relation with, Jesus himself. This relationship is given permanent significance in the recognition that they constitute those who share with Jesus the eschatological rule of the people of God. This secured the place of 'the Twelve' in the tradition of the Church, and established a principle expressed in later forms of Christian ministry: the sharing with Jesus in the divine 'government' of the new Covenant people of God. This view is reflected in later traditions (e.g. Lk. 22.30; Rev. 21.14) where significance

---

Order, (ET) ed. B. Botte (New York 1962). The Greek word for ministry is *diakonia*; use of a concordance will show that in the NT it refers to (a) practical service, (b) service at tables, (c) the ministry of the Twelve and their helpers, (d) the preaching and communicating of the gospel. The Greek term *leitourgia* is also relevant; cf. Rom. 15.16 and Hatch and Redpath's *Concordance to the Septuagint*, s.v. (Editors).

[1] The whole Church has a ministry, within which each member has his own particular ministry according to the gifts of the Holy Spirit (cf. 1 Cor. 12; Eph. 4.11f).

still attaches to 'the Twelve' as such and not simply because they were regarded also as apostles.

THE APOSTLE[1]

The significance of the apostle is established by St Paul. He is commissioned by the risen Lord and sees his own ministry (and that of apostles generally) as part of the 'advent' of the gospel; itself an event of eschatological significance in the proclamation of salvation open to all in Jesus Christ. The uniqueness of the apostle[2] is defined by the way in which, under the Spirit, he so conserves the tradition (of the words and works of Jesus) in his preaching that its true significance is recognized in its once for all historical character and its universal application: in short, it is seen to be 'gospel'. Consequently the apostle is recognized as the person through whom a church is established, and who has therefore a measure of responsibility for it and a certain authority over it. It is this same concern for the conservation of tradition in order to bring out the true significance of the gospel which underlies the concern for the 'apostolic' in later traditions within the NT, and forms one element in the development of a pattern of ministry which is (in this sense at least) apostolic.

APOSTLES, PROPHETS, AND TEACHERS

The priority of the action of the Spirit is recognized also in the way that the ministry of apostles is linked with that of prophets and teachers, constituting the ministry of the major 'charisms' in a Christian community (cf. 1 Cor. 12.28).[3] The community does not appoint prophets or teachers any more than it appoints apostles. They are all 'charisms' which are essentially God-given; to be recognized and accepted (and in some sense authenticated) by the community as such. Like the apostle, prophets and teachers express and interpret the

---

[1] A distinction should be drawn between the Twelve, whom St Luke (e.g. 6.13) and Revelation (21.14) call apostles, and the other apostles (Paul, Andronicus, Junias; cf. Rom. 16.7; 1 Cor. 15.5, 7). Cf. S. Freyne, *The Twelve: Disciples or Apostles* (Sheed and Ward 1968).

[2] No one after them is called an apostle in the NT, and none could witness as they did to the work of the incarnate Christ. Yet there is a sense in which the apostles can be said to have had successors; as early as 1 *Clement* 42.2–4 (dated *c.* 95, and therefore antedating some NT documents), it is stated that 'Christ comes from God, and the apostles from Christ ... and they appointed their first fruits, testing them by the Spirit, to be bishops and deacons of the future believers'. (For firstfruits, cf. 1 Cor. 16.15–16.)

[3] Cf. concordances to the NT s.v. *charisma, charizomai*.

tradition in a way which exposes the gospel and creates the Christian response to it (as, for example, in the work of the Christian prophet responsible for the Book of Revelation).

COMMUNITY LEADERS

Christian community leaders are variously designated 'leaders' (Heb. 13.7), 'elders' (*presbuteroi*, 1 Pet. 5.1; Jas. 5.14; Acts 11.30, etc.), 'presidents' (Rom. 12.8; 1 Thess. 5.12–13), 'teachers' (Gal. 6.6), as well as the more clearly specified 'overseers' (*episkopoi*, Acts 20.17, 28; Phil. 1.1; Tit. 1.5ff) and 'assistants' (*diakonoi*, Phil. 1.1; 1 Tim. 3.1ff).[1] 1 Cor. 16.15–16 contains several phrases implying functions of leadership; on the other hand there are some lists of ministries without any clear reference to such functions (e.g. 1 Cor. 12.28; Eph. 4.11).[2]

The relationships among these leaders and their standing vis-à-vis the elements of ministry already described cannot be easily or directly established. Some of these forms of ministry have their parallels in contemporary Judaism (see pp. 50, 300) and in the Qumran community,[3] but it has yet to be clearly established that they originate from such sources. The differences are usually as striking as the similarities, and there was in some Christian centres a period in which a later assimilation to Jewish forms of ministry took place.

Despite the differences in form, and the independent theological convictions behind them, there remains evidence of a movement towards unity which expressed itself in different ways. It is therefore not enough simply to draw attention to the fact that different traditions of ministry in the NT. Despite claims made for the adequacy of a 'pluriform' view of ministry, it is clear that the Christian communities represented in later

1 Scholars now generally agree that in the NT the terms *episkopos* and *presbuteros* do not indicate two different levels of ministry. Cf. A. E. Harvey, 'Episkopoi, Presbyteroi, Diakonoi', in *JTS* 25 (1974), pp. 318–32; D. Powell, 'Ordo Presbyterii', in *JTS* 26 (1975), pp. 290–329; J. G. Sobosan, 'The Role of a Presbyter', in *SJT* 27 (1974), pp. 142–3. On '*episkopos*' cf. a concordance to the LXX and commentaries on Jn. 10 and 1 Pet. 2. There is no sound evidence that the 'ordination' of the Seven in Acts 6 is the origin of the order of *diakonoi*. In short, the threefold ministry of bishops, presbyters, and deacons cannot be convincingly traced back to the NT.

2 The reason why priests are absent from this list is that in the NT no individual Christian or specially commissioned minister is called by this name. The whole Church has a priesthood (cf. 1 Pet. 2.9), and Christians as a body are designated 'kings and priests' (Rev. 1.6), but Christ alone fulfils the priestly offices of the old Covenant. Cf. P. Grelot, 'Le sacerdoce chrétien dans l'Ecriture', in *Bulletin du Comité des Etudes*, 38–9 (July–Dec. 1962) (an invaluable article); J. M. R. Tillard, *What Priesthood has the Ministry?*, Grove Booklets, No. 13.

3 See appended 'Note on the Qumran Documents' (p. 297).

NT documents rejected this possibility in favour of unifying different conceptions of the Christian community and its ministry.

One form of this movement is seen in the retention in the tradition of imagery which maintains the eschatological significance of ministry. The significance of 'the Twelve' has already been noted; the same concern can also be seen in the theological development of terms like 'shepherding the flock'. Much more is involved than simply the enrichment of appropriate images drawn from the OT. The development of such images implies that Church and ministry, by virtue of their relation with the risen Lord, participate already in the eschatological reality of the Kingdom proclaimed by the gospel. Such images continued to be used, even though by the end of the first century their original meaning had become somewhat obscured.

There was, secondly, the desire to create and preserve unity through placing particular emphasis on the priority of the action of the Spirit. St Paul himself demonstrates the unity of the Christian community on this basis (1 Cor. 12), but he shows that unity depends on more than the enthusiastic employment of the gifts of the Spirit. All such 'charisms' are indeed God-given, but there is also a God-given order in the assembly, and it is necessary to recognize, accept, and confirm particular charisms as well as giving particular priority to some.

The recognition of charisms within the community is therefore essential; though it is not clear from St Paul that an institutional form of ministry or a form of ordination plays any part in this. Equally, however, charismatics did not possess a ministerial autonomy such as institutional forms of ministry later developed. In the 'Pauline' churches recognized 'leaders' and charismatics appear to have exercised complementary functions rather than mutually exclusive ministries.[1] Such distinctions as are implied seem to have pastoral and preaching responsibilities rather than liturgical functions in view. It is only outside the NT that there is any evidence of a dialectical opposition of charismatics and ministerial office-holders on the basis of liturgical functions, and even here it is by no means clear what the situation is (cf. *Did.* 15.1). The charism of prophecy certainly existed and was recognized well after the NT period, alongside other recognized community leaders (who might be prophets themselves—e.g. Ignatius of Antioch); and this situation does not seem to change until the reaction to Montanism set in.

The third form of the movement towards unity is represented in the

---

[1] Accordingly there is no evidence that there was originally simply a charismatic ministry exercised by those possessing the spontaneous gifts of the Spirit, which only later 'hardened into offices'; nevertheless ministers were undoubtedly chosen for office on account of their gifts (cf. 1 Tim. 3.1ff).

NT mainly by St Luke, for whom the apostles, and what is historically shown to be 'apostolic', constitute the basis for the fundamental unity of the Church. The 'witness' of the apostles, like the 'witness' of the apostolic traditions, creates under the guidance of the Spirit the unity and authenticity of the Church. The apostles are unique, and can have no successors.[1] But the apostolic history shows that through the Spirit's action events constantly occur which constitute a 'new creation' for the Church. The appointment of the Seven (Acts 6) and the emergence of 'elders' (11.30) are new events, but in their context (the historical activity of the apostles) they are seen to be a theological assertion of the 'apostolicity' of these forms of ministry in the Church.

The same sort of pattern is apparent in writings closely related (theologically speaking) to Luke-Acts. In the Pastoral Epistles 'guarding' the tradition is the primary function of the ministry, and in 1 *Clement* the authenticity of Christian worship is held to depend on historic continuity with the apostles themselves (1 *Clem.* 40–4).

There is evidence that at this period church communities were convinced of the need for a decisive break with Gnosticism (see pp. 52–53). Consequently there was recognition of the need to express basic theological convictions in ways which made this separation apparent. The clearest instances of this in the NT period occur in the emphasis given to a doctrine of creation, the acceptance of history as involved in the Christian faith in God, and the development of a unified theology of Church, ministry, and sacraments on this basis. It is against this background that concern for the 'apostolic' and the historical verifiability of apostolic traditions becomes so important (by contrast with the gnostic emphasis on immediate and direct revelation). In this context particular emphasis came to be given to a tradition of ministerial appointment by 'ordination'; perhaps by contrast with the popularity of charismatic forms of ministry in gnostic communities.

This 'tradition' (discernible largely in Luke-Acts and the Pastoral Epistles) has three characteristics:

1. Ministerial appointment is by apostles (and subsequently by their successors, Tit. 1.5; cf. 1 *Clem.* 42, 44). Recognized forms of ministry originated from or were associated with the apostles (Acts 6.1ff; 11.30; 14.23).

2. The preferred form of authorization or appointment is by the imposition of hands.[2] This is associated with the operation of the Spirit

---

[1] But see p. 292, n. 2.

[2] *Epithesis ton cheiron.* It is to be distinguished from the verb 'to ordain' (*cheirotonein*), which means literally 'to vote by stretching out the hand'. Cf. the appended 'Note on Rabbinic Ordination'.

(cf. Acts 13.2; 20.28). A similar pattern is evident in the Pastoral Epistles, where, however, 'ordination' may mean 'recognition' of an existing ministry exercised in the Spirit (1 Tim. 4.14), or 'appointment' to such a ministry (2 Tim. 1.6).

3. The word 'succession' (*diadoche*) does not occur in the NT, nor is there, strictly speaking, a conception of succession attaching to the ministry of the Church. Nevertheless the Pastoral Epistles regard the transmission and preservation of sound doctrine in relation to the continuity of faithful witnesses as important (2 Tim. 2.2).

As far as the NT is concerned, then, the basic conceptions of ministry are rooted in an eschatological understanding of the Church and its mission and gospel. Under the pressure of historical circumstances (particularly the need for a decisive break with gnostic communities) the images of the early eschatological thought were expressed differently, that is in historical and sacramental terms. Eschatological immediacy proved too vulnerable a principle of continuity for Christians anxious to emphasize their distinctiveness from similar communities. So from the close of the NT period there is increasing emphasis on ministerial 'authorization' and recognition (ultimately by episcopal ordination) and, later, on the historic succession of bishops in the major sees. This particular emphasis on historical continuity increased not simply as an effective means of countering alternative claims, but because it enabled the communities concerned to express their conviction that a duly authorized and recognized ministry was one of the ways in which Christians could be assured that their own community really did participate in the life of the Kingdom of God through the Spirit of the risen Christ in its mission, ordering, and worship.

NOTE ON THE CONNECTION BETWEEN
CHRISTIAN AND RABBINIC ORDINATION[1]

Two Greek terms need to be distinguished. The word *cheirotonein*, which in later Christian writing signifies 'to ordain', means literally 'to vote by stretching out the hand'. It occurs twice in the NT (Acts 14.23; 2 Cor. 8.19); but it is not certain that the NT use refers to what Hippolytus and the Church after him understood by ordination (see pp. 301–2).

The second term is *epitithenai tas cheiras*, to lay on hands. The Hebrew equivalents occur in the OT in a number of connections, but in the Rabbinic literature of NT times the term *samakh* (lit. to 'lean on, apply pressure to'), used to describe the laying on of hands in order to appoint to office, is limited to the sacrificial cult and the ordination of a rabbi. From rabbinic texts it is clear that

---

[1] Cf. Daube, *NTRJ* (Athlone), pp. 224–46; J. Coppens, *L'Imposition des mains et les rites connexes* (Paris 1925).

the rabbis ordained their disciples to office by the laying on of hands (see p. 50). This rabbinic custom may shed light on the references to the laying on of hands in the NT. In St Luke the parallels are closer to passages quoted from the OT (cf. Acts 6.1ff), and only perhaps in the Pastoral Epistles is a direct rabbinic parallel possible (1 Tim. 4.14; 5.22; 2 Tim. 1.6 Cf. pp. 295–6, 309).

NOTE ON THE QUMRAN DOCUMENTS

The organization of the communities at Qumran has two particular parallels with the early Christian ministry.

1. *Mebaqqer.* Within the Qumran communities were a series of autonomous groups of no less than ten men under the rule of a 'Guardian' or 'Censor' (*Mebaqqer*). He controlled debate in the community assembly and in general acted as a pastor, an instructor, and a 'looser of bonds' (*MD* 6; cf. *Zad.* 13). The Greek synonym for this title is *episkopos*, and the Hebrew verb from which the title *mebaqqer* comes is used in the OT to describe the 'shepherding' of Israel by Yahweh (Ezek. 34.11f). The LXX translation uses the verb *episkopein*, and the passage in question was used frequently in the early Church to illustrate the work of a bishop (Acts 20.28; 1 Pet. 2.25; 5.2; 1 *Clem.* 16 etc.).

2. The elders. Within the organization of the community as a whole was a council of ten 'judges' and a community council consisting of twelve laymen and three priests. Their function was to assist the Guardian and the Priest of the community. The title 'elder' may possibly apply to the twelve laymen on the council, though this is not specifically stated in the documents.

2 The Tradition of Ordination in the Second Century to the Time of Hippolytus

FRANK HAWKINS

Beraudy, R., 'Le sacrement de l'ordre d'après la Tradition apostolique d'Hippolyte', in *Bulletin du Comité des Etudes*, 38–9 (July–Dec. 1962).

Botte, B., 'L'ordre d'après les prières d'ordination', in *Etudes sur le sacrement de l'ordre*. Paris 1957.

von Campenhausen, H., (ET) *Ecclesiastical Authority and Spiritual Power in the Church of the First Three Centuries*. A. and C. Black 1969.

Gore, C., *The Church and the Ministry*, 2nd edn rev. C. H. Turner. Longmans 1919.

Hanson, A. T., *The Pioneer Ministry*. SCM 1961.

Karrer, O., (ET) *Peter and the Church*. Herder/Nelson 1963.

Kirk, K. E., *Apostolic Ministry* (esp. essay of G. Dix).

Lecuyer, J., 'Épiscopat et presbytérat dans les écrits d'Hippolyte de Rome', in *RSR* 41 (1953).

Rahner, K., and Ratzinger, J., (ET) *The Episcopate and the Primacy.* Herder/Nelson 1962.

Streeter, B. H., *The Primitive Church.* Macmillan 1929.

See also bibliographies, esp. on Apostolic Succession, in *One in Christ*, 1970 (3).

The student might also consult:

Chavasse, A., *Le sacramentaire gélasien.* Tournai 1957.

Hope, D. M., *The Leonine Sacramentary.* OUP 1971.

From the second century the development of the tradition of ordination was related to the office and functions of the bishop. This represents the conclusion to that movement discerned within the NT period which related the origins and growth of traditions in general to the apostolic period.

The emergence of this 'episcopal' pattern of ministry is not accidental. Evidence of a movement to distinguish 'elders' or 'leaders' as '(presbyter-) bishops and deacons' during the last decades of the first century is clear not only from the NT but outside it also (Acts 14.23; 20.17ff; cf. Phil. 1.1; 1 Pet. 2.25; *Did.* 15.1f; 1 *Clem.* 42.4f). The reasons for the spread of this movement are theological as well as historical: the 'oversight' of the community and its 'service' reflect the continuing relation of the local Christian community under its leaders with the ultimate *episcope* of the Father and the permanent *diakonia* of Jesus Christ for the whole people of God.

At the same time the authority of charismatic ministries (particularly the prophets), while still recognized, was in practice increasingly subordinated to that of the presbyter-bishops. The defence of this institutional form of authority was its association with an apostolic tradition, and the means of this association was ordination by the imposition of hands with prayer. In this way the ground was established for a theological defence of presbyter-bishops as the exclusive leaders of the Christian community. By the middle of the second century, however, the plural form of leadership expressed in the council of the community's presbyter-bishops was making way for the principle of a single leader: the bishop in his own community (the so-called 'monarchical episcopate').

As far as can be discerned, the origins of this development lie in the theology represented in the epistles of St Ignatius of Antioch, written early in the second century. The theology of orders expressed in them is quite different from that of the 'Pauline' churches in the late first century, exemplified in Acts and the Pastoral Epistles. Ignatius shows no evident interest in the concept of tradition, nor in a particular significance of the apostolic period as such. He does not use a 'succession' type of argument, such as is found in 1 *Clement*. His main concern is for the unity of the Christian community: unity with the bishop is made both the focus and the guarantee of its own unity in Christ. This is underlined by the significance given to the bishop: he represents the divine Fatherhood to the community, he presides over the council of 'elders' (presbyters), and is assisted by the deacons. He is thus the focus for a harmony which preserves the worshipping and sacramental life of the community and establishes its unity in the divine unity itself (cf. *Magn.* 6, etc.). Even so, the significance of the bishop in an individual capacity is not stressed: he is indeed the 'type' of God the Father for his community, but on the same basis the deacons are a 'type' of Jesus Christ, and the presbyters of the apostles. He presides, but it is over a college of presbyters, on the pattern of Christ with his apostles. It is therefore a shared and mutually co-operative view of leadership and the exercise of authority which is being expressed.

The order of bishops, presbyters, and deacons is thus an innovation: it belongs to the history and the theological concerns of the second century. This particular pattern is however neither novel nor accidental in its theological basis: it is part of a pattern of development which has its roots deep in the NT. The growth of this new pattern in the second and third centuries took place on the basis of the gradual acceptance by the Church as a whole of the significance of the bishop as the Christian community-leader, as opposed to the collective leadership of the presbyter-bishops (or conceivably the charismatics; cf. *Did.* 13.1f). The main impetus for this change came from recognition of the need to combat the claims of gnostic communities and their teachers (cf. p. 295). This emphasis on the need to safeguard 'orthodox' teaching secured the connection of the bishop with the 'apostolic tradition' since he could be appealed to as a 'teaching authority'. At a later stage this argument was combined with an emphasis on the concept of succession (*diadoche*), particularly by Hegesippus and Irenaeus. It was developed as a counter-claim to the gnostic position on revelation relatively late in the second century. To this extent therefore the position (argued originally by C. H. Turner and followed by H. Küng, E. Schlink, and Y. Congar) can be stated thus: for the Church of the first three centuries succession does not mean primarily a direct sequence of persons, but the inner unity and continuity of apostolic doctrine in the Church.

Thus added to the pastoral, liturgical, and unitive concerns of the bishop is the desire of the whole community to participate in the mission of Christ not only in a creative way (in the existence of the community as such) but in terms also of the authentic interpretation of the tradition which creates a genuinely Christian community. In this sense the mission of the whole Church is seen to be founded on one gospel: the authentic and apostolic gospel of Jesus Christ, and the authenticity of this gospel is associated with the significance of the bishop as the single leader of the whole community.

There is one further aspect of this development which should not be overlooked: the growing emphasis on the use of OT typology in relation to the Christian ministry. There are references to the idea of a 'hierarchy' on the Jewish model, and a gradually increasing use of the language of priesthood (Greek: *hiereus*; later Latin: *sacerdos*) (apart from that used of Christ himself). Evidence for this goes back at least to the end of the first century (in 1 *Clement* and the *Didache*) and is also apparent in later second-century writings (e.g. Justin Martyr and the Epistle of Polycarp). By the end of the second century the use of this language of priesthood in connection with Christian worship and the argument for the succession of true apostolic doctrine *via* the sequence of bishops in the churches had together established the basis for an argument from the 'apostolic succession' of the Christian ministry. This view identified the content of 'apostolic' almost exclusively with the bishop, by contrast with the earlier view which identified 'apostolic' traditions with the witness of the whole community. Inevitably the interpretation of the liturgy of ordination was linked with the conception of the apostolic succession from about the third century. The background to this line of argument is not only the view about the Christian priesthood expressed by Clement of Rome but also what is said by Irenaeus about the true presbyter. Presbyters, he says, should be within the Church; they should have their succession from the apostles, and they should have received the 'gift of truth' (*charisma veritatis*; cf. *AH* 4.26.2ff).

In the second century, then, ordination seems to have included these aspects:

1. The rite itself recognized a vocation or calling to the office. This had to be recognized or authorized in the imposition of hands with prayer and in the acceptance of the candidate by the Church as a whole.

2. The ministry of each community was related to the one Church of Christ in its universal aspect through the consecration of the bishop by the bishops of other communities. The bishop was not consecrated by his own presbyterate (except perhaps in Alexandria; cf. W. Telfer, in *JEH* 3 (1952), pp. 1–13). The bishop himself did however recognize and authorize the ministry of the presbyters and deacons in his own church by ordination through the imposition of hands. In this way, both the internal

unity of the local community and its unity with the whole Church were secured through the primary association of ordination with the bishop. Equally, the concern of the whole Church with the mission of Christ to the world was established at the local level with the acceptance of the principle of territorial jurisdiction as a corollary to the theology of order. In this way the significance of the bishop was established geographically as well as temporally and historically by the argument from succession.

3. The association of ordination with the bishop contributed not only to the development of the theology of the 'one Catholic Church'; it expressed also an aspect of the one faith. Christian communities expressed their union in the one Church not only in the person of the bishop, but in the bishop as the president of a worshipping community which already presupposed a common faith.

4. The work of the Spirit in ordination was understood and expressed in a variety of ways. Resistance to gnostic influence led to an emphasis on the rite performed in the context of the Church rather than simple recognition of a charism within the community. This latter element survives in the approval of the candidate by the people in the ordination rite, but the emphasis is placed much more on the element of authorization.

5. Ordination was understood to be the occasion of receiving as well as publicly recognizing a gift of grace that enabled the recipient to exercise pastoral and sacramental functions in the Church (for example, presiding at the Eucharist). From this point onwards the status of the episcopally-based pattern of ministry was assured.

THE LITURGY
OF ORDINATION IN THE
APOSTOLIC TRADITION
OF HIPPOLYTUS

The *Apostolic Tradition* contains the oldest surviving liturgy of ordination (see pp. 57–9). It is known to us basically through its wide popularity as a model for subsequent church orders, particularly its ordination prayers. It is generally considered to give reliable (if limited) indications of the practice of the Roman church in the early third century. Its reliability rests on general conformity with what is known of the theology and practice of the second-century church, and on the assumption that Hippolytus would scarcely be commending to his church a liturgical model widely different from their own. The limitations are that it is not easy to distinguish tradition based on actual practice from what Hippolytus himself wishes to suggest as a model. It was also a period in which liturgical forms were by no means fixed; liturgical prayers in particular were improvised on the basis of a set pattern (cf. *Ap. Trad.* 10.3ff).

The tradition which is being commended by Hippolytus is then primarily a model commended for use. Candidates for ordination must first be approved by the Church as a whole; a prayer should be said for them, during which they receive the laying-on of hands. The elements of this tradition are present from the NT period, and subsequent development of the theology of ministry in the Church shows how they became normative (cf. *Ap. Trad.* 1.1ff; 38.2). The degree of improvisation in the prayers should not be over-emphasized. The inclusion of particular themes and 'types' (drawn largely from Scripture) is itself characteristic of liturgical prayers from the first century onwards (cf. 1 *Clem.* 59–62, 64). Hippolytus may well make use of a recognized pattern in defending a general tradition in danger of obscurity or neglect (cf. *Ap. Trad.* 1).

The first impression that the reader may gain from Hippolytus is the contrast between the ordinary domestic setting of the church community itself and the solemn language of its public prayers. The church building itself is apparently a house (16.1); the church community is subject to persecution since it has confessors (10.2), and many of the minor regulations reflect Jewish domestic laws. By contrast, the prayer for the consecration of the bishop reflects a serene and confident faith and hope in the God who 'from the foundation of the world hast been pleased to be glorified in them whom thou hast chosen' (3.2).

THE RITES OF ORDINATION

These include the consecration of a bishop and the ordination of presbyters and deacons. There are also rites providing for appointment to various minor orders.

The bishop is chosen and his election confirmed by the people together with the presbytery and bishops from other local communities. The bishops then proceed to the consecration of the candidate. They lay hands on him while the presbytery stands in silence, and all pray silently for the descent of the Spirit. One of the bishops then lays hands on the candidate and prays that the Spirit given by Christ to the apostles will now be poured forth on the candidate 'to feed thy holy flock and serve as thine high-priest ... and offer to thee the gifts of thy holy Church. And that by the high-priestly Spirit he may have authority to forgive sins according to thy command ... to loose every bond according to the authority thou gavest to the apostles' (3.3ff).

The bishop's office is understood primarily in liturgical terms, reflecting the understanding of *episcope* in the early second century (in for example Ignatius and 1 *Clement*). At the beginning of the third century, *Ap. Trad.* shows how the bishop had emerged from the corporate presbytery mainly by the concentration of liturgical functions upon him. Within the next century or so the bishop acquired the functions of government almost completely from the presbyterate, though at the same time the presbyterate itself began again to share increasingly in the bishop's liturgical responsibilities.

In *Ap. Trad.*, then, the consecration of the bishop has a threefold significance:

1. His acceptance by the people of his local community with its presbytery is an essential part of his ordination. The local community has to test and accept a candidate before he can exercise his episcopal ministry among them. In ordination therefore he is bound to them (and they to him) in the gift of his ministry.

2. The concern and recognition of the Church as a whole is expressed in the presence of neighbouring bishops to show that what is happening is not simply of local significance. The appointment of a bishop is seen to have its proper context within the one catholic Church. In this way the bishop's office itself is seen as one of the links which bind local communities in the one Church, and the evidence of *Ap. Trad.* marks a stage in this process between Ignatius (for whom the bishop is the focus of unity in the local community) and Cyprian of Carthage (for whom the bishop is a member of the collective episcopate of the catholic Church) in the third century.

3. The bishop is seen to have a particular status in relation to the activity of the Spirit of God in the Church. The Spirit is still the 'ruling Spirit' whose fresh creative act is sought to constitute the gift of grace in ordination, but the bishop's status is recognized in the prayer for the Spirit (3.3) in connection with the imposition of hands by one of the consecrating bishops (2.5).

A presbyter is ordained by the bishop laying his hands on his head, with the presbyters also touching him (8.1). The prayer used is probably the same as that for the consecration of a bishop except for the functions and ministerial gifts explicitly mentioned: to share in the presbyterate and to govern the people of God (8.2).

The presbyterate is a corporate body responsible for the government and administration of the local community. From the time that a single president came to be effectively distinguished from his fellow presbyters as 'the bishop' its corporate liturgical responsibilities tended to become centred on him, as the prayers of *Ap. Trad.* reveal. There are however indications that this was not always the case. The use of the same introductory prayer for the presbyters as well as for the bishop is itself a recognition of the organic relation between bishop and presbytery. There is also the reference in the ordination-prayer for presbyters to God's command to Moses to choose presbyters 'whom thou didst fill with the Spirit which thou hadst granted to thy minister [Moses]'. It is significant that there is no reference to the type of Moses in the prayer for the bishop, particularly as it was applied to the Christian ministry at least as early as 1 *Clement*. In 1 *Clement* Moses' appointment of presbyters is put forward as the biblical type for the succession of the presbyter-bishops from the apostles and also (more importantly) for the valid 'offering of the gifts' in the Church's worship in an explicitly priestly sense (1 *Clem.* 40–4). It is not clear therefore that the distinction which *Ap. Trad.* draws between the liturgical functions of the bishop and those of his presbyterate should be regarded as original or invariable. From the same point of view one may see more significance in the presbyterate joining with the bishop in the laying on of hands than just the natural right of the ruling body in the community. Ordination by laying-on of hands presumably belonged to the liturgical functions of the corporate presbyterate when this body consisted wholly of presbyter-bishops. With the increasing emphasis on the role of their president as 'the bishop' during the second century (for reasons already indicated) it would be natural for the bishop's liturgical position (already established in his presidency at the Eucharist) to gain increasing significance in the liturgies of ordination and penance.

It is also important to notice that the use of the term 'high priest' for the bishop (3.4) is not used with a view to describing an exclusive sacerdotal role, as the introduction to the ordination of deacons makes clear (9.1f). The idea of a Christian priestly 'hierarchy' was already established in the theology of the Roman church by the end of the first century (cf. 1 *Clem.* 40).

The evidence of *Ap. Trad.* does not bear out the view that the real distinction of bishop and presbyterate is one of liturgical function. The second-century evidence suggests that it is the significance which the office of bishop has in relation to the universal Church which effectively distinguishes it from the presbyterate, whose functions still relate primarily to the local Christian community.

The deacon is ordained by the bishop alone since, as the introduction shows, the function of the diaconate is 'not . . . for priesthood, but for the service of the bishop' (9.2). The deacon is not to be 'the fellow-counsellor of the clergy, but to take charge of property and to report to the bishop whatever is necessary' (9.3). It is possible to see in this relationship the ground of the importance possessed by the deacons in the church at Rome. The actual prayer is much less specific: 'whom thou hast chosen to minister to thy Church' (9.11). On the other hand it does emphasize the deacon's liturgical function: 'to bring up in holiness to thy holiness that which is offered to thee by thine ordained high priests' (ibid.).

Of the other orders for which instructions are provided in *Ap. Trad.* confessors appear to be the most important. If previously imprisoned, a confessor may become a deacon or be incorporated into the presbyterate without the imposition of hands (10.1). A candidate for consecration to the episcopate must however receive the imposition of hands in the usual way (9.2). Widows and readers are appointed but not ordained; the distinction being that 'ordination is for the clergy on account of their liturgical ministry' (9.5). Virgins and sub-deacons are named rather than appointed (13f), and the charism of healing is regarded as self-authenticating (15).

The rites and prayers of *Ap. Trad.* also provide evidence of the theological context in which church and ministry were seen in the second and early third centuries.

Biblical themes are used in the ordination prayers not so much as 'proof-texts' but as a way of communicating theological truths. Typical of this approach is the lack of any conscious division between Old and 'New' Testament material: the theme or type and the truth it conveys possess an essential continuity which to some extent transcends history. History is not ignored but its significance is secondary to the established and fore-ordained purposes of God. This is made clear in the way that Church and ministry in the present have a sacramental unity with those of the past, including the past of the old Covenant. The identity is not simply assumed, it is demonstrated in the type of the call of God in history, in the institution of the priesthood in history, and in the succession of those who received the Spirit originally bestowed on Christ and the apostles (cf. 3.2ff).

This view of ministry has implications for the significance of the Church's mission and its position in the world. It is assumed that the cosmos is 'hierocratically' ordered: based on the high priesthood of Christ. The Church has a special position by virtue of its relation to Christ in the power of the Spirit, not least because through its ministry it is included within a hierarchy of worship in the natural and in the supernatural order. This is not a view based ultimately on a desire to magnify the priestly role: it is the natural consequence for the second-century Church of belief in God as the Creator of all.

3 Theology and Rite A.D. 200–400

J. H. CREHAN, SJ

Crehan, J. H., 'Ministerial Priesthood: a survey of work since the Council' in *Theological Studies* 32 (1971) pp. 489–99.
Frere, W. H., in H. B. Swete, ed., *The Early History*.
Maclean, A. J., *The Ancient Church Orders* (CUP 1910), contains a valuable synoptic table and summary of ordination rites.

For information on the early Church Orders, see pp. 59–60.

1 THE THEOLOGICAL IMPORTANCE OF TYPOLOGY

Origen wrote that those Christians who devote themselves to sacred study might be considered high priests according to the order of Aaron, but not according to that of Melchizedek.[1] Awareness of this distinction in typology (which gives some ground for the later distinction in kind between ministerial priesthood and that of the baptized) does not prevent Origen from seeing Christ as fulfilling Aaronic typology[2] where Christ is said to stand between living and dead as Aaron did when he stopped the plague (Num. 16.48). Tertullian could identify high-priest and bishop.[3] So too the union of Christ's eternal priesthood with the ministerial priesthood on earth is expressed by Athanasius when he says that Christ presents to the Father those who come forward to himself in faith.[4]

Continued interest in the typology of Moses and his seventy-two helpers is found in the *Clementine Recognitions*, where Peter is made to say: '[Christ] chose us twelve first . . . , and then seventy-two other select disciples, that by this means the public might accept the typology of Moses and believe that he was the one about whom Moses spoke as the prophet to come.'[5] Variations in the reading of NT codices at Lk. 10.1 are due to the same factor, for scribes, aware that Christ's choice of seventy

[1] *Commentary on John*, preface.
[2] *Hom.* 26.3 on Joshua.
[3] *De Bapt.* 17.
[4] *Orat. 2 c. Arian.* 2.7. The words used are liturgical terms.
[5] *Recog. Clem.* 1.40 (GCS p. 32). Cf. p. 310, n. 7.

disciples (or seventy-two) was a fulfilment of Num. 11.16–29' hesitated whether to include or exclude the two who were counterparts of Eldad and Medad.[1] Melito said that Christ was *strategos* like Moses;[2] to a second century Asiatic like Melito, *strategos* would connote the power to command with authority. This corresponds well enough with what is asked for in the prayer of consecration for a bishop in the *Ap. Trad.*, which speaks of the new bishop receiving *principalis Spiritus* (in the Greek *hegemonikos*).[3] It may well be that the early Christian compiler of the *Ap. Trad.* (or his source) took the typology of Moses as more fitting to illustrate the difference between bishop and presbyter than that between Aaron and his sons, for after all the sons did succeed to their father, while most priests did not become bishops. There might alternatively have been a belief that the Seventy of Lk. 10.1 already were to the apostles in the same relation as presbyters to a bishop.

2 THE ENTHRONING OF A BISHOP

According to the *Canons of Hippolytus*, the enthroning of the bishop was the one act which distinguished his ordination from that of a presbyter.[4] The Council of Ancyra decreed that presbyters who shared in offering the sacrifice should also share in the honour of the *cathedra*.[5] In later usage, the term *synthronon* was brought in to describe the bench for priests on either side of the chair of the bishop, whether at the *bema* or in the apse. Tertullian's dictum that 'the difference between the ordained and the people is established by church authority and by the sacred rite of admission to where the priests sit in church' refers to this practice.[6] This *honor per ordinis consessum sanctificatus* no doubt came after the imposition of hands, but it was important. Eusebius twice says that James the Just was elected by the apostles to the episcopal throne of Jerusalem and he gives Clement of Alexandria as his authority.[7] The setting up of the *sella curulis* for a provincial governor in the forum of an Asiatic town was a solemn act which lends force to the language of the Christians even where it was not possible for them exactly to emulate the civil power.

---

[1] In the result, the MS tradition is almost evenly divided.
[2] Frag. 15 in SC 123, ed. O. Perler, pp. 241–4.
[3] *Ap. Trad.* 3.3. Dix translates unhappily 'princely Spirit'. On *Ap. Trad.* cf. pp. 57–9.
[4] Can. 4, PO 31.354. The *Canons of Hippolytus* are usually taken to date from *c.* 500, but the recent edition in PO settles for 340.
[5] Can. 1. The Council was held in 314.
[6] *De exhortatione castitatis*, 7.
[7] *HE* 2.1; 2.23.

3 THE IMPOSITION OF THE GOSPEL-BOOK

In Hippolytus' *Benedictio Moysis* Christ is seen as the Aaronic high priest, 'having taken upon himself in these last times the revelations and the truth, wearing his long robe and carrying upon his shoulders the two Testaments (the revelations being the old Law, and the truth, the gospel) in order that he may be seen to be priest perfect of the all-perfect Father'. The two shoulder stones of the high priest's robe were thus given typological importance.[1] Josephus tells how the one fixed on the right shoulder used to flash fire, whensoever God came down to be present at the Temple worship; the last time this happened was, he says, two hundred years before his own time.[2] The experience of the apostles at Pentecost was of the fire of the Spirit which sat upon each one of them.

At the close of the fourth century (e.g. in *Ap. Const.* 8.4), a rite is well established by which at the consecration of a bishop the Gospel-book is placed on the nape of his neck and held there by two prelates while hands are being imposed on him. The dialogue of Palladius on John Chrysostom, which was written in 408, tells how the clergy of Ephesus had recently chosen as bishop the eunuch of the tribune Victor, a most unworthy man who had once in a drunken revel garlanded himself with ivy and had carried chorus-girls on his shoulders round the room. On those shoulders where such creatures had been carried men now dared to rest the sacred book of the Gospels (PG 47.53). That the Scripture, inspired by the Spirit, should be used to symbolize the descent of the Spirit is not unexpected. The rite is encountered in the West in the *Statuta Ecclesiae Antiqua*[3] and from there it passed to the Pontificals. How much earlier than the days of Chrysostom the rite existed can only be conjectured, but there are some indications.

4 THE IMPOSITION OF HANDS

Ascension and Pentecost were one feast in antiquity and were not separated until *c.* 375–450. Yet in earlier documents such as the *Doctrina Addai*,[4] it is said of the apostles that 'they had received power and authority at the same time that he was received up'.[5] In the second-century *Acts of Peter*, the Apostles are described as 'those on whom Christ

---

[1] PO 27.144.
[2] *Ant.* 3.215–6.
[3] PL 56.887. This work dates from the end of the fifth century.
[4] *Syriac Documents*, ed. Vööbus (Stockholm 1960). The work is usually dated at about A.D. 400.
[5] Ibid. p. 13.

had imposed his hands'.[1] The Jewish manner of blessing was by such imposition of hands (see p. 296) and this is recorded of the ascending Christ (Lk. 24.50). If the descent of the Spirit was understood as the result of this imposition (and the identity of the feast with that of the Ascension would suggest this), then one might expect the rite to have been elaborated from a simple imposition of hands in the manner outlined above.[2]

5   CHRISTIAN TERMINOLOGY FOR ORDINATION (cf. p. 296)

The word *cheirotonein* was in common pagan usage to 'elect by show of hands', and it is used by Ignatius[3] and by Pope Cornelius[4] for appointing a deacon or bishop. But there is a Christian word, *cheirepithesia* used by the same Pope[5] for the imposition of hands that made a man a bishop. The same word is used (in the Greek version of the Acts) by the contemporary Council of Carthage (in 256) for the imposition of hands which reconciled a penitent. By the time of Nicaea (canon 19), the word has been simplified to *cheirothesia* with the parallel verb, *cheirothetein*. In the fourth century, perhaps because there were so many different impositions of hands, there can be seen a further change. In *Ap. Const.* 8.28, a distinction is made: 'A priest imposes hands (*cheirothetei*) but he does not ordain (*cheirotonei*)'. Already at Nicaea, the ruling on the reconciliation of Paulianist clergy was that they should be rebaptized, and then re-ordained (*cheirotoneisthosan*) by the bishop of the Catholic Church. Here the word would seem to have been used for the episcopal imposition of hands.[6] Chrysostom can distinguish the choosing of the Seven in Acts 6.1 from their *cheirotonia*.[7] By this time, the administrative act of election was felt to be quite separate from the sacramental act of imposition of hands. The Spanish bishops who answered Priscillian say: 'The consecration of a bishop belongs to a bishop, but his election stands

---

[1] Ch. 10; M. R. James, *The Apocryphal New Testament* (Clarendon Press 1924), p. 314.
[2] It is quite probable that the mosaics of the Constantinian churches at Jerusalem showed Christ with angels in glory above a line of expectant apostles, while between the two groups the Spirit was depicted as if sent by Christ, and hovering over the apostles. This is the design that recurs on the silver ampullae of Monza and Bobbio which were brought to the west by pilgrims in the sixth century prior to the destructive Moslem invasion.
[3] *Philad.* 10.1.
[4] In Eusebius, *HE* 6.43.10.
[5] Ibid. 6.43.9.
[6] Canon 19.
[7] *Hom. in Act.* 14.3.

with the canvassing of the people'.[1] The way in which confusion could arise appears from what Gregory Nazianzen relates of his own father who knelt as a catechumen before the bishop for an anointing of the ears when he ought simply to have stood and inclined his head. The bishop was put off by this change in routine and pronounced the formula of ordination instead of the usual blessing of a catechumen;[2] this *typos* of priesthood was clearly regarded as vital in the same way as the act of imposition of hands. Jewish art was allowed to depict the hand of God appearing from the sky. Chrysostom said: 'The man's hand is imposed, but God does all. In fact it is his hand which touches the head of the one being ordained when he is rightly ordained'.[3]

6 THE COLLEGIALITY OF PRIESTS WITH THE BISHOP

The term *bathmos* may not be technical where it is first used in 1 Tim. 3.13 for the *cursus honorum* which those ministering are said to enter upon, but at the Council of Sardica (*c.* 340) it is accepted as a recognized term for the ladder of promotion. The Latin term *ordo* is its equivalent. At Rome there was an *ordo publicanorum* and even an *ordo libertinorum* existed, but while these denoted a status, they did not suppose any great corporate spirit. Cyprian spoke tersely of 'deciding to call together the council of presbyters' in the words 'placuit contrahi presbyterium'.[4] (However this same word in its Greek original at 1 Tim. 4.14 is an abstract noun which signifies presbyterate and not a collective term for the college of presbyters, as D. Daube has shown;[5] the abstract sense was also defended by Calvin.)

Ignatius of Antioch uses *presbyterion* about a dozen times as a collective noun for the body of presbyters[6] and generates confusion for later times by comparing this body to the apostles. Sometimes (as in *Magn.* 6.1) Ignatius says that the bishop is in place of God, while the *presbyterium* represents the apostles, and the same idea may have been at work in the Clementine fantasy[7] that the apostles set up twelve presbyters in each church. The combined evidence of *Smyrn.* 8.2 and *Trall.* 3.1 makes clear

---

[1] PL Suppl. 2.1438. Sicut dedicationem sacerdotis in sacerdote, sic electionem consistere petitionis in plebe.

[2] Greg. Naz., *Or.* 18 (Funeral Oration on his father), 12, with scholion: PG 35.1000, with note 35.

[3] *Hom. in Act.* 14.3.

[4] *Ep.* 49.2.

[5] *NTRJ*, pp. 244–5.

[6] E.g. *Eph.* 2.4 and 20.

[7] *Hom. Clem.* 11.36 (GCS p. 172). On this spurious work, cf. art. 'Clementine Literature' in *ODCC* p. 304.

that Ignatius understood that only bishop or presbyter could hold the Eucharist. He also envisaged the possibility (in *Magn.* 3.1) that a bishop might be much younger than his presbyters. Other Greek Fathers use *hierateion* as the collective term, while Eusebius always prefers *presbeion*. From all this it would seem that the collegiate character of a body of presbyters in a particular church was understood principally as being on a minor scale what the apostolic college had been, while that college was represented on a major scale by the body of bishops in the world.

The developed theology of the priesthood can be studied in the second Oration of Gregory Nazianzen,[1] where he speaks of the priest 'sending up sacrifices to the altar on high and being priest along with Christ'. In Latin, Cyprian takes over from Tertullian the use of *sacerdos* alongside *episcopus* for 'bishop', and once at least he says that *presbyteri* share in the dignity of the *sacerdos*[2] (and see p. 300 on the language of priesthood). The heresy of Aerius (*c.* 300–70) as chronicled by Epiphanius (in the *Panarion* s.v.) consisted in saying that bishop and presbyter were the same in rank and honour. Jerome, while not agreeing with the heresy, borrowed some of its ideas to keep deacons in their place: 'When the apostle openly teaches that presbyter and bishop are the same, what is a server of tables and helper of widows doing by haughtily setting himself up over those at whose prayer the Body and Blood of Christ is made present? What does a bishop do that a priest does not?'.[3] In this climate of opinion, the sensitive caution of the versions of the *Ap. Trad.* can be better understood. The bishop alone imposes hands upon a deacon, since the deacon is not ordained for priesthood but for the service of the bishop. Presbyters join with the bishop however in imposing hands on a presbyter. Yet the presbyter does not confer the order; he merely 'seals' or confirms (*consignat*) what the bishop does.[4] Comparison with the OT would suggest that the practice (as in Num. 8.10) whereby the whole people lay hands upon the Levites (to signify that all share in the sacrifice the Levites make of themselves) was not without its influence on Christian liturgy here.

7 THE DEVELOPMENT OF THE THEOLOGY OF PRIESTHOOD

In 2 Cor. 5, 18–20, the apostles are said to carry out an embassy on behalf of Christ, beseeching men to be reconciled to God. When Chrysostom commented on these verses, he said outright that 'on behalf of Christ'

[1] PG 35.481.
[2] *Ep.* 61.3.
[3] *Ep.* 146.
[4] *Ap. Trad.* 8.1–8; see above, pp. 303–5.

meant 'in place of Christ, since we have taken upon ourselves what belonged to him'.[1] The work of reconciliation Chrysostom described as *hiketeria*, a supplication. The liturgy of Sarapion expressed this idea admirably, for it had a pause between the words of institution for the bread and those for the cup; during this pause, the priest had to say: 'We beseech thee through his sacrifice be reconciled to all of us and be merciful, O God of truth'.[2] This *katallage* or reconciliation was understood by Theodoret (writing on the same passage of 2 Cor.) as mediating between God and men. 'God made Christ the mediator of peace. He also entrusted to us the good tidings of these reconciliations. He ordained us ministers of this peace.'[3] The plural implies a two-way reconciliation, of God to men and of men to God. Bishops are called mediators of God and the faithful by the *Ap. Const.*[4] Sarapion's ordination prayer for presbyters asked that the presbyter 'may be an ambassador of (*presbeuein*) thy divine oracles and to reconcile thy people to thee ...', thus linking up with the prayer for reconciliation at the Eucharist.[5]

A further development prior to Augustine can be seen in Ambrosiaster's comment on 1 Tim. 4.14: 'The words at the imposition of hands are sacramental (*mystica*) and by them the elected one is sealed (*confirmatur*) for his task and receives authority that emboldens him to offer sacrifice to God in the place of Christ.'[6] On Eph. 4.11, Ambrosiaster is of the opinion that presbyters had initially been called bishops, but that 'as later presbyters were found unworthy to hold the first place, the arrangement was prudently changed, so that desert and not seniority (*ordo*) should make a man a bishop when he had been put in office by the judgement of several bishops, to prevent quick usurpations by the unworthy'.[7] The letter of Pope Julius, cited by Athanasius,[8] appealed to 'canons coming from the apostles' for the rule that a bishop had to be appointed by the bishops of the province from the body of the presbyters. This clearly supposes some ruling prior to the fourth Canon of Nicaea; Julius became Pope in 337, and there were men like Hosius who had been present at Nicaea able to correct him had he been mistaken in what was then a matter of controversy (as seen in the fourth Canon of Sardica).

---

[1] *Hom. in 2 Cor.*, 11.3.
[2] Text in *JTS* 1 (1900), pp. 105–6; see p. 200.
[3] PG 82.412.
[4] 2.25.
[5] N. 13; loc. cit., p. 266.
[6] CSEL 81.277.
[7] CSEL 81.100.
[8] *Apol. c. Arianos*, 1.30.

4 The Early History of the Roman Rites of Ordination

FRANK HAWKINS

Andrieu, M., *Les Ordines Romani du haut moyen âge*, vols. 3 & 4 (Louvain 1951, 1956), esp. introductions.

Beraudy, R., 'Les effets de l'ordre d'après les prefaces d'ordination du sacramentaire léonien', in *La tradition sacerdotale*, ed. Mappus (Paris 1959), pp. 81–107.

Bligh, J., *Ordination to the Priesthood*. Sheed and Ward 1956.

Botte, B., 'Le sacre épiscopal dans le rite romain', in *Questions Liturgiques et Paroissales* 25 (1940), pp. 22–32.

Martimort, A. G., ed., *EP*, pp. 489–503.

Porter, H. B., *The Ordination Prayers of the Ancient Western Churches*. AC SPCK 1967.

The text of the early Roman liturgy of ordination exists in three major recensions: the Leonine, the Gelasian, and the Gregorian (see pp. 224–227). The basic text is that of the Leonine Sacramentary, which contains rites for the ordination of bishops, deacons, and presbyters (in this order, reflecting the prestige of the diaconate at Rome). There are no prayers or directions for the minor orders in the book as it exists, other than a prayer for religious virgins.

In the Gelasian Sacramentary (and the *Missale Francorum* and the sacramentary of Angoulême) of the eighth century, the same basic prayers are found for the three sacred orders, together with prayers for the appointment of various minor orders. In these books the material of the Roman tradition is included with Gallican material originally independent of it.

The Gregorian Sacramentary (in a late eighth-century recension: the 'Hadrianic') and some of the *Ordines Romani* also contain texts of the prayers. The Gregorian agrees with the Leonine against the minor variations of the Gelasian, but has itself been subject to some revision and minor modification (e.g. prayers for a single candidate in each order).

In the opinion of H. B. Porter it is possible to gain reliable knowledge of the text of the Roman liturgy as it existed in the sixth and perhaps late fifth centuries. The extant ordination prayers all have the same pattern: a long 'consecration' prayer preceded by two shorter prayers. The second of these is a collect, while the first is either a bidding prayer (for presbyters and deacons), or else a first collect (for bishops).

The content of the longer 'consecration' prayers consists of carefully

313

developed reflections on selected biblical themes and 'types'. In relation to the *Ap. Trad.* of Hippolytus there is much common ground, though the prayers differ structurally quite considerably. There is development of the conception of the Christian priesthood with particular reference to OT types and models. There is also (except in the case of the deacon) much less explicit reference to the NT. The 'consecration' prayer for the bishop begins with God's relationship with Moses and the significance of the priestly vestments in relation to the Aaronic priesthood: 'The dignity of robes no longer commends to us the pontifical glory, but rather the splendour of spirits.... Whatsoever it was that those veils signified in radiance of gold, in sparkling of jewels, in variety of diverse workmanship, this may show forth in the conversation and deeds of these men' (Porter, p. 21). The contrast is between the 'vestments of the flesh' of the Aaronic order and the 'vestments of the Spirit' discerned in the words and deeds of the ministry of the Christian priesthood.

Similarly the 'consecration' prayer for presbyters makes it clear that the basic significance of the order is to be found in the OT dispensation. The concepts of a priestly hierarchy and succession are part of a natural order: as well as high priests there were orders of priests and Levites 'of a lesser order and secondary dignity to be their companions and help them in their labour' (ibid., p. 27). The spirit of Moses was 'spread out' through the seventy elders, while Eleazar and Ithamar, the sons of Aaron, participated also in the sacrificial worship of their father. The prayer mentions finally 'teachers of the faith' providentially given to support 'the apostles of thy Son as companions', and 'they filled the whole world with these secondary preachers' (ibid.).

In contrast the 'consecration' prayer for the deacon begins from the recognition that God orders all things through 'thy Word, Power and Wisdom, Jesus Christ thy Son our Lord' (ibid., p. 33). The prayer goes on to include the diversity of gifts within the Church as the Body of Christ, and concludes with particular mention of Christian discipline and conduct. Only in the references to 'the three grades of ministers' and 'the sons of Levi' is the typological approach of the other 'consecration' prayers evident.

It is clear, then, that the text has become less important from the point of view of what is actually said. The action of ordination and its basic significance speak largely for themselves in the context of the solemn public services of the Roman church. The text is simply part of the whole action: despite the formality of its contents and the somewhat involved typology, it is not conceived as a 'sacred text' which determines the Christian understanding of what is happening at an ordination at this time.

THE ORDINATION OF BISHOPS

The bishops consecrated by the pope were usually from his own province. They were elected in their particular locality, the election was subsequently confirmed at Rome (the election procedure was scrutinized and the pope's approval of the candidate given), and the consecration followed. This happened invariably on a Sunday, but not necessarily at any given time of year. In the Mass, after the Litany and Kyrie (which came after the Epistle as the formalized 'prayer of the people'), the pope recited the ordination prayers over the candidate and then embraced him. The newly consecrated bishop then joined the other bishops for the rest of the Mass.

The ordination of the pope was slightly different. The candidate (usually a deacon of the Roman church; and never a bishop before the ninth century) put on the papal liturgical vestments except for the *pallium*. At the Introit chant he prostrated himself before the altar. After the Litany the Bishops of Albano, Porto, and Ostia recited the three ordination prayers in turn. During the 'consecration' prayer the deacons held an open Gospel-book over the candidate's head. The book seems to have been a symbolic substitute for Christ himself; the action suggests a direct form of 'consecration' considered more appropriate to a pope than the laying-on of hands proper to bishops. The archdeacon then placed the *pallium* on the newly consecrated bishop, who proceeded to his throne and began *Gloria in excelsis*.

THE ORDINATIONS OF PRIESTS
AND DEACONS

An ordination was not necessarily held every year. When it occurred it was a solemn public occasion, held on one of the Saturdays in the Ember weeks. The candidates were presented to the people during the stational Masses on the Wednesday and the Friday. The names of those elected were announced shortly after the beginning of the Mass, and possible objections sought. Each candidate would have attested previously his fitness for ordination in respect of freedom from certain specified and grave sins.

Shortly before the reading of the Gospel, the archdeacon took the candidates and presented them to the pope, who then called on the congregation to pray. All then prostrated themselves during the singing of the Litany. The pope then laid hands on each candidate, and recited the ordination prayers for the deacons. These actions, which occur simultaneously in *Ap. Trad.*, have now become separated, presumably because of the numbers of candidates involved. Afterwards the new deacons received the Kiss of Peace and joined the deacons already present.

The candidates for the presbyterate were then presented. They prostrated themselves before the pope who then recited the ordination prayers over them. The new presbyters then went to join the presbyteral body already present.

THE APPOINTMENT OF MINOR ORDERS

There was no solemn ordination for minor orders. Acolytes and sub-deacons were simply admitted to their orders at the Communion by delivery of the appropriate instruments and with a blessing from the pope. Acolytes held a linen bag (for carrying the consecrated hosts to the priests at the Fraction), and the sub-deacons an empty chalice.

In the early Roman rites, therefore, the three classical elements of ordination as seen in the early Church still provide the basic structure. These elements however have undergone a process of formalization. The part that the people play in the election of candidates tends to move in the direction of simply having opportunity to object: a considerably less positive role than that envisaged in the third century and earlier. The prayer of the people too is expressed in the formal singing of the Litany rather than in the context of a period of silence as in *Ap. Trad*. Finally, the ordination prayers themselves have lost a good deal of the simplicity and directness of those provided by Hippolytus earlier.

5 Eastern Rites of Ordination

R. J. HALLIBURTON

TEXTS

The most orderly collection of ordination rites of the Eastern Churches is to be found in H. Denzinger, *Ritus Orientalium* (Wurzburg 1964), vol. 2, pp. 1–363. See also E. Martène, *De antiquis Ecclesiae ritibus*, lib. 1, c. 8, art. 11, Ordo 19, the Byzantine rite; Ordo 20, the Maronite rite; Ordo 21, the East Syrian rite; Ordo 22, the West Syrian rite and Coptic rite (Antwerp 1763, vol. 2, pp. 95–120, and Venice 1788, vol. 2, pp. 95–120); J. Goar (ed.), *Euchologion seu Rituale Graecorum* (Paris 1647; Venice 1730; phot. reprint, Graz 1960) on the Byzantine rite, with notes and variant readings; so too P. Trembelas, *Mikron Euchologion*, vol. 1 (Athens 1950), with information on the MSS.

Eastern liturgies, on the whole, tend to survive the centuries without great modification. On the transmission of texts see Brightman, *LEW* vol. 1; F. C. Conybeare, *Rituale Armenorum* (Clarendon Press 1905), esp. pp. 228–34. For modern rites of ordination in the Byzantine tradition see E. Mercenier and F. Paris, *La prière des églises de rite byzantin*, vol. 1, pp. 367–96 (2nd edn Chevetogne 1948).

See also A. Kokkinakis, *Parents and Priests as Servants of Redemption* (New York 1958), pp. 159–78; I. F. Hapgood, *Service Book* (New York 1922), pp. 307–32 for an account of services in the Russian tradition.

ORIGINS

For an understanding of the genesis of the Eastern rites of ordination, we have to turn on the one hand to the liturgy described in the text known as *Apostolic Constitutions* (representing the fourth-century Antiochene tradition) and on the other hand (though less significantly for our purpose) to the *Euchologion* of Sarapion, bishop of Thmuis in the fourth century (see pp. 60–61). In *Ap. Const.*, the rites for the ordination of a bishop or presbyter reproduce almost exactly those contained in Hippolytus' *Ap. Trad.* There are one or two notable modifications: e.g. in the ordination of a presbyter, other presbyters no longer lay on hands, and in the ordination of a deacon, not only is the example of St Stephen invoked, but also it is explicitly stated that the deacon will be eventually promoted to a higher rank. The text also provides for the ordination with laying on of hands of sub-deacons and lectors with appropriate prayers. In Sarapion, three prayers are provided for the ordination (here described as *cheirothesia* and *katastasis*) of bishop, presbyter, and deacon respectively. The prayers have the same simplicity as those of the *Ap. Trad.*, and there are certain related ideas: e.g. the typology for the ordination of presbyters is exactly that of Hippolytus' prayer. On the other hand it is important to note that the prayer for the ordination of presbyters is almost exactly reproduced in the ordination rite of the Abyssinian Jacobites and would suggest that Sarapion's *Euchologion* has a certain parental relationship to the developing rites of Eastern christendom.

DEVELOPMENT

It is virtually impossible to trace the development of these rites from their origins to the sixteenth century. The printed texts of the sixteenth and seventeenth centuries are on the whole based on MSS of comparatively recent provenance and it is principally the scholarly interest of western ecclesiastics that have made known to the western world rites which lived at the heart of the Eastern churches and survived virtually unknown to outsiders in the libraries of those whose care it was to administer them. Editors of the texts of the eucharistic liturgies (notably Brightman and Conybeare, op. cit.) provide most of the available evidence of the MS tradition behind the printed texts; and printed collections of the ordination rites (in e.g. Denzinger, op. cit.) enable the scholar to recognize the extent to which contemporary rites are closely related to their origins (notably to *Ap. Const.*) and to note the points at which they vary.

ORDERS AND ORDINATION

The Eastern churches of the Byzantine rite recognize five orders of ordained ministers: the three major orders of bishop, presbyter, and deacon, and two further orders of sub-deacon and lector (alternatively known as 'cantor' or 'psalmist'). There are also the orders of 'candlebearer' and 'deaconess'. The *Euchologia* provide also ceremonies for the appointment of officers of monastic communities (e.g. superiors, archimandrites, ecclesiarchs, cellarers, etc.), and for the appointment of archdeacons and archpriests. As in the Western church, ordination to the three major orders takes place during the Liturgy, deacons being ordained after the eucharistic prayers, priests at the Great Entrance and bishops at the Little Entrance (see pp. 211, 215). All are ordained by the laying on of hands with prayer. There is also a formulary common to the rite for all the orders as follows:

The divine grace which always brings healing to what is weak and supplies what is lacking, ordains the devout (subdeacon, deacon, priest) to be (deacon, priest, bishop) of.... Let us pray therefore that the grace of the Holy Spirit may come upon him.

At the ordination of a bishop, the candidate (at the Little Entrance) is led before the consecrating bishop (seated before the screen) and presented to the people. The consecrating bishop then asks him why he has come. He replies, 'For the laying on of hands for the grace of the episcopal office, because the clergy have elected me'. He is then brought closer to the consecrating bishop, who asks him to profess his faith 'on the properties of the Three Persons and on the incomprehensible divinity'. The bishop-elect then first reads the Nicene Creed. There follows the second long profession of faith in which the candidate affirms his orthodoxy on the doctrines of the Trinity and incarnation and his repudiation of all heresies. He then moves closer to the consecrating bishop and is asked once more to confess his faith on the subject of 'the Son, the Word of God and the two natures of Christ', which he proceeds to do, with the same assurances that he abjures all heretical notions. He also affirms his faith in the doctrine of Mary as Theotokos. He then receives the *epigonation* (on vestments, see pp. 480–5) and the pastoral staff 'to guide, protect and to chasten', and after the *trisagion* he is taken into the sanctuary and kneels down before the altar with arms crossed and head bowed on the holy table. The open book of the Gospels is placed on the nape of his neck and held in place by the co-consecrating bishops. Then the principal consecrating bishop recites three prayers, first 'Divine grace ...' (quoted above), and then two further prayers, one recalling St Paul's account of God's provision of the ministries of apostle, prophet, and teacher and praying that the duly elected candidate, now 'under the yoke of the gospel', may receive the grace of the Holy Spirit for the work of a bishop, and the second characterizing the dignity and work of a bishop (as occupying the throne of God himself in the Church, offering sacrifices for the people and following the example of the Good Shepherd, who gave his life for the sheep, and as being for his people a 'guide for the blind, and light to those in darkness, a teacher of the ignorant, an instructor of the children and a shining light in the world'), with prayer for grace to fulfil this office. He is then clothed with the *sakkos* and *omophorion* while the clergy and people acclaim him as 'Axios' (i.e. worthy, a reminder of the important part once played by the congregation in the election and approval of a new bishop). He and his consecrators then exchange the Kiss of Peace, and after an acclamation he is enthroned. He gives the blessing for the reading of the Epistle and is the first to receive communion, distributing communion to his consecrators and then to others present.

The ordination of presbyters and deacons follows the pattern of episcopal ordinations after the profession of faith. In both cases, the candidate is led to the altar and kneels, arms crossed and head bowed on the table as the candidate for the episcopate. The book of the Gospels is of course not laid on the candidate's neck. There follows the laying-on of hands, (in the case of priests, the bishop first covers the candidate with his *omophorion*), the prayer 'Divine grace ...', then the special prayers for each order. The candidate is then vested in the vestments of his new office (the priest's stole is put on, he is then girded with the priestly girdle and vested in the *phelonion*) to the acclamation 'Axios'. Priests after their ordination exchange the Kiss of Peace with the other priests and concelebrate with the bishop, communicating directly after him from the part of the host marked 'IS'.

6 Medieval Ordinations

J. H. CREHAN, SJ

Baisi, C., *Il ministro straordinario degli ordini sacramentali*. Rome 1935. A simpler treatment in *CDT*, vol. I, s.v. 'Abbot, Ordination by'.

Bieler, L., *The Irish Penitentials*. Dublin Institute for Advanced Studies 1963.

Crehan, J. H., 'The Typology of Episcopal Consecration', in *Theological Studies*, 21 (1960), pp. 250–5 (on the imposition of the book).

Crehan, J. H., 'The Seven Orders of Christ', *Theological Studies*, 19 (1958), pp. 81–93.

Ellard, G., *Ordination Anointings in the Western Church before 1000 A.D.* Cambridge, Mass. 1933.

Jedin, H., (ET) *Crisis and Closure of the Council of Trent*. Sheed and Ward 1967 (important for Trent's discussion of orders).

McNeill, J. T. and Gamer, H. M., *Medieval Handbooks of Penance*. New York 1938.

Vogel, C. and Elze, R., *Le pontifical romano-germanique*, ST 226–7, 269.

Wasserschleben, H., ed., *Die irische Kanonensammlung*. 2nd edn Leipzig 1885.

North of the Alps before 950 the rite of ordination developed in a way unknown to the conservatism observed at Rome and witnessed by the prayers in the Leonine Sacramentary and the regulations of *OR* XXXIV (in Andrieu's edition) which belongs to the middle of the eighth century.

About 950 the exuberant Spanish and Irish tradition, exemplified in the *Missale Francorum* (from Poitiers *c.* 760), the Egbert Pontifical (really from Evreux, *c.* 1000), that of Lanalet (tenth century, probably from Wells), and the Benedictional of Archbishop Robert (a Winchester book of 980), made its way to Rome in the wake of the Holy Roman emperors; it was embodied in the Romano-German Pontifical and in *OR* XXXV and XXXV B. A Germanic council of 800,[1] decreed that Roman use was optional for the liturgy of Holy Week, and this idea had been followed generally outside Italy.

The fusion of the two traditions into one composite rite and its subsequent elaboration in the course of the Middle Ages is illustrated in the adjoining table. The allocution came from the non-Roman tradition and was the equivalent of the presentation of the candidates to the people on the Wednesday and Friday before their ordination in that tradition. Since the Ember seasons were unknown outside the Roman tradition, the candidates had been presented to the people at the beginning of the ordination-rite itself and this address read, requesting their approval of those about to be ordained, to which the people originally responded with the acclamation, 'He is worthy'. The allocution was added to the simple Roman rite by the *Missale Francorum* (*MF*), and taken up in the Romano-German Pontifical (*RG*). There then followed the bidding, collect, and ordination-prayer from the Roman rite, and after that were inserted the bidding and ordination-prayer from the non-Roman tradition, termed the *consummatio* and *benedictio* respectively, so that candidates might effectively live up to their office. There is a slight variation from this pattern in the case of the episcopate, where the non-Roman bidding seems to have dropped out entirely, the ordination-prayers from the two traditions have been fused into a single consecration-prayer, and a further *benedictio* of unknown origin has been added to the rite. In all three rites the imposition of hands has become detached from the ordination-prayers and now takes place towards the beginning of the rite, at first in silence but increasingly accompanied by some imperative formula. The reason for this change of position seems to have been the growth in the numbers of candidates for ordination at any one time, which made it impractical to repeat the prayers for each one, and so hands were laid on each candidate individually, and then the prayers were said collectively while hands were extended over them all (see plate 17). In the course of the Middle Ages the rites were gradually enriched with many additional prayers and ceremonies, which varied considerably from place to place. Chief among these additions were anointings and the *traditio*

[1] MGH *Concilia aevi Karolini*, 1.212. On the early sacramentaries and missals, see pp. 65–8.

THE FUSION OF THE TWO TRADITIONS

	ALLOCUTION	PRAYER (after imposition of hands)	CONSECRATION
DEACON		Leonine 948–50 Old Gelasian 150–51	Leonine 951 Old Gelasian 152–4
	MF 21	*MF* 22	*MF* 23
		Robert 120 Claudius I.35 Egbert Lanalet stole blessed and given	Robert 120–1 Claudius I.36 Egbert Lanalet
	RG XVI.10	*RG* XVI.11 stole blessed *RG* XVI.13	*RG* XVI.14
PRIEST		Leonine 952–3 Old Gelasian 143–4	Leonine 954 Old Gelasian 145–6
	MF 27	*MF* 28–9 Robert 122	*MF* 30 Robert 123
		Egbert (stole given) Lanalet (stole given) Claudius I.38	Egbert Lanalet Claudius I.39
	RG XVI.22–4	*RG* XVI.28	*RG* XVI.29

	ALLOCUTION	PRAYER	CONSECRATION
BISHOP		Leonine 942 Old Gelasian 766–8	Leonine 947 Old Gelasian 769–70
	MF 35	*MF* 36–8 Robert 125	*MF* 39–40 * Robert 125–6 (with anointing of head)
		Egbert	Egbert
		Lanalet	Lanalet
	RG LXIII.1–12 and 28 *RG* LXIII.23–26 (sandals, dalmatic)	*RG* LXIII.34	*RG* LXIII.35 (with anointing of head)

CONSUMMATIO	TRADITIO	ANOINTING HANDS	BLESSING
Old Gelasian 155			**Old Gelasian 156**
MF 25			*MF* 26
	stolae evangelii		
Robert 122	Robert 121–2	Robert 122	
Claudius I.36	stolae Claudius I.37	Claudius I.37	Claudius I.36
Egbert			Egbert
Lanalet		Lanalet (after blessing)	Lanalet
	stolae *RG* XVI.15		*RG* XVI.18
Old Gelasian 147			**Old Gelasian 148**
MF 31		*MF* 33	*MF* 32
Robert 124–5	casulae Robert 124	Robert 123–4 (head also)	
Egbert	Egbert	Egbert (head also)	
Lanalet (at end)	Lanalet	Lanalet (head also)	Lanalet
Claudius I (at end)	Claudius I.40	Claudius I.39 (head also)	Claudius I.41
	RG XVI.36	*RG* XVI.35	*RG* XVI.37

ANOINTING	RING AND STAFF	ENTHRONING	BLESSING
	Old Gelasian 771		
		MF 40 f	
Robert 128	Robert 128–9 (staff first)	Robert 129	Robert 130
Egbert (hands and head)	Egbert (staff first)	Egbert	
Lanalet (head and hands)	Lanalet (staff first)	Lanalet	Lanalet
RG LXIII.36 (not always)	*RG* LXIII.38–9 (not always)	*RG* LXIII.41	*RG* LXIII.56–7
RG LXIII.37 (thumb)	*RG* LXIII.40 (staff)		

instrumentorum, the symbolic ceremony of handing over to the candidate some instrument representative of his function, a custom already practised in the case of the minor orders and drawn from the conferring of office in civil life.

It would seem that the bishop was always enthroned; even the Leonine consecration speaks of it. Where possible, references have been added to the section or page of the standard editions of the Pontificals cited in the table. The episcopal staff (where given) is called *cambuta*, a word of Celtic Latin origin. The Claudius Pontifical has no rite for bishops, but is probably the earliest of the English documents cited in this table.

The *cursus honorum* through the minor orders was gradually stabilized. Deacons had been the assistants of bishops, but now the diaconate became the next step below the priesthood. Pope Cornelius in 251 had deacons, sub-deacons and acolytes, exorcists, lectors and doorkeepers.[1] These eight ranks were reduced to seven for mystical reasons, for the idea spread that Christ in his life on earth had fulfilled seven offices: 'He was doorkeeper when he opened the door of the ark and closed it again. He was grave-digger (*fossor*) when he called forth Lazarus from the tomb, he was lector when he opened the book of Isaiah in the midst of the synagogue..., he was sub-deacon when he poured water in a basin and washed the disciples' feet. He was deacon when he blessed the chalice and gave it to the apostles to drink. He was priest when he blessed the bread and gave it likewise to them. He was bishop when he taught the people in the temple...'.[2] Here *fossor* has displaced the exorcist and there are no acolytes. Many other varieties of the list are found, the one quoted being probably from Lorsch, *c.* 750. The general idea that every order was a participation in the work of Christ was universally held, though the pictorial application might vary from place to place.

Anointing at ordination is first mentioned by Gildas, the poet of the last days of Roman Britain. He speaks of 'a blessing by which the hands of priests and deacons are hallowed'.[3] Ellard in his monograph on anointing took this as metaphorical, since the first liturgical evidence for anointing of hands is found in the *Missale Francorum* and the old Gelasian (756, where it is inserted for sub-deacons as an afterthought). Klauser and others have insisted that Gildas was speaking quite literally, and the fact that many Coptic ostraka bearing Christian epistles end with the words: 'God bless your holy hands' suggests that Egypt was the place of origin of the custom and that it spread along the established liturgical trade-route via Spain to Ireland, Cornwall, and South Wales.

---

[1] According to the letter in Eusebius, *HE* 6.43.
[2] *Chronicon Palatinum*, PL 94.1162.
[3] MGH, *Auctores antiquissimi*, 13.82.

A letter of Pope Nicholas I (858–67) to Rudolf of Bourges[1] in reply to his question whether deacons as well as priests should have their hands anointed at ordination says sternly that neither should. The archbishop is referred to a letter of Innocent I to Decentius of Gubbio,[2] which required that there should be no diversity in the manner of conferring orders. Pontificals in use at Cambrai, Senlis, Basle, Constance, and Rheinau at the time Nicholas wrote show that in these churches the hands of a priest were anointed, while at Mainz, Arles, and Bourges they were not. The anointing of kings had come into use in Visigothic Spain and at Iona by 700, and the anointing of the head of a bishop and the hands of a priest cannot have been long delayed thereafter in the western world. The prayer in the old Gelasian for the blessing of chrism (387) says: 'Thou didst give command to thy servant Moses that he should establish Aaron his brother as priest by the pouring of this oil, after he had been washed in water'. The words: 'oil with which thou didst anoint priests, prophets, kings, and martyrs' are found in many prayers.[3] The hearing of such words must have inevitably led to a desire to see anointing as part of the service of ordination, if indeed it was not that service which produced them. The abbot Regino of Prüm (in 906) in a canonical compilation directed that the oil whereby we are incorporated into Christ and with which kings and priests are anointed should be kept under lock and key; this he adduced from an undated Council of Tours.[4]

The *traditio instrumentorum* came into ordinations as a piece of feudalism. It is true that the Ethiopic of the *Ap. Trad.* says: 'To the lector who is ordained, the bishop shall deliver the Scripture and shall not lay hands on him'. This is copied in the Greek *Epitome* of the same work, while the *Statuta Ecclesiae Antiqua* (PL 56.888) have the book given to both lector and exorcist, the candle given to the acolyte, and keys to the door-keeper. The sub-deacon there receives an empty chalice and paten from the bishop and a water-jug and towel from the archdeacon. St

---

[1] PL 119.884.

[2] PL 20.552.

[3] The Euchologion of the White Monastery in Egypt (PO 28.393), the Latin and Ethiopic versions of the *Ap. Trad.* and the Gelasian Sacramentary.

[4] The prayer, *Consecrentur manus istae*, found in the *Missale Francorum*, in the old Gelasian (756), in the Egbert Pontifical and the Benedictional of Archbishop Robert, has the memorable phrase: *Ut quaecumque benedixerint benedicta sint, et quaecumque sanctificaverint sanctificentur.* The Coptic Euchologion of the White Monastery has a similar phrase in the prayer cited above for the blessing of oil; it says, in an equivalent Latin form: *Ut benedictione illud (oleum) benedicas et sanctificatione sanctifices.* These echoes from Egypt in Western liturgy (and they are not the only ones) suggest that the rite of anointing came to Gaul and Ireland from the East. Ellard claims that it reached Rome from Ravenna by 925.

Thomas could say, as if it was obvious: 'The conferring of a power is effected by giving to its subjects something which belongs to the proper exercise of that power.'[1] The Investiture struggle where bishops or priests were granted fiefs by kings and lords with a feudal rite must have speeded the acceptance of such ritual for the major orders as well as the minor. That regalists should claim coronation as a sacrament (a claim admitted by St Peter Damian) is not surprising when the king was invested with his crown in much the same way as the bishop with his ring and crozier. These are prescribed for the bishop by the Council of Toledo in 633 in Visigothic Spain, while the *Statuta* cannot be much later than 500, though their place of origin is unknown.

The *epistula ad Senarium* of John the Deacon[2] says: 'Acolytes receive the vessels in which the sacred elements are carried and have the task of ministering to the priests . . . . If they faithfully perform this task, they can go on to the rank of sub-deacon. For sub-deacons our practice is this, that when once a man has been given the sacred chalice in which the bishop is accustomed to offer the sacrifice of the Blood of the Lord, he is thereafter called a sub-deacon.' Senarius was a courtier of Theodoric the Great, and thus one is already in a Gothic climate. The 'vessels' which the acolytes carried were the *turres* in which the sacrament was reserved. The giving of the Gospel-book to the deacon is prescribed in the Spanish *Liber Ordinum* along with a prayer entitled *confirmatio*. This act is repeated in the Benedictional of Archbishop Robert, while in *Lanalet* it has been moved to the beginning of the deacon's ordination.

A developed theology of orders may be seen in an anonymous tract which was transmitted through the Dark Ages with the work of Jerome entitled *de septem ordinibus ecclesiae*.[3] Much of its argumentation is based on liturgical practice. Since a bishop receives communion at times from the hand of a priest (e.g. when he is ill), this argues a fundamental equality between them. Because a priest has power to consecrate the Body of Christ, he can also consecrate the chrism, which is a lesser act. Since also the Eucharist is greater than Mary the Mother of God, a simple priest can bless virgins, for Mary is the sister of virgins. The Council of Carthage in 390 had reserved the consecration of virgins to the bishop, but the so-called *Penitential* of Theodore of Tarsus declared that this was a Western custom not observed in the East. In the same vein the anonymous treatise said: 'Priests are themselves forbidden to take the

---

[1] *In IV Sent.* 24.2.3.

[2] Early sixth century, published by Wilmart in *Analecta Reginensia*, ST 59.176; also PL 59.399–408.

[3] It received a critical edition from Kalff in 1937 but it cannot be assigned to any definite place or time.

chalice from the altar of the Lord unless it be first handed to them by the deacon. This is on account of pride, so that though they have previously engaged in a holy ministry they may see themselves humbled after the consecration as they pay reverence to God's deacon'.

The *de VII Ordinibus* was followed blindly by Isidore of Seville,[1] and by the *Irish Collection of Canons*.[2] Priests as *consortes cum episcopis* (as para. 45 declares them to be) could on occasion presume to ordain another priest, as if they were substantive ministers of the rite and not accessories. Even the absence of a bishop did not deter some abbots from ordaining monks to the priesthood. Theologians and canonists in the Middle Ages discussed *pro* and *con*. Among those who were in favour of priests having such a power by delegation (as for the sacrament of confirmation) were Innocent III, Durandus, and Gerson. A Bull of Boniface IX in 1400 allowed the Abbot of St Osyth in Essex to ordain his monks to diaconate and priesthood. It is true that this was withdrawn in 1403 after protests from the Bishop of London. This was the period of the western schism and may be no more than a token of the canonical disturbances of the time, but Martin V in 1427 issued a similar grant to the Abbot of Altzelle in the diocese of Meissen.

Confusion generated by Levellers in the Church led to a desire to define more closely the true nature of priesthood and episcopacy. For St Thomas[3] investiture with the chalice was the act which conferred the priestly character, while the bishop, 'though he is given spiritual powers with regard to some sacraments at his consecration, does not receive a sacramental character'.[4] St Thomas thought that power over the body of Christ in the Eucharist was the principal thing about the sacrament and that power over the Church or Mystical Body of Christ (which was given to the bishop) was secondary. As he was tied to the number of seven sacraments, he could not allow for two sacraments of orders. Whereas his predecessors had regarded all the sacraments as so many means of healing the wounds of sin, he began a new line of thought by describing baptism, confirmation, and orders as three different ways of sharing in the priesthood of Christ. This was a development of the idea of sacramental character. Aquinas was translated into Armenian (*c.* 1340), and the Armenian decree of the Council of Florence (1439) adopted his views, applying them not to the whole Church but to Armenia.

The sacramental character was a theological construct arising out of the way in which the re-baptism controversy had been settled. If heretic

---

[1] *De officiis* 2.8; PL 83.789.
[2] (Wasserschleben) 3.5.
[3] *In IV Sent.* 25.1.2.
[4] Ibid. 24.3.3.

baptism is accepted by the Church, it must be that until the time when the Church does accept it for an individual who repents, that particular sacramental act was valid but unfruitful. More than the sacramental sign has been given to the individual, but not yet the grace of the sacrament. In other words, there is a middle term between sign and grace, and for sacraments which establish status this middle term is the character. Augustine had brought in the old distinction of Plato (in his aviary passage of the *Theaetetus*, 197c.) between having and using; to Cyprian's main argument that a heretic who has not the Holy Spirit cannot confer the Spirit, Augustine answered that it is one thing to have, and another to have and use. He worked this distinction in the question of Donatist baptism but he also applied it to orders.[1] Repentant Donatist clergy were to be accepted *in suis honoribus* without reordination, subject to the approval of the local bishop.

Severus of Antioch in 518 recalled what had happened there in Arian days: 'The ordination of Evagrius having been repudiated as unsound, Theophilus, bishop of Alexandria, writes to Flavian (the rival of Evagrius) to accept the clergy who had been ordained by Evagrius, saying thus: "Therefore in your days allow those who assemble apart by themselves to be united to the clergy under your religious self and to the whole people. If we are in communion with the devout Anastasius, bishop of the church of the Romans, and he gives the communion of clergymen to those who assembly by themselves and communicates with them all, you understand to what the conclusion points. Therefore, seeing that the reverend Anastasius, our fellow-minister, has communicated with them, I think it henceforth necessary that a concession on the ground of policy should be made to them in order that peace with our beloved fellow-ministers in the West may not be disturbed on account of anything that is wanting."'[2] Severus went on to urge his Monophysites that they should act in the same way with priests who came to them from the 'heresy of the Chalcedonians'. He added that Timothy Aelurus had done the same, saying: 'Regard them just as if they had received ordination from me'. Severus was thus in line with Augustine as to practice, though perhaps his theory would turn rather towards the notion of 'economy' than to the Platonic metaphysics of the West.

Theodore of Tarsus (d. 690) is often blamed for having brought into the West the idea of reordination, but the proposition found in his so-called *Penitential* to that effect is really the compilation of a priest of Northumbria after Theodore was dead. Certainly, Wilfrid had forced reordination on Chad in Theodore's time, and Eddius Stephanus

[1] *Contra Epist. Parm.* 2.13.28.
[2] *Select Letters* (ed. E. W. Brooks), II.302.

claimed that Chad's Celtic ordination had been the work of Quartodeciman heretics from Ireland. Many similar cases arose in the Dark Ages, and the feudal practice of having proprietary churches made it fatally easy to bring accusations of simoniacal ordination or consecration. Fulbert of Chartres in 1008 could still advise a perplexed archbishop[1] that simony does not invalidate an ordination, but in 1078 a Spanish council at Gerona taught that it did. The Exeter Pontifical (of 1420) incorporates a letter of an unknown bishop to his Primate describing the proper way to restore a priest who had been degraded for a simoniacal ordination: 'The canons forbid reordination; hence you must not reordain the deposed man but restore him to his grades *per instrumenta et vestimenta* (by tradition of the instruments and vestments which belong to those grades).' Archbishop John Pecham has left his mark on this Pontifical, and it may be he who inserted this ruling. A Council of Toledo is cited as authority, and it is probably the Council of 633 (can. 28), which has the same ritual.

Hugh of St Victor was the first medieval theologian to formulate clearly the three levels of sacramental action, the sign, the middle term, and the reality or grace conferred.[2] He did so in terms of the Eucharist, where the sign was the bread and wine, the middle term the real presence of the Body of Christ and the grace was that of union and peace. With this formulation Hugh was really extending to the other sacraments a distinction which had been slowly and painfully worked out in terms of baptism and orders. For orders the sign of commissioning was the imposition of hands, taken from the Jewish past of the Church. The middle term, which was at once sign and reality, was the ineffaceable character conferred; this was a reality but also had a sign-value, pointing forward to the grace of ministry which sanctifies the minister while he labours to sanctify others.[3] One might, of course, claim that the original sign of imposition of hands pointed to the grace conferred, for the Jews often picture the power of God as a hand coming out of the clouds upon Abraham as he sacrifices Isaac,[4] but the grace of priesthood was understood to be at a second level of symbolism; the hand signified a permanent commissioning, and this permanent ministry in its turn signified the grace of personal sanctification through that work.

The Eastern liturgical practice of placing the Gospel-book on the shoulders of a bishop at his consecration is not found in Andrieu's *OR* XXIV, which gives Roman usage of *c.* 750, but in the BM Codex of that

---

[1] PL 141.207.
[2] PL 176.140.
[3] Cf. Thomas Aquinas, *In IV Sent.* 26.3.2.
[4] See p. 310.

Ordo (Add MSS 15222), which Andrieu labels *OR XXXV*, it may be found inserted. The *Irish Collection of Canons* (dating from before 700) claims that Christ acted as bishop when he blessed the Apostles at the Ascension (see pp. 308–9). This idea is repeated in the *Bobbio Missal*[1] where the prayer for Pentecost (n. 307) says: 'We beseech thee, Lord Christ, giver of the Holy Spirit, on this day when thou didst enrich thy apostles with charismatic gifts of Holy Spirit in fire...'. The sending of the Spirit by Christ, rather than by the Father, would not be an idea welcome to Eastern theologians after the time of Photius, but it continued to make its way in the West. In the *Egbert Pontifical* one may read: 'Christ was bishop when he raised his hands and blessed his disciples and apostles in Bethania, and leading them forth was taken up to heaven.' This is repeated in the *Lanalet Pontifical*, which is slightly later in date than *Egbert*.

The *Questiones in Novum Testamentum* attributed to the Ambrosiaster says: 'Everyone knows that the Saviour appointed bishops to the churches, for before he ascended into the heavens he laid hands on the apostles and ordained them bishops'.[2] When the Council of Trent was busy with the subject of orders, Salmeron wanted to have a definition based on this tradition about bishops, but the closure was being applied to the conciliar debates, which were just coming to an end in 1563, and the matter got no further.

The theology of eucharistic ministry developed early. Jerome in his letters could write of those who 'with hallowed lips make (*conficiunt*) the Body of Christ',[3] and later[4] he explains this to mean: 'On the occasion of the prayers (of the priests) the Body and Blood of Christ are brought into being.' Basil[5] speaks of the priest, 'completing the sacrifice and distributing communion'. The idea that special importance and danger was involved in the exact recital of the words of institution at the Eucharist provided the Welsh language with one noun for priest (*periglawr* = *periculator*). The *Penitential* of Gildas has rules for the Mass-prayer that is called *periculosa* and these reappear in the *Penitential* of Cummean.[6]

Scotus made a notable contribution to the theology of orders, for he returned to the idea that imposition of hands gave power over the Body of Christ, though he added, with a Scotsman's caution, that the second

[1] 582, HBS 58, n.
[2] CSEL 50.185.
[3] *Ep.* 14.8.
[4] *Ep.* 146.1.
[5] *Ep.* 93.
[6] Cf. L. Bieler, *Irish Penitentials*. On the theology of consecration, see above, p. 207.

imposition of hands (which had been introduced into the rite from about 1025, with the words of Jn. 20.23) gave power to forgive sins. The Carmelite, Baconthorp, followed Scotus, and Thomas Netter (who answered Wyclif) did also. When Henry VIII compiled his *Defence of the Seven Sacraments* against Luther he accepted this theological opinion. Thus there was in England a considerable body of opinion supporting the idea that the essential part of the sacrament was the first imposition of hands, though Gabriel Biel could be cited for the contrary view that tradition of instruments was essential. Cardinal Pole accepted Biel's opinion. The Council of Trent began to consider Orders in January 1552 but the session was interrupted and the work was resumed in 1563. Then two new canons (4 and 8) were added to those originally drafted. The first of these new canons asserted the doctrine of sacramental character as conferred by orders. The sixth canon, after much controversy, was promulgated in the form of an assertion that the hierarchy was of divine origin in the Church, and this hierarchy consisted of bishops, presbyters, and ministers. Trent was as much concerned to round off the theological work of the Middle Ages on orders as to deal with the errors of its own day.

7 Reformation Churches

PAUL F. BRADSHAW

The medieval theology and practice of ordination were thrown into question by the Reformation. The Reformers rejected the hierarchical structure of the medieval ministry with its seven orders and the concept of the sacrificial priesthood as being contrary to the NT and sought to substitute a pure ministry of the word and sacrament. Some retained the office of bishop or superintendent but did not see it as constituting a separate order stemming from apostolic times. Where the office of deacon was retained it was concerned with the care of the needy, in accordance with what was seen as the scriptural pattern. In general the Reformers did not accept that ordination conferred grace or an indelible character, although some were prepared to term it a sacrament as it was a rite instituted by Christ. Faced with the complexities of the medieval ordination rites, they turned to the evidence of the NT to discover the essentials of ordination, and the following elements are found in varying degrees in the ordinations of most of the Reformation Churches:

(a) a thorough examination of the beliefs, morality, and authenticity of the vocation of each candidate, a process usually culminating in some form of 'election' or ratification of the choice of candidate by the whole church at the ordination itself and a public declaration by the candidate of his faith and intentions, generally in the form of set questions and answers;

(b) preparation for the ordination through fasting and prayer by the whole church;

(c) ordination within the context of the regular Sunday worship of the church accompanied by preaching on the duties of both minister and people;

(d) prayer, usually both by the congregation and by the ordaining minister, either before, during, or after the act of ordination itself, which was in most cases performed with the imposition of hands. Who was involved in the imposition of hands varied from church to church.

1 LUTHERAN

Examples of rites in B. J. Kidd, *Documents illustrative of the Continental Reformation* (OUP 1911), pp. 330–4; U.S. Leupold, ed., *Luther's Works* (ET) 53 (Philadelphia 1965), pp. 122–6; Emil Sehling, ed., *Die Evangelischen Kirchenordnungen des XVI Jahrhunderts* (Leipzig 1913), *passim*; E. E. Yelverton, *An Archbishop of the Reformation* (Epworth Press 1958), pp. 83–94, 131–41.

Luther could see no evidence in the NT for the office of bishop distinct from that of the presbyter, and hence some Lutheran churches (e.g. Sweden) retained the historic succession of the episcopate, others (e.g. Denmark) retained the office of bishop or superintendent but without the historic succession, and others (e.g. Germany) abolished the title of bishop altogether. Where the title was retained, the bishop was not regarded as having any inherent power to ordain but received this authority from the Church. Similarly Luther believed that every Christian was through baptism a priest with the duty to proclaim the word to those around him, and therefore ordination simply bestowed the functions of public preaching of the word, the administration of the sacraments, and the power of the keys—functions which belonged to the Church as a whole but which for the sake of good order were limited to those ordained.

Luther produced an ordination rite in 1535 which became the basis for the services of most Lutheran churches, including Braunschweig (1543), Mecklenberg (1552), Lüneberg (1564 and 1575), Mansfeld (1580), Hoya (1581), Henneberg (1582), and Lauenberg (1585). Its influence can also be seen in Bugenhagen's rites for Denmark (1537) and Laurentius Petri's rites for Sweden (1571). Typical features of these services were:

(a) prayer by the congregation for the candidate, usually in the form of a litany or the hymn *Veni Sancte Spiritus* introduced by a bidding and concluded with a collect;

(b) an address by the presiding minister on the qualities and duties required of a minister followed by a series of questions put to the candidate;

(c) imposition of hands by the presiding minister and other ministers accompanied by the recitation of the Lord's Prayer and an ordination prayer.

The rites concluded with a hymn and in most cases the Eucharist followed. The ordination of a bishop or superintendent was similar, but rather more elaborate.

2 REFORMED

Selected texts

John à Lasco, *Forma ac Ratio tota ecclesiastici ministerii in peregrinorum, potissimum vero Germanorum, ecclesia: instituta Londini in Anglia per Edvardum Sextum* (1555), pp. 29–56; W. D. Maxwell, *The Liturgical Portions of the Genevan Service Book* (2nd edn Faith Press 1965), pp. 165–74; Peter Hall, ed., *Reliquae Liturgicae* (1847) I, pp. 71–98, and *Fragmenta Liturgica* (1848) I, pp. 15–21; G. W. Sprott, ed., *The Book of Common Order of the Church of Scotland* (W. Blackwood 1901), pp. 13–30, and *Scottish Liturgies of the Reign of James VI* (2nd edn 1901), pp. 111–31; Westminster Assembly, *Propositions Concerning Church-government and ordination of ministers* (1647), pp. 24–9; Church of Scotland, *Ordinal and Service Book for use in the Courts of the Church.* 2nd edn 1954.

Studies

J. L. Ainslie, *The Doctrines of Ministerial Order in the Reformed Churches of the Sixteenth and Seventeenth Centuries* (T. and T. Clark 1940); J. J. von Allmen, 'Ministry and Ordination according to Reformed Theology', *SJT* 25 (1972), pp. 75–88; P. F. Bradshaw, op. cit., chs. 3 and 4; Gordon Donaldson, 'Scottish Ordinations in the Restoration Period', *Scottish Historical Review* 33 (1954), pp. 169–75; W. R. Foster, *Bishop and Presbytery: the Church of Scotland 1661–1688* (SPCK 1958); Duncan Shaw, 'The Inauguration of Ministers in Scotland: 1560–1620', *Records of the Scottish Church History Society* 16 (1966), pp. 35–62.

The Reformed Churches knew of four offices—pastors, teachers, elders, and deacons—which it was believed could be found in the NT, but only the first were strictly ministers of the word, although the others were often appointed in similar ways. Under Calvin at Geneva, when a new minister was required, the other ministers selected and examined a suitable candidate. If they approved him, they submitted him to the City Council for their approval and finally to the people. There followed a period in which inquiries could be made about the candidate and any objections lodged. If nothing was discovered against him, he was formally elected by the people and set apart with prayer by the other ministers, Calvin omitting the imposition of hands because of what he regarded as superstitious beliefs about its significance. The details of this procedure varied in other Churches. Thus under Valerand Pullain the ministers and elders first submitted nominees to the congregation, who chose either one of these or someone else to be examined by them. If he was found satisfactory, he was ordained by the ministers, and the imposition of hands was used. When a minister was required by the English exiles at Geneva during the reign of Queen Mary, the practice was for the congregation to appoint two or three candidates to be examined by the elders and other ministers. The examiners indicated who they thought was the most suitable, and a period of at least eight days was allowed for inquiries and objections. If no objections were made, the candidate was presented at a Sunday morning service by a minister, who was to preach about his duty, and in the afternoon the 'election' took place. There was no imposition of hands, but the minister who had preached was to pray 'as God shall move his herte' prior to the election, and afterwards 'geveth thankes to God with request of suche thinges as shal be necessarie for his office'. On their return to England during the reign of Queen Elizabeth I the Puritans tried unsuccessfully to secure changes in the Anglican practice so that it might conform more closely to this pattern.

In Scotland the procedure used by the exiles at Geneva was adopted and it appears that at first, as at Geneva, there was no imposition of hands. There was also in Scotland the office of superintendent, which seems to have been set up not as a type of permanent episcopacy but simply as a temporary expedient to organize the presbyterian system, to take charge of vacant parishes, and to ordain suitable ministers for them, although superintendents had no power of ordination inherent in their office but acted under the commission of the General Assembly of the Church. John Knox drew up a rite for their 'election' based upon a form used by John à Lasco for the exiled foreign congregations in London during the reign of Edward VI, although he substituted the giving of the right hand of fellowship for the imposition of hands. Later imposition of hands was introduced for the ordination of both ministers and superintendents under pressure from James VI, and in 1610 episcopacy was introduced, again under pressure from the King. New ordination rites for bishops and ministers were published in 1620, being a compromise between the former practice and the Anglican rites. An attempt in 1636 to impose the Anglican rites *in toto* was unsuccessful, and episcopacy was rejected and presbyterianism established. The Westminster Assembly in 1645 directed that a candidate was to be examined by other ministers and the consent of the congregation sought before his ordination. At the service there was to be a sermon on the duty of the minister and of the people, questions were to be put to both the candidate and the congregation, and then the ministers were to lay their hands upon the candidate while the ordination prayer was said. The service ended with a charge to the minister and the people, a prayer commending him and them to God, a psalm, and a blessing. These basic elements can be found in all modern rites of Reformed churches, and that of the Church of Scotland will serve as a typical example: after the ministry of the word, with appropriate lections, and the intercessions, there is a sermon and a statement on the nature of ordination by the Moderator before the ordinand answers a series of questions; then follows the ordination prayer accompanied by the imposition of hands by all the ministers present and concluded by the Lord's Prayer; the Moderator declares the candidate to have been ordained and all the ministers give him the right hand of fellowship; the congregation declare their support for him, the Moderator gives a solemn charge to the minister and the people, and the rite concludes with a prayer, psalm, and blessing.

3   ANGLICAN

Full bibliography in Bradshaw, op. cit., pp. 213–29. Text of Bucer's rite in E. C. Whitaker, *Martin Bucer and the Book of Common Prayer* (Mayhew-McCrimmon 1974), pp. 175–83. E. P. Echlin, *The Story of Anglican Ministry* (St Paul Publications 1974).

Ordination rites for bishops, priests, and deacons first appeared in 1550, their primary source apparently being a rite drawn up by Martin Bucer. Bucer had directed that, since there were three orders in the Church, changes should be made in his rite so that when a bishop was ordained it should be carried out 'more solemnly and at greater length' and when a deacon was ordained it should be simplified. As can be seen from the table (p. 336), this was what was done in the Anglican services. Additional elements which are adapted from medieval practice are indicated by capital letters. The services were preceded by a preface setting out the principles underlying their construction and the requirements of candidates for ordination. This stated that ministers should be admitted 'by publique prayer with imposicion of handes'. In view of the fact that the central petition for the candidates in Bucer's prayer before the imposition of hands has been deleted in the Anglican rite for priests,

Ordination

BUCER	DEACONS	PRIESTS	BISHOPS
Sermon	Sermon	Sermon	
'Veni sancte spiritus'		(see below)	(see below)
Introit: Pss. 40, 132 or 135		Introit: Pss. 40, 132 or 135	Introit: Pss. 40, 132 or 135
		Eucharist begins	Eucharist begins
Epistle: Acts 20.17–35; 1 Tim. 3; Eph. 4.1–16; or Tit. 1.5–9 Ps. 67		Epistle: Acts 20.17–35 or 1 Tim. 3	Epistle: 1 Tim. 3.1–7
Gospel: Mt. 28.18–20; Jn. 10.1–16; 20.19–23; or 21.15–17		Gospel: Mt. 28.18–20; Jn. 10.1–16; or 20.19–23	Gospel: Jn. 21.15–17 or 10.1–16
		'Come Holy Ghost'	Creed
	PRESENTATION	PRESENTATION	PRESENTATION
Final Inquiry for objections	Shorter Final Inquiry	Final Inquiry	Reading of King's mandate for consecration
			Oath of Royal Supremacy
			OATH OF OBEDIENCE TO ARCHBISHOP
			Bidding
	LITANY & Collect	LITANY & Collect	LITANY & Collect
	Eucharist begins		
	Epistle: 1 Tim. 3.8–13 or Acts 6.2–7		
	Oath of Royal Supremacy	Oath of Royal Supremacy	
Exhortation to candidates		Exhortation to candidates	ADDRESS TO ELECT
Examination & concluding prayer	Examination	Examination & concluding prayer	Examination & concluding prayer
Silent prayer		Silent prayer	'Come Holy Ghost'
Prayer		Prayer	Similar Prayer
Imposition of hands by ministers with blessing	Imposition of hands by BISHOP with special formula	Imposition of hands by BISHOP and PRIESTS with special formula	Imposition of hands by BISHOPS with special formula
	DELIVERY OF NEW TESTAMENT	DELIVERY OF BIBLE, CHALICE, AND BREAD	IMPOSITION OF BIBLE DELIVERY OF STAFF
	GOSPEL OF THE DAY		
Creed		Creed	
Eucharist	Eucharist	Eucharist	Eucharist
Prayer	Special Collect	Special Collect	Special Collect
Blessing	Blessing	Blessing	Blessing

turning it into a prayer for the congregation instead, and in view of the complete absence of any such prayer in the service for deacons, it would seem that in all three rites the litany with its special suffrage and concluding collect for the candidates was regarded as the essential 'publique prayer' of ordination.

The rites directed that candidates for the diaconate and priesthood should be vested in a 'playne Albe', and candidates for the episcopate in a 'Surples and Cope'. This met with strong criticism from some who saw it as perpetuating the medieval concept of the ministry, and when the services were revised in 1552 these directions were omitted. At the same time, apart from other minor changes, the delivery of the instruments of office was modified: priests received only the Bible and bishops did not have the Bible laid on their necks but given to them and no longer received the pastoral staff. The ordination services were now bound in a single volume with the Book of Common Prayer. No significant changes were made when the Prayer Book was revised in 1559 and in 1604, despite vociferous complaints from the ·Puritans. When the Prayer Book was revised in 1661 most of the significant changes in the ordination services were designed to exclude a Puritan interpretation of the rites: the preface was amended to make episcopal ordination a *sine qua non* for admission to the Anglican ministry; changes were made in the readings prescribed for each service to make it clear that bishops and priests were regarded as differing in order and not simply in degree; and additions were made to the formulas at the imposition of hands on priests and bishops which explicitly named the orders ,being conferred—no doubt to counter criticism advanced by both Puritans and Roman Catholics that the earlier rites did not recognize a clear distinction between the two orders.

Anglican orders were continually attacked by Roman Catholics as invalid. At first such attacks tended to centre on the allegation that sufficient consecrators could not be found when Matthew Parker was appointed Archbishop of Canterbury by Queen Elizabeth I and therefore his consecration and all subsequent ones were invalid. Fuel was added to this particular fire by the publication in 1604 of the 'Nag's Head Fable' which asserted that Parker had been consecrated in the Nag's Head Tavern, Cheapside, by a strange, illegal, and invalid rite, and the flames of controversy were later fanned by the discovery that there was no record extant of the consecration of William Barlow, Parker's chief consecrator. Subsequently little emphasis was attached to these historical doubts, but there remained allegations that the Anglican rites were defective in matter, form, or intention, although there was considerable diversity of opinion as to what constituted the essential requirements of an ordination rite in these respects. This culminated in the issue by Pope Leo XIII in

1896 of the Bull *Apostolicae Curae* which declared that Anglican orders were invalid through defects of form and intention in the 1550 rites for the priesthood and episcopate.

When an attempt was made to revise the Prayer Book in 1927, little was done about the ordination services, and it was not until towards the end of the process of revision that any significant amendments were suggested. A bidding, a period of silent prayer, and an ordination prayer (cast in 'eucharistic' form) were inserted before the imposition of hands in the ordination of deacons, the prayers before the imposition of hands in the other two rites were also cast in eucharistic form, and the litany was made optional, with a period of silent prayer to replace it when it was not used in the rite for bishops. Only when the services came before the House of Bishops for the last time did they think of inserting a petition for the candidates—'endue them with all grace needful for their calling'—into the prayer before the imposition of hands in the rite for priests so that it came closer to being a true ordination prayer. As the revised Prayer Book was rejected by Parliament, the 1661 services remain the official ordination rites of the Church of England. In the rest of the Anglican Communion revision has been extremely conservative, and some provinces have adopted the English rites almost without change. The only significant alteration in the PECUSA rites of 1792 was the inclusion of an alternative formula at the imposition of hands on priests, and when the services were revised in 1928 the only major changes were the addition of a new version of the hymn 'Come Holy Ghost' and a special litany for ordinations. Scotland and the CIPBC adopted almost all the proposals made in the unsuccessful English attempt at revision, with minor variations; South Africa has copied most of the Scottish amendments, and Canada has created an ordination prayer in the rite for the diaconate. The conservatism in the revision of ordination rites within the Anglican Communion is hardly surprising since they represent one of the bonds which binds Anglicans together, and indeed the 1958 Lambeth Conference pleaded for just such conservatism and suggested that suitable amendments were the mention of the particular order being conferred in the prayer before the imposition of hands and the addition of a declaration after the imposition of hands, in the manner of the Eastern Church, that the candidate was ordained to that particular ministry in the Church of God.

4 METHODIST

Selected texts

Order of Administration of the Lord's Supper and Baptism; the forms of Solemnization of Matrimony, and of the Burial of the Dead; together with the

Ordination Service: As used by the Wesleyan Methodists (1848), pp. 93ff; *The Book of Public Prayers and Services for the use of the people called Methodists* (1883), pp. 269–79; *The Book of Offices, being the Orders of Service authorized for use in the Methodist Church* (1936), pp. 58ff.

Studies

J. C. Bowmer, *Pastor and People: a Study of Church and Ministry in Wesleyan Methodism 1791–1858* (Epworth 1975). A. B. Lawson, *John Wesley and the Christian Ministry* (SPCK 1963), which contains the text of Wesley's rite in Appendix 2. Gerald F. Moede, *The Office of Bishop in Methodism* (Zurich and New York 1964). B. L. Semmens, *The Conferences after Wesley* (Melbourne 1971). E. W. Thompson, *Wesley: Apostolic Man—some reflections on Wesley's consecration of Dr Thomas Coke* (Epworth 1957).

Influenced mainly by two books, Edward Stillingfleet's *Irenicum* (1661) and Peter King's *An Enquiry into the Constitution, Discipline, Unity and Worship of the Primitive Church* (1691), John Wesley came to believe that bishops and priests differed only in degree and not in order. When therefore the English bishops would do nothing about providing a bishop for America, in 1784 he took it upon himself as an Anglican priest to ordain a 'superintendent' and 'elders' to serve in America, and later other 'elders' for Scotland, and eventually for England, adapting the Anglican ordination rites for this purpose. The most significant changes were the omission of the preface which spoke of the origin of the ministry and of the necessity for episcopal ordination, the deletion of all directions about vesture, the substitution of the terms 'elder' and 'superintendent' for 'priest' and 'bishop', and the removal of all references to 'consecration' in the rite for superintendents. In the formula said at the imposition of hands on elders the phrase from Jn. 20.23, 'whose sins thou dost forgive, they are forgiven; and whose sins thou dost retain, they are retained', was omitted. The rite for the diaconate was retained, and candidates were given a Bible instead of the NT. These services provided the basis of the ordination rites of Methodists in America, though in the course of time they have undergone various changes, among them the restoration of the terms 'bishop' and 'consecration' in Wesley's rite for superintendents and the substitution of the expression 'The Lord pour upon thee the Holy Spirit' for the words 'Receive the Holy Ghost' at the imposition of hands on both bishops and elders.

In England Wesley's services continued to be printed in subsequent editions of *The Sunday Service*, despite the fact that there were no deacons or superintendents in the Methodist ministry in England and the imposition of hands was not used until 1836, except occasionally for the ordination of overseas missionaries. The main features of the rite used for home ordinands were an examination, a token election (the admission to Connexion having taken place earlier in the day), prayer over the candidates, hymns, and additional extemporized prayer. The non-Wesleyan ordinations were generally of this same kind, although except for the United Methodist Free Churches, the 'election' was played down, and the United Methodist rite of 1913 dropped it altogether. In 1846 the Wesleyan Methodists replaced their service by one containing elements from all three of Wesley's rites but especially from those for elders and superintendents. Its main features were extemporized prayer, the reading of a number of prescribed passages of Scripture, the exhortation to the candidates and their examination from the rite for elders (with some minor changes), the bidding from the rite for superintendents, a period of silent prayer and the collect (slightly emended) from the rite for elders, and then came the prayers before the imposition of hands from both rites, the imposition of hands itself performed by the President of the Methodist Conference together with other ministers and accompanied by a formula adapted from the rite for elders, and the giving of a Bible. The service concluded with the final collect from the rite for superintendents and the Lord's Supper followed. This was slightly revised in 1882: the hymn 'Come Holy Ghost' was included, a hymn was sung immediately before the imposition of hands, and a charge was delivered by the ex-President of the Conference after the Lord's Supper. Further changes were made in the rite included in the 1936 *Book of Offices*. A fixed form was provided as an alternative to extemporary prayer, the examination was slightly modified, a new version of 'Come Holy Ghost' was substituted, and the collect, the prayer from the rite for superintendents, and the hymn before the imposition of hands were all omitted. The prayer before the imposition of hands was altered to conform with the version in the proposed Anglican rite for priests of 1927, including its inserted petition and eucharistic preface but, rather oddly, not the *Sursum Corda*. A new form of words accompanied the delivery of the Bible, and a declaration that the candidate had been ordained was added.

5 BAPTIST AND CONGREGATIONALIST

Selected texts

Book of Congregational Worship (1920), pp. 67–73; *A Manual for Ministers* (1936), pp. 132–9; *A Book of Public Worship* (1948), pp. 199–204; *A Book of Services and Prayers* (1959), pp. 90–6; Winthrop S. Hudson and Norman H. Maring, *A Baptist Manual of Polity and Practice* (1963).

These denominations may be classed together since they have a common origin in seventeenth century English Separatism and their ordination practice is derived from the Reformed tradition. Both view ordination as the recognition by the local congregation that a person has been called by God to the ministry and already has the necessary gifts and graces and as the setting apart of him to function as a minister within that particular congregation. Nevertheless, although this is the theory of ordination in both Churches, in practice they now involve the wider Church and not just the local congregation in the process, so that candidates are selected and examined by a council representing the wider fellowship of churches and at the ordination other ministers will be present, and one will preside. The practice of 're-ordaining' a minister every time he changed his pastorate, in strict accordance with the Independent principle, has also become obsolete.

According to the Savoy Declaration (1658) the elements of ordination were election by the congregation and separation by fasting and prayer; imposition of hands by the elders of the congregation was desirable although not essential. In the course of time Congregationalists generally abandoned the imposition of hands and often substituted the giving of the right hand of fellowship. At a modern ordination, after appropriate readings, the presiding minister speaks about the duties of the ministry, a representative of the congregation describes the process which has led them to invite the ordinand to be their minister, and the ordinand makes a statement about himself. He then answers a series of questions, and the congregation affirm their acceptance of him. After a hymn of the Holy Spirit the ordination prayer follows, accompanied by the imposition of hands performed jointly by representatives of the congregation and ministers from other congregations. This ends with the Lord's Prayer said by all. The presiding minister declares that the candidate is ordained and appointed pastor of that congregation, he delivers to him a Bible, and then the new minister receives the right hand of fellowship from representatives of both the local and the wider Church. A charge is given to the minister and to the congregation, and the service ends with the new minister giving his blessing to the congregation.

At a Baptist ordination the candidate is presented by the chairman of the deacons to the congregation and, after receiving vows from the candidate, the presiding minister declares him fit to be ordained. There follows a blessing of the candidate and the ordination prayer, accompanied by the imposition of hands by ministers and in many cases by representative laymen also. Charges are given to the candidate and to the congregation, and often a Bible is delivered to the candidate. The presiding minister welcomes the candidate into the ministry, and the Lord's Supper follows, presided over by the new minister.

8 Recent Developments

PAUL F. BRADSHAW

The most notable feature of recent developments is the growth towards a common understanding of the nature of ordination and a common structure in the rites between the different Churches.

1 THE INFLUENCE OF SOUTH INDIA

Selected texts

Order of Service for the Inauguration of Church Union in South India with the Form of Consecrating the first new bishops and the Order of Service for the Ordination of Presbyters (1947); *Church of South India, The Ordinal* (1958, 2nd edn 1962); *Services Proposed for use at the Inauguration of the Church of North India and the Church of Pakistan and the service for the ordination of presbyters in these united Churches* (rev. edn Madras 1957, 2nd rev. edn Madras 1960); *Proposed Scheme of Church Union in Ceylon* (3rd rev. edn, amended, Madras 1964), pp, 78–106; *Towards Reconciliation, the Interim Statement of the Anglican-Methodist Unity Commission* (1967), pp. 51–75; *Anglican-Methodist Unity, 1. The Ordinal* (1968); PECUSA, *Prayer Book Studies 20, The Ordination of Bishops, Priests and Deacons* (New York 1970), and *The Proposed BCP* (New York 1977).

Studies

Bradshaw, op. cit., ch. 11; T. S. Garrett, 'The Ordinal of the Church of South India', in *SJT* 12 (1959), pp. 400–13; *Worship in the Church of South India* (2nd edn Lutterworth Press 1965), ch. 9; 'Products of Nigeria's Liturgy Committee', in *SL* 5 (1966), p. 183; E. C. Ratcliff, 'The Ordinal of the Church of South India', *Theology* 63 (1960), pp. 7–15, *LS* pp. 173–82.

The first CSI ordination rites were simply revised versions of those proposed in 1927 for the Church of England. The significant differences were the omission of the preface, the substitution of a litany adapted from the Eastern Church for the Anglican one in all three rites, the inclusion of a period of silent prayer in the rites for the episcopate and diaconate as well as in that for the presbyterate, and modifications in the examination and readings. In the rite for the episcopate the giving of the pastoral staff was restored, the presentation was by presbyters instead of bishops, and they joined in the imposition of hands—a feature which caused concern to some Anglicans who feared that it implied that presbyters could consecrate bishops. The omission of the clause referring to the remitting and retaining of sins in the formula at the imposition of hands on presbyters also distressed some Anglicans, as did the use of the term 'presbyter' instead of 'priest'. However in 1955 the Church of England agreed to accept the validity of CSI ordinations, and several other Anglican provinces have done the same.

These services were adopted in the scheme of church union in Ceylon, with minor modifications, but in the scheme in North India and Pakistan it was decided to incorporate features from the ordination rite of the Church of Scotland. Since at the same time a revision of the ordination rites was being undertaken in South India, the two bodies worked closely together, with the result that the two sets of services were very similar in structure, though differing greatly in details. In the end, however, the Churches of North India and Pakistan adopted the CSI version for an experimental period. These rites are preceded by a preface which includes the statement that there are three essential elements in ordination—election by the people (the presentation of the candidates in the service representing the last step in this process), prayer, and the imposition of apostolic hands. All three rites are set within the Eucharist and follow the same basic pattern (italics indicate elements which were influenced by the practice of the Church of Scotland.)

(a) presentation of the candidates, *reading of the authorization of the diocese for the ordination*, and the assent of the people;

(b) after the ministry of the word (with proper lessons, sermon, creed, and hymn), the examination, preceded by a short *statement on the nature of ordination* by the bishop;

(c) a period of silent prayer, the hymn 'Come Holy Ghost', and the *ordination prayer with the imposition of hands during its central petition*;

(d) delivery of a Bible, *giving of the right hand of fellowship*, and a *declaration that the candidates are ordained*.

A novel expedient is employed when there is more than one candidate: instead of the whole prayer being repeated over each, or the imposition of hands being separated from the prayer, the prayer is said collectively over all and when the central petition is reached, that alone is repeated for each ordinand while hands are laid on him, and then the prayer is concluded. The rite for the episcopate includes the additional ceremony of the delivery of the pastoral staff.

These rites have become the basis for others:

(a) the scheme for union in Nigeria, which introduced some verbal improvements and a new ordination prayer for deacons, as well as the delivery of a chalice and paten to presbyters, this being done without any intention of imitating Roman Catholic practice, since the proposer was unaware of its existence in that Church.

(b) the proposed Anglican-Methodist Ordinal in England, although it differed from CSI in that the whole of the ordination, including the presentation, came after the creed, different proper lessons were

343

appointed, a fixed bidding introduced the period of silent prayer and a collect concluded it, and many minor changes in wording were made. The giving of the right hand of fellowship and the declaration that the candidates were ordained were omitted, and the newly ordained were to fulfil the liturgical functions of their order in the ordination Eucharist. Presbyters were not to join in the imposition of hands on bishops, and the giving of the pastoral staff was omitted. An abbreviated version of the exhortation to priests from the Anglican service was included as an optional element in the rite for presbyters, and a reminder of the commission to the apostles to remit and retain sins in Jn. 20.21–3 was included in the formula said at the delivery of the Bible to presbyters, since these words were no longer used at the imposition of hands as they were in the Anglican rite.

In *The Methodist Service Book* (1975), the 'Ordination of Ministers also called Presbyters' follows closely the sequence of the corresponding service in the proposed Anglican-Methodist Ordinal, though the Bible is delivered without formula and a declaration that the candidates have been duly ordained is added; in the ensuing Eucharist, the newly ordained simply receive communion.

(c) the ordination services in the PECUSA *Proposed Book of Common Prayer* (1977), though these are much more freely adapted and are also cast in modern language. They permit flexibility in various parts, particularly in the choice of readings. The term 'priest' is used instead of 'presbyter' and priests do not join in the imposition of hands on bishops. Other points worthy of note are that, following the new Roman Catholic rites, the ordination prayer for bishops is a free translation of the prayer from the *Ap. Trad.* (see pp. 301–5) and not the CSI prayer, and the giving of the *Pax* is allotted a prominent place in the rites, as it had in the ordinations of the early Church. The newly ordained are to fulfil the liturgical functions of their order in the ordination Eucharist.

2 ROMAN CATHOLIC

Text

Pontificale Romanum, De Ordinatione Diaconi, Presbyteri, et Episcopi. Rome 1968.

Study

J. D. Crichton, *Christian Celebration: The Sacraments* (G. Chapman 1973), ch. 8.

In the Apostolic Constitution *Sacramentum Ordinis* of Pope Pius XII (1947) the essential elements of ordination in the Roman Pontifical were defined as the silent imposition of hands and the central petitions of the original Roman ordination prayers, in preface form, for each order, and these features are made prominent in the new and drastically simplified ordination rites. All three services follow a common pattern, ordination being conferred within the Eucharist after the ministry of the word, for which a wide choice of readings is provided. These have as their main elements:

(a) the presentation of the candidates to the bishop and the declaration of assent to them by the congregation;

(b) a statement by the bishop on the duties of the particular order, and a very brief examination of the candidates;

(c) a bidding, litany, and collect, and the imposition of hands in silence on each candidate followed by the ordination prayer (even when there is only one ordinand);

(d) the delivery of the symbols of office, and the Kiss of Peace. The newly ordained then fulfil the liturgical functions of their order in the Eucharist.

The ordination prayers for deacons and priests are versions of the original Roman ordination prayers, and that for bishops is the prayer in the *Ap. Trad.* Deacons receive the stole, dalmatic, and the Gospel-book, and priests the stole and chasuble and the people's offering of bread and wine, in paten and chalice, to be used in the ordination Mass. The anointing of the hands is retained in the rite for the priesthood, and the anointing of the head in the rite for the episcopate. In the ordination of a bishop the presentation of the candidate is now performed by two priests instead of two bishops, the Gospel-book continues to be held over the candidate's head during the ordination prayer, the principal part of which is now said by all the consecrators, and the candidate receives as the symbols of office the Gospel-book, ring, and pastoral staff. The principal consecrator puts the mitre on the candidate but without formula.

3 LUTHERAN AND REFORMED

Selected texts

Inter-Lutheran Commission on Worship, *The Rite for Ordination* (Minneapolis/Philadelphia/St Louis 1977); Reformed Church of France, 'Ordination of a Pastor', *SL* 4, no. 4 (1965), see also *SL* 5 (1966), pp. 166–75; United Reformed Church, *The Manual* (1973), pp. 14–20.

The Lutheran Churches in Germany adopted a common form of ordination based on Luther's rite in 1951, and a rite has been prepared by the North American Inter-Lutheran Commission on Worship for trial use from 1977. The Reformed Churches of France and of Alsace and Lorraine together with the French Lutheran Evangelical Church and the Church of the Augsburg Confession have reached a considerable measure of agreement on the nature of the ministry and ordination, and have compiled a common ordination rite. After the ministry of the word, for which a choice of appropriate readings is provided, the presiding minister reads the declaration of faith of the Church and then asks the ordinand a series of questions. The ordination prayer follows, accompanied by the imposition of hands by the presiding minister, who may also be assisted by another minister and a lay representative. It may be followed by the Lord's Prayer. The new minister then exchanges the Kiss of Peace with the presiding minister and other ministers and preaches a short sermon. The service ends with a prayer of intercession and the blessing. The United Reformed Church, formed in 1972 by union of the Congregational Church in England and Wales with the Presbyterian Church of England, has not yet produced a common form of ordination but only a statement of the faith of the Church to be read aloud at ordinations and a series of questions to be put to the candidates.

4 OLD CATHOLIC

These Churches have attached the utmost importance to maintaining the apostolic succession and consequently use rites which follow closely the traditional *Pontificale Romanum*, although in the vernacular and with considerable freedom in the rendering of the actual texts of the prayers. They share a common form, although translated into the languages of the different countries, drawn up at the request of the Conference of Old Catholic Bishops in 1899. All the traditional orders, major and minor, are preserved. It is likely, however, that considerable revision will take place in the near future.

5 DEACONESSES AND MINOR ORDERS

Central Readers' Board, *Readers and Subdeacons* (new edn 1938). WCC Study No. 4, *The Deaconess* (Geneva 1966). Extensive bibliography in report of commission appointed by Archbishops of Canterbury and York, *Women and Holy Orders* (1966), pp. 40–4.

All the Reformation Churches discontinued the minor orders as having no foundation in Scripture, although some of the orders, especially that of Reader, have been reintroduced in many provinces of the Anglican Communion during the last hundred years. In 1972 the subdiaconate was suppressed in the Roman Catholic Church and the minor orders reduced to two—acolyte and lector—and called 'ministries' rather than 'orders'. Tonsure was replaced by a service of 'Admission to the Clerical State'. Like the major orders, these ministries are now to be conferred after the gospel and homily in the Eucharist, or during a service of the word. The rite consists of a bidding, a prayer, and the delivery of the appropriate symbol of office.

The office of deaconess has been revived in a number of Churches throughout the world since the middle of the nineteenth century. The Church of England adopted a common form for their admission, based on the rite for deacons, in 1924. The 1968 Lambeth Conference approved by a very small majority a resolution that deaconesses should be declared to be within the diaconate, but so far only PECUSA seems to have acted upon this. The admission of women to the full ministry of word and sacrament is a question which receives different answers not only in different Churches but also in the same Church in different geographical areas. In 1970 of the 239 member-churches of the World Council of Churches 70 declared that they favoured the ordination of women.

6   RITES OF UNIFICATION

Examples of the different types proposed are indicated in Bradshaw, op. cit., ch. 12. See also Anglican Consultative Council, *The Time is Now* (1971), and *Partners in Mission* (1973); Groupe des Dombes, 'Towards a Reconciliation of Ministries' in *Modern Ecumenical Documents*.

In schemes of union between non-episcopal Churches there has usually been no problem about the mutual recognition of ministries, but in the negotiations for union between Anglican and non-episcopal Churches it has generally been accepted that some rite is required which will enable the non-episcopal ministries to become fully accredited in the eyes of all Anglicans, and over the course of the years since negotiations began various suggestions have been made:

(a) that each Church should do to the ministers of the other Churches what it would do if those ministers were seeking admission to its ministry. In the case of the Anglican Church this would be episcopal ordination, and the non-episcopal Churches have consistently rejected this solution since it appeared to deny the reality of their former ordination.

(b) that non-episcopally ordained ministers should undergo con-

347

ditional episcopal ordination. This has been rejected on the same ground as the above.

(c) that there should be some form of mutual commissioning by all the Churches involved. This was suggested in South India (but abandoned), and in discussion with the Free Churches in England in 1925, in Australia, Iran, North India, and the USA. Underlying most of these proposals was the dubious concept of 'supplemental ordination', which was first advanced by the Anglican theologian O. C. Quick in *The Christian Sacraments* (Nisbet 1927), pp. 140–60. It started from the theory put forward by A. C. Headlam, later Bishop of Gloucester, in his Bampton Lectures *The Doctrine of the Church and Christian Reunion* (John Murray 1920), pp. 265, 291, that all ministries had been rendered imperfect and limited in authority through the division and disunity of the Church, and it suggested that this defect could be remedied by each Church bestowing on the others that element which they lacked. The concept was criticized by the 1948 Lambeth Conference: a man, it was maintained, either had received the commission of Christ or he had not, and the Church could only recognize the fact and not supplement it. A variation of this was the idea that each Church had a different ministry which could be conferred on the others to enrich them by the use of the normal ordination rite of that Church. This underlay a scheme of union drawn up by the Anglican Church and the United Church of Canada in 1946.

(d) that a rite of unification should be used in which God is asked to remedy whatever deficiencies there may be in any of the ministries rather than each Church claiming to bestow something on the others. This has tended to replace the idea of mutual commissioning in reunion discussions since 1948 and the rites suggested have had prayer of petition rather than an imperative commission as their central feature. Such was the basis of the rites used in North India and Pakistan and in Ceylon, and of the rites proposed in West Africa and in the Anglican-Methodist scheme in England. This last differed from the others, however, in that, as a result of criticism by some, the words to be used over each group of ministers were slightly different: the prayer over Anglican priests asked for the Holy Spirit *in* the office of presbyter while that over Methodist ministers asked for the Holy Spirit *for* the office. Moreover this was to be a 'two-stage' scheme, the integration of the ministries preceding the organic union of the Churches, whereas in the other schemes the rites were actions of the united Church. It retained, therefore, traces of the earlier idea of each Church bestowing something upon the other. The necessary ambiguity in such rites, since the deficiencies which God is asked to supply are not specified, has caused some to dissent from the method, and was one of the main reasons for the failure of the Anglican-Methodist scheme.

One alternative to the provision of any rite of unification is the method adopted in South India where a process of growing together of the ministries has been followed, but because of the necessity of retaining two classes of ministers for a period—those episcopally ordained who are acceptable to all and those not episcopally ordained who are only acceptable to some—in order to satisfy the consciences of some of the participants, this method has not won very wide approval outside South India.

V

THE DIVINE OFFICE

The student might well begin with Crichton, J. D., *Christian Celebration: The Prayer of the Church*. G. Chapman 1976 = *CCPC*. Chapter 3 gives a brief history of the Office. Fuller treatment of particular aspects of the subject can be found in the HBS collection.

Batiffol, P., *Histoire du bréviaire romain*. Paris 1911.

Baudot, J., *Le bréviaire*. Paris 1929.

Bäumer, S., tr. R. Biron, *Histoire du bréviaire* (Paris 1905) = Bäumer-Biron (especially valuable for its citation of texts).

Baumstark, A., (ET) *Comparative Liturgy*. Mowbray 1958.

Baumstark, A., *Festbrevier und Kirchenjahr der syrischen Jakobiten*. Paderborn 1910.

Baumstark, A., *Vom geschichtlichen Werden der Liturgie*. Freiburg 1923.

Baumstark, A., *Nocturna laus*. Münster 1957.

Bishop, W. C., *The Mozarabic and Ambrosian Rites*. AC 1924.

Bludau, A., *Die Pilgerreise der Aetheria*. Paderborn 1927.

Brightman, F. E., *The English Rite*. 2nd edn Rivingtons 1921.

Brinktrine, J., *Das römische Brevier*. Paderborn 1932.

Brou, L., *The Psalter Collects*. HBS 1949.

Callewaert, C., *Liturgicae institutiones: II. De breviarii romani liturgia*. 2nd edn Bruges 1939.

Callewaert, C., *Sacris erudiri*. Steenbrugge 1940.

Le Carou, P. A., *L'office divin chez les Frères Mineurs au XIIIe siècle*. Paris 1928.

Casper, J., 'La prière des heures canoniales dans les rites orientaux', *LMD* 21 (1950).

Cassien, Mgr and Botte, B., edd., *La prière des heures*. LO 35 (1963).

Cullmann, O., (ET) *Early Christian Worship*. SCM 1953.

Cuming, G. J., *A History of Anglican Liturgy*. Macmillan 1969.

Delling, G., (ET) *Worship in the New Testament*. DLT 1962.

van Dijk, S. J. P. and Walker, J. H., *The Origins of the Modern Roman Liturgy: The Liturgy of the Papal Court and the Franciscan Order in the thirteenth century*. DLT 1960.

Dugmore, C. W., 'Canonical Hours' in *DLW*.

Dugmore, C. W., *The Influence of the Synagogue upon the Divine Office*. 2nd edn AC 1964.

Egeria (Etheria). *See* Bludau, Férotin, Mateos, Pétré, Thibaut, Wilkinson.

Férotin, M. and Leclercq, H., 'Éthérie' in *DACL* V.

Fischer, B., 'Litania ad Laudes et Vesperas. Ein Vorschlag zur Neugestaltung der Ferialpreces' in *Liturg. Jahrbuch*, 1 (1951).

Gindele, P. C., 'Die römische und monastische Ueberlieferung in Ordo officii der Regel St Benedikts' in *Studia Anselmiana* 42 (1957).

Grisbrooke, W. J., 'A Contemporary Liturgical Problem: The Divine Office and Public Worship' in *SL* 8.3 (1971–2); 9.1–3 (1973).

Hanssens, J. M., *Nature et genèse de l'office des matines* (Analecta Gregoriana 57). Rome 1952.

Heiming, P. O., 'Zum monastichen Offizium von Kassianus bis Kolumbanus', *Archiv für Liturgiewissenschaft*, VII, I, (1961).

Jasper, R. C. C., ed., *The Daily Office*. SPCK and Epworth Press 1968 (the proposals of the Joint Liturgical Group).

Jungmann, J. A., ed., *Brevierstudien*. Trier 1958.

Jungmann, J. A., (ET) *Pastoral Liturgy*. Challoner 1962.

Leclercq, H., 'Bréviaire' in *DACL* II, pp. 1267ff.

Legg, J. W., ed., *Cranmer's Liturgical Projects*. HBS 1915.

Martimort, A. G., ed., *EP*.

Mateos, J., 'Les différentes espèces de vigiles dans le rite chaldéen', *OCP* 27 (1961).

Mateos, J., *Lelya-Sapra: Essai d'interprétation des matines chaldéennes*. Rome 1959.

Mateos, J., 'Les matines chaldéennes, maronites et syriennes', *OCP* 26 (1960).

Mateos, J., 'L'office paroissial du matin et du soir dans le rite chaldéen', *LMD* 64 (1960).

Mateos, J., 'L'office divin chez les chaldéens', in Cassien and Botte, op. cit.

Mateos, J., 'Quelques problèmes de l'orthros byzantin', *Proche-Orient Chrétien*, 11 (1961).

Mateos, J., *Le Typicon de la Grande Eglise*, Orientalia Christiana Analecta, 165–6 (1962–3).

Mateos, J., 'La vigile cathédrale chez Egérie', *OCP* 27 (1961).

Maxwell, W. D., *The Book of Common Prayer and the Worship of the Non-Anglican Churches*. OUP 1950.

Maxwell, W. D., *John Knox's Genevan Service Book, 1556*. 2nd edn Faith Press 1965.

van der Mensbrugghe, A., 'Prayer-time in Egyptian monasticism', in *SP* 1957.

Mercenier E., and Paris, F., *La prière des églises de rite byzantin* I. Amay 1937.

Moule, C. F. D., *Worship in the New Testament*. Lutterworth 1962.

Peaston, A. E., *The Prayer Book Tradition in the Free Churches*. James Clarke 1964.

Pétré, H., ed., *Ethérie: Journal de voyage*. SC 21 (1948) (Latin text with French tr. and introd.).

Porter, W. S., 'Cantica Mozarabica officii', *EL* 49 (1935).

Porter, W. S., 'Monasticismo español primitivo. El oficio hispano-visigotici'. *Hispania sacra* 10 (1957).

Porter, W. S., 'Studies in the Mozarabic Office', *JTS* 35 (1934).

Procter, F., and Frere, W. H., *A New History of the Book of Common Prayer*. Macmillan 1901.

Quiñones, Francis, Cardinal. A reprint of the first edn of Quiñones' Breviary was

351

edited by J. W. Legg (CUP 1888). The second edn was edited by J. W. Legg and reprinted, under the title *The Second Recension of the Quignon Breviary*, as HBS 35 in 1908. A commentary by Legg, entitled *Liturgical Introduction, with Life of Quignon, appendices, notes, and indices*, was published as HBS 42 in 1912.

Raes, A., *Introductio in Liturgiam Orientalem*. Rome 1947.

Ratcliff, E. C., 'The Choir Offices', in *LW*.

Righetti, M., *Manuale di storia liturgica: II. Il Breviario*. 2nd edn Milan 1955.

Roguet, A. M., (ET) *The Liturgy of the Hours. The General Instruction on the Liturgy of the Hours with a Commentary by A.M.R*. Sydney 1971.

Salmon, P., *L'office divin: histoire de la formation du bréviaire*, LO 27 (1959) = *DO*.

Salmon, P., *L'office divin au moyen âge: histoire de la formation du bréviaire du IXe au XVIe siècle*, LO 43 (1967) = *ODMA*.

Salmon, P., 'Aux origines du bréviaire romain', *LMD* 27 (1951).

Salmon, P., 'La prière des heures' in *EP*.

Salmon, P., *Les 'Tituli Psalmorum' des manuscrits latins* (Etudes liturgiques 4). Paris 1959.

Schmemann, A., (ET) *Introduction to Liturgical Theology*. Faith Press 1966.

Sehling, E., *Die evangelischen Kirchenordnungen des XVI. Jahrhunderts*. Leipzig 1902–13; 1955.

Strunk, O., 'The Byzantine Office at Haghia Sophia' (Dumbarton Oaks Papers 9–10). Cambridge, Mass. 1955–6.

Studia Liturgica 10 (1975), nn. 3–4, is devoted to the theme of 'Common Prayer'.

Thibaut, J. B., *Ordre des offices de la semaine sainte à Jerusalem du IVe au Xe siècle*. Paris 1926.

Wilkinson, J., ed., *Egeria's Travels: Newly translated with supporting documents and notes*. SPCK 1971 (the most recent English edition).

Winkler, G., 'Über die Kathedralvesper in den verschiedenen Riten des Ostens und Westens', *Archiv für Liturgiewissenschaft*, 16 (1974), pp. 53–102.

Winkler, G., 'Stundengebet (Offizium)', *Kl. Orientalisches Lexikon*. Wiesbaden 1975.

The divine office may be defined as a scheme of non-sacramental services to be celebrated or recited at intervals during the day (and night). Such a scheme was first fully elaborated in the second half of the fourth century, and it took varying forms in different places, a variety which was further complicated by the differences between 'cathedral' and 'monastic' usages (a distinction which is considered in detail later). The developed scheme could comprise anything between two and twenty-four 'hours' in the day. Probably the most familiar scheme is that of the historic Roman and Byzantine rites, comprising seven day hours and a night office, an arrangement which is monastic in origin and the fruit of a complex development; and even here the qualification has to be added that the basic Roman and Byzantine schemes are *not* in fact identical, first appearances to the contrary notwithstanding.[1]

1 The First Three Centuries

G. J. CUMING

Before the fourth century the evidence is scanty and ambiguous. It is often difficult to determine whether a writer is speaking of common or individual, private or public, prayer. It is also difficult to establish whether there was from the first a non-sacramental service distinct from the Eucharist: many scholars hold that in the early years of Christianity every service was a Eucharist, although others do not.[2] It is safest to assume that there was considerable variety over the years and from place to place. The Christians of Pontus whom Pliny reported to the Emperor Trajan (*c.* 110) had a morning meeting which seems to have been non-sacramental, and an evening meal which may have been an agape, a Eucharist, or both.[3] It may well have been the Emperor's prohibition of common meals in the evening which led to the transfer of the Eucharist to the morning and its union with the non-sacramental service. This union had become normal by the time of Justin (*c.* 150), and clear evidence for services other than the Eucharist remains hard to find until the fourth century. Much depends on the extent to which the Christian Church may be expected to have carried on the practice of the synagogue (see pp. 47–48).

Jesus and his disciples certainly conformed to ordinary Jewish practice in attending the synagogue. All four evangelists inform us that Jesus attended regularly and participated actively by teaching and preaching. Luke indeed describes Jesus as going to synagogue in Nazareth, 'as his custom was', reading the second lesson, and following it with the exposition (Lk. 4.16–27). Sometimes his visits are stated to have taken place on the Sabbath in a way that implies that he also attended on weekdays. After the ascension, the eleven apostles, Mary the mother of Jesus, and other women, 'persevered with one mind at the synagogue'. Peter and John go up to the Temple 'at the hour of prayer, the ninth hour'; on a subsequent occasion they are found teaching in the Temple at

---

[1] The Byzantine morning office corresponds to both the Mattins and Lauds of the historic Roman rite, and the Byzantine midnight office is an additional and subsidiary service. Cf. Mateos, 'Quelques problèmes'.

[2] A convenient summary of the two views can be found in A. Schmemann, pp. 40–43.

[3] Pliny, *Ep.* 10, 96. See pp. 51–2.

dawn, the first hour of prayer. Similarly, Paul is shown as beginning his evangelistic mission in every city he visited by going to the synagogue. Like Peter and John, he used his attendance as an opportunity for preaching.

How long Christians continued to attend Jewish synagogues and whether they continued to observe the three daily services on their own, are questions which the evidence does not allow us to answer. The concept of the Lord's Day is already discernible in the New Testament and the *Didache*; and later evidence points to worship on Saturday as well as on Sunday. More cannot be said.

It is not at all clear, either, to what extent Christians retained the structure and content of the Jewish services. Recognizable allusions to the actual words of the services in the NT are scanty, and the evidence needs handling with great caution. Not all the synagogue service is as old as the first century A.D. An apparent quotation from the synagogue service is evidence that the writer was brought up as a Jew, but not necessarily that he is alluding to contemporary *Christian* worship. Some parallels have a common source in the OT. The infrequency of such quotations is a further argument against their reference to Christian worship. The only convincing example is the Lord's Prayer, the first part of which bears a marked resemblance to the *Kaddish*, a prayer following the Bible readings. This provides a precedent for Christian adaptation of Jewish prayers.

Paul also provides very little evidence. 'In the twinkling of an eye' is very probably a quotation from the second Benediction, but that is all. In the Apocalypse, the Sanctus is sung, not by the seraphim, as in Isaiah, but by the four living creatures of Ezekiel; and the latter also appear in connection with the Sanctus in the *Yozer*, a prayer which leads up to the *Shema'*. The setting of the vision reflects the lay-out of the synagogue, with the elders grouped round the president, and the seven-branched candlestick in the middle.

The impression left is that the actual words of the synagogue services were no longer highly valued. Jesus' critical remarks about phylacteries and fringes (Mt. 23.5) sound like a direct attack on the *Shema'*, and this was certainly no longer in Christian use by the time of Tertullian. The Decalogue survived, at any rate in Pontus, according to one interpretation of Pliny's report: 'They bound themselves by an oath ... not to commit thefts, robberies, adulteries, not to break faith, not to refuse a deposit when demanded.'[1] There are later Christian texts in which parallels have been detected which point to a tradition which must have

---

[1] But see p. 52.

survived rather than been revived. In 1 *Clement* 59 (*c.* 100 A.D.) there are two parallels with the second Benediction, the source of the quotation in 1 Corinthians.[1] A set of prayers in the *Apostolic Constitutions* 7.32–4 (see p. 60) appears to be a more prolix version of the first three and last five Benedictions, which form the earliest, pre-Christian stratum of the '*Amidah*.

Justin Martyr (*c.* 150 A.D.) tells us that the Sunday service in his time began with readings from the prophets or the apostles; and the synagogue service also began with the readings. Before them came Pss. 148–50, which of course form the basis of Lauds.[2] The Eighteen Benedictions are in present day Jewish use now preceded by the psalm-verse 'Lord, open my lips . . .'; and though this usage cannot be dated, it seems much more likely that this is another pre-Christian element which the Church continued to use, than that it was first added to the Jewish service in the Christian era. Lastly, there is the Sanctus. This appears to have formed part of the Eucharist by the time of Origen; but it is quite possible that it entered Christian liturgy from the *Yozer* as part of the non-sacramental service. How it then made its way into the anaphora is wrapped in mystery.

A Christian community which kept fairly closely to the synagogue order of service might have had a rite which included psalmody, bible-reading and exposition, the Lord's Prayer, the Sanctus, the Decalogue, and some, at any rate, of the Benedictions. It is only to be expected that the Christian attitude to the synagogue service should reveal a certain ambivalence. The earliest Christians had grown up with it since childhood, and would instinctively continue to use it, just as they continued to use the OT. But they would also feel an increasing need to differentiate themselves from the Jews. This would lead, first, to the adaptation of Jewish prayers, and then to the substitution of Christian compositions; but it would not necessitate the abandonment of important biblical passages such as the Decalogue and the Sanctus.

The NT gives rather more guidance about specifically Christian principle and practice, exemplified in a saying of Jesus, 'Where two or three are gathered in my name, there am I in their midst'. The context shows that the purpose of the gathering is prayer. The routine of the first Christians included, besides teaching, fellowship, and breaking of bread, 'the prayers'. These were certainly common prayers, and the definite article seems to imply set forms of prayer. It is not clear whether there were Christian *times* of prayer. The *Didache* (8.3) enjoins that the Lord's

---

[1] C. W. Dugmore, *Influence*, p. 107 (but for 'Didascalia' read 'Apostolic Constitutions').
[2] A. Baumstark, *Comparative Liturgy*, p. 38.

Prayer should be recited three times a day, which suggests the three services of the synagogue. Hippolytus, Tertullian, and Cyprian alike regard morning and evening prayer as the norm, and also recommend prayer at the third, sixth, and ninth hours, because of their significance in the story of the crucifixion. Hippolytus (*Ap. Trad.* 35–6) further recommends prayer at midnight and cockcrow. All these, however, are times for private prayer; their adoption for common prayer belongs to the fourth century. The only public service of this kind referred to by Hippolytus is a morning service of instruction and prayer, and takes priority over private prayer. This is attended daily by the clergy, and when possible by the laity. For the content of common prayer, we have to rely on hints in the Epistles, for example, this passage from Colossians (3.16–17; see *supra* p. 155):

> Let the word of Christ dwell in you richly; in all wisdom teach and admonish each other; with psalms, hymns, and spiritual songs sing with grace in your hearts to the Lord ... give thanks to God the Father through (Christ).

Here Paul may be rapidly traversing the outline of a familiar service: the word, teaching, psalmody, and thanksgiving. Compare the account given by Justin, where reading is followed by teaching and exhortation, and, later, thanksgiving.

What were these 'psalms, hymns, and spiritual songs'? NT usage suggests that *psalmoi* and *hymnoi* normally refer to the OT Psalms, *odai* to Christian songs. Paul thus establishes a principle for common prayer: hymns need not be taken from the Bible. Contemporary evidence from Philo shows that Jews were singing both old psalms and newly-composed ones;[1] and if Jews were doing so, it is highly probable that Christians would do the same. One method of composition was to weave together biblical phrases from different passages. The Gospel canticles and the songs in Revelation are put together in this way. Several passages in the NT have been identified as Christian hymns; and the Odes of Solomon may be another example of the genre.

Another prominent feature was *homologia*, profession of faith, described in Heb. as a 'sacrifice of praise'. In Rom. the form 'Jesus is Lord' is implied; in 1 Jn., 'Jesus is the Son of God'. Some kind of credal affirmation was made, to which the writers could appeal, though it cannot have been very different from the hymn.

It has been suggested that Paul's characteristic opening, 'Grace to you and peace from God our Father and the Lord Jesus Christ', echoes the customary opening of the service. There are also indications of a

---

[1] *De vita contemplativa*, 80–7.

customary ending. In four of the earlier epistles, three phrases occur, always in the same order, though often separated by other matter:

The God of peace be with you all.
Greet one another with a holy kiss.
The grace of our Lord Jesus Christ be with you.

There are also traces of this sequence in other epistles. In every case the phrases occur close to the end of the epistle, which suggests that they also occurred at the end of the common prayers, which is precisely where we find the Kiss of Peace in Justin and Hippolytus.[1]

The author of Acts quotes a complete prayer uttered 'with one mind' after the release of Peter and John. This presumably reflects the type of prayer to which the author was accustomed; and it has often been pointed out that it anticipates the standard collect-form. This example lacks a doxology; surprisingly, since several are to be found in the Epistles. They are nearly always followed by 'Amen', which it is difficult not to regard as a congregational response.

It does not appear that there was any fixed order in which the component parts of the service normally occurred. Any order that existed in the early days was liable to be interrupted or completely overruled, by the prompting of the Holy Spirit. A possible reconstruction of the service would have to include: salutation, thanksgiving, intercession, Bible-reading, teaching and admonition, psalms (ancient and modern), doxology, Kiss of Peace, and dismissal. Room must also be found for the profession of faith, the Lord's Prayer, the Sanctus, and the Decalogue. It need not be assumed that all these elements were present in every service, but it is likely that some were normally present. Where later forms of daily common prayer differ most conspicuously from the practice of the first centuries is in the absence of the personal word, whether this takes the form of teaching, preaching, exhortation, admonition, or composition of new forms, and in the lack of opportunity for the exercise of extemporary prayer.

[1] See further G. J. Cuming, 'Service-Endings in the Epistles' (*NTS* 22 (1975), pp. 110–113).

2 The Formative Period
Cathedral and Monastic Offices

W. JARDINE GRISBROOKE

At the end of the fourth century, the account by the Spanish nun Egeria of her pilgrimage to the Holy Land includes a description of a fully developed daily office, as observed at that time in the Church of Jerusalem (see p. 64). The hours of the offices are stated, the basic structure and content of them are delineated, and the identity of those sections of the Christian community who participate in them, and to what extent, is revealed. The last point is of considerable importance. For Egeria tells us at which offices, and parts of offices, the clergy are present, at which the monks and nuns are present, at which the ordinary faithful are present. Making due allowance for the fact that in Jerusalem a large proportion of the congregation is composed of pilgrims, who then as now were inclined to assist at almost every liturgical function available in the place of their pilgrimage, her account reveals clearly which parts of the Jerusalem office in her time were primarily the concern of monks and nuns, and which were parts of the normal worship pattern of the ordinary clergy and laity. And this in turn reveals that already the daily offices in Jerusalem were of a hybrid character—partly public worship of the whole community, and partly the particular devotions of the monastic communities within it. It is indeed doubtful whether, once both the peace of the Church under Constantine and the establishment of organized cenobitic monasticism had taken effect, the daily offices anywhere in Christendom did not display this hybrid character: certainly there is no evidence of offices which do not display it to some extent, whether from the late fourth or from succeeding centuries.

It is only comparatively recently that historians of the liturgy have become aware of the basic problem which the history of the divine office presents for them—the fact that, in almost all its forms, it represents a compromise between two radically different patterns of worship, patterns which reflect two radically different *concepts* of worship. Historically, the problem may be stated in even sharper terms: it is the problem of the disappearance, more or less complete over a large part of Christendom, and everywhere to some extent, of what is for convenience called the 'cathedral office'—that is to say, that form of the divine office which developed from the original non-eucharistic public devotions of the Church—and its replacement in whole or in part by forms which derived from those which originated in the private devotions of monastic communities in the fourth century.

For practical purposes it is probably simpler to examine the monastic strand in the development of the divine office first. Although their first foundations were laid in the late third century, organized ascetic communities, and in particular organized cenobitic monastic communities, first came into prominence in the Christian Church as a whole as a reaction to the Constantinian revolution in the situation of the Church in the world, and therefore in the Church's reaction to the world.[1] This reaction can be described as due to the concern to emphasize 'the one thing needful' in a situation where it was in danger of being forgotten, or at least overlaid by other concerns. However that may be, the liturgical consequences of the monastic reaction to the change in the Church's situation *vis-à-vis* the world were drastic, and particularly in the realm with which we are concerned, the daily round of worship, the divine office.

Early monasticism was a lay movement—so emphatically that, for example, both St Antony and St Pachomius held that ordination was incompatible with the monastic profession. Early monasticism was also a departure from and rejection of not only the world, but also the Church, which it believed to have become too contaminated by the world.

The liturgical situation of the early monastic communities, consequently, was totally unprecedented. Nevertheless, monasticism did not develop a specific liturgical life of its own—at first. In the very early days the Church's liturgy was still regarded as the self-evident norm of corporate worship—the early monastic documents nearly all emphasize that monks should take part in the Church's worship when possible, above all in the Eucharist on Sundays, and, where it was the custom, on Saturdays also. And the first descriptions of specifically monastic worship leave one in no doubt that it followed the order of the normal public services of the Church. At the same time, however, the liturgical situation of the early monastic communities was wholly novel in this: they were to a large extent cut off, or rather cut themselves off, from the common worship of the Church.

The monks largely cut themselves off from the common worship of the Church because they cut themselves off from its common life in the world, in order to give themselves to constant prayer. The concept of constant prayer was in itself nothing new; what was new was the monastic understanding of it. 'If in the first early Christian view every undertaking

---

[1] Cf. W. J. Grisbrooke, 'A Contemporary Liturgical Problem: The Divine Office and Public Worship', *SL* 8 (1971–2) and 9 (1973), this issue being considered in 8, pp. 131–43.

could become a prayer... in monasticism prayer itself now became the sole undertaking, replacing all other tasks.'[1] This massive shift in spirituality was bound to lead to new forms of worship. And when these new forms did appear, they were not strictly speaking forms of worship, as the Church had hitherto understood it, at all. They were envisaged primarily as instruments to inculcate in the monk the discipline of continuous personal prayer: in other words, they were not forms of corporate worship, but forms of private prayer to be practised in common.

The novel concept of prayer was expressed in the monastic offices above all by an equally novel use of the Psalter. This was the invention of *recitatio continua*, the practice of reciting the whole Psalter, in its biblical order, over a given period of time and number of offices, without any reference to the hour, the day, or the season. The arrangements found in the early monastic rules differ widely: the Psalter may be recited in its entirety at one office, or it may be distributed over a day, or over a week, and so on.[2] In a few places the attempt was made to make this continuous recitation *really* continuous, the monks participating in it on a shift system,[3] but in the vast majority of monasteries the compromise was adopted of dividing the recitation between a number of offices at more or less regular intervals during the day and the night. So arose the pattern of the divine office which, with minor variations, came ultimately to be the norm in nearly all the historic rites.[4]

Ultimately the most widespread variant of this pattern came to comprise eight offices—a night office and seven day offices,[5] an arrangement for which scriptural warrant was sought and found in the Psalter itself.[6] The sources of this arrangement were twofold: the existing public worship of the Church, and the hours of private prayer recommended by a number of the early Fathers and observed in previous centuries by the more zealous members of the Christian community.

[1] A. Schmemann, p. 107.

[2] For the daily recitation of the Psalter in some early monastic communities, cf. A. Baumstark, *Nocturna laus*, pp. 156–66; Bäumer-Biron, *Histoire du Bréviaire*, pp. 182–5; and St Benedict's remark in his *Rule*, ch. 18.

[3] Cf. J. A. Jungmann, *Pastoral Liturgy*, p. 151, and the works there cited.

[4] The most notable exception is the Chaldean rite: cf. J. Mateos, 'L'office divin chez les chaldéens'.

[5] But cf. p. 353, n. 1: even schemes which appear basically identical may turn out not to be, on closer examination. Nevertheless, with this qualification, the statement in the text stands. The widespread diffusion of this scheme is probably due to the influence of St Basil the Great and John Cassian.

[6] Cf. Ps. 118 (119).64 for sevenfold prayer during the day, and the various references to prayer during the night in a number of psalms.

There is much evidence from an earlier period of regular prayer being required of the Christian morning and evening,[1] and some of it may most reasonably be interpreted as implying that these hours of prayer were not merely individual acts of devotion, but, where and when possible, corporate acts—that is, public worship.[2] These hours of prayer gave rise to the principal offices of Mattins or Lauds,[3] and Vespers, which are common, as we shall see, both to the cathedral and to the monastic rites. But the early Christians were exhorted to pray regularly at other times also. Well before the Constantinian period we find influential Christian writers advocating the performance of devotions of one kind or another at the common divisions of the Roman working day, the third, sixth, and ninth hours (9.00, 12.00, and 15.00 in modern terms), in addition to the observance of the morning and evening hours privately if it were not possible to join in their public observance.[4] Naturally enough, the monastic communities observed these lesser hours communally, just as zealous Christians had observed them in their families when possible at the earlier period. So arose the offices of Terce, Sext, and None. The other two lesser hours, Prime and Compline, appear to be of specifically monastic origin. Compline is in essence no more than a formalization of private prayers before retiring to bed. The origin of Prime is more obscure: according to John Cassian its incorporation in the official monastic round was for somewhat disedifying reasons.[5]

Pre-Constantinian writings also contain exhortations to pray during the night.[6] As with the lesser hours of the day, so with the night office: the

---

[1] Cf. especially Tertullian, *de Orat.* 25: in *recommending* prayer at the third, sixth, and ninth hours, he remarks on the fact that no reminder should be necessary of the *obligation* to pray morning and evening.

[2] Cf. Schmemann, pp. 65–6.

[3] The name Mattins (or Matins) has sometimes been used of the vigil or night office, and sometimes of the morning office. The former has variously been called Vigils, Nocturns or Mattins; where it has been called Mattins, another name has obviously been required for the morning office, hence 'Lauds', from the *laudate* psalms (148–50) so widely used at it.

[4] Cf., e.g., *Ap. Trad.* 41, and Tertullian, *de Orat.* 25.

[5] He says (*Institutiones*, 3.6) that it was instituted in order to prevent idle monks from going back to bed in the morning and sleeping until Terce. But J. Froger, *Les origines de prime* (Rome 1946) put forward the thesis that the office referred to by Cassian in this passage was not Prime but Lauds, a view strongly contested by J. M. Hanssens, *Nature et genèse de l'office des matines* (Analecta Gregoriana 57, Rome 1952). Cf. also L. Brou, a review of Froger, in *JTS* 48 (1947), pp. 240–1; F. Masai, *Archivium Latinitatis medii aevi*, 19 (1946), pp. 23–7; and O. Chadwick, 'The Origins of Prime', in *JTS* 49 (1948), pp. 178–82.

[6] A specific prescription of prayer at midnight and at cockcrow is to be found in *Ap. Trad.* 36. Clement of Alexandria (*Strom.* 7.7, 49, 2), Origen (*de Orat.* 12.2), Tertullian (*ad*

origin of this monastic observance appears to lie in the communal formalization of these originally private devotions. This last statement, however, requires considerable qualification, for the question of the origin and development of the night office, and of its relationship to the morning office is a complex one, which has given rise to much debate among liturgical scholars in recent years. Lack of space unfortunately precludes an examination of the problem here.[1] The one thing that is certain is that the liturgy, in this as in other areas, did not develop in accordance with the analytical theories of modern liturgical scholars; it developed in accordance with the needs, or the predilections, of those who worshipped through it, in whatever age or place.

It is time to turn from the origins and development of the monastic office to those of the cathedral office. The replacement of the cathedral office by the monastic office did not take place suddenly, nor did it take place everywhere to the same extent or at the same pace. Indeed, for some time the cathedral office continued to develop in many places along its own proper lines, often side by side with the assimilation of certain monastic features, the most common of the latter being the addition of a monastic-style course of psalms (sometimes with and sometimes without disturbance of the cathedral structure) and the addition of certain additional offices of monastic origin, the secondary nature of these remaining clear.

Development of this kind was both more involved and more protracted in the East than in the West. As early as the end of the fourth century it can clearly be seen taking shape at Jerusalem; its results survive to this day in the Chaldean rite, which preserves more of the structure and content of its cathedral office than does any other rite in Christendom;[2] and it can be traced in considerable detail in the Byzantine rite between the eighth and the fourteenth centuries, as the monastic office gradually and finally triumphed, although in the process it had itself assimilated many cathedral features. In the West the earliest forms of the divine office of which we have definite evidence already show monastic influence, although a strong basic cathedral stratum is to be found in some of them, part of which still survives at Milan, and, to a greater extent in the books, although less in actual use, in the Mozarabic rite at

---

uxor. 2.5), and Cyprian (*de Orat Domin.* 29) all speak of prayer during the night, but they do not expressly say 'midnight'.

[1] Cf., e.g., Hanssens, op. cit., and Botte's criticisms of Hanssens' thesis in *Questions Liturgiques et Paroissiales*, 36 (1955). Cf. also Jungmann, *Pastoral Liturgy*, pp. 105–57, and the works of J. Mateos listed in the bibliography for the light which can be thrown on the subject by the study of one Eastern rite.

[2] Cf. the article cited on p. 360, n. 4.

Toledo. There is little evidence of the Roman office before the sixth century, by which time it appears to have presented, not surprisingly, a combination of cathedral and monastic features.

The complexity of the evidence notwithstanding, it is possible to distinguish the essential features of the cathedral office from the monastic elements with which they are combined and by which they are obscured, in most of the historic rites. Three examples may suffice to illustrate this. It is possible clearly to disentangle the cathedral from the monastic elements in the Chaldean office to this day.[1] There is plentiful evidence of the differences between the cathedral and monastic offices in the Byzantine rite down to the early fifteenth century, when the cathedral office as such finally disappeared.[2] There is evidence of a Spanish cathedral office normally comprising but two hours side by side with evidence of a Spanish monastic office comprising at one time no less than twenty-four.[3] By applying the principle of comparison it is possible to deduce from this and similar evidence a basically universal structure and content of the cathedral office. And then, by applying the principle of comparison further still, it is possible to arrive at certain conclusions concerning the cathedral office in those rites, and notably among them the Roman rite, where the surviving evidence is not sufficient in itself.[4]

If we return to Egeria's description of the liturgy of the Church of Jerusalem in the last years of the fourth century (ch. 24) we find already in existence, as remarked upon earlier, a way of worship which displays a combination of cathedral and monastic elements. The psalmody with which the morning and the evening office both commence appears to be primarily the business of the monks and nuns; while some clergy attend in order to say the prayers which accompany the psalms, the bishop and the majority of the clergy only appear, and enter the assembly ceremonially, after the psalmody, to the singing of the 'morning hymns'. At the morning office, the episcopal and clerical arrival is followed by intercessions, a blessing of catechumens, a prayer over the people, and a concluding blessing. On Sundays the morning assembly for worship takes place before cockcrow. 'Fearing they may not arrive by cockcrow, they come early and sit down there [that is, in the atrium before the basilica of the Resurrection]. Hymns and antiphons are sung, and a prayer is offered after each hymn and antiphon.' What is more, we are

---

[1] Cf. the same article.

[2] Cf. pp. 368–9, and O. Strunk, art. cit.

[3] Cf. W. C. Bishop, 'The Breviary in Spain' in his *The Mozarabic and Ambrosian Rites*, pp. 55–97, and Jungmann, *Pastoral Liturgy*, pp. 122–51.

[4] Cf. Jungmann, *Pastoral Liturgy*, pp. 151–7, for the application of this exercise to the Roman rite.

told that the presbyters and deacons are already present, 'ready to celebrate the vigil'. At cockcrow, the bishop arrives, the church doors are opened, and all enter. The entrance is followed by three psalms, each followed by a prayer; and then the bishop reads the gospel, which is always part of one of the resurrection narratives. This is followed by hymns, a psalm with its prayer, and the blessing and dismissal. 'The bishop then returns to his residence.' At this point, the monks take over again, and 'psalms or antiphons' are sung until daybreak. What follows is not entirely clear from the text, but it certainly includes several sermons, the last of which is preached by the bishop, who returns at this point, and, apparently, the celebration of the Eucharist.

Allowing for the inevitable peculiarities of a great place of pilgrimage, the parallels with what is known of the cathedral morning office at other times and in other places are striking. In Chaldea, in Constantinople, in Spain, and in Gaul, the office commences with a number of psalms, and the word 'antiphon' is employed nearly everywhere to describe the groupings or divisions of this psalmody, the actual selection of which varies from place to place.[1] That this psalmody is of monastic origin seems clear from Egeria's description, and no evidence from elsewhere contradicts this supposition; rather it tends to support it. What are Egeria's 'morning hymns' with which the office proper, as distinct from this monastic prelude, commences? In the period with which we are dealing words like 'hymns', 'psalms', and 'antiphons' are somewhat vague and interchangeable.[2] Egeria's 'morning hymns' on weekdays occur at the same point as three psalms on Sunday. At this very point in every other cathedral office there are sung Psalms 148, 149, and 150. And these same psalms are described in evidence from Gaul as 'morning hymns'.[3] So universal was this use of them that even the monastic and monasticized offices retained it: and it survived as the universal use of the historic rites until it disappeared as a daily feature of the Roman rite with the reform of the breviary under Pope Pius X.[4] Moreover, this usage sheds light upon the origins of the cathedral office, for it is paralleled in

---

1 And not only from place to place: e.g. in Constantinople until 1204 secular and monastic churches had two entirely different arrangements—cf. the account given in the article by O. Strunk already referred to.

2 Cf., e.g. the varied uses of these words in the evidence considered in Jungmann, *Pastoral Liturgy*, pp. 122–57.

3 Cf. Jungmann, *Pastoral Liturgy*, pp. 148, 149.

4 Baumstark, *Comparative Liturgy*, p. 38, comments savagely on this particular aspect of Pius X's reform: '... to the reformers of the *Psalterium Romanum* belongs the distinction of having brought to an end the universal observance of a liturgical practice which was followed, one can say, by the Divine Redeemer Himself during His life on earth.'

the usage of the synagogue, a parallel which cannot reasonably be dismissed as a coincidence.[1]

There are other parallels among the several forms of the cathedral morning office which also cannot be regarded as coincidental. In nearly all of them the canticle Benedicite is sung either before or after these psalms; in nearly all of them they are or have been followed, at least on Sundays and feasts, by a reading (and in the Byzantine rite on Sundays this reading is a gospel of the resurrection);[2] in nearly all of them the service concludes with a NT canticle or canticles, prayers (usually in the form of a litany or of some derivative of it), and a blessing and/or dismissal. The basic structure and content of the cathedral morning office thus emerges clearly; clearly enough, indeed, to make it possible to reconstruct it in the one case—and in the light of later liturgical history how crucial a case!—in which almost no evidence of the cathedral office as such survives. The application of the principle of comparison leads us to discern the ancient Roman cathedral morning office in the Lauds of the monasticized Roman breviary, so far as structure is concerned, with the subtraction of those psalms preceding the OT canticle.[3]

Egeria writes of offices (probably on weekdays only) at the sixth and ninth hours, comprising 'psalms and antiphons', after which the bishop arrives, merely to say a prayer and give a blessing. The latter point in itself suggests that these offices are essentially monastic, although for local devotional reasons they were likely to have more popular appeal at Jerusalem.[4] And, indeed, all the surviving evidence leads one to conclude that the 'lesser hours' were nowhere part of the structure of the cathedral office—in some rites there is no mention of them at all, while in others, when they do occur, they do so irregularly.[5] (If confirmation of the

---

[1] Cf. Mateos, 'L'office divin chez les chaldéens', pp. 264-5, for a striking example of another, and closely related, parallel of this kind.

[2] For the complicated variety of current usage over the place of the gospel reading at mattins in the Byzantine rite, cf. Baumstark, *Comparative Liturgy*, p. 40, n. 1.

[3] But the application of the principle of comparison suggests that Psalm 50 (51) is also likely to have been part of the ancient office.

[4] The devotional interpretation of prayer at these hours in connection with the hours of the passion was already long established; cf. Botte 'Les heures de prière dans la "Tradition apostolique" et les documents dérivés' in Cassien and Botte, *La prière des heures*, pp. 105-7.

[5] The Byzantine and Chaldean rites offer good examples of the latter. In the cathedral rite at Constantinople an office called 'Terce-Sext' was celebrated on Lenten ferias, and a form of Compline during Lent and on a number of solemn days during the year; in the Chaldean rite, equivalents to Terce and Sext, what may be an equivalent to None in the beginning of Vespers, and Compline, are found on ferias in Lent, and Compline is also provided for certain festivals and saints' days.

secondary nature of the lesser hours is needed it can be found in the *Institutes* of John Cassian: even in the monastic office which he prescribes they are omitted on Sundays.)[1]

Indeed, the only offices which are found in the cathedral rite everywhere and every day are the morning and evening hours. Egeria tells us that the evening office at Jerusalem 'is here called *licinicon*, which we call *lucernare*', that is to say, the office of light. The name which she gives to the office which is later called Vespers or Evensong—that is, simply, the evening office—takes us back to the earliest definitive Christian evidence we have of specifically evening worship, and indeed beyond it.[2] The essential core of this service is the lighting of the lamps at eventide—a basically practical operation which was given a spiritual significance.[3] Egeria tells us that at Jerusalem, after the lighting of the lamps, 'psalms of light and antiphons' were sung at length. After this, the bishop entered with the clergy, and 'hymns and antiphons were sung'. These concluded, there followed lengthy intercessions, in a litanical form, a prayer over, and blessing of, the catechumens, and a prayer over, and blessing of, the faithful, and the dismissal. (Other devotions followed, which were clearly peculiar to the local situation, that of a great place of pilgrimage.)

The basic structure which Egeria describes can be discerned in the vespers of every cathedral office of which there is sufficient evidence, due allowance being made for the variations from time to time and place to place.[4] In one only of the historic rites have the vestiges of the *lucernarium* entirely—or apparently entirely—disappeared. And even in the Roman rite its traces can be discerned.[5]

Once again, what emerges clearly from Egeria's description, and from a comparative study of the other and later evidence, is the secondary

---

[1] Cf. O. Rousseau, 'La prière des moines au temps de Jean Cassien' in Cassien and Botte, p. 136.

[2] Hippolytus, *Ap. Trad.* 25 writes of a *lucernarium* in connection with an evening agape. But the association of evening worship with sunset or with the lighting of the lamps is far older than Christianity (cf. Exod. 30.7–8), and by no means confined to the Judaeo-Christian tradition.

[3] The theme of the spiritual significance of light is not, of course, confined to evening worship; it is equally, although in a different way, embodied in much traditional morning worship, both Christian and non-Christian.

[4] Cf., e.g., the accounts of Vespers in the several Eastern rites in J. Casper, 'La prière des heures canoniales dans les rites orientaux', in most of which the traces at least of such a structure can still be discerned.

[5] Supremely, of course in the blessing of the paschal candle on Easter Eve, even if this is not of Roman origin, but also in the selection of certain vesper texts in the pre-1969 breviary.

character, and the monastic origins, of the introductory psalmody.[1] The word 'introductory' calls for further comment. In the later Roman rite, until its recent reform,[2] and still to some extent, the psalmody appears not merely as an integral part of the office, but also as its major constituent. Such, indeed, is its place in the monastic concept of the office. When one turns, however, to any form of the cathedral office, it is abundantly clear that the 'antiphons' of psalms which consistently appear, in one way or another, at or near the beginning of each office, are not an integral part of it[3]—the psalmody which *is* integral to the office is far less in quantity, is selected and arranged on an entirely different principle, and is found in another and later place.[4] From Egeria's account it can reasonably be deduced that the introductory psalmody was originally an office in its own right, and a specifically monastic one at that: in those places, such as Jerusalem, where monastic communities worshipped in the public churches, and later were actually attached to them, and often eventually placed in charge of them, they naturally recited the monastic offices in church, with the result that the monastic morning and evening psalmody came in time to appear to be the first part of the cathedral morning and evening hours before which it was recited. But why, then, is preliminary psalmody of this kind found also in the cathedral offices of churches which were not served by a monastic community, nor had one attached to them? Yet again, it is Egeria who provides the clue. In Jerusalem large numbers of the faithful, and in particular of the many pilgrims, attended the monastic psalmody, treating it as a kind of community hymn-singing. And it seems that it was in this capacity that psalmody of this sort came to be prefixed to the cathedral office almost everywhere: its purpose was to edify the people before the service proper began.[5] And it does not seem too fanciful to suggest that the apparently rapid spread of this practice was in no little part due to the influence of the accounts of the services at Jerusalem brought back by returning pilgrims.

What could hardly have been foreseen by those who introduced this

---

[1] Cf. Jungmann, *Pastoral Liturgy*, pp. 157–62.

[2] Cf. pp. 386–8 infra.

[3] Perhaps the clearest example of this distinction is to be found in the old Byzantine cathedral office: cf. the works cited on p. 368, nn. 2 and 3. But note also that the introductory psalmody here, monastic though its origin may be, is arranged very differently from the corresponding psalmody in the Byzantine monastic office.

[4] This is true even in the example cited in the preceding note, which thus clearly demonstrates the secondary character of the introductory psalmody in the cathedral rite, even when that psalmody has apparently been arranged specifically for cathedral use.

[5] Cf. Jungmann, *Pastoral Liturgy*, pp. 157–62. It is much to be desired that someone would undertake a thorough study of this complex subject.

and similar monastic practices into the office in ordinary churches was that the time would come when these secondary monastic elements would assume such prominence as to obscure, and even to a large extent to supplant, the original primary elements of the office all over Western Christendom. But before examining this development we must take a brief look at the evolution of the Byzantine office during the middle ages.

Not until the beginning of the tenth century do we have sufficient evidence to reconstruct the Byzantine divine office with any certainty; and nowhere in Christendom was the office completely unaltered by monastic influence so late as this. Nevertheless, the early tenth century *Typikon of the Great Church*[1] reveals an office showing far fewer signs of monastic influence than one would expect, and retaining a distinctly cathedral scheme and structure of services. This essentially cathedral rite survived, although increasingly eroded, until the Latin conquest of Constantinople in 1204; and it found its last refuge in Salonika where, with the same qualification, it survived until the Turkish conquest of the city in 1430.[2]

The divine office of the post-medieval and modern Byzantine rite is an elaborate compromise between the cathedral and monastic schemes. In structure and arrangement it follows the monastic rite, although with a considerable assimilation of individual features of the cathedral office; in manner of performance it tends to follow the latter in general, although by no means in detail, with considerable adaptation to the preferences of monastic spirituality. Thus, for example, whereas the cathedral rite knew nothing of the lesser hours, with certain exceptions at particular seasons, the present Byzantine office has the eight (and in Lent twelve) hours of the monastic rite. On the other hand, whereas the early medieval cathedral office demanded public celebration with music and ceremonial, and the parallel monastic office could be—and apparently often was—recited to all intents and purposes without either, the present office, while it *can* be so recited, really requires celebration with these accompaniments.[3]

Lack of space unfortunately prevents any further account of the Byzantine office; those who are interested can find the information elsewhere.[4] However, it is important to note, because it might have some

[1] Critical text, with introduction, French translation, and notes, in J. Mateos, *Le Typicon de la Grande Eglise*, in the series *Orientalia Christiana Analecta* 165–6.

[2] Cf. O. Strunk, pp. 135–202.

[3] On the manner of celebration of the cathedral and monastic rites in medieval Salonika cf. the evidence of Symeon, archbishop of that city, cited in Grisbrooke, art. cit., in *SL* 8, p. 146, and at length in Strunk, art. cit.

[4] For the basic texts, cf. E. Mercenier and F. Paris, *La prière des églises de rite byzantin*, vol. 1. There is no satisfactory English edn; the most conveniently available texts may be

bearing on the problem of the renewal of the office in the West, that the Byzantine office, even in its hybrid post-medieval form, has retained its place and popularity in public worship, in this affording a striking contrast to the later fate of the Roman office in the West. It may be suggested that the principal reason for this (there are of course others as well, such as the problem of liturgical language) is that the Byzantine office did in fact retain so many elements of the cathedral office, whereas in the Roman rite practically every trace of the cathedral office disappeared or was almost totally obscured. In those Orthodox churches today in which, for practical reasons, the lengthy offices have to be curtailed, it is nearly always the most characteristically monastic elements which are omitted, and this, surely, is not without significance. Most notable among these omissions is that of the monastic *cursus* of psalms.

3 The Office in the West: The Early Middle Ages[1]

J. D. CRICHTON

The history of the divine office in the West from the fifth to the fifteenth century is very complicated. For centuries the office varied considerably from place to place. Furthermore, each of the elements that went to make up the office as it appeared at the end of the twelfth century has its own history. Then there are matters like the Christian interpretation of the psalms, which is assumed by the office, and the rationale of the original course of Scripture in the Roman office, both of which merit consideration.[2] Here we can deal only with the main lines of development.

For those unfamiliar with the Roman office as it existed in the Middle Ages and as it appeared in the reformed breviary of Pius V (1568), it may be helpful to detail its main elements. The daily course consisted of Vigils (eventually and misleadingly called 'Mattins') said before dawn. This was followed immediately by Lauds (*laudes matutinae*) to which was

those in I. F. Hapgood, *Service Book of the Holy Orthodox-Catholic Apostolic* (*Greco-Russian*) *Church* (Boston and New York 1906).

[1] The student who wishes to explore this period further will do best to turn to the writings of P. Salmon quoted in the bibliography and to *EP*.

[2] For the psalms see P. Salmon, *DO*, ch. 3, and for the scripture lessons his remarkable treatment in *DO*, ch. 4.

added, from monastic sources, the office of Prime. At the third, sixth, and ninth hours (9.00, 12.00, and 15.00) there were the offices of Terce, Sext, and None. Vespers was sung in the evening and Compline or night prayers, added like Prime from monastic sources, completed the daily course. Vigils consisted of psalms and lessons, from Scripture, the Fathers and, for saints' feasts, from hagiographical writings, in varying proportions. The lessons were divided by responsories, and units of the vigil office, consisting of psalms, lessons, and responsories, were called nocturns. Psalms were accompanied by antiphons, often drawn from the text of the psalms, and were sung in various ways until the seventh century when in Gaul the monks began singing the verses of the psalms alternately (the antiphon itself being placed at the beginning and end of the psalm).[1] The office of Lauds was made up of four psalms, one canticle (e.g. Benedicite), the *laudes* (Ps. 148—50), the Benedictus, and a concluding prayer. The lesser hours were made up of a hymn, three psalms, and a concluding prayer. Vespers had five psalms, the Magnificat and the concluding prayer. Compline had four psalms and its own characteristic pattern. All these offices had in addition a short reading.

In investigating the history of the office in the West between the fifth and eleventh centuries, the first factor we have to take into account is the existence of different offices in churches not only in different regions but sometimes even in the same city. Not for some centuries to come would there be an essentially uniform office. A second factor is that it took some time before each church or community felt that it had an obligation to recite all the hours every day. In Rome, for instance, there were at least three different kinds of church: the great basilicas, served from the fifth century by monastic communities; the title or presbyteral churches, served by other clergy; and the oratories of the martyrs where from time to time commemorative offices were celebrated. The office of the basilicas was monastic and that of the title churches was not. The former celebrated the full monastic daily round while the office of the latter consisted simply of morning and evening prayer. Thus in the fifth and sixth centuries the distinction between the monastic office (to be distinguished also from the Benedictine office) and the cathedral office was still maintained. The most important development in this period is the replacement of the cathedral by the monastic office. The divine office came to be thought of as the whole daily course from Vigils to Compline which the 'secular' clergy as well as the monks were now obliged to

---

[1] Cf. Salmon, *EP*, p. 823. How the antiphon mentioned in the *Rule* of St Benedict (ch. 9) was sung is not clear.

celebrate. But for some time the obligation was shared out among the churches of a single city. [1]

In the office of the basilicas, so far as it can be discerned, the whole of the Psalter was recited every week and was arranged as follows: with certain exceptions (to provide appropriate psalms for Lauds, for example), Pss. 1—108 were allocated to Vigils and Pss. 109—47 to Vespers.[2] There were daily Vigils (a monastic practice) consisting of twelve psalms and of four lessons in the winter and three in the summer. On Sundays there were eighteen or twenty-four psalms distributed over three nocturns, and nine lessons with nine responsories. For festal days there were only nine psalms (three to each nocturn) and nine lessons with eight responsories, the ninth responsory being replaced by the Te Deum. Lauds consisted of four psalms, one canticle, the 'praising' psalms (148–50) and the Benedictus. For Vespers there were five psalms specially chosen (i.e. appropriate to the hour) and the Magnificat. Ps. 118, divided into sections, provided the psalmody for the lesser hours. There were no hymns, no chapter or short reading, and no opening versicles and responses. Each office ended with '*preces*'[3] and, normally, the Lord's Prayer since in the basilicas the singing of the collect was reserved to the pope or his deputy.[4]

This office provided the basis for what eventually became the public prayer of the Western church. But we must not assume that the other great centres had an office of the same type at that time. If this Roman monastic office of Lauds and Vespers and the rest had no readings, even short ones, it is something of an anomaly. The evidence that the reading and all that followed it was the popular part of morning and evening prayer is strong.[5] We have to conclude then that in the Roman basilican office the lessons had already been incorporated, indeed transferred, into the vigil office.

Outside Rome, morning and evening prayer had their own distinctive character and, as J. A. Jungmann has shown, they were meant for the people and not only for clerics. In Spain the nucleus of morning prayer was the 'praising' psalms (148—50) (the one invariable element of morning prayer throughout the Church), the lesson (which, however,

---

[1] Cf. Salmon, *DO*, pp. 69–91; *EP* p. 810.

[2] Here and throughout the two succeeding sections of this chapter the LXX/Vulgate numbering of the Psalms is followed.

[3] Cf. pp. 377, 381.

[4] For this information about the basilican office see Salmon, *EP* pp. 819–20 and C. Callewaert, *De Breviarii Romani Liturgia*, pp. 51–63. The information about the lessons comes from the sixth century *Liber diurnus*, the relevant text of which is quoted by Callewaert, op. cit., p. 61.

[5] Cf. Jungmann, *Pastoral Liturgy*, pp. 151–62.

was sometimes omitted), the Kyries with petitions, the Lord's Prayer, to which according to the Mozarabic custom the people replied with Amen after each petition, and the blessing. To this was prefixed the more clerical part of the office, three psalms (3, 50, 56), sung in various ways, and the canticle, i.e. the Benedicite, sung responsorially. Yet even for this office the number of psalms used was small and there seems to have been no question of a regular *cursus*. There seem to have been only minor differences between the Spanish office and that of Southern Gaul, though the attempt of Caesarius of Arles to incorporate Terce, Sext, and None into his daily course witnesses to the fact that the process of monasticization was already under way.[1] The series of verses later known as *preces* formed part of morning and evening prayer in these regions.

We have now to consider the office prescribed in the Rule of St Benedict. Benedict, who grew up in Rome, and was familiar with the office of the Roman basilicas, adapted the latter to his purpose, though it was not his only source.[2] In spite of certain additions, his office was in some respects shorter than the Roman. At Vigils there were never more than twelve psalms, an arrangement he adopted from Cassian; there were only four at Vespers and three at Compline. Lauds retained the Roman pattern: four psalms, one OT canticle and Pss. 148—50, though one of the psalms (66) was clearly introductory. For Sundays and Festivals Vigils were rather lengthy: the first two nocturns had four lessons each, and there followed a third nocturn consisting of three canticles, and four NT lessons with their responsories.[3] The office concluded with the Te Deum and the singing of a gospel lesson.[4] Ferial Vigils had two nocturns of six psalms each, the first with three lessons and the second with only one short reading. In the summer, when dawn comes early, the scripture reading was reduced, the portions omitted being read later in the refectory.

The Psalter was distributed over the week, although Benedict altered the Roman *cursus*. He needed psalms for Prime and these (with the

---

[1] See Jungmann, *Pastoral Liturgy*, pp. 124–51, and for the Roman rite pp. 151–7. For other regions, at a rather earlier date, see the evidence he assembles at pp. 151–2. For the situation in Tours and Auxerre, where there was a similar monasticizing process, see Salmon, *EP*, p. 810.

[2] A convenient edition of the Rule in Latin and ET is J. McCann (tr. and ed.), *The Rule of St Benedict* (Burns Oates 1952). For the priority of the Roman office see Salmon, *EP*, pp. 819–20 (and his bibliography, p. 817), Callewaert, pp. 52–5, and the bibliography there given, and M. Righetti, pp. 492, 499–502, 504–5.

[3] This last nocturn suggests the shape of the Sunday Vigil of the non-monastic clergy of Rome.

[4] Does this derive from the Jerusalem custom of singing a gospel *de resurrectione* on Sunday morning? Cf. p. 364 supra.

exception of three used elsewhere) he took from Pss. 1—19 while for Terce, Sext, and None of the days from Tuesday to Saturday he took Pss. 119—27, used in the Roman *cursus* for Vespers. Moreover, he seems to have been the first compiler of a monastic office to make a systematic allocation of certain psalms (e.g. 117, 5, 35), on the ground of their appropriateness, to certain hours.[1] He divided long psalms into sections and replaced the responsorial manner of singing them by the antiphonal style,[2] or that called *in directum* which, as at Compline, meant with no antiphons at all.

The additions which Benedict made to the office could be described as evidence of sound liturgical sense. He added the opening versicles and responses to all the hours and, drawing on Milanese and perhaps Beneventan customs, included hymns likewise at all the hours. At Vigils, as also at Terce, Sext, and None, the hymn came at the beginning after the invitatory. At Lauds and Vespers it was placed after the short reading and this may be regarded as evidence of a desire to keep these hours in line with those of the ancient cathedral office. He is said[3] to have added 'the singing of the *Pater*' to these hours, though this may be doubted: it was, as we have seen, customary in Spain and Gaul, and it is improbable that it was missing from the Roman office. For the rest, the last part of these offices with the Benedictus or Magnificat, the short litany, and the Lord's Prayer, conforms to the cathedral pattern in general use in the West.[4]

Of all the monastic offices of the time Benedict's was the most reasonable and practicable. He provided a full daily office, including everything from Vigils to Compline, that a single community could undertake without undue strain. In this Benedict set an example that was slowly to be followed in the next two centuries. First, the practicability of his scheme led to the disappearance of other systems, like that of Columbanus whose office was much more burdensome than Benedict's. Second, the notion that a single community should make itself responsible for the whole of the daily *cursus* was by no means common in the fifth and sixth centuries. In Rome, such a *cursus* was to be found only in the basilicas where monastic communities had been brought in precisely to establish it. Certainly when in the sixth century the non-monastic clergy were pressed to assist at daily Vigils, they resisted: Vigils

---

[1] Cf. Bäumer-Biron, vol. 1, p. 248.

[2] That is, the singing of alternate verses by each of two groups of singers, or two sides of the choir.

[3] Cf. Salmon, *EP*, p. 820.

[4] Did these offices end with a collect? Salmon, *EP*, p. 820, says 'perhaps', while Righetti, p. 493, n. 31, says 'no'. There is no mention of it in the *Rule* (chs. 12, 13, 17).

were the business of monks.[1] However, the pressure was maintained, not only in Rome, where the 'suburban' bishops were required to give a guarantee that they would celebrate Vigils with their clergy, but also in Gaul. There, in the greater cities like Tours and Auxerre where there were several churches, the clergy attached to them undertook different parts of the office in turn. But the number of offices in different centres was not necessarily the same, and their content also differed widely.[2] What Benedict's office helped to bring about was the practice of the celebration of the same office in the same place by the same community. By a like process Vigils, or something corresponding to them, came to be regarded as a normal part of the office even for the non-monastic clergy. It was out of this situation too that the notion of *obligation* to the office arose, first for the community as a whole and then, much later, for individuals.[3]

All this came about through the example and experience of the Rule as it came to be known throughout Europe. And here largely non-monastic factors came into play. The political and military confusion of the time was such that the continuance of Benedict's work was seriously threatened. Monte Cassino itself was destroyed in 580–1, and other monastic communities suffered in various ways. A restoration—so early—of the Benedictine way of life was necessary and it was from a refugee monk of Monte Cassino that Gregory the Great learnt of the Rule. His adoption of it and his missionary policy were together to have decisive effects on the diffusion and propagation of the Benedictine office. As is well known, Augustine and his companions brought the Roman tradition of liturgy to England,[4] a policy endorsed a century and a half later by the Synod of Clovesho (747) which decreed that henceforth the Roman liturgy should be used in England and that the divine office should be 'the seven hours of prayer for the day and the night with the psalmody and chant belonging to them'.[5] The emphasis in this and other texts is heavily on the *Roman* aspect of the liturgy, and it is impossible to

---

[1] Cf. Salmon, *EP*, p. 818.

[2] Cf. Salmon, *OD*, pp. 22–5.

[3] For the history of this obligation see Salmon, *OD* ch. 1.

[4] If there is some doubt whether he brought the Gregorian Sacramentary and the *papal* liturgy (cf. H. Ashworth, 'Did St Augustine bring the "Gregorianum" to England?', *EL* 72 (1958), and other papers by this author), St Benet Biscop towards the end of the seventh century certainly brought back quantities of Roman books to Wearmouth and Jarrow and, more important still, secured the services of John the Chief Precentor of St Peter's.

[5] See Callewaert, op. cit., p. 64. Bede says that Benet gave to Wearmouth and Jarrow 'the order of singing, psalmody and ritual (*ministrandi*) according to the established Roman custom' (*Hist. Abb.* 6, ed. Plummer, p. 369; cf. *HE* 6.16, ed. Plummer, p. 241).

say now whether it was a pure Roman liturgy or the Benedictine recension of it. The eucharistic liturgy used by the Benedictines was then, as it always has been, that of Rome, while as a seventh century writer remarked, the Benedictine office differed but little from the Roman *cursus*; so perhaps the differences were not thought to be of much importance.[1]

It was this tradition that Boniface took with him to the continent and, with papal support, propagated first in Germany and then in France. He collaborated with Pepin in his efforts to restore regular and ordered worship to his realm. The Gallican liturgy was in a state of decadence and confusion, and Rome seemed to be the only source of a reformed liturgy. Consequently Roman books and Roman practices were introduced, and with them the Roman office. Boniface and Pepin paved the way for the decisive work of Charlemagne. At the same time Pepin's uncle Chrodegang of Metz went to Rome to collect Roman liturgical books.[2] On his return he began, with Pepin, the process of reform. They attempted gradually to eliminate the Gallican rite and replace it by the Roman. What was equally important, Chrodegang founded a community of canons regular, that is, priests living together according to a rule, which, though non-monastic, required them to celebrate the whole course of the office every day.[3]

In spite of the efforts of his predecessor the liturgical situation that Charlemagne inherited was still confused. Charlemagne, who saw his far-flung empire as a unity, regarded uniformity of liturgical practice as a necessary consequence. For him there was but one centre of unity, and that was Rome; and with the arrival of a further supply of liturgical books, he and his advisers (including the English monk Alcuin) set about the work of liturgical reform. For more than twenty years, by legislation and by pressure on bishops and synods, he sought to impose liturgical uniformity on his domains. As early as 789 he was insisting that all candidates for the ministry should study the Roman chant for both the Mass and the office, and in 805 he explicitly included the Roman *Ordo*, that is, the Roman way of celebration.[4]

But pressure from the monarch was one thing, and practice was another. There was resistance from ancient liturgical centres like Milan and Lyons,[5] and we do not know what the uncultivated clergy of the time

---

[1] Cf. Callewaert, op. cit., p. 63.

[2] Indeed, not merely did Chrodegang collect books; he also collected Pope Stephen II himself, whom he accompanied back to France.

[3] Cf. Callewaert, op. cit., p. 65.

[4] Cf. *MGH, Scriptores*, vol. 1, pp. 106, 131, as cited in *DACL* art. 'Charlemagne'.

[5] Cf. *DACL* art. cit.

made of it all. The fact that the legislation had to be repeated over years shows that the work of reform was accomplished only slowly and with difficulty.

Quite apart from a natural resistance to change there was a serious practical difficulty. It has been reckoned that at least ten books were necessary for the celebration of the office, among which were the Bible, the homiliary (the book of 'sermons'), the collectar, the antiphoner, the *ordo* and of course the Psalter.[1] A community, even perhaps a comparatively small one, could be expected to have most of these books, but what of the parish priest? However that may be, the next stage of the development of the office must be described as the organization of the liturgical books. This may seem to be no more than a material factor; its importance is that eventually it affected the shape of the office.

The office had always made use of the Bible, and in particular of the Psalter. The first new book to come into existence was the collectary or book of collects. The remote origins of this kind of book can be seen in the *Orationes* of the 'Gelasian' and 'Gregorian' Sacramentaries (see pp. 225–227), though the first examples of real collectaries are those of the eighth and ninth centuries. (Two well known English books are examples of complete collectaries, the Leofric Collectar and the collectary of St Wulfstan of Worcester.) These books came into existence to meet the needs of the celebrant. It was his function to conclude each office with a collect, and as there was a great number of them he could not be expected to know them by heart.

The first stage in the formation of biblical lectionaries came with the marking of Bibles in such a way that the reader would see where to begin and end. The second stage was probably the formation of *capitularia* giving references (*incipits* and *explicits*—beginnings and endings) to the passages to be read. The first known examples are Gallican, dating from the fifth to the eighth centuries, though Roman counterparts probably existed also.[2]

In the time of Caesarius of Arles a sermon was preached at the morning office, and the idea that there should be a sermon lasted for some time. One of the first collections of homilies for use during the divine office was drawn up by Bede.[3] But with the regular practice of daily Vigils the task of preaching became more burdensome and this gave rise to the

[1] Cf. Salmon, *ODMA*, pp. 30–1. The Leofric Collectar is ed. by E. S. Dewick and W. H. Frere, HBS 45; the Portiforium of St Wulfstan in HBS 56.
[2] Cf. Salmon, *ODMA*, pp. 27–8; M. Andrieu, III, pp. 25ff. Examples of the second stage appear not to survive for the office: those recorded are Mass lectionaries, but Salmon holds that they existed also for the office.
[3] Cf. Salmon, *ODMA*, p. 28.

production of books containing homilies, scriptural commentaries, and other readings from the Fathers. Hagiographical lectionaries for martyrs' and saints' days also became necessary. These contained the 'passions' or the 'legends',[1] read at Vigils, sometimes to the exclusion of Holy Scripture.

Although it was assumed that monks and even clerics would know the whole Psalter by heart, the addition of antiphons to the psalms made it necessary to compile the *psalterium liturgicum*. The psalms had to be arranged for the weekly and daily course, and as antiphons came into general use they too had to be included, although at first they were not written out with the psalms to which they belonged.

This effort at systematization was modest enough. It was destined for the use of communities, for no one at this time thought of a single cleric reciting the whole or even part of the office by himself. But uniformity was as yet far away. Not only were there the Roman monastic office and the Benedictine office existing side by side; there were also wide regional and even local divergences. Nevertheless, by the beginning of the ninth century the Roman office, or a version of it, was gradually making headway. It can be reconstructed with some probability from the writings of Amalarius of Metz (died *c.* 850) who was familiar with both the Roman and the Gallican traditions.[2]

Vigils were rather long with eighteen psalms, divided unequally among three nocturns, the second consisting of three psalms 'antiphonated' (i.e. with the antiphons sung between the verses of the psalms). There were twelve lessons with responsories, the Te Deum replacing the last responsory. This hour was preceded by the versicle and response and the invitatory, Venite, which was also antiphonated. Daily Vigils consisted of twelve psalms with six antiphons, three lessons, and three responsories. Lauds were the same as in the earlier Roman office (described above) with the addition of a short reading and the collect which had now definitely replaced the Lord's Prayer as the conclusion. Daily Lauds also included the *preces*. Prime had become part of the 'secular' office and now had extensive *preces*: Kyries, the Lord's Prayer, creed, the *Miserere* (Ps. 50) and a fixed collect. Vespers remained the same, with, at Rome, the addition of *preces*; and Compline was short and simple: four psalms, without antiphon, a versicle and the Nunc dimittis.

Clearly this is the old monastic office with additions. The Benedictine office had evidently been influential; a purely monastic office like Prime is

---

[1] From '*legenda*', 'something to be read'.

[2] Cf. Amalarii, *Opera omnia liturgica*, ed. J. M. Hanssens (Rome 1948–50), II, pp. 403–65; III, pp. 13–17, as cited in Salmon, *ODMA*, pp. 33ff. Salmon's reservations should be noted.

now regarded as an integral part of the daily *cursus*, and the short reading has come from the same source. It was also a clerical office, for the distinction between the cathedral and the monastic office to all intents and purposes no longer exists. This is the sort of office that Charlemagne sought to impose on the clerics of his empire, and it was this office which, in essentials, was to become the office of the Roman rite until the reform of 1912.

4 The Office in the West: The Later Middle Ages

J. D. CRICHTON

It has been thought until recently that the breviary originated as an abbreviation of the old choir office reduced to a portable compass for the benefit of the clergy who were becoming more mobile. Such a view is no longer tenable. First, by far the greater number of earlier 'breviaries' were monastic,[1] and second, they were books of from two to three hundred folios which could hardly be said to be portable.[2] Finally, they were *choir* books, regularly noted for singing. Certainly clerics did become more mobile in the twelfth century and no doubt the need was felt for what our forefathers called 'portasses' or *portiforia*. But that is to anticipate.

The origins of the book eventually called the breviary are to be found in a rather different set of circumstances. After the moral squalor and liturgical decadence of the tenth century,[3] and with the coming of the Gregorian reform in the eleventh, there was a movement towards a more worthy celebration of the liturgy and a search among clerics for a more regular style of life. It was an age marked by the foundation of communities of canons regular who accepted the obligation to maintain the daily prayer of the Church. These communities were often quite small and obviously could not celebrate it in any elaborate way. In monastic communities there was that small library of books which had to be collated, so to say, for the office of the hours, the seasons, and the feasts. Small communities of canons could hardly be expected to do this. Again, it was an age that looked for order, in public prayer as in

[1] See S. J. P. van Dijk and J. Hazelden Walker, pp. 32–34.
[2] See Salmon, *ODMA* p. 68.
[3] There were of course notable exceptions, such as the reforms of St Dunstan in England.

everything else. Out of this situation came the *ordo*, which in turn formed the nucleus of the 'breviary'.

Under the expert guidance of Pierre Salmon (*ODMA*, pp. 53–60) we can see how these primitive breviaries came into existence. The collectaries attracted other texts to themselves. Some give whole offices (apart from the lessons) which seem to have been intended as models. Others contain the Psalter with the necessary antiphons. In four of them Salmon has traced a certain progress, which leads to a group in which we find an *ordo* 'indicating for each day and each liturgical hour the texts that are to be sung with their *incipits*'. Its title is significant: *Breviarium sive ordo officiorum per totam anni decursionem*, which might be translated as 'A short conspectus or order for the offices of the whole year'. This, says Salmon, is no doubt the origin of the word 'breviary' for the book containing the divine office (*ODMA*, p. 60). All that remained to be done to produce the breviary properly so-called was to insert complete texts. When the full texts were incorporated into the *breviarium*, the modern book of that name was in sight. Yet there remained a problem. The lectionaries could not be inserted into any volume of manageable size, nor could the great variety of antiphons provided for optional use. Hence, inevitably, the lessons were shortened and the alternative antiphons eliminated. The consequent abbreviated lectionaries remained the weakest element of the office for many centuries.

A second factor in shaping the breviary of the thirteenth century was the re-organization of the papal chapel. The notion of a papal chapel seems to have originated under the influence of the Carolingian court. Under the Gregorian papacy of the eleventh century there was a further development. The papal chapel was attached to the old Constantinian basilica of the Lateran. Here and in St Peter's the old Roman office was maintained, though the office was not identical in both churches: liturgical variety was still accepted in Rome. In the Lateran the old Roman office was celebrated by the canons, known by the twelfth century as Canons Regular, while alongside, in the chapel of St Laurence, the pope and his chaplains celebrated their office. That in the time of St Gregory VII this was a traditional, i.e. Roman-monastic, office can be gathered from his rejection of Teutonic influences, prevalent before his time, which sought to reduce the psalmody.[1] Certain practices like the exclusion of three-lesson feasts in Lent and a more sparing use of antiphons are further indications of the early Roman tradition.

There were, however, striking differences in the style of celebration. Although the rich papal chapel can be presumed to have had the full

---

[1] Cf. M. Andrieu, I, p. 519, n. 1.

range of liturgical books, the celebration of the office must have been a good deal simpler than in the Lateran. The chaplains became the *curia* of the pope, and as years went by they had more and more curial work to do. Naturally, they could give less time to liturgical celebration. This trend increased considerably as the papal monarchy approached its apogee with Innocent III (died 1217). It is difficult to believe that the clerks of the curia had either the time or the skill to sing the offices with their sometimes difficult responsories and ever-changing antiphons.

Innocent was himself interested in liturgical matters, and a document of the last years of his reign marks another step towards the breviary. It is yet another *ordo*, known as the Ordo of Innocent III, which gives, in addition to the *incipits* of the Monte Cassino document referred to above, the rules and customs for the celebration of the office, and is described as 'a complete résumé of the choral offices with rules for its celebration'.[1] It was not yet a breviary, but it clearly provided the nucleus of the thirteenth-century book.

A further decisive stage was reached when the office of the papal chapel replaced that of the Lateran. This development came with the rising prestige of the papacy and can be traced even in the terminology that came into use at this time. At first called the *capella papalis*, it became the *curia romana* and finally *ecclesia romana*, and this is why the thirteenth-century breviary came to be known as the office of the *ecclesia romana*.[2]

Since the office of the papal chapel was the basis of the thirteenth-century office, which came to be known as 'Franciscan', it is a matter of some interest to discover what was its content. In general it was a monastic office in the old Roman basilican tradition and it has been described as 'the result of a mixture of Roman, Germano-Gallican and monastic customs'.[3] The age-old distribution of the psalms throughout the week remained the same. There was a modest collection of hymns and responsories, antiphons and lesser elements of the office were also to be found. What is surprising is that the lessons were *longer* than those of the lectionaries of the eleventh and twelfth centuries, thanks, we are told,[4] to the adoption of a smaller script. The place given to the reading of scripture is generous: whole epistles were read in a week and were sometimes allowed to run over two nocturns. The patristic texts were drawn from wider sources than those used earlier in the Roman office.

[1] Salmon, *ODMA*, p. 148. Salmon notes, however, Andrieu's opinion that it is perhaps to be dated to 1220.
[2] Cf. Salmon, *ODMA*, pp. 133–47.
[3] Salmon, *ODMA*, p. 151. This office can be reconstructed from an early Franciscan breviary belonging to the cathedral church of Assisi: cf. Salmon, *ODMA*, pp. 156–68, and van Dijk and Walker, *fere passim*.
[4] See Salmon, *ODMA*, p. 160.

The Benedictine Kyries and the Lord's Prayer were included in Lauds and Vespers though the collect had now to be the prayer of the day, a practice that reduced the corpus of prayers that had been in use formerly. Prime was lengthened by the inclusion of the Athanasian creed which remained there until 1960.

This office, although essentially clerical and monastic, does not deserve all the criticisms made of it both in medieval and in more recent times.[1] There were in fact causes for complaint. The calendar and its rules were over-complicated: octaves and commemorations were heaped up one on another. There was the steady erosion of the Sunday and ferial office by the offices of saints' days, and worst of all there was the addition of supplementary offices and other elements that made daily celebration a real burden. By the end of the twelfth century the Office of the Dead and that of the Blessed Virgin had to be recited on certain days in the week (unless there was a feast of a certain rank) *in addition* to the office of the day. As early as the ninth century the fifteen gradual psalms (119—33) had been added to Vigils and on certain days the seven penitential psalms (6, 31, 37, 50, 101, 142) were used. The second part of Prime, the *officium capituli*, was so extended that on ferial days the hour took longer to recite than Lauds. It was the *preces*, a string of psalm verses, prayers and intercessions, that were largely responsible for this lengthening, and on ferial days they formed part of Lauds, Vespers, the lesser hours and even Compline.

The final stage in the development of the breviary was reached when the prestige of the papacy was at its height. A book that appeared with the rubric '*secundum consuetudinem S. Romanae Ecclesiae*' (according to the custom of the Holy Roman Church) was *prima facie* likely to have a wide circulation, especially when what emanated from that church was identified with the apostolic tradition.[2] And it was substantially the office of the papal chapel that the Franciscans adopted and took with them as they spread throughout Europe.[3] Yet it is important to observe that this office was not *imposed* on western Europe by the Roman see. The Council of Vienne (1311–12) did no more than *allow* the papal entourage to follow the use of the papal chapel.[4]

In spite of the tendency to uniformity liturgical variety remained. Nor was there any central administrative authority, like the sixteenth-century Congregation of Rites, to produce authorized editions and to insist on

[1] See van Dijk and Walker, pp. 1–3.
[2] Cf. Salmon, *ODMA*, p. 169.
[3] The formation of the 'Franciscan' office can be traced in the pages of van Dijk and Walker, part 3.
[4] Cf. Salmon, *ODMA*, p. 169.

uniformity. The great religious families, the Benedictines, the Carthusians and others, as well as the great centres like Milan and Lyons, retained their own offices. In England there were the 'uses' of Salisbury, Hereford, and York whose books differed from one another, even if not very greatly. Within the general framework of the Roman calendar, local calendars assumed even greater proportions with the multiplication of saints' feasts. These often ousted the ferial office, and the course of the weekly psalmody was thus frequently interrupted. A number of feasts of all kinds had 'octaves' which involved commemorations during the eight days that followed, thus adding to the number of texts to be found before they could be said. On the other hand, the lessons tended to be shortened and the orderly reading of the Bible throughout the year became almost a formality. The use of the breviary had become an unalluring exercise and it is no wonder that Cranmer should have commented on the situation as he did in his introduction to the Book of Common Prayer: 'Moreover, the number and hardness of the Rules called the *Pie*, and the manifold changings of the service, was the cause, that to turn the Book only was so hard and intricate a matter, that many times there was more business to find out what should be read, than to read it when it was found out. Cranmer was not alone in his complaints, and well before he began his drastic revision of the office a reform was being projected in Rome itself. Meanwhile another, apparently material, factor had entered into the situation: the invention of printing. This made possible the diffusion of Quiñones' breviary, Cranmer's Book of Common Prayer, and the liturgical books of Pius V. Uniformity had now become a practical possibility.

5 The Office in the West:
The Roman Rite from the Sixteenth Century

J. D. CRICHTON

By the end of the Middle Ages there was widespread dissatisfaction with the divine office and an equally widespread desire for greater simplicity. The first book to meet this need was the breviary of the Spanish Cardinal Quiñones which although in many respects revolutionary was none the less commissioned by one pope, Clement VII, and authorized for use by another, Paul III. It did retain certain traditional features; notably, it provided for all the hours from Vigils to Compline. But it marked a complete break with tradition in its purpose. Up to this time the prayer of the Church had always been regarded, at least in theory, as a choral office, however many exceptions there may have been in practice. Quiñones' breviary was intended for private recitation by the individual cleric and this intention was implemented by the exclusion of most of the specifically choral and communal elements.

Keeping to the old principle of the weekly recitation of the Psalter, Quiñones laid down that it should in fact be recited every week irrespective of liturgical seasons or of any saints' feasts occurring. Apart from Fridays and Saturdays, the old practice of the allocation of certain psalms to certain occasions and feasts was abandoned. Each and every office consisted of no more than three psalms, to which for the night office (Mattins) Quiñones added three lessons: one from the OT and one from the NT, the third being either patristic or hagiographical (a traditional element). The scripture lessons were longer than in the medieval breviaries and the whole of the NT was read in a year, together with a great deal of the OT. In his allocation of the scriptural material Quiñones remained substantially faithful to tradition. In the first edition (1535) he suppressed antiphons and responsories, though some of the former were restored in the second edition (1536). Except for Lauds, which he combined with Mattins, hymns were retained but they were placed at the beginning of every office, including Vespers and Compline. The supplementary offices of the Dead and of the Blessed Virgin were suppressed and replaced by two commemorations. To all intents and purposes Quiñones had reduced the office to the recitation of the Psalter and the reading of Holy Scripture.[1]

---

[1] For a description of the Quiñones breviary, known also as the Breviary of Holy Cross (the dedication of Quiñones' titular church in Rome), see Jungmann, 'Why was Cardinal Quiñones' Reformed Breviary a Failure?', in *Pastoral Liturgy*, pp. 200–14.

The weaknesses of this office are obvious. The over-rigid arrangement of the Psalter did not allow of the use of psalms appropriate to certain hours and seasons (a principle as old as the fourth century), and the severe reduction of elements such as antiphons gave the office a certain monotony. Though it was used for the choir office, its purpose was the private edification of the cleric rather than public worship. Yet that it had a remarkable success for over thirty years shows that it did meet the needs of the time. But the suppression of so many choral elements and the evident, and revolutionary, change in the nature of the office caused scandal in certain quarters and the reform that followed on the Council of Trent was in conscious reaction to it. It exercised an immediate influence on the compilation of the Book of Common Prayer.[1]

The commission appointed by Pius V[2] to revise the liturgical books was determined to restore rather than to innovate, and the office they produced in the *Breviarium Romanum* of 1568 was in its main elements the old classical monastic office of the ancient Roman basilicas. Sunday Mattins consisted of eighteen psalms and twelve lessons, ferial Mattins of twelve psalms and three lessons, and Lauds of six psalms and one OT canticle. Even Compline retained its four psalms. Hymns, antiphons, and responsories were retained and all was held in a rigid system of rubrics that seemed to make variation impossible. The sanctorale was drastically reduced, for it was the intention of the revisers that the ferial office with its weekly course of psalmody should in fact be used. The supplementary offices were swept away and, as in Quiñones' book, replaced by one or two 'suffrages'.[3]

Such was the office offered to the secular clergy and to all who could not claim a breviary more than two hundred years old.[4] The invention of printing made its imposition a practical possibility and many who could have claimed exemption were daunted by the economic difficulty of printing books in comparatively small numbers. So it was that, like the *Missale Romanum* of 1570, the breviary of Pius V became the office of the Western church.

Apart from the lectionaries which remained inadequate, it was a noble office with roots reaching back to the fifth century. Unfortunately, it was

[1] Cf. pp. 390-3.

[2] For the commission of Pius V see T. Klauser, (ET) *A Short History of the Western Liturgy* (OUP 1969), pp. 124-9.

[3] The gradual and penitential psalms were included in breviaries, for private use, until the most recent reform, and the office of the BVM could be used if desired on certain Saturdays (and still can).

[4] Neither the Council of Trent nor the pope legislated about the obligation of *private* recitation of the office; local councils, canonists, and custom brought this about. The first *general* legislation was in the Code of Canon Law of 1918 (canon 135).

far too long and its proportions were wrong. Eighteen psalms for one office were psychologically too much, and unmanageable for a pastoral clergy who, in the centuries succeeding the Council of Trent, were to become far busier than they had ever been before. It is not surprising that they resorted to various devices to evade the burden: for example, by the (lawful) substitution of the office of saints' days for the Sunday office. Apart from devout priests, who have always tried to pray the office, the clergy for the most part found it a *pensum* or an *onus* rather than a prayer, and it played little part in their spiritual lives. Furthermore, in all this reform the notion that the office was the prayer of the *Church*, and that the laity were part of the Church, was completely overlooked. There was the language barrier of Latin, and the rubrics were still very complicated. Sunday Vespers in parish churches managed to survive into the early years of this century though on the whole both clergy and laity alike found the proliferating devotions of the post-Tridentine period more to their liking. The final judgement on this revised office must be that 'the reformers of the Breviary did not take sufficient account of pastoral needs and human possibilities'.[1]

Although Pius V intended his breviary to be definitive, his successors soon began to make additions and minor changes. A timid correction of the historical lessons was made by Baronius towards the end of the sixteenth century and in the seventeenth Pope Urban VIII had the hymns put into a classical straitjacket.[2] The greatest change, however, was wrought by the constant multiplication of saints' feasts which were inserted into the calendar. This process began as early as the pontificate of Gregory XIII, the successor of Pius V, and went on until recent times. Owing to defects in the rubrics, which looked so rigid, not only was it possible virtually to eliminate the ferial office with its ancient *cursus* of psalms and readings; the Sunday office too could be all but obliterated. Apart from Lent and Advent (and even here the Sundays were not wholly sacrosanct), it was lawful to celebrate comparatively minor feasts on Sundays, or even to choose votive offices.[3]

Over the next two centuries various attempts were made to reform the breviary, notably that instigated by Benedict XIV (1740–58), but they all

---

1 See J. D. Crichton, 'An Historical Sketch of the Roman Liturgy' in *True Worship*, ed. L. Sheppard (DLT 1963), p. 76. For the whole Tridentine period see the same essay, pp. 72–8.

2 The hymns of the medieval books were not in classical metre. The humanists thought them barbarous. Urban, well known in his time as a versifier in classical Latin, ordered four Jesuits to put the hymns into classical metre and diction.

3 For the history of this period see Bäumer-Biron, vol. II, pp. 117–23 and 294–8; cf. Salmon, *EP*, pp. 849–50.

came to nothing. The only exception was the Neo–Gallican reforms of the seventeenth and eighteenth centuries which, however irregular from Rome's point of view, produced some excellent results that have not been without influence on the most recent reform of the office. The only change of real importance was Pius X's redistribution of the Psalter through all the offices of the week (1912), reducing the number of psalms for Sunday Mattins to nine, to which were attached nine lessons, three from Holy Scripture, three from the Fathers (or from the legendary for saints' feasts), and three, also from the Fathers, which were called the homily (on the gospel of the day). Ferial days had nine psalms and three lessons, all from holy scripture. What was even more important, he improved the rubrics so that all the Sundays of the year took precedence over everything except the greater feasts. The pope had in fact brought about a reform of the whole temporal cycle and his work may be said to have begun the modern liturgical reform.

Complaints about the office had been made for centuries before the Second Vatican Council. But in the years before the Council the criticism was by no means all negative. Various projects for reform were put out in a number of liturgical periodicals, and the whole question of the office was discussed in the context of the pastoral needs and possibilities of the clergy. Some mitigation of the existing difficulties was made by the Decree on the Simplification of the Rubrics in 1955, and by the *Corpus Rubricarum* of 1960, which largely rationalized and clarified the rubrics of the missal and the breviary. Even after the Council further mitigations were made: the psalms for Mattins could be reduced to three, Prime was suppressed and only one of the lesser hours need be said.

The Council discussed and decreed a revision of the office which was comprehensive and in some ways radical. Its findings can be summarized as follows:

1. Lauds and Vespers are the two most important offices of the day and are to be celebrated as such.

2. 'The hour known as Mattins' is to be adapted so that it can be said at any time of the day; the psalms are to be fewer in number and the lessons longer.

3. Prime is to be suppressed, and of the other lesser hours (Terce, Sext, and None) only one need be said.

4. Compline is the prayer for the end of the day and is to be revised accordingly.

5. The Psalter is to be distributed over a longer period than a week.

6. The scripture lectionary is to be improved, and the passages to be read

are to be longer. There is to be a better selection of patristic readings and the acts of the martyrs and the lives of the saints are to be in accord with historical truth.

7. The hymns are to be restored to their original (non-classical) form and the selection extended.

8. Offices are to be said at the right time of day (Lauds in the morning and Vespers in the evening) and the parish clergy are exhorted to see that Vespers is celebrated on Sundays with the people.[1]

The revisers have been faithful to these principles and injunctions. The main features of the Divine Office published (in Latin) in 1971 are as follows (for a fuller account see Crichton, *CCPC*, pp. 62–118):

1. It is called *The Liturgy of the Hours* to emphasize the New Testament injunctions to 'pray always', to recall to people that 'the purpose of the office is to sanctify the day and all human activity', and perhaps to indicate that the office is a communal celebration, and not merely a form of private prayer for the edification of the clergy. It must be confessed however that the title sounds a little odd in English and the translators have opted for 'The Divine Office'.[2]

2. No office has more than three psalms (the third in Lauds and Vespers is a canticle, the former from the OT and the latter from the NT).

3. The old 'Mattins', originally a night office, is replaced by an 'Office of Readings' which is not tied to any particular hour. It is meant primarily, it would seem, for the clergy and for religious whose order or congregation has no office of its own. It consists of three psalms and two lessons. The first lesson is taken from Holy Scripture, the second from the Fathers or other ecclesiastical writers, with the exception of saints' days when an extract from the saint's writings (if any) or from a contemporary biographer or near-contemporary writer is read. On Sundays (except during Lent) and feast days the office ends with the Te Deum, which is recited after the final responsory, as it was in many places in the earlier Middle Ages. The invitatory (with 'proper' antiphons) has been retained and is to be said before the first office of the day whether this be the Office of Readings or Lauds.

4. The Psalter is distributed over four weeks, although during the

---

[1] Constitution on the Liturgy, 89–94.
[2] See the approved translation (Collins, Dwyer and Talbot Press 1974). The typical edn in fact bears both titles, and 'The Liturgy of the Hours' appears in the ET as a subtitle. The quotation is from the General Introduction to the Breviary, 11.

greater seasons (e.g. Christmastide and Eastertide) and on the greater feast days psalms appropriate to the occasion are allocated.

5. All psalms have their antiphons throughout the day and the week; in the Office of Readings there are but two responsories, and short responsories are given for Lauds, Vespers, and Compline.

6. In form Lauds and Vespers have been assimilated to each other—the revisers have thus continued a process begun by the breviary of Pius X. These offices are made up as follows: opening versicle and response, hymn, psalms, short reading (which may be extended in public celebrations), short responsory, antiphon, Benedictus or Magnificat, intercessions, the Lord's Prayer, collect, blessing and dismissal.

7. The old and unsatisfactory *preces* have been replaced by 'prayers' or intercessions at Lauds and Vespers. These vary from day to day and over the year cover almost every conceivable need.

8. The Lord's Prayer has been restored to the offices of Lauds and Vespers but the revisers did not think fit to include the *supplicatio litaniae* (the Kyries, etc.), always found in the Benedictine office and probably pre-dating it.

9. As in Quiñones' breviary, the hymn has been put at the beginning of every office. This involves a change in Lauds, Vespers, and Compline. The revisers' view is that since hymns sum up the meaning of the season, feast, or hour they are best placed at the beginning of the office.[1] The hymnary has been greatly extended. Not only have hymns been added from old sources, but each region or country may use its own authorized collections.

The new calendar of 1969,[2] with its reduction in the number of saints' feasts, and a simpler and more efficient set of rubrics that prevent the Sunday and ferial course of psalms and Scripture from being obliterated by such feasts, has made possible a simpler office. The Sunday and ferial offices are now those most frequently used, and the daily course of scripture lessons and psalmody is rarely interrupted. The scripture lectionary, which has been drawn up with the advice of professional exegetes, is much better than the old one, although sometimes it is difficult to discern the principles of selection.[3] The NT, apart from the

[1] Cf. General Instruction, 173.
[2] *Calendarium Romanum* (Vatican Press 1969).
[3] This is particularly so for the OT, and it is impossible to pass a definitive judgment until a supplementary volume is issued containing, among other things, the rest of the OT lectionary.

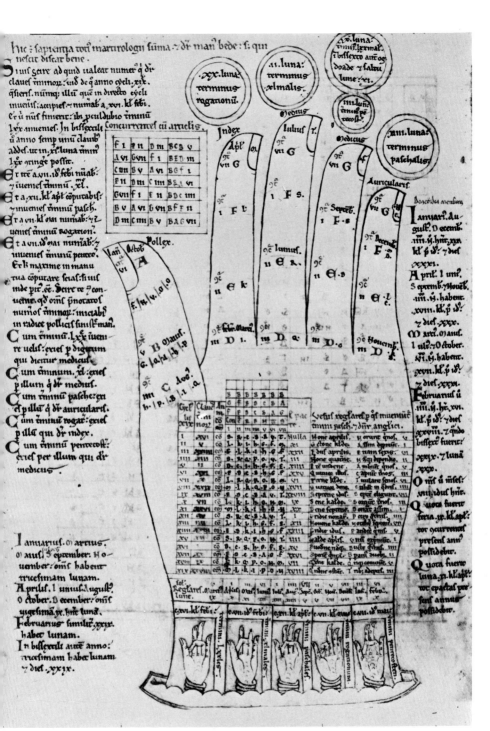

18 Computistic Hand, for calculating the date of Easter and other observances
from an Augustinian house on the border of England and Wales,
of the latter half of the twelfth century
(see p. 407)

19 Cantors
Two Franciscan cantors
behind a lectern
supporting *antiphoner*
or *graduale*, illustrating
a Franciscan psalter
from northern France
c. 1270

hic tibi cantori sunt cuncta

sequentia presto. Que circulo

annorū modulantt ordine pulchro.

Alleluia

Beatus uir Stephanus.
Alleluia

Iustus Iohannes

ut palma florebit in caelo.
Alleluia

20 Early plainchant notation
from the Winchester
Troper *c.* 1050, giving
the chant for sequences
for the feasts of
St Stephen and St John
(see p. 447)

Gospels which are reserved for the Eucharist, is read in its entirety in the year; almost all parts of the OT are drawn on, though much is omitted. The revisers have drawn on a very wide range of Fathers and ecclesiastical writers, but have not admitted recent authors.[1] One notable feature of the book is that, apart from the greater feasts, the daily offices (except the Office of Readings for which the collect of the day is used) all have their own collect.

One unfortunate feature of the book is its inevitable bulk, and consequent expense. Yet it has proved to be popular with the clergy who appreciate the comparative brevity of the offices, the clear pattern of the Sunday and ferial offices and the addition of daily intercessions and their quality. Whether it will prove to be popular with the laity only experience and time will tell.

In reviewing this long and complicated history it is a matter for regret that the formation of the divine office led to the submergence of the old and popular offices of morning and evening prayer. The main reason for this was the monasticization of the office which seems to have been inevitable. In the disturbed conditions of the early Middle Ages it was only monasteries and similar communities that could sustain the daily prayer of the Church. This task they performed nobly, and through the ages they kept alive the notion that common prayer is an essential function of the Church. It was the monks too who devised certain features of the office hymns, antiphons and responsories—that through the centuries have given life and variety to that prayer. Perhaps, given the conditions of the times, complication was unavoidable, but it was complication that became the chief enemy of public prayer. The Divine Office of 1971 has done much to simplify and rationalize the office, and the revisers, working within the brief given them by the Second Vatican Council, could perhaps do no more. They have emphasized by word and example that morning and evening prayer are the two principal offices of the day, and have made it possible for them to become so in fact. They have provided the form and the means for the restoration of these offices to the normal worship of the Church and it remains for the Church, clergy and people, to use what is provided.

[1] Except for extracts from the documents of Vatican II and a few papal texts.

6 The Office
in the Church of England

G. J. CUMING

The first reformed offices to emerge from the Reformation were Lutheran (see pp. 396–7). The desire for reform of the Breviary soon spread to England. Soon after the appearance of Quiñones' books, Archbishop Cranmer drew up the first of two schemes for a reformed daily office which have survived in manuscript (see plate 3). Compared to Quiñones', Cranmer's scheme is extremely radical, retaining only parts of Mattins and Lauds, altering the shape of Vespers, using parts of Prime on Sundays only, and omitting Compline and the lesser hours altogether. It was already common practice to say all the hours in two groups, and Cranmer's scheme is the logical next step. C. H. Smyth has produced arguments for assigning this scheme to 1538.[1] At this time Henry VIII was negotiating with the Lutherans, and the reduction to two services fits well into this context (see p. 396).

In a Preface which is heavily indebted to that of the first edition of Quiñones, Cranmer defines his chief object as follows: 'The thread and order of holy Scripture shall be continued entire and unbroken', with the minimum of non-biblical additions. To this end, three scripture lessons are appointed for Mattins and two for Vespers; on Sundays and holy days a fourth lesson is added at Mattins, dealing with the saint or Sunday in question (the manuscript contains a number of such readings, apparently composed by Cranmer himself). The lectionary is detached from the church year and begins on 1 January with Genesis, Isaiah, and Matthew at Mattins, and Genesis and Romans at Vespers; this arrangement is close to that of Quiñones. The lessons consist each of one chapter, continuing all through the year without any interruption, even on Christmas Day. In this way the OT (and Revelation) is read once a year, the NT (except Revelation) three times. The lessons are to be read in English, from the pulpit, and not within the chancel. Three psalms are to be read at each service, which requires some adjustment by subdivision; the Psalter is thus spread over a month instead of a week. All antiphons, responsories, invitatories, and *capitula* are omitted, which gives the service an appearance of extreme simplicity; hymns, however, are retained. At this stage, apart from the lessons and the Lord's Prayer, the services are still in Latin, even though an unofficial English translation of the Hours of our Lady had run into several editions by 1538. Collects are

---

[1] *Cranmer and the Reformation under Edward VI* (CUP 1926), pp. 74–7.

appointed by season rather than by Sunday, as in Brandenburg–Nürnberg; and on Sundays Te Deum, the fourth lesson, and Quicunque vult may be omitted to make room for a sermon.

The Lutheran negotiations proved abortive, and so did this scheme. The second, and equally abortive, scheme in the manuscript is harder to date; it may be part of the Catholic backlash of 1540–1. Certainly it displays a more conservative approach, and is little more than an adaptation of the second edition of Quiñones. All the traditional services are retained, and are set out exactly as in the Breviary, though there are indications that Cranmer intended them to be said in three groups. The internal structure of the services largely follows that of Quiñones, except that Cranmer inserts a lesson into Vespers and keeps the *preces*. The lectionary still follows the church year, not the civil calendar. The OT lessons at Mattins are now both taken from the same book. Quiñones' breviary had become very widely used, and Cranmer may well have prepared this version when it became apparent that the more radical scheme stood no chance of acceptance.

By 1543 the political and religious climate once more allowed steps to be taken towards breviary reform, this time publicly and officially. Convocation ordered that 'every Sunday and holy day throughout the year, the curate of every parish church, after the Te Deum and Magnificat, should openly read unto the people one chapter of the New Testament in English, without exposition; and when the New Testament was read over, then to begin the Old'. This order implies that the people were expected to attend Mattins and Vespers.[1] The prohibition of exposition is in strong contrast to Lutheran orders, in which Bible-reading is normally followed by exposition. At the same time it was announced that 'all ... portuises (i.e. breviaries) ... should be newly examined, corrected, reformed, and castigated from all manner of mention of the Bishop of Rome's name, from all apocryphas, feigned legends, superstitious orations (i.e. prayers), collects, versicles, and responses; and that the names and memories of all saints which be not mentioned in the Scripture, or authentical doctors, should be abolished'.[2]

The reform was at last fully carried out, after a change of sovereign, in 1549, with *The Book of Common Prayer*, a title which suggests that its contents were originally intended to be confined to the daily office. In this book the Anglican services of Mattins and Evensong make their first

---

[1] This expectation was in fact in accordance with normal practice in England in the later Middle Ages.

[2] Wilkins, *Concilia*, vol. 3, pp. 861–3.

official appearance, in what was to be their essential and permanent form, though they were subsequently to be expanded by additions at the beginning and end. Here Cranmer reverts to his first scheme in providing only two services, but Mattins is now made up of elements from Mattins, Lauds, and Prime, while Evensong is produced by fusing Vespers and Compline. The lesser hours once again disappear completely.

The orderly reading of Holy Scripture remains the chief function of the office, and is again carried out according to the civil calendar, but now there are only two lessons at Mattins, and again two at Evensong. This still allows for the great bulk of the OT to be read once a year, and the NT three times, except for Revelation, of which only two chapters are read. The number of holy days is reduced to twenty-five (apart from those dependent on Easter and Whitsun), but they are provided with proper lessons when suitable passages are available, and the lectionary is so arranged that after a holy day the *lectio continua* is resumed where it was left off without any omission, in contrast to modern practice, where the occurrence of a holy day causes a gap in the *lectio continua*. The Psalms are again spread over a month, but Cranmer now departs from the strict rule of saying three at each service, and instead aims at producing sixty approximately equal portions. Even so, twenty-six of them contain three psalms.

The whole service is now in English, and everything is said aloud. Much of the work of translation had already been done in *The Great Bible* (1538) and *The King's Primer* (1545), each of which summed up some fifteen years of work in its field. Anthems, responds, and invitatories are 'cut off', as promised in the Preface, and so now are all hymns, though Cranmer only abandoned these with reluctance, because of the difficulty of translation, being aware that his own verses lacked 'grace and facility'. The result of these omissions is to make the new service seem starkly bare and simple compared with the medieval rite. The longer lessons and the total absence of short sentences of scripture must have produced an impression of monotony on those who were accustomed to the rich variety of the Breviary, even in the debased form which was actually used; and this will have been only partially offset by a less frequent repetition of the Psalms.[1]

The central block of Psalms–Lesson–Canticle–Lesson–Canticle forms the classic Anglican pattern, differing alike from the Roman structure and from the Lutheran. The result was particularly felicitous at Evensong, with Magnificat placed as a sort of hinge between the OT and the NT, and old Simeon hailing the revelation of salvation in the NT

[1] Cf. the table in Cuming, *History*, p. 71, for the way in which Cranmer arrived at the order and content of the BCP offices.

lesson with Nunc dimittis. Cranmer's experiments had already brought him very near this pattern, and now his desire to give the two services an identical structure settled its final shape. Doubtless Quiñones had provided the original inspiration, and the Lutheran orders may also have made their contribution, but most probably Cranmer arrived at this pattern simply by putting into practice his principle of letting nothing interfere with the orderly reading of Holy Scripture. This is set forth at length in the Preface, a revised version of that in the first manuscript scheme, but now, of course, in English. The application of the principle removed a great deal of secondary material, and left the lessons and canticles standing next to each other.

It was not necessary to sacrifice all the secondary material. Cranmer kept several features which recur in most of the services: the Lord's Prayer and the traditional versicles by way of introduction, and the Kyrie and second Lord's Prayer as epilogue. To these he added the Apostles' Creed from Prime and Compline, the suffrages from the Bidding of the Bedes (as in the second manuscript scheme), the collect of the day from Lauds, and one memorial collect each from Lauds, Prime, Vespers, and Compline. As an afterthought, Quicunque vult was restored from Prime, but only on six days in the year. Despite the radical treatment of the structure, the services were entirely derived from the medieval service-books, and contained nothing that can have offended the most hardened traditionalist. There are, however, two notable omissions besides the cutting-off of antiphons and the like. One is the private repetition of 'Hail, Mary' before Mattins, Prime, and Compline, together with the memorials of St Mary at Lauds and Vespers. The other is the penitential section found in Prime and Compline.

The Marian devotions were never replaced, but the lack of any penitential section was remedied in 1552, when a lengthy form was prefixed to both Morning and Evening Prayer (as they were named in the *BCP* of that year). In Prime and Compline the confession and absolution come almost at the end of the service, but in Quiñones a confession is placed at the beginning of Mattins. However, in view of the markedly reformed character of the new material, it is more likely that its position was suggested by Martin Bucer's services for Strasbourg and Cologne, especially as the latter, unlike most reformed services, includes an absolution. The new section is a mosaic of phrases from Bucer, Peter Martyr, Poullain, à Lasco, and the Bible. Nevertheless, in the midst of all this, the compiler suddenly slips in a familiar phrase from the Breviary: 'But thou, Lord, have mercy upon us'. The section comprises sentences of Scripture, an exhortation setting forth the reasons for public worship, and forms of confession and absolution.

In the 1552 Book the obligation of saying the office was made explicit: where 1549 had merely said 'An Order for Mattins daily through the year', 1552 adds a direction 'All priests and deacons shall be bound to say daily the Morning and Evening Prayer, either privately or openly, except they be letted by preaching, studying of divinity, or by some other urgent cause'. At the same time, an attempt was made to encourage the attendance of the laity: parish priests are to toll a bell before the services 'that such as be disposed may come to hear God's word and to pray ...'; and the services are to be said 'in such place of the church ... as the people may best hear', rather than 'in the quire'. Thus the first steps were taken which ultimately led to making the office the chief religious exercise on Sundays of the laity of the Church of England.

Between 1559 and 1645 Mattins followed by the Litany and Ante-Communion became the standard Sunday morning service, while Evensong was said during the afternoon. There is not much evidence from this period as to how far the clergy complied with the requirement of daily recitation throughout the week. George Herbert 'brought most of his parishioners, and many gentlemen in the neighbourhood, constantly to make a part of his congregation twice a day'; but it may be that we are told this because it was exceptional. When the Litany was not said, the practice grew up of adding after the third collect the prayers printed after the Litany (the prayers for the King and the clergy, the 'Prayer of St Chrysostom', and the Grace). This practice was enjoined by rubric in the Scottish Book of 1637 , and the 1662 revisers carried the process a step further by printing the prayers at this point, with the addition of the prayer for the Royal Family. The Office was thus encased in sections of penitence and intercession, but still contained no provision for preaching. Hymns were not yet permitted within the service, though allowed by the Injunctions of 1559 before its beginning and after its end. This permission was unofficially extended in two ways: by singing the psalms in metrical versions to metrical tunes, and by the inclusion of more elaborate choral compositions, which soon acquired the name 'anthem'. After 1662 the addition of the 'State prayers' brought the anthem within the service, thus providing official sanction for the introduction of hymns. This became more and more common during the eighteenth century, and finally received judicial recognition in 1792; but no attempt was made to reintroduce hymns into the text of the Prayer Book.

By the beginning of the twentieth century, Mattins and Evensong had taken two forms: on Sundays the Prayer Book text was supplemented by hymns, a sermon, and a blessing; on weekdays the text would receive no additions, and might even be confined within its 1549 limits, omitting the penitential introduction and the 'State prayers'. There was also an increasing tendency to widen the scope of the latter section. This tendency was fully expressed in the abortive revision of 1928, when forty-five prayers from various sources were added for use in supplementing or replacing the 'State prayers'. At the same time seasonal introductory sentences were added, and an alternative exhortation, confession, and absolution were provided, though the core of the office remained almost untouched. Much of this work had been pioneered by the Scottish Episcopal Church. The lectionary was reconstituted on the basis of the church year, and forms of Prime and Compline were printed in an appendix, the latter service having been widely, if unofficially, revived.

The passing of the Prayer Book (Alternative and Other Services) Measure (1965) led to the issue of Morning and Evening Prayer in a slightly revised form, authorized in 1967 ('Series Two'). Sentences are kept, but there is no exhortation, and the confession and absolution are new. In 1963 a Joint Liturgical Group had been formed, on which all the major Churches of the British Isles were eventually represented, and in 1968 it produced an ecumenical *Daily Office*. A new lectionary was provided, with shorter daily portions, the OT being spread over two years, and the NT over one. The evening office has only one lesson; the Psalter is recited four times a year instead of twelve; and each weekday service has its own canticle. There is no penitential section in the morning office, and only one invariable collect for each service. The intercessions are arranged on a completely new and less formal pattern, in place of the traditional series of collect-form prayers. This Office was adopted by the Church of England with minor alterations as an alternative to the traditional form: it bore the title *Morning and Evening Prayer, Second Series (Revised)* and was authorized in 1971; a version in modern English ('Series Three') was authorized in 1975.

7 The Office
in the Lutheran, Reformed,
and Free Churches

D. H. TRIPP

The first reformed offices to emerge from the Reformation, as has been said above, were Lutheran. Luther's *Deutsche Messe* of 1526 includes directions for rudimentary morning and evening services made up of psalms, a chapter from the OT at Vespers and the NT at Mattins (in both Latin and German), a German hymn at Mattins and a Latin hymn and Magnificat at Vespers, the Lord's Prayer (privately), a collect, and *Benedicamus Domino*.[1] A similar pattern was enjoined by Johann Bugenhagen in his forms for North Germany (e.g. Brunswick 1528), though he restores the *preces* before the collect; in the monastic section of his Order for Denmark (1537) he anticipates the Book of Common Prayer in joining Compline to Vespers.[2] Brandenburg–Nürnberg (1533) has an interesting conflation with the synaxis of the Mass, for use when there is to be no communion, consisting of psalms, epistle, hymn, gospel, Te Deum, and three collects.[3] The otherwise unimportant Order for Calenberg-Göttingen achieves an 'early service' (*Frühmesse*) very similar to Cranmer's Mattins: versicles, Venite, psalms, OT or NT lesson, Te Deum, NT lessons, Benedictus, collect, and *Benedicamus Domino*.[4] Many of the Lutheran *Kirchenordnungen* follow Luther's pattern, some experiment in combining services (as Cranmer did later), and some make no provision at all.[5]

Put forward as a collection of interesting suggestions, the Lutheran revision of the office in Germany soon fell into disuse, except in some Pietistic circles. Scandinavian Lutherans had more considered forms of the office, but these were abandoned in the early seventeenth century (Sweden, 1614). It is important to note that, for both Lutheran and Reformed Churches, the devotional function of the office was transferred to the Christian home and to the study (which was also an oratory) of the Christian pastor, as well as to the school.

The Lutheran office had fallen into neglect long before Frederick William III of Prussia (1797–1840) tried to arouse interest in it as in all

[1] E. Sehling, *Evangelische Kirchenordnungen*, vol. 1.
[2] Ibid., vol. 6 (i).
[3] Ibid., vol. 11.
[4] Ibid., vol. 6 (ii).
[5] This paragraph was supplied by Dr G. J. Cuming.

liturgical matters. It was, however, inevitable that a living Christian community should eventually produce some version of the office, and this occurred in the midst of the Lutheran revival of the second half of the nineteenth century. Forms of morning and evening prayer were devised by Theodor Kliefoth in northern Germany and by the Bavarian Wilhelm Löhe, the founder of the great 'Home Mission' movement, of a deaconess order and of a major programme of social work, of which Neuendettelsau is the centre. This last case is symptomatic of the way in which the office repeatedly asserts its vitality in the context of religious orders.

It is impossible to divide the different traditions clearly here, for most of the new Protestant religious houses, and their rites likewise, are the fruits of ecumenical contacts. Some of the new communities use a very simple type of office: the Brethren of Common Life in Reformed Switzerland and Lutheran Bavaria; the Imshausen Community near Bebra; the *Christusbruderschaft* at Selbitz in Upper Franconia (Bavaria). Fuller versions are used by the Evangelical Sisters of Mary at Darmstadt (in a United Evangelical area, founded under the spiritual direction of a Methodist), and also by the sisters of the Castell Circle in the Schwanberg Castle near Kitzingen (the headquarters of the Christian Girl Guides of Bavaria) as well as by the French communities at Grandchamp and Pomeyrol.[1]

The best known Protestant religious community is that of Taizé in Burgundy. The Taizé Office (published as *L'Office de Taizé* in 1963, in ET in 1966, and in a revised form as *Louange des Jours* in 1971) has a simple ground-plan but also extensive provision for seasonal and optional adaptation. Terce, Sext, None, and Compline are simplified versions of the corresponding elements in the old Roman secular breviary. There is a form of Vigil for the eves of Sundays and feasts. The principal hours are the morning and evening offices, each of which follows the basic order: Introduction–Psalmody–Readings–Homily or Silence–Responsory–Hymn–Versicle–Prayers–Blessing. Seasonal propers affect the content of the offices in great detail, and there is no recurrent Psalter throughout the whole year as in the Roman rite. The material is from many sources, and much is of new composition.

Practical and creative interest in the office is not confined to monastic circles, and versions for more general use are by no means unknown. The Swiss group '*Eglise et Liturgie*' have produced an *Office divin de chaque jour*, edited by R. Paquier and A. Bardet, issued in 1953 (Neuchâtel; 3rd edn 1961). Not dissimilar are the *Stundengebet* of the Brotherhood of St

---

[1] A convenient summary in English of the major examples will be found in Olive Wyon, *Living Springs* (SCM 1963), ch. 3.

Michael (3rd edn Kassel 1953) and the *Allgemeine evangelische Gebetbuch* (1955), which closely resemble the day hours of the new Roman *Liturgy of the Hours*. They lack, however, the Office of Readings, and the readings in the day hours are substantial. Again comparable, but closer to the older Roman Breviary, are the *Gebetsgottesdienste* issued as the second volume of *Agende für evangelisch-lutherische Gemeinden* (Berlin 1960). It is noteworthy that at least this last version of the office has been adopted for domestic use by devout Lutheran families. In similar ways, Lutheran traditions of the office have been effectively revived in Sweden (*Tidegärd*, Peters and Adell) and in Denmark (Monrad–Moller's *Tidebog*).[1]

The Free Churches properly so called have their origin in the radical wing of the Protestant Reformation. Most worship in this tradition has been free from prescribed forms, the governing liturgical principle being dependence on the guidance of the individual believer by the Holy Spirit, without recourse to traditional or regulated structures such as the divine office. This principle has always been preserved within the Free Church traditions, even where the Churches concerned are 'Free' in that wider sense that embraces Presbyterian or Connexional (Methodist) varieties of church life. Churches of these latter types, which have always included established liturgical systems within their practice, have in Anglo-Saxon Christianity and elsewhere come to be classed with the Free Churches, so that the phenomenon of the 'Free Church' is by no means simple or uniform.

The radical wing of the Reformation owes much to the movements of dissent which flourished before the sixteenth century. This may explain why Anabaptist and similar groups seem not to have considered the office as patient of revision or purification. Their normal or non-sacramental worship was a free composition of extempore prayer and Bible-reading with exposition.

English Puritan Churchmen of the sixteenth and seventeenth centuries, other than Independents, were inclined to revise the office rather than to abandon it, as witness the conferences at Hampton Court and the Savoy.[2] The failure to achieve complete comprehension at the Restoration and the subsequent sundering of traditions after the upheavals of the Stuart period resulted in a Dissent that had no place for the Book of Common Prayer. In such a setting the office was reduced to

---

[1] For Sweden see *SL* 1 (1962), p. 74f.
[2] See E. C. Ratcliff, 'The Savoy Conference and the Revision of the Book of Common Prayer' in Nuttall and Chadwick, *From Uniformity to Unity* (SPCK 1962), pp. 89–148; A. G. Matthews, 'The Puritans' in N. Micklem, *Christian Worship* (Clarendon Press 1936), ch. 9; H. Davies, *Worship and Theology in England. I, 1534–1603* (Princeton and OUP 1970), esp. chs. 7 and 9.

freely formulated private devotions, and every congregational service was now a service of preaching, with or without the addition of the Lord's Supper. As Puritan Christianity was driven by events into cultural isolation on the same terms as Independency, so its liturgical life changed accordingly.

At various times in the eighteenth and nineteenth centuries, individual Congregational ministers produced variants of the Anglican office for local use. Their duration and influence seem to have been slight, but one recurrent fact may be noticed. Apart from a renewed interest in psalmody, which is largely inspired by the example of Anglican worship, the influence of the Church of England's office may be seen in the Free Church habit of using a sermon, usually with two accompanying hymns, as the last section of a service. The older tradition was to place the sermon in the middle of the service, after the scripture lesson: so it was given a central but not isolated place in the scheme. The Anglican custom of attaching a sermon at the end of Morning or Evening Prayer (to which preaching was extraneous before the current revisions) encouraged an imitative tendency in Free Church circles, so that the sermon took on the appearance of a climax, to which the readings and prayers were merely 'preliminaries'. Other details of the Anglican office have influenced Reformed and Free Church preaching-services, from Osterwald (Neuchâtel 1713) and Bersier (Paris 1874) to the recent service-books for English Baptist and Congregational Churches.[1]

Within the Congregationalist development we note the place of John Hunter's *Devotional Services for Public Worship* (8th edn Dent 1903). Hunter's orders for Sunday and weekday use, if employed systematically, would produce a Reformed equivalent of Luther's scheme. The general outline of each service is that of the Anglican office, with longer introductory intercessory prayers (at least most of them written by Hunter), and with provision for a sermon and hymns as an integral part of the worship, usually as its climax.

Hunter's book was very influential, chiefly as an ideas-book for Free Church ministers who wanted to enlarge their liturgical vocabulary; it had the virtue of being thoroughly identifiable with the tradition within which it was to be used. More enigmatic was the *Divine Service* (OUP 1919) of Dr W. E. Orchard, Hunter's successor as minister at the King's Weigh House in London. Orchard's office contains much more material of Anglican or Roman origin. His ten Sunday morning and evening services assume a *pensum* of Psalms for each day, and the outline of

---

[1] See A. E. Peaston and W. D. Maxwell, *The Book of Common Prayer.* . . . See also H. Davies, *Worship and Theology in England* (OUP and Princeton) vols. IV (1962) and V (1965), chapters on Free Churches.

Cranmer's Common Prayer is clearly to be seen, despite the great quantity of new or newly edited matter fitted into it. As 'Daily Offices' Orchard offered simplified versions of Prime, Vespers, and Compline from the Latin Breviary. Heavily influenced by Orchard is a very similar collection of material in *A Free Church Book of Common Prayer* (Dent 1929), which, however, omits the Roman Vespers, and in its Sunday office moves the psalms to a position between the lessons.

The Scots Churches, developing the ideas and resources made available by the Church Service Society, have produced new versions of the office. Movement in this direction began with the Society's *Euchologion* (1867) and *Daily Offices* (1893), and continued in the United Free Church's *Book of Common Order* (1928) and the Church of Scotland's *Prayers for Divine Service* (1929).[1] In recent years a new ordered form of daily worship has grown up to answer the needs of the Iona Community whose members gather for spiritual renewal in prayer and work on the island.

The only English Free Church attempt to create a new form of the office *qua* office is in Dr Nathaniel Micklem's *Prayers and Praises* (Hodder and Stoughton 1941, 1954). In morning and evening devotions there appears a seven-part order: invitatory; psalm; hymn; reading; prayers; hymn; doxology. Its catholic dignity and evangelical simplicity make this the most valuable Free Church contribution in the field of the office.

The Free Churches have had a hand in the compilation of the proposals of the British Joint Liturgical Group (see p. 395), and there is some interest in the Taizé Office and the new Roman Liturgy of the Hours. On both sides of the Atlantic there is considerable appreciation of a Lutheran product, a daily office designed explicitly for the private use of the clergy, J. W. Doberstein's *The Minister's Prayer Book* (1959, British edn Collins 1964). The plan of this is similar to Micklem's, except that there is less use of hymnody, the readings are solely biblical in the morning, but include a more modern text in the evening, and there is added a noon-tide devotion. This last is made up of: invitatory; hymn for the week; text for the week; spiritual reading on some aspect of the ministry; prayer and benediction.

Of the Free Churches (in a wider sense), Methodism has been closest to the Anglican tradition in respect to the office. The Wesleys and their clerical colleagues, being in Anglican orders, were subject to and observant of the rubrics as to daily recitation of the Common Prayer. Wesley's lay itinerant helpers were not so bound, either by Anglican Canon Law or by Methodist legislation, but they were expected to follow

[1] See W. D. Maxwell, *An Outline of Christian Worship* (OUP 1936), pp. 168–70.

a discipline of scriptural, patristic, and other devotional reading, with prayer and meditation attached, as is explained in Questions 29 and 48 of the *Large Minutes* (to be found in editions of Wesley's *Works*). Methodist congregations were expected to take part in the worship of their parish churches, their distinctive services being supplementary to this. When, after Wesley's death, Methodists became more and more independent of the Anglican parish structure, they were encouraged by the Conference to use at least an abridgement of the Anglican office, or, at the very least, the lessons from it.

This 'abridgement' was the form of the office included in Wesley's Sunday Service (1784 and many later edns to 1936). In America, these versions of Morning and Evening Prayer fell almost at once into desuetude. In Britain and the Empire, Evening Prayer soon became very rare. Morning Prayer has been used in Wesleyan churches, albeit in increasingly fewer places, to the present day. It has also been adopted in some places since the union of the British Methodist denominations in 1932, especially where West Indian Methodists are numerous. In Wesley's prayer book *The Sunday Service*, in both Morning and Evening Prayer the Lord's Prayer is said only once (after the absolution), the canticles are replaced by their Prayer Book alternatives (Pss. 100, 98, and 67) although Te Deum is retained, and the Prayer for All Conditions of Men and the General Thanksgiving are incorporated into the closing prayers. Venite is omitted from Morning Prayer. In 1882 (*Public Prayers and Services*, used until 1936), Venite and Benedictus were restored, the Prayer for the High Court of Parliament was added to the closing prayers of Morning Prayer, and Evening Prayer was omitted altogether. The Nicene Creed was added as an alternative to the Apostles', for use when the communion was to follow. This version of Morning Prayer was retained in the 1936 *Book of Offices*. The less frequently used and now largely forgotten *Divine Worship* (1935) offered a variety of responsive services, comparable with, and in an appreciable measure derived from, the Anglican office. Throughout this process, the use of psalmody has decreased, the number used at any single service being now one psalm proper to the day, and the available selection being restricted to the fifty psalms at the end of the *Methodist Hymn Book* (1933). In 1975, the unofficial Methodist Sacramental Fellowship published *Forms for the Divine Office*, which comprised both 'private' and 'communal' orders for a 'primary' and a 'second' office each day.[1]

From the middle of the nineteenth century, attempts to produce ecumenical liturgies have been made, mostly with little effect. The

[1] See further A. R. George, 'Private devotion in the Methodist tradition' in *SL* 2 (1963), pp. 223–36, and G. S. Wakefield, *Methodist Devotion* (Epworth 1966).

Catholic Apostolic Church, the rite of which reached its final state about 1880 after forty years of growth, possessed an office consisting of Morning, Fore-noon, Afternoon, and Evening Prayer, derived from various sources. Its interest is chiefly in the attention to ancient sources which it aroused in Free Church, Church of Scotland, and Lutheran circles.

A collection of 'Orders for Morning and Evening Worship' was issued by the Church of South India in 1958, and in a revised form incorporated into the *Book of Common Worship* which the Synod authorized in 1962. The needs both of a daily congregational non-eucharistic worship and also of a daily office, at least for the clergy, are here catered for. The first order is simply the Ante-Communion, or Liturgy of the Word, of the South Indian Eucharist. The second order is in essence the English Common Prayer, with such additions as seasonal introductory sentences and a variable doxological section before the confession (distantly reminiscent of the East Syrian *Lakhumara*), and numerous alterations in detail. By great dexterity, both morning and evening orders are combined in one text. A sermon may follow the second canticle, before the creed. The third order is typical of British Free Church adaptations of the Anglican office. Sentences, prayers of adoration and confession, and a hymn introduce two lessons (OT and NT), which are themselves separated by the psalms or psalm of the day. A canticle or lyric leads into the creed and the intercessions and thanksgivings, which end with the Lord's Prayer. Hymns and prayers of dedication and benediction conclude the service. A sermon may precede the creed or follow the hymn after the Lord's Prayer. The Psalter is recited essentially in course (except on Sundays and various special days), over a two-month cycle. Two Psalters are provided, one virtually complete, the other more selective.

The great Churches of the Reformation have been rediscovering their inheritance in the office; the Free Churches and in some measure the 'Younger Churches' have been assimilating the value of having an office of a formal kind; there is yet to begin a thorough dialogue on the profound problems about the nature and principles of this area of worship which have aroused discussion among Roman Catholics. Without such dialogue, even the course of development so far must remain significantly incomplete.[1]

[1] For examples of recent discussions of the Office, see J. A. Lamb, 'The liturgical use of the Psalter' in *SL* 3 (1964), pp. 65–77; the exchanges between W. van der Syde and J. D. F. Anido in *SL* 4 (1965) no. 3, and 5 (1966) nos. 1 and 3; W. J. Grisbrooke, in *SL* 8 (1971–2) no. 3, and 9 (1973) nos. 1 and 3; D. H. Tripp, 'Ecumenical notes on the new Breviary' in *One in Christ* 8 (1972) no. 4.

VI

THE CALENDAR

1 The History
of the Christian Year

PETER G. COBB

GENERAL

Denis-Boulet, N. M., (ET) *The Christian Calendar*, Faith and Fact Books. Burns Oates 1960.
McArthur, A. A., *The Evolution of the Christian Year*. SCM 1953.
Weiser, F. X., *Handbook of Christian Feasts and Customs*. New York 1958.

THE WEEK

Sunday

Rordorf, W., (ET) *Sunday* (SCM 1968) (with extensive bibliography).
Rordorf, W., *Sabbat und Sonntag in der Alten Kirche* (Traditio Christiana 2). Zürich 1972.

THE PASCHA

'Festum festorum' (St Leo, *Sermo* 47 *in Exodum*).

HOLY WEEK

Davies, J. G., *Holy Week. A Short History* (Ecumenical Studies in Worship No. 11). Lutterworth 1963.
Greenacre, R., *The Sacrament of Easter* (Studies in Christian Worship 4). Faith Press 1965.
O'Shea, W. J., *The Meaning of Holy Week*. Collegeville Minnesota 1958.
Schmidt, H. A. P., *Hebdomada Sancta*, 2 vols. Rome 1956–7 (with bibliography).
LMD 41 (1955), *La semaine sainte*; 45 (1956), *Restauration de la semaine sainte*; 67–8 (1961), *La liturgie du mystère pascal*.

PENTECOST: THE FIFTY DAYS OF EASTER

Cabié, R., *La penecôte: L'évolution de la cinquantaine pascale au cours des cinq premiers siècles*. Tournai 1965.
Gunstone, J., *The Feast of Pentecost* (Studies in Christian Worship 8). Faith Press 1967.

THE CHRISTMAS/EPIPHANY CYCLE

Botte, B., *Les origines de la noël et de l'épiphanie*. Louvain 1932.
Botte, B. et al., *Noël-épiphanie, retour du Christ* (LO 40). Paris 1967.

Gunstone, J., *Christmas and Epiphany* (Studies in Christian Worship 9). Faith Press 1967.

LMD 59 (1959), *Avent, Noël, Épiphanie.*

RECENT REFORMS OF THE CHRISTIAN YEAR

Jasper, R. C. D., ed., *The Calendar and Lectionary: a Reconsideration by the Joint Liturgical Group.* OUP 1967.

McArthur, A. A., *The Christian Year and Lectionary Reform.* SCM 1958.

THE WEEK

SUNDAY

The Lord's Day, in the words of the Second Vatican Council, is 'the foundation and nucleus of the whole liturgical year' (*Constitution on the Sacred Liturgy*, 106). It was on 'the first day of the week', according to the Jewish calendar, that our Lord rose from the dead (Mk. 16.2 and parallels) and it was no doubt for this reason that his followers met every eighth day for common, and almost certainly eucharistic, worship thereafter (cf. Jn. 20.26). St Paul takes it for granted that Christians will meet every first day of the week (1 Cor. 16.2), and the author of Acts speaks of such an occasion in stereotyped phraseology (Acts 20.7). 'The first day of the week' continued to be the usual expression for Sunday in Syriac-speaking circles but it was superseded by 'the Lord's day' in Greek-speaking communities very early on (Rev. 1.10; Ignatius, *ad Magnes.* 9.1; *Didache*, 14.1) and by its equivalent '*Dominica*' in the Latin West (Tertullian, *de Cor.* 3.4). Justin Martyr, about the year 150, alludes to weekly eucharistic worship in terms of the pagan week in which each day had a tutelary planet: 'On the day of the sun, all who live in towns or in the country gather together in one place...' (1 *Apol.* 67), and the Emperor Constantine, in making the Christian day of worship a civil day of rest in 321, referred to it as '*dies solis*' (Eusebius, *Vita Const.* 4.18).

The earliest reason given for celebrating Sunday is that it is the day of the resurrection (*Ep. of Barnabas*, 15.9), but in the Jewish understanding of the week the first day commemorated creation and this idea was taken over even by Gentile Christians: 'We assemble on the day of the sun because it is the first day, that on which God transformed the darkness and matter to create the world, and also because Jesus Christ our Saviour rose from the dead on the same day' (Justin, 1 *Apol.* 67). From early on too, Sunday has strong eschatological overtones: it is also the eighth day 'on which God inaugurated a new world' (*Ep. of Barnabas*, 15.8), 'the image of the age to come' (Basil, *de Spir. Sanct.* 27); it 'prefigures eternal rest' (Augustine). Later writers tended to multiply the number of historical events which Sunday commemorated. Thus Theodulf, one of the leading Carolingian reformers, in his Capitular to the clergy about 800, a book which circulated widely in the Middle Ages, wrote: 'On it God established light; on it he rained manna in the wilderness; on it the Redeemer of the human race voluntarily rose from the dead for our salvation; on it he poured out the Holy Spirit upon his disciples...' (*Capit.* 24; PL 105.198).

We do not know of a Sunday on which the Eucharist was not celebrated. Attendance at the weekly assembly was regarded as obligatory even in times of persecution: 'We have to celebrate the Lord's Day. It is our rule.' 'We could not live without celebrating the Lord's Day.' Such is the witness of the martyrs of Abitina (*Bibliographica hagiographica latina*, n. 7492) and Chrysostom says 'To abstain from this meal is to separate oneself from the Lord: the Sunday meal is that which we take in common with the Lord and with the brethren.' (*in Epist.* 1 *ad Cor. Hom.* 27; PG 61.227). It was always a day of joy (*Didascalia*, 21; Connolly, p. 178); no one was allowed to fast (Tertullian, *de Cor.* 3; Cassian, *Institutes*, 2.18) or to kneel (Tertullian, *de Orat.* 23; Canon 20 of Council of Nicaea). It became a day of rest after 321 when Constantine closed the law-courts and stopped the crafts working on it. It was *the* Christian festival. It was reckoned after the Jewish manner as starting from dusk on the Sabbath (Cassian, ibid.; Augustine, *Ep.* 36 *ad Casulanum*) and, because of its unique importance, developed a vigil office (cf. Acts 20.7–10). This is attested in the East by Egeria in the fourth century (24.8–11) and in the West by various Frankish councils from the sixth century. Popular participation in this vigil has always been more marked among the Orthodox, particularly the Russians, than in the West. In Rome ordinations anciently took place during the Sunday vigil (*Ap. Trad.* 2; Leo, *Ep.* 9, *ad Dioscurum*). Baptisms, when they no longer took place only at the Easter or Pentecost vigil as they did in the time of Tertullian (*de Bapt.* 19) and Hippolytus (*Ap. Trad.* 20), were usually on a Sunday, and it is because of this that the rite of *Asperges*, widespread in the West since the ninth or tenth century, has always been confined to Sunday.

From the ninth century certain saints' days were allowed to take precedence over the Sunday in the West and the Book of Common Prayer continued this tradition. In the modern Roman Church this reached enormous proportions until a reverse trend was inaugurated by Pius X in 1911. The East has maintained the privileged position of Sunday more consistently; only a few feasts, and those connected with the 'mysteries of Christ' are celebrated on a Sunday. The Protestant Churches have usually confined their corporate worship to Sundays and consequently celebrate the Epiphany and the Ascension, for example, on the nearest Sunday. Often, however, their Sundays are given over to special observances, Education Day, Family Day, and such like, which in traditional terms would be called Votives (see C. Seidenspinner, *Great Protestant Festivals* (New York 1952)).

THE SABBATH

Although Sunday seems to have superseded the Sabbath completely as the weekly day of worship within the first generation of Christians, there are hints in the NT and elsewhere that there were Judaizing groups within the Church who wanted to observe the Sabbath (Col. 2.16; cf. Gal. 4.10f., Eusebius, *HE* 3.27). The Sabbath was accorded a certain privileged place in the week: it was 'a day never to be kept as a fast except in the Passover season' (Tertullian, *de Ieiun.* 14; Egeria, 27.1), and by the middle of the fourth century it was a day on which the Eucharist was regularly celebrated in certain areas (*Test. Dom.* 1.22; Cassian, *Institutes*, 3.2) even during Lent (Canon 49 of Council of Laodicea *c*. 363; Egeria, 27.8). For centuries the Church in Rome and North Africa resisted the innovation of a liturgical Sabbath and went to the opposite extreme of making it a fast day, but that they were in a minority is shown by the fact that the historian Socrates, in the mid-fifth century, thought they had ceased to observe an ancient tradition by not having a Saturday celebration (*HE* 5.22). In the West, at least from the time of Alcuin (d. 804) the Saturday Mass has been a Votive of our Lady (L. Gougaud, (ET) *Devotional and Ascetic Practices in the Middle Ages* (Burns Oates 1927), pp. 66–74).

WEDNESDAY AND FRIDAY

The early Christians set aside two days of the week as fast-days after the tradition of the Jews but on different days from theirs, Wednesday and Friday instead of Monday and Thursday (*Didache* 8.1; Tertullian, *de Orat.* 19; *de Jejun.* 2). By the middle of the third century, a historical reason had been adduced for the choice of the particular days: Wednesday because it is the day of the Lord's betrayal, and Friday because it is that of his crucifixion (*Didascalia*, 21; Connolly, pp. 180–4). In the West the fasts became abstinences and then the Wednesday one disappeared altogether except in Lent. In the event only the Ember Days preserved the ancient ascetic character of Wednesdays and Fridays.

From their inception, the Wednesday and Friday fast-days may have been marked by a liturgical synaxis: it is said to have been so in Origen's time (Socrates, *HE*, 5.22) and it was certainly the case in Rome under Leo the Great. The natural development of celebrating the Eucharist on them seems to have taken place first in the East (Basil, *Ep.* 93 to Caesaria; *Egeria*, 27.5–7).

It was no doubt because of the character of these days, both privileged and penitential, that Gregory the Great during the barbarian invasions suggested that the Sicilian bishops should order a litany of intercession to be sung every Wednesday and Friday (*Registrum Epistolarum*, 11, Ep. 31; Ewald and Hartmann, 2.301). In medieval England these days were marked by the singing of a litany, usually in procession, and Cranmer continued the tradition in the BCP.

THE EASTER CYCLE (see plate 18)

Originally, when this Feast of Feasts emerges into the light of history in the second century, it is a unitive commemoration of the death and resurrection of our Lord, a nocturnal celebration of a single night, constituting the Christian Passover. It was also, or soon became, the normal occasion for converts to be initiated into the Christian Mystery (Tertullian, *de Bapt.* 19). Thus it combined the commemoration of both the death and the resurrection of Christ and the celebration of both baptism and the Eucharist.

It is the only feast of the Christian Year which can plausibly claim to go back to apostolic times.[1] This for two reasons: first that it must derive from a time when Jewish influence was effective, i.e. during the first century A.D., because it depends on the lunar calendar (every other feast depends on the solar calendar); and, second, that for three centuries the Church tolerated its celebration on different days, in Asia on 14 Nisan, elsewhere on the Sunday after 14 Nisan, because it was acknowledged that there was apostolic authority for both. (For the Quartodeciman controversy see Eusebius, *HE* 5.23–5; Socrates, *HE* 5.22; Epiphanius, *con. Haer.* 1). It has been held, on the basis of 1 Cor. 5.7, that St Paul knew of it but the allusion is too isolated to build much on.

At first the vigil was preceded by a single day's fast, the only day of the year when 'the religious duty of fasting is general and as it were official' (Tertullian, *de Orat.* 18; cf. *ad Uxorem* 2.4), but when every Friday became a half-day fast, the one before the Pascha naturally became extended and an integral part of the Paschal fast. Irenaeus tells us, 'Some think they ought to fast one day, others two, others even more, some count their day as forty hours, day and night. And such variations of observance did not begin in our own time, but much earlier in the time of our predecessors' (Eusebius, *HE* 5.24), and although by the time of Hippolytus, a two-day fast had become the accepted rule (*Ap. Trad.* 20.7,

[1] But see M. Richard, 'La question pascale au 2ᵉ siècle', *L'Orient Syrien*, 6 (1961), pp. 179–212.

407

29.2) the Saturday fast still retained a certain pre-eminence. The third century saw the extension of the fast, at least for the pious, from two days to six (*Didascalia* 21; Connolly, pp. 189–90) and the introduction, at least in some places, of a vigil on the Friday as well as the Saturday night (*Didascalia*, ibid.; *Test. Dom.* 2.12).

By the end of the fourth century, probably in large part on account of the influence of Cyril of Jerusalem,[1] Good Friday was widely kept as the commemoration of the cross. It was marked in Jerusalem by the veneration of the relic of the cross during the morning and by a three-hour service of readings and hymns from midday to 3 o'clock in the afternoon (*Egeria*, 37.1–7). Chrysostom, preaching in Antioch in 388, speaks of 'the day of the cross' on which the passages from the Gospels relevant to the cross were read; and Augustine in 400, following St Ambrose,[2] writes of the *Triduum*, 'the three most sacred days'. 'The observance of these days has been enjoined ... by Councils ... and the whole Christian world has arrived unanimously at the persuasion that this is the proper mode of observing the Pascha' (*Ep.* 55.14.24, 27). Fifty years later, however, Leo the Great's sermons show that Good Friday was still unknown in Rome.

(1) HOLY WEEK

Palm Sunday

The distinctive feature of Palm Sunday in fourth-century Jerusalem was the palm procession from the Mount of Olives back into the city which took place in the afternoon (*Egeria* 31). This was imitated first in Spain in the fifth century and then in Gaul by the seventh. It was known in England at the turn of the century; Aldhelm in 709 mentions the singing of Hosanna (*de Laud. Virg.*, PL 89.103): and finally it was accepted in Rome itself in the twelfth century. Primitively it always began at some place outside the main church; at Canterbury, for example, it began at the parish church of St Martin and made its way to the cathedral with a station at the city gate. In the early Middle Ages its focus seems to have been the Gospel book but that was later supplemented by relics and finally, in England and Normandy at least, by the Host itself. In Germany the Palmesel, a wooden ass on wheels, bearing on its back the figure of the Saviour, was used.

Maundy Thursday

This, as J. G. Davies remarked, is 'one of the most complex days of the whole ecclesiastical year'. It is a combination of three elements: the

---

[1] See Dix, *Shape*, pp. 349ff.
[2] *Ep.* 23.12–13.

commemoration of the Last Supper, the reconciliation of penitents, and various preparatory rites for the Holy Saturday baptisms, notably the consecration of the oils. The footwashing took place on Holy Saturday in Milan at the time of Ambrose (*de Sac.* 3.4, 5, 7) and that is possibly its original position. Maundy Thursday was the first weekday in Holy Week to have a Eucharist. In Jerusalem in the fourth century in fact there were two according to Egeria (35) and such was the case in Africa in Augustine's time. In the Roman and Sarum tradition there was only one, although the Gelasian Sacramentary has three.

GOOD FRIDAY

The two most striking features of the Good Friday liturgy in the West are the Veneration of the Cross and communion from the reserved sacrament, the so-called Mass of the Pre-Sanctified. For the former we are probably indebted to the liturgical genius of Cyril of Jerusalem. Egeria gives a vivid description of it (37.1–3). The dissemination of relics of the true cross led to its adoption in the West; it was known, for example, in Rome in the eighth century. Ironically it disappeared from the Jerusalem rite at the beginning of the seventh century when the city was sacked by the Persians, but was transferred in a new form to 14th September, the Feast of the Exaltation of the Cross. Alone of the Eastern rites, the Syrian has preserved it.

The Mass of the Pre-Sanctified can in some ways be said to go back at least to the second century. On weekdays when no mass was celebrated the people communicated from the reserved sacrament at home. It is not known when the custom was transferred to church but the earliest documentary evidence for it is from the beginning of the seventh century from Constantinople. The Orthodox now have the Mass of the Pre-Sanctified every Wednesday and Friday evening in Lent but not on Good Friday itself. In the eighth century in Rome there was still no communion at the papal liturgy although there was in the suburban churches. Strangely, what must have been a provision to meet the demands of the faithful for communion was restricted at the beginning of the thirteenth century to the celebrant alone, although in some countries, in Germany and Spain for example, general communion continued.

HOLY SATURDAY AND EASTER EVE

The most primitive feature of Holy Saturday, as we have seen (p. 407), is the total fast that was kept on that day. It was a completely aliturgical day: the Eucharist was never celebrated in either East or West.

The celebration of the Pascha began with a lengthy vigil. 'Watch all night in prayers, supplications, the reading of the prophets, of the Gospel and of psalms in fear and trembling and continual supplication until three in the morning...' (*Didascalia*, 21; Connolly, p. 189). This vigil is 'the mother of all vigils' to quote St Augustine (*Sermo* 219), no fewer than twenty-three of whose sermons for the occasion have survived. During it the whole history of salvation is rehearsed in readings and song. In the Byzantine rite the readings still take place during the Saturday afternoon. Originally the entire Passion may have been read. This was certainly the case at Rome in the fifth century and at Antioch at the end of the fourth. The Vigil culminated in the joyous celebration of the Eucharist after midnight.

In the course of time the vigil, at least in the West, developed three new features: the baptism of catechumens, the lighting and blessing of the paschal candle and the blessing of the new fire. Easter Eve was the time *par excellence* for baptism as early as Tertullian (see p. 91), but it was only in the fourth century that the number of baptisms of adults was very large. The baptismal theme was preserved in the Western rites by the continuance of the blessing of the font but was lost in the East as the font was blessed each time baptisms were performed. The revised Roman Holy Week rites (1955) include the striking innovation of an annual renewal of baptismal promises at the vigil on the part of the whole congregation.

The blessing of light stems ultimately from the Jewish blessing of the lamp on the eve of the Sabbath, which was taken over by the Christians (e.g. *Ap. Trad.* 26.18). The blessing of the Paschal candle was popular in the West and is found in Africa, Spain, Gaul, and Italy from the fourth and fifth centuries, but the papal liturgy until the eleventh century began with the readings. More and more honour was paid to the single candle used by the lectors at the Easter vigil; elaborate praises of it, *laus cerei*, survive from the end of the fourth century, the *Exultet* of the present Roman rite being a Gallican version (see plate 22); a cross was to be inscribed on it according to the 'Gelasian' Sacramentary and the insertion of five grains of incense to represent the five wounds of Christ was common from the fourteenth century.

The blessing of the new fire and the procession of light were originally distinct from the blessing of the candle. Egeria mentions the carrying of fire from the Holy Sepulchre into the church at the beginning of the weekly Saturday vigil (24.4), but no significance is attached to the striking of new fire. The ceremonial blessing of new fire on Easter Eve comes about in N. Europe, some crediting it to St Patrick (L. Gougaud, *Christianity in Celtic Lands* (Sheed and Ward 1932), pp. 279ff), but there is evidence of such a blessing of fire in Jerusalem itself.

(2) PENTECOST
THE FIFTY DAYS OF EASTER

The fifty days of Easter constitute the oldest season of the Church's year, corresponding to the Jewish 'feast of Pentecost which is the holy feast of seven weeks' (Tob. 2.1; see p. 51) from the Feast of Unleavened Bread to the Feast of First Fruits. Tertullian refers to it several times (*de Orat.* 23.2; *de Idol.* 14.7; *de Bapt.* 19.2; *de Ieiun.* 14.2). It is a fifty-day long Sunday—the Latin version of St Athanasius' letters actually calls it *magna dominica*, the great Sunday—and consequently neither fasting nor kneeling was allowed during it (Tertullian, *de Cor.* 3.4; *Egeria*, 41; Nicaea, Can. 20).

The Ascension was commemorated on either Easter Day itself following the Lucan and Johannine narratives (Lk. 24.50–3; Jn. 20.21f; *Ep. of Barnabas* 15.9; Aristides, *Apology* 2; Tertullian, *adv. Jud.* 13, but cf. *Apol.* 21) or the fiftieth day (Eusebius, *de Sol. Pasch.*, PG 24.699). It was not until the second half of the fourth century that the Ascension was commemorated as an historical event on the fortieth day and the gift of the Spirit on the fiftieth. These commemorations resulted from various tendencies: the influence of the chronology of Acts (see, for example, John Cassian, *Collatio* 21.20; PL 49.1194); the development of the theology of the Spirit by the Cappadocians, which led to the desire for the institution of a feast to highlight the role of the Third Person; and perhaps the influence of the Holy Places. Egeria, however, celebrated the Ascension, not on the Mount of Olives, but at Bethlehem (42) (see P. Devos, *Anal. Boll.* 1968, pp. 87–108). The commemoration of the Ascension on the fortieth day led to the splitting of the season into two, even fasting being permitted after it. The first week of Pentecost was very early given a pre-eminence which also derogated from the unity of the season. In Egeria's time, there was a daily Eucharist in that week, largely owing to the bishop's giving his mystagogical lectures (see pp. 61, 65) to the newly baptized then, whilst in the others there was a Eucharist only on Wednesday and Friday. The last day of the season was early given a vigil as it was the second annual occasion for baptism, but the final blow to the integrity of the season was the giving of an octave to it, as if it were a commemorative feast of the descent of the Spirit. Originally the week after Pentecost was the time to resume fasting and penitential exercises (*Egeria*, 44.1; Leo, *Serm.* 78–81). This explains the ceremonial genuflexions at Vespers on the Feast of Pentecost in the Orthodox rites. The octave, established in Rome by the seventh century, still anomalously contained the Ember Days. Perhaps more logically, the C of E keeps only the Monday and Tuesday as Red Letter Days, followed by the Ember Days. The Orthodox Churches also keep an octave, but the fiftieth day is now observed as the feast of the Holy Trinity, one of the Twelve Great Feasts; it is the following day, the Monday, which is kept as the Day of the Spirit.

(3) DEPENDENT FEASTS

THE SUNDAY AFTER PENTECOST

Again there is divergence between East and West as to the mystery which is celebrated on this day. The Orthodox keep it as a feast of All Saints, whilst the West observes it as the Feast of the Holy and Undivided Trinity. Votive Masses of the Holy Trinity were extraordinarily popular in the Middle Ages in the West, even on a Sunday, and gradually, encouraged particularly by the Benedictine Order, a formal feast was set up on this Sunday in spite of official reluctance. It was not until 1499 that Alexander VI abolished the commemoration of the Sunday in the Mass and Office and raised the rank of the feast. It was customary in the Sarum Use, as in most of northern Europe, to number the Sundays after Trinity rather than after Pentecost, and the C of E continues this somewhat eccentric tradition.

CORPUS CHRISTI

This feast, which is peculiar to the Western Church, was occasioned by the vision of an Augustinian nun, Juliana, in Liège in 1246. It was first celebrated there, and made a universal feast by Urban IV, a former archdeacon of Liège, in 1264.

LENT

Lent, *Quadragesima* in Latin, *Tessarakoste* in Greek, is referred to for the first time, although most certainly not as an innovation, in Canon 5 of the Council of Nicaea. It seems basically to be a combination of two elements, an extended fast before the Pascha and a regulated period of preparation for baptism, both elements having previously varied in length. The number of forty was determined by the length of our Lord's fast in the wilderness.[1]

The actual length of Lent varied considerably, depending on how the forty-day period was calculated, whether it excluded Sunday or Saturday and Sunday, and whether it excluded Good Friday and Holy Saturday or the whole of Holy Week. Athanasius apparently alludes to a six-week

---

[1] Coptic sources in fact suggest the fast was originally related, not to the Pascha but to Epiphany. See L. Villecourt 'Les observances liturgiques et la discipline du jeûne dans l'église copte', *Muséon*, 38 (1925), p. 266. Cf. R. Coquin, PO 31, p. 328.

Lent, beginning on a Monday and including Holy Week, whilst Egeria, some fifty years later, states quite specifically that in Jerusalem Lent, in which she included the Great Week, lasted eight weeks because Saturday and Sunday were not fast days (27.1). This latter arrangement was known in Cyprus (Epiphanius, *AH* 3.2, 22; PG 42.828) and in Antioch (Chrysostom, *ad Populum Antiochenum*, *Hom.* 20; PG 49.197). At Rome the earliest custom was to observe a three-week fast, but this may have been a fast of three alternate weeks in a six-week period (A. Chavasse, 'La structure du carême', *LMD* 31 (1952), pp. 82–4; cf. G. G. Willis, *Essays in Early Roman Liturgy*, AC SPCK 1964, pp. 101–4; Duchesne, p. 243 and note). Certainly by the time of Leo (440–61) there was a six-week Lent beginning on a Sunday and lasting until Maundy Thursday.

It is only in the 'Gelasian' Sacramentary that Ash Wednesday is named as *caput jejunii*. By the time of Gregory the Great, the three Sundays before Lent, Septuagesima, Sexagesima, and Quinquagesima, had emerged in Rome. In the Western tradition, therefore, the forty days of Lent are counted from Ash Wednesday and include Holy Week but not the Sundays, whilst in the Eastern tradition Lent begins on the Monday after Western Quinquagesima and goes up to the Friday before Palm Sunday, thus excluding Holy Week but including Sundays. As in the West, Lent, the Great Fast, has a pre-Lenten season, actually of five weeks, the last, Cheese-fare Week, with limited fasting and some Lenten liturgical features.

With the decline in the number of adult baptisms and the consequent atrophying of the catechumenate, the baptismal aspect of Lent declined in prominence. On the other hand, the penitential character of the season was emphasized; it permeates the ninth-century Lenten *Triodion* of the Orthodox Church, for example; and in the West it became increasingly common from the tenth century for all the faithful, not just those doing public penance, to take part in penitential exercises such as the Ash Wednesday ashing.

East and West differ, however, in their liturgical observance of Lent. The Orthodox celebrate the liturgy on Saturdays and Sundays only and have the Mass of the Pre-sanctified on Wednesday and Friday evenings. The West originally had Masses only on Wednesday and Friday, then Mondays were added to the fifth century, then Tuesdays and Saturdays and finally, under Gregory II (d. 731), Thursdays. From the turn of the fifth century, no feasts or festivals were celebrated in Lent, except the Annunciation, which in the East even now can be observed on Good Friday or Easter Day itself. Lent has been a closed season for marriages since the fourth century in both East and West (Canon 52 of Council of Laodicea, *c.* 363).

THE CHRISTMAS/EPIPHANY CYCLE

Attempts have been made to see Epiphany as the Christianization of the Feast of Tabernacles, the third great Jewish feast (see A. Schmemann, *Introduction to Liturgical Theology* (Faith Press 1966), pp. 123–5 and refs.). Both celebrations included the all-night vigil, the lighting of fires and the procession of lights, the waters of life, the palm branches and the allusions to the sacred marriage (see E. G. Selwyn, *JTS* 13 (1912), pp. 225–36), but the theory is by no means proved.

Both Christmas and Epiphany are, partly at any rate, an attempt to counter pagan festivities connected with the winter solstice, which in the West was reckoned to be on 25 December, and in the East, in Alexandria, on 6 January. 25 December had been fixed as the date for observing the birthday of the sun, *Natalis solis invicti*, in 274, only sixty-two years before the first evidence of the Christian celebration of Christmas in Rome (Philocalian Calendar). Constantine encouraged the adaptation by the Church of various features of sun-worship, and the institution of the feast may owe something to him and to his building of St Peter's on the Vatican Hill, where the sun was already worshipped in the Mithras-cult (see N. M. Denis-Boulet, *Rech SR* 1947, pp. 385–406). In the East 6 January was connected with the virgin-birth of Aion/Dionysus (Epiphanius, *AH* 51.2; GCS 31.284) and with legends of epiphanies in which gods made themselves known to men. Pliny the Elder even tells of Dionysus revealing his presence on that day by changing the water in springs and fountains into wine (*Natural History*, 2.106, 31.13).

Christmas and Epiphany became widely celebrated only in the fourth century and their popularity undoubtedly owes much to the contemporary Christological controversies and the need to combat Arianism.

Epiphany is almost certainly the older of the two festivals and was probably from its origin a celebration both of Christ's nativity and the events connected with it, and of his baptism and first miracle at Cana (Cassian, *Conferences* 10.2; PL 49.821). McArthur argues from the fragment of a sermon, possibly by Hippolytus, preserved at the end of the *Ep. of Diognetus* (11.3–5), that such a unitive festival existed as early as the end of the second century or the beginning of the third. Although the name indicates its Greek origin, the first indisputable reference to it, in Ammianus Marcellinus' *History* (21.2), is to its celebration in Gaul in *c.* 361. The reference unfortunately, however, provides no evidence as to the content of the celebration. At Jerusalem, according to Egeria's account (which is, however, incomplete), the main content was the nativity; there is no reference to the baptism or to the miracle at Cana

(25.6–12), yet Jerome (d. 420), who spent forty-five years in the East, twenty-four of them in Bethlehem, says that baptism was the main content (*Comm. in Ezek.* 1.1; PL 25.17). By the time of his death, however, Christmas had been introduced into the East, in Antioch by 386 (Chrysostom, *in diem natalem DNJC*; PG 49.351), in Cappadocia by 370 (Gregory of Nyssa, *in diem luminum*, ed. Jaeger, 9.221) and in Constantinople itself by 380 (Gregory Naz., *Orat.* 38).

Unlike the feast of the Epiphany, Christmas originated in the West, probably at Rome itself, where Epiphany does not seem to have been celebrated before the early fifth century (Coeburgh, *R Bén.*, 1965, pp. 304ff), although it was well established by the time of Leo. Christmas also seems to have been the original feast in North Africa. Augustine in 412 complains that the Donatists have not added the festival of the Epiphany like everyone else (*Serm.* 202; PL 38.1033). The Epiphany was, however, known earlier in Gaul and Spain and even in north Italy, where it was a three-fold commemoration of the Adoration of the Magi, our Lord's baptism and the miracle at Cana (Paulinus of Nola, *Poema* 27; PL 61.649), whereas in Rome the Magi seem to have been its only theme in the mid-fifth century.

It would seem then that an originally unitive festival has become divided in different ways in East and West: Christmas is the feast of the nativity in both, to which the East adds a commemoration of the adoration of the Magi; Epiphany is a celebration of the Lord's baptism in the East and of the visit of the Magi in the West. The other two themes associated with Epiphany, the baptism and the marriage at Cana, are commemorated on the Sundays after Epiphany in the West. In the Byzantine liturgy there is no mention of Cana but nuptial imagery is used of baptism.

In the East, as early as the Cappadocian Fathers, Epiphany became a normal day for baptism, whilst in the West, at least up to the time of Leo, baptism was never administered then, although Leo did preach on the subject at Christmas. In Gaul, however, which was much influenced by the East, Christmas/Epiphany did become a baptismal season, and it is significant that it is in Gaul that we first hear of a forty-day period of preparation for it.

Advent

This is an entirely Western institution, which owes its origins to Gallican and also Roman traditions. A three-week period of preparation for Epiphany is evidenced by Hilary of Poitiers (d. *c.* 367) in Gaul, and by the Council of Saragossa in 380 in Spain. In the fifth and sixth centuries this period was lengthened to forty days and calculated back from Christmas. Bede records that St Egbert and St Cuthbert fasted for forty days *'ante natale Dei'* (*HE* 3.27, 4.30). In Rome, originally only a single day's fast before Christmas was known (Philastrius of Brescia, *Div. Haer.* 149; CSEL 38. Cf. Augustine, *Ep.* 65). Advent there seems to have grown out of the December Ember Days, 'the fast of the tenth month' (Leo, *Serm.* 12; PL 54.168). Approximating to the Gallican season, it became longer and more penitential in character. Gregory the Great fixed its length at four weeks but the 'Gelasian' Sacramentary provides for six Sundays before Christmas. The BCP and the Roman Missal of 1570 have only a four-week Advent, but the propers for the Sunday next before Advent in the former and for the Eighteenth and Twenty-third Sundays after Pentecost in the latter have various Advent references. As late as the twelfth century Advent was still regarded as a festal season in which white vestments were worn and the *Gloria in Excelsis* sung. It was only as the theme of the Second Coming, first a marked feature in the Bobbio missal of the late seventh century, came to dominate the season that it approximated more and more to Lent. It is noteworthy that the *Dies Irae* was originally written for the Sunday before Advent. The Orthodox Church has a fast preparatory to Christmas, beginning on 15 November.

DEPENDENT FEASTS

The days immediately after Christmas have, from the fourth century, been devoted to what Durandus in the thirteenth century calls *'comites Christi'*, the companions of Christ, members of his family, notably his mother, and the early martyrs. Gregory of Nyssa's writings show that 26 December was dedicated to St Stephen, 27 to St James and St John, 28 to St Peter and St Paul and 1 January to St Basil, the champion of Orthodoxy. In the West 28 has been reserved for the Holy Innocents since the fifth century and St John has been commemorated alone since the Leonine Sacramentary, whilst 1 January was the most primitive feast of our Lady.[1] By the beginning of the seventh century 1 January was observed rather as the octave of Christmas and later still as the Circumcision of our Lord. This last title appears first in a lectionary from Capua in 546 and was widely adopted in Gaul before finally being accepted in Rome itself in the ninth century. The Feast of the Holy Name (2 January) appeared in some liturgical books in the fourteenth century.

The most important, and one of the oldest, feasts dependent on Christmas is the *Presentation of Christ in the Temple*, *Hypapante* (the

---

[1] The Byzantine and Syro-Jacobite rites have a feast of our Lady on 26 December.

Meeting), as it is known in the East and indeed in the Gregorian Sacramentaries. It was celebrated in Jerusalem at the time of Egeria (26) on the fortieth day after Epiphany, i.e. on 14 February, 'with special magnificence... all things are done with the same solemnity as at the feast of Easter'. Introduced to Constantinople under the Emperor Justin at the beginning of the sixth century, its observance was ordered by Justinian on 2 February 542 as a thanksgiving for the end of a plague and from there it spread throughout the East. The earliest reference to the Candlemas Procession is from Constantinople, from the year 602 when the historian Theophanus the Confessor notes that the Emperor Maurice took part in it barefoot (*LP* 1.376). We know that it was accepted soon after at Rome as the Christian counterpart of the ancient expiatory procession, the *Amburbale*, which accounts for its penitential character—until 1960 violet vestments were worn for it in the Western Church. The Gallican and Mozarabic rites knew nothing of the feast however.

The Feast of the Nativity of John the Baptist on 24 June is also dependent on the date of Christmas (Lk. 1.36), and St Augustine was probably right in stating that its purpose was to replace the ancient pagan rites in connection with the summer solstice (PL 38.301; *Sermones post Maurinos reperti*, ed. G. Morin 1930, pp. 231, 592). *The Conception of the Baptist* came to be celebrated on 24 September, thus matching the Annunciation at the other equinox.

The observance of *the Annunciation of our Lord* may be alluded to in the homilies of Proclus of Constantinople in 430, but the first indisputable evidence of the feast is from the West in the 'Gelasian' Sacramentary, which interestingly gives it the same lections as were used on the ancient Marian feast of 1 January. By the eighth century it had become a universal observance in the West, although Spain kept it on 18 December to avoid keeping it in Lent.

RECENT REFORMS OF THE CHRISTIAN YEAR

REVISION OF THE ROMAN CALENDAR

Even before Vatican II, the twentieth century saw various attempts to reform the Calendar, notably by Pius X and John XXIII, but it was the *Constitution of the Sacred Liturgy* (nn. 102–11), faithfully implemented by the Calendar of 1969, which did so decisively. The Council decreed that 'the proper of time must be given the preference which is its due over the feasts of the saints so that the entire cycle of the mysteries of salvation may be suitably recalled' (108). Sunday therefore takes precedence over all but a very few solemnities and has absolute precedence over every kind of feast in Advent, Lent, and Eastertide.

The Paschal Triduum, beginning with the evening Mass of the Lord's Supper on Maundy Thursday, centring on the Easter Vigil and ending with Vespers on Easter Day, is the climax of the whole Liturgical Year. The integrity of Eastertide is reaffirmed by suppressing the octave of Pentecost so that Whitsunday is clearly the last of the sacred fifty days, and by numbering the Sundays 'of Eastertide' rather than 'after Easter', Low Sunday being Easter 2 not Easter 1. Lent begins on Ash Wednesday and ends on Maundy Thursday, the title 'Passion Sunday' being transferred from the fifth to the sixth Sunday in Lent. It is a period of preparation for the celebration of the paschal mystery; its main themes, reflected in the lections, are baptismal and penitential.

The Christmas cycle is also reformed; the celebration of Christmas/Epiphany runs from Christmas Eve to the Sunday after Epiphany (or after 6 January if it is kept on a Sunday), that Sunday being the feast of the Baptism of the Lord. The Sunday after Christmas is the feast of the Holy Family and the octave day of Christmas is marked by the restoration of the most primitive feast of our Lady, the Solemnity of Mary, Mother of God. Advent remains a season of four weeks but is to be kept in a spirit of joyful expectancy; the penitential element is reduced. The last week of Advent, from 17 December, is taken up with the preparation for the coming of Christ in his nativity, Mary, Joseph and John the Baptist being prominent.

The rest of the year is regarded as 'ordinary time' and its weeks are numbered from 1 to 34; the numbering of Sundays 'after Epiphany' and 'after Pentecost' is dropped. This helps to assert the independent status of such weeks and emphasizes the 'extra-ordinariness' of the two cycles of Easter and Christmas.

The Proposals of the Joint Liturgical Group

The proposals of this ecumenical group, set up in 1963, are important in that they have been adopted *in toto* by most of the British Free Churches and experimentally, with some modifications, by the C of E. Unlike the reforms of the Roman Catholic Church, they depart radically from the traditions of the early Church and show little appreciation of the theological meaning of the Christian year as a means of participating in the mystery of Christ. Pentecost is given a new prominence by becoming a third focus of the Christian Year. Presupposing the fixing of Easter, which the Vatican Council also encouraged, the Group proposed a season of nine Sundays before Easter and six after, and also a season of twenty-one Sundays after Pentecost. The controlling factor in adjusting the length of the seasons has been less their intrinsic nature and purpose than considerations of lectional convenience. The pre-Christmas season for example has been lengthened in order to allow for readings covering salvation-history from creation to the nativity. As the Standing Liturgical Commission of the American Episcopal Church has pertinently remarked, 'the inherent fallacy' of such a reconstruction is its 'approach to the Christian Year on a pedagogical rather than a kerygmatic basis' (*Prayer Book Studies* 19 (Church Hymnal Corporation, New York), p. 10). In the *Proposed BCP* (1977) the PECUSA year is seen to consist of two cycles of feasts only, dependent on Easter Day and Christmas Day.

2 The Sanctoral

KEVIN DONOVAN, SJ

GENERAL SURVEYS

Butler, A., *The Lives of the Saints*, ed. and rev. by H. Thurston and D. Attwater, with suppl. vol. Burns Oates 1926–49.

Calendarium Romanum. Vatican City 1969. Text and commentary.

DACL, vol. 8, s.v. 'Kalendaria'.

Denis-Boulet, N.-M., (ET) *The Christian Calendar*. Faith and Fact Books. Burns Oates 1960.

Eisenhofer, L. and Lechner, J., (ET) *The Liturgy of the Roman Rite*. Herder and Nelson 1961.

Jounel, P., 'Le sanctoral', in *EP*.

LMD 52 (1947), pp. 59–88.

Jungmann, J. A., 'A Feast of the Church', in *Pastoral Liturgy* (Challoner 1962), pp. 387–407.

SPECIAL TOPICS

Linguistic: *TDNT*, s.v. '*Hagios*' and '*Martus*'.

Origins

Delehaye, H., *Les origines du culte des martyrs*. 2nd edn Brussels 1933.

Delehaye, H., *Sanctus, essai sur le culte des saints dans l'antiquité*. Brussels 1927.

Delehaye, H., (ET) *The Legends of the Saints*. G. Chapman 1962.

Frere, W. H., *Studies in Early Roman Liturgy. I. The Kalendar*. AC OUP 1930.

Gaiffier, B. de, 'Réflexions sur l'origine du culte des martyrs', in *LMD* 52 (1947), pp. 19–44.

The Calendar

Klauser, T., 'Christliche Märtyrerkult', in *Gesammelte Arbeiten*. Münster Westf. 1974.
These last two works bring Delehaye's approach up to date.

Texts

Baumstark, A., (ET) *Comparative Liturgy* (Mowbray 1958), pp. 174–99 gives full information on the earliest texts and their modern edns. The article from *DACL* cited above gives a useful selection of actual texts.

Early Middle Ages

Quentin, H., *Les Martyrologes historiques*. Paris 1908.
See the various Roman sacramentaries, and the discussion in:
  Hope, D. M., *The Leonine Sacramentary* (OUP 1971), pp. 38–53, 78–90.
  Chavasse, A., *Le sacramentaire gélasien* (Paris 1958), esp. pp. 273–422.

Late Middle Ages

Convenient edns of several calendars and martyrologies in HBS publications. HBS also published the Mass of Sweden.
Jounel, P., *LMD* 63b (1960), comments on medieval developments.
BCP and calendar: Lowther Clarke, W. K., *LW* pp. 201–44.

Medieval cult of relics

Morris, C., 'A critique of popular religion; Guibert of Nogent on *The Relics of the Saints*', in *Studies in Church History*, vol. 8 (CUP 1972), pp. 55–60.
Bethell, D., 'The making of a twelfth-century relic collection', ibid. 61–72.

> For all the saints who from their labours rest,
> Who thee by faith before the world confessed,
> Thy name, O Jesu, be for ever blest. Alleluia!

Late and lyrical, the words of this well-known hymn sum up the age-old Christian attitude to saints, those men and women who witnessed to God's work in Christ by the quality of their own lives, and above all by their death. It is to the martyrs that we must look for the origins of the present sanctoral: but there has been a long development since then. The main stages are the broadening of the concept of martyrdom/witness to include, first, confessors—those who suffered imprisonment and torture, but not actual death, for the name of Christ—and later, ascetics, virgins, and bishops who confessed Christ without being imprisoned. A further stage in the elaboration of a complete sanctoral is the process whereby a purely local list of saints is broadened till it takes on the characteristics of a truly universal calendar. The Roman Church, with its claims to universality, has carried this process to a logical conclusion in the recent General Roman Calendar (1969); but it has found it necessary to prune drastically the number of saints. The present brief essay can do little

21 Gospel Cupboard. Mosaic showing a cupboard used to house the texts of the Gospels in the mausoleum of Galla Placidia, Ravenna, fifth century

22 San Clemente, Rome (1), the choir with *ambones*, paschal candlestick, and pulpit for singing the *Exultet* (see pp. 410, 475)

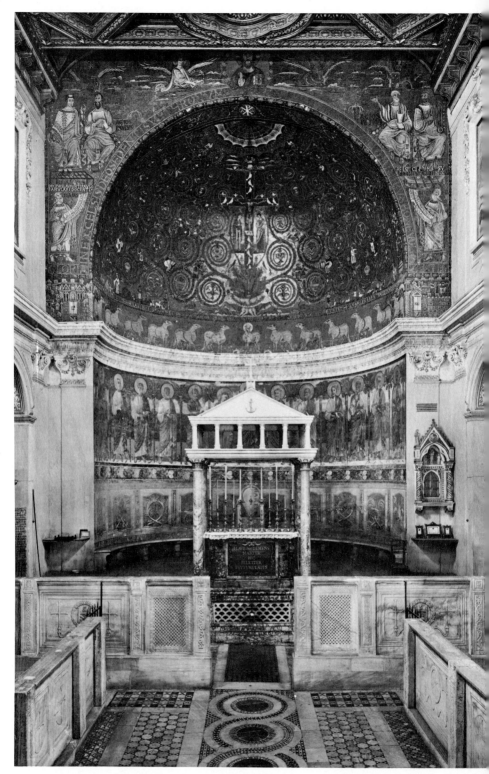

23   San Clemente, Rome (2) showing apse with mosaics, bishop's throne, presbyters' bench, and altar with canopy, eleventh-century in its present form (see p. 475)

more than trace the origin of the cult of the martyrs from its NT roots to its elaboration in the local lists of the major sees. These gradually become fused, and we shall confine ourselves to the subsequent history of the main Western calendar, that of the Church of Rome. Some Christians have seen the elaborate machinery of saints' days as detracting from the unique mediatorship of Christ. Popular aberration there may have been: but if we look to the age of martyrs, we shall see the veneration of brave and holy Christians in its earliest and purest form.

THE ORIGINAL CULT OF MARTYRS

The Christian practice of honouring martyrs comprises a number of original features, both semantic and ritual. The word *martus* was in current use, both for a legal witness and, more generally, for any witness to facts. The first stage towards a Christian usage was to apply it to the contents of the gospel proclamation: but the circumstances in which the witness to Christ took place would, as with Jesus himself, often lead to the arrest and death of the martyr (a term applied to Christ in Rev. 1.5 and 3.14).

> Stephen (Acts 22.20) is not called a witness because he dies, but he dies because he is a witness of Christ, and because of his evangelistic activity .... The term is reserved (in Rev.) for those who prove the final seriousness of their witness by suffering death. (Strathmann in *TDNT* 4.49.4)

At this date, it does not yet mean all that we understand by the term 'martyr'. The dignity and glory of a death for Christ is, however, clear in the NT, where the teaching that the servant cannot be above the Master was a constant reminder of what might be in store for the believer. Death for Christ's sake was already seen as sacrificial in some sense. Frequently we find St Paul glorying in his sufferings, but asserting that nothing can come between himself and Christ (e.g. Rom. 8). His language in Phil. 2.17 anticipates that of Ignatius of Antioch (mart. *c.* 107):

> Grant me no more than to be a sacrifice for God while there is an altar at hand. Then you can form yourselves into a choir and sing praises to the Father in Christ Jesus that God gave the bishop of Smyrna the privilege of reaching the sun's setting when he summoned him to its rising. It is a grand thing for my life to set on the world and for me to be on my way to God, so that I may rise in his presence .... It is not that I want merely to be called a Christian, but actually to *be* one. (*ad Rom.* 2 and 3; LCC 1.103)

The full development of the term 'martyr' to mean the Christian who sheds his blood as a witness to Christ and to the reality of the resurrection is reached by the middle of the second century. *The Martyrdom of Polycarp* is evidence that the Christians of Smyrna venerated the memory

of their bishop with an annual service of joy held at his tomb. After the
body had been burned,

> We later took up his bones, more precious than costly stones and more
> valuable than gold, and laid them away in a suitable place. There the Lord will
> permit us, so far as possible to gather together in joy and gladness to celebrate
> the day of his martyrdom as a birthday, in memory of those athletes who have
> gone before, and to train and make ready those who come hereafter. (*Mart.
> Polyc.* 18; ET LCC 1.156)

The ancient world paid special respect to the dead, and Roman law
protected tombs: they were not to be disturbed, and were to be located
outside city boundaries. Details of ceremonies might vary in different
parts of the Empire, but it was normal for the family to visit the tomb of
dead persons annually on their birthday, strew flowers and perfume, and
hold a meal in their honour. The main Christian novelty was to meet on
the day of death, regarding this as the true birthday (*natalis, genethlia*):
for the follower of Christ, death is now the entry into risen life. A further
development in the case of martyrs like Polycarp was for the Christian
community as a whole to assemble. From sources like the *Didascalia* (ed.
Connolly, p. 252) and *Ap. Const.* (Funk 6.20; see p. 60) it is clear that
these meetings were held in the cemeteries, and included readings
(possibly also from accounts of a martyr's death), psalms, hymns and the
Eucharist.

The meaning of such a ceremony is not in doubt. The *Martyrdom of
Polycarp* is quite explicit, for some members of the Jewish community at
Smyrna had suspected that the Christians' desire to 'have fellowship with
his holy flesh' would lead them to 'abandon the Crucified and begin
worshipping this one'. The author retorts:

> We can never forsake Christ, who suffered for the salvation of the whole world
> of those who are saved, the faultless for the sinners, nor can we ever worship
> any others. For we worship this One as the Son of God, but we worship the
> martyrs as disciples and imitators of the Lord, deservedly so, because of their
> unsurpassable devotion to their own King and Teacher. May it be also our lot
> to be their companions and fellow disciples (ibid. 17).

Later writers will repeat this assertion that sacrifice is offered to God, but
not to martyrs: the martyrs are not gods or heroes like a Hercules or a
Romulus, writes Augustine at the end of the *City of God* (22.10)—thus
anticipating the answer to an objection of the nineteenth century.
However, sacrifice is offered in their memory—the sacrifice of the Body
of Christ, of which they are now part. Augustine adds a precision not met
with in earlier writers: he distinguishes between prayer for the dead and
prayer to the martyrs (*in Joh.* 84.1; *Serm.* 159.1 and 284.5). Here too

there has been a natural progression from the days when the martyrs were commended to God along with other departed Christians, or when the dead were invoked by the living 'because we know you in Christ' (cf. Delehaye, *L'origine*, ch. 4). Even Plato (*Symposium* 202e) speaks of the intercession of the dead, and this was particularly true of parents. Orestes, in Aeschylus' *Choephoroe* (475ff), invokes the help of his father Agamemnon, and the mother of the Gracchi tells her sons, 'you shall invoke your mother as a god' (Nepos, fr. 12). What more natural then that Christians should commend themselves to the departed in this way? In the course of time, the custom of praying to the dead was restricted to prayer to martyrs. Apart from epigraphic evidence, conveniently assembled in Delehaye, there are hints of invocation in Hippolytus' apostrophizing of the Three Children in the Fiery Furnace (*in Dan.*, 2.30, GCS).

Cyprian had what might be described as a mutual prayer pact with Pope Cornelius, should either of them be called to God through martyrdom (*Ep.* 60.5, CSEL). Besides Cyprian's letters (e.g. *Ep.* 61.2), and the information contained in the controversy *de lapsis*, we are particularly well-informed about the attitude of contemporary Christians towards their martyrs, from North African sources such as the authentic *Acta* of the trial of the martyrs from Scillium. Again, we only have to read Tertullian's brief letter *ad Martyres*, or his longer *ad Nationes* and *Apologeticum* ('the blood of martyrs is the seed'; *Apol.* 50.13) to appreciate the dignity in which martyrs were held, and the warnings against the presumptuous courting of martyrdom. When in prison awaiting trial or death, those arrested for being Christian were visited and consoled by other members of the community. The pagan satirist Lucian has a sarcastic parody of this in his account of Peregrinus, the man who got rich on the strength of being imprisoned (*Death of Peregrinus*, ch. 11). This exaggeration at least serves to high-light the respect paid to 'confessors'—those who confessed Christ before the judge, but were deprived of the final glory of martyrdom. Such confessors were often granted special privileges in the matter of ordination and of reconciling to the Church the *lapsi*, brethren who had denied their faith in the face of persecution. After death, confessors were not infrequently given the veneration hitherto reserved for martyrs. Hippolytus, who died in exile in Sardinia, is one of the first and best known examples. Again a natural development: Cyprian himself held that the important thing in martyrdom was the disposition of the will, and his contemporary Denis of Alexandria compared those who died ministering to the plague-stricken with those who died a martyr's death. However, this extension of the concept of martyrdom was the thin end of the wedge, the beginnings of what Delehaye characterized as the degradation of the idea of martyrdom. We may close this section on the age of the martyrs by noting the importance of the great persecution in the 50s of the third century, which claimed Laurence, Cyprian, and so many others. There had been persecutions before—sporadically under Nero and Domitian, with some reluctance under Trajan, with ferocity at Lyons towards the close of the second century. But the evidence of the earliest liturgical records suggests that the wave of persecutions under Valerian, which forbade Christian worship and systematically picked on bishops and church leaders, aroused a wider enthusiasm for the martyrs, and ultimately laid the foundations of the sanctoral.

The Roman *Depositio martyrum* of 354 is our earliest extant example of a local list of martyrs. Similar lists exist for the region of Antioch, Carthage, and elsewhere. After a detailed survey of the evidence, Baumstark concluded:

> The primitive *Sanctorale* may everywhere be reduced to a double *stratum* of which both elements are strictly local: (1) the *Memoriae* or *mnemai* of the local martyrs and (2) those of the local bishops. In both cases the observance was inseparably attached to their tombs. (Baumstark, *Comparative Liturgy*, p. 180)

Today we are familiar with Calendars which for the most part endeavour to combine this early local quality with that of universality. This development began in the Constantinian era.

THE EXTENSION OF THE SANCTORALE
AFTER CONSTANTINE

With the Peace of Constantine and the cessation of active persecution, martyrdom became, for the time being, a thing of the past. The cult of the martyrs, far from declining, now gained in external solemnity. Basilicas were built near or above earlier simple tombs, splendid processions were held, special preachers delivered panegyrics. The martyr's 'birthday' now became a popular holiday, meeting the need that ordinary people have for tangible reminders of religion and opportunities to celebrate—a need formerly met by the official state religion. This was recognized by church leaders. It was no accident that the Roman *Depositio Martyrum* opens with 25 December, formerly the birthday of the Unconquered Sun, but now to be the birthday of Christ. Constantine celebrated the dedication of his Jerusalem basilica on the same day as the dedication of the old Roman temple of Jupiter Capitolinus. The anniversary days of a dedication provided additional local feasts. At Jerusalem, the festivities lasted a week, and on the second day, which coincided with the original date of the discovery of the true cross by Helena, the Holy Wood was specially venerated; this feast gradually spread throughout the Christian world with fragments of the cross itself.

In this period when Christianity might seem threatened by its new-found status as a popular and even imperial religion, the inevitable reaction occurred with the flight to the desert. Originally offering safe hiding from persecution, the Thebaid and other centres now became a refuge for an increasing number of hermits and monks. Paradoxically, these uncompromising ascetics became a source of fascinated admiration for pious tourists. At their death, and sometimes well beforehand, these athletes of Christ were accorded the honours which had hitherto been reserved for martyrs and confessors. The life of St Anthony by Athanasius is symptomatic of the interest shown towards those whose voluntary austerities seemed to equal the torments of the original martyr-witnesses. This is the period when virgins and pastoral bishops came to be regarded as having shown a similar witness in their lives, and to deserve appropriate honours after their death. After the Council of Ephesus, reflection on the newly vindicated status of the *Theotokos* led to the establishment of a full liturgical cultus of Mary, with its four great feasts, which originated in the East, but soon spread to the West. Two of them (The Nativity of BVM, and the *Dormitio* or Assumption) evolved from the Dedication of basilicas in her honour at Jerusalem. The other two (Annunciation, and Purification or Presentation of the Lord) are in direct dependence on the date selected for the birth of her Son. Other feasts clustered around Christmas—those of the earliest witnesses to Christ such as St Stephen (see p. 416). This is rather typical of the way NT personages entered the sanctoral, for there was not often a stable local tradition connecting name, place, and date, as there was at Rome, although it is not certain whether 29 June represents the date of the translation of Peter and Paul or of the institution of a feast in their honour.

The first well-attested case of a translation is that of St Babylas, the martyr of Antioch whose body was translated by Gallus Caesar (351–4) to the suburb of Daphne, in order to silence a prominent oracle of Apollo. Julian the Apostate moved him back ten years later in an effort to revive the oracle; twenty years later, Babylas was on the move again, this time to a new basilica erected by Bishop Meletius, who was himself soon to be brought back from his deathbed in Constantinople and buried with a panegyric by Chrysostom in the same basilica. In the meantime, the imperial city, not rich in local martyrs, had received the relics of Timothy, Andrew, and Luke; others were soon to follow, including a Bishop Paul, before long confused with the Apostle. The mighty Justinian appealed in vain to Pope Hormisdas for relics of Laurence and the Roman apostles, but had to be content with the *brandea* or *sanctuaria* sent him instead. These were cloths which had touched the tombs of the dead apostle, and were felt to have the same healing power as the cloths which had touched Paul when alive (Acts 19.12). The East was less particular about dividing relics than was Rome. Gregory Nazianzen believed that even a small portion of relics was as valuable as the whole body (*contra Julianum*, 1.69; PG 25.589), but Gregory the Great could snub the empress who asked for the head of St Paul with the remark 'It is not the Roman custom' (*Registr.* 4.30). Gregory himself maintained the traditional principle of requiring name, place, and day for an authentic cult. Ambrose had been less exacting. He was involved in more than one 'invention' of relics, as the discovery of the lost bones of martyrs was not inappropriately called. The most famous of these was the case of the skeletons of Gervasius and Protasius which came to light in 386 at Milan as the result of a vision. It is possible that Ambrose did thus discover martyrs whose tombs had been neglected in times of persecution. The same can hardly be credited in the case of relics of Gamaliel, Cornelius, and Stephen which were revealed at Jerusalem by means of a dream. Gervasius and Protasius offer a case of a cult introduced on insufficient evidence, although this did not prevent it from spreading far and wide as portions of their relics were generously distributed. Stephen is a case of doubtful relics being wished upon a genuine martyr. But what are we to say of holy Job, whose tomb was also discovered in the late fourth century? No wonder the Third Council of Carthage (397) deplored the setting up of altars as a result of dreams. (For a list of Inventions, see *Egeria*, pp. 281–3, with the striking parallels between some of these and Plutarch's account of the discovery of the bones of Theseus.) With the influx of pilgrims to the Holy Land, the cult of OT personages, well-known in the time of our Lord (Mt. 23.29; cf. Heb. 11), received fresh impetus. This was particularly true in the East, where they were in some sense local figures, and feasts of saints from the OT are still a feature of oriental church calendars. In the West, there was a Gallican feast of Elijah, but little in Rome beyond the references to Abraham and Melchizedek in the Canon. The Celtic church inserted a long list of patriarchs from Abel onwards into the commemoration of the dead (cf. Stowe Missal, HBS 1906). The sanctoral of the early Roman sacramentaries was also fairly resistant to the introduction of non-Roman feasts.

THE ROMAN SANCTORAL IN THE MIDDLE AGES

By the end of the fourth century, virtually all the types of feast that are now found in the sanctoral had become established. In the succeeding centuries new saints were added, while changes in devotion led to the introduction of fresh feasts of our Lord and of Mary. There continued to be borrowing from one region to another. Rome and Constantinople might enjoy increasing prestige, but there was as yet no centralized liturgical authority. Not surprisingly, considerable diversity existed between neighbouring dioceses, although something like national calendars tended to emerge. In the present section we shall follow the fortunes of the local sanctoral of Rome as it gradually becomes the calendar of the whole Western Church. It is not necessary to rehearse again the migrations of the 'Gelasian' and 'Gregorian' sacramentaries to the lands of the Franks, and their return, enriched with non-Roman features (see pp. 225-6). The Curial Missal which eventually emerged was spread abroad by papal legates and Franciscan friars. During this period there were additions, here an Augustine, there the characteristically Gallican feast of All Saints. However, the core of the sanctoral remained unmistakably Roman, the Rome of the martyrs. It was Gregory VII (1073-85) who made the first major additions, Roman again, but now decidedly the Rome of the popes, some thirty of whom were added to the calendar. Gregory's regulations about canonization also inhibited the introduction of new saints into local calendars, yet the reservation to Rome of the right to canonize paved the way for a real break-through. Three years after his murder in 1170, Thomas à Becket of Canterbury was canonized, and his feast incorporated into the Roman sanctoral—a northerner, a modern, and junior by nearly 600 years to the next most recent saint, Gregory the Great. This step opened the way for the great increase of saints in the middle ages. Anthony of Padua was canonized within a year of his death, Francis and Clare within two, Elizabeth of Hungary after four. The Roman calendar was fast becoming universal. New feasts of a theological (Corpus Christi) or devotional turn (Precious Blood, Seven Dolours of BVM) were also added.

Besides the relatively restrained sanctoral of the Mass and office books, there was a much more diverse compilation, represented by the various martyrologies. These all stem from the *Martyrology of Jerome*, a late sixth-century Gallican recension of an earlier pseudonymous document which fused the local traditions of Rome, Syria, and Africa. The venerable Bede was the first to add to Jerome's martyrology, filling in some of the gaps with entries drawn from biblical and patristic sources. This tradition was continued in the ninth century by Florus of Lyons, and Ado of Vienne. The latter was not blessed with the spirit of historical criticism, and he introduced many spurious saints and legendary details. Although Usuard of St Germain later in the century eliminated some of these, many more survived. Since Usuard's work was widely diffused throughout the Benedictine order and cathedral chapters, it became the virtual basis for the first Roman Martyrology issued by Gregory XIII in 1584. It was about as reliable as many of the pious legends incorporated into the third nocturn of Mattins. Hardly more accurate, but infinitely more readable, are some of the martyrologies from the western fringes of Christianity. A late example, the twelfth-century metrical *Martyrology of Gorman*, includes saints from the OT and NT, the East, Rome, Anglo-Saxon and Celtic sources. The entry for 24 June conveys something of the delightful familiarity with the saints typical of this work:

> The vigil of John Baptist: Felix and Johannes, perfect men; my Coe, gentle sad; Lucia with them and Festus. Arion, joyous Faelan, secret Etheldreda, Senchan's children and Senan's, to direct me for my leader. (*Martyrology of Gorman*, HBS 1895)

Familiarity, but of a different sort, characterizes the Waning of the Middle Ages, to borrow the title of Huizinga's masterly survey (Pelican 1955). The tale of aberrations is endless and horrifying—a Charles VI of France distributing the ribs of his ancestor St Louis during a banquet, a St Eutropius being credited with causing as well as curing the dropsy. The grosser side of medieval superstitions and the criticisms voiced by a Wyclif, a Gerson or an Erasmus, are no part of our story, except insofar as they led to curtailments of the sanctoral, some total, some benign.

> The Reformation attacked the cult of the saints, and nowhere in the whole contested area did it meet with less resistance .... When, therefore, Catholic Reform had to re-establish the cult of the saints, its first task was to prune it: to cut down the whole luxuriant growth of medieval imagination and establish severer discipline, so as to prevent a reflorescence. (Huizinga, op. cit., p. 170)

THE REFORMERS AND TRENT

Any examination of the Reformers' attitude must begin with Martin Luther. Always loth to introduce violent change into the liturgy, he defended the use of images, but became progressively more reticent about saints' days. If he mentioned the Purification and St Michael in the *Deutsche Messe*, by the time he compiled the *Instructions for the Visitors of Parish Pastors* in Electoral Saxony (1528) he could write: 'The days of Annunciation, Purification, Visitation, St John the Baptist, St Michael's, Apostles' Day, Magdalene—these have already been discarded and could not conveniently be restored' (Luther's *Works*, ET (Philadelphia 1958) 40.298). Yet in the same work he was emphatic on the value of the example of the saints in arousing the people to faith and good works. The Augsburg Confession (n. 21) excludes the veneration of saints. It was

Calvin who argued most comprehensively against the man-made character of canonization, and against the practice of invocation, notably in *Institutes*, 3.20.21-7. Invocation is both unscriptural and blasphemous, for it threatens the unique status of Christ as mediator. The sanctoral disappeared from the continent, but survived in Sweden and England. Olaus Petri (see p. 253) retained most scriptural feasts, those of apostles and several others, although he suppressed Corpus Christi. Brilioth judged that 'the limit of the calendar was to a large extent only on paper' (*Eucharistic Faith and Practice* (SPCK 1930), p. 246). Laurentius Petri officially had seven saints' days, but after the failure of the Red Book of John III and the increasing influence of Calvinism, the sanctoral waned. In England the first two Prayer Books of Edward VI drastically curtailed the Sarum Calendar, but retained some two dozen saints' days, mostly of apostles. The Book of 1662 added over sixty names, but as black letter days, without special commemorations. King Charles the Martyr, the Birth and Restoration of Charles II, and Papists' Conspiracy were included as Red Letter days, but were dropped by an Order in Council in 1859. The Tractarians were in favour of a richer sanctoral, while those who were in the more Evangelical tradition of the Puritans continued to have grave reservations about the whole question of invoking the saints. It is perhaps regrettable that no official machinery exists in the West outside of Rome for recognizing the outstanding Christian witness of men like John Wesley or Albert Schweitzer. Meantime, what of Rome itself since the days of Trent?

Although the Fathers of Trent had singled out a number of abuses in the celebration of the Mass, such as the lighting of a special number of candles in honour of particular saints, the real task of revising the service-books, and with them the sanctoral, was left to a papal commission. This, unwittingly, inaugurated an era of centralization without parallel in earlier times; it also made for a more uniform calendar. The number of saints' days in the 1570 missal of Pius V was reduced to about 130. Within three centuries it had more than doubled. The periods of most rapid increase were the years of the Counter-Reformation itself, and the first half of the present century. The preponderance of founders and members of religious orders among the new saints is significant, and rather too many have reached heaven on an Italian passport.

The new General Roman Calendar of 1969 had in some measure to repeat the work begun at Trent, in order to prevent the sanctoral from engulfing the office of the season, particularly Lent. The number of saints was again reduced, but the aim was also to provide a selection that would be more truly representative. Accuracy and universality were the guiding principles. Any saint of doubtful historicity was excluded—one thinks in this connection of the enormous popularity of St Philomena in the last century. As far as possible, feasts were restored to their traditional dates, the day of the death, of the translation of relics, or of the dedication of an important church. Universality was sought for both in space and time. Every continent is represented, although Africa, Asia, and the Americas less abundantly so than Europe and the Mediterranean basin. All the periods of the Church's history make a contribution, from the NT to modern times. However, more than half date from the sixteenth century or later. All in all, it still remains a largely male clerical gathering. The classification has been simplified, and consists of solemnities, feasts, and memorials. There are fourteen solemnities; but if we exclude those of the Trinity, of our Lord (six, including Christmas) and BVM, this leaves SS Joseph, John Baptist, Peter and Paul, and All Saints. Of the twenty-five feasts, only that of Laurence involves a non-biblical saint. Memorials, unlike solemnities and feasts, do not usually have proper lessons, but all the collects have been specially rewritten. A novel feature is to make the observance of many memorials (92 out of over 150) optional: those which are obligatory are of more universal import. Provision is also made for supplements of local saints.

Having reached an appropriate place at which to conclude this short account of the sanctoral, a better ecumenical statement of the place of saints in the life of the Church could scarcely be found than these words from the *Brief Summary of Christian Doctrine* (n. 24) of Martin Bucer:

> We teach that the blessed saints who lie in the presence of our Lord Christ and of whose lives we have biblical or other trustworthy accounts, ought to be commemorated in such a way, that the congregation is shown what graces and gifts their God and Father and ours conferred upon them through our common Saviour and that we should give thanks to God for them, and rejoice with them as members of the one body over those graces and gifts, so that we may be strongly provoked to place greater confidence in the grace of God for ourselves, and to follow the example of their faith.

ADDITIONAL NOTE

This chapter has inevitably stressed the RC contribution to the continued development and renewal of the sanctoral. The Orthodox Churches for the most part preserve the traditional Calendars of local churches, in which early saints predominate. *The Festal Menaion* (ET Mother Mary and K. T. Ware, Faber 1969) has an important introduction explaining the Christological significance of the greater saints' days. The position in other churches tends to be that of a few ancient saints or none at all. Hence the meagre remarks in the Joint Liturgical Group's booklet on *The Calendar and Lectionary* (ed. R. C. D. Jasper, OUP

1967) which indicate that the time is hardly yet ripe for a comprehensive treatment from an ecumenical point of view. Something of the background to this situation emerges from the chapter on Calendar Conflict in the second volume of Horton Davies' monumental account of *Worship and Theology in England* (Princeton UP 1975). This contains a good survey of the differing Catholic, Anglican, and Puritan attitudes to the commemoration of saints. Further information may be gleaned from A. E. Peaston's work on *The Prayer Book Tradition in the Free Churches* (Clarke 1964).

Currently, however, a major reconsideration of the whole issue is taking place in the Anglican Communion. Bishop Frere's *Some Principles of Liturgical Reform* discussed the cultus of English popular saints and the issue of historicity as far back as 1911. The 1928 Prayer Book contained a considerably revised Calendar. The Anglican Communion is now revising the Calendar province by province, which results in divergences in the dates of some common commemorations and even feasts. A valuable Report was produced by a Commission appointed by the Archbishop of Canterbury after the Lambeth Conference in 1948 entitled *The Commemoration of Saints and Heroes of the Faith in the Anglican Communion* (SPCK 1957) which warned of the danger of adding to the Calendar 'the names of people who were worthy rather than heroic and so lowering the idea of holiness to a more comfortable level' and suggested that there was much to be learnt from the Roman Catholic process of canonization especially its very rigorous examination of the virtues of a candidate's life. Most of the provinces agree in adding certain early saints such as Justin and Anselm but content themselves with including significant figures in their history 'for the information and devotion of the faithful ... without thereby enrolling or commending such persons as Saints of the Church', as the Preface to the Calendar of the Canadian Prayer Book (1962) puts it. The Church of England has not yet authorized a definitive Calendar. The latest report from the Liturgical Commission (GS 292, SPCK 1976) puts forward a very ecumenical list, including not only a number of Anglicans, Caroline divines, Evangelicals, and Tractarians, but also Counter-Reformation saints and Protestant heroes. Among the Anglicans, there are several who are common to a large part of the Communion: Cranmer, Laud, Herbert, the Wesley brothers, Simeon, Keble, and Hannington. The most recent are Bishop Edward King and Florence Nightingale. The revised and expanded Calendar of the PECUSA *Proposed Book of Common Prayer* (1977) includes modern missionaries, some of them martyred, and such recent American bishops as Phillips Brooks and Charles Henry Brent.

VII
THE SETTING OF THE LITURGY

1 Ceremonial

HUGH WYBREW

Andrieu, M., *Les Ordines Romani du haut moyen-âge*. Louvain 1931–61.
Dix, G., *Shape*.
DLW, articles on 'incense' and 'lights'.
Jungmann, J. A., *MRR*.
Klauser, T., (ET) *A Short History of the Western Liturgy*. OUP 1969.

It is usual to distinguish in liturgical worship between rite and ceremonial, as though the latter were a dispensable adornment of the former. In reality, the two are inseparable. The rite, understood as a form of words, has to be performed, and the way in which it is performed is its ceremonial. No celebration of a sacrament can be without ceremonial, although it may be performed with extreme simplicity or great complexity.

In the historical development of Christian worship, ceremonial has come to have theological implications, as well as devotional significance. To illustrate this fact, the present section will concentrate on the different ways in which the Eucharist has been celebrated in the Catholic and Orthodox traditions, and in those of the Reformation.[1]

THE PRE-NICENE EUCHARIST

The Eucharist before the Peace of the Church was usually celebrated in small house-churches. That did not mean it was a casual performance, even in the first century. The first letter of Clement, about A.D. 96, compares the bishop, presbyters, and deacons at the Eucharist with the high priest, priests, and levites of the Jewish Temple (40, 41). That presupposes that all was done with decency and order by the various orders which made up the worshipping Body of Christ, including the order of laity.

The ceremonial of the early Eucharist was largely functional, designed to secure the decent performance of the essential action of the service.[2]

[1] The reader will be helped if he reads this section in conjunction with the section on the Eucharist.
[2] Cf. Dix's description in *Shape*, pp. 103–5.

After the ministry of the word, a linen cloth was spread on the altar, and the bread and wine brought by the people were collected by the deacons, and the requisite amount placed on the table. The bishop, with the presbyters, laid his hands on the oblations in silence. The eucharistic prayer followed, after which the bread was broken by the deacons for distribution in communion. Although in essence a practical action, this had come even in Paul's time to be given a symbolic significance: participation in the one loaf is a sign of the unity of the Body (1 Cor. 10.17). In due course, symbolic actions were to become far more prominent in the Eucharist.

THE DEVELOPMENT OF CEREMONIAL

When Christianity became a recognized religion in the fourth century, its worship moved out of the private house-church into the public basilican church. The bishops became public figures, soon invested with the dignity of magistrates. Christian worship rapidly became a public performance, and its ceremonial became correspondingly more elaborate.

Some of the features of the public celebration of the Eucharist were borrowed from civil practice. When bishops were given the status of magistrates, they adopted also the practice of having lights and incense carried before them when they entered and left the church. In time similar honour was paid to the book of the Gospels, which had come to be regarded as a symbol of Christ himself.

Both lights and incense were used in connection with religious observances in the ancient world. Lights were of course a practical necessity, but by the fourth century were hung before Christian altars with a votive and honorific significance. Incense was not used ceremonially in the first three centuries of the Church, because of its associations with pagan cults and Emperor-worship, although it figures prominently in the visions of the Revelation to John, which seem to reflect Christian worship. From the fourth century its honorific use spread rapidly, and in the East it came to be given propitiatory significance, as in the OT. It was perhaps this understanding which underlies the censing of the church before the Eucharist described by Dionysius the Areopagite about A.D. 500.[1]

Actions of a deliberately symbolic kind began to be used in the Eucharist in the fourth century. The lavabo, or ceremonial washing of the bishop's hands before the eucharistic prayer, is first mentioned by Cyril

[1] For the use of lights in worship, cf. C. E. Pocknee, 'Candles, Lamps and Lights', in *DLW*. For the use of incense, cf. W. J. Grisbrooke, 'Incense', also in *DLW*.

of Jerusalem.[1] It is explained as symbolizing the purity required of those serving the altar, and Ps. 26.6, quoted by Cyril, was then or later recited by the celebrant as his hands were rinsed.

CEREMONIAL DEVELOPMENT IN THE EAST

In the East the Eucharist rapidly came to be performed with a degree of ceremonial splendour which the West achieved only much later. The *Liturgical Homilies* of Narsai witness to this development in the East Syrian church in the middle of the fifth century.[2] They describe a rite celebrated by priests and deacons splendidly vested, at an altar richly adorned. On it stand a cross and the book of the Gospels, and around it lamps shine. The deacons carry liturgical fans, and the smoke of incense fills the air. At the consecration of the sacrament, the priest signs the oblation three times, and bows three times. At the communion, the sacrament is escorted from the sanctuary by the priests and deacons with splendour and glory. The description is reminiscent of a medieval Corpus Christi procession.

Behind this development lies the theology of the Eucharist first clearly set out in Cyril's *Mystagogic Catecheses*. The Eucharist is terrifying in its holiness, and to be approached with fear and trembling. Its consecration is effected by the invocation of the Holy Spirit, to transform the bread and wine into the Body and Blood of Christ. The ceremonial setting of the rite as described by Narsai gives fitting expression to this theology, which had already produced in Cyril's time an elaborate method of receiving the sacrament.

This understanding of the Eucharist passed into the Eastern tradition generally, and influenced the development of its liturgy. The elaboration of ceremonial found in Narsai spread before long to Constantinople. There, in the glorious Church of the Holy Wisdom, built by Justinian in the sixth century, the Eucharist was celebrated with the splendour befitting the chapel of the Byzantine Emperors. The Great Church of Constantinople became the model for the whole Byzantine Church.

The ceremonial high-spot of the Byzantine Eucharist, or Liturgy, came to be the so-called Great Entrance, the procession in which the elements are brought from a side-altar to the altar at the offertory.[3] The remote origin of this procession seems to have been the Eastern custom of collecting the oblations of the people at the door of the church as they came in. Sufficient bread and wine were then transferred to the altar by

---

[1] *Myst. Cat.* 5.2. See p. 195.
[2] *The Liturgical Homilies of Narsai*, ed. R. H. Connolly (CUP 1909).
[3] See p. 211, and R. Taft, *The Great Entrance* (Rome 1976).

the deacons after the ministry of the word. By the fifth century this procession had in some places acquired considerable prominence. Theodore of Mopsuestia interprets it as representing Christ, going forth to be crucified, to be laid upon the altar as in the sepulchre. Behind this understanding of an originally practical movement lies a view of the unconsecrated bread and wine as already symbols of the dead body of Christ. Though this curious theological notion was never accepted in the Byzantine tradition, the procession of the Great Entrance became the chief ceremonial moment of the Byzantine Liturgy for the congregation, from whom the sanctuary was cut off by the screen separating it from the nave.

The later ceremonial development of the Byzantine Liturgy was heavily influenced by the tradition of interpreting the movements of the rite symbolically, first observed in connection with the Great Entrance. By the eleventh century, the Liturgy was commonly held to represent symbolically the whole life of Christ. This tradition, which at first attached itself to existing movements, originally of a practical nature, finished by creating actions of a purely symbolic kind. This tendency was particularly marked in the preparation of the elements, which from the eighth century took place before the Liturgy began, in a preliminary rite called the *Proskomidia* (see pp. 214–5 and plate 14).

The ceremonial of the Byzantine Liturgy was given its more or less final form in the fourteenth century, and is basically that of the modern Orthodox Liturgy.

WESTERN CEREMONIAL DEVELOPMENT

In the West ceremonial developed less swiftly. The classical Roman Mass of the seventh century, described in the *Ordo Romanus Primus* (see p. 68), retains much of the direct simplicity of the early Eucharist. Lights and incense accompany the entry of the bishop and the chanting of the gospel. The chief ceremonial moments in the rite are still essentially practical. At the offertory the people bring their gifts of bread and wine to the chancel rails, where they are collected by deacons. The consecration is performed with no external action, save that of elevating the bread and wine at the final doxology in a gesture of sacrificial offering to God. The breaking of the bread is still a reality, for communion is still general.

But Rome was a conservative church, and soon the initiative in Western liturgical development passed to the church in the Carolingian Empire. The temperament of the Franks was quite other than the sober, restrained mood of the Romans. Under their influence, the severe, practical Roman Mass became more richly ornamented. Censing was extended to the altar at the beginning of the Mass, and to the oblations and the altar at the offertory. The sign of the cross was used in connection with the eucharistic prayer.

This ceremonial development can be seen in some of the later Ordines, which adapted the Roman rite to local customs prevailing in Frankish lands. In this form it was adopted in Rome itself, and in the later Middle Ages became general throughout the West. Local 'uses', originating in certain important cathedral churches, were only variants of this common form. In England the 'use' of Sarum (Salisbury) became the most influential.

The most significant ceremonial development in the West came in the thirteenth century, with the elevation of the Host after the words of consecration in the Canon of the Mass. Introduced in France, to give expression to the theological opinion that the Host was consecrated when the relevant words of the institution narrative had been read, the elevation of the Host, gradually followed by that of the chalice, filled the devotional gap which had been left when the second part of the eucharistic prayer began to be recited in a low voice at Rome in the seventh century. Rapidly it became the focal point of the Mass for the congregation, which had widely ceased to communicate save once a year. To this moment were attracted all the ceremonial resources of the medieval church. Lights were held in front of the Host, so that it might be better seen. Incense was offered, to honour the presence of Christ in the consecrated elements. Bells were rung, both to warn people of the approaching consecration and elevation, and at the elevation itself, so that those unable to be present in church might know the moment of consecration. The elevation became for the West what the Great Entrance had been for centuries in the East—the focal point of popular devotion, and the ceremonial high-spot of the rite.

But by the end of the Middle Ages the solemn Eucharist had ceased to be the typical form of the celebration in the West. In the East there remained only one way of doing the Eucharist: the solemn sung Liturgy, in which clergy, choir, and people all participated. In the West the development of the Low Mass revolutionized the ceremonial of the Eucharist. The solemn Mass required the participation of all the orders of the Christian community, and each had their proper role to play. The spread of the custom of celebrating private votive Masses, and the devotional habit of each priest saying Mass daily, required a simpler way of doing the service, in which one priest could say the whole rite by himself. By the eleventh century, this development had produced the ancestor of the modern Missal, a book which contained all the parts of the

Mass previously contained in separate books used by the different participants.

By the sixteenth century, the Low Mass was regarded as the typical form of the Eucharist. The people knelt throughout, and their part was performed by a single server, making the responses to the priest. Wherever possible, of course, the solemn Mass was still performed on Sundays and feast-days. But the prevalence of the Low Mass caused its ceremonial to be imported into the solemn Mass, so that the celebrant had to read every part of the service himself, even though it was also being sung by one of the other ministers or by the choir.

The ceremonial of both the said and the solemn Mass—'Low' and 'High' Mass—was fixed in every detail by the Missal of Pius V in 1570, and remained the only way of doing the service in the Roman Catholic Church until 1969.[1]

CEREMONIAL IN THE REFORMATION TRADITIONS

The sixteenth-century Reformation produced varying degrees of change in the ceremonial of public worship, particularly of the Eucharist. The theology of the medieval Mass was attacked by all the reformers, whose own theology was given expression in revised rites, all of which restored communion to a central place.

The Lutheran reformation was perhaps the most conservative in this respect. It retained the broad lines of the Mass, with the omission of such parts as seemed doctrinally unacceptable, and the introduction of elements thought to be lacking. The notion of consecration was kept, and the sign of the cross and the sacring bell were widely used, together with kneeling at the consecration, and for receiving communion. But everything which expressed the notion of sacrifice was cut out, above all the offertory.[2]

The Calvinist reform treated the Mass as beyond redemption, and made no use of the traditional rite. Eating the bread and drinking the wine were the central act of the service, in a setting in which exhortation is the dominant note. Ceremonial was deliberately reduced to a minimum. Communion was often received sitting, either at the table or with the people remaining in their places.[3]

In England reform began in an apparently conservative way with the Prayer Book of 1549. The form of the Mass was retained, though its ceremonial was greatly simplified. The elevation of the Host was cut out,

1 Cf. J. D. Crichton, 'Mass, High' and 'Mass, Low', in *DLW*.
2 See pp. 252–3.
3 See pp. 261–2.

with all that had accompanied it. The preparation of the bread and wine was drastically simplified, in order to remove any notion of sacrifice. As in other reformed rites, communion was made an essential part of the service, and was received kneeling.

Reform became openly more radical in the second Prayer Book of 1552. The communion service of that book set out to give expression to the belief that the Eucharist was a meal eaten to commemorate the death of Christ. All traces of medieval ceremonial were removed. The service took place at a table set length-wise in the chancel or nave of the church. The bread and wine were placed on it before the service began, and nothing further was done with them until they were distributed in communion. Any bread and wine remaining could be consumed at home by the minister.

The revision of the Prayer Book in 1662 modified this rite in a conservative direction. The table was to be set altar-wise in the chancel. There was a formal setting of the bread and wine on it at the offertory. During the prayer of consecration the priest was directed to take the paten and the chalice into his hands at the appropriate words of the institution narrative, to break the bread, and to lay his hand on the bread, and on the vessels containing wine to be consecrated.[1]

In practice Anglican eucharistic ceremonial came to vary greatly in different churches. From the seventeenth century onwards, a movement existed which sought to restore a good deal of the ceremonial abolished in the sixteenth century. Lights and even incense were used in some places, and genuflecting to the sacrament was not unknown. But it was the nineteenth century which brought with the Tractarian Movement a more widespread revival of ceremonial. Some churches, while using the Prayer Book rite, performed it with the ceremonial laid down in the Roman Missal. Others used an adaptation of the 'Sarum' ceremonial. By the beginning of the twentieth century it was largely only churches in the Evangelical tradition who retained more or less the way of celebrating Holy Communion as prescribed in the Prayer Book. Most others had been influenced by the catholic revival at least to the extent that the celebrant stood facing East, and not at the north end of the holy table.

MODERN EUCHARISTIC CEREMONIAL

The way in which the Eucharist is now celebrated in many churches of the West is the result of the Liturgical Movement, which began in the Roman Catholic Church in the latter part of the nineteenth century, and

---

[1] See pp. 264–6 and 270. For the ceremonial directions of the successive revisions, cf. *The English Rite*, ed. F. E. Brightman (Rivingtons 1921), vol. ii, pp. 692–3.

has influenced most Western Christians. Its fruits have been seen most clearly in that Church since the second Vatican Council, which initiated sweeping reforms both in the text of the Mass and in the way it is celebrated. The traditional ceremonial of 'High' Mass is rarely performed. Normally the Eucharist is celebrated in such a way as to emphasize that it is a community celebration, in which all take an active part. The priest faces the people across the altar, and ceremonial is relatively simple (see plate 15). Many celebrations are characterized by a certain informality, and movements are only those which are necessary for the performance of the service. Communion is received, usually still in one kind only, at every celebration, by those present.

In the Anglican Church, too, the Liturgical Movement has had much influence. It has succeeded in restoring the Eucharist to its central position in many parishes, and has also modified the way in which it is celebrated. Revised rites have been produced in recent years in all provinces of the Anglican Communion, and they are generally celebrated in a way which emphasizes their community character. Change has been both more gradual and less uniform than in the Roman Catholic Church. While it is true to say that the ceremonial of the Eucharist in many churches is not radically different from that of the modern Roman Mass, older forms of ceremonial, both Anglican and Roman, persist in others.

The Protestant churches have also been affected by the Liturgical Movement. It has produced a greater appreciation of liturgical worship, and a number of new eucharistic rites. These have all marked a return to the sources of Christian worship, going behind the traditions of the Reformation, which were worked out by reaction from the late medieval tradition.

The Liturgical Movement in all Churches has grown out of a study of the basic principles of eucharistic worship. Although these principles have been formed in the light of early Christian worship and theology, the movement has not been simply an attempt to re-create early ceremonial. While much has been learnt from the past, new ways of doing the Eucharist have been evolved, and are being evolved, which are appropriate to the communities worshipping together. They are all characterized by simplicity of movement and action, and are designed to make the basic significance of the rite stand out clearly for those taking part in it.

2 Music and Singing in the Liturgy

J. GELINEAU, SJ

Corbin, S., *L'Eglise à la conquête de sa musique*. Paris 1960.
Dearnley, C., *English Church Music 1650–1750*. Barrie and Jenkins 1970.
Douglas, W., *Church Music in History and Practice. Studies in the Praise of God*. New York 1937.
Fellowes, E. H., *English Cathedral Music*. Rev. edn, Methuen 1974.
Gelineau, J., *Voices and Instruments in Christian Worship*. Burns Oates, and Collegeville, Minn. 1964.
Hutchings, A., *Church Music in the Nineteenth Century*. Jenkins 1967.
Le Huray, P., *Music and the Reformation in England 1549–1660*. Jenkins 1967.
Long, K. R., *The Music of the English Church*. Hodder and Stoughton 1972.
Müller, K. F., and Blankenburg, W., *Die Musik des evangelischen Gottesdienstes*. Leiturgia: Handbuch des evangelischen Gottesdienstes, vol. 4. Kassel 1961.
Quasten, J., *Musik und Gesang in den Kulten der heidnischen Antike und christlichen Frühzeit*. Münster in W. 1930.
Routley, E., *Church Music and Theology*. SCM 1959.
Routley, E., *The Musical Wesleys*. Jenkins 1968.
Routley, E., *A Short History of English Church Music*. Mowbrays 1977.
Routley, E., *Twentieth Century Church Music*. Jenkins 1964.
Routley, E., *Words, Music and the Church*. Jenkins 1969.
Scholes, P. A., *The Oxford Companion to Music*. Ninth edn corrected. OUP 1960.
Stefani, J., 'Bibliographie fondamentale de musicologie liturgique', *LMD* 108 (1971), pp. 175–89.
Westrup, J. A., ed., *New Oxford History of Music*, vol. 2. OUP 1954.

Christian assemblies have at all times and in all places read the Scriptures, prayed, and sung. The Christian liturgy was born singing, and it has never ceased to sing. A good number of the elements of present-day liturgy appeared on the scene only gradually—for example, the feast of Christmas, or church buildings. Others are met with only in a particular cultural area—the iconostasis, or stained glass windows. Singing, however, must be regarded as one of the fundamental constituents of Christian worship. This fits the fact that Christian worship is the public proclamation of the *mirabilia Dei* and of the good and joyful news, an act of thanksgiving, praise, and blessing for the freedom won for us by the resurrection. It is an Amen, an unceasing Alleluia (Rev. 19.4), a Yes to the new Covenant, a hymn of glory to God the Father.

The Church used music and singing in its worship well before it began to ask itself questions about why and wherefore, and such questioning was at first sporadic and empirical, connected with matters of discipline, devotion, and even polemics. It is not till the modern period that we first meet any systematic attempt at theological reflection on the matter. Here too, many different approaches are possible. This chapter will confine itself to three of them, namely those afforded by a Christian understanding of man, by the history of music in the liturgy, and by an analysis of ritual activity.

I

What do singing and music add to the worshipper in the Christian assembly, which is one of faith?

1. Singing and music take pride of place after words and gestures among all the signs and symbols which make up liturgy. To sing a psalm or the Trisagion, to ring a bell or play the organ—these are every bit as much rites as are the reading of a lesson, the saying of a prayer, a procession, or even the breaking of bread. As with any other rite, the purpose of singing and music is to awake meaning and induce an attitude.

The first and most distinctive characteristic of singing would appear to be that of musical time. Singing places a man before God as a creature existing in time. Whether it be the Byzantine Liturgy, the Roman Mass or Anglican Evensong, a large part of the service consists in singing of various sorts. The different chants mark off the order of service (Introit, Kyrie, Gloria, etc.). Augustine goes so far as to say:

> Apart from those moments when the Scriptures are being read or a sermon is preached, when the bishop is praying aloud or the deacon is specifying the intentions of the litany of community prayer, is there any time when the faithful assembled in the church are not singing? Truly I see nothing better, more useful or more holy that they could do.
>
> (*Ep.* 55.18-19; PL 33.204)

2. The liturgy is the shared activity of a people gathered together. No other sign brings out this communal dimension so well as singing. Bodily movements can be synchronized but remain juxtaposed. Many individual voices, however, can actually be fused together, so that when they blend and follow the same rhythm, only one voice is heard—that of the group. This brings out a very strong feeling of unity and of belonging. It even touches on the essential mystery of the Church as *koinonia*. From the time of Ignatius of Antioch down to our own day, singing with one voice has remained a privileged way of expressing unity in diversity. Shortly after becoming bishop of Constantinople, John Chrysostom preached these words to his flock:

The psalm which occurred just now in the office blended all voices together, and caused one single fully harmonious chant to arise; young and old, rich and poor, women and men, slaves and free, all sang one single melody.... All the inequalities of social life are here banished. Together we make up a single choir in perfect equality of rights and of expression whereby earth imitates heaven. Such is the noble character of the Church.

(*Hom.* 5; PG 63.486–7)

3. The Christian liturgy can be celebrated without singing or music: but this is to mutilate it. The liturgy is a 'festal gathering' (Heb. 12.22). A festival implies singing, music, and dancing. A given piece—a Christmas carol, or a National Anthem—may serve as the symbol for a particular celebration. The canticle of Moses, celebrating the deliverance of Passover, became the 'new song' of the Lamb (Rev. 5.9; 15.3–4) and, as such, the symbol of all who have been definitively saved by the One who 'makes all things new' (Rev. 21.5). The eucharistic feast of those who anticipate the coming of the Kingdom is a 'sacrifice of praise' (cf. Ps. 50.14; Heb. 13.15), which needs singing if the sign is to be really complete. In the Psalms, the *todah* (confession—thanksgiving—praise) which, together with the Jewish *berakah* (blessing), makes up the biblical background of the Christian Eucharist, is often associated with music, including the use of instruments (e.g. Ps. 33.1–3). This context of musical praise is found in the assemblies of the people, in the Temple liturgies, and in the proclamation of the Name.

4. A distinctively Christian use of music in the liturgy is met with in the kerygmatic and evangelistic aspect of worship. Following the prophets and even Jesus himself, Christian preachers have made use of rhythm and even melody, in order to proclaim the gospel. This was the style of preaching adopted by Melito of Sardis in his homilies, Ephrem the Syrian in his *madrâshê* and Romanos Melodus in his *kontakia*. A refrain sung by the assembly often punctuated the strophes of the preacher. Even today, the *praeconium pascale* and the prefaces of the Western liturgies take on a rhythmo-melodic form thanks to the musical recitative.

Missionaries of all periods have made use of hymns to teach and spread the Christian faith. The charge of seducing the people by means of hymns has been levelled at heretics from Bardesanes and Arius down to the most modern of sectaries. Popular hymns played a great part in the religious reforms of Luther, Calvin, Wesley, and the Catholic Counter-Reformation. None of this should surprise, since singing adds new power to a text thanks to rhythm and melody. Attempts have sometimes been made to banish all singing from church, either because of its use in heretical propaganda, or on the grounds that it represents a concession to human weakness granted under the old Covenant. To one such objection, the author of the fifth-century *Quaestiones et responsiones ad Orthodoxos* answers:

> The apostle Paul calls the canticle the 'sword of the spirit', because it provides a weapon for those who virtuously fight against the invisible spirits; for the word of God, taking possession of the spirit when sung or spoken, has power to drive away the demons.
>
> *(Qu.* 107; PG 6.1354)

5. If we consider singing and music from the point of view of the worshipper, the emphasis has varied in different periods. The Fathers stressed the ease which singing brings to prayer, and the manner in which it sweetens and tempers the rigours of the law. Thus Basil can write:

> The Holy Spirit sees how much difficulty mankind has in loving virtue, and how we prefer the lure of pleasure to the straight and narrow path. What does he do? He adds the grace of music to the truth of doctrine. Charmed by what we hear, we pluck the fruit of the words without realizing it.
>
> *(Hom. in Ps.* 1; PG 29.211)

Some solitaries, like the abbot Pambo, protested against the way music invaded prayer, but the mainstream of monastic spirituality expects music to add a certain sweetness and savour to the text, provided that the mind is attentive to the meaning of the words, according to the adage *mens concordet voci.*

To-day, the emphasis is less on the powers of liturgical singing as an aid to teaching. These powers retain their importance, but it is the poetic and cathartic quality of music which is stressed. Western liturgy has suffered in the past from an excess of rationalization, and singing during a celebration brings an important corrective. Melody can allow a text to unfold in a way which allows time for contemplation. Music appeals to the emotions rather than to reason, and this too is important when we remember that the Spirit appeals to the whole man.

6. Up till now, we have lumped music and singing together. It is, however, important to distinguish them without separating them. Compared with 'pure' music—instruments and wordless humming, etc.—singing has a privileged position in the Christian liturgy because of its connection with the revealed word. Only singing can combine explicit confession of faith in Christ with musical expression. All music can indeed be religious or sacred, but only that music is specifically Christian which articulates the Christian faith.

It would, however, be wrong to oppose liturgy and music. It is true that the early Church as a whole, and the majority of Eastern Churches today, have excluded all instrumental music from the liturgy. This reserved attitude is to be explained on socio-historical grounds. A balanced attitude to instrumental music sees the instrument as an extension of the human voice and body. Man is widening his capacity for song when he accompanies singing or even plays without actually singing. Hence music, like singing or any other human activity, can become a ritual. It gets its meaning from the celebration as a whole, provided that it in some way prepares for, accompanies, or prolongs the word and the sacrament. It is as signs of, and for, faith that singing and music enter into the sacramental economy of Christian worship.

II

How has the Church used singing and music in its liturgy? A brief historical review will throw light on this aspect of the question.

1. A search through the NT to discover musical allusions will prove disappointing. Today, music is a discipline with a separate existence, and singing is clearly distinguished from mere speech. These distinctions did not obtain in the cultural milieu of the early Church. Hebrew and Greek have no separate word for music. The frontier between singing and speaking was far less precise. As soon as speech turned to poetry, or when public and ceremonial speaking was involved, rhythmic and melodic features were incorporated which today would be classified as musical or at least pre-musical. Music and singing could be present even though none of the vocabulary associated with musical performance might be met with.

Besides this general point, one can go further and recognize an intense lyrical quality in the life of the apostolic Church, particularly in its liturgical assemblies. The Church was born with the proclamation to all nations of the mighty works of God (Acts 2.11). When the Book of Revelation describes the many groups which sing Amen, Alleluia, Holy, and other hymns to God and to the Lamb, the author is using his own experience as a model for the practice of heaven. Other NT texts reflect this lyricism. The canticles in the opening chapters of Luke, and those passages of Paul which are definitely hymnic, witness to the creativity of the early Christian communities. It is quite by chance that we learn that Paul and Silas, when in prison at Philippi, spent the night hours 'praying and singing hymns to God' (Acts 16.25). There is the advice of the Epistle to James: 'Is any one cheerful? Let him sing praise' (Jas. 5.13). The Pauline corpus contains positive injunctions on the question of singing in the Christian assembly. As well as the oft-cited references in

Colossians (3.16) and Ephesians (5.19) there is Paul's acceptance of the right of each worshipper at Corinth to propose a hymn, provided it be intelligible and edifying in the Spirit (1 Cor. 14.13–17, 26).

Two characteristics of Christian singing emerge from the NT. It must be filled with the Holy Spirit, and it must be the expression of a conscious faith. It is not a question of making music for its own sake, but of expressing the word of God.

2. The first three centuries of the Church have left us many references to singing during the assembly, and also a relatively large number of hymn-texts. Pliny speaks of the *carmen* to Christ of the Christians of Bithynia (cf. p. 51). Even if this is more probably a baptismal profession of faith, the lyrical dimension is not excluded. Hippolytus describes the *Lucernarion* (*Ap. Trad.* 26). There is abundant evidence from Africa, Egypt, and the East that the Church of the martyrs was rich in song.

Some of the fragments of hymns which have survived from this period emanate from gnostic circles: The Hymn to Jesus, or the Hymn of the Soul (see p. 52). Others, like the *Phos hilaron*, which has been preserved in the evening service of several oriental liturgies, or the earliest kernel of the *Gloria in excelsis*, are the remains of a creative activity which was abundant in the second and third centuries (Eusebius, *HE* 5.28). This early hymnology, like the prayer of the martyrs, bore a strongly Christological character. In form, it avoided classical metres and remained closer to the poetry of the Bible and to rhythmic prose. By the time of Clement of Alexandria the isosyllabic tendency of Christian hymnody is emerging. This gives it a popular character, and underlines the priority given to the words of the text, rather than to poetic or musical experiment. Contrary to the accepted opinion, there is in fact no evidence to suggest that the early Christians sang the Psalms in their worship once the separation from the synagogue was complete. The Psalms were rather read, along with the rest of the Bible. The first clear reference to the singing of the Psalms is to be found in a fragment of the *Acts of Paul* (ed. C. Schmidt and W. Schubart (Hamburg 1936), p. 50). During the third century, several authors confirm that certain psalms were used, particularly during the agape or the Lucernarion. The congregation replied with an Alleluia to the verse read by the cantor or reader.

3. After the peace of Constantine, the fourth and fifth centuries witness the elaboration and organization of the liturgy. From the point of view of singing, the most noteworthy feature of this period is the spread of responsorial psalmody throughout the whole of the Christian world. A verse from the psalm is chosen to serve as refrain for the congregation between the verses of the soloist. This way of singing the Psalms, besides

being popular, had a considerable religious value, whether at Antioch under Chrysostom or at Milan under Ambrose. Countless bishops of the period commented on the Psalms for their people. Psalms were sung on every possible occasion—between the readings at the Eucharist, during the vigils, during the morning and evening offices, during processions, and even in the fields or at home.

For a time, ecclesiastical hymnody suffered something of a set-back. Biblical songs were preferred, and Basil voiced this mood when he contrasted human formulae with the songs of the Spirit when replying to the charge of innovation which had been levelled at the office he compiled for Neo-Caesarea (*Ep.* 207.4; PG 32.763). However, in spite of the prohibitions of several local councils, hymnography soon began to find new vitality thanks to the genius of Ephrem the Syrian and the pastoral concern of Ambrose, the father of Western hymnody. In their different ways, they both perfected the popular model of a hymn made up of strophes and isosyllabic lines, whether in metrical form or not. It was to have an endless posterity.

During this period there was developed a significant variant of responsorial psalmody, namely antiphony, a term first met in the fifth century. To begin with, the assembly was divided into two choirs or choruses, which in turn repeated the refrain called *onyâtâ* (Chaldean), *hypakoi* (Byzantine), or *responsorium* (Latin). Gradually, non-biblical texts were used in the refrains. The rudimentary aspect of a concert or game provided by this alternation of two choirs also spread into virtually all the liturgical families. This explains the generalized practice of singing in two choirs or sides in much of the Church's ritual music, as well as providing the clue to the structure of many of the traditional forms which derive from this practice.

4. Confessional and political divisions in the East, and the barbarian invasions in the West, reduced the extent of popular participation in the liturgy. It was now that cenobitic monasticism provided fresh impulse to the life of the liturgy, as can be seen in the local churches of Palestine or certain western towns from the sixth century. The older responsorial psalmody loses its vigour. In the East, the psalm-refrain develops into the *troparion*, a text which retells the mystery of a feast with poetic freedom, and introduces a note of contemporary praise or petition. As the *troparion* increases in length, so the number of psalm-verses recited diminishes. John, Cosmas Melodus, both monks of Jerusalem, and their successors continued to enrich Christian hymnography. In the West, a different pattern emerged. The number of psalm-verses was not reduced, but the refrain was no longer repeated after each verse. Gradually, the verses

were recited alternately by two choirs, and the whole psalm was preceded and concluded by an antiphon almost always taken directly from Scripture. Ecclesiastical singing eventually became the almost exclusive preserve of monks and clerics. Poets and skilled chanters are met with, and music receives an ever-increasing place in the liturgy. In the eighth century, choir-schools are found from Mesopotamia to Spain, and even in Rome, which had remained hitherto soberly conservative. In the time of Gregory the Great, the *schola* was a training ground for readers; after the Syrian popes, it becomes the *schola cantorum*.

At this time, the art of the *psaltes* or chanter consisted in adapting received musical models to the various texts. They remained close to recitative, and the tones for reciting were classified according to eight modes which corresponded to the eight weeks from Easter to Pentecost. Such a classification was originally ritual rather than musical.

5. The Frankish chanters of the turn of the eighth century, perhaps in Metz, may be credited with the greatest revolution in the history of Christian singing. They introduced a melodic 'repertoire', and with it, a concentration on music as such. They began with the *cantilena Romana* and the texts of the antiphonary as this had been fixed by Gregory the Great. On this basis they elaborated a sumptuous melodic version whose prestige was such that it gradually spread throughout the whole West. This phenomenon was made possible by the emergence, at about the same time, of a primitive form of musical notation which enabled the tunes of this oral composition to be more or less fixed and handed on in writing. Spreading like ripples in a pool, the melodies of what we now call Gregorian chant cross Europe in manuscript form. By the thirteenth century they have even supplanted the indigenous Roman chant known as Old Roman—a somewhat debatable appellation, since a certain amount of evolution had occurred in the intervening period (see plate 20).

Gregorian plainchant is not the only instance of a new-found focus on music itself. First the Byzantine theorists, and then their disciples in the West, began to apply to chants and melodies used in the liturgy the musical theories of ancient Greek music as this was refracted by men like Boethius. It is in this period that the first tentative efforts are made in diaphonic music and counterpoint, and these too pass into the liturgy. As the texts of the antiphonary had largely been fixed by Gregory, the creative vein produced the whole series of tropes, proses, and sequences. Another category where production continued unabated was that of the *Ambrosiana*, strophic hymns which sometimes retained the *metrum* of classical metre, and sometimes abandoned it in favour of *rhythmum* or tonic speech accent. A special mention among this vast corpus must be given to those proses and sequences which survived right through the Middle Ages and gave rise to the *Kirchenlied* of German-speaking countries (*Victimae pascali, Veni Creator*, etc.). In the Roman Catholic Church, these pieces were often the only really popular part of the liturgical repertoire, the rest being the preserve of semi-specialist chanters or even professional musicians.

6. With the advent of the *Ars nova*, the history of liturgical singing becomes virtually identical with that of western music. What J. A. Jungmann called 'the centrifugal force of music in the liturgy' makes its effect, for better and for worse. The better leads to the production of masterpieces of sacred music. The worse will be the increasing divorce between the practice of the trained musician and the popular taste he will tend to despise; between an *ars musica* which continues to evolve, and a sclerotic and deformed *cantus ecclesiasticus*; between concert performances in church and the deep meaning of the rites. In the baroque period, sacred music conjures up a world of princely courts, great churches, and opulent monasteries rather than of ordinary parishes and simple faithful.

This protracted alliance between culture and religion benefited music much more than it did liturgy. But there were also some noteworthy attempts to redress the balance. Pride of place must be given to that of Luther and those other Reformers who restored life and dignity to the liturgical singing of the congregation. The Catholic attempt to rediscover the true worth of congregational singing was slower, less radical, but still not negligible. A good example would be the Masses of Henri Du Mont in so-called 'musical plain-chant' which were, for nearly three centuries, almost the only popular liturgical chants used in French parishes.

7. The age of the Enlightment marks the summit and also the end of this particular evolution. The nineteenth century sees the beginnings of a rupture between sacred and profane music. This concept of 'sacred music' which is now elaborated for the first time implies an understanding of church music as something grave, archaic, and unaffected by the contemporary world. The reform initiated in the Roman Church by Pius X is particularly significant. Palestrina is the model, and above all, a Gregorian chant freshly rediscovered amid an uncritical admiration for an idealized medieval Christendom. From now on, 'modern' music develops outside the life of the Church. On the rare occasions when the Church and contemporary music meet, it will be through the organ repertoire or elaborate choral works.

8. The liturgical renewal which developed slowly but surely in the twentieth century had something of an archaeological flavour to begin

with. But sooner or later, it was bound to call into question the whole purpose of singing and music in the liturgy. If Christian worship really is a symbolic activity in which an assembly expresses its faith, then it follows that any singing or music must belong to the believing people as a whole, and not remain the special preserve of a chosen few, be they clerics or musicians. Again, if rites are a cultural as well as a religious phenomenon, then the language and the musical form used to clothe them must be both practicable and meaningful for each different culture and for each given assembly. From these basic principles has stemmed the whole radical evolution in Christian worship, which has crossed confessional boundaries. In this matter of worship, the clock cannot now be put back.

ADDITIONAL NOTE
ON THE ENGLISH TRADITION
BY THE EDITORS

In England the complexities of the Sarum Rite (see pp. 236–7) were matched by exceptional magnificence in polyphonic composition in the hands of Tallis, Taverner, Sheppard, Tye, White, and others. These, as the Reformation progressed, applied their talents to the fixed texts of the new vernacular liturgy, and other works ('anthems') to enrich its relative austerity. This tradition was continued by their successors, Byrd, Gibbons, Morley, Weelkes, and Tomkins, who were also leading composers of secular music. The high quality of their music, coupled with the survival and fresh flowering of choral foundations in cathedral and collegiate churches with their twice daily choral offices, assured the continuance of the tradition despite the disruption of the civil war. So at the Restoration, Humfrey, Locke, Blow, and Purcell, leading composers of the day, were able to develop this tradition and adapt it to new styles, with such success that, after Handel, secular music took second place to church music; while the entirely male choirs of the foundations safeguarded the future of boys' singing. The tradition continued through the nineteenth century, at varying depths of banality, with honourable exceptions among the works of the Wesleys, until the so-called English renaissance of the early twentieth century brought new life to ecclesiastical and secular music alike, through the work of Stanford, Wood, and others; after which nearly every leading British composer has added something to the liturgical repertory.

The 1549 liturgy, following Cranmer's pioneer litany of 1544, was given a monophonic setting by John Merbecke in 1550. Soon a polyphonic equivalent was developed (a type of *falso bordone*), thus giving rise to the method of psalmody known as the 'Anglican chant'.

III

Those parts of the liturgy which are sung or set to music are constitutive elements of the total ritual celebration. They may make up a separate rite in themselves (as in the case of an acclamation or a hymn), they may accompany a rite (as in the case of a processional), or they may be integrated into a rite (as the recitative is integrated into the preface). There are different ways of classifying this musical activity. One may consider it according to its function—a hymn to reflect on the word, a litany for the intercessions, a processional for the offertory. Or one might adopt more formal criteria, and label a piece as responsorial, antiphonal, strophic, with or without refrain etc. The more traditional classification by genre could be adopted—psalmody, antiphon, hymn etc. Another starting point would be to consider the person who executes the piece— celebrant, deacon, cantor, choir. A further tool of analysis would be the musical style—homophonic, polyphonic, concertante; or the idiom— modal, diatonic, atonal.

In the section which follows, the system of classification will be based on the axiom that the main characteristic of singing in Christian worship is to act as a support for the words. Hence we shall study the relation of words to music in the different ritual situations which confront us in the liturgy. In this way, our analysis will not be confined merely to set forms or to obvious functions. The fundamental conviction behind such an approach is simple. The liturgy is primarily an activity, an action. It consists in the actual performing, rather than in the set of things or pieces or rituals to be performed. Hence, in each ritual situation, we should be looking for the real human and religious dimensions which give significance to the particular musical activity.[1] In the liturgy, every musical 'action' will involve three things: a 'significant' human act, a symbolic and ritual context, and a given musical form. This classification may be illustrated by means of a diagram, where it will be seen that the relative importance given to the verbal and the musical elements varies in inverse proportion.

WORD ←————————————————————————→ MUSIC

Chant
'Verbo-Melodism'

Meditation	Hymn
'Psalmody'	*'Lied'*
Proclamation	
'Cantillation'	Acclamation
Ordinary speech	
	Vocalise, *Jubilus*, Instruments

[1] Cf. G. Stefani, *L'acclamation de tout un peuple* (Paris 1967).

1. Starting from the 'ordinary speech' end of the curve, the first form of rhythmo-musical recitation we reach is 'proclamation'. It is the activity in which an individual, or more exceptionally a choral group, conveys a message to the assembly. The ritual situations are those of reading a passage from the Bible, a prayer, a preface, or a blessing. The word being proclaimed remains in the foreground. Such elements of rhythm and melody as are introduced do not constitute a musical form independent of the words. The rhythm is that of ordinary speech, stylized to some extent. It is a type of recitative, either pre-musical (indeterminate pitch) or musical (precise notes). This form of recitative is very characteristic of Judaeo-Christian worship, where it is especially used in the reading of the Bible. Musicologists employ the term 'cantillation' to describe it, and at the same time to distinguish it from other forms met with in music (*stilo recitativo, secco, accompagnato*).

Liturgical cantillation in living languages may pose problems where this style of singing has virtually disappeared. This is the case in western culture, apart from exceptions like children's story-telling or learning by rote. When cantillation is employed in modern music, there is almost always an instrumental accompaniment. Yet in spite of cultural difficulties, there remain occasions in the liturgy when the proclamation of Scripture needs to be solemn, and when something in the nature of a revised form of cantillation will be called for.

2. Meditation, musically speaking, is that activity in which those who are celebrating consciously savour a text thanks to the use of rhythmic cadences and a more or less formalized tone pattern. The collective recitation of the Lord's Prayer, or of intercessions and versicles, may take this form. In Christian worship, psalmody has been the most typical form of meditation, and in its biblical sense this always implies rumination upon words which are pronounced aloud. In this way, each person is 'informed', possessed almost, by the inspired words he pronounces.

Traditional psalm-singing has often combined several different musical activities. The responsorial psalmody of the early Church combined the recitation of the verses by the psalmist with the meditation of the assembly as it repeated the refrain. Later, with the introduction of alternate recitation by two choirs or continuous '*in directo*' recitation by all, a whole psalm could serve as the text for meditative recitation by the entire assembly. The development of troparia and antiphons combined recitative with something much closer to genuine chant (see 3 below). Psalmody in the strict sense must be distinguished from the singing of metrical psalms. Here the versification, regular strophic pattern and specific melodies constituted a sub-class of hymn. True psalmody

451

remains a species of cantillation in which the biblical text is given forth in a manner which respects its poetic structure (e.g. parallelism), thanks to a melodic pattern or tone which can be adapted. The use of modern languages, and the development of the practice of meditation during worship, may call for fresh musical solutions. But psalmody in some form remains indispensable in the liturgy, providing it with an approach to prayer that is both active and yet contemplative.

3. The activity we have called 'chant' introduces a genuinely musical expression, while always adhering completely to the words of the text. In a Gregorian antiphon, for example, the melody can be identified: it has a complete musical shape. And yet this shape evolves organically from the sentences, words, and syllables of the spoken text. The term 'verbo-melodism', or word-melody, has been used to describe this sort of singing, in which the music is never there for its own sake, but always remains subservient to the meaning and affective quality of the text.

In many ways, chant may be considered the form of singing which is best adapted to Christian worship. The monodic tradition of the early Church made use of extensive vocalization and of the full palette of modal colour. Later, harmony was added, as in the Slav liturgy. Today, the rhythmic possibilities offered by the heightened recitatives of African chant and Negro Spiritual are being explored.

4. With the hymn we move to the side where the musical element is more predominant. By hymn we mean in particular the isosyllabic *lied* with strophes, and perhaps a refrain. The melody has its own architecture, based on the laws of rhythm and modality. Its overall structure may stem from the literary strophe (number of lines and feet), but it is the melody which seems to lead, both because of its regular rhythm and its cadences. The best examples of hymn offer an admirable balance between music and text. The latter changes, the former is continually repeated, so that this interplay of stability and change produces a characteristic progression in time and mood. Western culture created this form of 'closed time' which contrasts with the endless melody of the Orient. The western Christian tends to consider the hymn as the ideal form of congregational singing, both from a musical and popular point of view. It corresponds to those ritual situations when the congregation acts as a group, whether to reply to the word of God or to utter praise and entreaty. The hymn acts as a mirror in which the congregation can see itself. However, the drawback of the closed form is sometimes felt in situations when the ritual activity ought to take precedence over the actual singing.

5. Acclamation develops from the human cry, developed and stylized. A

shout or cry is man's vital response to an intense situation. The ritual situations which involve acclamation are important—the cry for help of an oppressed people (Maranatha, Hosanna), the prayer of intercession (Kyrie eleison), the heart-felt ratification of covenant and revelation (Amen), the joy of a people which is saved (Alleluia). Acclamations represent high points of the activity of the assembly. They express solidarity in faith and conversion. They are a religious experience. In this type of activity, the notional content of the words being uttered is of less importance than the vocal and corporal activity itself. This explains why it is possible to retain liturgical acclamations in Hebrew, Greek, or Latin. Their phonetic qualities and their traditional character outweigh the possible absence of precise rational meaning.

Social tolerance to the expressive value of shouts and cries varies enormously according to the cultural and sociological background of different assemblies. And yet to reduce ritual acclamations to a sort of shapeless mumble is to destroy their whole point. Singing gives them style and a hieratic quality. Polyphony lends grandeur and richness. But always, their impact depends more on rhythm than on melody.

6. Finally, at the musical extreme of our diagram, we come to pure vocal music without any words, the *jubilus*. Whether in monody or in polyphony, there are compositions in which the text is not necessarily considered as a form of discourse but serves rather as a starting-point for the play of voices (e.g. a motet or a vocal fugue). The limit is reached with instrumental music where there are no voices. Yet such situations are not to be excluded *a priori* from the Christian liturgy, even if ecclesiastical authorities have often intervened in a negative manner. Such cases of pure music fit in with those festive moments of the celebration when the action does not need words, as in a procession. There are also poetic and contemplative moments, when music can prolong the spoken word and take us further into the mystery. There are moments of pure gift, as with the organ music which can introduce or conclude a ceremony. For the musician, playing an instrument can become a means of prayer in so far as it is an activity done before God in faith.

Christian liturgy calls on all the resources of sound through which man can express his faith in the worshipping assembly. It even preserves musical forms which contemporary culture has neglected or been unable to assimilate. Man at prayer needs such forms. But the liturgy can also be open to new sources of sound, like electronic music. There is a place in worship even for the unexpected. It is the whole man who must worship: not only with his mind, but with his voice, and even with his body too, with the rhythm of dance and instrument which prolongs his bodily activity. Finally, amid the great diversity of rites, languages, cultures, and confessions within Christianity, music remains a privileged meeting point. When the liturgy is sung or set to music, the Christian assembly is more inviting. To those separated by the unfortunate divisions of the past, or who are unable to surmount their own isolation, music offers a sign of reconciliation and of communion.

3 Hymnody in Christian Worship

ALAN DUNSTAN

Bett, H., *The Hymns of Methodism*. 3rd edn Epworth 1945.

Dearmer, P., *Songs of Praise Discussed*. OUP 1933.

Dunstan, A., *These Are the Hymns*. SPCK 1973.

Frost, M., ed., *Historical Companion to Hymns Ancient and Modern*. Wm Clowes & Son 1962.

Hodges, H. A., and Allchin, A. M., *A Rapture of Praise*. Hodder and Stoughton 1966.

Julian, J., *Dictionary of Hymnology*. John Murray 1907.

Manning, B. L., *The Hymns of Wesley and Watts*. Epworth 1942.

Northcott, C., *Hymns in Christian Worship*. Lutterworth 1964.

Parry, K. L., *Companion to Congregational Praise*. Independent Press 1953.

Patrick, Millar, *Four Centuries of Scottish Psalmody*. OUP 1949.

Phillips, C. S., *Hymnody Past and Present*. SPCK 1937.

Rattenbury, J. E., *The Eucharistic Hymns of John and Charles Wesley*. Epworth 1948.

Rattenbury, J. E., *The Evangelical Doctrines of Charles Wesley's Hymns*. 3rd edn Epworth 1954.

Routley, E. K., *The English Carol*. Herbert Jenkins 1958.

Routley, E. K., *The Music of Christian Hymnody*. Tideforth Press 1957.

Routley, E. K., *Hymns and Human Life*. John Murray 1952.

Routley, E. K., *Hymns Today and Tomorrow*. DLT 1966.

Singing a 'new song to the Lord' was a characteristic of early Christian worship and has attended many forms of spiritual renewal in the history of the Church. In his comment on Ps. 148, Augustine wrote: 'Know ye what a hymn is? It is a song with praise of God.... A hymn then containeth these three things: song and praise, and that of God.'[1]

[1] Quoted in Julian, p. 640.

I

Psalms and hymns and spiritual songs are enjoined in Ephesians and Colossians, and Paul and Silas occupied the night in gaol at Philippi by 'praying and singing hymns unto God'. Perhaps the psalms and canticles of the OT formed part of their praise; but it seems likely that Christians very quickly produced their own distinctive hymnody. Various passages in the NT have been identified as quotations from hymns, notably Eph. 5.14 and the 'kenotic' hymn in Phil. 2.6–11.

The Sanctus, the Gloria in excelsis and the Trisagion are almost Biblical; the Te Deum and the evening hymn translated by John Keble as 'Hail gladdening light' are of an early date, and the latter is referred to, on a point of doctrine, by St Basil in the fourth century. The expressive hymns written in the fourth century by St Ephrem in the East and St Ambrose in the West had a great influence. Egeria mentions that hymns were sung at every office she attended in Jerusalem, and it was probably through the early monastic offices that hymn-singing began to form a regular part of Christian worship. Five manuscripts, collected by Clemens Blume, and published in the *Analecta Hymnica Medii Aevi*, have been taken to represent what was in general use in the Benedictine order before the ninth century. The hymnal belonging to the cathedral church in Canterbury illustrates tenth-century practice with hymns for the offices, special seasons, and festivals of saints. The hymns in the Sarum Breviary reveal both a dependence on earlier sources and the new trends and practices of the later Middle Ages; by that time, *Pange Lingua* had joined *Vexilla Regis* in the hymns for Passiontide.

With the Carolingian period, a new type of hymn-singing arose—the sequences which belonged to the Mass rather than the offices. Liturgically and musically, these arose from the Alleluia with which the variable scriptural passage ended; on festive occasions, the last syllable was extended over a long musical phrase, and gradually words were substituted for the syllable. When independent hymns were written to fulfil the same function in the Mass, they were also called the 'sequence'—'Come thou Holy Paraclete' is a modern translation of one such hymn.

Both for the offices and for the sequence, hymns tended to be simple, objective, and doctrinal. But there were other occasions of hymn-singing. There were the hymns of the Church in controversy, the Arians and their opponents singing such in their processions. There was the ecstatic hymnody represented by the collection that Abelard made for Heloise. The devotional poems of Bernard of Cluny were by no means intended for singing; yet excerpts from *Hora Novissima* represent for many modern congregations their closest acquaintance with the hymnody of the Middle Ages.

Erik Routley has claimed of the Middle Ages:

> We have examples of every sort of hymnody that we shall find in later times. We have liturgical hymnody, ecstatic hymnody, controversial hymnody and devotional hymnody, the last three over and against the first, and firmly excluded from the offices of the Church. What the Reformation did was to harness the forces which produced the hymnody of devotion and controversy and ecstasy, and develop a new kind of congregational hymnody, sternly disciplined and immensely powerful.[1]

II

Certainly, the Reformation saw the beginning of hymn-singing as we now understand it. Hitherto, as we have seen, it was generally restricted in church to those who sang the offices and the Mass. Now it became an essentially congregational activity. So far as the Churches of the Reformation are concerned, it remained—almost until the liturgical movement of this century—the only active way in which the people participated in the service. The C of E provided in the Prayer Book considerable occasions of involvement in services. But during the centuries of widespread illiteracy, it was probably during the metrical psalms—'lined out' by the clerk—that the worshippers were most conscious of taking part in the worship.

Hymn-singing blossomed in Lutheran Germany—where already there was a distinctive tradition of church music. The conservative nature of Lutheran liturgical revision facilitated the use of hymns. For in general the Sunday morning service consisted of the Ante-Communion; an introit and gradual were retained, but in the place of the old propers, German hymns were sung. Martin Luther was himself a writer of hymns and composer of tunes—of which 'A safe stronghold our God is still' is the most celebrated example. Luther was followed by such writers as Rinkhart and Gerhardt, and the seventeenth and eighteenth centuries are both marked by new bursts of hymn-writing. Since the Sunday service included the pre-Reformation selection of epistles and gospels, chorales and voluntaries alike began to be 'proper' to particular Sundays and festivals. Luther himself had said 'I would fain see all arts, especially music, in the service of him who made and created them', and his object was fulfilled in the development of the chorale.

Within Calvinism, the 'new song' took the form of psalmody. In

1 Routley, *Hymns and Human Life*, pp. 31–2.

Geneva itself, the psalms proved an exciting discovery, and the Psalter, with all its diversity of mood and aspiration, became the sole vehicle of the people's praise. Rediscovery of the richness of the Psalter itself was one reason for this; another was the belief that only strict paraphrases of Scripture were appropriate for public worship. The Reformed service was again modelled upon the medieval synaxis, but adaptation was far more radical than in Lutheran Germany, and the old table of epistles and gospels tended quite quickly to disappear. Martin Bucer's Strassburg Liturgy refers to the singing of psalms before and after the sermon, and it also refers to the use of a psalm or hymn (i.e. a metrical version of another passage of Scripture) 'instead of the introit'. The same form provides for a psalm or hymn 'according to the occasion' in place of the creed, thereby anticipating the English Dissenting tradition of expressing belief through hymnody. *The Forme of Church Prayers* (Geneva 1542) provides for the singing of psalms during the administration of the sacrament.

The Geneva Psalter of 1562 appeared a year after the death of Louis Bourgeois, who contributed so many of its most enduring tunes. But these were known and sung by the English exiles who fled to Geneva during the reign of Mary Tudor; and it was therefore this strand of Protestant hymnody that exercised the most direct influence in England in the two centuries that followed the Reformation. Cranmer's first Prayer-Book (see pp. 264–5) had left the medieval introits in place; and although the 1552 Book still allowed the possibility of singing parts of the service, there was no appointed place for psalms and hymns. The re-enactment of that book in 1559 was, however, accompanied by Royal Injunctions, one of which stated:

> that in the beginning or at the end of common prayers, either at morning or evening, there may be sung a hymn or such-like song ... in the best sort of melody or music that may be conveniently devised, having regard that the sense of the hymn may be understood and perceived.[1]

This led to the publication in 1562 of the '*Whole Book of Psalmes*' (Sternhold and Hopkins), which reigned supreme in English worship until the production in 1696 of the New Version by Nicholas Brady and Nahum Tate.

In Anglican worship, the metrical psalms were commonly used before and after the sermon. In the parish churches they were often the only form of singing; in cathedrals, they took their place (after the Restoration) alongside anthems and settings of canticles. The metrical psalms were usually bound together with the Prayer Books, thus constituting a quasi-official but widely-used appendix.

[1] Gee-Hardy, *Documents*, p. 435.

Within the Presbyterian and Puritan traditions, the psalms and paraphrases were emphatically the only music permitted, and they were unaccompanied. They were led by a 'precentor'—a new lay office in Protestantism. John Knox's *Forme of Prayers* decreed the singing of psalms 'in a playne tune' (not plain-song!), and both he and the 'Middleburg' Puritans suggested Ps. 103 for use after the sacrament. In Scotland, the texts of the metrical psalm were regarded as sacred in themselves, although the tunes were not; hence arose the curious custom of 'practice-verses' with which to learn the tunes.

In the years that followed the Reformation, both in the C of E and the Puritan congregations, the metrical psalm became a regular and expected ingredient of worship. Such singing was never obligatory; but in Anglicanism, it became as much part of regular Sunday worship as the services of the Prayer Book itself.

III

The eighteenth-century flowering of English hymnody did not immediately affect the worship of the C of E. But it represented a new enthusiasm for hymns, and a new concept of the purpose which they were to serve.

This cannot be better illustrated than by reference to two famous prefaces. First, that of Isaac Watts to his *Psalms of David imitated in New Testament Language*. Watts was concerned that the OT should be used and interpreted in the light of the NT, and that the Psalms in particular should become *Christian* praises:

> It is necessary to divest *David* and *Asaph* etc. of every other character but that of a *psalmist* and a *saint*, and to make them *always speak the common sense of a Christian*. When the Psalmist describes Religion by the *Fear* of God, I have often joined *Faith and Love* to it. Where he talks of sacrificing *Goats and Bullocks*, I rather chuse to mention the sacrifice of *Christ, the Lamb of God*. When he *attends the Ark with shouting in Zion*, I sing the *Ascension of my Saviour into heaven*, or *His presence in His Church* on earth.[1]

Hence, Ps. 72 becomes

Jesus shall reign where'er the sun
Doth his successive journeys run.

In his metrical Psalter, he was confined to certain standard metres already in general use for singing. But to the verses he gave a smoothness and a literacy that did not destroy their simplicity. Tate and Brady's version of Ps. 90, which began

[1] Quoted in Manning, p. 180.

O Lord the Saviour and Defence
Of us thy chosen Race,
From age to age thou still hast been
Our sure abiding place,

now gave way to the unforgettable

Our God, our help in ages past,
Our hope for years to come,
Our shelter from the stormy blast,
And our eternal home.

In no other writer are the themes of natural and revealed theology so nicely balanced. Ps. 19 bears the title 'The Books of Nature and Scripture compared'. A Passiontide hymn, restricted on the whole to Watts' own Independent tradition, deserves to be as well-known as 'When I survey':

Nature with open volume stands
To spread her Maker's praise abroad;
And every labour of his hands
Shows something worthy of a God.

But in the Grace that rescued man,
His brightest form of glory shines,
Here on the Cross 'tis fairest drawn
In precious blood and crimson lines.

Here his whole nature stands complete;
Nor wit can guess, nor Reason prove
Which of the letters best is writ,
The Power, the Wisdom, or the Love.

Beside the paraphrases are the hymns for the Lord's Supper (from which the above-quoted verses are taken), and hymns 'composed on Divine Subjects' which, though unquestionably biblical, were not paraphrases and relied upon no single passage of Scripture. This, as much as his work on the Psalter, makes Watts a hymn-writer in the modern tradition. Much of his work has passed into oblivion; a hymn with the title 'Papist idolatry reproved; a psalm for the 5th of November' could hardly have survived. But the *Divine and Moral Songs* for children were admired for more than two centuries, and the conclusion of his hymn on the Trinity might almost have been written in this generation:

Where reason fails
With all her powers,
There faith prevails
And love adores.

459

The second preface is that which accompanied the *Collection of Hymns for the use of the people called Methodists*, published in 1780. Here Wesley wrote:

> The hymns are not carelessly jumbled together, but carefully ranged under proper heads, according to the experience of real Christians. So that the book is, in effect, a little body of experimental and practical divinity.[1]

John Wesley went on to claim that no such hymn-book had yet been published in the English language. He had not been responsible for the writing of many of the hymns, so his claim was not 'inconsistent with modesty'. But, he asked:

> In what other collection of this kind have you so distinct and full an account of scriptural Christianity? such a declaration of the heights and depths of religion, speculative and practical? strong cautions against the most plausible Errors; particularly those that are now most prevalent? and so clear directions for making your calling and election sure; for perfecting holiness in the fear of God?

He was proud of the standard of the English and devoted a whole paragraph to justification of its excellence. But this was always subservient to the main purpose of the book:

> When Poetry thus keeps its place as the handmaid of Piety, it shall attain not a poor perishable wreath, but a crown that fadeth not away.

These prefaces are quoted at length because they represent a new *raison d'être* for hymnody, and suggest a quite new way of using hymns. This new use of hymns was to flourish from the end of the eighteenth century in all the churches of the Dissenting tradition, but particularly among the people called Methodists who do not quite belong to that tradition. B. L. Manning wrote:

> Hymns are for Dissenters what the liturgy is for the Anglican. They are the framework, the setting, the conventional, the traditional part of divine service as we use it. They are, to adopt the language of the liturgiologist, the Dissenting Use.[2]

To this we must return. For a moment we may linger with this new discovery of hymnody, and on the effect that the 1780 Collection has had in Christendom. To quote Manning again:

> This little book—some 750 hymns—ranks in Christian literature with the

[1] Quoted in successive editions of *Wesley's Hymns* and *The Methodist Hymn Book*.
[2] Manning, p. 133.

Psalms, the Book of Common Prayer, the Canon of the Mass. In its own way, it is perfect, unapproachable, elemental in its perfection.[1]

The book of experimental divinity was, of course, to be expanded and to contain many more of the 4000 hymns with which Charles Wesley is credited. The doctrines of the Christian Faith are contained here, and the seasons of the Christian Year, but they are arranged in terms of experience: the Goodness of God, For Believers Rejoicing, For the Society Meeting, The Lord's Supper, and so forth. They are full of the joy of worship. Thus the hymn 'Meet and right it is to sing', which is based upon the Sanctus:

> Vying with that happy choir,
> Who chant thy praise above,
> We on eagles' wings aspire,
> The wings of faith and love:
> Thee they sing with glory crowned,
> We extol the slaughtered Lamb:
> Lower if our voices sound,
> Our subject is the same.

They sing of conversion, as in the famous 'And can it be':

> Long my imprisoned spirit lay
> Fast bound in sin and nature's night;
> Thine eye diffused a quickening ray—
> I woke, the dungeon flamed with light;
> My chains fell off, my heart was free,
> I rose, went forth, and followed thee.

They accompany the Lord's Supper, as 'Jesus, we thus obey':

> With high and holy bliss
> Thou dost our spirit cheer,
> The house of banqueting is this,
> And thou hast brought us here.

They are never straight paraphrases, but are more like a kaleidoscope of texts:

> No man can truly say
> That Jesus is the Lord,   (1 Cor. 12.3)
> Unless thou take the veil away   (2 Cor. 3.16)
> And breathe the living word;   (Jn. 20.22; Matt. 4.4)
> Then, only then, we feel
> Our interest in his blood,
> And cry with joy unspeakable   (1 Pet. 1.8)
> 'Thou art my Lord, my God!'   (Jn. 20.28)

[1] Manning, p. 14.

And, unlike Watts, Wesley was able to use a variety of unusual metres.

With all this came three further developments. First, others began to write hymns with similar intent: James Montgomery, Augustus Toplady, Thomas Kelly among them, and of course Newton and Cowper. Secondly, collections of hymns began to appear, like the *Olney Hymns*. Thirdly, devotional poems written between the Reformation and the eighteenth century began to be discovered as hymns—Ken and Baxter, Herbert and Crossman. This was a gradual process, and not until the end of the nineteenth century were the treasures of the seventeenth fully explored. The age of Wesley and Watts remained singularly creative in the matter of hymnody. When Philip Doddridge wanted to preach on some special subject, he would often write a hymn to go with it, a hymn in which the congregation might respond to his sermon.

IV

The nineteenth century saw the full integration of hymnody into Christian worship in Britain. The Methodists became, by degrees, a separate denomination, and what had hitherto served for its less formal extra-liturgical gatherings now became a kind of service-book for the Church. The Congregational Union began to authorize collections; of these the most distinguished was commonly known as 'Barrett' after the name of its editor (*Congregational Church Hymnal*, 1887). The Church of Scotland broke away from its strict adherence to psalms and paraphrases. And others followed with hymn-books which had varying degrees of official approval.

Hymns were introduced into the worship of the C of E through the influence of the Evangelical movement, although the Tractarians were to take new directions in hymnody through the translation of ancient Greek and Latin hymns. John Mason Neale was, more than any other single person, responsible for the translation and adaptation of such hymns. But in 1819, the production by Thomas Cotterill of his *Selection of Psalms and Hymns* for use in St Paul's, Sheffield, led to an action in the diocesan court at York. Archbishop Vernon Harcourt then promised to sanction a further edition provided any hymns of which he disapproved were cut out. From this time onwards a spate of hymn-books was seen in the Church of England; they tended to represent different party-interests within the Church and to be devised as companions to the Prayer Book, providing hymns for the various occasions of worship enjoined in that book. The best-known and most lasting of these collections was *Hymns Ancient and Modern* first published in 1861, and last revised in 1950. In the twentieth century, the *English Hymnal* became its most serious rival; *Songs of Praise* was less widely used in churches, but became almost the standard book in the state schools. The most recent major collection is the *Anglican Hymn Book*, replacing two earlier Evangelical collections.

Within Anglicanism, hymns have been intended as adornments to worship, and essentially as supplementary to the Prayer Book. The services of that book were complete in themselves, but by the end of the nineteenth century hymns had become as familiar as the metrical psalms had been in past centuries, and in the same way were accepted as normal additions to public worship. In the offices of Morning and Evening Prayer, a hymn was commonly sung at the place provided for the anthem, and befoie and after the sermon when such was added. Office hymns began to appear under Tractarian influence; such hymns were originally intended for the medieval offices, but now they were introduced at Mattins and Evensong. The use of an office hymn was always more popular at Evensong than at Mattins; it was frequently inserted between the first lesson and Magnificat, although Percy Dearmer urged that it should be sung before the psalms. Hymns were compiled, too, for use in 'processions'—both the formal kind described in *The Parson's Handbook*, and for the simple walk-in of the choir before service.

Dearmer wrote in some detail about the use of hymns at the Eucharist, and his words reflect common uses at the end of the century:

> If we are to use hymns at the Eucharist in strict accordance with precedent and authority, we shall not have to depart from the present general custom. A hymn may be sung (1) for a procession (when the Litany is not so used); (2) for the Introit because this is before the commencement of the service; (3) for the Sequence between the Epistle and Gospel—an excellent place from the liturgical point of view—because there is here a necessary interval; (4) at the Offertory, because there is a break in the service; (5) during the Communion, for the same reason; (6) during the Ablutions, because it is at the end of the service, and for the best practical reasons. Thus six hymns may be sung in all, or fewer, according to the needs of the church.[1]

Few men have done so much for Anglican hymnody as Dearmer, but the reasons which he gives for the singing of hymns at certain points in the liturgy reveal very clearly his attitude to the hymns. Always, they were regarded as embellishments to the service, as a means of edification for the people whilst other activities were in process.

In what Manning called the 'Dissenting Use', it was otherwise. It is, in fact, impossible to understand such a way of worship without reference to the hymns. With no appointed forms of praise and penitence, hymns

---

[1] P. Dearmer, *The Parson's Handbook* (Humphrey Milford 1913), pp. 220–1.

often supplied that need. Manning claimed that Dissenters recited no creed, because their hymns were full of the form of sound words as in Wesley's:

Let earth and heaven combine,
Angels and men agree
To praise in songs divine,
The Incarnate Deity:
Our God, contracted to a span,
Incomprehensibly made man.

But if hymns were meant to supply partially-felt liturgical needs, they were chosen, above all, to reflect the congregation's meditation upon and response to the preached word of God on a particular Sunday. Hymns became part of a constantly renewed liturgy. The 'hymn-sandwich' is an unfair and pejorative description of such acts of worship, though it must be recognized that ideals of hymn-choosing were not invariably of the highest.

There is then a sharp distinction to be drawn between the *use* of hymns in the C of E and their use in Nonconformity, although a large body of hymns has been common to both. The distinction is less marked with the growth of liturgical forms among the Free Churches and with new thinking about liturgy in the C of E. During the last decade, supplements to the older hymn-books have been appearing. The newer and smaller collections have, in part, been culled from the wide range of experimental hymnody that the decade has witnessed. Many such hymns reflect the theological and liturgical ideas of the times; thus there has been a steady flow of hymns expressing the 'social gospel'; hymns designed specifically for the parish communion; and hymns meant to accompany those liturgies which have substituted 'you' for 'thou' in their prayers.

But the most striking development has been the new interest in hymnody among Roman Catholics. The Roman Catholic Church has never been without its hymn-writers; Caswall and Faber were prolific contributors to nineteenth-century hymnody, and the few hymns of Newman have been heard throughout Christendom. But in English-speaking countries, until recent times, hymns tended to be outside the mainstream of worship, and those sung to be always by Catholic authors. New collections like the *New Catholic Hymnal* have drawn heavily on Watts and Wesley, Herbert and Baxter, and the current English form of the Mass makes specific provision for hymns—at the entrance, the offertory, and during and after communion. Hymnody plays a part in modern Roman Catholic worship that is akin to the part played by psalmody in the churches of the Reformation period.

We have looked at some length at the tradition for which hymns have been integral to public worship, and at that in which their status has been no more than quasi-official. But in both the Anglican and Free Church traditions (and perhaps in the future in the Roman Catholic Church) hymns have *seemed* to the worshippers as important as the other element in worship. Through hymnody, the people have been able to participate physically in worship; through hymnody, they have learned much of their theology; through hymnody they have grown to adore their Lord.

4 The Language of Worship

GEOFFREY WAINWRIGHT

In the twentieth century, language has attracted much interest from philosophers and from anthropologists. In philosophy, it is sufficient to mention such diverse examples as L. Wittgenstein and the Anglo-Saxon practitioners of linguistic analysis, the importance of *die Sprache* in the existentialism of M. Heidegger, and P. Ricoeur's work on the hermeneutic of symbols. In anthropology, B. Malinowsky observed the difference between the 'social' and the 'magical' (i.e. ritual) uses of language, C. Lévi-Strauss has devoted attention to linguistic structures as part of the whole psycho-social process of imposing forms upon content, and M. McLuhan has explored the relation between the 'medium' and the 'message'. Furthermore, our century has seen important developments in the sciences of language proper, with F. de Saussure and N. Chomsky among the outstanding names. Liturgists may find insights from these secular disciplines which will help them to understand the functions of language in worship.[1]

To give a few examples. First, language is not to be understood apart from the community which uses it and the activities and self-understanding of that community; liturgical language is the language of the historical Church at worship—a Church which in every age believes itself to be the people of God in the world, with the duties of praise and witness laid upon it. Second, there is the notion of a 'universe of

[1] A. C. Thiselton, *Language, Liturgy and Meaning* (Grove Books 1975); H. Schmidt, 'Language and its function in Christian worship' in *SL* 8 (1971–2), pp. 1–25; R. Chapman, 'Linguistics and liturgy' in *Theology* 76 (1973), pp. 594–9; J. H. J. Westlake, 'The problems of modern vernacular liturgy' in *SL* 6 (1969), pp. 147–57; D. B. Stevick, *Language in Worship: Reflections on a Crisis* (New York 1970). The February 1973 number of *Concilium* contains several articles on the language of worship.

discourse': users of a common language presuppose the existence of a shared world of beliefs, ideas, and experiences which enables words and phrases to convey intended meaning between speaker and hearer; Christian worshippers share with one another *and with God* a common history focused in Jesus Christ and a common interest in the continuing battle of grace against sin. Third, there is the recognition of a multiplicity of 'language games': the games have their own rules, techniques, and aims; in Christian worship, we are not playing the game of scientific description or of everyday social conversation, nor even the game of theological discourse, but rather the game of the community's conversation with the God who is our creator and redeemer; this game has its ontological rules (at the level of the objective difference and relation between man and God), it includes technical 'moves' whose efficacy has been proved in past play, and the present enjoyment and permanent 'point' of the game lie in a growing communion of man with God. Though human language is used in worship, Christians believe that this language becomes the sign and medium of a reality which goes beyond the purely human, viz. the encounter between man and God. In worship we have the peculiar situation that one partner in the conversation, though in some sense he hears and speaks, is the transcendent God. In worship, where we listen to God and talk to him, a characteristic linguistic 'register' will be in operation even at the phenomenologically observable level.

Liturgical language may now be viewed from four angles, of which the first is theological, the second historical, the third social and pastoral, the fourth aesthetic.

1 THEOLOGICAL

Worship is grounded in the human creature's vocation to communion with God: man is made in God's image, in order to 'glorify God and to enjoy him forever' (Westminster Shorter Catechism). By divine grace, the symbols of human communication become the expression and vehicle of the traffic between man and God in which saving communion consists. God spoke through the prophetic message of the OT, 'Thus saith the Lord'; now the divine Word has been made flesh (Jn. 1.14), and in these last days God has spoken to us through a Son (Heb. 1.1f). Conversely, the Bible presents God as listening to the words of men who call upon him, and in the NT this prayer is made 'through Jesus Christ' (Rom. 1.8; 2 Cor. 1.20) or 'in his name' (Mt. 18.19f; Jn. 16.23f). The Hebrew *dabar* means thing, act, event, as well as word; and God and men 'speak' also through actions, [1] and speech is also an 'act'. Significant actions, however, depend on a context of interpretation, which can to a greater or less extent be put into words; and verbal symbolism itself is more supple and subtle than the dramatic and material symbolism which it may sometimes replace (though often only at the expense of a 'cerebral' reduction of human possibilities) or preferably (according to the incarnational and sacramental principle) accompanies. It is in any case the *words* of worship that I am writing about here.

Within the linguistic register of worship, there are at least six 'sub-registers' which correspond to different aspects of the communion between man and God. This variety may produce some 'unevenness of tone', but at its best the combination will be rich and satisfying.

(a) ADORATION

Adoration is an acknowledgment of God's transcendence made possible by the fact that he is also self-giving. Here human language is stretched to its upper limits. A sign of this is that at the high moment of adoration, the Sanctus in the eucharistic liturgy, our worship is joined with that of 'angels and archangels and all the company of heaven', God's nearer servants who with unceasing tongue cry 'Holy, holy, holy'. The language of adoration pays homage to the surpassing majesty of God and sings his amazing love for his creatures and his unexampled grace for sinners. At times, adoration will pass over the linguistic horizon into eloquent silence.

(b) PROCLAMATION

The readings from the Bible [2] and the sermon, if they are to communicate the word of God to man, will appropriately themselves share the sharpness of a two-edged sword, piercing to the division of joints and marrow (cf. Heb. 4.12; Rev. 1.16). Their language must surprise, must open the hearers afresh to God's revelation, allow God creatively to break through the banalities of existence that the language of cliché reflects. God speaks only 'where and when it pleases him' (Augsburg Confession), but since he does not spurn human co-operation in the presentation of his message and of himself, that co-operation should be of the best linguistic quality possible.

(c) THANKSGIVING

The chief ground of our thanksgiving to God is God's saving

---

[1] R. Grainger, *The Language of the Rite* (DLT 1974); cf. Mary Douglas, *Natural Symbols* (2nd edn Penguin 1973); R. Bocock, *Ritual in Industrial Society* (Allen & Unwin 1974).
[2] J. H. J. Westlake, 'The liturgical use of modern translations of the Bible' in *SL* 8 (1971–2), pp. 98–118.

intervention in Jesus Christ. God's marvellous deeds through the man of Nazareth are recalled in the manner of a solemn recital, not in the way a newspaper reports a *fait divers*. Our thanksgiving is at the same time a confession of faith: it declares our belief that we ourselves are included in the scope of God's redeeming action and have been touched by it. Modern Western liturgies have restored the 'thanksgiving series' that characterized the ancient *eucharistia*.

(d) COMMITMENT

Worship expresses our turning from sin and the offering of ourselves in obedience to God, whose service is perfect freedom. The appropriate linguistic register is that of the deepest personal relationships: trust, mercy, asking and receiving forgiveness, yielding, sacrifice.... Here language assumes a strongly 'performative' function: as these things are spoken, they happen; until they are spoken, they are not fully real.

(e) PETITION AND INTERCESSION

It is here that liturgical language may come closest to the language of the television news programme. For it is the world of famine and plenty, of war and peace, of work and play, of individual tragedies and triumphs, which is being presented to God in compassion and hope and set in relation to the coming of his Kingdom.

(f) EXPECTATION

Even now, men in Christ may glimpse and taste their final filial destiny in the purpose of God. The language of worship takes on a visionary cast. Its figures will be chiefly those of the messianic feast, which dominates the biblical imagery of the 'enjoyment of God'.[1]

2 HISTORICAL

The question is that of the languages that have been used in Christian worship. The principle admitted in one way or another by all the Churches is that the language of worship should be intelligible by the worshipping community: the use of a 'foreign' tongue, insofar as it excludes the rational understanding, offends against the ontological 'rule' that God is to be loved with man's whole being, including his mind; and this is therefore *not*, despite the desires of some modern reactionaries concerning the use (say) of Latin, a Christian way to achieve the sense of

[1] G. Wainwright, *Eucharist and Eschatology* (Epworth 1971).

'mystery' in worship. Historically, however, the matter has not been so simple.[1]

In first-century Aramaic-speaking Palestinian Jewry, the language of Bible reading and liturgical prayer was Hebrew; in the Hellenistic Dispersion, however, the liturgical language was Greek. The earliest Aramaic-speaking Christians seem to have worshipped in their own tongue,[2] and some of their key words passed over to the Greek-speakers: *Abba* (Rom. 8.15f; Gal. 4.6), *Maranatha* (1 Cor. 16.22; *Did.* 10.6). When Christianity spread round the Mediterranean basin, the language of worship was Greek in the Hellenistic areas, and apparently Latin in Roman North Africa (in the third and fourth-century Church in Rome, the social shift from Greek to Latin preponderance was followed before too long by a corresponding change in the liturgical language). The early Church also used Syriac, Coptic, Armenian, Georgian, and Ge'ez in worship in the respective linguistic localities. In the late ninth century, Pope John VIII approved the use of 'the Slavonic language' in the Byzantine liturgy in the regions evangelized by SS. Cyril and Methodius.

But, as part no doubt of the conservatism that characterizes the phenomena of worship, liturgical language later did not keep step with changes in social language. In three different ways there came about a gap between the language of worship and the language of society. First, linguistic evolution: the liturgy remained fixed in patristic Greek; in Ethiopia, Ge'ez turned into Amharic, but the liturgy was left behind; as the modern Slav languages developed, the liturgy continued to be celebrated in Staroslav or 'Church Slavonic'; Latin was still used in church, while the people began to speak Italian, Spanish, and French. Second, military and political changes: despite the spread of Arabic by conquests, the Churches of the Levant and Egypt maintained, to varying degrees, Greek, Syriac, or Coptic as their liturgical language. Third (and this is a somewhat different case), importation: Syriac was taken to the Malabarese in India; with a few exceptions (some of them in the peculiar circumstances of Eastern Europe), the ordinary Roman practice from medieval times up to Vatican II was for its missionaries and representatives abroad to introduce the Roman rite in the Latin tongue[3]

---

1 C. Korolevsky, (ET) *Living Languages in Catholic Worship* (Longmans 1957); T. Klauser, 'Der Übergang der römischen Kirche von der griechischen zur lateinischen Liturgiesprache' in *Miscellanea G. Mercati* vol. I (ST 121, 1946), pp. 467–82; C. Mohrmann, *Liturgical Latin: its origin and character* (Burns and Oates 1959).

2 J. Jeremias detects numerous Semitisms behind the NT texts of the eucharistic institution narratives and thinks transmission may have taken place in both Hebrew and Aramaic, leaving open the question which was original: see (ET) *The Eucharistic Words of Jesus* (SCM 1966 = 3rd German edn 1960), pp. 160–203.

3 This was the case already in the evangelization of the Germanic nations, where the

(though Uniat Churches were allowed to keep their accustomed rite and liturgical tongue upon submission to Rome).

In the West, the Reformers, recovering the importance of Scripture, preaching, and intelligent faith for all, brought their followers to the use in Bible reading and worship of a language 'understanded of the people' (the phrase is from the XXXIX Articles of the Church of England). Luther's *Deutsche Messe* was published in 1526 and his Bible translation was completed in 1534. The English *Book of Common Prayer* was introduced in 1549 and, in its second form, in 1552; the Great Bible of 1539 prepared the way for the Authorized Version of 1611. Calvin's Genevan *Forme des Prières* appeared in 1542, and his revision of his cousin Olivetan's French Bible in 1551.

Faced by the Protestant 'threat', the Council of Trent[1] anathematized 'any who should say that the Mass ought to be celebrated only in the vulgar tongue' and declared it 'not expedient that the Mass should be celebrated everywhere in the vulgar tongue' (Session 22, ch. 8 with Canon 9). While echoes persisted of the medieval argument that the three languages in which Pilate wrote what he wrote, Hebrew, Greek, and Latin, were the only ones fit for use in divine worship, the Tridentines justified the use of Latin chiefly on the grounds of its universality (it is true that in the sixteenth century Latin was still the international language of educated western culture), and of the dangers of doctrinal error arising from the translation of liturgical texts. Thus a formulation of August 1562: 'The Latin language, which is used for the celebration of Mass in the Western Church, is in the highest degree appropriate, seeing that it is common to many nations.... There would also be a great danger of various errors arising in many translations, with the result that the mysteries of our faith, which are in fact one, would seem rather to differ.' Pius XII argued similarly in his encyclical of 1947 on the sacred liturgy, *Mediator Dei*: 'The use of the Latin language prevailing in a great part of the Church affords at once an imposing sign of unity and an effective safeguard against the corruption of true doctrine' (n. 64). The last point raises the difficult systematic questions of doctrinal authority and of the adequacy of human language in the formulation of divine truth.

In their modern missionary work, the Orthodox have translated the Byzantine liturgy into Japanese and Eskimo, for example. Protestant

---

military, political, and cultural prestige of the *imperium* also helped in the introduction of Latin. For the agonizing story of the struggle for the use of Mandarin Chinese in the seventeenth and eighteenth centuries, see F. Bontinck, *La lutte autour de la liturgie chinoise aux XVIIᵉ et XVIIIᵉ siècles* (Louvain 1962).

H. Schmidt, *Liturgie et langue vulgaire: le problème de la langue liturgique chez les premiers Réformateurs et au Concile de Trente* (Analecta Gregoriana 53, 1950).

missionaries have introduced worship in the modern European languages (Christianity often accompanied the colonizing power), but chiefly in the native vernaculars of Africa and Asia. In the 'home' countries, however, the Protestant Churches have in the twentieth century become increasingly aware of the fact that their classical liturgical speech, dating largely from the sixteenth century, is now behind the times when viewed in relation to the general evolution of the national languages; and they are facing such questions as those raised in our next section. While Vatican II preserved the normative status of Latin in the liturgy, it gave prudent encouragement to some translation of the liturgy for use in modern vernaculars (*Constitution on the Sacred Liturgy*, 36), and local episcopal conferences have widely exploited their authority in this matter. Roman Catholic problems of linguistic adaptation are not quite the same as those for Protestants, since for Catholics the passage, ecclesiastically if not culturally, is straight from the Latin to (say) modern English, without the intervening 400 years of Cranmer and King James' men.

3 SOCIAL AND PASTORAL

Today we face the problems of maintaining a number of bipolar tensions between legitimate *desiderata* in liturgical language:

(*a*) *Traditional and contemporary:* Christianity has a history and a memory, and the psychological power of traditional associations is great; but archaisms in liturgy may threaten intelligibility. Christianity intends to actualize the gospel in every situation; but worship should not fall into the language of barber's-shop conversation.

(*b*) *Sacral and secular:* Christianity has its specialized vocabulary because of its particular experience of God's acts in the world, and the linguistic 'registers' of worship are in part determined also by the fact that the awe-inspiring God is a partner in the conversation. But God is claiming the *whole world* for his Kingdom, and Christian worship is man in Christ exercising his role as the priest of *all creation* (as the Orthodox theologians are fond of saying). In the 'post-Christian' West or in 'missionary' areas, how much notice should be taken, linguistically, of the 'fringe attender' (cf. 1 Cor. 14.23ff)?

(*c*) *Plural and common:* Varied levels and styles of education and the variety of social and cultural experience make it difficult to find a common vocabulary which is rich enough for the purposes of worship and yet does not preclude understanding by particular social or cultural groups.

471

(*d*) *Fixed and free:* According to Justin Martyr (*c.* 150), the liturgical president extemporized the great eucharistic prayer (*hose dunamis autoi,* 1 *Apol.* 67), but various North African councils around A.D. 400 document the fact that the later moves towards complete fixity were due at least in part to the need to ensure the doctrinal orthodoxy of new prayers even when written down;[1] other factors making for fixity are the social need for formality in large assemblies and the psychological need for the regularity which confirms relationships. But what is the place for improvization in the Spirit?[2]

(*e*) *Written and spoken:* Books play their part in achieving the degree of fixity thought desirable (by whom? But that is to raise the question of authority, which it is not my business to treat here). But liturgy is essentially *spoken and heard.* How are modern liturgical authors to master the relation between the written, the read, and the spoken word? Poets, dramatists, and actors might help them.

The reader may see for himself how the much-debated question of 'Thou' or 'You' as an address to God in modern English liturgical compositions shares in several, if not all, of the tensions just mentioned.

4 AESTHETIC[3]

In the space available I can do no more than invite the reader to savour some prayers from the *Book of Common Prayer,*[4] and then to analyse their aesthetic perfection. Take, for example, the collect for purity at the opening of the Communion service:

> Almighty God, unto whom all hearts be open, all desires known, and from whom no secrets are hid: Cleanse the thoughts of our hearts by the inspiration of thy Holy Spirit, that we may perfectly love thee, and worthily magnify thy holy Name; through Christ our Lord. Amen.

Or the collect for aid against all perils, from Evening Prayer:

---

[1] The *Ap. Trad.* of Hippolytus proposes prayers as 'models'. See R. P. C. Hanson, 'The liberty of the bishop to improvise prayer in the eucharist' in *VC* 15 (1961), pp. 173–6.

[2] On glossolalia in worship, see W. J. Samarin, *Tongues of Men and Angels: the religious language of Pentecostalism* (Collier-Macmillan 1972).

[3] R. Speaight, 'Liturgy and language' in *Theology* 74 (1971), pp. 444–56; D. L. Frost, 'Liturgical language from Cranmer to Series 3' in R. C. D. Jasper, ed., *The Eucharist Today* (SPCK 1974), pp. 142–67; I. Robinson, *The Survival of English* (CUP 1973), pp. 22–65 ('Religious English').

[4] Stella Brook, *The Language of the Book of Common Prayer* (André Deutsch 1965); C. S. Lewis, *English Literature in the Sixteenth Century* (Clarendon Press 1954), pp. 215–21, 598f.

Lighten our darkness, we beseech thee, O Lord; and by thy great mercy defend us from all perils and dangers of this night; for the love of thy only Son, our Saviour, Jesus Christ. Amen.

Or again, the prayer of humble access in the Communion service, with its 'We are not worthy so much as to gather up the crumbs under thy table'.

Notice how the total effect is achieved through a variety of things such as rhythm, parallelism, balance, word pairs, contrasts, biblical echoes, archetypal ideas, and the discreet use of affective language. Memorable prayers in the fixed parts of the liturgy allow the worshippers to be disencumbered from books and to relish the spoken words.

It is no mistake that the poet Patrice de la Tour du Pin should have been given an important part in the translation of the Roman Catholic liturgy into French. It is a pity that no poet was a member of the Church of England Liturgical Commission.

5 The Architectural Setting of the Liturgy

PETER G. COBB

Addleshaw, G. W. O., and Etchells, F., *The Architectural Setting of Anglican Worship*. Faber 1948.
Anson, P. F., *The Building of Churches* (New Library of Catholic Knowledge, vol. 10). Burns and Oates 1964.
Biéler, A., (ET) *Architecture in Worship*. Oliver and Boyd 1965.
Bouyer, L., *Liturgy and Architecture*. Notre Dame 1967.
Briggs, M. S., *Puritan Architecture and its Future*. Lutterworth 1946.
Davies, J. G., 'Architectural Setting', *DLW* pp. 21–30.
Davies, J. G., *The Architectural Setting of Baptism*. Barrie and Rockliff 1962.
Debuyst, F., 'Architectural Setting (Modern) and the Liturgical Movement', *DLW* pp. 30–41.
Debuyst, F., *Modern Architecture and Christian Celebration* (Ecumenical Studies in Worship 18). Lutterworth 1968.
LMD 63 (1960) *Bâtir et aménager les églises: le lieu de la célébration.*
LMD 70 (1962) *La dédicace des églises.*
Lockett, W., ed., *The Modern Architectural Setting of the Liturgy*. SPCK 1964.
Minchin, B., *Outward and Visible*. DLT 1961.

There is no peculiarly Christian type of architecture because Christian worship does not centre on a cult object or require a fixed altar which have to be housed in a special way. 'We have no temples; we have no altars', as Minucius Felix said in the third century (*Octav.* 32). Christians themselves are the living stones of the new Temple, indwelt by the Holy Spirit (1 Pet. 2.4–10; cf. 1 Cor. 3.16, 6.19; 2 Cor. 6.16f; Eph. 2.19–22). Consequently Clement of Alexandria can say, 'What I am calling a temple is not a building but a gathering of the elect' (*Strom.* 7.5; cf. Hippolytus, *in Dan.* 1.17; GCS 1.28). Christians gathered and continue to gather for worship in various types of building, some purpose-built and exclusively used for worship, some borrowed for the occasion.

Acts indicates that the early Christians assembled for the Eucharist in private houses, 'breaking bread from house to house' (Acts 2.46), often in an upper room like that at Troas mentioned in Acts 20.7ff (cf. Rom. 16.5; 1 Cor. 16.19). As the communities grew and became richer, they acquired houses for their permanent use. Efforts have been made to identify such house-churches in Rome[1] but the only notable house-church so far discovered is at Dura Europos in Syria (fig. 1), where two rooms were knocked into one in 232 for the eucharistic assembly and another room turned into a baptistery with canopied font and elaborate wall paintings.[2] At the opposite end of the Roman Empire in England, a villa was reoccupied in the fourth century and some of its rooms adapted for Christian worship.[3]

When Christianity became the state religion, the numbers of Christians vastly increased and the dignity of bishops was enhanced. Consequently 'Christianity under Constantine had to find a new architecture of a higher order, public in character, resplendent in material and spacious in layout' (R. Krautheimer, *Early Christian and Byzantine Architecture* (Penguin 1965), p. 19). Eschewing pagan architecture, the Church adopted the basilica, an essentially secular form of assembly hall. The Christian basilica, like its secular counterpart, varied from region to region but basically it is a three-aisled building, with the nave higher than the side aisles and lit by clerestory windows; it is longitudinally arranged with an apse at one end opposite the entrance doors. From contemporary descriptions (e.g. Eusebius, *HE* 10.4.37–45) and from some surviving examples, notably at Ravenna, it is obvious that the basilica, though simple in form, could be awe-inspiring in its magnificence, with its marble revetments and splendid mosaics in the apse and on the triumphal arch. It is not easy to reconstruct the layout of the essential furniture in the basilica, the altar-table, the ambo, and the bishop's throne. The font was housed in a separate baptistery.) The altar

[1] E.g. E. Mâle, (ET) *Early Churches of Rome* (Benn 1960), pp. 42–8.
[2] C. H. Kraeling, *Excavation at Dura Europos Final Report 8, Part 2: The Christian Building* (New Haven 1967). See plate 4.
[3] G. W. Meates, *Lullingstone Roman Villa* (Heinemann 1955).

was usually on or near the chord of the apse but, especially in North Africa, it was often much lower down the nave. Almost invariably it was dignified by a *ciborium* and protected by low barriers, *cancelli* (fig. 2). There is some evidence that curtains were hung between the columns of the ciborium or from a beam across the church which may have completely veiled it from sight but not necessarily during the liturgy itself.[1] The reading-desk might be fixed to the chancel barrier but more commonly it was an ambo, a separate structure, in the midst of the basilica (fig. 3), sometimes linked to the altar area by a *solea*, a processional passage-way. When the elaboration of liturgical music led to the need for a choir, the singers stood round the ambo or in the solea and this led to the kind of arrangement in San Clemente (plate 22) and Santa Maria in Cosmedin in Rome, where the solea has been widened for the schola and the ambo forms part of one side of it. The *bema*,[2] or *exedra*, a raised platform for the reading of the Scriptures and for the choir in the body of the basilica, was another arrangement, possibly derived from the Jewish synagogue to be found in Syria, where evidence of it survives (fig. 4), but probably elsewhere as well. The bishop's throne was situated on the bema but otherwise was generally placed at the back of the apse, with or without a *synthronos* for the other clergy, depending on the size of the basilica (figs. 3, 5; and plate 23).

Gregory the Great was responsible for erecting an altar over the actual tomb of St Peter (fig. 5) thereby forging a link between eucharistic worship and the veneration of the relics of the martyrs of immense theological and liturgical significance. This arrangement with the altar over the resting-place of the relics, the *confessio*, to which access could be had from the main body of the building, though not new, now spread very rapidly throughout the West. There is a fine example of a *confessio* in the Anglo-Saxon basilica at Wing in Buckinghamshire, although it is not known whose body, if any, once rested there.

There was a significant development of the basilica in the East too, but it was connected, not with the internal arrangements, but with the architectural shell. Under the influence of the example of the Emperor Justinian's building of Hagia Sophia in Constantinople, the East adopted the dome. At first this hardly altered the ground-plan of the basilica (e.g. Hagia Eirene in Constantinople, fig. 6) but it tended to lead to a more

[1] See J. Lassus, *Sanctuaires chrétiens de Syrie* (Paris 1947), pp. 206f; D. Rock, *Church of our Fathers* (John Murray, new edn 1905), vol. 1, pp. 153–5; E. J. Yarnold, *Heythrop Journal*, 13 (1972), p. 264.
[2] See D. Hickley, 'The Ambo in Early Liturgical Planning', *Heythrop Journal*, 7 (1966), pp. 407–27. R. Taft, 'Some Notes on the Bema in the East and West Syrian Traditions', *OCP* 34 (1968), pp. 326–59.

centralized building (fig. 7). The sense of space and the upward 'pull' of the dome, accentuated by its elaborate mosaic decoration, usually culminating in the figure of the Pantocrator at the top, gave a completely different feel to such a building from that in a Western basilica with its very strong emphasis on the horizontal perspective. It undoubtedly contributed to the survival of a more corporate sense of the People of God in the East whereas Western architecture emphasized its hierarchical nature.

Nothing could be in greater contrast to the classical one-roomed basilica with its single altar than the medieval church with its many rooms each with its own altar (fig. 8). This was the product of various factors. Clericalism, in the sense of a growing feeling of obligation on the part of the ever-increasing number of priests to say Mass individually each day, on the one hand, and the popular demand for Requiem Masses, on the other, led to the proliferation of altars and consequently to the partitioning of the body of the church building and the construction of transepts and of coronas of chapels. The monasticizing of the clergy meant that provision had to be made in most cathedrals and the larger parish churches for a place for them to sing the office, which led to further enclosures in the nave, lengthened chancels and often separate choirs. Further the cult of relics necessitated the construction of vast crypts, and later side chapels, to house them, and ambulatories and processional ways to display them. Veneration of the saints was also responsible for the erection of painted and carved reredoses and retables behind the altar, which led to the removal of the bishop's throne (which had already been duplicated by a seat in choir in any case) to the side of the sanctuary. The ciborium—or what was left of it, the tester—was often moved from over the altar to a position over the principal shrine behind it.[1] The decline in lay communion with all its consequences, especially the abandonment of the offertory and communion processions, facilitated such changes in the design of church buildings, whilst the shift of devotional interest to the visual aspects of the Mass, particularly the elevation of the Host, actually encouraged them.[2]

The development of the chancel screen, the rood-screen, or *pulpitum*, as the stone ones are often called, has never been satisfactorily explained.[3]

[1] See E. Bishop, 'On the History of the Christian Altar', *Liturgica Historica* (Clarendon Press 1918), pp. 20–38.

[2] The growth in complexity of a medieval church is well illustrated by Canterbury Cathedral (fig. 9), for which see: R. Willis, *The Architectural History of Canterbury Cathedral* (Longman 1845); A. E. Henderson, *Canterbury Cathedral Then and Now* (SPCK 1938).

[3] F. Bond, *Screens and Galleries* (OUP 1908).

It is parallelled by the development of the iconostasis in the East.[1] Torcello, near Venice, exemplifies what was probably a typical screen in an eleventh- or twelfth-century Byzantine church and is clearly a prototype of the Western rood-screen. The iconostasis, which effectively cuts off the entire altar area from the sight of the laity, is a comparatively late development reached in the sixteenth century in Russia and spreading from there to the rest of the Orthodox world, but never adopted by the non-Chalcedonian churches. The rood-screen never entirely cut off sight of the altar, although the rood loft, which often accommodated an organ and singers, and the tympanum behind the rood itself completely filled in the chancel arch in the smaller churches. The pulpitum in the cathedral and large monastic churches was, however, a solid stone screen pierced only by one or two doorways. Its origin and purpose may be different from that of the rood-screen as some monastic churches have both.

The Reformers were well aware that the medieval church buildings they inherited embodied an understanding of the Christian community and its worship which they rejected. As Martin Bucer said, 'That the choir should be so distantly separated from the rest of the temple, and the service, which pertains to the whole people and the clergy, be set forth in it alone, is anti-Christian'.[2] The logic of their thought demanded a one-roomed assembly place. In some countries, e.g. Scotland, chancels were pulled down or walled off, but in England the usual arrangement was to preserve the chancel and its screen and use it exclusively for celebrations of the Holy Communion for the people as well as the clergy whilst the nave was used for Morning and Evening Prayer and preaching. When churches were built designedly for the reformed liturgy of the Church of England (e.g. St James, Piccadilly, fig. 10) they were essentially one-roomed buildings of a size to enable all present both to hear and see everything clearly. 'The Romanists, indeed, may build larger churches,' wrote Sir Christopher Wren, 'it is enough if they hear the Murmur of the Mass and see the elevation of the Host, but ours are to be fitted for Auditories'.[3] The eighteenth-century church interior[4] was dominated by the pulpit, often a three-decker to accommodate the clerk as well as the parson, placed usually in the middle of the north wall or not infrequently in front of the altar, and surrounded by pews. These last had been almost unknown until the fifteenth century. Galleries were a common feature,

---

[1] J. Walter, 'The Origins of the Iconastasis', *ECQ* 3 (1970–1), pp. 251–67.
[2] Quoted in Addleshaw and Etchells, p. 249.
[3] Quoted in Addleshaw and Etchells, p. 249.
[4] E.g. Chislehampton, Oxon; Ravenstonedale, Cumbria.

added to increase the seating capacity of the building without enlarging it.

In his churches Wren maintained the medieval tradition of siting the font symbolically, near the main entrance to the church, but other eighteenth-century churches had fonts elsewhere and some even had portable ones. The Lutherans on the Continent, with the same ideal of a single-roomed, chancel-less building, generally grouped together all the three essential pieces of furniture, altar, font, and pulpit, the focus of the main liturgical acts, in the Prinzipalstück.

Architecturally the nineteenth century was dominated in Britain by the Gothic Revival, an aspect of the contemporary romanticization of the Middle Ages. Gothic architecture was regarded as the only possible Christian form; Georgian, for example, was condemned as the 'ne plus ultra of Wretchedness'. Churches were restored or built[1] according to an imagined medieval ideal. Three-decker pulpits and galleries ('flying pews') were anathema to the Ecclesiological Society, which more than any other group dictated the fashion,[2] whilst chancels were regarded as a necessity. An artificial symbolism dictated church design rather than the needs of a worshipping community. It is significant that J. M. Neale and Benjamin Webb, two of the founders of the Society, published a translation of Durandus' treatise on the symbolism of church-buildings. Although its proponents sought their inspiration in the Middle Ages, they were men of their time. They were influenced by contemporary Roman Catholic churches on the Continent which had been rearranged or built so that all could see the principal altar where the Sacrament was reserved and where the drama of the Mass was enacted (fig. 11). Consequently high altars were raised on steps, screens were light and open, and chancels were wider and shorter than their medieval counterparts (e.g. fig. 12; cf. fig. 8). In ancient churches some medieval remains were actually removed—the *pulpita* of Durham and Ely were destroyed and almost all the chancel tympana from parish churches—in the interests of improving visibility. Thus although the Gothic Revival was responsible for the return of the basic two-roomed medieval arrangement, the nave for the people and the chancel for the clergy and now a lay choir, it nevertheless tried to use it as one entity.

The Gothic Revival continued to determine the building and arrangement of churches in England until the middle of this century, largely because of the failure of the Liturgical Movement to make much

[1] Perhaps the finest example is St Giles, Cheadle, Staffs. by Augustine Pugin. See P. Stanton, *Pugin* (Thames and Hudson 1971), pp. 100–10.
[2] J. F. White, *The Cambridge Movement* (CUP 1962).

headway there. This Movement, with its rediscovery of the corporate nature of the Church's worship, has led to a revolution in church architecture. Churches built under the influence of the Liturgical Movement are again basically one-roomed buildings, much more centralized, some even circular, with the congregation on three sides of the altar (see plates 15 and 16).

The revolution owes much to the insights of modern architecture with its stress on functionalism, and also to developments in the theatre. Just as seventeenth- and eighteenth-century churches reflected Baroque opera-houses, so twentieth-century churches reflect contemporary theatre-in-the-round. The simultaneous disappearance of the chancel arch and the proscenium arch is no coincidence. But essentially the revolution is the result of the attempt to express architecturally the corporate nature of the People of God (rather than its hierarchical aspect) and to articulate in space the structure of the eucharistic action (fig. 13).[1]

The corporate nature of the worshipping community demands that the altar and lectern be much more in the midst of the people so that they can hear and see everything. They are often positioned on three sides of the altar and the president sits or stands facing them; the choir has been moved to one side or even placed in a gallery at the back of the building as in many eighteenth-century churches. A common feature is a central lantern which serves the same purpose as the dome of an Orthodox church. Artificial lighting, a circle or corona of lights once traditional in Anglo-Saxon as well as Orthodox churches, can be used in a similar way to draw the congregation together.

The renewed understanding of the eucharistic rite has also had a profound influence on the layout of the buildings. The twin parts of the Eucharist, the ministry of the word and the ministry of the sacrament, are often given architectural expression by creating two foci in the church, an ambo as well as an altar. The altar, usually now a much squarer and smaller piece of furniture than before, is not uncommonly dignified by a ciborium or baldaquin as in the basilica, but the ambo can normally be accentuated only by lighting. Ideally the church has a single altar so that, where reservation of the Sacrament and the practical needs of weekday celebrations with a small congregation necessitate the incorporation of one or even two further altars in the church-complex, they are housed in virtually separate buildings, as is the font wherever possible. Some designers however have tried to place the font in the main body of the

[1] For other examples see R. Maguire and K. Murray, *Modern Churches of the World* (Studio Vista 1965).

church in such a way that its relation to the altar in space reflects the relation of baptism to the Eucharist in theology.[1]

Thus the recovery of a more patristic understanding of the Church and of the liturgy has led to the return in many new churches of features of the early basilicas—the president's chair behind the altar (sometimes even in an apse and with a synthronos for the concelebrating priests), the ciborium over the altar, a single ambo for the entire ministry of the word, the corona of lights and the separate baptistery. Most Christian communities, however, have inherited treasured medieval or Gothic Revival buildings from the past, but many of these have been successfully re-ordered in accordance with the insights of the Liturgical Movement without vandalism. Usually the chancel has constituted the greatest problem: either it has been turned into a virtually separate chapel for weekday worship or it has been cleared of choir stalls and the altar brought much nearer the people.[2]

---

[1] See the explanation of the layout of St Paul's, Bow Common, by its architects in their book: Maguire and Murray, op. cit., pp. 90–3.

[2] For discussion of the problems and examples of re-ordering see G. Cope, ed., *Making the Building Serve the Liturgy* (Mowbray 1962).

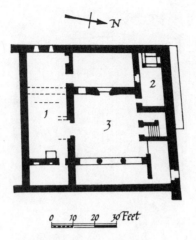

1 Plan of Dura Europos House Church

   1 Eucharistic Assembly Room with dais
      at east end
   2 Baptistry
   3 Open courtyard

2 Liturgical layout of a fifth-century African basilica

481

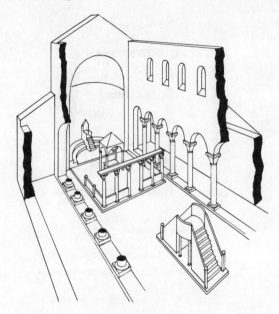

3   Liturgical layout of a sixth-century Greek basilica

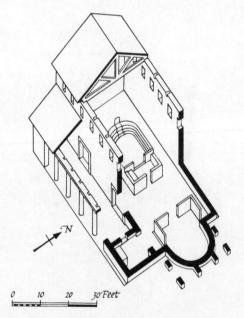

4   Fifth-century Syrian basilica

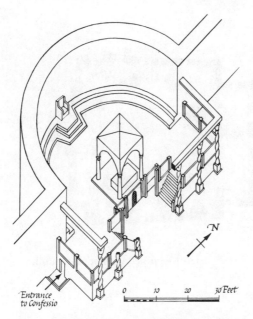

5   St Peter's, Rome, *c.* 600
Reconstruction of altar and *Confessio* by J. B. Ward-Perkins

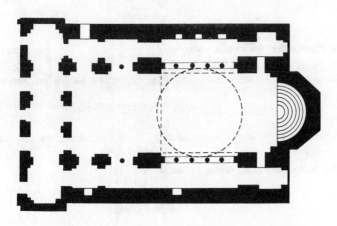

6   H. Eirene, Constantinople, as in the sixth century
From Thomas F. Mathews, *Early Churches of Constantinople*
(Pennsylvania State University Press, University Park, PA 16802, 1971)

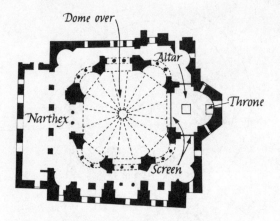

7   Eighth-century Orthodox Church

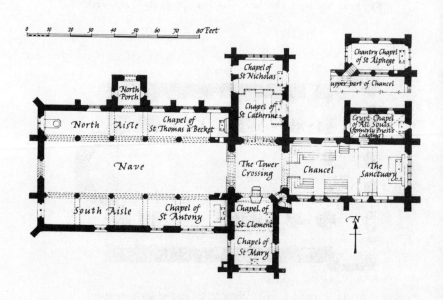

8   St Alphege, Solihull
There was a tenth altar in the Rood Loft under the Tower

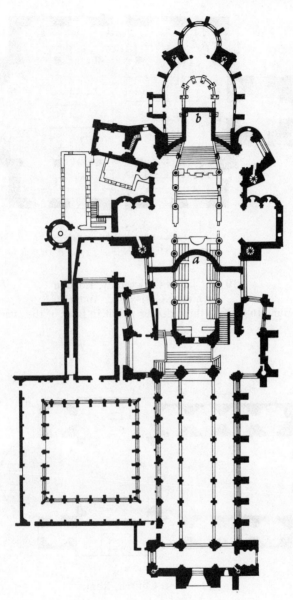

9   Canterbury Cathedral
Showing extent in (a) 1077 and (b) 1110
before final extension in 1184
to accommodate Becket's shrine

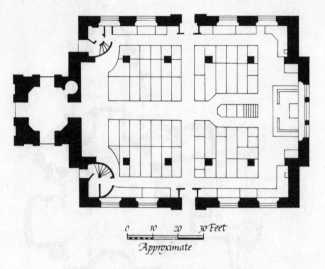

0   10   20   30 Feet
Approximate

10   St James's, Piccadilly, London
Architect: Christopher Wren
Built 1684, with three-decker pulpit in front of the altar

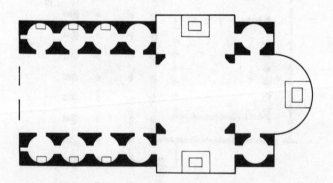

11   Gesù Church, Rome

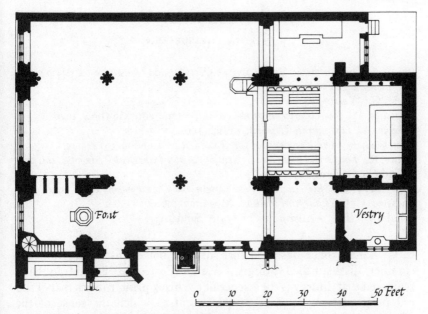

12   All Saints', Margaret Street, London, 1850–9. Architect: William Butterfield

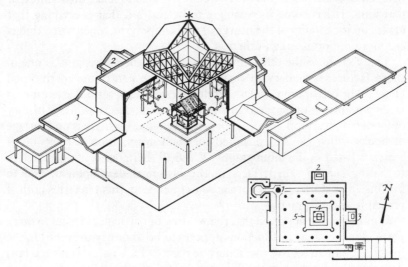

13   St Paul, Bow Common, London, 1956–60
     Architects: Keith Murray and Robert Maguire

1	Font	4	Altar with Ciborium
2	Lady Chapel	5	Corona of lights
3	Reserved Sacrament Chapel		

487

6 Vestments

W. JARDINE GRISBROOKE

Braun, J., *Die liturgische Gewandung im Occident und Orient nach Ursprung und Entwicklung*. Freiburg 1907.

Cope, G., 'Vestments' in *DLW*.

Dearmer, P., *The Ornaments of the Ministers*. 2nd edn Mowbray 1920.

Flüeler, A., *Das sakrale Gewand*. Zurich 1964.

Fortescue, A., *The Vestments of the Roman Rite*. London 1912.

James, R., *The Origin and Development of Roman Liturgical Vestments*. 2nd edn Catholic Records Press 1934.

Norris, H., *Church Vestments: their Origin and Development*. Dent 1949.

Pocknee, C. E., *Liturgical Vesture*. Mowbray 1960.

Roulin, E., (ET) *Vestments and Vesture*. Sand 1931.

E. C. Ratcliff once observed that 'liturgy, not circus, is my subject'. Another distinguished liturgist, Adrian Fortescue, is said to have remarked that 'liturgy is the science of the black print, rubrics that of the red print'. It is a measure of the extent to which the sense of the wholeness of the liturgical celebration has been recovered in recent years that few of their successors today would feel able to make distinctions of that kind. It has come increasingly to be realized that everything that makes up the totality of the liturgical act is important, albeit some things are more important than others.

The vesture of the officiating ministers and their assistants is one of those factors, secondary in themselves, which contribute to the total effect of the celebration, and is therefore deserving of serious attention. It is not possible, in the space available, to give a full description and history of Christian liturgical vesture; nor is it necessary, for there is no shortage of books which can be consulted for such information, a selection of which is listed in the bibliography. We shall therefore confine ourselves to noting certain salient facts in the historical development, and to making an attempt to draw out the consequences of them in terms both of principle and of practice.

It must first be observed that the wearing of particular clothes to mark particular occasions or functions appears to be so nearly universal in the history of human society that it may be regarded as a natural cultural law, departure from which is not only psychologically unhealthy, but also in practice all but impossible: if, for example, the celebrant of the Eucharist today decides to wear 'ordinary clothes', they immediately cease, psychologically, to be ordinary clothes, and become another form of symbolical ecclesiastical garb, their very ordinariness making an extraordinary theological or sociological point. Second, it must be noticed that in more than one religion there is a tendency for the formal ordinary dress of a formative period of that religion to become ecclesiastical vesture, and so to survive long after it has disappeared from use in any other context, attracting to itself in the course of historical development a symbolism and a rationale which have little or nothing to do with its origins, and under the influence of which changes then take place in the vesture itself.

The history of Christian vesture is a notable case in point. Its basic stratum—to all intents and purposes what have come to be called in the West 'the eucharistic vestments'—is derived from the formal secular dress of the Roman Empire in the first six centuries of the Christian era; the only one of these garments which almost from the beginning appears to have had a particularly Christian meaning attached to it is the long white tunic, the *tunica alba* or alb, which was seen to be highly appropriate as a symbol of the purity and wholeness acquired by the Christian in baptism. Certain of the minor garments of this basic stratum were indeed in origin symbolical, but their symbolism was a secular one, indicative of a certain rank or office, which was then Christianized after the leaders of the Christian community had taken to using them when they were given equivalent secular rank after the peace of the Church in the fourth century. From the same period comes the first definite evidence of the provision of garments specifically for liturgical use, as distinct from the reservation of 'best clothes' for such a purpose, and some of this evidence suggests that the design and ornamentation of these garments was distinctive of their liturgical significance. In case one is tempted to regard this development as due to the influence of pagan usage, it is worth noting that one of the charges levelled by the Emperor Julian the Apostate against the Christians was that they dressed up in special clothes to worship God!

During the Middle Ages the origins of these vestments were lost sight of, and so an ecclesiastical rationale was found for them in terms of a more or less complicated system of symbolism, some of it simple and reasonably obvious, some of it—and more and more of it as time went on—abstruse and artificial, and most of it varying, of course, from one part of Christendom to another. In the West three basic strands of this symbolism may be traced. First, there is the tendency, especially evident among the liturgists of the earlier middle ages, to try to find a biblical rationale for almost all the externals of Christian worship, and in particular to find types of the impedimenta of the Christian cultus in the cultus of the old Covenant. Certain modifications and additions to the vestments were made under the influence of this school of thought, almost all of which have since disappeared. Second, there is the tendency, especially marked in the later Middle Ages, to interpret almost everything connected with the liturgy, and especially the Eucharist, in terms of the details of the passion; this too had certain practical consequences which have by now to all intents and purposes disappeared. Third, there is the tendency, pronounced through most of the medieval centuries, to moralism, which led to the interpretation of the vestments in terms of a symbolism of virtues and graces, an interpretation which survived until 1969 in the vesting prayers of the Roman rite, one of the many sets of such prayers which originated in the Middle Ages all over Christendom.

The centuries which followed the Counter-Reformation saw the vestments, like so much else, regarded simply as part and parcel of an immutable liturgy, the expression in worship of an immutable Church, and this not unnaturally led to their being treated rather as 'ornaments' than as 'clothes', with unfortunate results upon their construction and decoration aesthetically—if, that is, one is judging them as 'clothes'. Not until recent years have they again been regarded primarily as 'clothes', and their design influenced by this, for the difference between vestments of the baroque period and of the period following the Gothic revival was largely no more than one of fashion and historical and aesthetical preference.

Meanwhile, in most, although not all, of the Churches which originated in the Reformation, or derived from such Churches at a later period, the traditional vestments were abandoned, or greatly reduced, because they had come to be regarded as an integral part of a rejected cultus embodying a rejected doctrine. Some of the more extreme manifestations of the reformed traditions rejected special ecclesiastical garb altogether, but most did not, or returned to it when their first reforming ardour had burnt out. But in this, as in so many other matters, they rejected the primitive, which they thought to be medieval, and retained things that were medieval, which they thought to be compatible with what they fondly imagined to be primitive. During the Middle Ages, apart from modifications and additions to the basic stratum of vesture, two other strata arose and developed. The first was a development from the basic stratum, comprising mainly linen garments such as the various forms of surplice and rochet derived from the alb, and found more convenient for certain functions. The second was not really ecclesiastical at all, and certainly not liturgical; it comprised a range of garments which originated in the academic dress of the medieval universities and came to be used in church, at certain functions and by certain functionaries, owing to the close association between the ecclesiastical and academic worlds. From these two developments arose the whole of what came to be called 'choir habit' and 'clerical dress', and from these are derived the various forms of ministerial vesture worn in those post-Reformation traditions in which the traditional liturgical vestments have been rejected.

'Liturgical vestments comprise a special case of ceremonial clothing and are, therefore, part of a complex pattern of communication. They serve both to express the nature of the occasion when they are worn and to distinguish the respective role and rank of each participant.'[1] In addition, as we have seen, they have over the centuries acquired symbolical significance of various kinds—spiritual, theological, and, inevitably if regrettably, controversial in certain contexts. 'However, on all sides, it is recognized that whatever particular meanings vestments have acquired, there must, from time to time, be an appraisal of the symbolism of vesture and its relevance and effectiveness in the total communication pattern of worship.'[2]

The first criterion to be observed in such an appraisal is aesthetic. If liturgical garments are 'to express the nature of the occasion when they are worn', they must be beautiful, for it is of the very essence of worship that it should both reflect and acknowledge the beauty of God, as it is revealed in his mighty works of creation and redemption. Standards of beauty vary, of course, with taste and fashion, but it must always be borne in mind that the beauty of clothes resides principally in form and colour and texture, and only secondarily in ornamentation, and that the latter must therefore always be kept subordinate to the former. Judged according to this criterion the traditional vestments, in their original and early medieval forms, and in the forms which some—still all too few— modern designers are producing,[3] are highly satisfactory, while far too many of their later developments and derivatives are not.

The second criterion is theological and historical. An essential element in the nature of Christian worship is its witness to the unchanging and abiding value and power of God's mighty works in Christ, and it follows that the vestments should reflect the continuity of Christian worship, rather than the discontinuities which at times have afflicted it.

The third criterion is functional. In any large gathering of people for a specific purpose it is necessary to distinguish those who have particular functions to perform within it. This may be done in various ways, one of

[1] G. Cope, 'Liturgical Vestments', in *DLW*, p. 380.
[2] Ibid.
[3] Supreme among these is Sr Augustina Flüeler, of Stans, Switzerland, whose work is a model of what is needed, and whose important book on the subject is listed in the bibliography. There is no English equivalent.

the simplest and most effective of which is distinctive dress or items of dress. The liturgical assembly is such a gathering, and the liturgical vesture should clearly indicate the diverse functions within the assembly of those who wear it.

What consequences follow from the application of these criteria? First, any move towards the abandonment of distinctive liturgical vesture (except in extraordinary circumstances in which other considerations may take precedence) is folly. Functionally, it can only create confusion; theologically and historically, it can only suggest a contempt for the continuity of the Christian worshipping tradition which is pastorally intolerable; aesthetically, the 'ordinary dress' of the western and westernized societies of our time, whether formal or informal, must surely rank among the least attractive forms of clothing which the human race has ever devised. Second, if distinctive liturgical vesture should be retained, then it should be recognizably related to Christian liturgical vesture of the past: there is neither need nor excuse for attempting to invent something novel. The theological and historical ground of this assertion is obvious: the functional and aesthetic grounds are equally sure, but require a little expansion.

The historic vestments comprise in fact three categories of garment: under-clothes, over-clothes, and insignia of function or office. The basic alb, with its accompaniments (where necessary) and derivatives, is common to all ministers, 'clerical' or 'lay', exercising a particular function in the assembly, and is also the 'under-clothing' for those whose 'over-clothing'—chasuble, dalmatic or tunicle, cope—further distinguishes the function which they are performing. The latter purpose is also served in a different way by items such as the stole, the pallium, and the mitre, which are indicative of office as well as of function. Aesthetically, these three categories of garment include all the basic forms of ceremonial social clothing (other than military dress and its derivatives): it is not merely undesirable but also impossible to invent forms of such clothing which do not fall into the same fundamental structural groups (and this is true, incidentally, of other cultures as well as our own), without departing from the realm of what is natural and becoming in dress. And the more closely these garments approach to their classical liturgical form, the more natural and the more becoming they are. Within these limitations, which are far from constricting, there is room for a great deal of variety. But there is no room at all either for philistinism or for puritanism, nor for allowing the presuppositions and prejudices derived from some of the less edifying accidents of church history to overrule the imperatives of what is theologically fitting and pastorally elevating.

PART THREE

Pastoral Orientation

I

THE UNDERSTANDING
OF LITURGY IN THE LIGHT
OF ITS HISTORY

GEOFFREY WAINWRIGHT

Worship is a thread that is always being woven into the Church's historical tapestry. At any given period and place, the liturgy must be seen together with doctrine, evangelism, and holiness of life as composing the present and local image of the Church. The details and style of that picture will vary with time and space. Yet the present and local Church is of a piece with a Church which stretches back in time to Jesus Christ and which has been implanted in all parts of the globe. My concern is to show the liturgy in both its continuities and its varieties. On the way, I shall be dropping hints—with our contemporary work of liturgical revision and composition in view—as to what may be regarded as a proper kind of relationship between the constant character of the liturgy and its particular manifestations.

I THE CHRISTOLOGICAL CONSTANTS

Worship is a human glorification of God and a divine glorification of man: in and through our giving glory to God, God himself is changing us from glory into glory. For the Christian, this saving encounter of fellowship between God and man takes place 'in Jesus Christ'.[1] Precisely because we are being conformed to *Jesus Christ* (which is our glory), our worship takes its origin and fundamental pattern from the Jesus Christ to whom the NT bears the closest, and therefore most authoritative, witness we have. The constant reading of the NT within worship illustrates the fact that the Church recognizes Jesus Christ, and the Scriptures which bear witness to him, as the norm of its liturgy as of all its life. The constant Christological reference of Christian worship may be demonstrated with respect to both content and structure:

(a) CONTENT

(i) The Lord's Prayer, whose recitation is seldom absent from any major

---

[1] See E. Schillebeeckx, (ET) *Christ the Sacrament of Encounter with God* (Sheed and Ward 1963).

service, provides the *doctrinal* norm for Christian worship. Its address expresses the basic relationship between Christians and God: 'Our Father'. 'Abba' was the way in which Jesus characteristically spoke to God (Mk. 14.36; Mt. 11.25f=Lk. 10.21; Mt. 26.42; Lk. 23.34, 46; Jn. 11.41; 12.27f; 17), and Christians are allowed to share that privilege (Rom. 8.15f; Gal. 4.6). All Christian worship must have that tone of both reverence and intimacy sounded by 'Abba'.[1] The first petitions of the Lord's Prayer indicate that Christian worship is first and foremost a glorification of God and a prayer for the coming of his Kingdom: 'Hallowed be thy name, thy kingdom come, thy will be done...'. The second half of the Lord's Prayer shows that God's Kingdom includes certain divine benefits towards God's children: God feeds us, forgives us our sins, delivers us from evil. The constant saying of the divine office expresses an attempt to live permanently in filial communion with God.

(ii) What have come to be called the 'sacraments' place the saving activity of Jesus within the broad *cultural* context of the whole of humanity. Thus baptism takes up the universal practical and symbolic significance of water as the medium of washing, an instrument of death and new life: baptism is the sign of participation in the redemption wrought by the death and resurrection of Jesus Christ (Mk. 10.38f; Lk. 12.50; Rom. 6; Col. 2.12; Tit. 3.5-7). The universal practical and symbolic significance of eating and drinking is taken up by the meal-words and meal-deeds which abound in the ministry of Jesus (e.g. Mk. 2.15-19; Mt. 11.19=Lk. 7.34; Lk. 15.1f; Mt. 8.11=Lk. 13.29; Mt. 22.1-10=Lk. 14.15-24; the 'feeding miracles' and the meals which the risen Lord shared with his disciples): the Eucharist is the sacrament of feeding on the bread of God and of drinking the cup of salvation (Jn. 6.51-8; 1 Cor. 10.16f), all in anticipation of the banquet of the final Kingdom when the Messiah will sit at table with his people.[2] Jesus healed men of their diseases, and he commanded his followers to do the same (Mt. 10.1, 8; Lk. 9.1f; 10.9; cf. Acts 3.1-10; 4.30; 5.14-16; 28.8f; 1 Cor. 12.9, 28, 30): the sacrament of the sick (Jas. 5.14) is a present sign of that total salvation of body and soul—*sozo* means both to heal and to save—for which mankind looks and by which the nations will finally be healed (Rev. 22.2).

(b) STRUCTURE

(i) The constant basic structure of the principal act of worship, the Eucharist, links the Christian community of every time and place to the

---

[1] See J. Jeremias, *The Prayers of Jesus* (SCM 1967).
[2] See G. Wainwright, *Eucharist and Eschatology* (Epworth Press 1971).

Jesus Christ of the NT. The scriptural institution narratives present Jesus (if we may be allowed to follow the telescoping of seven actions into four which the later liturgies accomplished)[1] as (1) taking the bread and wine, (2) giving thanks to God over them, (3) breaking the bread, and (4) distributing the bread and wine to the disciples for them to eat and drink. Although the fraction has sometimes been stressed as a sign of the 'breaking' of Christ in death, yet it is the taking of the elements, the thanksgiving, and the communion which have constantly emerged as the central features of the sacrament (ignoring the medieval Western aberration which made the elevation of the host for the people's contemplation a practical high-point of the Mass—almost a surrogate communion). *Doctrinally*, the Eucharist is a focal instance of man living as he ought in the world: man is putting the material creation ('taking' the bread and wine) to its proper use as the occasion (the 'thanksgiving') and medium (the 'eating and drinking') of his own fellowship with God. It is through the work of Jesus Christ and in communion with him that men are enabled to live as God's sons in the world, and the Eucharist is therefore celebrated 'in remembrance of him'.

(ii) *Culturally*, the use of water in baptism, and of bread and wine at the Eucharist, has maintained itself almost universally; the use of oil has continued in 'confirmation', ordination, and the sacrament of the sick in the Orthodox and Catholic Churches. In modern times, however, there has been some call, particularly in Africa and Asia, to replace the 'Mediterranean' or 'European' bread and wine by local food and drink at the Eucharist. One respects these suggestions as attempting to express the way in which the sacrament both assumes and informs daily life. But, leaving aside the exceptional circumstances of the prison-camp or the jungle, it would appear preferable, for several reasons, to retain the use of bread and wine as one of the constants of Christian worship: they keep clear the original reference to Jesus Christ, whom the NT presents as instituting the sacrament with these elements (Mt. 26.26–8; Mk. 14.22–4; Lk. 22.19f; 1 Cor. 11.23–6); the bread and wine have rich symbolic associations in the Scriptures; their almost universal use in the Church up to now constitutes a precious ecclesiological bond in time and space.

Another cultural constant in the structure of Christian worship has been the use of the laying on of hands as a central act in various connections: ordination, 'confirmation', penance, prayer for the sick. The most general sense of this gesture appears to be the transmission of power (a 'blessing'); the specific meaning is determined by the context and the accompanying words. The NT, like the OT, knows the laying on

---

[1] G. Dix, *Shape*, p. 48.

of hands in several contexts (Mk. 5.23; 6.5; Acts 6.6; 8.17f; 9.17; 13.3; 19.6; 1 Tim. 4.14; 5.22; 2 Tim. 1.6; Heb. 6.2; cf. Mk. 16.18): it seems right that the Church should continue to make sacramental use of this action which is easy and natural to embodied humanity, its Christological reference being verbally stated on each occasion.

In the use of oil, the reference to Jesus Christ the anointed king and priest is never far away.

2   THE HISTORICAL VARIABLES

Since Newman's great *Essay*, it is impossible for any thinking Christian to deny that there has been development of doctrine in the course of the Church's history. It is also clear that worship has played some formative part in the evolution of dogma. Take four examples, whose value may be variously appreciated among different Christians.[1] First, the doctrinal recognition of the divinity of Jesus Christ must have been aided by the worshipping Church's experience of the presence of the One in whose name it gathered (Mt. 18.20): Jesus Christ was both invoked (1 Cor. 16.22) and acclaimed (Phil. 2.10f) as 'Lord'.[2] Second, the use of the threefold Name in baptism was claimed to establish both the distinct personality (already Tertullian, *Against Praxeas*, 26) and the full divinity (Athanasius, *Letters to Serapion*, 1.29f; Basil, *On the Holy Spirit*, 24ff) of the Holy Spirit. Third, the practice of infant baptism helped at least to consolidate the doctrine of original sin: one of Augustine's arguments against the Pelagians appealed to the administration to infants of baptism *in remissionem peccatorum*. Fourth, when the Roman Catholic Church came to proclaim the dogmas of Mary's immaculate conception (1854) and her assumption (1950), the preparatory and subsequent justification advanced by the theologians included an appeal to liturgical feasts and phrases: the festivals of 8 December and 15 August were of long and official observance, and ancient and authorized liturgical texts call the Mother of Christ 'spotless' and 'queen of heaven'.

While worship has thus unmistakably played a formative part in the development of dogma, it is also true that doctrine, contrariwise, has contributed to historical changes in the liturgy. Centuries of belief have left their deposit in prayers and ceremonies which, after being introduced in a gradual and almost incidental way, have continued to be used by later generations. There have also been times when, more deliberately, doctrinal motives have been at work in the fashioning of new rites or in

[1] See M. F. Wiles, *The Making of Christian Doctrine* (CUP 1967), pp. 62–93.

[2] On *Maranatha* (1 Cor. 16.22), see G. Wainwright, *Eucharist and Eschatology*, pp. 68–70. On the pre-Pauline hymn of Phil. 2.5–11, see R. Deichgräber, *Gotteshymnus und Christushymnus in der frühen Christenheit* (Göttingen 1967), pp. 118–33.

the revision of old. We shall look in a moment at ways in which *doctrine* makes for variability in the liturgy.

But *culture* also makes for variability in the liturgy. We shall look soon at examples of this. At this point I wish simply to indicate the creative role which, contrariwise, the Church's worship has played in the shaping of human culture, particularly in Europe. It is sufficient to mention the medieval cathedrals of the West, the icons of the East, the altar-pieces of the Florentine school, the passion music of Bach, the language of the Book of Common Prayer and the Authorized Version of the Bible—or even the Christmas presents, the Shrove Tuesday pancakes and the Easter eggs which testify to the way in which the liturgical calendar has coloured the annual rhythm of a whole society.

It is time now to look at ways in which both doctrinal and cultural factors bring change and variety into the liturgy.

(a) DOCTRINE

(i) From the point of view of *content*, it is the sermon which most consistently introduces an element of variability into the liturgy. While the one gospel of Jesus Christ remains constant, yet it has to be preached afresh in each new situation—and that in terms which will render it both intelligible and relevant to hearers in a particular time and place; hence its sermonic expression will vary with the historical and geographical circumstances and indeed with every preacher's reflection on the Christian message.

Sometimes, new liturgical 'propers' have been specially composed in order to keep pace with doctrinal development. Thus in the medieval West an increasingly 'realistic' understanding of the eucharistic presence went hand in hand with new forms of popular devotion to the Sacrament until the feast of Corpus Christi emerged—and Thomas Aquinas (tradition credits him with their authorship) finally wrote a series of propers for Mass and Office. More recently, Pope Pius XI decided that the universal rule of Christ needed stronger emphasis and in 1925 he instituted the feast of Christ the King (the last Sunday in October; now moved to the Sunday before Advent), with its own set of propers.

On occasion, doctrinal developments and their liturgical expression have come under challenge. This was especially the case at the time of the Reformation. Led by Luther, the Reformers' chief attack—made in the name of Scripture—fell upon the sacrificial character of the Mass in its medieval form and practice. From the viewpoint of his radical doctrine of justification by faith alone, Luther saw the medieval Mass as a human 'work': and a work which threatened the sufficiency of Calvary to boot. In his reformed service, all that smacked of oblation had been removed, and the sacrament appeared entirely as a divine gift, to be received in faith: in the *Deutsche Messe* of 1526 the words of institution are no longer sung in the tone of prayer (as in the *Formula Missae et Communionis* of 1523) but in the gospel tone. Ironically, Luther's very stress on the words of institution shows him to be still the prisoner of the Middle Ages.

Lately, there are other examples of milder reform of content which is better called revision. In connection with infant baptism, there has occurred in recent years in practically all the Western Churches a certain dissatisfaction—partly anthropological, partly theological—with the idea that godparents or sponsors act as the mouthpiece of the candidate: this was the practice in the traditional Roman Catholic rite (and the Lutherans maintained it, and so too, though with some explanation in the text, did the Anglicans), where the baptismal interrogations were addressed to the infant and the sponsors simply spoke for him. In the 1969 Roman Catholic rite of infant baptism, the questions are now addressed to the parents and godparents concerning their own faith (not the child's), and they are exhorted to bring the child up in the faith. Here the Roman Church is falling into line with what has been the practice in many Presbyterian, Congregational, and Methodist Churches for several generations.[1]

(ii) As far as liturgical *structure* is concerned, the case of 'confirmation' is an excellent example of the way in which doctrinal development has in turn affected the liturgy. From patristic times onwards, certain post-baptismal ceremonies in the Western Church, notably the imposition of hands and the anointing of the forehead, were reserved, especially under Roman influence, to the bishop as the guardian of the Church's unity. With the growth of the Church in numbers and the increased preoccupation of the episcopate with civil affairs, it happened that often years could elapse between baptism (administered in infancy by a presbyter) and episcopal 'confirmation'. Eventually, 'confirmation' came to be regarded, doctrinally, as a separate sacrament (it is certainly listed among the seven by the Second Council of Lyons, 1274). The medieval service-books recognized the separation ever more definitely. The Reformers were left to make of 'confirmation' something quite different from what its origins would suggest: it came to be seen and practised in Protestantism as above all the occasion—following catechesis—of a personal profession of faith on the part of one baptized in infancy.

Infant baptism was responsible for historical variation at the other end

---

[1] The 1975 C of E Report, *Series 3: Infant Baptism* made the parents and godparents 'answer the questions both for themselves and for their children'. The 1977 draft *Initiation Services* make the shift more complete.

of the initiation structure also. The multiple ceremonies of the catechumenate—which originally accompanied the instruction of adult candidates over an extended period—came to be condensed into a few minutes before the baptismal rite proper, from which they were now practically indispensable. Elements of this remain in the Roman revision of infant baptism of 1969.

Doctrinal development affected the structure of the Eucharist, too. In the medieval West, the stress on the sacrificial character of the Mass led to such an inflation of the 'offertory' that a veritable 'little canon' grew up at that point in the service, where it persisted in the Roman Catholic rite until the reforms that followed Vatican II. The sixteenth-century Reformers cut out the offertory prayers on doctrinal grounds. They also shaped their own eucharistic rites so as to express their own doctrines of the Eucharist. In general, the purpose and effect was to make communion itself (now restored to both kinds for the people as well) the chief act.[1] Of Cranmer's Communion Service in the 1552 Prayer Book, for instance, E. C. Ratcliff wrote thus:

> The liturgical action of the Lord's Supper, according to Cranmer's later conception of it, consists in the eating of bread and drinking of wine in thankful remembrance of Christ's death. It is possible to reject this conception as inadequate or mistaken; but rejection neither requires nor justifies refusal to acknowledge the skill and felicity with which the rite embodying the conception is constructed. The several parts of the rite succeed each other in a logically inevitable order which deserves the admiration of all students of liturgy.[2]

One doctrinally conditioned structural feature of Cranmer's 1552 service which has remained rather characteristic of the Anglican tradition to this day (though not in the Scoto-American stream) is the worshippers' self-oblation after the communion ('And here we offer and present unto thee, O Lord, ourselves, our souls and bodies...').

Ordination rites have also varied with doctrine. Thus the Reformers jettisoned words and acts which bespoke a sacerdotal view of the ordained ministry. In the Second English Ordinal of 1552, the only 'instrument' to be 'delivered' to the 'priest' is the Bible: paten and chalice have gone, for the primary ministry is now that of preaching and teaching.

[1] Why, since the twelfth and thirteenth centuries, had the chalice commonly been withheld from the laity? Had an increasingly 'realistic' understanding of the presence made mishaps ever more insupportable? There will have been an interplay between the practice of communion *sub una* (infants were often communicated under *wine* alone) and the emerging doctrine of concomitance whereby it is held that Christ is totally present under each separate species.

[2] 'The liturgical work of Archbishop Cranmer' in *JEH* 7 (1956), pp. 189–203=*LS*, pp. 184–202.

(b) CULTURE

(i) The *content* of worship has been variously affected by cultural factors. In tracing some 'laws of liturgical evolution', A. Baumstark detected a primary movement from 'austerity' to 'richness'.[1] As the ceremonies and prayers proliferated, it was natural that the expansions should take on local colouring and express the genius of the people. Thus there is a remarkable difference in style between Roman and Gallican prayers: whereas the Roman style is 'pregnant', 'precise', 'simple', 'sober', the Gallican and Mozarabic is 'elaborate', 'effusive', 'picturesque'.[2] It was often the later developments which held their place when, on account of the 'weakness of the flesh', a certain amount of pruning was felt to be necessary in the rites: Baumstark pointed out that, when there had been a secondary and reverse movement in favour of abbreviation, it was the Scriptures which were no longer read in their ancient quantities (pericopes were curtailed in the Office, the OT lessons practically disappeared from the Mass . . .), while the Psalms and scripture canticles often largely gave way in the Byzantine Office to the poetical compositions that were originally written to accompany them. In the West Syrian rite, the ancient and rather concise Anaphora of St James was supplemented in the sixth and seventh centuries by new anaphoras which were much more prolix and which dwelt on themes that captured the Syrian imagination (so, for example, the description of the heavenly choir before the Sanctus, and the long descriptions of the final judgement attaching to the mention of the second advent in the anamnesis); later, however, yet more formularies, but of an extreme brevity, were produced, and in the thirteenth century Bar-Hebraeus even made an abridgement of the Anaphora of St James.

Another way in which local culture has brought varied material into the liturgy has been the cult of the saints, where the particular devotion has often been regional. In 1955, Pope Pius XII cashed in on the popular 'labour' celebration of May Day to make May 1st the feast of St Joseph the Worker.[3]

---

[1] A. Baumstark, (ET) *Comparative Liturgy* (Mowbray 1958), pp. 15–30.

[2] E. Bishop, 'The genius of the Roman rite' in *Liturgica Historica* (Clarendon Press 1918), pp. 1–19.

[3] J. A. Jungmann (ET, *The Early Liturgy*, DLT 1960, pp. 145–9) links the old *litania major* of 25 April (dropped from the calendar of 1969) with the Roman *Robigalia* (for the aversion of wheat rust), the procession of 2 February with an old Roman *amburbale* (sacrificial procession round the city), the feast of the *cathedra Petri* on 22 February with an old Roman feast in honour of the dead (at which an empty chair was left)—and of course 25 December as Christmas Day with the *dies natalis Solis Invicti*, the 'birthday of the unconquered sun'. Cf. *supra* pp. 414, 417.

(ii) Cultural factors also make themselves felt in the *structure* of the liturgy. A prime example is the magnification of the Great Entrance in the Byzantine Eucharist: the bringing in of the elements is decked out with imperial ceremonial as the entry of the divine Ruler; and fans and lights and incense continue to attend the sacred species throughout the service.

In the initiation rite described in *Ap. Trad.*, the bishop's Kiss of Peace to the neophytes and the cup of milk and honey at their first communion may well be derived from ancient pagan initiatory practices—which, in these cases, lent themselves easily to Christian interpretation.[1] In the cultural situation of the Middle Ages, it is not surprising that the tap on the cheek in 'confirmation'—which was probably in origin a form of the Kiss of Peace—came to be interpreted in terms of courageous combat, corresponding to the idea of 'confirmation' as a *robur ad pugnam*, a 'strengthening for the fight'.

3 THE MODERN WESTERN LITURGICAL MOVEMENT

We have seen how the liturgy, in respect of both content and structure, has always been governed by certain basic Christological constants and yet has exhibited considerable variability of detail as doctrine has both developed and been reformed and as cultural circumstances have changed. How does the twentieth-century Western Liturgical Movement, whose effects have been felt particularly since the Second World War, fit in with these patterns? Our answer may be arranged under six heads and a conclusion.[2]

(a) THE BIBLE

The Liturgical Movement has undoubtedly sought to 'return to the Scriptures', which are the closest and best witness we have to Jesus Christ. In terms of the structure of the eucharistic liturgy, there has been widespread reform of the lectionary leading to the reintroduction of an

---

[1] See J. A. Jungmann, *The Early Liturgy*, pp. 128, 139.

[2] On the RC side, see the valuable composite volume assembled by J. P. Jossua and Y. Congar, *La Liturgie après Vatican II* (*Unam Sanctam*, 66 (Paris 1967)). For a Swiss Reformed viewpoint: J. J. von Allmen, *Worship: its theology and practice* (Lutterworth 1965), and 'The theological frame of a liturgical renewal' in *The Church Quarterly* 2 (1969–70), pp. 8–23. For a Methodist viewpoint: G. Wainwright, 'The risks and possibilities of liturgical reform' in *SL* 8 (1971–2), pp. 65–80, and 'The Methodist Service Book 1975' in *Epworth Review* 3 (1976), pp. 110–18. For a brief history of the early stages of the modern movement, see J. H. Srawley, *The Liturgical Movement: its origin and growth* (Mowbray 1954). For the American scene, see J. F. White, *Christian Worship in Transition* (Nashville 1976), esp. chs. 4, 6, 7.

OT lesson as a regular feature and the matching of OT, Epistle, and Gospel according to a coherent theme for each Sunday (whereas the old Epistles and Gospels had often fallen out of phase). In the Roman Church, a new Lectionary accompanied the Missal of Paul VI: its large number of 'ordinary Sundays' marks a departure from a long traditional system which most Anglican and Protestant Churches are fundamentally continuing to follow—and that in a tidier way than has often been the case in the past—in numbering their Sundays 'before' and 'after' the high points of the Christian year. In Britain, pioneering work was accomplished by A. A. McArthur in *The Evolution of the Christian Year* (SCM 1953) and *The Christian Year and Lectionary Reform* (SCM 1958); the *Calendar and Lectionary* produced in 1967 by the Joint Liturgical Group has now been adopted, with variations of detail, by the major Anglican and Protestant Churches in the British Isles. In general, the Scriptures are now being allowed to bear their own witness within the liturgical context more clearly than had long been the case; though an awareness of the *fragilitas carnis* has caused several new liturgies to permit the OT lesson and the Epistle to be considered as alternatives.

On the doctrinal plane, the best work of contemporary biblical scholars has been drawn upon in order to ensure that balance and perspectives are as scriptural as possible. The whole range of God's mighty acts comes to expression in many new anaphoras. Eschatological and pneumatological themes have reappeared in liturgies from which they had almost vanished. An important contribution of biblical theology has been the interpretation of liturgical 'memorial' (OT root *zkr*) as having both a Godward and a manward aspect in such a dynamic way that the liturgy involves—by God's gracious ordinance—the making present for man of at least the *saving power* of the original events of redemptive history.[1] All this is part of a proper willingness to submit to the scriptural and Christological constant.

(b) THE FATHERS

The *retour aux sources* has also included a return to that patristic period which has usually been regarded as possessing a normative status second only to the apostolic age (the sixteenth-century Reformers certainly regarded the early Fathers with great respect,[2] though later Protestants have sometimes transferred that respect to the Reformers themselves). Different traditions have found a meeting ground in the Fathers.

Study of the *Mystagogical Catecheses* of Cyril of Jerusalem, Ambrose,

[1] For 'memorial', see G. Wainwright, *Eucharist and Eschatology*, pp. 64–8 and (for bibliography) p. 177, note 204.
[2] See H. O. Old, *The Patristic Roots of Reformed Worship* (Zürich 1975).

John Chrysostom and Theodore of Mopsuestia has in various ways aided both the understanding and the re-structuring of the process of Christian initiation: the most splendid achievement in this respect has been the Roman *Ordo Initiationis Christianae Adultorum* (1972).

With regard to the Eucharist, study of ancient anaphoras has greatly influenced the recovery of the 'great prayer of thanksgiving' which has taken place not only in the Protestant Churches but also in the Roman Catholic Church.[1] Eucharistic Prayer II in the new Roman rite is clearly based on the prayer in Hippolytus, *Ap. Trad.*,[2] Eucharistic Prayer III turns to Gallican and Spanish sources for inspiration,[3] and Prayer IV to the Ancient Eastern liturgies.[4]

In the new Roman Catholic *Liturgy of the Hours* (1971–2), the highlighting of Lauds and Vespers was motivated by the rediscovered early primacy of the so-called 'cathedral office' (the public prayers of morning and evening) as distinct from the monastic office.

(c) THE CHURCH

Our century has witnessed an ecclesiological renewal. The recovery of a sense of 'the Church' can be traced in the writings of O. Dibelius (*Das Jahrhundert der Kirche*, 1927) and D. Bonhoeffer (*Sanctorum communio*, 1930) in German Lutheranism, of E. Mersch, H. de Lubac and Y. Congar in French-speaking Catholicism, of A. M. Ramsey (*The Gospel and the Catholic Church*, 1936), R. N. Flew (*Jesus and his Church*, 1938), and L. Newbigin (*The Household of God*, 1953) among English theologians. Institutionally, there is the evidence of the Faith and Order movement and then of the World Council of Churches, of the encyclicals *Mystici corporis* (1943) and *Mediator Dei* (1947) of Pius XII and then of the Second Vatican Council and its great Constitutions on the Church and on the Liturgy. The Liturgical Movement has in fact drawn on, and contributed to, the ecclesiological renewal.

The revised rites of initiation have brought out the fact that Christians

---

[1] See I. Pahl, 'Das eucharistische Hochgebet in den Abendmahlsordnungen der Reformationskirchen' in *Questions liturgiques et paroissiales*, 53 (1972), pp. 219–50; and, for the RC Church, P. Tihon, 'Theology of the Eucharistic Prayer' in L. Sheppard, *The New Liturgy* (DLT 1970), pp. 174–93; P. Jounel, 'La composition des nouvelles prières eucharistiques' in *LMD* 94 (1968), pp. 38–76.

[2] B. Botte, 'The short anaphora' in Sheppard, pp. 194–9.

[3] L. Bouyer, in Sheppard, pp. 203–12. This prayer owes much to the proposals, themselves deeply patristic, of C. Vagaggini, (ET) *The Canon of the Mass and Liturgical Reform* (DLT 1967).

[4] J. Gelineau, in Sheppard, pp. 213–27. See also A. Houssiau, 'The Alexandrine Anaphora of St Basil', ibid., pp. 228–43: the proposal to adopt Alexandrine Basil as a *fifth* prayer did not in fact carry.

are a royal priesthood charged with showing forth the wonderful deeds of the God who called them out of darkness into his marvellous light: the very words of 1 Pet. 2.9f are incorporated in the 'confirmation' service of the British Methodist *Entry into the Church* (1974), and the theme of Christian witness in the world finds an explicit place in many recent revisions of baptism and confirmation. From the Eucharist also, the worshippers are 'sent forth' into the world. This recovery of the missionary character of the whole Church marks a return to an authentic NT viewpoint.

So, too, does the recovery of the Church as a community in which each member has a ministry to fulfil within the body. The Liturgical Movement has sought to give expression to this truth in the ordering of the worship assembly. It has fostered the active participation of the whole gathering: intercessions are often said in litany form; simple chants have been composed for the people's acclamations; communions have become more frequent among Catholic worshippers, and communion *services* in Protestant Churches; 'Protestant' hymns have been introduced into Catholic worship. Lay members of the congregation have been appointed, whether formally or informally, to functions within the cult. The isolation of the Catholic priest at his altar and the Protestant preacher in his pulpit has largely given way to a view of the minister as president of the liturgical assembly.

(d) ECUMENISM

The modern Liturgical Movement has stretched across denominational boundaries. Starting from rather different doctrinal and practical positions, Churches have noticeably converged as they have tried to reform and revise their worship in the light of the Scriptures and of what they have sensed to be the most authentic tradition and character of the Church. Total agreement has not yet been reached, even on matters concerning the doctrinal and practical 'constants'. But the use, as far as may be, of similar liturgies will undoubtedly contribute towards the achievement of a fuller common understanding: the formative power of the liturgy is a proven reality. Where ecclesiastical unity has already been attained, as in the CSI, it is now clear that the widespread use of a *Book of Common Worship* is playing an important part in cementing the bonds of fellowship.[1]

---

[1] The liturgical compositions for the new Church of South India (1947) were the first great production inspired by the Liturgical Movement. They excited the admiration of liturgists and have been widely influential in Anglicanism and English-speaking Protestantism. See T. S. Garrett, *Worship in the CSI* (2nd edn Lutterworth 1965).

(e) SYMBOLISM

Through depth psychology, the studies of anthropologists, and the work of modern artists, writers, and philosophers, we are nowadays very conscious of the importance of symbols. Since worship is a privileged area of verbal, material, personal, and dramatic symbols, it is only fitting that contemporary liturgists should have devoted attention to the matter.[1] On the Catholic side, they have succeeded in disencumbering the liturgy from much of the minor ceremonial that had become attached to it, in such a way that the great, constant, elemental symbols now stand out in all their power: witness the revised Roman rite of the Easter Vigil, in which also the element of personal recommitment has been made verbally explicit in the introduction of a renewal of baptismal vows. On the Protestant side, a few steps have been taken to enrich the material and dramatic symbolism of a long denuded cultus: witness the giving of the lighted candle suggested in some new baptismal rites, or the standing for the reading of the Gospel in Churches where that custom was previously unknown. That warmly human gesture, the Kiss of Peace, has caught on widely in various forms.

(f) CULTURE

The great archetypal experiences and figures come to concrete expression in a variety of culturally conditioned symbolic and practical forms. Hence the question is raised: how far should the Christian liturgy accommodate itself to the varying socio-psychological patterns of communication and behaviour which are observable in different human contexts? The whole problem is thus raised of cultural 'adaptation' in an 'incarnational' religion which is particular in its historical origins and universal in its claims. In recently evangelized areas, the matter is complicated by the need for a theological evaluation of the pre-Christian religiously-based culture whose symbols it may be a question of taking over.[2] In general, the Liturgical Movement has tended to encourage greater local variation in symbolic expression than had long been the case in 'romanized' and even 'curialized' Catholicism[3] or in a Protestantism suspicious of all symbolism other than verbal. The advantage of 'localization' is that the

---

[1] For example, G. Cope, *Symbolism in the Bible and the Church* (SCM 1959). Also three essays in *La Liturgie après Vatican II*: M. D. Chenu, 'Anthropologie de la liturgie'; M. Carrouges, 'La liturgie à l'heure de Ionesco'; P. Colin, 'Phénoménologie et herméneutique du symbolique liturgique'.

[2] G. Wainwright, 'The localization of worship' in *SL* 8 (1971–2), pp. 26–41.

[3] In his *Short History of the Western Liturgy* (ET OUP 1969), T. Klauser characterizes the period in the RC liturgy between Trent and Vatican II by the heading 'rigid unification and rubricism'.

worshippers are enabled to feel 'at home' in the liturgy, and the spirit of the gospel and of the liturgy may, through them, more easily penetrate the surrounding society.[1] All this must remain within the limits set by the Christological constants.

CONCLUSION:
THE ACCUSATION OF ANTIQUARIANISM

It has been the implied thesis of this chapter, and indeed of the whole book, that the liturgy cannot be properly understood apart from its history. The general value of historical explanations in the case of human realities is, in the particular case of the Christian liturgy, enhanced by the unique importance which Christianity attributes to its historical Founder and by the Christian's sense of belonging to a continuing community which stretches through time and space. Nevertheless, students of liturgy are sometimes accused of being mere antiquarians: it is alleged that they are often interested in the past simply 'for its own sake'—or if they do apply themselves to present composition, then it is with a view to the 'restoration' of long outdated features of the cult. It is said that the whole work of official liturgical revision since the Second World War is irrelevant because it is theologically behind the times.

To take an example: J. L. Houlden has argued that the C of E's Series 3 Eucharist remains caught in an 'historical-cum-mythological approach' to the Christian faith which lags far behind 'current theology'.[2] But *which* current theology? And what if the historical-cum-mythological approach were at least *a* proper approach to the Christian faith—and one particularly suited to the very nature of the liturgy as *dromenon* or 'drama'? Worship will necessarily express a theology, but the Church's worship must not be tied to one particular theological school (there are so many, and they are often so ephemeral). The 'theology' expressed in worship must be as broadly acceptable as possible to the present Christian community and as faithful as possible to what is sensed to be authentic in the past. This is because the liturgy is a public act by which the worshippers identify themselves with a continuing community and enter into the 'myth' of that community—a 'myth' which is rooted in the

---

[1] A classic study was A. G. Hebert, *Liturgy and Society* (Faber 1935). See also B. Wicker, *Culture and Liturgy* (Sheed and Ward 1963), and G. Wainwright, 'Christian worship and western culture' in *SL* 12 (1977), pp. 20–33. A deliberate attempt to start from the culture was made in the US United Methodist booklet, *Ritual in a New Day* (Nashville 1976).

[2] In R. C. D. Jasper, ed., *The Eucharist Today: Studies on Series 3* (SPCK 1974), pp. 168–76.

history of Jesus Christ to which the Scriptures bear witness. There should be no fear that the liturgy will petrify: for, while ever the people gather in faith, worship is an occasion when the living Lord breaks in to inspire, to correct, and to lead men on in that fellowship with God which is the human vocation.

II

WORSHIP AND THE PASTORAL OFFICE

D. H. TRIPP

William Ralph Inge, Dean of St Paul's Cathedral, was once asked if he studied liturgiology. No, he did not; nor (he added) did he collect postage stamps. The Dean spoke for many people, but with less than his usual wisdom. Even the great Harnack could not see the history of worship as the arena of a worthwhile theological discipline. Students of liturgy may respond to such views by pointing to three simple facts.

In the first place: without the practice of worship there would be no theology at all. There can be no talking *about* God where there is no talking *to* God. When 'God' means no more than a *primum mobile* in metaphysics or a portmanteau expression for the unexplained in conversations with our children, it is time for God-language to be abandoned. As things turn out, religious experience repeatedly breaks out of such limitations, and can only be described as encounter with God who speaks and hears: and that encounter is worship.

In the second place, worship is the one activity in which all Christian people join. They are all affected by it, and all in some measure find their expression in it. It is amusing to notice that worship is given the least specialized attention in denominations which make most of preaching—and preaching, whatever else it may have been in addition, has always been a liturgical act. In every Christian seminary, theological study gives pride of place to liturgical documents of the synagogue and the early Church: *Torah*, prophets, psalms, letters, Gospels. Obvious but ignored is the fact that, were it not for redaction for synagogue use, there would be no OT, and that the NT similarly grew up around letters read out at gatherings on the Lord's Day, which day in turn gave birth to the Gospels.

In the third place, worship is the context in which Christian people must surely be expected to be most sincere. The vows of initiation, marriage, ordination; prayer for friend and enemy; thanksgiving: if we do not utter these cordially and advisedly, when *can* we be taken seriously?

These remarks suggest a value in the study of worship, at least on an academic level. Our interest in this part of our book is to relate worship to the practical concerns of pastoral work.

'It is the duty of a bishop', said the medieval Roman pontifical, 'to judge, to interpret, to consecrate, to ordain, to offer [the Mass], to baptize, and to confirm'. Of seven functions listed, six are 'liturgical' (although with administrative and disciplinary associations), and only one is administrative in itself, and even that has liturgical associations, for 'judgement' is related to the exercise of clerical character and communicant status. A similar order of priorities, although with predictable adjustments, may be found in Protestant sources. 'Our preaching should be so near to prayer that it would require only a very slight transposition to turn our words into words of prayer. It is certainly an abridgement of our ministry for a preacher to think of himself primarily as a teacher. The centre of the congregational sermon is an act of our priesthood, which we share with all believers, but which must first become manifest in us.' So a Lutheran, Hans Asmussen.

Both of the traditions cited here are derived ultimately from the New Testament, and more specifically from 1 Tim. 2.1: '*First of all*, then, I urge that supplications, prayer, intercessions, and thanksgivings be made for all men.' The pastoral office is a matter of worship. In all his functions, the priest or minister is the apostolic teacher (as in Titus), the Church ruler (as in Gregory the Great's *de cura pastorali*), the shepherd—and the liturgist.

By the very nature of Christian worship, a study of its pastoral dimensions is obliged to look beyond the situation of the pastoral office. The clergy exist to glorify God in the care of his Church and its mission. At the Last Supper, Christ handed his apostles a cup, as he said: 'This is my blood of the covenant, which is poured out for many' (Mark 14.24). For *many*; for the sake of all mankind. The disciples were to consider, in this moment, more than themselves, more even than the totality of the Church that was to be: the many, the *hoi polloi* who are the intended beneficiaries of the cross. The Church's worship is inseparable from its mission, and indeed from the whole problem-ridden range of its relationships with its God and with the world it has to live in.

It is nonetheless necessary to begin with the Church, the Church as it is, for it is in and with the Church that the pastoral office has to be directed to the world. The Church, of course, is a single organic entity, a body to which all its members are indispensable; but we begin with some consideration of the laity in isolation and go on to the clergy in isolation, for, as things are, laity and clergy often exist and work and think in isolation.

This part of our book is intended less to convey information than to stimulate reflection. We now offer therefore a series of twenty-four theses, with some attached remarks.

WORSHIP AND THE LAITY

1. *Christian worship realizes the true status of the laity, and requires the laity to exercise it*

The reaffirmation in recent generations of the dignity of the laity[1] as the *laos tou theou*, the chosen race, the royal priesthood, the holy nation, the corporate guardian of the faith, has been both wholly justified and wholly beneficial, especially for liturgical life. Indeed, this reaffirmation of a major biblical principle owes its currency largely to the Liturgical Movement.[2] Augustine's appeal to his people to see themselves in the oblation upon the altar, the *plebs tua sancta* of the Roman Canon, the scattered and gathered bread in the *Didache*: all these things have come back into prominence. Even if these themes did not originally enjoy the importance they now have, they are nevertheless indispensable insights of Christian belief. Even in the ages of greatest clerical domination the clergy and the laity exchanged greetings, and the celebrant humbly asked his people to pray for him before he ascended the altar steps.

2. *Christian worship manifests the spiritual significance of the 'world', within which the laity work out their vocation*

Christian worship is not an aerial waltz of disembodied spirits. It is spiritual because the Holy Spirit, the Lord, the Lifegiver, hovers over human chaos and there imposes an ordered reflection of Christ. By his working, the constituent elements of the world, matter, space, time, and mind, are hallowed, for they are offered in the persons and prayers of the people whom God has made his own in this world by the incarnation of the Son. Even if the offertory at the Eucharist was not seen in this light until the present century, it may reasonably be so understood as one point where this implication of our worship may be noticed.

Clearly, clergy and laity alike are involved in the 'world'. However, it is chiefly the laity who carry the burden of secular responsibilities, and it is chiefly they who appreciate the value of the sanctification of worldly

---

[1] On the laity, see the various studies of the WCC, and such works as C. C. Eastwood, *The Royal Priesthood of the Faithful* (Epworth Press 1963), and *The Priesthood of All Believers* (Epworth Press 1960), and works there listed.

[2] See J. H. Srawley, *The Liturgical Movement* (Mowbray 1954), B. Koenker, *The Liturgical Renaissance in the Roman Catholic Church* (Chicago 1954), H. G. Hardin, J. D. Quillian, J. F. White, *The Celebration of the Gospel* (Nashville 1964 and London 1965), etc.

things, provided that it can be expressed in a convincing and modest fashion.

3. *In Christian worship, there is an intractable element of strangeness, both for unbelievers and for worshippers*

However helpful it may be to illustrate the nature of worship by comparisons with family life, daily employment, social or civic celebration, the etiquette of the throne-room, or whatever else may at the time seem to be especially splendid and yet utterly simple and obvious, there remains in it a sense of doing something different in kind from all other activities.

This is not merely a question of the *kind* of liturgy that is available. Whether the rite in which you are sharing is the Holy Liturgy of St John Chrysostom or a Quaker silence—and we know quite well that most of us find the spiritual directness that we need only at one or another place in the spectrum of Christian practice—you are doing something not entirely paralleled in any other sphere of life.

It is not only unbelievers who find worship strange. Perhaps it is only in times of decadence that this sense of alienation from worship occurs on a large scale, but it is not confined to our modern world. The Roman augur smiled, and for centuries the Hebrew prophets had occasion to denounce the moral incongruity between the cultic devotion and the social behaviour of their people. Much attention has been given to the present form of this alienation, known for the time being as 'secularization'. This process may be uniquely forceful at this stage of history, or it may be a recurring disturbance of the corporate mind. However it may be explained—and original sin has something to do with its negative aspects—it must be taken into account here. On the positive side, the present trend affirms the reality and value of this-worldly experience, the validity of senses and sciences, what in religious terms may be thought of as the complete presence of God in every moment and aspect of his creation, not only in the explicitly religious acts and thinking hitherto recognized. On the other hand, a feeling, vague in its beginnings but rapidly becoming oppressive and sharp, that we can get along very smoothly with everything important without taking time to address a problematic God, a tacit assumption that responsible action must be on purely human levels, leads many people to relegate worship to the category of marginal or even self-indulgent behaviour. A two-edged turn of events![1]

[1] Apart from H. Cox, *The Secular City*, see also W. Vos, ed., *Worship and Secularization* (=*SL* 7/2–3, 1970), H.-J. Auf der Maur, *Common Prayer Today* in *SL* 10 (1974), pp. 167ff. Compare also Plutarch on the oracles!

Clergy are in some measure protected from this alienation by their professional business, so that they do not share in it so quickly. It is only in the twentieth century that clergy in the West have begun to feel the impact of humanism and the natural sciences to the degree expressed, for example, by Voltaire in his *Lettres philosophiques*. Most lay people are not so shielded. By the commitment of their vocations, they are exposed to the alienating factors of social development. This is at once a privilege and a particular burden of the lay state.

Worshippers who are daily faced by a world that is hard to reconcile with their Christian professions clearly have a right to find in their worship not only a haven from the weekly grind, and not only a stirring challenge to faithfulness, but also an encounter with a God who has so loved the world, this secular world, that he gave his Son for it. At the very least, this must affect our preaching.

We have described this sense of strangeness as intractable. Attempts have been made to produce expressions of worship entirely attuned to the temper of the age. Some Lutheran pastors in the Germany of the Enlightenment tried to do this, with strange and instructive results. K. R. Lang's formula for the distribution of the eucharistic elements was: 'Enjoy this bread. The Spirit of devotion rest upon you, with his (or its) full blessing. Enjoy a little wine. The power of virtue does not lie in this wine, but in yourselves, in religious instruction, and in God.' One Graff devoted a Christmas Day sermon (which he was proud to publish) to the sturdy outdoor life of shepherds and the inadvisability of wearing fur caps![1] The same sort of thing was suggested among Roman Catholics and Anglicans, but the relative fixity of their liturgical systems restrained the wilder flights of fancy from such public display. In more recent times, the liturgies of the German Christians were aimed at the same target.[2] The inexorable progress of events tries and breaks almost all such experiments, and makes clear the transience of the fashions of thought which gave them their being. The heart of Christian belief cannot be fitted into the thought-forms of any age—not even the thought-forms of the Hellenistic age which saw its beginning—and in every generation Christian worship which states this belief adequately must seem, and be, in some measure out of fashion. This is a strain on the minds of Christian worshippers. It also reflects their liberation from the secular dogmas of their time.[3]

---

[1] William Nagel, *Geschichte des christlichen Gottesdienstes* (Berlin 1962), pp. 148f.
[2] Walter Birnbaum, *Das Kultusproblem und die liturgischen Bewegungen des 20. Jahrhunderts*, II (Tübingen 1970), pp. 113ff.
[3] Cf. V. A. Demant, *The Religious Prospect* (F. Muller 1939), pp. 11ff.

4. *The theological, devotional, and liturgical needs of a laity equipped for mission require constant recalculation*

These needs are very real, and are different from, not less than, the corresponding needs of the clergy. Any limit that must be set to the provision of help and instruction in these fields is set, not by any lay stupidity, but simply by the fact that lay people have many responsibilities. These responsibilities dictate a sense of priorities not always appreciated by the professional clergy. (This suggests that the relationship between pastoral work and worship so badly but so typically expressed in the English saying 'A house-going parson makes a church-going people' is utterly topsy-turvy. A more just and necessary bond between them is in the education of the clergy in the people's approach to worship.)

This difference in priorities may appear in surprising ways. For example: the clergy often like a service to be quick and short—not that they have a low regard for worship, but because they have come to understand a collect, a litany, an entire order of service as a unit of thought. They go at the work swiftly, then, so as to embrace it, as a unity, tidily with the mind, just as a musician dislikes slow playing of music if it loosens the architectonic continuity of the piece. Many lay people are deeply offended by a quick service. They do not want worship to be repetitious, verbose, or merely slow; but they have set time aside for the praise of God (usually with more effort and at greater cost than the clergy ever guess), and it is only fitting that in that time the inwardness of the act of worship should be allowed to unfold itself, without hurry or interruption, in such a way as to draw into itself the understanding, the affections, and the will.

Helmut Thielicke, in his little book *Leiden an der Kirche*, has examined in some detail the effects of clerical education: a world of interests, a style of thought, even a language (and certainly a voice!) peculiar to the profession and isolating it from the world of laity. Clerical pretence of any sort is a grave psychological and spiritual impediment to worship, and is no cure for the divergence of clerical and lay interests. It must be possible, without strain or affectation, to find room in worship for concerns and responsibilities which claim the attention of the local congregation.

It should not now be necessary to observe that the great majority of Christian worshippers are lay people. The early East Syrian Church seems to have consisted exclusively of celibates, and in medieval Europe the perpetuation of Christian worship was often possible only because of the vitality of monastic communities. Such situations, although they may

515

have to recur in the future, are clearly exceptional. It is, for all that, never unnecessary to make efforts to ensure that the worship of the Church can be truly an act of the laity, for all the factors in the situation are constantly changing.

5. *Alienation from worship may be experienced chiefly in terms of period, of class, of language or, most fundamentally, of belief*

The strangeness of worship is sometimes put down to changes in social habits and social assumptions. Worship has been despised as obsolete, or admired for its archaic and nostalgic associations; in either case, it has been radically misunderstood, or, we ought rather to say, the commentators have not entered into the action. Similar to such remarks is the suggestion that the Christian liturgy is a natural vehicle of expression for only a limited class of society: women, the elderly, the discontented but articulate artisan class, the more conservative of the *petite bourgeoisie* (these have all been favoured candidates)—in fact, any class but that which the commentator will admit to belonging to. Much more common is the charge that worship is couched in a language that is not natural, either because it is too old or because it is too technical, or because it is simply meaningless. (Linguistic problems are discussed elsewhere in this work, pp. 465–73.)

These different allegations all refer to worship as the activity of a more or less defined community. Alienation from worship is alienation from that community. Most fundamental is alienation from the faith on which that community is built. An example from fiction may express this better than any exposition. In Thomas Hardy's *Jude the Obscure*, the children of Jude Fawley and Sue Brideshead have met a hideous death, hanged by the eldest child because he knows that their parents cannot support them. Jude and Sue hear in passing the cathedral organist at practice: it was the anthem from the seventy-third Psalm, 'Truly God is loving unto Israel'.

6. *In Christian worship, this sense of alienation is to be confronted, not fled from or succumbed to*

It would be quite possible, and indeed it has been done, to press on with the practice of Christian worship without the slightest regard for the mental and social pressures of the time. Such a policy might, subjectively, be heroic. It would certainly be reassuring for some people. Objectively, it would make the liturgy look like an ivory tower, a refuge from the streaming reality of change. It would, of course, be equally possible to adapt the content of worship to the fashions of thought and feeling, in an attempt to make every imaginable participant feel at home without any effort; we have noted above the kind of thing this can lead to (see thesis 3).

One motive for both these courses of action is fear for the peace of mind of the laity. On one occasion, the old will be kept rigidly unchanged for fear of unsettling the faith and confidence of the people. On another occasion, the difficulties and angularities of the faith will be smoothed down at every turn, lest the people find it hard to take. In both cases, the fear does less than justice to the steadiness, adaptability, and discretion of lay people.

WORSHIP AND THE PASTORATE

7. *One function of the pastoral office is to identify Christian worship*

The Spanish pilgrim Egeria, in her picture of the Jerusalem liturgy, describes how the day's worship began unofficially with devotions before dawn. Anyone could attend; but they were in essence private devotions, derived from the ancient midnight office which was the progenitor of Mattins, and most of those present were ascetics. The corporate worship of the day, designed for the whole Church, began with Morning Hymns, or what the Western Church would call Lauds. The corporate nature of this stage of the proceedings, its character as being in every sense the act of the Church as a whole, was signalized by the presence of the bishop, who now made his first appearance. He might, for all one knew, have been present at the earlier prayers; but he did not step forth in his hierarchical character until it was time to involve explicitly the total membership of the Church.[1]

Since the Reformation, and especially since the Ecumenical Movement began to renew interest in differing theologies of ministry, the questions of valid ordination and its implications for the life of the Church, particularly in the presidency of the Eucharist, have been given an extended but not yet a final airing. Too often the arguments have hinged upon the tacit and unfounded view that the issue at stake is the personal piety and spiritual experience of the minister. The real importance of this discussion is the need felt by the body of Christians at large (since Ignatius of Antioch at least) for the pastoral ministry to serve as a recognizable sign of the spiritual unity of the Church. When the Church breaks bread together, it acts in unison through space and time. To show that this is so, the president of the celebration has tended to be an acknowledged representative of the wider body of the Church. Whether locally elected or sent from afar, he acts with authority conferred (by whatever means) in the name of Christ and his Church Universal.

[1] *The Pilgrimage of Egeria*, 24. See p. 64. Comments in J. A. Jungmann, *Pastoral Liturgy* (ET Challoner 1962), pp. 113ff.

'Where the bishop is, there is the Catholic Church', according to Ignatius. This principle can be applied without ambiguity or qualification only within a defined community which agrees in recognizing a defined ministry. For some Christians, this is indeed the situation: there is one Church, one ministry, with established areas of jurisdiction, one communion. For others, the matter is not so simple. They admit the possibility of the one Church being divided into distinct and conflicting communities, with differently constituted ministries as well as diverse rites. As a worshipping community, the Church is obliged to say where it stands on these questions. Can we ascribe any unitive theological meaning to the worship, sacraments and ministry of a divided Christendom?[1]

Within a given communion, the role of the ministry in identifying a liturgical act as the Church's act has many pastoral applications. Above all, the communion of the sick, prayer with the imprisoned or disabled and the like, as being led by the representative of the whole body, serve to show and to strengthen the standing of the patient or prisoner in that body. Even on a purely psychological level, this is of such importance that one might invite the theologians to consider whether the reality of the Church and the awareness of belonging to it are together the *res et sacramentum* of each sacrament.

The minister, as the leader of this or that part of the Christian body, serves to mark out a gathering as a gathering of the body. He does so more particularly as a bearer of the gospel, which function is after all what makes him the leader in the Church. For the most part, the roles of the preacher and of the liturgical president have been closely linked. This is usually most practical, and is quite fitting. It is not, however, absolutely necessary. In the Greek Church, for example, it is not rare for the celebrant of the Liturgy to be a farmer, elected by his village; the preaching will be done, perhaps, by a layman, the local schoolmaster. Yet, even in such a case, the priest himself (though never a preacher) is a bearer of the gospel by his presbyteral ministry.

8. *The liturgical and kerygmatic functions of the clergy are equally necessary and mutually complementary*

It used to be (and perhaps still is) commonly said that Catholic clergy were priests and Protestant clergy were preachers. This epigram does indeed give a fair sketch of the respective emphases and interests of the two types of tradition, but it does not do justice either to history or to the

---

[1] See (from a large literature) the studies listed in R. P. C. Hanson, *Groundwork for Unity* (SPCK 1971) and L. Hodgson, *Church and Sacraments in Divided Christendom* (SPCK 1959).

nature of the Christian ministry. Quite apart from the fact that OT prophets included priests among their number, the Christian ministry is not modelled on either prophetic or priestly roles as found in the Jewish Church, but on the new function of an apostle, a messenger of Jesus Christ the Risen. If one must use the terms of (hieratic) priesthood and (didactic) prophethood, then an apostle is both priestly and prophetic.

Although he did not see himself as responsible for baptism (1 Cor. 1.14), Paul certainly presided at the Eucharist (Acts 20.1–12) and his description of the Eucharist (1 Cor. 11.26) is exactly parallel to his description of the work of preaching (e.g. 1 Cor. 2.1–5). The preaching of the gospel is incomplete and indeed gravely distorted without the 'visible words' of the sacraments, without provision for the proclamation/hearing/response in the celebration of the Word made flesh, without the sanctifying acts of God divinely instituted to accompany the words of his messengers.

Likewise, sacramental acts are impossible without accompanying doctrine. They must mean something, and that meaning cannot attach to them unless it is declared. Even where symbolism of movement, colour, light, and scent expresses profundities beyond the reach of words (and these are usually profundities of emotion rather than of concept), the symbols themselves are ambivalent or even demonic without the accompanying doctrine (the 'myth', in some contexts) to determine their moral and metaphysical direction. A great French author once wrote that a priest coming silently to the altar said more to him than any sermon could. Sermons may be impossible for some worshippers to relate to; but if they had not already learned their catechism...?

9. *Worship, in any tradition, is affected by the personality and attitude of the clergy*

Worship-systems like those of the Free Churches, in which so much depends on the extemporization of the appointed preacher, are obviously deeply affected by the views and characters of those who lead the services. It is equally true that even the most rigidly prescribed systems cannot conceal the individual behind the universal. If the clergy are bored or embarrassed by worship, or if they regard it as a vehicle for their own importance, that fact will sooner or later emerge.

The doctrine of the *ex opere operato* efficacy of the sacraments was designed, at least in part, to meet the problems set by this situation. What is involved in the meeting of God with his Church is his faithfulness, not the quality of his ministers. Even a sordidly immoral cleric, or one acting in conscious hypocrisy, could not stand between the divine promise and those who approach in faith.

Such a doctrine is a reassurance for the laity, and at the same time a sharp challenge to the clergy. Since God will not be thwarted by our unworthiness, we have all the more reason gratefully and humbly to put ourselves in accord with our sacred functions.

10. *Especially in the sphere of worship, the part of the clergy is to feed the Church, not to assert the separate dignity of their order*

In the Church's life, there can be no dichotomy of *plebs* and *ordo*. It is, in scriptural metaphor, a body whose limbs and organs are to serve one another; every member has its own *taxis*, its own place in the economy of things. This commonplace is particularly relevant to worship.

When the clergy of any Church recite the divine office, or its equivalent, they are not only enjoying a special personal fellowship with God. They are expressing the praises and petitions of the whole body. If they have to do this alone, as the parochial clergy are often obliged to do, they are, so to speak, the minimum congregation for that worship at any given moment. The recurrent danger is that the clergy may see themselves as acting instead of the Church at large, or as supplying the defects of the laity. There is indeed a ministry of extended worship, a place for those who have more time for worship and prayer than others, and can therefore give voice to the devotion of the Church and of the world. Such work has traditionally been done by religious orders (in which lay members have had at least as significant a place as their clerical fellows). Consideration should also be given to such a role being played by retired lay people in their additional leisure hours. Either by sharing in the Office with their pastors or by some other means, they too might find their vocation in speaking for the Church.

Whether in the vocalizing of the adoration of the people of God or in the presidency of their communal celebrations, the pastoral ministry is best considered, not as a privileged class, but as a gift to the Church. Its work is to feed the Church with sound doctrine, to make manifest the presence of Christ in his Spirit, to identify each service as an act of the universal company of believers, to give cohesion and articulation to its life and its prayers. The individual members of the ministry are privileged to belong to it, but their incorporation into it is only incidental to its nature as a constantly renewed divine aid to the Christian community as a whole.

11. *The clergy exercise their function most properly in the pursuit of Christlikeness*

In a volume of essays from the Munich theological faculty, published in a Europe still shattered by war (*Aus der Theologie der Zeit*, ed. G. Söhngen,

Regensburg 1948), Joseph Pascher contributed a sensitive essay on 'Pastoral care, seen from the altar'.

> Our pastoral care [he wrote] is the responsibility of shepherds, carried out at the behest of, in discipleship to, and in mystical union with Christ, the 'Shepherd and Bishop of our souls' (1 Pet. 2.25). There can be no doubt, then, that our responsibility as shepherds must find its principles in the example of Christ, if it is to be valid. Christ-like pastoral care is also, necessarily, always successful in the most profound sense, and successful pastoral work is never valid before God if it is not Christ-like.... Every Christian will agree automatically that Christ's supreme expression of his shepherd's care was his sacrifice on the cross.... The cross was an act of love for mankind and set free a sinful race, it healed the sick and gave life—because it was a total dedication to God. The very heart of this unique event is this: the face of the Redeemer is, in the all-decisive moment, not turned to those who need redemption, but to God.... Pastoral care must then be, in the last analysis, care for God's honour and glory. Yet we must agree that the best fulfilment of the task occurs when the one to whom the flock are entrusted and the flock themselves are at one, before God, united with the central act of Christ's pastoral care in the worship of the Church.

In the work and relationships peculiar to the clergy there are many and various occasions for sharing Christ's sacrificial devotion. Consorting with the tempted, the despairing, the bored, with those deeply disturbed by alienation from their faith, the pastor cannot escape from sharing their disturbance, whatever degree of spiritual detachment he has attained. It is as a shepherd who stands (and even sleeps!) between the flock and the wolf that he goes to and from the Office, the pulpit, and the sanctuary.

WORSHIP AND THE BODY

12. *Worship is a necessary realization of the marks of the Church*

The central act of Christian worship includes an act of communion, in which participants are *one*. In every part of their worship, Christians act as those who have been dedicated, brought into God's possession, by the sacrifice of Christ and the indwelling of the Spirit, and so are *holy*. This worship is open to all, and offered on behalf of all: it is *catholic*. It is continuous (*because* of its development) with the life and missionary endeavours of the first Christians: it is *apostolic*.

Worship is not the sole valid or necessary way in which the Church acts out its calling, but it is a necessary way. The Christian community cannot meaningfully exist without addressing itself to the God whose reality and nature are the foundation of its being.

13. *Worship reveals the unity of Christians, and also their disunity; it is a necessary aspect of the quest for new unity*

In the early centuries of the Christian era, it was not unusual for congregations in a large city to send one another fragments from their consecrated breads, the *fermentum*, at the time of communion. In recent centuries, this has been restricted to the sick and mid-week communicants (except that it was once revived, probably unconsciously, by the Primitive Methodists), but it was a cogent symbol of unity. Other such symbols have always had some place in the liturgy—the Kiss of Peace, the greeting of the congregation before prayers, the shaking of hands at the church door after the service, and so on—and they reflect an important feature of the community whose members are enjoined to accept one another graciously, as God in Christ has accepted them.

It is only too obvious that Christian disunity is grievously mirrored in, and also bitterly exacerbated by, disunity in worship, whether in the breakdown of table-fellowship, in the deliberate divergence of ritual practice, or even in polemical utterances in hymns or prayers.

Where Christians cannot conscientiously adopt any more positive policy, one can ask only that imprecation and insult be kept out of divine service, for they have no place in any Christian life. Most Christians would go further, and agree that a direct pursuit of unity is both right and a duty.

All prayer for unity is a contribution to this end. More direct is the increasing practice of special united services expressly intended to further unity. These are chiefly associated with the name of Paul Couturier.[1] The service itself is a 'preaching-service', usually with lessons, address, and intercessions devoted to themes of unity. Sharp discussion has surrounded the question whether it is morally defensible for people to pray together for unity when they do not agree on the nature of the unity which is sought. If Christians could pray together only when in a state of perfect harmony, common prayer for anything would be as rare as elephants' wings. In Couturier's approach, however, the emphasis is on the unity which God wills, in the way that he wills. His will must always transcend our intentions and understandings; and in any case the way to unity as seen by Couturier is above all the shared quest for Christlikeness. Unity is essentially a matter of holiness. The as yet unrevealed ecumenical implications of the charismatic movement may well point in the same direction.

Common prayer for unity requires more than the occasional special united service. If such special events are to mean very much, they have to

[1] See G. Curtis, *Paul Couturier and Unity in Christ* (SCM 1964).

be surrounded by a variety of common action (for example, Christian social action) and to take place in a relationship of growing trust and understanding.

14. *Diversity of rites is both inevitable and desirable*

One of the major phenomena of liturgical history is a dialectic of uniformity and diversity. Sometimes it has been a canonist like Balsamon or an administration (like a Tudor government) that has tried to impose uniformity, but silent instinct has also moved in this direction: one thinks of the unofficial standardization of the use of Sarum in pre-Reformation England, or of the experience of some denominations after a Church union. In the case of British Methodism after its union in 1932, it was tacitly assumed by many that Wesleyan practice would be quietly dropped in favour of non-Wesleyan custom in many fields.[1]

The antithesis of this dialectic—or perhaps we should call it the thesis, for recent scholarship suggests that the oldest pattern is one of local diversity—is a recurrent move toward diversity. Difference in locality, in culture, naturally make for this.[2] Not dissimilar, but more subtle, are the needs of differing psychological types. Even within inflexible liturgical systems, this has been seen. The medieval Latin rite, even at its most rigid, provided for those who needed magnificence (as in the Papal High Mass) and for those who needed austerity (as in the cold simplicity of some monastic rites). There are those who can only worship in an 'alone to the alone' setting, while others can only relate to the larger group; for the former there is the Low Mass, the early morning celebration, and for the latter there is the Parish Communion, the big evening preaching-service....

It would be pleasant to come up with a neat and comprehensive solution to this tension, but that would be too much to expect. Christians cannot expect divine provision for human need to be neat and simple, for God cannot be tied down to systems. At the same time, Christian community cannot allow itself to be dissipated by cultural and psychological differences. In the liturgy, there can be something for everybody, and something for everywhere, but there will also have to be something in it that asks for a stretching of the personal or the national sympathies and instincts.

The tension between uniformity and diversity will, so far as one can see, never be resolved, for the creativity of the Christian community has

---

[1] This information is derived from ministers serving in the Methodist Church of Great Britain in the years following the 1932 Union.

[2] See G. Wainwright, 'The localisation of worship' in *SL* 8 (1971–2), pp. 26–41.

never completely paused, let alone stopped, and must be expected to go on.

This creativity is part of the inherent liveliness of the Church. A helpful approach to the whole problem is that of the French Dominican I.-H. Dalmais,[1] who has recommended that differing rites be seen as different manifestations of the same vitality, manifestations that are complementary, and so by their very divergence show that that vitality is one.

15. *The work of the hierarchy is to guide creativity and select from it*

Every Christian community has within it the hierarchical principle, whether it appears in hierarchs (pope, bishops) or in hierarchical groups (Conference, Synod, Assembly) or even in the will of the people.

On a very few occasions, hierarchies have been liturgically creative. Even when this happens, it is generally found on inspection that the core of the creative work came from one or two individuals. It was a Cranmer who laid the foundations of the Common Prayer, although amendment by select committees worked wonders—until the process could go no further, and the master-piece of 1662 was followed by the catastrophe of 1689.[2] The chiselled beauty of texts in the Latin Sacramentaries, at their best, reveals the hands of a few masters, perhaps of St Leo the Great and some of his school. The relationship between liturgical tradition and the individual talent has not yet been studied as it deserves.

16. *The growth of worship should be conscious, but not contrived, and based on considered principles*

Worship develops, and liturgies change. This is largely inevitable. There is no reason why the process should be left to chance, or left to the uncritically applied urges of the moment, however important current insights may be. When ritual practice alters, the nature of worship as an action of the whole person in the Spirit requires that the alteration be a conscious and considered movement.

The whole of our present study touches upon the pastoral priorities which govern the maintenance or the development of worship: providing a means for the meeting of God and man (so far as human arrangements can help this), balancing the established with the new, being true to the Christian community and its creed but still opening the way to worship to not-yet-believers as far as may be, combining the different elements of

[1] Cf. 'Signification de la diversité des rites au regard de l'unité chrétienne' in *Istina* 7 (1960), pp. 301–18.
[2] Cf. T. J. Fawcett, *The Liturgy of Comprehension, 1689* (Mayhew-McCrimmon AC 1973).

worship as justly and as smoothly as can be managed, reconciling law and freedom, exercising the ministerial and the common priesthood, using the best available material because only the best will do, not readily taking refuge in ambiguities or compromises, and on a basis of steady scholarship.[1]

Bishop Frere warned his fellow Anglicans against 'incongruous' alteration of the liturgy. He drew attention to the ill effects of combining practices that were, duly considered, incompatible (as, for example, Reformed and medieval Latin elements, the simple and the profuse, or practices of markedly different national traditions). This warning is usually sound, both on aesthetic grounds and indeed for the sake of consistency; but there are exceptions, for Christians cannot live in isolation, and will always affect one another (as Frere himself knew). Perhaps the danger he recognized was really that of *contrivance*, of doing things for effect, to impress. The antidote to contrivance is a combination of restraint, common sense—and very hard work.

17. *Worship instructs in the Faith*

Worship sanctifies the Church and its members by instruction in the Faith. It is committed to being orthodox both by its nature as a response to the gospel and also by the moral need to be true to God,' for the sake of honouring him. The Eastern Church is wise to think of heresy as blasphemy.

One of the oldest and most certainly permanent constituents of the liturgy is the provision for the reading of the Bible, usually with its exposition. Hymn, prayer, and psalm similarly state, at least by implication, the beliefs which underlie them. Those who take part in worship become formed in the expression of doctrine, and have opportunities to meditate upon it, if they choose. Every Christian liturgical scheme has this effect upon its users, whether it is 'free' (and even the freest Church uses hymns, which are not usually all composed *ex tempore*) or prescribed. The degree of didacticism will vary from time to time and from place to place. The liturgies of the Reformation, for example, were often instructive to the point of weariness, but this was after all a reaction to a period in which preaching had not had an adequate place in the Church's principal acts of worship.

Christian worship goes far beyond the level of didactic instruction. The faith is, as recent theology has been at pains to show, [2] far more than a

---

[1] W. H. Frere, *Some Principles of Liturgical Reform* (London 1911); cf. G. Wainwright, 'Risks and Possibilities of Liturgical Reform' in *SL* 8 (1971–2), pp. 65ff.

[2] Cf. John Baillie, *The Idea of Revelation in Recent Thought* (New York 1956). The situation may have changed; it has not developed very much.

collection of facts; it is a living relationship with God in which cognition has a regulative place but the total dedication of the person is the essential event. Worship not only holds out for our notice the nature of this relationship for our cognition to grasp. It also puts this relationship into practice. We learn the unity of God by commerce with the one God. We learn the triunity of God by being incorporated into the life of the Trinity.

By continued participation in worship, we learn the 'proportion of the faith'. Not everything important can be said in a prayer or sung in a hymn, and turning the statements of the faith into song does not remove them from the troubled world of doubt and question,[1] but the cardinal doctrines are those which can be confessed by the simplest Christian and made the stuff of liturgy and meditation. It is also important to notice how the liturgy, by shunning the preoccupations of any period, and by pointing up the directness of our access to God, is a firm bulwark against superstition.

18. *In their worship, Christians live their life which is hidden with Christ in God*

In an age when moral conformity is publicly challenged on all hands, the moral affirmations implied by Christian rites can be disturbing. Not that worshippers are anxious to leave the holy place in a hurry to get to their next sin, but because, especially in Anglo-Saxon lands, they fear that their being there is a claim to a moral excellence that they know they have no right to claim. When pressed, they often explain that they go to church because they know their failings well enough to seek divine help in fighting them. It would be helpful if we encouraged one another to explain our worship as a grateful conversation with Christ who so transforms our life that, for him, no acknowledgement could be too much. In colloquial terms: we don't go to church because we deserve to, but because God deserves that we do that much for him, at least.

By their contact with Christ in their assembling for him, Christians live progressively in dependence on him, and grow in Christlikeness. This works both on a psychological and on a sacramental level. Psychologically, there occurs a repeated 'reinforcement' of the new identity created by acceptance of the faith and membership in the faith-community. Sacramentally, there is a deepening of the union between the believers and the Lord whom they are obeying and by whom they are

---

[1] Cf. a witty remark, by Wittgenstein or one of his commentators (perhaps following *Tractatus* 7: *Wovon man nicht sprechen kann, darüber muss man schweigen*), to the effect that what cannot be said cannot be sung, either.

being prepared for the eternal world, the union in the Spirit who infuses into their being the power of the resurrection.

The sacramental growing together of the Head and members of the body in turn adds to the conscious spiritual lives of the worshippers. The various acts in which the liturgy has spread out to touch common life (marriage, death) and the recurrent texts of the preaching-service and the Eucharist come to acquire more and more interest and significance, and offer raw material for meditation and other ways of mental prayer. Where there is spiritual growth, there will be found profit even in the boredom and uncertainty which worshippers sometimes experience: they may begin as temptations, but may become stepping-stones to new fields of prayer.[1] (This is also relevant to prayer for unity; see thesis 13.)

19. *The worshipping community is committed to the quest for healthy relationships among its members*

Our Lord's injunction to leave our offering at the altar if we remember that our brother has any complaint against us, and go off to seek peace with him before we return to the altar is quite clear and direct. It seems likely that this lies behind the general feature of the eucharistic liturgy in every area: the Kiss of Peace, which in the English Reformation became the invitation to all who 'are in love and charity with your neighbours'. A community which gathers for the feast of love cannot consistently condone lack of love among its ranks.

Modern pastoral theology is much concerned with relationships, being naturally and rightly influenced by recent advances in individual and social psychology.[2] The liturgy certainly draws people together and creates a relationship between them, and involves them in the shared search for harmonious community. It also, however, turns their gaze away from one another towards the glory of God, and this has much to teach us about healthy relationships. We are to care for one another, on

[1] See Benedikt Reetz, *Liturgie und Streben nach Vollkommenheit* (Salzburg 1951 = *In viam salutis*, III); Jacques and Raissa Maritain, *Liturgy and Contemplation* (ET G. Chapman 1961); P. Grammont, a paper of the same title in L. Sheppard, ed., *True Worship* (Helicon and DLT 1963); G. Diekmann, *Personal Prayer and the Liturgy* (Melbourne and London 1969); P. Toon, *Knowing God through the Liturgy* (Grove Booklets 33, 1975). On ascetical experience as a source of dogmatic theology, especially with relation to worship, see C. Vagaggini, *Il senso teologico della liturgia* (4th edn Rome 1965), ch. 22.

[2] Contrast P. E. Johnson, *Pastoral Ministration* (Boston and London 1955), etc., with M. Thornton, *Pastoral Theology, A Re-orientation* (2nd edn SPCK 1958). Useful complementary views in P. T. Forsyth, *Positive Preaching and the Modern Mind* (2nd edn London 1909) and in J. A. Jungmann's papers as collected in *Pastoral Liturgy*. See also *La Maison-Dieu*. A pioneer work was K. Borgmann, ed., *Volksliturgie und Seelsorge* (Kolmar-im-Elsass, no date but about 1942). NB Vagaggini, pp. 753ff.

Christian principles, but not to let our vision stop with the creature, for we shall do most justice to the creature when we know and revere the Creator. There is room within the praying fellowship for those who respond to intimate groups, for those who respond to big assemblies, and also for those who cannot respond to groups very much at all. The renewed interest in the liturgy does not entail any sort of devotional collectivism or any licence for pious regimentation!

20. *Worship may be judged aesthetically, but creates its own aesthetic*

Students of the fine arts have a high regard for a quality which worship certainly ought to have: sincerity. Aesthetic, and particularly literary criticism, when applied to (say) a liturgical text, shows that sincerity is not as simple as it first appears. A sincere prayer is more than a prayer off the top of the head. A prayer written for other people to use will start with the heartfelt purpose of the first author, but it will grow before it is sent into the common stock of material, by being pruned or expanded to meet the needs of those who will use it, by being polished to make a just use of the resources of the language in which it is used (a well-translated liturgy is a new creation), and above all by re-examination against the canon of faith.

The aesthetic principles of worship have not yet been definitively reviewed, but one could go a long way with the principle that a well-composed prayer would have something definite to say, and something worth saying to God, who does not have to have everything spelled out! One thinks of the newspaper report of a meeting addressed by Bishop Gore, who concluded the proceedings with 'probably the finest prayer addressed to a Boston audience. . . .'

WORSHIP AND SECULAR SOCIETY

21. *The worship of the Church expresses moral claims upon the structures of society*

By a natural process, paralleled in most religions, Christian liturgy extended to most of the critical phases of human life. Marriage, motherhood, and death have had their own liturgical concomitants from ancient times. Birth has not been so marked, for the most part, but the 'churching of women' or thanksgiving after child-birth and the preference for speedy baptism among paedobaptists or infant dedication among 'anabaptists' have suggested an instinct for some such provision. With rare exceptions such as the votive mass *ad barbam tondendam* (corresponding to the pre-Christian Roman usage of dedicating the first shavings of a patrician youth), Christian custom has made little allowance for puberty rites. Although, in Teutonic and Anglo-Saxon lands especially, confirmation has tended to be seen in this light, adolescence celebrations have mostly been left to secular arrangements. Observances of this sort meet a deep-felt need arising from the experience of social life, and serve in their various ways to hallow life by revealing in its midst the presence of God and the claims of his creative design.

Other occasions have been thought suitable for religious observance, in addition to these *rites de passage*: the ratification of treaties, the inauguration of monarchs, the graduation of students, the onset of plague or war, the swearing-in of military recruits . . ., even the naturalization of aliens.[1] When the Church has been sufficiently prominent in the community, it has been called upon to provide the appropriate forms, and it has obliged on many occasions. There are obvious dangers in such developments. The Church may seem to have no function beyond providing supernatural sanction for the *status quo*, and Godhead may be reduced to a sense of awe before the forces of social cohesion, while the secular may lose its own proper autonomy and worth. Nonetheless, when society and Church are required to say something of what they believe about the purpose of human life, which they must in such cases, and they have certain convictions which they share, it would be wrong to refuse. A refusal would suggest that life and death, family and city, work and peace mean nothing to God. Any course of collaboration with the state or other social organs is fraught with ambiguity and the smell of compromise, which is the price to be paid for doing anything in a sinful world.

Social life is never perfect, or even free from serious imperfections. The presence of the worshipping community in the midst of imperfect society is a lasting witness to a conviction, however inchoate, that something better is possible and necessary. In baptism, men and women become (or, if you will, are manifested as) the children of God. As God's children, they have a right to justice, mercy, compassion, to a dignity which government does not always find it convenient to acknowledge. As God's children, they are trustees for their citizenship, and owe justice, mercy, and compassion to their neighbours. At the offertory, material things are put upon the table for God's use in his self-communication to man; if material things are capable of such honour, they cannot consistently be used as instruments of injustice, either through wastage or privilege.

The liturgy has often been described as non-political, and indeed the expression of political views in the setting of divine service has called forth great wrath, at least in English-speaking countries. Anti-Christian

[1] See Paul Einzig, *In the Centre of Things* (Hutchinson 1960), pp. 95–6. Cf. the 'vocational services' in S. Morison, *English Prayer Books* (CUP 1945), pp. 120–32.

organizations, with perhaps clearer sight, have on occasion regarded worship as a very political, even a subversive activity. So in a sense it is. If all men are entitled to come to the communion on the same basis, where is the distinction between nobles and commons? If all men are welcome—as sinners—where is the ruthless optimism that several forms of political 'idealism' depend on?

Pliny sent to execution—as he thought, to oblivion, *duci iussi*—those who would not burn incense before the image of Trajan, for he had been given to understand, and correctly, that such an act was beyond the possible accommodation that could be expected of a Christian. It is ironical that such a confrontation should take place in the reign of perhaps the wisest and best of the Caesars; but that was typical of the political conundrum of Christianity. The best of absolutist governments will make its idolatrous claims most sternly, and most sternly will Christians have to decline to yield to them. The worshippers of the high King of the universe indeed have their earthly loyalties, and treasure them. But these loyalties are all conditional. Worship of God questions, at least by inference, all political claims to absolute obedience and all dreams of administrative finality or infallibility.

22. *Worship points to hope for secular society*

Henry II, King of England, could not endure Thomas of Canterbury, who qualified his allegiance to his monarch and all the claims of State 'saving the honour of God'. The King saw the problem truly, but not its meaning.

By challenging every deification of the State (or of any class or pressure group, or method or structure), the witness of the liturgy holds open the door of hope for progress. Progress is not automatic, and is repeatedly mixed with regression; but our tomorrows are in the keeping of the God whom we worship. Monarchs can repent, and the poor have the good news preached to them.

23. *Worship is a means of healing*

Christian liturgical acts have always included prayers for the healing of the sick, and, at certain times, these have attracted much interest.[1] Apart

[1] For complementary studies of healing as a distinct ministry, see E. Frost, *Christian Healing* (2nd edn Mowbray 1949) and L. D. Weatherhead, *Psychology, Religion and Healing* (3rd edn Hodder & Stoughton 1955); C. W. Gusmer, *The Ministry of Healing in the Church of England: an ecumenical-liturgical study* (Mayhew-McCrimmon AC 1974). On worship and the healing of society in general, see, e.g. P. T. Forsyth, *The Church, the Gospel and Society* (Independent Press 1962); A. G. Hebert, *Liturgy and Society* (Faber

from this specialized ministry, worship as a whole has a curative work to fulfil. Anxieties and joys alike may be offered in prayer, and there is no need, as there is no justification, for any self-deception when there is a place in worship for confession. Before God, there is no compulsion to repression. Christianity is, as has been said in Freudian language, a religion of the ego, not of the super-ego.

More profoundly, worship testifies to *normality*, a right balance of things which, although we are far from it in the way we do things, still undergirds and augments our limited efforts to do the right. The Southern slave who sang 'I know where I'm going' was not condoning slavery or any of the inhumanity meted out by race to race, but was expressing the sense of direction that in time made slavery morally impossible.

Even the imperfections of the Church, which its worship makes all the more obvious, have a place in this healing function. A disunited Church is a nonsense; but even the nonsense itself reminds us that division is not the last word about human community. The visible Church is touched with the compromises of the world in which it lives, but if the Church can still rejoice in the Lord who is preparing his Bride, so can the world at large, although in very different terms.

24. *Worship is fed by a healthy culture, and itself enriches and corrects cultural growth*

The linguistic achievements of the Roman chancery and post-Renaissance Europe and the musical wealth of many periods have left the Church's liturgy more amply expressed than it was before. This is never a final accomplishment, for every life-style and cultural pattern wears out: only its best can survive to build up the outward continuity of the worshipping community. There are also dangers here, for adoration can be lost in admiration, and Puritan reactions (Athanasius, Benedict, Robert Harrison and Robert Browne . . .) are periodically needed, and the underprivileged as well as the well-educated have to be provided for.

As worship creates its own aesthetic, it also expands the language and sympathies of any culture in which it is maintained. One need point only to the maturation of the German language after Luther's Bible and the sixteenth-century chorales, to the bond between the Latin liturgy and the poetry and architecture of Europe.[1]

1935); P. T. R. Kirk, ed., *Worship: its Social Significance* (Industrial Christian Fellowship, 1939); Josef Pieper, *Leisure the Basis of Culture* (ET Faber 1952)—important!; J. G. Davies, *Worship and Mission* (SCM 1966).

[1] See G. Wainwright, 'Christian worship and western culture' in *SL* 12 (1977), pp. 20–31.

EPILOGUE

Our twenty-four theses have picked out for (admittedly cursory) comment some of the ways in which worship poses the problems of the lay and pastoral members of the Church, and similarly of the Church's internal life and its work within society. Fundamental to all these and to all related topics is the theological dimension of worship, which is discussed elsewhere in this book, but must also be our last theme here.

By its worship, the Church affirms (despite opposition from the world at large and also from within its own life) its utter dependence upon the reality of God. For worship as understood in Christian faith, God is not an external and remote principle, nor a merely internal depth of awareness. God is, and lives, confessed by man or not. By his loving action among and with and upon us, focused in worship, he takes us up into his own life, so that in the Son, by the power of the Spirit, we are and make to the Father a spiritual sacrifice of praise, in which our whole being, at once sacred and secular, finds its fulfilment here and for ever.

Worship is totally worthwhile.

INDEX OF SUBJECTS

533

INDEX OF PERSONS